Critical Theory and Performance

Critical Theory and Performance

Edited by
Janelle G. Reinelt and Joseph R. Roach

Ann Arbor

THE UNIVERSITY OF MICHIGAN PRESS

1995   1994   1993   1992   4   3   2   1

Library of Congress Cataloging-in-Publication Data

Critical theory and performance / edited by Janelle G. Reinelt and
Joseph R. Roach.
    p.   cm.
  Includes bibliographical references and index.
  ISBN 0-472-09458-0 (alk. paper). — ISBN 0-472-06458-4 (pbk. :
alk. paper)
  1. Theater—Philosophy.   I. Reinelt, Janelle G.   II. Roach,
Joseph R., 1947–
PN2039.C75   1992
792'.01—dc20
                                            92-16197
                                              CIP

Contents

General Introduction

To take up a book on critical theory and performance is immediately to encounter the topography of *post*. There are postmodernism, poststructuralism, post-Marxism, postfeminism, postcolonialism—all designating a departure from something prior. Of course, the use of the prefix *post* is incrementally problematic: in the case of *postmodernism* and *poststructuralism* it indicates that there once was a monolith called "modernism" or "structuralism" that is now definitively defunct; in the case of *post-Marxism* and *postfeminism* it marks as "over" certain political theories that are in fact changing but vitally alive. As for *postcolonial*, any informed observer would be justified in wondering what possible accuracy it might have in this presently quite colonial world.

By way of introduction to critical theory and performance, *postmodernism* offers a good starting point. The term reappears frequently in the essays that follow, but it has no chapter of its own. Perhaps this is so because postmodernism represents neither a category nor a method but, rather, as Jean-François Lyotard has observed, a "condition." The condition it represents reflects the collapse of categories themselves, an implosion that has been attributed to the media-saturated powers of capitalistic production and consumption. Postmodernity has been described as a culture of "hyperrepresentation" in which objects lose their authenticity and become indefinitely reproducible and representable as commodities. "Eclecticism," Lyotard writes, "is the degree zero of contemporary general culture: one listens to reggae, watches a western, eats McDonald's food for lunch and local cuisine for dinner, wears Paris perfume in Tokyo and 'retro' clothes in Hong Kong; knowledge is a matter for TV games."[1] Even nature, which it was once art's theoretical purpose to imitate, becomes a fabrication, a representation of itself, as in the television commerical that shows various species of marine animals joyously applauding petrochemical conglomerates for rescuing the environment from toxic spills. Postmodernism embraces simulations; it distrusts claims to authenticity, originality, or coherence. Postmodernism appropriates the popular debris of retrospective styles; it vacates modernist belief in progress and the perpetual avant-garde. Postmodernism inspires pluralism; it deflates master narratives and totalizing theories.

As editors of this volume, we acknowledge the impact of postmodernism—and of the pluralistic eclecticism it inspires—on critical theories of performance as well as on performances themselves. Performance research and practice both have found in postmodernity a positive stimulus to creative work, an opening out and up of imaginative possibility whereby the emotive and cognitive, the popular and the esoteric, the local and the global can come into play. In his study of the development of performance art, for instance, historian of the American avant-garde Henry M. Sayre substitutes the category-resistant term *undecidability* for pluralism in order better "to describe the condition of contingency, multiplicity, and poly-vocality which dominates the postmodern scene."[2] In one of the most quoted essays of the last decade, anthropologist Clifford Geertz welcomes the emergent "genre blurring" among collapsing disciplinary categories, and he places performance, which he terms symbolic action, at the head of an agenda for the "refiguration of social thought."[3]

The exhilaration produced by the blurring of genres cannot be denied, but it makes our necessary task of developing a taxonomy, of organizing the contents of this book and introducing them, a kind of performance in its own right, one that certainly encourages us to leave room for improvisation, but also one that compels us to make choices. We take note here of the ongoing critique of postmodernism by such theorists as Jürgen Habermas, Fredric Jameson, and Christopher Norris, one of the burdens of which is the slackness of its politics amid its play of shimmering surfaces.[4] In face of the postmodern multiplicity of performance research, we accept responsibility for the politics of the categories we have constructed.

These politics intensify most sharply, predictably enough, as we approach the most contested boundaries. Feminism, for example, became a plural section in our first discussions, but equal representation of its divergent positions exceeds not only our grasp but also our reach. We also chose not to develop separate categories on the basis of racial, ethnic, or national differences, though, of course, work pertaining to ethnicity appears throughout the collection. Similarly, we chose not to make a category out of theories of gay male and lesbian performances, though several essays pertain to these topics, including one on the politics and representation of AIDS. We do not intend to efface important differences, but neither do we wish to create taxonomic ghettoes to contain them. We did not include a section on the pure aesthetics of performance, transcending the realm of ideology, because we could not imagine one.

Each of the eight sections below begins with an introduction to the major critical theories pertinent to what we inclusively call performance. Each introduction also includes the identification of seminal texts and key terminology, and each is followed by several essays that demonstrate how the critical theory is used by practitioners in the field. Each of the essays collected here, however, might have found an appropriate place in more than one of our sections. There is no doubt that a different taxonomy would have produced a different book, but the present plan seeks to provide a preliminary map to the field as it looks to us today. Three categories—Marxism, feminism(s), and, arguably, cultural studies—derive from an explicitly doctrinal yet interdisciplinary position or set of positions. Others—semiotics, psychoanalysis, and history—organize themselves around their respective disciplinary practices and methodologies. Still others—deconstruction, hermeneutics, and phenomenology—represent philosophically based strategies of reading and interpretation. This is not to say that the discipline of history is without a doctrinal aspect or that Marxism lacks a philosophical basis; on the contrary, it is to recognize that categories overlap in complex networks of influence and affiliation.

We have sought to recognize such affiliations—and at the same time to open up a space for taxonomic improvisation—in three ways. First, we have sometimes included essays with a methodological base in one field within categories organized around another. The essays by Kate Davy (in "Feminism[s]") and David Román (in "After Marx"), for example, share the topic of gender critique in performances by gay male artists. While Ellen Donkin's theater historical essay joins the section on feminism(s), Marvin Carlson's consideration of Mikhail Bakhtin's theories of dialogic play resides in "Theater History and Historiography"—and so forth. Second, we have provided what we hope is a rigorous system of cross-referencing in which the keywords are appropriately glossed and indexed. Third, we have invited two of our contributors, Herbert Blau and Sue-Ellen Case, to conclude the volume by writing summary essays under the rubric of "Critical Convergences," momentary sites where ideas come together but do not come to rest.

Much of the turbulence generated by performance and performance scholarship, which has proved productive and frustrating by turns, stems from the divisions created by the diverse institutional sites of research in the field. These include departments of theater, performance studies, communication, literature, media studies, and anthropology—and their respective professional associations. The dialectics that they produce include theory versus practice, history versus theory, dramatic text versus stage performance, performance (as a high culture form like most performance art) versus theater (as a popular form like circus), and theater (as a high culture form like the production of classic plays) versus performance (as popular culture, including rituals and social dramas). Some of these divisions, such as the almost completely separate institutional development of both dance research and musicology, may explain omissions from this book, which we hope future scholars will address.[5]

While it clearly emphasizes the extraliterary, the collection contains a number of essays concerned with traditional dramatic texts. The range and diversity of performance genres do, however, enter the collection in juxtaposition to and in potentially subversive dialogue with canonical and other texts: a Hmong shaman, a *King Lear* in the mode of Indian *kathakaḷi*, stand-up comics, a circus sharpshooting act, jazz, and performance art— all exert pressure on the dominant status of the text as the privileged object of critical theory and on the exclusivity of high culture forms as its central domain. Yet, while this collection goes beyond the canon, it also remains canonical since part of the appeal of the new theory is its ability to enhance and revitalize traditional texts. Theory has also, we believe, inspired new ways of creating texts and performance events, or, at least, created a new climate for their inception, and some of the essays discuss this work. Indeed, we see an inherently political character to the performance analysis that has emerged from critical theory; it revises, challenges, rewrites, interrogates, and sometimes condemns received meanings.

We have collected these essays, however, with a sense that they belong to a particular tradition. Theory, as a discursive literature devoted to fundamental principles, has had a longer history in the academic study of theater than in almost any other discipline in the humanities. Venerable anthologies such as Barrett Clark's collection of dramatic theory and criticism introduced generations of theater students to Plato and Lodovico Castelvetro, August Schlegel, and Emile Zola—broad reflections on general theories of art and literature—at a time when English departments emphasized New Criticism, the close reading of particular literary masterpieces.[6] Many theater departments require a course in theory, separate from dramatic literature and theatrical history. In theater and drama studies, the search for general structural principles across a variety of historical periods and genres has produced some significant theoretical statements.[7] Moreover, theatrical performance has assembled an impressive array of theoretical writings concerning stage practices, including, for example, Richard Wagner and Adolph Appia on the social and aesthetic role of the total work of art, Vsevolod Meyerhold and Bertolt Brecht on the political implications of that role, and (prophetically) Antonin Artaud on its disintegration into fragments of autonomous gesture and obsolete languages in a culture with "no more masterpieces."[8] Many of the theatrical practitioner/theorists, such as Constantin Stanislavski in acting and Robert Edmond Jones in stage design, have exerted a continuing day-to-day influence on the curriculum and pedagogical approaches of theater programs.[9]

Our collection does not prove that there is nothing new under the sun. There has been a theory explosion, and it has had important consequences for both theater studies and other humanities as well. First, it has enlarged the conception of performance in ways not envisioned in the traditional study of drama and therefore reduced some of the separation of specialites between theater history, theory/criticism, and theater practice, a trend strongly reflected by the movement between categories in this collection.

Second, the "new" theory has returned the humanities to philosophy: performance history and criticism, along with other humanities disciplines such as English, modern languages, and history, have returned to a fundamental examination of the underlying assumptions that govern their own methodology in particular and their understanding of objects of inquiry in general. Both epistemological and metaphysical questions have been reopened, and they have forced a reassessment of all that has "gone without saying" for too long. Some of these fundamental issues have involved the nature of representation and its relationship to a reality it doubles/produces/defies; the exact relationship is precisely the question. The twin problems of agency and subjectivity, what constitutes them and how they work, also return studies of performance to philosophical questions of the nature of the self, to what used to be called "philosophical anthropology." In fact, much of the "new theory" derives from the work of philosophers (or perhaps "post-philosophers"): Jaques Derrida's critique of metaphysics, Paul Ricoeur's phenomenology, J. L. Austin's speech/act theory, and Jean François Lyotard's conception of the postmodern all constitute traditional philosophical thought or its undoing by philosophers. Of course, philosophy has always spilled over into other discourses (some think it colonizes all academic disciplines); to this list we can add, among others, Lacan's revision of Freud, Raymond Williams's and Fredric Jameson's revisions of Marx, and Foucault's epistemological critique. Even to begin to make such a list is to realize how intensive and productive the theory explosion has been.

Finally, the new theory has provided a methodology and an impetus to specify the meaning of an old cliché: a text is different on the stage than it is on the page. Theory has done so principally by radically questioning the idea of what a text is. Semiotics, for example, has provided notions of multiple sign systems coinciding in performance. The difference between a playscript and a performance text can be theorized and articulated. The audience can finally be interrogated as to its role in the production of meaning. There are concrete reasons why a show differs from night to night, venue to venue, cast to cast. Perhaps most important, performance can be articulated in terms of politics: representation, ideology, hegemony, resistance.[10] In a way, theory gives theater back again to the body politic.

Ironically, the history of the discipline of theater studies is one of fighting for autonomy from English and speech departments, insisting on a kind of separation from other areas of study. It was necessary, politically necessary, to claim this distinctiveness, even at the expense of becoming somewhat insular and hermetic—a result that unfortunately became true of many departments of theater. Now, however, it is even more necessary to recognize and insist on the interdependency of a related series of disciplines and also on the role of performance in the production of culture in its widest sense.

J. G. R. and J. R. R.

NOTES

1. Jean-François Lyotard, "Answering the Question: What Is Postmodernism?" in *The Postmodern Condition: A Report on Knowledge*, trans. Geoff Bennington and Brian Massumi (Minneapolis: University of Minnesota Press, 1984), 76.

2. Henry M. Sayre, *The Object of Performance: The American Avant-Garde since 1970* (Chicago and London: University of Chicago Press, 1989), xiii.

3. Clifford Geertz, "Blurred Genres: The Refiguration of Social Thought," in *The American Scholar* 49 (1980), reprinted in *Critical Theory since 1965*, ed. Hazard Adams and Leroy Searle (Tallahassee: Florida State University Press, 1986), 514–23.

4. Jürgen Habermas, "Modernity: An Incomplete Project," in *The Anti-Aesthetic: Essays on Postmodern Culture*, ed. Hal Foster (Port Townsend, Wash.: Bay Press, 1983); Fredric Jameson, *Postmodernism, or, The Cultural Logic of Late Capitalism* (Durham, N.C.: Duke University Press, 1991); Christopher Norris, *What's Wrong with Postmodernism: Critical Theory and the Ends of Philosophy* (Baltimore: Johns Hopkins University Press, 1990). See also Jonathan Arac, ed., *Postmodernism and Politics* (Minneapolis: University of Minnesota Press, 1986).

5. For the stimulating dialogue between dance scholarship, theater history, and performance theory, see Susan Leigh Foster, *Reading Dancing: Bodies and Subjects in Contemporary American Dance* (Berkeley: University of California Press, 1986);

and Philip Auslander and Marcia B. Siegel, "Two (Re)Views of Susan Leigh Foster's *Reading Dancing*," *TDR: A Journal of Performance Studies* 32, no. 4 (1988): 7–31.

6. Barrett H. Clark, *European Theories of the Drama* (1918; rev. ed., New York: Crown, 1965); and Bernard F. Dukore, *Dramatic Theory and Criticism: Greeks to Grotowski* (New York: Holt, Rinehart, and Winston, 1974).

7. See, for example: Bernard Beckerman, *Dynamics of Drama: Theory and Method of Analysis* (1970; reprint, New York: Drama Book Specialists, 1979); Michael Goldman, *The Actor's Freedom: Toward a Theory of Drama* (New York: Viking Press, 1975); Manfred Pfister, *The Theory and Analysis of Drama*, trans. John Halliday (Cambridge and New York: Cambridge University Press, 1988).

8. Key modernist texts are anthologized in Eric Bentley, ed., *The Theory of the Modern Stage: An Introduction to Modern Theatre and Drama* (Harmondsworth: Penguin, 1968); and E. T. Kirby, ed., *Total Theatre* (New York: Dutton, 1969).

9. For a comprehensive survey of theatrical theory, which charts the boundaries of the subject, see Marvin Carlson, *Theories of the Theatre: A Historical and Critical Survey from the Greeks to the Present* (Ithaca and London: Cornell University Press, 1984).

10. For a collection of essays that acknowledge the political articulations of performance, see Sue-Ellen Case and Janelle Reinelt, eds., *The Performance of Power: Theatrical Discourse and Politics* (Iowa City: University of Iowa Press, 1991).

Cultural Studies

Introduction

Artistic Lady in a Box (a Club Woman Type): Mr. Webb, is there
any culture or love of beauty in Grover's Corners?
Mr. Webb: Well, ma'am, there ain't much—not in the sense you
mean. Come to think of it, there's some girls that play the piano
over at High School Commencement; but they ain't happy about it.
No, ma'am, there isn't much culture; ... Robinson Crusoe and the
Bible; and Handel's Largo, we all know that; and Whistler's
Mother—those are just about as far as we go.
—Thornton Wilder, *Our Town*

Mr. Webb speaks of two meanings of culture, both of which are germane
to a definition of cultural studies. The first meaning is made explicit by
the helpful Artistic Lady, who associates culture exclusively with an empa-
thetic response to aesthetic forms, a "love of beauty." Mr. Webb, who edits
the local newspaper, understands without elaboration on her part that she
confines the meaning of culture to a few elite, Eurocentric forms—from
which he derives his short, apologetic list. The second meaning of culture
resides in the comic irony of the wider context of Mr. Webb's answer to
her narrow question: the New Hampshire village of Grover's Corners, as
Wilder's play repeatedly demonstrates (through enactments of material
household economies, familial and kinship relations, weddings, and funerals), is rich in social structures and practices, in the rituals of both daily
life and hallowed occasions; rich, that is, in precisely those tradition-bearing
forms of organized behavior that articulate the limits and the possibilities
of collective human experience—in a word, *culture.*

Practitioners in the field of cultural studies—which might be thought
of more as a point of intersection for various kinds of interdisciplinary
work than as a unitary approach—accept something much closer to Mr.
Webb's second, social meaning of culture, while at the same time they find
that they must still somehow reckon with the persistence of the aesthetic
one. John Fiske, for instance, speaking for cultural studies as it first developed in Britain, begins his definition of culture by saying what it is not:

> The term "culture," used in the phrase "cultural studies," is neither
> aesthetic nor humanist in emphasis, but political. Culture is not con-
> ceived of as the aesthetic ideals of form and beauty to be found in
> great art, nor in more humanist terms as the voice of the "human
> spirit" that transcends the boundaries of time and nation to speak to
> a hypothetical universal man (the gender is deliberate—women play
> little or no role in this conception of culture). Culture is not, then,
> the aesthetic products of the human spirit acting as a bulwark against
> the tide of grubby industrial materialism and vulgarity, but rather a
> way of living within an industrial society that encompasses all the
> meanings of that social experience.[1]

Culture, then, is not general and universal but local. Culture is not innocent and neutral but partisan. Culture is not transcendent but material and historical.

Also implicit in Fiske's understanding of cultural studies is the Marxist idea that culture is the occasion and the instrument of struggle between contending groups with differing amounts of power or, at least, with different kinds of power. Theorists frequently divide cultural productions into three levels or zones of consumption: mass culture, high culture, and popular culture. Such a division includes the complementary idea, implicit in the question posed by the Artistic Lady in a Box in *Our Town*, that culture may serve to exclude as well as to include different kinds of people for different kinds of purposes. Understanding without prompting the limitations she intends (culture often operates on the level of what Fredric Jameson has called "the political unconscious"),[2] Mr. Webb comes up with a revealingly ethnocentric list of cultural examples drawn exclusively from high culture forms: an operatic aria turned into a Protestant hymn, an English novel showing the entrepreneurial ascendance of a white man marooned among his future colonial subjects, the King James version of the Bible, the masterpiece of a painter who believed in "art for art's sake," and the modest pianistic accomplishments of acceptably "finished" young ladies.

Editor Webb's privileged shortlist, his canon of classics, erases as it enunciates. Excluded from his account of local culture are the vestiges of "Early Amerindian stock, Cotahatchee tribe," mentioned earlier in the scene by another character, and the denizens of "Polish Town.... You know, foreign people that come here to work in the mill, coupla Canuck families, and the Catholic Church." In Grover's Corners such minority cultures tend to be effaced by the dominant culture's normalizing love of "beauty." Culture is what makes "our" town not "their" town. Yet implicit in the ironic framework of *Our Town* is a more positive notion of what benefits membership in a given culture may include, not the least of which is the enabling solidarity created by the circulation of shared values within the signposts and boundary markers of a symbolic social economy.

The interdiscipline of cultural studies, generally speaking, investigates the various kinds of boundaries—inclusive, exclusive, and negotiated—that human societies construct. It features prominently the exploration of cultural difference and otherness, including differences based on social class, gender, and ethnicity. As a transatlantic term, *cultural studies* has particularly nuanced meanings associated with its usage in several disciplinary contexts: media studies (mass culture), literary studies (generally high culture), and performance studies (generally popular culture, with the elusive exception of performance art, and performative behavior in daily life). In any event, cultural studies resists the view of art and life as autonomous experiences and insists, instead, that they are inextricably entangled in history and that they are both products of and productive of dynamic cultural processes.

British cultural studies, following the pioneering work of Raymond Williams (beginning with *Culture and Society* in 1958), tends to focus on the cultural boundaries defined by social class. Noting that *culture* is one of the "two or three most complicated words in the English language," Williams strove to relate the *material* productions of culture (institutional continuities of physical practices such as manufacture) to its *signifying* and *symbolic* systems (such as literature and media).[3] The convergence of material productions with signifying systems inheres in the fundamental nature of theatrical performance, a definitional truth to which Raymond Williams's career as a professor in Drama adds the logic of disciplinary affiliation. A similar convergence characterizes media culture as explored in the work of Stuart Hall (*Culture, Media, Language* [1980]) and John Fiske (*Television Culture* [1978]). In recognition of the importance of Marxist critical theory to cultural studies, the section entitled "After Marx" contains a number of explicit and implicit cross-references. Bruce McConachie, for instance, applies Raymond Williams's strategy of locating and explicating "keywords" to the term *production* in both its theatrical and economical meanings, and Philip Auslander looks at stand-up comedy in light of its class-conscious consumers, an approach suggestive both of the work of Williams and of the method of class analysis developed by the French social theorist Pierre Bourdieu (*Distinction: A Social Critique of the Judgement of Taste* [1984]).

In addition to distinctions founded on culture and class, cultural studies explores boundaries defined by ethnicity, intercultural encounter, and social circulation. Such an approach frequently looks to cultural anthropology for its theoretical paradigms. In recent American literary and textual studies, the word *culture* has entered into the lexicon of the "New Historicists," the term used to describe a loosely confederated group of literary scholars and intellectual historians associated particularly with the Berkeley journal *Representations* (see the introduction to "Theater History and Historiography"). Speaking of what he regards as the most powerful binary opposition exerted by a culture—constraint and mobility—Stephen Greenblatt calls for a "cultural poetics," a method of interrogating canonical literary texts (Shakespeare appears frequently in his work) in light of their social position as both boundary markers and mediums of exchange:

> A culture is a particular network of negotiations for the exchange of material goods, ideas, and—through institutions like enslavement, adoption, or marriage—people. Anthropologists are centrally concerned with a culture's kinship system—its conception of family relationships, its prohibitions of certain couplings, its marriage rules— and with its narratives—its myths, folktales, and sacred stories. The two concerns are linked, for a culture's narratives, like its kinship arrangements, are crucial indices of the prevailing codes governing human mobility and constraint. Great writers are precisely masters of these codes, specialists in cultural exchange.[4]

This New Historicist paradigm suggests a continuous interaction between canonical texts by "great writers" and the everyday cultural experience of constraint and mobility. It is limited, however, by its emphasis on high culture texts (and the experience of solitary reading) to the neglect of popular performance (and the experience of public participation).

Far more systematic than New Historicism in its interdisciplinary exchanges with cultural anthropology, performance studies has recently developed ethnographic and intercultural perspectives on a variety of public events and practices. Indeed, the profusion of kinds of performance—from Yoruban dance to street carnivals, from performance art to the performative practices of everyday life—epitomizes the interdisciplinary ferment characteristic of the approach of performance studies. In Richard Schechner's encompassing definition (see Dwight Conquergood's essay), performance consists of "restored" or "twice-behaved behavior," behavior that is repeated, reinstated, or rehearsed. The concept of restored behavior embraces theatrical performances, sacred and secular rituals, and social displays of many kinds, from sporting events to shamanism. Such performances lend themselves particularly well to interpretation by means of ethnographic description, a methodology developed by cultural anthropologists to represent indigenous societies.

Ethnography literally means "writing culture." Like the cultural anthropologist Clifford Geertz, ethnographers of performance value "local knowledge."[5] Cognizant of the critique of Claude Lévi-Strauss by poststructuralists (see "Semiotics and Deconstruction"), contemporary ethnographers tend to reject the monolithic "primitive mind" of structuralist anthropology. In other words, they do not insist on structural oppositions of nature and culture (on the binary model of Saussure's structuralist linguistics) in the myths and kinship patterns of non-Western peoples. Nor do they accept the nostalgic narrative of the disappearance of static "native" and "organic" cultures before the onslaught of "civilization." In a challenge to the Lévi-Straussian idea that authentic human differences recede, like tropical rain forests, in the global leveling of commodity culture, ethnographer James Clifford sets forth an alternative consequence of cultural encounter: "organic culture reconceived as inventive process or creolized 'interculture.'"[6] Such a "Caribbean" model argues that all cultures are potentially dynamic, adaptive, and interactive. Characteristic of what is now generally called postmodernism, therefore, contemporary cultural studies asserts the constructedness, and thus the negotiability, of any boundary— linguistic, geographic, or social. Performance lends itself readily to such a strategy of interpretation.

The contributors to this part of the book reflect the intercultural approach to performance within the theoretical rubric of cultural studies. First, in his account of the Franco-Anglo-Indian reception of a multinational production of *King Lear,* Phillip Zarrilli introduces some of the complex issues of translated conventions in cross-cultural performance. Then the essays by Dwight Conquergood, Sandra Richards, and James Moy variously treat performance as a contested borderland in the construction of, respectively, Hmong-American, African-American, and Sino-Japanese-American relations. Finally, Richard Schechner takes up the provocative question of carnival in the global village: local cultural production in a postmodern world increasingly dominated by the mass media.

Performance provides the hermeneutics of culture in each case, and not surprisingly so, even in the view of anthropologists. "By their performances ye shall know them," wrote Victor Turner, in the belief that cultures express themselves most fluently by means of performance.[7] A key Turnerian concept in support of this belief is *liminality*, the state or process of living on the margins, of crossing the boundaries, of literally being at the "threshold" of culture's inside/outside, which he associated particularly with performance and performers (see also Marvin Carlson's "Theatre and Dialogism" in "Theater History and Historiography").

Borderlands traditionally exist as sites of political contestation, risk, and risk taking. This fact, which renders the liminal performer socially vulnerable, also makes the refugee the cultural epitome of the postmodern condition. Dwight Conquergood's article on shamanistic performance is based on his fieldwork in Hmong refugee communities in Thailand and Chicago. The vulnerability of the shaman (healer) in performance is not only social but physical, a metonym (an object substituted for its signified) representing the rigors of liminal experience generally. The shaman not only performs to heal the sick but also to assert, not without risk to himself, the dignifying perimeters of his culture in the face of external threats of humiliation from the dominant social order. Certain similarities appear in the performances of internally marginalized subcultures, including those testing the margins of gender and sexuality (see "Feminism[s]").

Two essays in this section interweave different kinds of performances (text-based and actor-based) from geographically distant cultural traditions to support the feasibility of theater as a mediator across boundaries of historical and cultural difference. Their interpretive strategy is based on the concept of *métissage* (or "braiding"), not a melting pot but a tactful weaving together of separate strands. Zarrilli, whose materials derive from his fieldwork in India, takes up the multilateral negotiations for the translation of Shakespeare's *King Lear* into the performance mode of the dance-drama called *kathakaḷi* (or "story play"). His intercultural reception-study of this special production spans subcontinental Kerala and the Edinburgh Festival. Richards reads intertextually the plays of Ntozake Shange, an African-American, and Femi Oṣofisan, a Nigerian. She identifies these playwrights—great writers in Greenblatt's sense—as masters of the code of Yoruba ritual, guardians of its "sacred stories," as circulated through the intercultural exchange of the African diaspora.

Métissage has its dangers, as the contributors to this collection realize. Performance dramatizes culture on the margins, but it can all too readily be appropriated in support of the continuing imposition of marginality. Representation easily becomes misrepresentation. The question of racial and cultural stereotypes raised by Moy in his article on playwrights Henry David Hwang and Philip Kan Gotanda draws attention to the deeply problematic issues inherent in the idea of intercultural performance. Constraint (or racist monologue) can operate with at least as much power as mobility (or interactive dialogue). The very process of theatrical representation may knowingly or unknowingly impose the cultural values of one group upon the members of another—caricaturing them, even as it claims to respect their difference, erasing them, even as it purports to celebrate their existence. Zarrilli alludes to the controversy surrounding Peter Brook's *Mahabharata,* a problematic attempt to "universalize," through international performance, the local knowledge of the Sanskrit epic. In a similar way, Moy critiques two Asian-American playwrights who, in their earnest attempts to "deconstruct" racial stereotypes, may in fact have reproduced them in even more insidiously popular forms.

Critical theory—in the work of such diverse thinkers as Edward Said, Renato Rosaldo, and Gayatri Chakravorty Spivak—has addressed this key issue of the construction of the cultural "Other." "Orientalism," as Said defines it in his mordant study of the production of Western knowledge about the non-West, splits the world into a "we-they" dichotomy in which "they"—say, the Palestinians—subsist as a political nullity.[8] The Oriental becomes the essentialized Other, a provocation for the fantasies of Western authors, not the least ornate of which is the myth of an exoticized and feminized sexuality. Moy finds just such a provocation in Hwang's *M. Butterfly:* the fantasized Song Liling, who flutters tantalizingly on the threshold between genders, between cultures, and between orifices. Similarly, Renato Rosaldo reasserts the postmodern ethnographer's claim that borderlands, such as the ones that Moy's Asian-American dramatists ambiguously traverse, are always political. Rosaldo, in his moving discussion of Chicano narratives, argues that "we" must listen carefully to both the voice of the Other and other voices, "especially if they use unfamiliar idioms and speak to us from socially subordinate positions."[9] The construction of "us" in this context presents as vexed a problem as the construction of "them." For whom does an author speak when using the first-person plural? Who are *we*? (See also "Psychoanalysis.") This problem of positionality— the assumption of authority from which cultural position (or positions) one is entitled to speak—provokes Spivak's question about permission: "Can the subaltern speak?" It also motivates her double-edged answer: "Clearly, if you are poor, black, and female you get it in three ways."[10]

Richard Schechner's concluding essay returns to the central issue of our general introduction: the politics of postmodern representation, here expressed in mass-media appropriation of local versions of street theater (Tiananmen Square, the Berlin Wall, Mardi Gras, Spring Break at Daytona Beach). This time the setting is a unitary global interculture, a kind of United Nations of the carnivalesque. Carnival supposedly turns the world upside down, but, more often in Schechner's reckoning, the world (or its politically dominant institutions) is turning carnival right side up. The critique of such domination takes some surprising turns. Even the pluralism (the welcoming of multiple voices and positions) implicit in Schechner's dizzying itinerary and explicit in the organization of this collection of essays has recently come under attack as yet another means of mystification and hence denial of human difference, this time in the name of open-ended human diversity.[11] Mobility and constraint, negotiation and appropriation, inclusion and exclusion, identity and difference—these oppositions come less often in tidy pairs of either/or than in tangled bundles of perhaps/ but. Such questions currently animate debate in cultural studies, and no doubt they will continue to do so for as long as boundaries exist, which is to say for as long as cultures exist.

J. R. R.

NOTES

1. John Fiske, "British Cultural Studies and Television," in *Channels of Discourse: Television and Contemporary Criticism*, ed. Robert C. Allen (Chapel Hill and London: University of North Carolina Press, 1987), 254.

2. Fredric Jameson, *The Political Unconscious: Narrative as a Socially Symbolic Act* (Ithaca: Cornell University Press, 1981), 20.

3. Raymond Williams, *Keywords: A Vocabulary of Culture and Society*, rev. ed. (New York: Oxford University Press, 1983), 87–93.

4. Stephen Greenblatt, "Culture," in *Critical Terms for Literary Study*, ed. Frank Lentricchia and Thomas McLaughlin (Chicago and London: University of Chicago Press, 1990), 229–30.

5. Clifford Geertz, *Local Knowledge: Further Essays in Interpretive Anthropology* (New York: Basic Books, 1983). For the paradigmatic instance of what Geertz calls "thick description" of a local cultural performance as a "text," see "Deep Play: Notes on the Balinese Cockfight," in *The Interpretation of Cultures* (New York: Basic Books, 1973), 412–53.

6. James Clifford, *The Predicament of Culture: Twentieth-Century Ethnography, Literature, and Art* (Cambridge and London: Harvard University Press, 1988), 15.

7. Victor Turner, cited in *By Means of Performance: Intercultural Studies of Theatre and Ritual*, ed. Richard Schechner and Willa Appel (Cambridge and New York: Cambridge University Press, 1990), 1.

8. Edward Said, *Orientalism* (New York: Pantheon Books, 1978), 26–27.

9. Renato Rosaldo, *Culture and Truth: The Remaking of Social Analysis* (Boston: Beacon Press, 1989), 148.

10. Gayatri Chakravorty Spivak, "Can the Subaltern Speak?" in *Marxism and the Interpretation of Culture*, ed. Cary Nelson and Lawrence Grossberg (Urbana and Chicago: University of Illinois Press, 1988), 294. See also Spivak, *In Other Worlds: Essays in Cultural Politics* (New York: Methuen, 1987).

11. Ellen Rooney, *Seductive Reasoning: Pluralism as the Problematic of Contemporary Literary Theory* (Ithaca and London: Cornell University Press, 1989).

For Whom Is the King a King? Issues of Intercultural Production, Perception, and Reception in a *Kathakaḷi King Lear*

Phillip B. Zarrilli

The Interculture of Production

It has become commonplace to assume that "culture" is both reflected within and simultaneously invented by the webs of signification knit into the performative moment. Performance as a mode of cultural action is not a simple reflection of some essentialized, fixed attributes of a static monolithic culture but an arena for the constant process of renegotiating experiences and meanings that constitute culture. Critical theorist Susan Bennett expands this notion of the interactive state of flux in the relationship between culture and performance when she writes that

> both an audience's reaction to a text (or performance) and the text (performance) itself are bound within cultural limits. Yet, as diachronic analysis makes apparent, those limits are continually tested and invariably broken. Culture cannot be held as a fixed entity, a set of constant rules, but instead it must be seen as in a position of inevitable flux.[1]

It is also a commonplace of the postmodern condition that we cannot credit metanarratives like the concepts of "culture" or discrete "performance traditions" within "cultures,"[2] that we indicate our awareness of such incredulity by using quotation marks, and then we go ahead and use such dangerous words laden with the baggage of their metanarratives because we recognize that "there are times when we still need to be able to speak holistically of Japanese or Trobriand or Moroccan culture in the confidence that we are designating something real and differentially coherent."[3]

If "culture" and "cultural performances" as fixed metanarratives have been quoted out of existence, where is "culture" and where are "its performances" to be located in a postmodern world? Ethnographic historian James Clifford asserts that

> the world's societies are too systematically interconnected to permit any easy isolation of separate or independently functioning systems. . . . Twentieth-century identities no longer presuppose continuous cultures or traditions. Everywhere individuals and groups improvise local performance from (re)collected pasts, drawing on foreign media, symbols, and languages.[4]

Indonesian novelist/playwright/poet Putu Wijaya describes the super-human effort required to exist in this jumble of identities prompted by a "world dominated by the media, by consumption, and by global cultural flows"[5] when he writes:

> To discuss an Indonesian poet does not merely mean to discuss the poetry of the man because the poet also writes prose, essays, drama, critiques, travelogues... articles about the economy, philosophy... gossip, pornographic stories... and so forth. Nor can we write of the joys and sorrows in the life of a teacher only from the perspective of his work at school because he also raises chickens... is a councilman for his neighborhood... as well as being... a law student, a Moslem scholar... a fan of pornographic movies, a royal servant, a gambler and a shaman.
>
> ... The above descriptions present a complex but also superhuman phenomenon.... Complex because we find that cultural roles are inexorably entwined with one another so that no characteristic stands alone. The phenomenon is labelled "super" because we sometimes have a difficult time imagining that people can have so many roles and statuses in life.[6]

While sharing Clifford's point of view and appreciating Putu's ironically poetic self-definition, I would qualify both by suggesting that, even if individual and group identities are being shaped in an interculture of juxtaposition and disjuncture, the reflexive awareness of and attention to this condition is primarily part of the discourse of an educated and/or artistic elite. Although twentieth-century identities no longer necessarily *presuppose* continuous cultures or traditions, there are nevertheless many contexts within which either "the world" or at least some more framed and circumscribed arenas of experience are imagined as continuous, and where tradition is cast in the role of maintaining and authorizing a particular form of continuity within that particular experiential arena.

Given the provocative choice by James Clifford of interpreting our postmodern condition and the breakdown of metanarratives with either a Lévi-Straussian "narrative of entropy or loss... [as] an inescapable, sad truth" or "a more ambiguous 'Caribbean' experience... reconceived as inventive process or creolized 'interculture,'"[7] I have chosen the latter. I will examine the relationship between performance and interculture by focusing primarily on one experiment—a recent South Indian *kathakaḷi* dance-drama version of Shakespeare's *King Lear*.

On 28 July 1989, I attended the inaugural performance of a South Indian dance-drama (*kathakaḷi*) version of Shakespeare's *King Lear* (*Kathakaḷi King Lear*) on the proscenium stage of the Victorian styled V. J. T. Hall, Trivandrum, Kerala, India. The European premiere took place on 2 September 1989, at the Festival of Rovereto, Italy, followed by two and one-half months of performances in the Netherlands, France, and Spain. A second international touring production appeared in Singapore as part of its Twenty-fifth Independence Day celebrations and at the Edinburgh Theatre Festival in August 1990.[8] Australian playwright/director David McRuvie and French actor-dancer Annette Leday originally conceived *Kathakaḷi King Lear*, which was coproduced by their Association Keli (Paris) with the internationally known Kerala State Arts Academy (Kerala Kalamandalam, Cheruthuruthy, Kerala, India). Scripted by McRuvie in English and originally translated by Iyyamkode Sreedharan (poet and secretary of the Kerala Kalamandalam) into Malayalam (the regional language of Kerala, *kathakaḷi*'s home state), *Kathakaḷi King Lear* was choreographed and staged collaboratively by McRuvie, Leday (who also played Cordelia), and a group of highly regarded senior *kathakaḷi* artists: K. Kumaran Nayar (King Lear), C. Padmanabhan Nayar (King Lear), Kalamandalam Gopi (France), K. P. Krishnankutty Poduval (percussion), T. K. Appukutty Poduval (percussion), Madambi Subramaniam Namboodiri (vocalist).

With its Western content, its highly conventionalized *kathakaḷi* mise-en-scène and techniques, its collaborative process of conceptualization and realization, and its performances in continental Europe, Edinburgh, Singapore, and Kerala, *Kathakaḷi King Lear* was certainly intercultural in both its production and reception. Prompted in part by my agreement with and desire to pursue Susan Bennett's assertion that "production and reception cannot be separated, and a key area for further research is the relationship between the two for specific cultural environments, [and] for specific types of theatre,"[9] I will use *Kathakaḷi King Lear* as the primary example through which to analyze the relationship between production, perception, and reception in a postmodern intercultural world.

What is Kathakaḷi?

Kathakaḷi is one among many indigenous performing arts of Kerala, India. At the historical moment of its emergence as a distinct genre of performance during the late sixteenth and early seventeenth centuries, it was given the new name *kathakaḷi*, denoting a hybrid formed by borrowing from a number of Kerala's traditional arts. The name *kathakaḷi* literally means "story play" and refers to the performance of dramas written by playwright/composers in a highly florid Sanskritized Malayalam based on India's epics and *puranas*—first the Ramayana, then the Mahabharata, and later from the *Bhagavata Purana*.[10]

On a bare stage using only a few stools and an occasional property, three groups of performers collectively create *kathakaḷi* performances: actor-dancers, percussionists, and vocalists. Traditionally constituting an all-male company of actor-dancers,[11] the performers use a highly physicalized performance style embodied through years of training to play a variety of roles, including kings, heroines, demons, demonesses, gods, animals, and priests. Each role is easily identifiable to a Malayali audience as a particular character type with its own inhering characteristics by the codified makeups and elaborate, colorful costumes. The actor-dancers create their roles by using a repertory of dance steps, choreographed patterns of stage movement, an intricate and complex language of hand gestures (*mudrās*) for literally "speaking" their character's dialogue with their hands, and a pliable use of the face and eyes to express the internal states (*bhāva*) of the character. The percussion orchestra consists of three types of drums (*ceṇṭa*, *maddaḷam*, and *iṭekka*), each with its own distinctive sound and role in the ensemble, and brass cymbals, which keep the basic rhythmic cycles around which the dance-drama is structured. The two onstage vocalists keep the basic time patterns on their cymbals and sing the entire text, including both third-person narration and first-person dialogue in a vocal style where elaboration and repetition are common characteristics. Performance traditionally began at dusk, and it took all night to perform a thirty- to forty-page text.

Kathakaḷi's dense performance structure provides many opportunities for narrative and performative elaboration on the basic story/text, enhancing the realization of the aesthetic ideal of *rasa*—tasting or savoring the major moods unfolded in the drama. *Kathakaḷi* has always appealed to a wide cross-section of Malayalis. The easily recognizable characters, colorful makeup and costumes, and those scenes played with broad dramatic action, mime, and dance combine to make *kathakaḷi* entertaining and pleasing for the general audience, which knows the stories well but is not attuned to reading its nuances. Its more subtle and codified modes of performance appeal to connoisseurs in the audience educated to appreciate these nuances.

Kathakaḷi King Lear

From its inception, *Kathakaḷi King Lear* was intended to be more than a superficial dressing up of Shakespeare's Lear in colorful *kathakaḷi* costumes as an exotic novelty for Western audiences. Rather, it was to serve as an intercultural experiment in production *and* reception, opening in Kerala for Malayali audiences and then touring continental Europe. Leday and McRuvie wanted the production to speak equally to both its original audiences. For Malayalis the production was intended to provide a *kathakaḷi* experience of one of Shakespeare's great plays and roles. Assuming that many in the European audience would know Shakespeare's play, the production was intended as an accessible way of experiencing *kathakaḷi* and the aesthetic delight of *rasa*. For Leday and McRuvie, *kathakaḷi's* "rich means of expression and its intensity of effect" seemed an appropriate performative means through which to "find a theatrical expression for the larger-than-life dimension and explosive power of the play."[12]

Following theater semiotician Patrice Pavis, the lengthy process of adaptation and translation that created *Kathakaḷi King Lear* might best be described as a series of *reelaborations* of text, gesture, and choreography into a new frame.[13] The process began with McRuvie's reelaboration of the *King Lear* text to conform with *kathakaḷi's* theatrical criteria in length, action, and number of characters—a process that radically transformed the original. The typed English adaptation ran barely twenty pages for the two-hour-plus performance. The action focused exclusively on Lear and his three daughters. The Gloucester subplot was completely cut, as were Kent,

Fig. 1. *Kathakaḷi King Lear.* Goneril (right) bows before her father as Cordelia (left) asks herself, "What shall Cordelia speak? Love, and be silent." Photo credit: Annette Leday and David McRuvie.

Cornwall, and Albany. Only eight characters appeared, including Lear, his three daughters (Cordelia, Goneril, and Regan), the King of France (in a somewhat expanded role), the Fool, mad Tom, and a soldier. Each of the nine scenes—(1) King Lear Divides His Kingdom (fig. 1); (2) The Departure of Cordelia and France; (3) At Goneril's Palace; (4) At Regan's Palace; (5) The Storm (figs. 2, 3, 4); (6) The Return of Cordelia and France; (7) The Reconciliation of Lear and Cordelia; (8) The Battle (fig. 5); and (9) The Death of Lear (fig. 6)—was organized around one or two major dramatic actions. The first scene, for example, enacted the division of the kingdom and banishment of Cordelia. The second scene dramatized the wedding and departure of Cordelia and France in which Cordelia expresses her sorrow at leaving her father and pledges herself to her husband.

McRuvie rendered his English adaptation into a somewhat simplified version of the three major components of a traditional *kathakaḷi* performance script: narrative passages (*śloka*) in third person describing the context of the action, dialogue passages (*padam*) sung by the onstage vocalists and spoken by the actors through hand gestures, and passages (*āṭṭam*) delivered in gesture language and mimetic dance by the actors but not sung by the onstage vocalists. The *śloka* and *padam* were then translated into Malayalam and set in the appropriate musical mode for the vocalists and/or rhythm for the percussionists.

The production ensemble also carried out a series of specific spatial, gestural, choreographic, and musical reelaborations of McRuvie's translated text to fit *kathakaḷi*'s theatrical conventions—a process that required reinterpretation of a number of *kathakaḷi* conventions as well as the creation of one new role (*vēṣam*). Since the *vēṣam*, literally "dress, mask, disguise," which is the "whole outward appearance, shape,"[14] determines not only the

Fig. 2. *Kathakaḷi King Lear.* In the midst of the storm mad Tom is discovered by Lear and the Fool. Lear: "Unaccommodated man is not more but such a poor, bare, forked animal as thou art." Photo credit: Annette Leday and David McRuvie.

external contours but also the internal nature of each character an actor plays, the decision on each *vēṣam* was the actor's beginning place in trying to create roles for which there was no tradition to follow.[15] A few roles were obvious and easy to select: the heroic King France, who marries Cordelia, defeats her evil sisters, and attempts to return Lear to his throne, had to be played as a *pacca*, the primarily green-colored, ideal, heroic, kingly type of character. Cordelia, the devoted, loving, chaste daughter, had to be played as a female *minukku*, or "radiant" type, whose makeup has a golden hue. Mad Tom was played as a *tēppu* with a smeared black face, a special category for characters close to animals in nature.

   The selection of *vēṣam* for the other major characters, including Goneril, Regan, the Fool, and Lear, generated considerable controversy in Kerala. For Lear the "knife" (*katti*) *vēṣam* was selected since its mixture of green and red symbolized his combination of kingly and turbulent attributes. In keeping with *kathakaḷi* convention, the role of Lear was split into two parts, each to be played by a senior *kathakaḷi* actor: the fully costumed Lear who appears at the opening of the play in court through the moment in the storm scene when he removes his crown and ornaments to become like mad Tom and the partially costumed mad Lear on the heath. For Goneril and Regan the *kari vēṣam*, typically used for demoness roles, was selected, and each was costumed in black and blue, respectively, symbolizing their primitive nature. Finally, for the Fool, no *kathakaḷi vēṣam* existed; the brahman clown (*vidūṣaka*), however, who serves as the king's court fool in the tradition of staging Sanskrit dramas (*kūṭiyāṭṭam*)—from

21

Fig. 3. *Kathakaḷi King Lear.* Lear is revealed after he has removed his ornaments and crown to be like mad Tom at the Kalamandam dress rehearsal. A great deal of controversy was raised when Kumaran Asan appeared bareheaded and virtually without makeup. Photo credit: Kunju Vasudevan Namboodiripad.

which *kathakaḷi* historically derived much—provided a model adapted for the production.

Appropriate ways of enacting each role and scene were developed in the collaborative rehearsal process. Beginning with the basic *vēṣam* in which each role was to be played, the spatial, choreographic, gestural, and musical elements were carefully reelaborated to fit the nonindigenous narrative and the peculiarities of the story's characters. Vasudevan Namboodiripad, former superintendent of the Kerala Kalamandalam, who served as an advisor for the production, explained that Leday and McRuvie made sure that the production was more than a superficial appropriation of *kathakaḷi* conventions and techniques:

Thought had to be given to not only the outer structure of *kathakaḷi*, but also to the inner structure and nuance. For example, for King Lear's initial entrance with his "curtain look" (*tiranōkku*) [i.e., gradual revelation of a character behind a hand-held curtain], you retain the visible structure of the look but you may change the inner structure of the nuance of expression in the look. The ultimate purpose of the curtain look is kept, but these subtle changes are made. Otherwise, it is just a copy of the same scene from any other curtain look of any other play in the repertory. To accomplish this, you must have people like Padmanabhan Asan [playing Lear] who have the capacity

Fig. 4. *Kathakaḷi King Lear.* For the Trivandrum performances and tour, more of the original costume and makeup were kept for Kumaran Asan's mad Lear. The trial scene in which Lear says, "Anatomize Regan; see what breeds about her heart." Photo credit: Annette Leday and David McRuvie.

to analyse the character's inner state or condition (*bhāva*). From this analysis every phrase must be worked out in detail.[16]

This sensitivity to the nuance of expressive interpretation was one reason for the decision that Leday would play Cordelia. McRuvie explained his view of the centrality of the Cordelia role to me: "What makes *King Lear* great is a great king, which is rare. Second in making the king is the Fool. But the one thing that can ruin it is Cordelia."[17] To McRuvie's decidedly Western eye, potential disaster threatened if one of the young male actors specializing in female roles (*strivēṣam*) were to act the "delicate role of Cordelia" in what McRuvie correctly characterized as "their boyish quality . . . that becomes kind of campy."[18]

The lengthy process of reelaboration created a completely new performance text that would provide both Malayali and European audiences with a new performance experience—a *kathakaḷi*-style production of Shakespeare.

Production, Perception, and Reception

Although *Kathakaḷi King Lear* was originally reelaborated for continental European and Malayali audiences, in fact, it played for audiences in four quite different cultural locations on its two tours: not only Kerala and continental Europe but also Singapore and Edinburgh. Both between and within each set of cultural boundaries there are "different viewing publics,"[19] each of which brought to the production not only their own native cultural

23

Fig. 5. *Kathakaḷi King Lear.* Goneril and Regan in battle. Photo credit: Annette Leday and David McRuvie.

assumptions but also an increasingly global flow of ideas, images, and information all of which affected their expectations about what they would experience, their perceptions and categories for understanding that experience, and therefore how they received and responded to *Kathakaḷi King Lear.* How are we to understand reception of *Kathakaḷi King Lear* among such diverse audiences?

Phenomenologist Maurice Natanson explains that our perceptions are shaped by a consciousness that posits horizons of probabilities, which constitute expectations.[20] In performance, expectations are created in four interdependent ways: (1) the daily experiences and cultural assumptions that inform the experience each spectator brings to the performance; (2) performance experiences similar to or different from the one that each is having now; (3) expectations created by publicity, word of mouth, etc.; and (4) what happens within the frame of the performance one is attending. In this fourth mode, a set of expectations is created as the performance is enacted.

The way in which *kathakaḷi* structures an audience's experience creates the possibility for a particular range of meaning very different from other genres of performance, whether that is American psychological realism or Japanese *noh.* Likewise, the way in which a Shakespeare play and its characters create the possibility for a particular range of meaning is very different from other types of dramas such as the *kathakaḷi* play *Naḷa Caritam* or *Peter Pan.*

As theater semiotician Marco De Marinis, following Umberto Eco, asserts: "Production and reception are strictly linked even though they obviously do not altogether coincide...[and that] a [performance] text

Fig. 6. *Kathakaḷi King Lear.* Lear: "She's gone forever." Photo credit: Annette Leday and David McRuvie.

postulates its own receiver as an indispensable condition not only of its own, concrete communicative ability, but also its own potential for meaning."[21] We have seen how *kathakaḷi*, as a genre of performance, postulates both a general audience and one of connoisseurs educated to receive a range of cultural meanings implicit in the conventions used to enact its stories. Each specific *kathakaḷi* play-in-performance articulates a specific set of meanings for both these generic audiences as well as its particular audiences. Like other adaptations of *kathakaḷi*, such as P. K. Devan's one-hour performances for tourists in Ernakulam, Kerala,[22] *Kathakaḷi King Lear* postulated its own receiver in the process of reelaboration described above and possesses its own potential for meaning different from other *kathakaḷi*.

When *kathakaḷi* performances of Indian epic stories are held for Kerala audiences, it may often be said with reception theorist Anne Ubersfeld that the "signs refer to what corresponds to them in the experience of the spectator. The fictional universe set before him [*sic*] summons up the referential universe of the spectator, that of his personal as well as his cultural experience."[23] In intercultural performance, however, codes and conventions easily read by those within one culture may be opaque to those outside.

Those working interculturally have evolved a number of different production strategies for deaing with this fundamental problem. Peter

Brook's recent production of India's great epic Mahabharata demonstrates one strategy. For Brook "art means extracting the essence from every detail so that the detail can reveal itself as a meaningful part of an inseparable whole."[24] Brook problematically assumes that if one can erase all the cultural codes in the way of reaching a hypothetically universal "reality of zero" common to all humanity, then "geography and history cease to exist."[25] Brook works with an international acting company whose style attempts to reach this zero state of communication by removing any cultural marks that might require of the audience the ability to read any special cultural codes. Consequently, "to tell [the Mahabharata] we had to avoid evoking India too strongly so as to not lead us away from human identification, but also we had to nevertheless tell it as a story rooted in Indian earth."[26]

If Brook erases distinctive cultural codes in his attempt to be universal, Leday and McRuvie chose to challenge their European audiences by maintaining as much of kathakali's structure and technique as possible.[27] Given the fact that Kathakali King Lear was originally reelaborated for two quite different audiences, played in four quite different geographical/cultural contexts, and has conventions or content that are nonindigenous to one or more of its audiences, I want to ask the following questions: Who was the receiver postulated by the production? What potential meanings were implicit in the production? What meanings were read into the production? Specifically, how was the production received?

European Reception: From "Curiosity" to "Bewitching Ritual" to a "Moving Performance"

For anyone seeing something from outside one's own "culture" for the first time, there is bound to be some degree of difference in assimilation and understanding of what is being seen and heard between an indigenous and nonindigenous audience. Moreover, as Anne Ubersfeld explains,

> when he is faced with signs which he does not understand to which he cannot give a name (objects, gestures, discourse), which do not refer to anything in his experience, or, more simply, which pose a problem for him, the spectator's own inventiveness is stimulated: it is up to him to manufacture the relationship between the sign and its intelligibility, or its relationship to the world.[28]

The West has a long and continuing history of manufacturing a variety of meanings for nonindigenous customs, persons, or cultural artifacts/performances it could not (or did not wish to) understand. Historically, the West took this experience of difference and encapsulated it in a series of discourses on the cultural Other.[29] In the Western-initiated colonial drama of subjugation and domination, India was cast in several key roles. Most important, as South Asian historian Ronald Inden relates, for empiricists and rationalists that role was "THE unchangeable" and/or "THE absolutely different" (and therefore inscrutable and dominatable), and, for romantics, the "SPIRITUAL or IDEAL" Other.[30] As the period of colonial expansion reached its final climax at the turn of the nineteenth century, this drama of subjugation and domination was played out symbolically rather than literally at the "World's" Fairs[31] and even at Coney Island and other amusement parks where exotic Indian nautch dancers were featured in the Durbar of Delhi. Our abilities to read, understand, assimilate, and even participate in Indian performance have been shaped by these discourses of Otherness, which feed both our imagination of Otherness and the way we describe it.[32]

Kathakaḷi King Lear generated all these responses and more. On continental Europe, the original production was received with great and near universal acclaim by French dance critics, who filled their columns with information on kathakaḷi interspersed with comments ranging from F. C.'s vacuous but appreciative "a splendidly colorful show,"[33] to Pichot's more adamant expression of appreciation—"a dazzling marriage" of kathakaḷi and Shakespeare filled with "intensity, energy, and extravaganza."[34] Not surprisingly, in Shakespeare's home, responses focused on the production as a specific interpretation of Shakespeare's Lear rather than on kathakaḷi per se. The colorfully opinionated British theater press greeted the Edinburgh Festival performances with less than universal praise. They reaped everything from Michael Billington's cynical scorn ("Empty gestures of a frustrating Lear")[35] to Charles Spencer's appreciative evocation of the production as both exotic and mysterious ("Hypnotic power of an Indian Lear")[36] to Randall Stevenson's grudging appreciation ("Beat of a different drum"), which marvelled that even if "Shakespeare transformed into the traditional, colorful, highly stylised dance drama of Kerala . . . doesn't sound entirely promising . . . [it is] one of the most enthralling performances of the Festival."[37] The one near universal point of agreement among most of the British press was that Kathakaḷi King Lear had, as Tom Morris put it, "little to do with Shakespeare."[38]

Beyond the general praise and blame, there were those like the reviewer from the Cannes-Matin/Nice-Matin who found the production inscrutible and difficult to decode: "we do not have all of the keys to this code, which allows us only sporadically to decipher them."[39] For the writer from La Presse de la Manche the only pleasure of the production was the spectacle of the costumes: "The costumes are the main attraction of the show at least for the western audience, incapable of understanding the complex language of the hand and face gestures, somewhere between mime and a sign language conversation."[40] For Sergio Trombetta from La Danse this inscrutability made the spectacle fascinating: "The interplay of the dance, the facial expressions and the hands remain impenetrable and fascinating."[41]

Some like Grandmontagne writing for Le Telegramme responded to the difficulties of reading the production by inventing kathakaḷi as a timeless, Jungian, dreamlike world:

Without any training, you can appreciate this theater by allowing yourself to be invaded by the music, by the rhythms; by marvelling at the splendid, glittering, colorful costumes, the make-up that completely re-sculpts the actors' faces and makes them timeless even while accentuating the expression of each individual character....

You can, without any training, be subjugated, letting the music intoxicate you.[42]

Pierre Gilles responded similarly, finding in the production a realization of an Artaudian reverie in which "the drama of the aging King Lear . . . [was] promoted to the ranks of the sacred, rendered to the 'primitive destination' of theater—which Artaud sought—and, therefore, to the universal."[43]

The most extreme problem with response is when either too many demands are made on the spectators so that they withdraw their participation or audience members are unwilling to make any attempt to respond to the performance and therefore withdraw their participation.[44] It appears that the latter may have been the case for John Percival of the *London Times*, who, in a remarkably snide, nothing short of racist, tongue-in-cheek commentary entitled "Lear's heath at half blast," ungenerously wrote of the vocalists as "two fellows with skirts, bare chests and cymbals," of Tom as a "dirty little chap," of the adaptation as "crippling," and the production as a "curiosity."[45]

If, for some, *Kathakaḷi King Lear* was inscrutable—or all spectacle—for others, the production communicated at more than a level of surface exoticism. I think it an oversimplification to assume with Bennett that "audiences are at best 'fascinated' with performances that do not fall into their cultural experience, performances that resist or deny the usual channels of decoding."[46] Randall Stevenson provides a balanced and sensible account of his fascination with *kathakaḷi*'s spectacle, his simple enjoyment of its exciting moments of obvious and colorful action, as well as the subtler way in which the performance affected him:

> From the opening moment, when the screen brought on to signal scene changes drops to reveal magnificently poised and costumed performers, *Kathakaḷi* offered spectacle and simple excitement. The two onstage percussionists add a mesmeric heartbeat to every move and turn onstage—creating a devastating prelude to the storm, for example—while the singers who chant the narrative fill in tone and colour for every scene. More subtly, what seems "simple" spectacle quickly communicates a great deal of emotion. Stylized movement, minute repeated hand gestures, progressively indicate Lear's poised withdrawal, even before Goneril's ecstatic devil dance steals a vision of insanity and the stresses which create it.

The argument I want to make regarding the kind of European reception of *Kathakaḷi King Lear* represented by Stevenson's review depends upon a prior understanding of the Malayali reception.

Malayali Reception: From "Bouquets to Brickbats"

Although *Kathakaḷi King Lear* was coproduced by the premiere Kerala State government arts school, featured some of the most distinguished performers of the *kathakaḷi* stage, played well over thirty performances on its continental tour and at Edinburgh, and, with the important exceptions noted above in the British press, was generally appreciated and praised on tour, *Indian Express* journalist Paul Jacob recalled one year after the original production that it opened in Kerala to "no great critical or popular acclaim."[47] As early as the January 1989 experimental staging of four scenes at the Kerala Kalamandalam, the production aroused considerable controversy in Kerala, a situation reflected in the *Hindu* staff writer's report that "comments from the spectators . . . came out in the form of a mixed bag of bouquets and brickbats."[48]

In Kerala during the final months of rehearsal before the production opened, I read and heard the artistic and aesthetic "brickbats" thrown at the production. Debated both within rehearsals as well as in the public and press, the controversy swirled around the following five issues all having to do with the "sense of appropriateness" (*aucityam bodham*) in *kathakaḷi*: (1) Were non-Indian, nonepic, nonmythic stories like Lear appropriate for the *kathakaḷi* stage? (2) To what degree was the title character of Lear kingly? (3) Was the selection of the *katti vēṣam* appropriate for Lear, or should the heroic *pacca* have been selected? (4) During the storm scene, was it appropriate to have Lear "realistically" remove part or all of his kingly accoutrements and typifying makeup, or should his relative "nakedness" have been imagined by the audience? (5) Was it appropriate to borrow the clown's (*vidūṣaka*) makeup and costume directly from *kūṭiyāṭṭam?*

All five issues are part of a continuing "internal cultural debate"[49] within the *kathakaḷi* cultural community over the limits of experimentation within the tradition.[50] Since the dawn of the modern institutional era of *kathakaḷi*'s history with the founding of the Kerala Kalamandalam by the great Malayali poet Vallathol in 1930, *kathakaḷi* has been adapted both by practitioners from within the tradition and by artists and entrepreneurs from without. Some of these adaptations are responses to an increasingly intercultural, global artistic economy such as *Lear*, while others have been shaped by the complex contemporary sociopolitical and economic realities within Kerala itself.[51] As there are wide differences of opinion on these issues, my task here is to represent several parties to the debate, situate each point of view so that the terms of argument informing each is clear, and discuss how this internal debate shaped perception and reception of *Kathakaḷi King Lear*.

Given limitations of space, I want to explore Malayali response to the production primarily through the eyes of one of the most visible and certainly the most outspoken champions of a radically conservative interpretation of the *kathakaḷi* tradition, Appakoothan Nayar, one of the founders of the Margi Kathakali School in the capital city, Trivandrum. An engineer by training who holds a graduate degree from the University of

Michigan, Appakoothan Nayar is the architect of the uniquely styled Kerala Kalamandalam theater where *kathakali* is regularly performed. His response to *Kathakali King Lear* was straightforward and blunt: "I could not stand it. . . . Even though there are thirty performances abroad, after five years, nobody here will remember it. It will die a natural death."[52] To understand Appakoothan Nayar's negative response to *Kathakali King Lear,* it is necessary to explain the aesthetic that informs his point of view.

Appakoothan Nayar differentiates between two levels of aesthetic realization. The first and "lower" aesthetic he calls "sensual" or "worldly" because it limits reception to the feelings of the five senses. Such reception is a simplistic and immediate sensual response, i.e., "when you see [touch, taste, feel, etc.] a thing you like it, but it doesn't go to the mind." An example is the appearance of an everyday character like the elephant mahout in *Kamsavadham,* where the spectator's simple recognition of the character could be characterized as sensual, immediate, and based on what one sees in daily life.

In contrast is what Appakoothan Nayar calls an "aesthetics of the mind," i.e., an act of reception that resonates long beyond the immediate apprehension of the five senses. It is an aesthetic built on the cultivation of the aesthetic sensibilities of the connoisseur's tasting and savoring of *rasa.*[53] This interpretation of *kathakali's* aesthetic as "of the mind" is derived from *kutiyāttam* and the classical Sanskrit drama tradition. Sanskrit scholar Barbara Stoler Miller calls the aesthetic of the most celebrated Sanskrit poet, Kalidasa, an "aesthetic of memory" and identifies Sanskrit theater as a "theater of memory."[54] In many Sanskrit dramas such as Kalidasa's *Sákuntala* and Bhasa's *The Vision of Vasavadatta,* the act of remembering is both a literal mode of reconciling and relating love-in-separation and love-in-union and remembrance of a "deeper metaphysical kind."[55]

> Indian epistemologists hold that whatever we perceive by means of the sense organs leaves an impression on the mind. Memory occurs when a latent impression is awakened. Indian literary theorists define memory as a recollection of a condition of happiness or misery, whether it was conceived in the mind or actually occurred. In what is considered one of the key passages of Sanskrit aesthetics, the tenth-century Kashmiri philosopher Abhinavagupta explains what Kalidasa means by "memory." It is not discursive recollection of past events, but rather an intuitive insight into the past that transcends personal experience, into the imaginative universe that beauty evokes.[56]

In *kathakali* this aesthetic of mind is accomplished through extended narrative and performative elaboration of the basic story and playtext. An example from the first of Unnayi Warrier's famous series of four plays, *Nala Caritam,* will illustrate the process. The first of the Nala plays dramatizes the budding love of King Nala and Damayanti from the moment they hear of each other's perfection and beauty. The play opens with a scene intended to awaken Nala's imagination to Damayanti's beauty. The sage Narada is visiting Nala when he suggestively implants the idea in Nala's mind that he should "waste not [his] birthright," i.e., it is time to consider marriage. Having implanted the idea of marriage in Nala's mind, Narada goes on to describe Damayanti in florid poetic terms:

> In Kandinapur there lives a beauty,
> A gem among women,
> Damayanti by name.
> Even the *devas* have fallen in love with her.
> But mark me.
> Jewels rightfully belong to kings.
> The *devas* may claim only *yagnas* (sacrifices) offered in their
>   honour.
> Perfect one, paragon among kings,
> Strive to win this jewel for your wife.[57]

The poetic conceits imbedded in this *padam* provide opportunities for the actor to embody each image through gesture language, thereby serving as the vehicle for the creation of an image of Damayanti not only in Nala's mind but also in the mind of the spectator.

There follows an interpolation (*āṭṭam*) in which Narada assures Nala that he will win Damayanti since she already has set her heart on him alone. Immediately after Narada's departure, Nala enacts the following *sloka* in which the actor embodies Nala's state of mind at that moment: "Having heard Narada's words, and the words of other travellers, Nala's mind, already immersed in thinking about Damayanti, became pained by his longing for her."[58] This is a moment of consummate "interior" acting in which he embodies *cinta bhāva* [one of the thirty-two transitory states (*sañchāri bhāva*) of the *Nāṭyaśāstra*], best translated as a state of "reflecting." Nala's reflections on Damayanti cause him pain because he is unsure whether he will actually realize union with her. The actor, lingering over these moments of reflection, must take sufficient time to allow his elaboration of Nala's inner mental state to be relished by the audience. Unlike the semiotically more complex reading of an actor's delivery in hand gestures of the specific dialogue of the text, reception of this particular scene does not depend upon technical knowledge but on an audience that knows the story as well as the actors and therefore possesses a similar set of associations regarding Nala's character, state of mind, and the possible associations conjured in that state.

Returning to Appakoothan Nayar's point of view, it is precisely moments such as this which are the epitome of the aesthetic that informs his point of view about *kathakaḷi* in general and his critique of *Kathakaḷi King Lear* in particular. For Appakoothan Nayar the two major problems with *Kathakaḷi King Lear* are its all too brief two-hour running time and its nonepic characters. In contrast to *King Lear*, where everything is cut short, Appakoothan Nayar is proud of the fact that the recent Margi production of Warrier's *Naḷa Caritam* expanded its running time to thirty total hours to allow more performative elaboration than usual. Appa-koothan Nayar told me how one friend commented: "If you go on like this it will come to 365 days."

To which he said:

> "It will go on to one thousand days!" And this is precisely why I don't like *Kathakaḷi King Lear.* The potential for elaboration *must* be there. In most [new] *kathakaḷi* they simply translate the text into gestures and say, "that's *kathakaḷi.*" But that is *not kathakaḷi!* You must take the text and see how much scope there is for expansion and decoration.

From Appakoothan Nayar's perspective, it is impossible to elaborate nonepic stories because the characters are "not fit for *kathakaḷi.*" Unlike epic characters, who "never existed" and therefore must be created in the imagination of the spectator, Lear, like Jesus, Karl Marx, or Franklin Roose-velt, is for Appakoothan Nayar a historical figure who at one time existed and for whom therefore one already has a set of associations.

> Although one has images of epic characters, the image is not supported by any visual comparison because the characters never existed. Ravana is supposed to have ten heads and twenty hands—can he ever have existed in any stage of human evolution?[59] Lear's features you know because he was a human being. But in the case of Ravana, he is the concretization of a concept. . . . The concretization of the abstract is there [in ritual and theatrical arts] in order to reach the abstract.[60]

For Appakoothan Nayar *kathakaḷi* is a metaphysical theater of the imag-ination where the spectator "creates [each character] in his mind," and for Appakoothan Nayar the spectator's ability to freely imagine, or "take in his mind," a Lear was disrupted because, he says, "I have that [previous] image [of Lear] in mind."

Lest Appakoothan Nayar's metaphysical theater of the imagination be perceived as unproblematic, I want to situate his discourse in the larger debate over the role of the past in the Indian present by reflecting on the astute observation by South Asian poet and scholar A. K. Ramanujan: "In a culture like the Indian, the past does not pass. It keeps on providing paradigms and ironies for the present, or at least that's the way it seems."[61] On the one hand, Appakoothan Nayar's argument against *Kathakaḷi King Lear* is constructed from an aesthetic paradigm of the past—the *rasa* aesthetic—and his institution is an attempt to insure that this aesthetic remains central to *kathakaḷi*'s creativity in the future. It is a paradigm written for and from the privileged position of the traditional patron/connoisseur for whose pleasure *kathakaḷi* was originally created. While his is an inventive form of intercultural discourse in its use of the Western intellectual icons of history and evolution as part of its argument against experimentation, it is a reactionary one that stakes exclusive claim to interpreting what is or is not appropriate within the tradition and what qualifies as a legitimate form of experimentation. Appakoothan Nayar's critique implies a denial of the validity of experiments attempting to reach audiences other than connoisseurs. Such experiments range from *Kathakaḷi King Lear* to populist adaptations with little elaboration for Malayali mass audiences at annual temple festivals to the 1987 production of *Humanity's Success* (*Manavidyam*), the latter of which was a dramatized critique of imperialist aggression authored by Iyyemgode Sreedharan (translator of *Kathakaḷi King Lear*), staged primarily for leftist political audiences.[62]

Aesthetic Congruence and Kingly Dissonance

Although *Kathakaḷi King Lear* evoked little aesthetic delight in Appakoothan Nayar and some other *kathakaḷi* connoisseurs, for at least some among the European and Malayali audiences the subtlety of *kathakaḷi*'s interior acting *was* communicated. I refer especially to the penultimate and ultimate moments of pathos in the production—the seventh and ninth scenes of the production in which Lear is first reunited with Cordelia, then dies from grief over her loss.

> *His crown having been placed beside him by the Fool, Lear slowly wakes. Cordelia stands back, but the fool urges her to present herself to Lear. Lears sits up.*
> Lear: I do not know whether I am alive or dead. I do not remember these clothes.
> *Cordelia:* Sir, do you know me?
> Lear: I fear I am not in my right mind, but I think you are my child.
> *Cordelia:* Yes! I am, I am your child!
> Lear: You have cause to hate me.
> *Cordelia:* No cause, no cause.
> Lear: Forgive me, I am old and foolish.
> *They embrace. The Soldier appears. He claims Cordelia and the Fool as prisoners.* [After their departure] *Lear picks up his kiridam [crown].*[63]

In the battle that ensues during the eighth scene, Regan orders her soldier to kill his prisoners, Cordelia and the Fool. The order sends France into a wild fury, played out in *kathakaḷi*'s typical stylized battle choreography as he slays both Regan and Goneril. As the final scene opens, the vocalists create a transition from the cacophany of battle with its loud-sounding drums to the pathos of loss and death as they sing the opening *śloka* in a slow rhythm, reporting what has happened, and telling what will happen: "The young Queen and the King's Fool have been brutally murdered. The old King finds his beloved daughter dead. He dies from grief and so ends his terrible suffering." Even though the Western audience cannot understand what the vocalists are singing, the pathos carried by the music alone sets the appropriate mood. The hand-held curtain is lowered to reveal Cordelia's body.

> *Lear enters in full* katti vēṣam. *He walks slowly but stands very straight. Lear approaches Cordelia. He turns her head and recognizes her. He screams with grief. He falls down beside his daughter.*
> Lear: I know when someone is alive or dead. My child is as dead as earth.

In spite of reservations about certain aspects of the production, reviewers of the Edinburgh performances in particular focused much of their positive commentary on Lear's pathos over the loss of Cordelia. Although Tom Morris, writing in the *Times Literary Supplement*, responded to most of the production with "remote fascination," it was different with the closing scene: "at Lear's cry over the dead Cordelia, magical and spot-lit, there is a frightening and uninterrupted moment of agonized theatrical communication." For Randall Stevenson of the *Independent*, who responded positively to the shape, contours, and variety of the entire production, the closing scene in which Lear dies of grief was also a profoundly moving moment:

> Lear's concluding rhythmic keening over Cordelia, picked up by the percussion, provides almost the first remotely human sound from performers rather than the accompanying singers.
> It both wrings the heart and moves the performance forward into another dimension: towards the awesome, elemental world from which Shakespeare's original vision was compounded.

Among Malayalis who responded at least in part favorably, V. Kaldharan acknowledged that both Kumaran Nayar and Padmanabhan Nayar were "successful in portraying the full depth of King Lear's sorrow (*karuṇa rasa*)."[64]

I would suggest that the emotive resonance that Stevenson describes was a moment of aesthetic congruence where at least some among the Edinburgh audience experienced the resonance of aesthetic delight similar to if not the same as a Malayali connoisseur's arousal of *rasa*. As steeped in Shakespeare as a Kerala audience in the Mahabharata and Nala story, at least some in the Edinburgh audience share a common knowledge of Lear's mental state equal to that of the actors playing the roles. The knowledgeable audience "knows" that Lear's mental state moves from his deranged wandering, forgetfulness, and impromptu ravings to one of the dawn of remembrance when he awakes from his sleep.

McRuvie's sparse text allows the *kathakaḷi* performer the performative time necessary to embody through internal acting the appropriate *bhāvas*—in scene 7, *cinta bhāva*, "reflection," or "remembrance." Lear, in a dreamlike state of forgetfulness, awakens to Cordelia and the Fool. In the process of remembering, he gradually remembers Cordelia, his loss of her, his foolishness in rejecting her, and the mental agony of their separation. Although the tone and specific dramatic context and circumstances are quite different, Lear's act of reflection, or remembrance, is similar to that of Nala. The scene is that moment of classic Western recognition in which Lear realizes his loss. It makes possible the Western audience's experience of Lear as a tragic character.

As staged at Edinburgh, the entire final scene could be characterized as Lear's grieving cry over the loss of his beloved daughter. When Lear returns in the final scene to discover the dead Cordelia, he is resplendent in his full costume and makeup. With only one line "spoken" during the entire scene, Padmanabhan Nayar was free to elaborate, through interior acting, *śoka bhāva*—that is, the pathos of his loss—and the moment-by-moment search for any signs that she might still be alive. Since he was playing Lear as a *katti*-type character considered less refined than the idealized kingly *pacca* roles, he was permitted by convention to utter sounds. In his brilliant elaboration of this long dramatic moment, Padmanabhan Asan chose to make full use of the psychophysical means of embodiment in the *kathakaḷi* repertory, subtly uttering whimpers through the control of his breath and manifesting other signs of the grief of loss such as trembling. The sounds and signs of Lear's grief gradually draw out of him his own life force (*prāṇa-vāyu*) so that he collapses beside his daughter, dead of grief.

The narrative and mimetic simplicity of these scenes meant that it was unnecessary for the Western audience to be able to read *kathakaḷi*'s codified gesture language to follow or appreciate the action. Given the familiar trajectory of both the Lear story and the narrative of pathos, at least some in the Edinburgh and European audiences savored *karuṇa rasa*—pathos—the closest emotional tone in Indian theater to Western tragedy.

Kathakaḷi King Lear's success at communicating pathos is not unproblematic. The positive reception of Padmanabhan Nayar's empathic cry of loss over Cordelia unquestionably assumes a modernist paradigm of the main character's emotional state as the essence of the pleasure of dramatic reception. It was also a problem for some in the Malayali audience—how could one appreciate a play in which the predominant *rasa*, or flavor of aesthetic delight, is pathos and in which the king does not act like a King? Understating the case somewhat, Malayali reviewer Vinita noted, "It is unusual to conclude a *kathakaḷi* on a tragic note."[65]

But even more problematic was Lear's behavior. *Kathakaḷi* actor Nelliyode Vasudevan Namboodiri, who played the role of the Fool in the original experimental staging of the storm scene and Goneril on the second tour, described his problems with understanding Lear: "When Lear's older daughters tell him they love him so much, and Cordelia says she can only give half her love, he believes all these things. It is difficult to believe that Lear, at 80 years of age, with all his life experience, would respond this way to his daughters!"[66] V. Kaladharan raised the same problem in his *Mathrabhumi* article, noting that even master percussionist Krishnankutty Poduval, who helped conceive the production, was puzzled by the fact that

Lear would "forgo his daughter who is prepared to share her love between her father and her husband."[67] Given the fact that social convention dictates that a daughter will naturally give her love to her husband and that tragedy and the individual human weaknesses that prompt Lear's downfall have little resonance in Kerala culture, where human kinship was historically idealized and related to maintenance of the cosmic order, Lear's behavior toward Cordelia appeared naive, to some Malayalis, even silly. As Kaladharan concluded, for those in the audience for whom Lear could *not* be perceived as a king, "the theme which is important for a Western audience becomes totally awkward for an Indian audience."[68]

Conclusion

Although *Kathakaḷi King Lear* was conceived ideally as an intercultural project to be performed for Kerala and European audiences, the commercial realities (over thirty performances abroad and two in Kerala), the Western Lear narrative, and McRuvie's directorial eye naturally shaped the production for a primarily Western theatergoing public. In doing so, it may not have been as well received by Malayali audiences as Western audiences, but it brought to its Western audiences an integrity hard to find in a number of other intercultural experiments. In contrast to Peter Brook's naturalized Mahabharata, which "flattened" the Indianness of the epic's cultural markers and suppressed any use of India's codified performance techniques,[69] Leday and McRuvie's project intentionally kept an active tension between a simplified Western narrative played in a fully codified theatrical and choreographic reelaboration of that narrative.

As Daryl Chin argues, in the increasingly intercultural world in which we live where "the interconnections of the geopolitical structure are so intricate and so intertwined that there is no way out of the dilemma of [inter]dependence. And that dependence . . . means that diplomacy must be vigilant."

> Interculturalism can so easily accommodate an agenda of cultural imperialism. This is what happens when Lee Breuer tosses disparate elements together pell-mell as an indicator of disintegration; this is what happens when Robert Wilson's staging overwhelms Heiner Müller's text; this is what happens when Peter Brook distorts the narrative structure of Indian mythology and of Chekhovian dramaturgy. The sense of imposition is omnipresent in these enterprises.[70]

Kathakaḷi King Lear was an intercultural project that did not impose meaning. With its collaborative process of creation and its respect for the *kathakaḷi* aesthetic, it "allow[ed] meaning to arise from the material."[71] This was so even if the meaning and pleasure communicated were part of a modernist paradigm and even if they did not reach some hypothetically universal realm of communication.

NOTES

1. Susan Bennett, *Theatre Audiences: A Theory of Production and Reception* (London: Routledge, 1990), 101.

2. Jean-François Lyotard, *The Postmodern Condition: A Report of Knowledge* (Minneapolis: University of Minnesota Press, 1984), xxiv.

3. James Clifford, *The Predicament of Culture: Twentieth-Century Ethnography, Literature, and Art* (Cambridge: Harvard University Press, 1988), 230.

4. Ibid., 231, 14.

5. Arjun Appadurai and Carol A. Breckenridge, "The Situation of Public Culture," in *Modern Sites: Consumption and Contestation in a Postcolonial World* (in press), 3.

6. Putu Wijaya, "Indonesian Culture," trans. Ellen Rafferty (unpub. MS, 1986).

7. Clifford, *Predicament of Culture*, 14–15. See also Arjun Appadurai, "Disjuncture and Difference in the Global Cultural Economy," *Public Culture* 2, no. 2 (1990): 1–24; Appadurai and Breckenridge, "Situation of Public Culture"; Appadurai and Breckenridge, "Why Public Culture?" *Public Culture* 1, no. 1 (1988): 5–9; Roy Wagner, *The Invention of Culture* (Chicago: University of Chicago Press); and other articles in *Public Culture*.

8. The second production, no longer associated with the Kerala Kalamandalam, used a new Malayalam translation, several new cast members, and some revisions in the staging. My analysis of the European performances is based on viewing a videotape of the Edinburgh production and the numerous reviews of the continental and Edinburgh performances.

9. Bennett, *Theater Audiences*, 114. See also Marco De Marinis, "Dramaturgy of the Spectator," *TDR: A Journal of Performance Studies* 31, no. 2 (1987): 100–114.

10. The two great Indian epics (Ramayana and Mahabharata) and puranas (a diverse collection of wisdom and stories which "become the bibles of popular Hinduism" [William Theodore De Bary, *Sources of Indian Tradition* (New York: Columbia University Press, 1958), 1:323]) are the sources of most traditional modes of storytelling and performance. Of the eighteen major and eighteen minor puranas, the *Bhagavata Purana* is the most popular and widely circulated. Especially dear to devotees of Visnu, this purana tells the story of the life of Lord Krishna.

11. On women *kathakaḷi* performers, see Diane Daughterty and Marlene Pitkow, "Who Wears the Skirts in Kathakali?" *TDR: A Journal of Performance Studies* (in press).

12. Annette Leday and David McRuvie, *Kathakaḷi King Lear* (program) (Paris: Keli, 1989), 1.

13. Patrice Pavis, "Dancing with *Faust*: A Semiotician's Reflections on Barba's Intercultural Mise-en-scène," *TDR: A Journal of Performance Studies* 33, no. 3 (1989): 37–57.

14. Rev. H. Gundert, *A Malayalam and English Dictionary* (Mangalore: C. Stolz, 1872), 995.

15. The actor uses the *vēṣam* to cover and thereby "transform" himself when he assumes a role. For a discussion, see Pramod Kale, *The Theatric Universe: A Study of the Natyasastra* (Bombay: Popular Prakashan, 1974), 58–59.

16. Personal interview, 9 December 1989.

17. Personal interview, 29 September 1989.

18. McRuvie was referring to the fact that actors who play female roles receive special training in three modes of expression used exclusively for playing many

female roles: a coy, "pretended" shyness; a pouting contempt; and, similarly, a pouting anger. In all three modes of expression, there is clearly a set of quotation marks put around each emotional state which says, "This is pretended" or "I don't really mean this." Therefore, when a female character is enacting this special shyness toward her beloved, the subtext is, "I'm just acting shy and you can really have me." Although there are a few strong and less submissive female roles played in which shyness, contempt, and anger are expressed more directly without the quotation marks, they are the exception rather than the rule. Consequently, McRuvie's hesitancy about using a male *kathakali* actor for the role of Cordelia.

19. Bennett, *Theatre Audiences*, 101. See also Marvin Carlson's important essay on the "local habitation" of performance, "Local Semiosis and Theatrical Interpretation," *Theatre Semiotics* (Bloomington: Indiana University Press, 1990).

20. Maurice Natanson, *Phenomenology and the Social Sciences*, vol. 1 (Evanston, Ill.: Northwestern University Press, 1973).

21. Marco De Marinis, "Dramaturgy of the Spectator," 102.

22. See Phillip B. Zarrilli, "Demystifying *Kathakali*," *Sangeet Natak* 43 (1979): 48–59.

23. Anne Ubersfeld, "The Pleasure of the Spectator," *Modern Drama* 25, no. 1 (1982): 131.

24. Jean-Claude Carriere, *The Mahabharata* (New York: Harper and Row, 1987), xiv.

25. Richard Schechner, "Talking with Peter Brook," *TDR* 30, no. 1 (1986): 55.

26. Ibid., 68. For a critique, see Rustom Bharucha's "Peter Brook's 'Mahabharata': A View from India," in *Theatre and the World* (Columbia, Mo.: South Asia Publications, 1990), 94–120.

27. Similar to Brook, Barba seeks a form of metacultural communication, but, rather than erasing cultural distinctions, he has his group of international actors each keep her distinctively enculturated movement vocabulary while developing the mise-en-scène, thereby seeking to real "culture . . . through cultures" (Pavis, "Dancing with *Faust*," 53).

28. Ubersfeld, "Pleasure of the Spectator," 133.

29. For a comprehensive overview, see Edward Said's *Orientalism* (New York: Pantheon Books, 1978).

30. Ronald Inden, "Orientalist Constructions of India," *Modern Asian Studies* 20, no. 3 (1986): 401–46.

31. See Burton Benedict, *The Anthropology of World's Fairs* (Berkeley: Lowie Museum of Anthropology, 1983); and Robert W. Rydell, *All the World's a Fair* (Chicago: University of Chicago Press, 1984).

32. One of the earliest performance examples of our mystification of India is Ruth St. Denis's creation of her 1905 "Radha" where she danced the role of this "SPIRITUAL OTHER." See Joan Erdman, "Performance as Translation: Uday Shankar in the West," *TDR: A Journal of Performance Studies* 31, no. 1 (1987): 64–88.

33. F. C., "'Le roi Lear' en Kathakali!" *Progres* (21 November 1989).

34. Nadine Pichot, "Le Roi Lear en Theatre Kathakali: Intensite, force et feerie," *Semaine Côte d'Azur* (8 December 1989).

35. Michael Billington, "Empty Gestures of a Frustrating Lear," *Guardian*, 17 August 1990.

36. Charles Spencer, "Hypnotic Power of an Indian Lear," *Daily Telegraph*, 17 August 1990.

37. Randall Stevenson, "Beat of a Different Drum," *Independent*, 18 August 1990.

38. Tom Morris, "*A Midsummer Night's Dream*," *Times Literary Supplement*, 24 August 1990.

39. "L'histoire du 'Roi Lear' Contée en Kathakali," *Cannes-Matin* (*Nice-Matin*), 26 November 1989.

40. "Le Roi Lear Version Kathakali: Un Spectacle Haut en Coleurs," *Presse de la Manche*, 9 November 1989.

41. Sergio Trombetta, "Le Roi Lear," *Danse*, 3 October 1989.

42. Cl. Grandmontagne, "Le 'Roi Lear' par le Theatre Kathakali: Deroutant Mais Superbe," *Telegramme*, 9 October 1989.

43. Pierre Gilles, "L'automne Indien du Roi Lear," *Ouest France*, 15 September 1989.

44. Ubersfeld, "Pleasure of the Spectator," 133.

45. John Percival, "Lear's Heath at Half-Blast," *Times* (London), 17 August 1990.

46. Bennett, *Theatre Audiences*, 103.

47. Paul Jacob, "King Lear Coming Again," *Indian Express* (Kochi ed.), 5 August 1990.

48. "'King Lear' in Kathakaḷi," *Hindu*, 13 January 1989.

49. D. Parkin, *The Cultural Definition of Political Response* (London: Academic Press, 1978).

50. The paradigmatic past is present for the *kathakaḷi* actor each time he approaches any important role on stage. The "sense of appropriateness" guiding his acting is imbibed first and foremost from his teacher, from the traditional method of playing each role taught in training, from observation of senior actors (especially his own teacher) playing the role on stage, and, finally, from one's own understanding of what is appropriate in each dramatic context.

The degree to which performers feel responsible for creating only what they interpret as appropriate to the context is illustrated in the great *kūṭiyāṭṭam* actor Guru Ammannur Madhava Chakyar's account of how and why he "modified slightly" his enactment of Bali's death scene in *Balivadham* ("The Death of Bali"). After recounting his family's traditional right to perform the play, he recalls how, "of all the actors I saw in my childhood, Kitangur Rama Chakyar, who took the role of Bali, remains indelibly engraved in my memory. His Bali was unrivalled indeed" (G. Venu, *Production of a Play in Kūṭiyāṭṭam* [Irinjalakuda: Natankairali, 1989]: iv). Eventually, as he grew older and matured as an actor, "the rare fortune of acting Bali descended" on him and, in his words, he was

> emboldened to [make the slight modification] by the training I received from Bhagavatar Kunjunni Tampuran of the royal family of Kodungalloor. I went to Tampuran, who had done deep research in the art of drama, to learn the art strictly according to the principles laid down by Bharata [author of the authoritative *Nāṭyaśāstra*]. I was his student for two years. He taught me also the minute details of climacteric breathing. This particular training took about forty days. The various Svasas [breaths or internal winds] . . . are controlled, one after another, appropriately to make the death-throes realistic. This is the essence of my modification. (v)

Although *Kathakaḷi King Lear* was a new production for which no precedents had been set for particular roles, nevertheless there was very real pressure felt by some of the actors that they might be severely criticized for transgressing the boundaries of appropriateness. This was especially true of junior actor Balasubramaniam, who was playing the role of the fool in a *vēṣam* over which controversy raged to and past the official opening production.

51. For a discussion of specific adaptations, translations, and transformations

that have shaped *kathakaḷi* to suit a particular audience, see Phillip Zarrilli, *The Kathakaḷi Complex* (Delhi: Abhinav, 1984).

52. Personal interview, 24 October 1989.

53. On *rasa*, see Rachel Van M. Baumer and James R. Brandon, *Sanskrit Drama in Performance* (Honolulu: University of Hawaii Press, 1981), 209–57; and V. K. Chari, *Sanskrit Criticism* (Honolulu: University of Hawaii Press, 1990).

54. Barbara Stoller Miller, *Theatre of Memory: The Plays of Kalidasa* (New York: Columbia University Press, 1984).

55. Ibid., 40.

56. Ibid.

57. V. Subramanya Iyer, trans., *Naḷa Caritam Attakatha* (*Journal of South Asian Literature*) 10, nos. 2–4 (1975): 211–48.

58. Trans. M. P. Sankaran Namboodiri.

59. Ravanna and Raman are adversaries in one of India's two great epics, the Ramayana. Ravanna is the ten-headed demon-king of Lanka who captures Raman's wife, Sita, and whom Raman rescues with the help of the devoted monkey-god, Hanuman.

60. P. C. Namboodiri made the same point when he contrasted the historical characters who appeared in a locally initiated and produced World War II *kathakaḷi* [Hitler (the evil red beard), Roosevelt, Chiang Kai-shek, and Stalin (the heroic beneficient "green" character type)] with epic characters: "They are real human beings you have seen either in motion pictures or in photos. But you don't know what Shiva is. People can only imagine what is his exact nature. The costumes fit only such characters. So realism in that [historical] way is not appropriate to a dance-drama like Kathakaḷi" (quoted in Judith Lynn Hanna, *The Performer-Audience Connection* [Austin: University of Texas Press, 1983], 162).

61. A. K. Ramanujan, "Classics Lost and Found," *Contemporary Indian Tradition: Voices on Culture, Nature, and the Challenge of Change* (Washington, D.C.: Smithsonian Institution Press, 1989), 133. For a provocative study of the manipulation of the past in the creation of the present, see David Lowenthal, *The Past Is a Foreign Country* (Cambridge: Cambridge University Press, 1985).

62. On the political Left's attempts to demystify the traditional ritual arts and use them for political means, see Wayne Ashley and Regina Holloman, "From Ritual to Theatre in Kerala," *TDR* 26, no 2 (1982): 59–72.

63. David McRuvie, *Kathakaḷi King Lear*, MS, 1989.

64. V. Kaladharan, "The Problems Raised by King Lear Kathakaḷi," *Mathrabhumi*, 13 August 1989.

65. Vinita, "The Heart-rending King Lear," *Deshabimani*, 5 February 1989. The only Sanskrit drama in which it could be argued that pathos plays a major role is Bhasa's play *Urubhangam*. In the *kūṭiyāṭṭam* repertory, the style of acting Bali's death is filled with pathos and may have served Padmanabhan Nayar as a model.

66. Personal interview, 25 September 1989.

67. Kaladharan, "Problems Raised by King Lear Kathakaḷi."

68. Ibid.

69. Pavis, "Dancing with *Faust*."

70. Daryl Chin, "Interculturalism, Postmodernism, Pluralism," *Performing Arts Journal* 12:1–3 (1989): 174.

71. Ibid., 175.

Performance Theory, Hmong Shamans, and Cultural Politics

Dwight Conquergood

> Shamanism is the oldest technique of theatrical performing.
> —Richard Schechner, *Ritual, Play, and Performance*

In two widely cited essays, "The Sorcerer and His Magic" and "The Effectiveness of Symbols," Claude Lévi-Strauss analyzes in a remarkably performance-sensitive way the curing practices of North and South American shamans. He demonstrates the efficacy of these healing performances through a rigorous and highly original analysis of the mythic underpinnings and symbolic dimensions of medical practice, "ours" (Western scientists) as well as "theirs" (Cuna shamans). Through concrete case studies of shamans, these essays make important contributions to performance theory.[1] Indeed, Richard Schechner draws on Lévi-Strauss's subtle discussion of the skeptic-turned-shaman Quesalid as an examplar of the epistemological predicaments and postmodern paradoxes of performance. "Quesalid did not become a great shaman because he cured his patients," Lévi-Strauss insists in a deconstructive reversal, "he cured his patients because he had become a great shaman."[2]

Unfortunately, the brilliance and deconstructive force of this insight get lost in Lévi-Strauss's structuralist project. The story of Quesalid, the reluctant shaman, is deeply subversive, contradictory, and potentially poststructuralist. It relentlessly undermines and confuses the distinction between the "real" and the "made up," categories that Quesalid, for all his ontological struggles, can never quite stabilize. At the end of the narrative, Quesalid comes to accept the reality of his performances as he "carries on his craft conscientiously, takes pride in his achievements, and warmly defends the technique of the bloody down against all rival schools." But Lévi-Strauss, who as narrator identified with the early, doubting Quesalid, admiring "the radical negativism of the free thinker" and referring to him as "our hero," at this point distances himself from Quesalid's development as a performer: "He seems to have completely lost sight of the fallaciousness of the technique which he had so disparaged at the beginning."[3] The word *fallaciousness* belies Lévi-Strauss's sensitive analysis of the effectiveness of performed myth and symbol for the patient. Although he can understand with great subtlety how Quesalid cured his patients through performance, he does not understand how Quesalid, too, was persuaded by his own performances.

What is missing from Lévi-Strauss's discussion of Quesalid is a performative appreciation for historical process, how practices cumulatively interact and develop through time, reconstituting agent and agency and reconfiguring context. He notes that Quesalid "carries on his craft" but is surprised when Quesalid's stance and attitudes toward that craft are no longer the same as they were at "the beginning" of his performance practice. The structuralist approach blinds him to the ways in which Quesalid was "carried," caught up, and changed by performing his craft. Lévi-Strauss is excellent with the single case study of a performance, such as the Cuna shaman's song for a woman experiencing difficult childbirth, but the limitations of his method are revealed when he deals with Quesalid's performance career over time. At the end of the story Lévi-Strauss is still stuck where Quesalid was at the beginning, in a "fallaciousness"/foundationalist view of performance technique, but it is clear that Quesalid has moved on.[4]

Although I am situating Lévi-Strauss's work on shamanism within performance studies, he did not, connecting shamanism instead to psychoanalysis. In one passage, however, he explicitly acknowledged the shaman as performer:

> In treating his patient the shaman also offers his audience a performance. What is this performance? . . . we shall say that it always involves the shaman's enactment of the "call," or the initial crisis which brought him the revelation of his condition. But we must not be deceived by the word *performance*. The shaman does not limit himself to reproducing or miming certain events. He actually relives them in all their vividness, originality, and violence.

For all his ambivalence about the word *performance*, Lévi-Strauss powerfully articulates shamanic practice with performance theory. After this brief and tantalizing foray into performance theory, he refocuses on psychoanalysis, proposing that it "can draw confirmation of its validity, as well as hope of strengthening its theoretical foundations and understanding better the reasons for its effectiveness, by comparing its methods and goals with those of its precursors, the shamans and sorcerers." Although Lévi-Strauss respectfully compares these two traditions of healing, shamanism and psychoanalysis, he treats them hierarchically instead of dialogically. The assymetry is revealed by casting shamanism in the role of "precursor" to the modern, "developed" psychoanalysis, a clear example of what James Clifford calls a "temporal setup" and Johannes Fabian dubs "chronopolitics."[5]

In order to distance myself from this evolutionist ideology that would celebrate the primordial, originary nature of shamanism but locate it before, behind, and subordinate to contemporary performance, I will draw on ethnographic fieldwork with living, practicing Hmong shamans whose performances are a vital and contested part of the current refugee diaspora and struggle for identity. These shamans are not ghostly precursors or avatars of theater in the West, they are our contemporaries, and their performances stretch and challenge more than they romantically confirm received notions about theater and aesthetics or about the boundaries between performance and politics.

In this way I hope to resist the problematic practice of appropriating premodern and non-Western performances as sources of inspiration or revitalization for bourgeois theater. This trend resembles the imperialist practice of "discovering" natural resources in the colonies and shipping them back to the capital as raw materials for processing and manufacture. Christopher Innes's *Holy Theatre: Ritual and the Avant-Garde* charts the romantic fascination that "primitive ritual" has held for Western theater practitioners. Unfortunately, the promise of cultural critique, signaled in the title of the first chapter, "The Politics of Primitivism," is not delivered. Instead of critiquing the complex interplay between desire and domination which is inscribed in Western representations of and returns to primitive ritual, Innes simply reinscribes the imperialist ideology of "primitivism" that underpins Western practices of domination and exploitation. He refers, without irony, to the shaman as "the witch doctor."[6]

In *Gone Primitive: Savage Intellects, Modern Lives* Marianna Torgovnick conducts a much more "hard-hitting critique" of the politics of primitivism: "The tropes and categories through which we view primitive societies draw lines and establish relations of power between us and them, even as they presuppose that they mirror us." "The idea of the primitive," she argues, deploys "a rhetoric of control, in which demeaning colonialist tropes get modified only slightly over time; and a rhetoric of desire, ultimately more interesting, which implicates 'us' in the 'them' we try to conceive as the Other." Michael Taussig, professor of Performance Studies at New York University, provides the most sustained and unflinching political critique of primitivism in his study of the colonialist image of the "wild man," often figured as the shaman. In *Shamanism, Colonialism, and the Wild Man: A Study in Terror and Healing*, he documents with gruesome detail the colonialist mythology of the primitive that enabled white colonists in South America both to seek out the shamanic performances of shamans *and* to torture and terrorize Indians as savages. He argues: "Going to the Indians for their healing power and killing them for their wildness are not so far apart. Indeed, these actions are not only intertwined but are codependent."[7]

The shamanic performances of Hmong refugees I have been privileged to witness in Thailand and Chicago are not, I hope to make clear, timeless relics of prehistoric performance preserved in the cultural deep freeze of Hmong isolation from modernity in their remote mountaintop villages in Laos. As William Smalley makes clear, Hmong history has been a series of adaptations, contacts, and adjustments to other cultures.[8] Shamanism is a theatrically sophisticated, complex, and contextually nuanced performance practice enmeshed in the current cultural politics of Hmong people struggling to cope with the post–Vietnam War devastation of refugee upheaval, displacement, dispersal, and domination. Hmong shamans have more to teach performance theorists about what Clifford calls "critical cultural politics" than about primal roots of theater. I believe with Clifford that identity is "conjunctural, not essential," an idea that resonates with Bakhtin's powerful insight that meaning emerges most richly through dialogue and encounters, along borders and intersections.[9] By placing Hmong shamanic performance in metonymic tension with performance theory, I hope to open more space in cultural studies for an ethnography of cultural performance which features the politics of performance.

Performative Restorations

Shamanic performance displays on many levels what Schechner in *Between Theater and Anthropology* calls "twice-behaved behavior" or "restored behavior," the fundamental characteristic, he argues, of all performance. "Restored behavior," he explains, "is symbolic and reflexive: not empty but loaded behavior multivocally broadcasting significances. These difficult terms express a single principle: The self can act in/as another; the social or transindividual self is a role or set of roles." In concert with the opening up and pluralizing of identities, performance as restored behavior plays with time: "Restored behavior offers to both individuals and groups the chance to rebecome what they once were—or even, and most often, to rebecome what they never were but wish to have been or wish to become." Emphasizing the "restoration" qualities of performance encourages "revision," change, and improvisatory adjustments to contingency: "That's what theater directors, councils of bishops, master performers, and great shamans do: change performance scores." In *Theatre of the Oppressed* Augusto Boal has developed the revolutionary potential of a restoration, processual view of performance as a revisioning, reassembling, and reworking of social reality.[10]

A Hmong shamanic performance is an intricate assemblage of dynamically orchestrated image and action. Every performance is loaded and layered with incandescent palimpsests, multiple exposures, superimposed doublings. The restoration of behavior occurs simultaneously on at least four levels: Hmong shamans (1) re-present the patient's affliction, (2) reenact their own initiatory crisis, (3) relive the myth of Shee Yee ("*Siv Yis*" in Hmong), the first shaman, in the context of refugee diaspora and relocation in the West, (4) reconstitute their displaced tradition of healing within this contested space of domination and struggle. Although these multiple restorations are cathected and concurrent, for the purposes of discussion I will discuss them separately.

1. *Performing the patient's affliction.* The performing art of the shaman is precarious, strenuous, and intimate. In *Woman, Native, Other,* Trinh Minh-ha writes particularly of the intimate quality of the shaman's performance:

> They derive their power from *listening* to the others and *absorbing* daily realities. While they cure, they take into them their patients' possessions and obsessions and let the latter's illnesses become theirs. Their actions imply a personal investment. . . . The very close relationship these healers maintain with their patients remains the determining factor of the cure.[11]

Shamans enter into a dialogical relationship with their patients. The patient does not become the object of medical treatment but a coperformer in his or her own healing. Such intimacy leads to vulnerability on the part of the shaman as much as the patient.

In his life story, *I Am a Shaman*, published as ethnopoetry, Paja Thao describes how he and other shamans take on the afflictions of their clients during ecstatic performance ("shaking"):

> When you shake to carry away the bad things with you
> You feel heavy
> You do not see
> You slow down as you climb the steps to the sky
> Your speech slows down
> You feel tired
> You work very hard
> So they must pay you a little
> THIS IS THE WAY OF CARRYING AWAY AN AFFLICTION[12]

Thao's performance is both mimetic and appropriative. It is purgative for his patients because it convincingly mimes their listlessness, depression, and heaviness of spirit. Like Quesalid, Thao "presents them with their sickness in a visible and tangible form."[13] Through mirroring and thereby objectifying the diffuse, subjective feelings of the patient, Thao turns them inside out. The shaman's dramatic performance functions as a condensation symbol that collects, absorbs, and, most important, displays affliction. The logic of shamanic performance is that making a spectacle of something is a strategy for control and subjugation. It is the same logic as Bentham's panopticon, the relationship between the gaze and power, surveillance and subordination, discussed at length in Michel Foucault's *Discipline and Punish:* it is not so much that seeing is believing as that seeing situates the observer in a power relationship over that which is watched, inspected, surveyed. Foucault argued that power that could not be sighted (seen), located at originary sites, was most insulated from resistance.[14]

Thao describes vividly the intricate scenography and staging of another spectacular performance when the shaman "lays down his life on the ground" to rescue "the soul which sinks deep into the ground." This depressing malady is a severe and chronic form of soul loss which is imaged as the soul sinking deep into the ground and falling into a watery abyss. The shaman's restoration of this condition is a theatrical tour de force:

> When you lay down your life on the ground
> The people put one big jar of corn on your chest
> > And one big jar of water
> > And the top grindstone
> > And the sick one sits on the grindstone
> All pressing down on the chest of the shaman[15]

The prostrate shaman, pressed to the ground by this multitiered edifice of heavy weights, reproduces the debilitating illness and depression of the patient. The heavy jar of corn pressing down on his chest makes it difficult to breathe. The heavy jar of water adds to the weight of the big jar of corn and dramatically symbolizes the watery depths into which the soul is sinking and drowning. And the top grindstone pressing down on top of the water jar richly evokes the grinding pressure and crushing effect of chronic illness. But through the dramatic reversal of performance the final weight added on top of the grindstone is the patient, "the sick one sits on the grindstone." A stunning stage picture of weighted down inertia and passivity is subtly deconstructed by placing the patient on top of the grindstone, a position of empowerment, not paralysis. The participatory staging and environmental scenography not only "set things in the theatrical sense, they iconosize in the mythic-religious sense."[16]

This dramatic performance enacts the release from the heaviness of despair as the patient literally surmounts the weights while the shaman takes his place underneath. The shaman's performance reassembles and reconstructs the patient's situation in other ways:

> Two men stand at your head and feet striking gongs
> And a four-hands pig by your side
> Then you shake three times
> The sick one sits on top of the water jar
> The people carefully steady the water jar while he shakes
> If the water splashes on the shaman it is bad
> THE WAY OF THE SHAMAN FOR SAVING THE SOUL WHICH SINKS
> DEEP INTO THE GROUND IS LIKE THIS

The shamanic performance both reverses the vertical hierarchy and threatens stasis with movement. It repositions the patient from crushed underneath to triumphantly astride his problems and converts prone passivity to active agency. Friends and neighbors must steady the water jar as the entire structure of weights is destabilized by the powerful shaking of the shaman: "When he is lying down on the ground / He does not feel the heavy weights on his chest / Because he has the spirits to help him."[17] How heartening it must be for the audience, and particularly the sick one balancing himself on top of the weighted-down shaman, to experience viscerally the shaman's irrepressible power as he defiantly shakes and heaves, resisting all that would pull one down and debilitate.

But we are reminded again that the same performance that empowers the patient exposes the shaman to danger. Substituting himself for the sick one, the shaman now is vulnerable to the afflictions of the patient, concretely symbolized by the heavy water jar that he quite literally has taken on himself: "If the water splashes on the shaman it is bad." Indeed, the extremity of the shaman's exertions is revealed in the aftermath to this exhausting performance:

> Then the people take the shaman to the altar-bench
> He is stiff

Fig. 1. Masked shaman performs healing ritual in Chiang Kham Refugee Camp, Thailand, 1987. The ring of rattles he grasps will help him trap runaway souls. Photo credit: Dwight Conquergood.

The people flex his arms and legs
They spray water from their mouth on him
Then he begins to shake and speak to the spirits

The length of time it takes to recover underscores how taxing the performance has been for the shaman. Thao explains:

When you lay down your life on the ground
With weights on your chest
You have to stay at home for thirteen days
If someone calls you to shake
You do not go
After thirteen days you can go[18]

When shamans perform the affliction of their patient they are simultaneously empowered and acutely vulnerable. They embrace death to regenerate life. To control life-threatening disorder they release themselves into an out-of-body trembling ecstasy, an exquisitely controlled chaos. They hang suspended between earth and heaven, betwixt and between human and spirit. They are both present and absent. The veil that shadows their face (figs. 1 and 2) signifies that they have left the side of reality that is seen. They are structurally invisible, and yet they fill the room with their charismatic presence. The shaman's performance deconstructs and reconstructs, balancing among opposites, reversals, and paradoxes.[19]

47

Fig. 2. Elderly shaman with finger rattles sits on special shaman's bench—the winged charger that will carry him skywards into the spirit world—in Chiang Kham Refugee Camp, Thailand, 1987. Photo credit: Dwight Conquergood.

2. *Performing the initiatory crisis.* In addition to performing the patient's malaise, the shamanic performance recapitulates the initiatory sickness through which all shamans derive their healing power. People do not themselves choose to become a shaman. They are chosen by special spirits who want them to become shamans by experiencing first an illness that is interpreted by another shaman as the sign of their calling. As Thao explains,

> I became a shaman not because it was my will
> But because it was the will of my shaman spirits
> The shaman spirits came to me
> To make me a shaman
> The spirits make you sick
> To let you know
> That you must be a shaman
> It is not for you to choose
> And then to do
> The way of becoming a shaman
> Comes from the spirits
> You must follow them
> They will make you sick
> Until you become a shaman[20]

48   The sickness comes from the spirits who will keep calling the chosen

one to become a shaman until he or she starts performing the vocation by calling on the shamanic spirits to cure the sick. Jacques Lemoine explains this intricate process: "They [the spirits] will make him sick in a strange way, with fever, attacks, shivering and pain, until he calls for a shaman who will diagnose his illness as the vocation." Moreover, the persistent spirits "will not leave him alone until he starts calling them regularly."[21] When a performing Hmong shaman calls on the spirits to help cure an afflicted patient, he or she recapitulates and reverses the initiatory affliction through which these same spirits called him or her to shamanism. The interplay between sickness, calling, and curing in the context of shaman and patient is a highly complex set of doublings and transformations.

For many shamans their intiatory illness is remembered as a harrowing and profound encounter with the forces of death. An elderly shaman in Chicago recounted that when he was nineteen years old, he became gravely ill and was unconscious for ten days. In a dream he saw his soul travel to the jagged, rocky cliffs then descend to the depths of the earth. During this time he said his soul learned many things. A shaman came and divined that he was indeed far gone, that his soul was already at Step Nine on the Twelve Step ladder ascending from earth to sky. He was laid out on a table, and the shaman beat the gong and called back his departing soul. As his soul was called back, he remembered the sensation as feeling "like a leaf that floats up from the bottom of the lake." As he recounted this part of the story, he gestured with his hand to mime the upward floating movement of a fragile leaf.[22]

When shamans perform, they are highly vulnerable. They conquer death through dangerous encounters with destructive forces. Accompanied by a host of helping spirits, the shaman leaves the side of reality that is seen and journeys into the invisible world of spirits and supernatural forces. There he or she will search for lost or kidnapped souls, do battle with evil ogres, and bring back runaway souls. This threshold crossing between two worlds is, like most transitional experiences, risky and intense. Because of their acute vulnerability while in trance performance, Hmong shamans are attended by assistants who help balance their bodies as they leap back and forth between the altar bench and the ground and act out the dramatic struggles in the spirit world (figs. 3 and 4). Particularly near the close of a performance, when the shaman removes the mask, attempts to wind down while assistants lightly slap and massage his or her back—what Schechner calls the "cool-down" phase of performance—one can see just how strenuous the passage has been. This cool-down phase can be seen along with vivid footage of shamanic trance performances in the documentary *Between Two Worlds: The Hmong Shaman in America*.[23] The special power of the shaman comes from this presence achieved through an absence, this performative ability to leave one reality, enter and participate fully within another reality, and then return.

The shaman's interpretive reenactment of his or her initial sickness in the performance of healing pushes Schechner's idea of performance as a *"restoration* of behavior" to performance as *"restorative* behavior." By re-

Fig. 3. Assistant balances rattle-wielding shaman with arms spread
in ecstatic flight. Ban Vinai Refugee Camp, Thailand, 1985. Photo
credit: Dwight Conquergood.

enacting ("restoring") the experience of critical vulnerability, shamanic performance becomes charged with restorative power. The shift from
restoration to restorative emphasizes the transformational dynamics of
performance.

3. *Performing the role of Shee Yee, the first shaman.* At the beginning
of all performances, Hmong shamans invoke the name of Shee Yee, who
in Hmong cosmology is the first shaman who delivered the world from
sickness and death and bequeathed to future shamans the legacy of healing.
Many times, in both Thailand and Chicago, I have heard shamans chant
at the opening of their performance, "Shee Yee . . . Shee Yee." This chant
does more than commemorate the name of a powerful ancestor. As Charles
Johnson makes clear, contemporary shamans actually stand in for Shee
Yee, act out his role:

> Shee Yee is the greatest of Hmong mythical magicians, and the chief
> or patron saint of Hmong shamans, with whom they identify them-
> selves when performing their sacred functions. (Whenever Hmong
> shamans go on their ride into the spirit world to search for a lost
> soul, *they tell the spirits that they are Shee Yee.*)

Through this theatrical disguise, they reenact the power and precarious
struggles of the first shaman. The story, for example, of "Shee Yee's battling
evil spirits with his saber is simulated in modern practice by the shaman,
who brandishes a saber during some ceremonies in order to frighten away
evil spirits."[24] Contemporary Hmong shamans restore the behavior of their
spiritual mentor and, through this dissembling, achieve their power. This

50

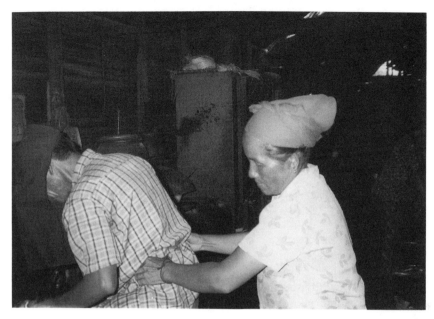

Fig. 4. A wife, who is herself an accomplished shaman, "spots" her shaman husband, who leaps between bench and dirt floor in one of the longhouses of Ban Vinai Refugee Camp, 1987. Photo credit: Dwight Conquergood.

is a wonderful example of the efficacy of theatricality, what Victor Turner calls performance as "making, not faking."[25]

The Hmong example of the story of Shee Yee helps us understand how the power of a myth is constituted through performance. Anthropologist Edward Bruner states this point clearly:

> It is in the performance of an expression that we re-experience, re-live, re-create, re-tell, re-construct, and re-fashion our culture. The performance does not release a preexisting meaning that lies dormant in the text. Rather, the performance itself is constitutive. Meaning is always in the present, in the here-and-now, not in such past manifestations as historical origins or the author's intentions. Nor are there silent texts, because once we attend to the text, giving voice or expression to it, it becomes a performed text, active and alive.[26]

When contemporary Hmong shamans perform the role of Shee Yee, they are reviving and reinterpreting an ancient myth to redress an immediate crisis of soul loss, attack by evil ogres, or affliction from offended nature spirits.

Hmong shamanic performance also helps us understand the different levels on which a myth can be performed. Although a long and fascinating oral narrative—transcribed and titled by Johnson, "Shee Yee and the Evil Spirits"—circulates within Hmong culture, the story of Shee Yee is performed typically through the figural enactments of practicing shamans. During 1985 I lived in Ban Vinai refugee camp for the Hmong in Thailand. Although I never came across a storytelling session where someone recited

51

the Shee Yee myth in verbal form, I was awakened almost every morning before dawn by the drumming and chanting of shamans acting out the role of Shee Yee.[27]

Even though shamans embody and improvise within the role of Shee Yee, instead of orally reciting the myth of the first shaman, much can be learned by taking a close look at the verbal narrative. There are multiple episodes in the story, but I will focus on the central section where Shee Yee is pursued by the nine evil spirit brothers, who proclaimed: "If we could only kill the damned Shee Yee, we would have a better life, and be free to eat earth people without fear or trouble." Shee Yee eludes and resists the attacks of the evil spirits through shape shifting and a remarkable series of transformations. He triumphs over the evil spirits through the arts of performance, disguise, guile, and deception. Indeed, one of the evil spirit brothers complains: "Shee Yee is a crooked liar, a mean trickster."[28]

Outnumbered nine to one, Shee Yee protects himself through multiple metamorphoses and plural identities. As a tactical response to each renewed attack, Shee Yee takes on yet another identity: he "took the form of a water buffalo," then "disguised himself as a cloud," then "turned himself into a drop of water," then "changed himself into a deer," then "changed himself into a rat," then "turned himself into a caterpillar," until, finally, he "disguised himself as a very tiny red ant."[29] From water buffalo to very tiny red ant, from cloud to water droplet—the direction of the transformations is from big to small, from brute force to the guileful ruse of the weak. His performative transformations recall the opportunistic tactics of the weak, described by Michel de Certeau as "'ways of operating': victories of the 'weak' over the 'strong' . . . clever tricks, knowing how to get away with things, 'hunter's cunning,' maneuvers, polymorphic simulations, joyful discoveries, poetic as well as warlike." What de Certeau calls the creative "art of making do" is quite literally an art of performance, the ability to improvise in everyday life. He describes it performatively as "an art of being in between," the ability to inhabit "the other's place" but "without taking it over in its entirety, without being able to keep it at a distance." The multiple identities and fluid role shiftings of de Certeau's tactical tricksters partake of the identity paradoxes of the performer, described by Schechner as the "not me" and the "not not me."[30] De Certeau is useful for performance theory because he links theatricality to issues of power and domination within everyday situations of resistance.

Shee Yee changed himself into the tiny red ant in order to elude an evil spirit that had changed into a cat in order to catch and eat Shee Yee when he was in his rat form. All these transformations, beginning with the water buffalo, had been defensive moves, retreats and dodges from the stronger powers of the evil spirit brothers. Significantly, it is in his weakest and tiniest form, the red ant, that Shee Yee switches from a defensive to an offensive stance: "He quickly and fiercely bit the cat on the testicle."[31] This intervention enabled Shee Yee to escape the cat and return home to his wife. It also marks a structural turning point in the narrative: Shee Yee turns from passive to active agent and initiates a new transformation of identity in which he no longer retreats into rat burrows but emerges slyly on the attack.

His switch from the hunted to the aggressor is marked by a gender reversal: "Shee Yee changed into a beautiful, well dressed girl, and . . . he pretended to be a young girl."[32] This "gender play," to borrow Margaret Drewal's felicitous term,[33] was anticipated when he bit the cat on the testicle. The evil spirit disguised as the cat was the "kind of evil spirit" that "is always attracted to nice looking women and tries to seduce them." In a double role reversal, Shee Yee, dressed as a young woman, aggressively flirts with the evil spirit seducer, still disguised as a cat, and seductively disarms and destroys him. Shee Yee then "changed into another girl" and boldly advanced to the cave that was home to the entire family of evil spirits. When the evil spirit mother spied Shee Yee approaching, she exclaimed: "There comes a pretty young girl. My, isn't she beautiful!"[34]

The scene in the home of the evil spirit family is rich with gender play, sexual farce, and dramatic irony. Shee Yee disguised as the young girl announces to the family that s/he has come to marry the eldest son. The eldest son, it turns out, was the one who had disguised himself as the lecherous cat that Shee Yee killed. The other brothers, however, found his battered body, patched him up, and "made him alive again." When he returned home with a terrible headache, Shee Yee ran to him and, savoring the irony of the situation, said: "'Oh, darling! Today is the day I have come here to marry you. I love you very much! . . . But when I marry you, you must not go and fight with Shee Yee any more. I don't want him to beat your brains out again!' And Shee Yee pretended to cry and cry." The evil spirit quickly forgot about his headache, "thinking of how he would soon enjoy going to bed with his new wife, this pretty girl." For most of this scene, Shee Yee, brilliantly playing the role of "this pretty girl," both attracts and defers the amorous advances of the evil spirit, insisting all the while: "I like men a lot" and "you alone will sleep with me" but "do not touch me yet."[35] Finally, while feigning solicitousness and serving the family of evil spirits gathered around the dining table, Shee Yee destroys them with hot boiling pork fat.

The elaborate constructions and deconstructions of gender enabled by Shee Yee's gender play are ideologically complex and merit a sustained analysis from the perspective of feminist critical theory.[36] For the purposes of this essay, the myth clearly features Shee Yee, the first shaman, as a consummate performer with an extensive repertoire of roles. He fights against evil and ultimately triumphs with tactics that are "poetic as well as warlike."[37] Of all his many roles and masks, his most developed, sustained, and artful performance is that of a woman. It is in the role of a woman that Shee Yee vanquishes the evil spirits. Kenneth Burke argues that "the profoundest way of symbolizing a change in identity is in the symbolic change of sex."[38] Shee Yee's change of sex, which is structurally connected in the narrative with his empowerment and triumph, underscores change, process, and transformation as the vital qualities of performance. Augusto Boal points to the "enormous efficacy of the transformations" celebrated in performance: "Theater is change and not simple presentation of what exists: it is becoming and not being." He argues that "mimesis" actually means "re-creation." Stephen Tyler argues for a performative, processual, postmodern theory of representation that privileges "kinesis" over "mimesis," and Renato Rosaldo privileges cultural "improvisations" and argues for "putting culture into motion."[39] When Hmong shamans perform today they, like Shee Yee, and as Shee Yee, wage battle against the forces of death by exploiting the recreative power of performance to resist closure, undermine oppressive structures, and revision reality in more life-enhancing ways.

4. *Performing a displaced tradition.* The fertile idea that performance is restored behavior gets radically politicized in the context of studying shamanic performance traditions of Hmong refugees in the West. The Hmong word for "refugees" is *neeg tawg rog* ("war-broken people"), or the more evocative phrase *tawg tsov tawg rog* ("broken before the tiger, dispersed by the war").[40] These words capture the explosive, shattering heartbreak of displacement from home and the spirit-numbing anxiety of relocation and exile on the margins of a dominant culture. In the refugee situation of upheaval and disintegration, cultural performance, particularly shamanism, has been a powerful resource for shoring up and restoring Hmong identity. Jacques Lemoine makes this observation about Hmong refugees resettled in the West: "all their choices, even their political mistakes, have been dictated by the same collective urge to preserve Hmong ethnicity. . . . For they did not come to our countries only to save their lives, they rather came to save their selves, that is, their Hmong ethnicity."[41]

Shamanism takes on new political meanings when performed in a Chicago apartment, in a culture where a Judeo-Christian ethos combines with positivist science and the legal system to displace, oppress, and erase a healing performance practice that entails ecstatic trance, belief in spirits, and animal sacrifice (figs. 5, 6, and 7). Mary Strine usefully sorts out "the *act* . . . and the *fact*" of performance practice. By the "fact" of performance she means the political implications of a performance, "the multiple affiliations that hold the performance text in place as a significant (and signifying) form of cultural expression."[42] Restorations of the *act* of Hmong shamanic performance in the West constitute radical distortions of the *fact* of shamanic performance. Violently severed from the multiple affiliations and web of meanings that held shamanic performance significantly in place in the mountain culture of Southeast Asia, shamanism performed in a Chicago apartment becomes at best a bizarre figure of ignorance and the occult, or, at worst, signifies moral transgression (devil worship) or illegal behavior (butchering of animals within city limits).

The political response to Hmong shamanism in the West has not been subtle. In his racist book on Hmong refugees, *The Yellow Rainmakers: Are Chemical Weapons Being Used in Southeast Asia?* investigative reporter Grant Evans associated shamanism with "village rumours and superstition" and used it to brand the Hmong as ignorant peasants steeped in a paleolithic mentality. The aim of the book is to discredit Hmong allegations of the

Fig. 5. Veiled shaman talks to the spirits in front of an altar he has set up inside his Chicago apartment, 1988. Photo credit: Dwight Conquergood.

use of chemical weapons ("yellow rain") during the Vietnam War. His rhetorical masterstroke for debunking these persistent Hmong reports of chemical warfare was to depict them as "shamanism writ large."[43]

In the spring of 1988, I was invited to attend a meeting of concerned Hmong leaders and elders in Chicago who had gathered to view a home video circulating within the U.S. Hmong community. The video consisted of the oral testimony of a Hmong shaman in Lansing, Michigan, who recounted how a fundamentalist Christian minister had entered his apartment with an interpreter and torn down his shaman altar. The minister then removed the altar along with all the performance equipment—gong, rattles, divination buffalo horns, joss sticks, spirit paper, etc.—to the church. The old shaman told of his pain and deep sense of loss, financial as well as spiritual. The custom-made shaman drums and rattles, for example, are costly in Laos or Thailand and are almost impossible to replace in this country. The elderly shaman had carried his cherished equipment with him when he escaped from Laos and had performed with it in the refugee camp in Thailand during the years he awaited resettlement in Michigan. It had taken imagination, effort, and some expense to build the eight-foot-high altar inside his Lansing apartment. Shamans build a household altar not just as a mise-en-scène for performance but as the resting place for their helping spirits during all the time they are not performing. The Christian minister destroyed property as well as committing an act of metaphysical violence against the old man. Instead of being intimidated, the Hmong leaders were angry and had made the video to protest this aggression and galvanize resistance to forced assimilation.

Within this context of domination, the practice of shamanism becomes

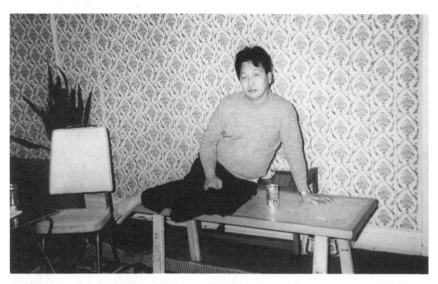

Fig. 6. Unmasked, shaman relaxes on special bench in postperformance repose,
Chicago, 1988. Photo credit: Dwight Conquergood.

an act of resistance.[44] Here are the reflections of Yang Lau, an elderly
Hmong shaman in Milwaukee:

> If all of the Hmong were to become Christians we would lose Hmong
> culture forever. We Hmong who believe in Hmong culture still have
> shamans. . . . Now I'm very old but I hope my children and the gen-
> eration following won't forget Hmong culture. I tell you this to remem-
> ber for the future generation. . . . A long time ago we were born to
> have shamans. My grandfather was a shaman and my father was a
> shaman also. . . . I want to pass this on to the future generations so
> that they will know about the shaman. This is all I have to say.[45]

The quietly firm resolve underneath the meditations of this articulate old
man illustrates how "performance as a site of cultural memory" can transcend nostalgia and become a site of political contestation and struggle.[46]

In defiance of the hegemonic forces of assimilation, some Hmong are
deploying shamanic performance as a political symbol of cultural resistance.
A number of Hmong cultural societies have sprung up across the country.
The Hmong society in Chicago is called *Dab Ohuas* (Work of the Spirit).
The Chicago founder of this society features its association with shamanism:
"Without Shee Yee [the first shaman] it is impossible to conduct *Dab Ohuas*
and without *Dab Ohuas* Shee Yee has nothing to do." The Milwaukee
branch of *Dab Ohuas* actually took the name Society of Shee Yee. It has
become incorporated as a nonprofit service organization, and its logo is
the gong of the shaman. The leader of the Chicago Hmong community
named his third son born in this country Shee Yee.

The defamiliarizing effect of wrenching dislocation sharply reveals the
cultural underpinnings that render established performance practices
meaningful by holding them in place and brand others transgressive because

Fig. 7. Sacrificed pig is ritually displayed alongside patient (the author), seated behind the elevated shaman. This shamanic ceremony of soul cleansing and renewal was performed for me on the occasion of my return to Refugee Camp Ban Vinai, Thailand, in the summer of 1987, where I had lived and conducted ethnographic fieldwork during 1985. Photo credit: Xiong Houa.

they are out of place, displaced. Displaced traditions are perceived as disorderly, dangerous, and dirty—filth that collects in the margins. In *Purity and Danger*, Mary Douglas argues that "dirt is essentially disorder," or "matter out of place." The restoration of a displaced performance tradition within a dominant culture intensifies the magnitude of the politics of performance. Margaret Drewal defines performance as "re-presentation with critical difference."[47] In the refugee context of re-presenting shamanic healing performances, the difference is indeed "critical," in the manifold meanings of that word.

The Other as Performer

Although a potential resource for resistance, the restoration of performance practices, especially shamanism, in the West renders the Hmong people vulnerable to discursive displacements in mainstream writings and publications about them. Reporting, interpreting, and documenting the Other are constituent moments in "the politics of representation" and control. Casting subordinate groups as performers of "tribal rites," a pervasive motif of colonialist discourse, is a primary way of constructing their Otherness. The image of the Primitive as Performer draws on and expands the "antitheatrical prejudice" that is deeply seeded in Western culture.[48] Associated with feelings, emotions, and the body, performance—especially ecstatic and/or divinatory performance—is constructed in opposition to scientific reason and rational thought. Particularly when linked with archaic

57

custom and premodern belief, performance is branded as regressive and transgressive within societies dominated by an evolutionary ideology of progress and development. Taussig argues that the performance practices (spells, sorcery, shamanism) condensed in the colonialist constructions of "magic became a gathering point for Otherness in a series of racial and class differentiations embedded in the distinctions made between Church and magic, and science and magic." He further notes that "shamans are deeply implicated in and constituted by this colonial construction of determinism's Otherness in which savagery and racism are tightly knotted.[49]

Grant Evans constructs the Hmong in *The Yellow Rainmakers* as superstitious peasants but then historically contextualizes their irrational behavior by sweeping them into a long tradition of performing primitives:

> All through history there have been outbreaks of mass hysteria—in the sense of large numbers of people being driven to behave in unusual antisocial fashion. In the Middle Ages in Europe there were outbreaks of dancing mania. There was the strange phenomenon of the Children's Crusade. In pioneer America there were the religious manifestations of the "Shakers" and the "Holy Rollers."

For Evans, the strange, manic, hysterical, childlike, antisocial, dancing, ecstatically performing Other is the negative mirror of "We of the west," who "pride ourselves on the effectiveness of our application of science to human affairs."[50] Evans's writings about the Hmong epitomize a postcolonialist rhetoric of domination that positions performance against, beneath, behind, in opposition to, and as threatening to progress, order, and enlightenment.

This Other as Performer trope has been used against the Hmong since their early encounters with the West, first with missionaries and then with the Central Intelligence Agency (CIA). Both groups legitimated their practices of conversion, coercion, and exploitation by constructing shamanic performance as a spectacle of primitivism. The missionary Isobel Kuhn, a prolific writer as well as dedicated evangelist, imaginatively situates Hmong shamanism within a reinforcing context of darkness, demons, death, and the forest primeval:

> It is a rainy, dreary night in a little Miao [*sic*] village tucked away in the folds of almost unexplored mountains in North Thailand. From the thick forest which still closely encircles the little shanties, one had proof that human beings have only recently hacked out a clearing from primeval growth. Big jagged stumps jutting up amidst the shanties, still fresh looking, tell us where they got the materials for their wooden huts, with their long shaggy grassed roofs. But a scourge has struck the little settlement and all day long the gong! gong! of demon exorcism has been going on. Not a house in the village but is calling on the demons this dismal night.

Kuhn dehumanizes the shaman-performing Hmong by describing an audience member's response in animalistic imagery: "'Be quiet,' growls her mate." At the same time she suffuses the scene with romantic sentimentality and pathos: "the little figure on the mat in the corner moans with misery, and outside, the wet night drips its tears ceaselessly in soft splashes."[51]

Kuhn's scenic blending of romantic exoticism and barbarity—fascination and repulsion—is mirrored in *Journey from Pha Dong*, a CIA film that depicts the recruitment and training for guerilla warfare of the Hmong in Laos. The anonymous voice-over narration explains: "This film is concerned with how a people learn to win a war." Over visual images of Hmong villagers awkwardly assembling and handling CIA-supplied weapons, the omniscient narrator comments: "This man has never seen a modern rifle. . . . They can get anything apart, but putting it back together again is something else. The spirits of their ancestors who fought so well for the Hans might be slightly embarrassed. There is a limit to what they can learn now, they are taught simple things. They begin with the M-1 rifle. They are difficult to train." This representation of the Hmong as childlike simpletons and technological primitives is reinforced by spectacular scenes of performing shamans with ecstatic chanting and animal sacrifice. Even the educated Vang Pao, anointed by the CIA to lead the Hmong guerillas, is described as someone who still "half-believes himself in the spirits and spells of their animism."[52]

More recently, the Hmong have entered the discursive space of the West in newspaper and law journal articles that report their legal difficulties as refugees contesting assimilation and struggling within a dominant culture.[53] These articles often display shamanic performance as a spectacle of Otherness. As an ethnographer who has worked with the Hmong, I was called to testify as an expert witness for a Hmong friend whose courtroom trial was sensationalized in the press when he asked the judge if a rooster could be sacrificed in a divination ceremony to establish his innocence, according to Hmong forensic practices. The *Chicago Tribune* made this story newsworthy by developing the Primitive as Performer motif:

> Two Hmong tribesmen from Laos who had wanted their trial to include the Hmong custom of sacrificing a rooster were convicted in an ordinary jury trial Wednesday of beating a man during a traffic dispute. . . . The Xiongs had asked Judge Michael S. Jordan . . . to have a rooster sacrificed in the courtroom and to have drops of the rooster's blood placed in glasses of water. . . . The Xiongs suggested that the complainant and the Xiongs all swear to tell the truth and then consume the blood and water. Hmong tribesmen believe a person who lies after this ceremony will soon die and that the rooster will take the liar's spirit so that the liar can never be reincarnated as a human.[54]

This incident, which had enormous consequences for my friend Bravo Xiong, who received a felony conviction, was discursively staged in the press with all the titillating details that would both attract and repulse middle-class readers while underwriting their superiority over the new immigrants, the "tribesmen": animal sacrifice, blood drinking, unnatural death, reincarnation (with the suggestive hint of human-animal minglings in some reincarnations), and latent sexual sadism and kinkiness in the symbolism of a cock-killing in a public courtroom. This journalistic representation draws on many of the same fetishistic constructions of "primitive art."[55]

The exhibiting of the Hmong, and other ethnic Others, in print and electronic media as exotic performers is a contemporary response to and containment of the "problem" of diversity, difference, and demographic change which is transforming the sociological landscape of late twentieth-century America. Cultural cohesion (if that ever was achieved) and hegemony are perceived as threatened by, if not unraveling under, the pressure of large numbers of refugees and immigrants, many of them from the Third World, who have entered this country since the repeal of racist quotas in 1965 immigration legislation and the 1980 Refugee Act. This contemporary staging of the Other as Performer has interesting ideological resonances with nineteenth-century People Shows, and particularly Frank Hamilton Cushing's remarkable staging of Zuni culture for New England middle-class and elite audiences when he assembled a troupe from the pueblos and "brought rich travelling theater eastward in 1882."[56] Attention to the complex cultural politics of performance—as ambivalent front, slippery site, and shifting intersection of domination and resistance, appropriation and contestation—promises to invigorate performance theory by grounding it in praxis.

NOTES

1. Claude Lévi-Strauss, *Structural Anthropology*, trans. C. Jacobsen and S. G. Schoeff (New York: Basic Books, 1963), 167–85, 186–205. Lévi-Strauss demonstrates how to conduct ethnographically sensitive performance analyses of historical texts. His brilliant performance analysis of the Cuna Shaman's song for a woman experiencing difficult childbirth (186–97) is based on an archival text, not participant observation research. Lévi-Strauss excavates the dramaturgy embedded in the text, a kind of textual archaeology of performance practice.

2. Lévi-Strauss, *Structural Anthropology*, 180; Richard Schechner, *Between Theater and Anthropology* (Philadelphia: University of Pennsylvania Press, 1985), 121, 125, 130–31.

3. Lévi-Strauss, *Structural Anthropology*, 178. Quesalid learned from other shamans backstage how to hide a puff of down in his cheek, bite his gums to make them bleed, then suck from the afflicted place on the patient's body and, through theatrical sleight of hand, pull out the bloody mess from his mouth and present it as the palpable evil he had drawn forth from the sick one.

4. Marshall Sahlin's *Islands of History* (Ann Arbor: University of Michigan Press, 1985) is an exemplar of cultural studies research at the conjuncture of ethnography and history. See particularly his discussion of "performative structures," a concept that features the creative, constructed, and fluid nature of social forms. Many anthropologists are now productively combining ethnographic with historical research methods. See Clifford Geertz, *Negara: The Theatre State in Nineteenth-Century Bali* (Princeton: Princeton University Press, 1980); and Smadar Lavie, *The*

Poetics of Military Occupation: Mzeina Allegories and Bedouin Identity under Israeli and Egyptian Rule (Berkeley: University of California Press, 1990). Both Geertz's and Lavie's studies explicitly draw on and contribute to the performance paradigm in cultural studies.

5. Lévi-Strauss, *Structural Anthropology*, 180–81, 204. On dialogical treatment, see Mikhail Bakhtin, *The Dialogic Imagination*, ed. Michael Holquist, trans. C. Emerson and M. Holquist (Austin: University of Texas Press, 1981); James Clifford, *The Predicament of Culture: Twentieth-Century Ethnography, Literature, and Art* (Cambridge: Harvard University Press, 1988), 16; and Johannes Fabian, *Time and the Other: How Anthropology Makes Its Object* (New York: Columbia University Press, 1983), 144.

6. Christopher Innes, *Holy Theatre: Ritual and the Avant-Garde* (New York: Cambridge University Press, 1981), 16. For postcolonial critiques of the politics of representation, see Bill Ashcroft, Gareth Griffiths, and Helen Tiffin, *The Empire Writes Back: Theory and Practice in Post-Colonial Literature* (New York: Routledge, 1989); Michel de Certeau, *Heterologies: Discourse on the Other*, trans. Brian Massumi (Minneapolis: Minnesota University Press, 1986); Christopher Miller, *Blank Darkness: Africanist Discourse in French* (Chicago: University of Chicago Press, 1985); and *Theories of Africans: Francophone Literature and Anthropology in Africa* (Chicago: University of Chicago Press, 1990); V. Y. Mudimbe, *The Invention of Africa: Gnosis, Philosophy, and the Order of Knowledge* (Bloomington: Indiana University Press, 1988); Edward Said, *Orientalism* (New York: Pantheon, 1978); and Tzvetan Todorov, *The Conquest of America: The Question of the Other*, trans. Richard Howard (New York: Harper and Row, 1984).

7. Marianna Torgovnick, *Gone Primitive: Savage Intellects, Modern Lives* (Chicago: University of Chicago Press, 1990), ix, 11, 245; Michael Taussig, *Shamanism, Colonialism, and the Wild Man: A Study in Terror and Healing* (Chicago: University of Chicago Press, 1987), 100.

8. William Smalley, "Stages of Hmong Cultural Adaptation," in *The Hmong in Transition*, ed. Glenn L. Hendricks, Bruce T. Downing, and Amos S. Deinard (New York: Center for Migration Studies, 1986).

9. Clifford, *Predicament of Culture*, 147, 11; Bakhtin, *Dialogic Imagination*; and *Speech Genres*, ed. C. Emerson and M. Holquist, trans. Venn W. McGee (Austin: University of Texas Press, 1986), 140.

10. Schechner, *Between Theatre and Anthropology*, 52, 36–38; Augusto Boal, *Theatre of the Oppressed*, trans. Charles A. MacBride and Maria Odila-Leal MacBride (1979; reprint, New York: Theatre Communications, 1985).

11. Trinh Minh-ha, *Woman, Native, Other: Writing Postcoloniality and Feminism* (Bloomington: Indiana University Press, 1989).

12. Dwight Conquergood and Paja Thao, *I Am a Shaman: A Hmong Life Story with Ethnographic Commentary*, trans. Xa Thao (Minneapolis: University of Minnesota, Center for Urban and Regional Affairs, 1989), 10. Contemporary ethnographers sensitive to the performance dimensions of verbal art argue that oral narrative should be transcribed in poetic form instead of prose paragraphs. The lineation of poetic verse captures better than prose the rhythms and pacing of oral discourse. See Elizabeth C. Fine, *The Folklore Text: From Performance to Print* (Bloomington: Indiana University Press, 1984); and Dennis Tedlock, *The Spoken Word and the Work of Interpretation* (Philadelphia: University of Pennsylvania Press, 1983).

13. Lévi-Strauss, *Structural Anthropology*, 176.

14. Michel Foucault, *Discipline and Punish*, trans. Alan Sheridan (New York: Pantheon Books, 1977).

15. Conquergood and Thao, *I Am a Shaman*, 8, 7.

16. Schechner, *Between Theatre and Anthropology*, 179.

17. Conquergood and Thao, *I Am a Shaman*, 7, 8.

18. Ibid., 8, 9.

19. This discussion builds on and extends my analysis of shamanic performance in "The Dramaturgy of Healing," in Conquergood and Thao, *I Am a Shaman*, 62–68.

20. Ibid., 2.

21. Jacques Lemoine, "Shamanism in the Context of Hmong Resettlement," in Hendricks, Downing, and Deinard, *Hmong in Transition*, 341.

22. Conquergood and Thao, *I Am a Shaman*, 49. See also Joan Halifax, *Shamanic Voices: A Survey of Visionary Narrative* (New York: Dutton, 1979).

23. Schechner, *Between Theatre and Anthropology*, 16, 99; Dwight Conquergood and Taggart Siegel, producers, *Between Two Worlds: The Hmong Shaman in America* (video documentary).

24. Charles Johnson, ed., *Dab Neeg Hmoob: Myths, Legends and Folktales from the Hmong of Laos* (St. Paul, Minn.: Macalaster College, Department of Linguistics, 1985), 73 (emphasis added), 75.

25. Victor Turner, *From Ritual to Theatre: The Human Seriousness of Play* (New York: Performing Arts Journal Publications, 1982), 93; see also *Anthropology of Performance* (New York: Performing Arts Journal Publications, 1986).

26. Edward Bruner, "Experience and Its Expressions," in *The Anthropology of Experience*, ed. Victor Turner and Edward Bruner (Urbana: University of Illinois Press, 1986), 11–12.

27. Charles Johnson, "Shee Yee and the Evil Spirits," in Johnson, *Dab Neeg Hmoob*, 23–59. See Dwight Conquergood, "Health Theatre in a Hmong Refugee Camp," *TDR: A Journal of Performance Studies* 32, no.3 (1988): 174–208.

28. Johnson, "Shee Yee," 38, 45–46.

29. Ibid., 39–40.

30. Michel de Certeau, *The Practice of Everyday Life*, trans. Steven Rendall (Berkeley: University of California Press, 1984), xix, 30; Schechner, *Between Theater and Anthropology*, 123.

31. Johnson, "Shee Yee," 40.

32. Ibid., 41.

33. Margaret Drewal, *Yoruba Ritual: Performers, Play, Agency* (Bloomington: Indiana University Press, 1992), 172.

34. Johnson, "Shee Yee," 41.

35. Ibid., 43, 44.

36. Sue-Ellen Case, *Performing Feminisms: Feminist Critical Theory and Theatre* (Baltimore: Johns Hopkins University Press, 1990). Although I have neither observed myself nor read reports from other researchers of cross-dressing among Hmong shamans, transvestism and bisexuality are found commonly in shamanic traditions in other cultures. See Mircea Eliade, *Shamanism: Archaic Techniques of Ecstasy*, trans. Willard R. Trask (New York: Pantheon Books, 1964), 125, 258, 352. Eliade states that this "ritual androgyny" is a symbolic way of underscoring the shaman's role as "intermediary" as well as the "need to abolish polarities" (352). For two contrasting case studies that explore the problematics of men performing women, see Joseph Roach's insightful analysis of eighteenth-century *castrati*, "Power's Body: The Inscription of Morality as Style," in *Interpreting the Theatrical Past: Essays in the Historiography of Performance*, ed. Thomas Postlewait and Bruce McConachie (Iowa City: University of Iowa Press, 1989), 99–118; and Morris Meyer's provocative

study of transsexuals, "I Dream of Jeannie: Transsexual Striptease as Scientific Display," *TDR: A Journal of Performance Studies* 35, no. 1 (1991): 25–42.

37. de Certeau, *Politics of Everyday Life*, xix.

38. Kenneth Burke, *Attitudes toward History*, 3d ed. (Berkeley: University of California Press, 1984), 211.

39. Boal, *Theatre of the Oppressed*, 28,1; Stephen Tyler, *The Unspeakable: Discourse, Dialogue, and Rhetoric in the Postmodern World* (Madison: University of Wisconsin Press, 1987); and Renato Rosaldo, *Culture and Truth: The Remaking of Social Analysis* (Boston: Beacon Press, 1989).

40. Jean-Pierre Hassoun and Michel Mignot, "Le terme 'refugie' dans les langues Hmong et Vietnamienne," *Asie du Sud-Est et Monde Insulindien* 14 (1983): 7–24.

41. Lemoine, "Shamanism," 337.

42. Mary Strine, "Between Meaning and Representation: Dialogic Aspects of Interpretation Scholarship," in *Renewal and Revision: The Future of Interpretation*, ed. Ted Colson (Denton, Tex.: Omega, 1986), 70.

43. Grant Evans, *The Yellow Rainmakers: Are Chemical Weapons Being Used in Southeast Asia?* (London: Verso, 1983), 194,124.

44. James C. Scott, *Domination and the Arts of Resistance: Hidden Transcripts* (New Haven, Conn.: Yale University Press, 1990).

45. Conquergood and Thao, *I Am a Shaman*, 74.

46. For a discussion of Hmong refugees' confrontations with the U.S. legal system, see Dwight Conquergood, "Roosters, Blood, and Interpretations: Cultural Domination and Resistance in the Courtroom," in *Culture and Communication*, ed. Edith Slembeck (Frankfort: Verlag für Interkulterelle Kommunikation, 1991), 149–60.

47. Mary Douglas, *Purity and Danger: An Analysis of Concepts of Pollution and Taboo* (1966; reprint, London and Boston: Routledge and Kegan Paul, 1969); and Margaret Drewal, "The State of Research on Performance in Africa" (paper delivered at the 1990 meeting of the African Studies Association, Baltimore).

48. Michael J. Shapiro, *The Politics of Representation: Writing Practices in Biography, Photography, and Policy Analysis* (Madison: University of Wisconsin Press, 1988). On "tribal rites," see Michel de Certeau, "Ethnography: Speech, or the Space of the Other: Jean de Léry," in *The Writing of History*, trans. Tom Conley (New York: Columbia University Press, 1988), 209–43; and Jonas Barish, *The Anti-theatrical Prejudice* (Berkeley: University of California Press, 1981).

49. Taussig, *Shamanism*, 465.

50. Evans, *Yellow Rainmakers*, 181.

51. Both *Miao* and *Meo* are racist terms, which are deeply insulting to Hmong people (Isobel Kuhn, *Ascent to the Tribes: Pioneering in North Thailand* [1956; reprint, Singapore: Overseas Missionary Fellowship Books, 1991], 110).

52. The exact date and circumstances of production of this CIA film are unknown. Through the Freedom of Information Act, however, the film is available through the Southeast Asian Refugee Studies Program, Center for Urban and Regional Affairs, University of Minnesota.

53. See, for example, David Jordan, "Hmong Sentenced to Learn Our Ways," *Albany Park News*, 5 July 1988, 1–2; Mike Royko, "A Fine Opportunity to Learn Our Culture," *Chicago Tribune*, 1 July 1988, 3; and Julia Sams, "The Availability of the 'Cultural Defense' as an Excuse for Criminal Behavior," *Georgia Journal of International and Comparative Law* 16 (1986): 335–54; "The Cultural Defense in the Criminal Law," *Harvard Law Review* 99 (1986): 1293–1311.

54. Terry Wilson, "Two Hmong Convicted of Beating Motorist," *Chicago*

Tribune, 5 May 1988. For a more detailed discussion of this case, see Conquergood, "Roosters, Blood, and Interpretations."

55. See Sally Price, *Primitive Art in Civilized Places* (Chicago: University of Chicago Press, 1989).

56. Curtis M. Hinsley, "Zunis and Brahmins: Cultural Ambivalence in the Gilded Age," in *Romantic Motives: Essays on Anthropological Sensibility,* ed. George W. Stocking, Jr. (Madison: University of Wisconsin Press, 1989), 169–207.

Under the "Trickster's" Sign: Toward a Reading of Ntozake Shange and Femi Ọṣọfisan

Sandra L. Richards

As numerous commentators have observed, when Africans were forcibly transported to the "New World," they did not travel alone. Systems of thought, technology, aesthetics—in short, cultures—traversed that Middle Passage, transforming and being transformed by the environment and other cultures with which the slaves came into contact. Though continental as well as diasporan Africans have been required to adapt their perspectives in order to rationalize the West's brutal impact, many aspects of traditional cultures continue to thrive. Activists like W. E. B. DuBois and Marcus Garvey projected Black Pride and Pan-African perspectives within a political arena; writers from the Harlem Renaissance, Haitian Indigenism, and Cuban Negrism movements of the 1920s and from the Paris-based Negritude movement of the 1930s gave artistic expression to those viewpoints, while scholars like Melville Herskovits, Janheinz Jahn, William Bascom, Jean Price Mars, and Fernando Ortiz conducted many of the early investigations documenting a continuity of culture between Africa and its American diasporas. Within the field of drama, recognition of this continuity is more recent.[1] The work of Amiri Baraka, Paul Carter Harrison, Larry Neal, James V. Hatch, Errol Hill, and Eleanor Traylor—the first three primarily creative writers and the latter three primarily scholars—has been important in consciously mapping in broad terms some of the parameters of a tradition.[2]

The present work participates in what might be characterized as a second-generation critical move that, in capitalizing upon earlier studies, seeks to connect *specific* African cultural practices with their literary reformulations in the Americas.[3] Given the significant variables involved, this line of inquiry is necessarily in an infant stage of development, needing many more focused studies in order to identify with greater precision the intertextuality of African and African-American literatures. This essay links one contemporary African-American playwright with a Nigerian dramatist through their use of Yoruba religious practices as a paradigm for dramatic structure. It argues that, through a creative deployment of the principles of Sixteen Cowrie and Ifá divination, Ntozake Shange and Femi Ọṣọfisan construct dramaturgies that empower audiences, challenging them to impose an interpretive hegemony that can extend from the symbolic to the socio-political order. Additionally, it suggests that the figure of Ọṣun, who is said to have taught mankind Sixteen Cowrie divination, serves as an appropriate representation of the ways in which African women, on the continent and in the diaspora, conceptualize feminism.

Methodological Assumptions

Before discussing the dramatic appropriations which Shange and Ọṣọfisan effect, I want to outline some of the assumptions underlying my orientation. A critical approach that seeks to name continuities between Africa and the Americas must remain historically and contextually grounded. Thus, we must acknowledge that the postulation of a purely African identity is impossible: scholars like Cheikh Anta Diop, St. Clair Drake, and Martin Bernal have convincingly argued that African and Afroasiatic peoples contributed significantly to classical Western civilization.[4] Furthermore, colonialism is a fact that we, as descendents of and as still subjugated peoples, cannot escape, no matter how strong our longings for an Eden in which we are fully human; complete retreat from the West is neither possible nor desirable. But even while acknowledging our embeddedness within Western traditions, we must insist upon the autodynamic quality of our cultures. African peoples developed systems of thought which continue to govern contemporary production. In deploying critical tools from precolonial traditions, we must ask how these traditions have changed over time in accordance with the changed material conditions and perceptions of adherents. In addition, we must ask to what extent present cultural practices advance our well-being, to what extent they may need to be reinterpreted so as to allow us, as Amilcar Cabral phrased it, "to return to the upward paths of [our] own culture."[5] As Hortense J. Spillers observes, "Traditions are not born. They are made. We would add that they are not, like objects of nature, here to stay, but survive as *created social events* only to the extent that an audience cares to intersect them."[6]

In discussing this intersection, the critic must attempt to fashion an appropriate vocabulary by situating the artist within the more narrow biographical and larger discursive contexts. Within the latter resides the challenge of identifying those elements more allied to African traditions, those more linked to Western, and those constituting a synthesis of traditions. Equally important, the critic must pinpoint imaginative revisions of these traditions and take into account the various ways in which specific audiences— of directors, designers, performers, and managers as well as observers— produce meanings, often in opposition to the author's expectations.

The present essay attends to redeployments of specific African traditions, leaving unaddressed at this point the ways in which Shange and Ọṣọfisan manipulate their Western identities.[7] Readers may recognize within the discussion parallels both with Western and other, non-Western practices of representation. That recognition suggests that a complex of reading strategies is operative: as educated elites, Ntozake Shange and Femi Ọṣọfisan create in relation to their dual heritage; the majority of their audiences in America, Africa, or Europe may interpret their work in relation to the single tradition of which they are cognizant; and a portion of these observers are, it is hoped, beginning to develop a "diaspora literacy," enabling them to sight the various layers of intertextuality.[8]

Contexts

Ntozake Shange and Femi Ọṣọfisan are contemporaries. It is unlikely, however, that the two have met or that Shange is familiar with the latter, who, among American audiences, is overshadowed by his predecessor, Nobel Prize winner Wole Ṣoyinka.

Born in New Jersey in 1948, Shange was brought up in a middle-class environment in which Pan-African values were inculcated and artistic expression encouraged. Knowledge of American racism came early, for at age eight she was one of the first black children to integrate the St. Louis public school system. But because her parents maintained an international set of friends and nurtured her precocity, Shange grew up aware of a larger frame of reference wherein skin color was not a badge of stigmatization. Emergence into adulthood occurred during the turbulent period of the Vietnam War and the Black Power/Black Arts and women's movements.

Shange's familiarity with Yoruba culture may be dated to the early 1970s, when radical, political activists in Boston and New York introduced her to Yoruba religions through the study of dance.[9] Both Pearl Primus and Mercedes Baptista commanded significant respect among African-American dancers at that time: not only had Primus incorporated blues and spiritual motifs into her modern dance choreography of the 1940s, but she was also the first African American to research and concertize West African dance in the United States.[10] Journeying periodically from Brazil to New York's Clark Center, Baptista taught Afro-Brazilian dance, itself a Yoruba–Dahomean-based synthesis of African, Portuguese, and Amerindian cultures. Leaving New York in 1973 to join the Bata Koto dance group headed by Trinidadian Gloria Toolsey and African American Luisah Teish of San Francisco,[11] Shange also studied with Raymond Sawyer, who had trained in techniques pioneered by Primus and Dunham. The famous choreographer-anthropologist Katherine Dunham had established a basic vocabulary for black dance instruction based upon her field research in Haiti; it emphasized the transmission of knowledge of the social function of dance as well as mastery of technical form. Through the technique Shange would have been exposed to some of the basic concepts of Haitian *vodun*, which synthesized the belief systems of the peoples of Yorubaland, Dahomey, and the Congo with Roman Catholicism. In addition, she associated with other dancers and musicians who practiced *santería*, the distinct form that these religions took among African slaves in Cuba.

Undoubtedly, the literary examples of Amiri Baraka, Ishmael Reed, and Zora Neale Hurston should not be overlooked as factors conditioning Shange's appropriations of Yoruba cultures. Valuing Black folk practices as a point of origin for their artistry,[12] all three employ conjuring as both formal device and subject matter. Indeed, with it, Hurston established the conditions of literary authority for African-American women writers.[13] A general belief in the transformative power of language would find specific corroboration in Yoruba culture's sophisticated acknowledgment of language as a multivalent, ambiguous force. Seemingly, Shange's opposition to racism and imperialism, rejection of Western cultural hegemony, and commitment to recuperating marginalized folk traditions of "New World" Africans and of women in general were born out of this early background.

In contrast, Femi Ọṣọfisan was born in a Yoruba farming village in western Nigeria in 1946, some four months before his father died, leaving the family economically vulnerable. Educated in Ibadan and Paris, initially by relatives and later through government scholarships, Ọṣọfisan received an Oxbridge education, which functioned to enable Britain to continue its dominance, even though decolonization was clearly inevitable. He was also exposed to the Negritude movement pioneered by Senghor, Césaire, and Damas and to the example of the Mbari Club, dominated by Wole Ṣoyinka, J. P. Clark, and Christopher Okigbo. Though the latter disavowed the Negritudinists' self-conscious proclamation of black worth, the two artistic movements concurred in deploying—and in the process revalidating—indigenous themes.

As a youth, Ọṣọfisan had been subject to both Yoruba and Christian perspectives, but systematic study of Yoruba culture seems to have occurred first as a part of the process of writing a dissertation on the origins of drama in West Africa. He came of age in the chaotic, early post-independence period when self-rule had exploded into civil war (1968–70), a condition mirrored on the African continent as other nationalist struggles were followed by military coups and countercoups. His commitment to the poor, appreciation of the pivotal position in African development occupied by educated classes, and materialist impatience with those traditions that impede human agency appear to be the consequences of this early background.

The Theoretical Frame

Common to Yoruba worship, Brazilian *candomblé*, Haitian *vodun*, and Cuban *santería* is a metaphysics centering on the concept of a life-force that pervades all elements of the universe. Known in Yoruba as *àṣẹ*, this power-to-make-things-happen is a morally neutral energy that manifests itself in discrete entities often in opposition to other distinct entities. Women are thought to possess an additional "bird power" (*ẹyẹ*), a prophetic ability that, like *àṣẹ*, allows them to accomplish whatever they wish.[14] Though force fields often compete with each other, coexistence and equilibrium are also possible. Human communities are assumed to strive to replicate the natural order so that, while harmony represents a desired objective, considerable latitude is allowed for difference and tension. Concepts related to human agency or identity and difference are instantiated in seminal narratives whose signification is replicated throughout the social order. Thus, for example, an individual is said to kneel and choose his destiny in the spirit world; in assuming physical form, he forgets that knowledge and uses divination, sacrifice, and ritualized dance as devices to discover the life he was meant to lead. But, in the divination process especially, the individual supplicant remains supremely active, for it is she or he who formulates the

problem, selects the most applicable among a variety of explanatory scenarios presented, and chooses to make sacrifice.

Central to the divination process are three gods. Ọrunmila is said to
know the secret of existence of both humans and divinities, for he is present
whenever a human is created and his or her destiny sealed. His geomantic
system of divination, which remains in use today, is known as Ifá. Encoded
within two hundred and fifty-six "volumes," or *odu*, each with its own
distinct divination signature and related to a specific Yoruba deity, Ifá's
discourse is intensely poetic.

Ọ̀ṣun, as she is known in Yorubaland, Cuba, and Brazil, or Erzulie,
as she is called in Haiti, is regarded as the source of power for most of
the Yoruba male-dominated cults because she is reputed to have rendered
the original male gods impotent and plunged the world into near-chaos
when they refused her admission to their deliberations.[15] Through her
actions, Ọrunmila is said to have learned the necessity of making sacrifice,
which reestablishes the unity of natural and supernatural elements. Other
divination verses assert that Ọ̀ṣun learned the art while living with Ọrunmila, and, when he discovered that his wife was divining for clients in his
absence, he banished her from his home. Known as Sixteen Cowrie divination, Ọ̀ṣun's system of prophecy, unlike Ifá divination, is open to female
as well as to male diviners. It is also the preferred system in the Americas.
In that Ọ̀ṣun's Haitian equivalent, Erzulie, is associated with desire beyond
satiation, this godhead is said to represent the human capacity to conceptualize and to dream, creating both art and the very idea of divinity.[16]

While Ọ̀ṣun encompasses a necessary animating force, and Ọrunmila,
or Ifá, speaks the truth, the god who presides over its decoding in either
system is Eṣu. Functioning as a "special relations officer," or liaison, between
heaven and earth, who exacts retribution on both wayward humans and
gods, Eṣu is also represented as a trickster who seemingly delights in engen-
dering chaos.[17] Said to be both small and large in stature, male and female
in gender, Eṣu is the embodiment of paradox. He functions in part as "a
generating symbol who promotes change by offering opportunities for
exploring what possibilities lie beyond the *status quo.*"[18] As his central
position on the divination tray attests, Eṣu

> challenges, shatters, and redraws the structures of life. In so doing,
> both [Eṣu and his Fon counterpart, Legba] reveal the sacredness of
> ambiguity itself and enlarge the total pattern of meaning that is soci-
> ety, shaping it more closely to the design of the cosmos itself.[19]

Knowledge of that design, however, whether articulated as a religious or
scientific narrative, is a social construction reflective of man's apprehensions
at a given point in time.

Within the Yoruba performing arts one locus for the manifestation of
àṣẹ is the spectacle. Encompassing the ideas of mental images, mystical
visions, and even generations, or lineages, the spectacle is said to constitute
a periodic (re)introduction of a "mysterious, permanent dimension of reality

which, until revealed, is shut off from human view."[20] In unmasking a transcendent reality, the spectacle strives to increase the collective life-force, or potentiality of all those present, by reasserting the link between the living community, departed ancestors, the yet-to-be-born, and the entire cosmos.

Supernatural contact is valued even in secular entertainment because experience is posited more in holistic than categorically distinct terms. Research on Yoruba secular performance traditions or on African story-telling indicates that principles of categorization are more fluid in these discourses than in Western thought. That is, genres are determined not so much by the presence (or absence) of formal properties as by the effect of that property. Not only may a dramatic event contain sequences that are intended as representational and others that are presentational, but it may also include segments that are liminal, that is, neither material nor super-natural. The application of an analytical label to a given sequence varies, dependent upon its contextual placement in relation to other units and, even more important, upon individual audience members' beliefs.[21] Thus, the dynamic interaction of material-performer-audience is foregrounded within this cultural framework.

The aesthetic means employed to enhance the collective life-force are varied. Dance, mask, totem, the spoken word, chant, and song may com-mingle; tragedy, comedy, and pathos may mix within a single, dramaturgic event because they stimulate different, affective responses that together constitute an experiential totality. A polyphony of narratives, shifting per-spectives, and complementary oppositions with the potential of resolution into equilibrium may feature prominently in the spectacle. Clearly demar-cated openings and closings, seriality, repetition, discontinuity, interlocking of energies or values, and density of meaning may also signify the active presence of àṣẹ, or life-force.[22]

Shange's Spell #7

In structure and potential effect *Spell #7* replicates the divination process, wherein a supplicant is offered a number of poetic narratives from the volume prescribed by the divining instruments and then asked to choose the scenario that best speaks to his or her need. Shange's text functions like an *odu*, or book, on the construction of black identities within an exorcised space, freed of the dominant culture's stereotypes. Thus, the performers present a series of narratives whose tones vary and whose relationships to each other initially appear tenuous. There is Fay, for ex-ample, a Brooklyn housewife, who, contrary to the societal categorizations allotted black women, is not a prostitute but is looking for a fun night out on the town. Alec wants a day of national apology for the dehumanization blacks have suffered at white hands, while Lily dreams of brushing an abundant head of hair from which pomegranates, ambrosia, and Ishmael Reed essays flow.

Two narratives placed at the end of each act threaten to rupture the whimsical or contained quality of most of the other scenarios.[23] They instigate instances of an interlock of conflicting energies whose resolution is problematic, heavily dependent upon audience members' imposition of an interpretive choice. I am referring to Sue-Jean, who kills her boychild named "myself" and thinks herself perpetually on the verge of giving birth, and to Maxine, who buys gold from South Africa in atonement for black people's willful perversions. Both women arrest processes of self-discovery, opting instead to remain in a liminal state on the verge of creative action. Their narratives exemplify what critic Barbara Christian terms "contrariness,"[24] for they are structured so that audiences are likely to be engaged by elements of the familiar and yet disturbed or repelled by the transgression of behavioral norms. Sue-Jean's and Maxine's histories challenge audiences to consider valuable energies that lie outside communal boundaries, energies that, if fully acknowledged, would disrupt these norms and force their redefinition. Thus, within these moments of contrariness Eṣu is potentially at work.

Furthermore, Maxine's monologue is followed by another interlock of oppositional energy, for the master of ceremonies reemerges to reassure spectators that they will love his "Black" magic. He initiates among cast members the refrain "bein colored & love it." Stage directions indicate that the chant is supposed to be handled like a celebratory moment in a Black church. But this is an extremely hard moment for performers to achieve, occurring, as it does, immediately after Maxine's anguished confession that she has been stripped of her childhood belief that Black people were immune to certain immoral practices because "surviving the impossible is sposed to accentuate the positive aspects of a people."[25] She has introduced the suspicion that salvation will never come, that the victims of oppression will become as inhumane as their oppressors, but the cast, like members of a church choir, must deploy language as a percussive instrument and perhaps dance as a vehicle for the manifestation of the invisible in order to massage into being a moment whose force, or emotional signification, will counteract the effect of Maxine's narrative. Whether they accomplish that task depends upon how the audience reads or interacts with what they are doing. Shange comments obliquely upon this foregrounding of audience response when she answers complaints that the production was "too intense":

> both *spell #7* & *boogie woogie landscapes* have elements of magic or leaps of faith / in typical afro-american fashion / not only will the lord find a way / but there *is* a way outta here. this is the litany from the spirituals to Jimi Hendrix' "there must be some kinda way outta here" / (xiv)

Thus, the near-final moment of *Spell #7* is left open, dependent on the triangulation of material-performer-audience at any given performance.

It is further complicated by the reappearance of the minstrel mask, reminding spectators that whatever vision they have chosen within the symbolic realm of theater must compete against the dominant culture's definition of blackness awaiting their exit from the performance space. Faced with that distorted grin, individuals may succumb to despair or project a will (àṣẹ) to somehow make life different. As the divination supplicant is required to make sacrifice, that is, to carry out magical-material acts designed to affirm his new perceptions, so too is a *Spell #7* audience challenged to envision and enact some realignment of social relations. But, whereas in the religious context the instability of interpretation may be masked by specific prescriptions and institutional pressures toward priestly self-preservation, in this theatrical appropriation of Yoruba divination, the spectators' freedom remains painfully apparent.

Oṣọfisan's Once Upon Four Robbers

Spectators' active production of meaning is even more directly acknowledged in the Oṣọfisan text, where their opinions are solicited and, in fact, determine a mode of formal closure. For those familiar with contemporary Nigerian history, the play's very title signals a contradiction of customary expectations: the drama seems to belong to the fairy tale genre, but, rather than being situated in some distant past, it concerns a more current phenomenon, that of armed robbery and the public execution of criminals. Though the playwright provides a narrative thread that holds together various plot elements, the extended roles-within-roles assumed by various actors create the impression of a text whose stitching becomes looser as the play progresses. Thus, rather than utilizing a critical mode that assumes an eventual harmony of elements, one may more appropriately read the text in relation to the divination paradigm, which projects a gallery of competitive social stances vis-à-vis a given problematic.

Presented in *Once upon Four Robbers* is an *odu* of episodes concerning the issue of solidarity. But, whereas in divination poetry each scenario constitutes a whole and contradiction arises from the juxtaposition of different narratives, Oṣọfisan employs a dialectical method of dramatization throughout. The consequence is that conflict and rupture are encoded within an individual *ẹsẹ*, or episode, as well as in the relationship among the various episodes. This discussion focuses on aspects of the text's self-reflexiveness, which simultaneously constitutes an aesthetic as well as social critique and defies fairy-tale conventions regarding moral clarity.

The drama begins with a narrator chanting and soliciting from listeners the formulaic call-and-response, which initiates a storytelling session and affirms the active interplay of all those assembled. His song promises a tale "ancient and modern" about "Dangerous highwaymen / Freebooters, source of tears,"[26] who approach him for protection from modern men who commit all manner of crimes in their rush to acquire money and property. As spectators join in singing the refrain, actors and musicians, scattered throughout the auditorium, drift onstage, greet each other, and casually go about choosing costumes and roles. Thus, by ironically juxtaposing two classes of criminals at the very outset, the text signals its concern with probing the nature of crime in a peripheral capitalist economy such as Nigeria's. In addition, by constructing an illusion of reality in front of viewers, it insinuates an intention to assert an equation between the fabrication of art and the fabrication, or alterability, of the world art is assumed to represent.

From this brief introduction flows a story about a band of robbers set adrift by their leader's public execution. Anticipating that a group of three men and one woman mean to rob him, an old man named Aafa upbraids them for not following an honest occupation. Their scornful miming of advertisements for day laborers indicates that, for those not in a position to "steal government files, award contracts—alter accounts—collude with aliens ——" (17), death by public execution represents a shame no greater than a life of unending, abject poverty. Aafa promises them a gift that will make them rich provided they pledge never to steal from the poor, rob only in public places, and resist killing another person. His talisman is a song to which they must each contribute a memorized verse; when sung, it will mesmerize listeners, causing them to dance and leave their property untended.

The band finds that the old man's magic does indeed work. Predictably, one of their members becomes greedy and attempts to steal from the others.[27] The ensuing argument about loyalty results in Major's being shot, the other thieves fleeing for safety, and the military police pocketing the original victims' money. Alhaja's attempt to rescue Major at the subsequent execution raises anew the issue of solidarity: she pleads for their colleague, Angola, to forgive Major and join in singing the song that will enchant the public and allow them all to escape. Simultaneously, the presiding officer presses ahead with his intention to kill the robber Hasan, who is also his brother. At the point where the robbers finally start to sing and the army prepares to shoot, Aafa reappears. He freezes the action, and encouraging spectators to speak, asks them to decide an appropriate ending for the play.

Setting serves as an important sign of the text's preoccupations, for events occur in a marketplace. Once a site for the exchange of goods and services, it has become a locus for an intense, economic struggle in which capital has been fetishized and functions as the yardstick of human worth. Power to consume and to enforce an oppressive hierarchy are the objectives toward which virtually all—the traders, soldiers, and thieves—strive.

But, for the Yoruba, the marketplace has traditionally meant more than a simple commercial locus. It also serves as a trope for the entire social network in which a human being is necessarily situated. Not only must people frequent this place in order to sustain themselves, but the gods also visit it often in order to feed their need for human contact. Usually located either in the center of town or at an outlying crossroads accessible to a number of villages, the marketplace is a favorite spot for Eṣu, who mediates the intersections of stability and disorder and of the human and the supernatural.

And Eṣu does indeed appear in the personage of Aafa. As storyteller, he initiates an illusion and participates in its making. He offers art as a deceptive, seductive medium that can function as a vehicle for individual self-aggrandizement and collective anesthesia or as a provocative agent introducing new circumstances and renewed definitions of self for practitioners and consumers alike. Just as the robbers must decide whether and how to insure the cohesiveness of their social unit, audiences are challenged to grapple with questions that inextricably link the symbolic with the material: Within the illusory world of the play, should the thieves be shot? Within the realm of observers' daily lives, what constitutes an appropriate definition of robbery in a society in which a few grow inordinately rich at the expense of the majority? How should such constructs as compassion and brotherhood operate within a social order? What is a proper, i.e., effective, relationship between their debates about art and their capacity to determine the directions of their sociopolitical existence?

Unlike the narrator of a fairy tale, this storyteller/text offers no happy ending. Rather, the "trickster" Eṣu is again at work, insisting upon sacrifice, enforcing the recognition that with choice comes responsibility: stage directions indicate that, should observers vote to execute the robbers, their deaths are to be mimed in slow, jerky movements with martial music blaring away at an annoyingly loud level. Should the audience choose to spare them, the thieves sing their song, enchanting and robbing both the spectators onstage and those seated in the auditorium. The playwright has reported that, in most instances, Nigerian audiences opted to free the robbers, but certainly one can imagine a situation where no clear consensus emerges from discussion. In such a case, the actors would presumably be relieved of the obligation to impose either of the scripted endings, for the artistic enterprise aims not so much for the interpretive tidiness of closure as for dialogue among an assembled community of performers and spectators. As the presence of Aafa/Eṣu signifies, closure is itself an illusion. Each person, as a member of a complex social network, is challenged to impose meaning upon events, but that interpretation is always subject to chance and change.

Divination and Feminism

Given spatial constraints, the subject of feminism/womanism is largely outside the scope of this essay.[28] I do want to note, however, that, like Oṣofisan, Shange not only utilizes divination as dramatic structure but also incorporates some of its gods into her plays as characters. The "passion flower of southwest los angeles," who lures and then rejects men in *for colored girls who have considered suicide when the rainbow is enuf*, is perhaps the most stunning example of Shange's revision of *vodun's* sacred lore surrounding Erzulie.

More important perhaps than concrete instances of imaginative redeployments is the fact that such usage signals a concept of feminism which significantly departs from those definitions advanced by white European and American theorists. Because Yoruba is a nongendered language, traditional Ifá hermeneutics has remained relatively free of gender bias;[29] thus, to a certain extent, Shange—as well as Oṣofisan—is guided or constrained by its perspectives. The mythologies of Ọṣun and Erzulie argue for gender complementarity, for, as Maya Deren observes in the case of Erzulie,

> Vodoun does not idealize women, per se, as the principle of fecundity. Neither does it give preferential emphasis to the maternal womb over the phallic principle, either as cosmic origin, or in the prevalent psychology reflected in ritual. . . . But if Vodoun denies women this distinctive role as a separate cosmic element, . . . [it] has given women, in the figure of Erzulie, exclusive title to that which distinguishes humans from all other forms: their capacity to conceive beyond reality, to desire beyond adequacy, to create beyond need.[30]

But set against religious discourse is Yoruba social praxis whose oppressive patriarchal character can be attributed in part to contact with Islam and Christianity.[31] Nonetheless, historical studies of Yoruba women like that of Niara Sudarkasa and observations of African-American life-styles by essayists like Alice Walker document the extent to which the stance encoded in archetypal lore, though greatly attenuated by contemporary sociohistorical conditions, remains vital for significant portions of African and African-American communities.[32] Consequently, the challenge for a critical reader is to attempt to calibrate the effect of countervailing variables within a given text.

Conclusions

Divination as encoded in Ifá and Sixteen Cowrie offers a compelling mode of reading and comparing dramatic texts within the literatures of Africa and its American diasporas. As argued above, the paradigm favors multiple narratives, discontinuity, and paradox with the possibility of interpretive cohesion arising out of the spectator's imposition of meaning. When applied to literary texts like novels, the figure of Eṣu has been interpreted so as to privilege the critic, who is said to perform a parallel function to that of the god.[33] But, while such privileging may be suspect at the level of theory, the collaborative nature of theater production and the texts by Shange and Ọṣofisan demonstrate its utter untenability within the domain of live performance. Given the objective of redefining constricting social relations coupled with the space allowed for audience intervention, these texts possess the potential to function as a counterhegemonic discourse.

While this essay has purposefully limited its arena of textual investigation, discussion of the Yoruba theoretical frame suggests that aspects of the paradigm may be appropriately applied to other playwrights in Africa and the diaspora. Consideration of issues of intertextuality points to the care with which we must move in pursuing studies of individual authors and in undertaking comparative reviews. Given the adaptations African peoples have made in confronting a myriad of geographical and sociohistorical terrains, the eventual compilation of such comparative analyses will give entirely new meaning to the term *world drama*.

NOTES

1. While forms such as minstrelsy or plays like William Wells Brown's *Escape; or, A Leap to Freedom*, long considered the first drama written by an African American, or Marita Bonner's *The Purple Flower* can be said to offer evidence of continuity; though W. E. B. DuBois articulated his theory of "double consciousness" in the first decade of this century, realism has exerted such a strong hold on the American dramatic imagination that, with the exception of Langston Hughes, African-American playwrights prior to the 1960s largely ignored Africa as an originary point for positive identity.

2. Obviously, it is impossible to provide an extensive citation here; the following texts will nevertheless offer a solid introduction to the area: Paul Carter Harrison, *The Drama of Nommo: Black Theater in the African Continuum* (New York: Grove Press, 1972); and, most recently, "Mother/Word, Black Theatre in the African Continuum: Word/Song as Method," in *Totem Voices: Plays from the Black World Repertory*, ed. Paul Carter Harrison (New York: Grove Press, 1989), xi–lxiii; LeRoi Jones [Amiri Baraka], *Home: Social Essays* (New York: William Morrow, 1966); and *Blues People: Negro Music in White America* (New York: William Morrow, 1963); Larry Neal, "Some Reflections on a Black Aesthetic," in *The Black Aesthetic*, ed. Addison Gayle, Jr. (New York: Doubleday, 1971), 13–16; and *Visions of a Liberated Future: Black Arts Movement Writings* (New York: Thunder's Mouth Press, 1989); also essays by Hatch, Traylor, Thompson, and Bentson in *The Theatre of Black Americans*, vol. 1: *Roots and Rituals / The Image Makers*, ed. Errol Hill (Englewood Cliffs, N.J.: Prentice-Hall, 1980).

3. *The Signifying Monkey* by Henry Louis Gates, Jr. (New York: Oxford University Press, 1988) is perhaps the most outstanding example, but other critics such as Femi Euba and Diedre Badejo are also using Yoruba practices to inform their analyses. See, for example, Euba's *Archetypes, Imprecators, and Victims of Fate: Origins and Developments of Satire in Black Drama* (New York: Greenwood Press, 1989); and Badejo's "The Goddess Òṣun as a Paradigm for African Feminist Criticism," *Sage: A Scholarly Journal on Black Woman* 6, no. 1 (1989): 27–32.

4. Cheikh Anta Diop, *The African Origin of Civilization: Myth or Reality?* trans. M. Cook (Westport, Conn.: L. Hill, 1974); St. Clair Drake, *Black Folk Here and There: An Essay in History and Anthropology*, vol. 1 (Los Angeles: Center for Afro-American Studies, University of California–Los Angeles, 1987); and Martin Bernal, *Black Athena: The Afroasiatic Roots of Classical Civilization*, vol. 1: *The Fabrication of Ancient Greece, 1785–1985* (New Brunswick, N.J.: Rutgers University Press, 1987).

5. Amilcar Cabral, "National Liberation and Culture," in *Unity and Struggle: Speeches and Writings*, trans. Michael Wolfers (London: Heinemann, 1980), 143.

6. Hortense J. Spillers, "Cross Currents, Discontinuities: Black Women's Fiction," in *Conjuring: Black Women, Fiction, and Literary Tradition*, ed. Marjorie Pryse and Hortense J. Spillers (Bloomington: Indiana University Press, 1985), 250.

7. See, for example, my article "Wasn't Brecht an African Writer?: Parallels with Contemporary Nigerian Drama," in *Brecht in Asia and Africa*, vol. 14: *The Brecht Yearbook*, ed. John Fuegi et al. (Hong Kong: International Brecht Society, 1989), 168–83.

8. The term has been coined by VèVè A. Clark, who states, "Diaspora literacy is the ability to read and comprehend the discourses of Africa, Afro-America and the Caribbean from an informed, indigenous perspective," in her article "Developing Diaspora Literacy: Allusion in Maryse Condé's *Hérémakhonon*," in *Out of the*

Kumbla: Caribbean Women and Literature, ed. Carol Boyce Davies and Elaine Savory Fido (Trenton: Africa World Press, 1990), 304. Although to my mind the point is implicit in Clark's comments, I am explicitly arguing that, since the sixteenth century at least, the Western presence has been implicated within indigenous perspectives.

9. Personal interview, 11 January 1991.

10. Primus, like her more famous contemporary Katherine Dunham, was also a dancer-anthropologist; she had been preceded in the effort to have African dance viewed seriously by the West African Asadata Dafora, who presented dance from the Mende people of Sierra Leone during the 1920s. See, for example, William Moore, "The Development of Black Modern Dance in America," in *Black Tradition in American Modern Dance,* ed. Gerald E. Myers (Durham, N.C.: American Dance Festival, 1988), 15, 17.

11. New Orleans native Luisah Teish later became a priestess of Ọ̀ṣun in the Yoruba Lucumi tradition. She is also the author of *Jambalaya: The Natural Woman's Book of Personal Charms and Practice Rituals* (San Francisco: Harper and Row, 1985).

12. Shange reports absorbing different lessons from these three mentors: from Baraka, an appreciation of the ritual of language; from Reed, a global sense of black history and permission to change the syntax to change the mood; and, from Hurston, a demonstration that long fiction could be successfully sustained by a female character (personal interview, 11 January 1991).

13. Marjorie Pryse, "Zora Neale Hurston, Alice Walker, and the 'Ancient Power' of Black Women," in Pryse and Spillers, *Conjuring,* 11.

14. Rowland Abiodun, "Woman in Yoruba Religious Images," *African Languages and Cultures* 2, no. 1 (1988): 3.

15. Abiodun, "Woman," 3.

16. Maya Deren, *Divine Horsemen: The Voodoo Gods of Haiti* (New York: Dell, 1970), 138.

17. Note that numerous critics such as Ogundipe and Pelton argue that the trickster designation denotes negative Christian influence and obscures Eṣu's divine functions. See, for example, Ayodele Ogundipe, "Eṣu Elegbara, the Yoruba God of Chance and Uncertainty: A Study in Yoruba Mythology" (Ph.D. diss., Indiana University, 1978); and Robert D. Pelton, *The Trickster in West Africa: A Study in Mythic Irony and Sacred Delight* (Berkeley: University of California Press, 1980).

18. Pelton, *Trickster,* 133, quoting Joan Westcott, "Sculpture and Myths of Eshu-Elegba, the Yoruba Trickster," *Africa* 32 (1962): 336–53.

19. Pelton, *Trickster,* 150.

20. Diedre LaPin, "Story, Medium and Masque: The Idea and Art of Yoruba Storytelling" (Ph.D. diss., University of Wisconsin–Madison, 1977), quoted in Henry John Drewal and Margaret Thompson Drewal, *Gẹlẹdẹ: Art and Female Power among the Yoruba* (Bloomington: Indiana University Press, 1983), 1.

21. Kacke Gotrick, *Apidan Theatre and Modern Drama: A Study in a Traditional Yoruba Theatre and Its Influence on Modern Drama by Yoruba Playwrights* (Göteborg, Sweden: Graphic Systems AB, 1984), 115–19; LaPin, "Story, Medium and Masque," chap. 2.

22. Drewal and Drewal, *Gẹlẹdẹ,* 1–7.

23. Sandra L. Richards, "Conflicting Impulses in the Plays of Ntozake Shange," *Black American Literature Forum* 17 (1983): 73–78.

24. Barbara Christian, *Black Feminist Criticism: Perspectives on Black Women Writers* (New York: Pergamon Press, 1985), 31–46.

25. Ntozake Shange, *Spell #7*, in *Three Pieces* (New York: St. Martin's Press, 1981), 51; hereafter page citations are indicated in parentheses within the text.

26. Femi Ọṣọfisan, *Once upon Four Robbers*, 2d ed. (Ibadan, Nigeria: BIO Educational Services, 1982), 74. All subsequent references are from this edition; page citations are indicated in parentheses within the text.

27. Ọṣọfisan returns to these plot elements in his *Eṣu and the Vagabond Minstrels* (Ibadan, Nigeria: New Horn Press, 1991).

28. For a rigorous discussion of which term more accurately registers Black women's perceptions, see Carol Boyce Davies and Elaine Savory Fido's introduction and Sylvia Wynter's closing comments to Davies and Fido's anthology, *Out of the Kumbla: Caribbean Women and Literature*; also Kathleen M. Balutansky's review of this anthology, "Naming Caribbean Women Writers," *Callaloo* 13 (1990): 540–43.

29. Gates, *Signifying Monkey*, 30.

30. Deren, *Divine Horsemen*, 137–38.

31. While Ọṣọfisan is virtually unique among his male contemporaries in representing women as actors or agents of Nigerian events, he also betrays some of the patriarchal attitudes characteristic of his culture. For further discussion, see chapters 2 and 7 of my book *Ancient Songs Set Ablaze: The Theatre of Femi Ọṣọfisan* (forthcoming).

32. Niara Sudarkasa, "'The Status of Women' in Indigenous African Societies," in *Women in Africa and the African Diaspora*, ed. Rosalyn Terborg-Penn, Sharon Harley, and Andrea Benton Rushing (Washington, D.C.: Howard University Press, 1987), 25–42; and Alice Walker, *In Search of Our Mother's Gardens* (New York: Harcourt Brace Jovanovich, 1983).

33. Gates, *Signifying Monkey*, chap. 1, passim.

David Henry Hwang's *M. Butterfly* and Philip Kan Gotanda's *Yankee Dawg You Die:* Repositioning Chinese-American Marginality on the American Stage

James Moy

> One thinks one is tracing the outline of the thing's nature over and
> over again, and one is merely tracing around the frame through
> which we look at it. . . . A *picture* held us captive. And we could not
> get outside it, for it lay in our language and language seemed to
> repeat it to us inexorably.
>
> —Wittgenstein

The point of intersection of the popular unconsciousness and the self-conscious, seriously intended work of art has always been problematic. The extent to which socially conscious drama, for example, can emerge from the morass of the bourgeois perception of the world is questionable at best.[1] For over a hundred years now popular representations of Asian populations in America have remained at a level perhaps best described as stereotypical. Employing various strategies, Anglo-American playwrights have offered the Chinese in America as collections of fetishized parts and as exotics. In the nineteenth century, for example, in seeking to provide sympathetic views of the Chinese, Bret Harte and Mark Twain, both serious writers, could offer finally little more than a stereotypical character consisting of fragments that articulated the most obvious aspects of difference. Some fifty years later Eugene O'Neill, often regarded as the father of American playwriting, seeking to provide a positive image of "Oriental wisdom" in contrast to a corrupt Western commercialism, could do little more than demonstrate a tourist view of an exotic "heathen" Orientalist China.[2]

Not until the new cultural awareness of the 1960s did this situation change, as playwrights produced conscious attempts to dispel stereotypes. As Asian-American playwrights emerged, then, the earlier comic or exotic treatments offered by whites were replaced by Asian self-representations. Rarely popular with the dominant culture audiences, some of these plays did provide incisive examinations of what it is to be Chinese in a familiar yet alien land. Notable among these are Frank Chin's *Year of the Dragon* (1974) and *The Chickencoop Chinaman* (1972), the first Chinese-American offering on a major New York stage; David Henry Hwang's *F.O.B.* (1979), *The Dance and the Railroad* (1981), *Family Devotions* (1981), and *M. Butterfly* (1988); and Benny Yee and Nobuko Miyamoto's *Chop Suey* (1980),

Fig. 1. John Lithgow as Rene Gallimard and B. D. Wong playing Song Liling in *M. Butterfly*. New York City, 1988. Photo credit: Joan Marcus.

a musical comedy that invited its audiences to look beyond the surface realities of colorful Chinatown.

Significantly, Hwang's *M. Butterfly* won the Tony award for best American play of 1988. In addition, 1988 saw successful runs of Philip Kan Gotanda's *Yankee Dawg You Die* in San Francisco, Los Angeles, and Chicago, with an off-Broadway production in New York during 1989.[3] Both of them written by Asian-Americans, these plays feature Chinese characters as major figures and have received generally favorable press in America.

Against the backdrop of the Vietnam War, China's Cultural Revolution, and the events of May 1968, *M. Butterfly* relates the true-life tale of French diplomat Rene Bouriscot's twenty-year affair with a Beijing Opera performer. The liaison results in the birth of a child and a trial for espionage. Through the character Rene Gallimard, Hwang stages Bouriscot's story. At Gallimard's trial it is revealed that his lover was not only a spy but also a man. Accordingly, the audience is left to ponder how a sophisticated Western member of the diplomatic service could fall victim to so amusing a case of gender confusion. Responding to this question, Hwang uses Giacomo Puccini's *Madama Butterfly* (1904) as a point of departure for the diplomat's first encounter with his "mistress," which takes place at a performance of scenes from the Puccini opera in the German ambassador's residence in Beijing. Gallimard compliments the performance: "You were utterly convincing. It's the first time . . . I've seen the beauty of the story."[4] In response, Song Liling, the soon-to-be lover, assails the silliness of the Western stereotypes:

It's one of your favorite fantasies, isn't it? The submissive Oriental woman and the cruel white man.... Consider it this way: what would you say if a blond homecoming queen fell in love with a short Japanese businessman? He treats her cruelly, then goes home for three years, during which time she prays to his picture and turns down marriage from a young Kennedy. Then, when she learns he has remarried, she kills herself. Now, I believe you would consider this girl to be a deranged idiot, correct? But because it's an Oriental who kills herself for a Westerner—ah!—you find it beautiful.(4)

Despite this harangue, Gallimard proceeds to entrap his "butterfly." We look on as he manipulates the emotions of Song Liling, all the while unaware that he himself has fallen into a trap of his own delusions regarding their relationship: "I stopped going to the opera, I didn't phone or write her,... and, as I wickedly refused to do so, I felt for the first time that rush of power—the absolute power of a man" (7). As Gallimard feels the "power of a man," Song explains, "all he wants is for her to submit. Once a woman submits, a man is always ready to become 'generous,'... Now, if I can just present him with a baby. A Chinese baby with blond hair—he'll be mine for life!" (12). Gallimard's conquest of his butterfly complete, he applies his newfound wisdom to the conduct of international policy: "If the Americans demonstrate the will to win, the Vietnamese will welcome them into a mutually beneficial union.... Orientals will always submit to a greater force" (9–10). This, of course, was the mistake of the Vietnam War:

And somehow the American war went wrong.... Four hundred thousand dollars were being spent for every Viet Cong killed; so General Westmoreland's remark that the Oriental does not value life the way Americans do was oddly accurate. Why weren't the Vietnamese people giving in? Why were they content to die and die and die again? (13)

As he had miscalculated the Vietnamese will to resist, so Gallimard had fallen hopelessly in love with a Song Liling created in his own imagination. When Song reveals his deception, Gallimard dismisses him, "You, you're as real as hamburger. Now get out! I have a date with my Butterfly." Gallimard explains that he is "a man who loved a woman created by a man. Everything else—simply falls short.... Tonight, I've finally learned to tell fantasy from reality. And, knowing the difference, I choose fantasy." Gallimard's fantasy collapsed the Orient into one indistinguishable mass, annihilating the differences between Chinese, Vietnamese, and Japanese, offering a vision of

slender women in chong sams and kimonos who die for the love of unworthy foreign devils. Who are born and raised to be the perfect women. Who take whatever punishment we give them, and bounce back, stengthened by love, unconditionally. It is a vision that has become my life.

As Gallimard's unworthy life interpenetrates that of his imaginary lover, he realizes that the only course open to him is the same as that chosen by Puccini's Cho Cho San, since "death with honor is better than life ... with dishonor." As the diplomat commits suicide, Song, making explicit an ironic role reversal, declares Gallimard his butterfly as the lights fade to black (16).

Although there is a curious conflation of "imperialism, racism and sexism,"[5] Hwang's indictment of the West is clear. If not clear through the development of Gallimard's character, then Song's words make Hwang's attack explicit:

> The West has a sort of international rape mentality.... The West thinks of itself as masculine—big guns, big industry, big money—so the East is feminine—weak, delicate, poor ... but good at art, and full of inscrutable wisdom—the feminine mystique.... Her mouth says no, but her eyes say yes. The West believes the East, deep down, *wants* to be dominated—because a woman can't think for herself. (15)

Resonances of Puccini's *Madama Butterfly* likewise permeate Philip Kan Gotanda's *Yankee Dawg You Die*. Where Hwang's *M. Butterfly* cinematically spans some twenty years, the Gotanda piece examines the first year in the evolving relationship between a young aspiring Japanese actor, Bradley Yamashita, and an older more established "Chinese" actor. While Hwang's *Butterfly* has a cinematic feel, Gotanda's piece uses a stereotypical cinematic portrayal of a Japanese soldier to fix the general reception of Asianness in the popular consciousness. The opening scene of *Yankee Dawg You Die*, which attacks this standard portrayal of the Japanese, sets the tone for the rest of the play. The lead character in the piece, Vincent Chang, is a Chinese actor who is later revealed to be a Japanese man, having changed his name to find work after World War II. In the industry, then, he is a Japanese man who pretended to be a Chinese actor so that he could get work portraying Japanese stereotypes.

If *M. Butterfly* merely attacks the Anglo-American system of representing Asianness, *Yankee Dawg You Die* reinforces the attack with a discussion of its impact. Bradley, for example, exposes the effects the mediated castration of the Asian male has had on his life while accusing Vincent of perpetuating it:

> Vincent.... All that self hate.... *Where does it begin?* You and your Charley Chop Suey roles.... you think every time you do one of those demeaning roles, the only thing lost is *your* dignity.... Don't you see that every time you do a portrayal like that millions of people in movie theatres see it? *Believe* it. Every time you do any old stereotypic role just to pay the bills, you kill the right of some Asian child to be treated as a human being. To walk through the school yard and not be called a "chinaman gook" by some kid who saw the last Rambo film. (33–35)

Gotanda sensitively measures the depth of the Asian-American desire to find role models. Bradley's misplaced identification with Neil Sedaka, a Jewish pop singer with a Japanese sounding name, causes Yamashita to mistake him for America's first "Japanese American rock 'n' roll star" (27). Finally, failing to locate an adequate human model for behavior, Gotanda seems to suggest that many Asian Americans have turned to the Japanese movie monster Godzilla as a source of cultural pride and perhaps even identification (41–44). Gotanda's piece shifts back and forth between the issue of identifying proper role models on one hand and the pragmatics of employment in the theater/film industry on the other. The desire to show "real" Asians is always suspended in tension with the Orientalist stereotype required in the industry. And the latter usually wins out. Vincent's claim to being a "leading man" is repeatedly undercut by vignettes that display the mechanics of his stereotypical portrayals. Early on in the play, Bradley complains that the only roles open to Asians are "waiters, viet cong killers, chimpanzees, drug dealers, hookers, sexless houseboys. . . . They fucking cut off our balls and made us all houseboys on the evening soaps. 'Get your very own neutered, oriental houseboy!'" (36). Accordingly, this piece seems more overt than M. Butterfly in its attack on the theatrical institutions that work to subjugate the representations of the Orient.

Vincent makes clear his cognizance of his complicity within this theatrical institution by relating an early episode in the life of Martin Luther King, Jr.:

> They came and took him away. Told him they were going to kill him. He said he never felt more impotent, more like a slave than that night. After that, he realized he had to fight not only the white man on the outside, but the slave inside of him. . . . It is so easy to slip into the ching-chong chinaman. (60)

Central to Yankee Dawg You Die, then, is the issue of how one must deal with this imperative that would seduce Asian Americans into the kind of cultural complicity required to "survive." To allow one to surrender to the cultural hegemony of Anglo dominance. In response to this question Gotanda offers the contrast between the older Vincent Chang who has "sold out" by accepting stereotypical roles and Bradley Yamashita, the aspiring young actor full of radical rage with demands that Asians be allowed realistic stage presences.

Again, since both plays are clearly popular with Anglo-American audiences, one is inspired to wonder whether the acceptance of these plays signals, finally, an end to the marginalization of Chineseness, or Asianness in general. Even a superficial examination of the social text reveals that this is not the case. A close interrogation of the playscripts reveals an interesting system of literary subversions with significant impact for the social.

Obviously, both Gotanda's Yankee Dawg You Die and Hwang's M. Butterfly set out to dispel stereotypical representations of Asianness.

Fig. 2. Sab Shimono playing Vincent Chang (left) and Marc Hayashi as Bradley Yamashita in Chicago's Wisdom Bridge Theatre Company's 1988 production of *Yankee Dawg You Die*. Photo credit: Jennifer Girard.

While Gotanda makes explicit the aim in his text, Hwang has said that he set out to do a "deconstructivist *Madame Butterfly*."[6] Toward this end Hwang employed a strategy described in an interview/essay appropriately entitled "Smashing Stereotypes":

> I am interested in cutting through . . . all the crap about the way people write about characters from the East. I mean, when these people are written about, it's always in this inscrutable poetic fashion. It's so untrue, and kind of irritating. So my tendency is to go to the other extreme and make it so slangy and contemporary that it is jarring.[7]

Hwang's hope, then, is to offer a truer view of Asianness within the space created by the tension between the audience's stereotypical knowledge and his "slangy and jarring" contemporary reality.

Still, both plays seem to be scathing indictments of the Western need to demean, stereotype, and psychologically control the Orient and its representations. There are, then, two possible explanations for their popularity. Since it is clear that Asians remain marginalized, one must conclude that either Anglo-American audiences harbor a strong heretofore unexploited masochistic tendency or the authors of these pieces have somehow managed to neutralize or deflect their explicit attack on Anglo-American sensibilities. Given the limits of enlightened liberal self-guilt, one must conclude the reasons for this popularity will be found in the latter.

If Hwang sought to locate a new potential vision for Asianness sus-

pended in tension between the stereotypical and his jarringly contemporary reality, then the characters he deploys to do so are of crucial importance. Unfortunately, they more often seem to subvert his stated intention. The specifically Asian technical aspects of Hwang's *M. Butterfly*, the kurogo, for example, serve not as characters but, rather, exist as mere absent presences without voice who silently move stage properties about the acting area. Matters get worse as Asian characters are given voice. Comrade Chan (and the other characters played by the same actor) is perhaps even more stereotypical and cartoonish than the worst of the nineteenth-century stereotypes. Chan, then, serves as a sort of caricature of the stereotype whose "jarring" language alienates while fixing a provisional position for this traditional view of the Orient.

With the traditional stereotype thus disfigured and in place, the character of Song Liling is of paramount significance, because it is within the space of the tension between this role and the stereotype that a new hoped for vision of Chineseness or Asianness will emerge. And it is here that Hwang's project falls apart. For here he offers at best another disfigured stereotype. As racial and sexual confusion are collapsed into one character, Song Liling exists as a vehicle of massive self-doubt. S/he claims to be working as a spy for the state while admitting that he enjoys the life of a transvestite. While s/he stands in for the role of the victimized Chinese character, the claim is made false as his manipulation of Gallimard is revealed through the role reversal at the end of the play. Accordingly, s/he finally comes across as little more than a disfigured transvestite version of the infamous Chinese "dragon lady" prostitute stereotype.[8] After proudly revealing his manhood to Gallimard, s/he covers up with great embarrassment as his Armani slacks are tossed offstage. This pattern of subversion establishes not an articulation of Asian desire, but, rather, it affirms a nefarious complicity with Anglo-American desire in its constitution of Otherness, both sexual and racial. Moreover, with the displacement of the action into the neutralized alien space of France, the author deflects any need for consideration of actual race relations in America. Within this confused indeterminant anamorphic site at the intersection of race and gender, only obvious questions can be apprehended. As audiences leave the theater, then, racial/sexual identity is not an issue; instead, most are simply incredulous about how for twenty years Gallimard could have confused Song's rectum for a woman's vagina.

Gotanda also uses what could be called jarring contemporary language to demythologize stereotypical portrayals of Asianness, which are fixed in the first scene of the piece. A somewhat more mature writer, he successfully contrasts the attitudes of the two actors confronting the imperatives of working in an industry that is essentially racist. Vincent Chang is revealed to be a Japanese man pretending to be Chinese to gain employment, but the clear linkage between racial disguise and economic imperative makes this acceptable. Indeed, it serves to emphasize the handicaps under which Asian-American performers must work. Difficulties arise when it becomes evident that Vincent is gay and obviously ashamed of this situation. In light of America's gay/lesbian liberation movement, this collapse of race and gender confusion is almost enough to crush the unwitting Chinese/ Japanese/closet gay Vincent Chang into the space of aporia, subverting the most positive aspects of the play before it. Between the cinematic stereotype and this disfigured Chinese actor, little space exists for a new "real" Asian American since it is suggested that Bradley, too, will succumb to Chang's fate. Indeed, before the end of the play the once radical Bradley has already accepted stereotypical roles, had a nose job, and been warned that within thirty-five years he may be just like Chinese actor Vincent Chang (60).

Clearly, most problematic are the stage characters that both Hwang and Gotanda deploy to replace the earlier stereotypical portrayals. Their positions in tension with traditional standard portrayals create the site for a new Asian stage presence. Unfortunately, at this site for the emergent new image of Asianness the figures self-destruct at the very moment of their representation, leaving behind only newly disfigured traces. By interrogating David Henry Hwang's M. Butterfly and Philip Kan Gotanda's Yankee Dawg You Die one can see the genesis of a new representational strategy, one in which the words offer a clear indictment of the cultural hegemony of the West, while the characters empowered to represent and speak on behalf of the Chinese or Asians are laughable and grossly disfigured. Thus marginalized, desexed, and made faceless, these Asian characters constitute no threat to Anglo-American sensibilities. Instead, these figures provide a good evening's entertainment and then float as exotic Orientalist fetishes articulating Anglo-American desire now doubly displaced into the new order of stereotypical representations created by Asian Americans.

Most troubling is the possibility that this rupture at the site of representation could be strategic, intentional. A way of exploiting a jarringly contemporary Orient in a manner quite common in the fashion industry. In a public forum like the theater, writers must ultimately seek validation in the marketplace. And the market being appealed to here is clearly Anglo-American.

The popular acceptance of these disfigured Chinese characters despite their Asian-American authorship does not signify an assimilation of the Chinese or Asianness into the American mainstream but, rather, a mere repositioning of their marginality and the creation of new "play" figures for the West. It would appear that both writers have fallen into the trap of complicity that Martin Luther King, Jr., had admonished against, for it seems that while their mouths say no their eyes say yes.[9]

NOTES

1. For a detailed treatment of this, see Donald M. Lowe, *History of Bourgeois Perception* (Chicago: University of Chicago Press, 1982).

2. See my article "Mark Twain and Bret Harte's *Ah Sin:* Locating China in the Geography of the American West," in *Frontiers of Asian American Studies: Writing, Research, and Commentary,* ed. Gail M. Nomura and Stephen H. Sumida (Pullman,

Wash.: Washington State University Press, 1989), 187–94; and "Eugene O'Neill's *Marco Millions:* Desiring Marginality and the Dematerialization of the Orient," *Drama* (published in Chinese), Central Institute of Drama (Beijing), 1988.

3. *M. Butterfly* premiered on 10 February 1988 at the National Theater in Washington, D.C., and opened in New York City on Broadway on 20 March 1988 at the Eugene O'Neill Theater. All references to the playscript are from the first publication of the piece, which appeared as an insert (with independent internal pagination) between pages 32 and 33 of *American Theatre* (July–August 1988); hereafter this playscript will be referred to as *M. Butterfly* and cited in the text. Philip Kan Gotanda's "Yankee Dawg You Die," was provided by the Wisdom Bridge Theatre Company of Chicago, which produced the piece during the fall of 1988; hereafter referred to as *Yankee Dawg You Die* and cited in the text.

4. *M. Butterfly,* 4. The use of Puccini's *Madama Butterfly* (1904) for a point of departure is intriguing given that the Italian opera was an adaptation of an earlier American play entitled *Madame Butterfly* (1900) by John L. Long and David Belasco.

5. David Savran, *In Their Own Words* (New York: Theatre Communications Group, 1988), 127.

6. David Henry Hwang, *M. Butterfly* (New York: New American Library, 1989), 95.

7. Gerard Raymond, "Smashing Stereotypes," *Theatre Week* (11 April 1988): 8. See also Savran, *In Their Own Words,* 117–31.

8. For a treatment of this stereotype as it developed in the American cinema, see Renee E. Tajima, "Lotus Blossoms Don't Bleed: Images of Asian Women," in *Making Waves: An Anthology of Writings by and about Asian American Women,* ed. Asian Women United of California (Boston: Beacon Press, 1989), 308–17.

9. It is interesting to note here that, in responding to "leftist element[s], which might accuse me of selling out," Hwang has said, "I think the [Chinese-American] community by and large is very success oriented and is more likely to embrace one of their own on the basis of having got to Broadway, no matter what the play was—as long as it was not horribly critical of the Chinese-American community" (Raymond, "Smashing Stereotypes," 8).

Invasions Friendly and Unfriendly:
The Dramaturgy of Direct Theater

Richard Schechner

> ... old authority and truth pretend to be absolute, to have an
> extratemporal importance. Therefore, their representatives ... are
> gloomily serious. ... And thus these personages come to the end of
> their role still serious, although their spectators have been laughing
> for a long time.
>
> —Mikhail Bakhtin, *Rabelais and His World*

> The role of the revolutionary is to create theatre which creates a
> revolutionary frame of reference. The power to define is the power
> to control. ... The goal of theatre is to get as many people as
> possible to overcome fear by taking action. We create reality
> wherever we go by living our fantasies.
>
> —Jerry Rubin, *Do It!*

What is the relation between "the authorities" and "the people" when the
people occupy public streets, squares, plazas, and buildings? Do carnivals
encourage giddy, drunken, sexy feelings and behavior, or does the very
action of taking spaces, of "liberating" them, make people giddy? Is it
accidental that official displays consist of neat rectangles, countable cohorts,
marching past and under the fixed gaze of the reviewing stand, while
unofficial mass gatherings are vortexed, whirling, full of shifting ups and
downs, multifocused events generating tension between large scale actions
and many local dramas? And why is it that unofficial gatherings elicit,
permit, or celebrate the erotic, while official displays are so often associated
with the military?

Festivals and carnivals belong to comic theater, comic in desire, even
if sometimes tragic in outcome. When people go into the streets en masse,
they are celebrating life's fertility. They eat, drink, make theater, make love,
enjoy each others' company, put on masks and costumes, erect and wave
banners, and construct effigies not merely to disguise or embellish their
ordinary selves or to flaunt the outrageous but also to act out the multiplicity each human life is. They protest, often by means of farce and parody,
what is oppressive, ridiculous, and outrageous.

Sometimes street actions bring about change—as in Eastern Europe
in 1989. But mostly such scenes, both celebratory and violent, end with
the old order restored. The old order sponsors a temporary relief from
itself. Obeying strict calendars and confined to designated precincts, carnival allows the authorities to keep track of such relief while readying the
police. Despite such preparations, rebellions swell to almost musical cli-
maxes around sacrilized dates—anniversaries of the deaths or funerals of

heroes and martyrs or of earlier popular uprisings (as in China) or the Christmas season and the approach of the New Year (as in Eastern Europe). To allow people to assemble in the streets is always to flirt with the possibility of improvised rebellion.

Incipient revolutions are carnivalesque. This is because both revolution and carnival propose a free space to satisfy desires, especially sexual and drunken desires, a new time to enact social relations more freely. People make, costume, and act in ways that are "not me" and almost always excessive relative to ordinary life. They drink, fuck, loot, burn, riot, murder, and practice rough justice on those they feel have wronged them. But, sooner or later, either at a defined moment—when the church bells ring in Ash Wednesday, when school begins again after spring break, when a new government is firmly in power—the liminal period ends and individuals are inserted or reinserted into their (sometimes new, sometimes old, but always defined) places in society.

René Girard argues that "the fundamental purpose of the festival is to set the stage for a sacrificial act that marks at once the climax and the termination of the festivities." Festive sacrifice is necessary to innoculate society against "falling into interminable violence." Roger Caillois goes further: "In its pure form, the festival must be defined as the paroxysm of society, purifying and renewing it simultaneously. The paroxysm is not only its climax from a religious but also from an economic point of view."[1] The potlatches of Native Americans on the Pacific coast in the late nineteenth century are clear examples of what Caillois was talking about. The public destruction of goods was both a display of wealth and an act of violent dissipation. After a great potlatch there was nothing left but to get back to amassing the resources needed to stage another. Unlike the Roman Saturnalia where a scapegoat slave was sacrificed or the Athenian theater of Dionysus where actors pretended to suffer and die, potlatchers gave up the real thing: the material substance of their wealth.

Caillois regarded modern European carnivals "as a sort of moribund echo of ancient festivals." In modern times state apparatus guarantees social solidarity. With rare exceptions today's festivals and carnivals are not inversions of the social order but mirrors of it. "Lords of Misrule" are not drawn from the lower or oppressed classes or enabled to rule (even for a day). But unofficial culture worms its way back into public outdoor spaces. There is a long history of unofficial performances "taking place" in (seizing as well as using) locales not architecturally imagined as theaters.[2] Over the past thirty years performance experimenters have used outdoor spaces—courtyards, streets, walls, beaches, lakes, rooftops, plazas, and mountainsides—for purposes aesthetic, personal, ritualistic, and political. And, while modern Western dramatists abandoned the public squares of Renaissance theater for the living room, kitchen, bedroom, motel, and office, the emerging festival theater repositioned itself in places where public life and social ritual have traditionally been acted out. Doubtlessly, there has been a mutually fruitful exchange between art performances and politically radical symbolic public actions. By the 1960s these

Fig. 1. Tiananmen Square, 17 MAY 1989. The
Gate of Heavenly Peace with Mao's portrait in
the background. Photo: AP/Wide World.

Fig. 2. The "Goddess of Democracy and
Freedom" in Tiananmen Square, 30 May 1989.
Photo: AP/Wide World.

actions constituted a distinct liminoid/celebratory/political/theatrical/rit-
ual genre with its own dramaturgy, mise-en-scène, role enactments, audience participation, and reception. This theater is ritual because it is
efficacious, intending to produce real effects by means of symbolic causes.
It is most theatrical at the cusp where the street show meets the media,
where events are staged for the camera.

The democracy movement focused in Beijing's Tiananmen Square in
May and June 1989 is a rich example of these exchanges. Tiananmen
Square's one hundred acres can hold hundreds of thousands of people. It
is the symbol of official power, as Red Square had been in the former Soviet
Union or the White House or Capitol building is of the United States. Before
the triumph of the Communists in 1949, Tiananmen Square was much
smaller. The focus of power was on Tiananmen Gate, the Gate of Heavenly
Peace, the southern entrance to the Forbidden City (fig. 1). "Until China's
last dynasty fell in 1912, it was through this gate that the main axis of the
emperor's power was believed to run, as he sat in his throne hall, facing
south, the force of his presence radiating out across the courtyards . . . ,
passing through the gate, and so to the great reaches of the countryside
beyond. . . . During the Cultural Revolution of 1966 [to 1976] the gate,
dominated now by an immense colored portrait of Chairman Mao Zedong,

became a reviewing stand in front of which marched the Red Guards, a million or more strong."[3] Clearly, the creation of Tiananmen Square was intended to refocus ceremonial—that is, theatrical—power from behind the Forbidden City's walls to the big open space, a more fitting symbol of what the new order promised. The image of Mao, the new emperor, was mounted in front, gazing out over the square and from there to all of China. Power was no longer to radiate from secret forbidden places but to be displayed for all people to see and share. The nation itself was renamed the People's Republic of China. And what the students who came to Tiananmen Square in 1989 demanded, more than anything, was what they called "transparency"—an openness in government operations corresponding to the open square that symbolized the new China.

There were precedents for such actions in the dramatic May Fourth movement of 1919 and in the more recent democracy movements of 1978 and 1986. Joseph Esherick and Jeffrey Wasserstrom argue strongly that the 1989 democracy movement was political theater:

> Even when improvising, protesters worked from familiar "scripts" which gave a common sense of how to behave during a given action, where and when to march, how to express their demands, and so forth. Some of these scripts originated in the distant past, emerging out of traditions of remonstrance and petition stretching back millennia. More were derived (consciously or unconsciously) from the steady stream of student-led mass movements that have taken place since 1919.[4]

The struggle in China, before it became violent, was over who would control the means and style of information. The question became: Would official culture or the democracy movement write the script? The theatrical stakes were even higher in May because fortune laid ceremony atop ceremony. Hu Yaobang died on 15 April, close to the anniversary of the May Fourth movement; Soviet president Mikhail Gorbachev was set to arrive in Beijing on 15 May, and the leadership wanted to impress him. The students also wanted to impress Gorbachev, but with a different show. If Chinese officials wanted Gorbachev to see an orderly China under their control, the students wanted him to see a powerful and seething people's movement akin to those taking place in Eastern Europe and his own country. On 15 May about eight hundred thousand people gathered in Tiananmen Square, even as Chinese officials steered Gorbachev around Beijing, pretending that this vast spectacle at the very core of power was not occurring. Official public ceremonies were held at the Beijing airport, a nonplace historically.

Within the overall dramaturgy of the 1989 demonstrations were particular molecules of theater. Student leader Wuer Kaixi in his 18 May confrontation with Premier Li Peng put on what Esherick and Wasserstrom describe as "one of the best acts." Wuer "appeared in his hospital pajamas [on hunger strike]. . . . He upstaged the Premier by interrupting him at the very start. And props: later in the session, he dramatically pulled out a tube inserted into his nose (for oxygen?) in order to make a point. Especially for the young people in the nationwide television audience, it was an extraordinarily powerful performance." The dramatic meeting the next day between hunger striking students and Communist party secretary Zhao Ziyang had the quality of a tragic perepeteia (reversal) and anagnorisis (recognition). Speaking through tears, Zhao said, "I came too late, I came too late . . . but the problems you raised will eventually be solved." And, of course, on 30 May the "Goddess of Democracy and Freedom" made her appearance (fig. 2)—a multivocal figure resembling the Statue of Liberty, a Bread & Puppet Theatre effigy, a "traditional Bodhisattva, . . . [and] the giant statues of Mao that were carried through the square during . . . the sixties."[5] Before the goddess the crowds had been sagging, but she brought many back to the square. Students freely adapted costumes and slogans from non-Chinese sources, including a banner proclaiming "We Shall Overcome."

Esherick and Wasserstrom theorize that the struggle in Tiananmen Square was between official ritual and student theater. But this distinction is too rigid. As Victor Turner and I have pointed out, the relation between ritual and theater is dialectical and braided with plenty of entertainment and social critique in many rituals and with plenty of ritual process in theater.[6] The struggle in Tiananmen Square before the entrance of the tanks was not between rigid ritual and rebellious theater but between two groups of authors (or authorities), each of whom desired to compose the script of China's future and each of whom drew on both theater and ritual. The students took Tiananmen Square, the center stage and ritual focus of Chinese history, thereby upstaging official culture. When Deng Xiaoping, Li Peng, and the generals of the People's Liberation Army felt their authority slipping, they radically shifted the basis of the confrontation from theater and ritual to military force. But, even after the slaughter of 3–4 June, there were moments of high theater, such as when an unarmed man, his fate since unknown, stood his ground in front of a column of tanks.

And, despite the orderliness of their demonstrations and the seriousness of their intentions, the students acted up a carnival. Their mood of fun, comradeship, irony, and subversion enraged and frightened China's officialdom. Students camped out willy-nilly, they sang and danced, they spoke from impromptu "soapboxes," and they granted interviews to the world press. They unfurled sarcastic, disrespectful banners, including one depicting hated Premier Li Peng as a pig-snouted Nazi officer. Even the hunger strike, in which thousands participated, had the feel of melodrama. The Chinese government called this behavior "*luan*," or chaos, a word that in certain of its uses implies dissipation and drunkenness. The Chinese leadership feared that the virus of *luan* would spread: Tiananmen Square is a very bright stage visible all over China. From the government's point of view, *luan* acted out in Tiananmen Square could not be ignored anymore than the Nixon administration could, nineteen years earlier, ignore the ever more carnivalesque anti–Vietnam War demonstrations invading Washington. Meaningful theatrical *luan* is a potent weapon.

From the mid 1960s, protests against the Vietnam War and in favor of what University of California activists in Berkeley called "free speech" had pitched scores of American campuses into chaos. Much of the theory underlying these actions was developed by Jerry Rubin and Abbie Hoffman. By "theater" Rubin and Hoffman clearly meant a lot more than orthodox drama or even "guerrilla theater." According to Hoffman, "Drama is anything you can get away with. . . . Guerrilla theater is only a transitional step in the development of total life-actors." Or, as Rubin put it, "Life is theatre and we are the guerrillas attacking the shrines of authority. . . . The street is the stage. You are the star of the show and everything you were once taught is up for grabs." The Yippies, which Hoffman and Rubin helped to form, emphasized more than the Chinese the Bakhtinian/Rabelaisian mode.[7] In October 1967, a massive demonstration in Washington, D.C., against the Vietnam War climaxed in an effort to "exorcise" and "levitate" the Pentagon. I was not alone in pissing on the Pentagon steps in a gesture of contempt and defiance. In the spring of 1968, Hoffman, Rubin, and others planned a "Festival of Life" for the August Democratic Party National Convention in Chicago. The Festival was conceived as both something disruptive to the Convention and constructive of a new way of life. According to an ad in the spring 1968 *TDR*, the festival would feature "guerrilla theatre, a mock convention, and happenings." All who participated would be provided with "costumes, paint, and props." Of course, what happened in Chicago's Grant Park was instead a "police riot."

The violent, the political, the carnivalesque, and the erotic were linked again in May 1970 after the bombing of Cambodia, an escalation of the Vietnam War, triggered protests. On 4 May—an ironically appropriate date given what happened in China—the National Guard, called out to repress a protest at Kent State University in Ohio, shot four students dead. Schools everywhere went on strike, students marched, and a massive rally was called for Saturday, 9 May, in Washington. But, despite the occasion—a protest against bombing in Cambodia and murder at home—the march on Washington quickly turned into a carnival. At dawn Nixon, like Zhao, visited the students, attempting to make peace with them. As he spoke, some students taunted him with shouts of "Fuck Nixon! Trash Nixon!" raising garbage can lids with his face embossed on them. The demonstrations began with speeches reminding the activists of the contingent causes of their assembling in the nation's capital. But soon, warmed by the sun and more tuned in to Woodstock Nation than "verbalism," many youths stripped in the hot sun, smoked dope, made out, and jumped naked into the Lincoln Memorial Reflecting Pool (fig. 3). The frolic—with its characteristic whirling choreography, the dispersal of orderly ranks into many intense and volatile small groups, the show of private pleasures satisfied in public places—subverted and mocked the neo-Roman monuments and pretensions of imperialist Washington. Washington that day felt very much like Beijing in 1989. And, although there was no single massacre as in Tiananmen Square, the American "big chill" from the mid 1970s into the 1990s accomplished the same end. Nixon and Agnew were driven from

Fig. 3. Swimming in the Lincoln Memorial Reflecting Pool, Washington, D.C., 9 May 1970. Photo credit: Fred W. McDarrah.

office, as Deng Xiaoping and Li Peng might be, but social systems do not rest on one person or even a dozen.

The system of communist domination of Eastern Europe and the USSR and the cold war between that system and the North Atlantic alliance were symbolized by the Berlin Wall. Existing for only twenty-eight years (1961–89), the 103-mile-long wall lacked architectural grace or ornament. Like the Bastille, it not only symbolized a hated regime and physically helped preserve it, but also it was demolished as soon as that regime fell. During its twenty-eight years more then five thousand went over, under, or through the wall—climbing, leaping, ballooning, gliding, tunneling, and ramming. At least another five thousand were captured, and 191 were killed trying. Ugly and mean, the wall disgusted and attracted people, including presidents John F. Kennedy and Ronald Reagan, who used it as a theatrical backdrop for communist-bashing speeches. Still others knew it as a tourist "must."

The events leading to the destruction of the wall—and the collapse of communism throughout East Europe—are complex. The system was imposed from without, sustained by military force, and failed to deliver the material goods people desired. There were many revolts and several major uprisings crushed by Soviet armies or the clear threat of Soviet intervention. When in the mid 1980s Gorbachev began restructuring the USSR, Eastern Europeans saw an opportunity, but the actual license for radical change was not issued until Gorbachev's declaration on 25 October 1989 that the USSR had no right to interfere in the internal affairs of its Eastern European neighbors. He may have been driven to this position by events. The social drama began in the summer of 1989—shortly after the brutal crushing of the democracy movement in China—when Hungary opened its border to East Germans. This meant that people who wanted to leave the German Democratic Republic (GDR) had a way out—and many thousands took it at rates unequalled since the building of the wall.

Throughout September and October the East German government—led by one of those who authorized building the wall, seventy-seven-year-old Erich Honecker—shilly-shallied regarding the exodus. Clearly, the GDR lacked the means to stem the outgoing tide. Meanwhile, the festival that always accompanies a "revolution from below" had begun. "A carnival atmosphere greeted the first large convoy of jubilant East Germans to arrive today in this city [Passau, West Germany] on the Danube in southeastern Bavaria," reported the *New York Times*. "Hundreds of onlookers watched and cheered as five buses unloaded an estimated 700 East Germans who were welcomed with speeches, free balloons, bananas, beer and soft pretzels. . . . A similar welcome was given to East Germans arriving at five tent cities set up by the West German Red Cross in nearby towns." As if following a Bakhtinian script, headlines in the *New York Times* proclaimed: "Exodus Galls East Berlin / Nation's Sovereignty Seems to Be Mocked."[8] But the climax was not yet reached; the streets of Berlin were still relatively quiet and empty.

Then, as in China earlier in 1989, an important date sparked street protests. Friday, 6 October, was the GDR's fortieth anniversary. Ordinarily, one could expect a rectangular parade of military muscle and hardware in front of and below rigidly saluting generals and commissars mounted on a viewing stand. As in China that May, globe-hopping Gorbachev was scheduled to make an appearance, and, as in China, the official celebration turned sour. "Honecker faces the birthday party," the *New York Times* continued, ". . . humiliated, derided, and threatened." Gorbachev was seized on by both sides, soon becoming a contradictory sign. Addressing "an elite congregation gathered in the glittering Palace of the Republic . . . [he] assailed demands that Moscow dismantle the Berlin wall," while earlier many Berliners hailed him with shouts of "Gorby! Gorby!" a known code for the reforms they were demanding from Honecker's government.[9] On 9 October more than fifty thousand demonstrated in Leipzig. On 18 October Honecker was replaced by his "protégé," fifty-two-year-old Egon Krenz, a man who had just paid a praising visit to Li Peng and Deng Xiaoping.

The East German people replied with more demonstrations. In Dresden on 19 October, fifty thousand staged a silent candlelight march. The next day several thousand took to the streets of Berlin. People were openly disrespectful of Krenz. Asked about the new leader,

> a retired factory hand, speaking in the pungent accent and mocking vocabulary of the Berlin working class, nearly exploded with derisive laughter. . . . "From him?" he asked with a snort. "After he went to China to congratulate them for the blood they spilled? After he rigged our last election? After being the boss of State Security? The sparrows on the roof wouldn't believe him."[10]

Ferment was spreading. On 23 October three hundred thousand marched in Leipzig demanding change, including the legalization of opposition parties and an independent labor movement. Smaller demonstrations took place in Berlin, Dresden, Halle, Schwerin, and Magdeburg. The police did not crack skulls, and people grew bolder. Political debates erupted in the streets of East Berlin. Meanwhile, big demonstrations were starting in Prague. Not only were East Germans challenging their leadership, the once docile press, in print and on TV, were giving open coverage to the emergent debates.

The big demonstrations grew more and more festive. Three hundred thousand again marched in Leipzig on 30 October. The "old city center was virtually taken over for three hours by people of every age and from every walk of life. . . . The center [was filled] with cheers, jeers, and chants from all sides."[11] On 2 November the East German government dropped its ban on travel, and thousands crossed into Czechoslovakia on their way west. On 7 November the East German cabinet resigned, but the politburo—the core of official power—held fast. By 8 November more than fifty thousand East Germans a day were streaming from Czechoslovakia into the Federal Republic of Germany (FRG), where, according to law, they instantly became citizens. Then, on 9 November, the East German government opened its borders.

Once the announcement was made "a tentative trickle of East Germans testing the new regulations quickly turned into a jubilant horde, which joined at the border crossings with crowds of flag-waving, cheering West Germans. Thousands of Berliners clambered across the wall at the Brandenburg Gate, passing through the historic arch that for so long had been inaccessible to Berliners of either side."[12] The Brandenburg Gate, like Beijing's Tiananmen Gate, is heavily symbolic. Erected in 1888–89 at the western end of the Unter den Linden, soon dubbed Germany's Arc de Triomphe, the gate celebrates the military prowess of Prussia and the unity of Germany.

On 9 November, in a flash, the Berlin Wall's symbolic value was reversed. What had been avoided or surpassed became the chosen place of celebration. Because it had been such a terrifying barrier, it was now where people acted out how totally things had changed. People couldn't wait to climb it, sit on it, pop champagne and dance on it, and chip away souvenir chunks of it (fig. 4). Formerly murderous East German border guards went out of their way to show how friendly they were. The wall was a media bonanza. Dominating the front page of the 10 November *New York Times* was a four-column photograph of "East Berliners dancing atop the Berlin Wall near the Brandenburg Gate." The same picture, or others very like it, appeared on front pages around the world. Again and again television showed people clambering onto and over the wall.

The wall was not "interesting" everywhere along its 103-mile route. The focus was on the segment in front of the Brandenburg Gate or bifurcating Potsdamer Platz, which, before the wall, was the center of Berlin, among the busiest intersections in Europe. Just as Tiananmen Square was the necessary stage for China's democracy movement, so the wall at these places was where Berliners focused the "unparallelled celebration that swirled through Berlin day and night." "Cheers, sparkling wine, flowers and applause greeted the new arrivals. . . . At the Brandenburg Gate . . .

Fig. 4. On the Berlin Wall in front of the Brandenberg Gate, 10 November 1989. Photo: AP/Wide World.

hundreds of people chanted, 'Gate open! Gate open!'" A middle-aged East German woman broke through a police cordon to give flowers and a "vigorous kiss" to a young West German cop as "the crowd roared." "A festival air seized the entire city. West Berliners lined entry points to greet East Berliners with champagne, cheers, and hugs. Many restaurants offered the visitors free food. A television station urged West Berliners to call in with offers of theater tickets, beds, dinners, or just guided tours." The popular Hertha soccer team gave away ten thousand free tickets for its Saturday game. That giddy weekend the West German government gave every visitor from the east one hundred marks of "greeting money" for spending in West Berlin's glittering shops. "In an unprecedented step for a place with the most rigid business hours in Western Europe, West Berlin banks will be open on both Saturday and Sunday for East Germans wishing to pick up cash."[13] It was only a matter of time before the East German state collapsed into the arms of the West.

It could have ended otherwise. Craig R. Whitney reports that "there was a written order from Honecker for a Chinese solution."[14] But the politburo overrode its aging boss. Once events are in the saddle, the speed of the reversals is breathtaking. A faltering regime in China suddenly reasserts itself; a seemingly invincible state in East Germany crumbles like dust.

Hindsight discloses the "inevitability" of events. But "what if" haunts all such talk. What if the Chinese leadership had not sent in the army? What if the East Germans had? At what point does a regime lose control of its military? There are too many variables for anyone to answer these questions. What can be known is that, when oppressed or angry people sense a weakening official power, they take to the streets. Their carnival can last only so long; every Mardi Gras meets its Ash Wednesday. Whether that Wednesday will see a new order or the return of the old cannot be known in advance.

China and East Germany in 1989 or the United States in 1970 are examples of festivals where the outcome was unknown. The excitement of such social dramas—not unlike what grips whole populations during some sports matches, especially those like the World Cup, where teams and nations are closely identified—is rooted in the tension between known patterns of action, stunning instantaneous surprises, and a passionately desired yet uncertain outcome. At the other extreme are festivals where written dramas are enacted. Here the excitement derives from immersing oneself in a known flow of events. One of these festivals, the Ramlila of Ramnagar, India, offers an intriguing variation on the theme of the critique of ordinary reality. In most carnivals the revolution is from below: the underdog, or the top dog disguised as underdog, rules. But in Ramlila the critique is from above. For a month Ramnagar is the place where Hindu gods and mythic heroes walk the earth and rule the realm.

The epic story tells of Rama's birth, his boyhood education, his exile, the kidnapping of his wife, Sita (also a god), his war against the demon-king Ravana, his victory and triumphant return home to his rule as India's ideal king. During Ramlila, Vibhuti Narain Singh is celebrated by hundreds of thousands of devoted spectators as the "Maharaja of Banaras," representative of Shiva and worshipper of Rama. Never mind that the maharaja was stripped of both princely title and kingdom shortly after Indian independence in 1947. The maharaja is the principal spectator and occasional participant in the reenactment of Rama's life. Spectator-participants regard Ramlila month as time-out from their daily grind. When the boy actors enact the roles of gods, spectators regard them as divine. Inversions abound. Ramlila is a time when rich persons dress simply and eat street food while poor persons dress beyond their means and enjoy expensive, voluptuous sweets; when the maharaja bows down before the boy actors feeding them with his own hand; when the barely literate farmer playing the demon-king Ravana is honored by all; when slick lawyers and gruff shopkeepers, books in hand, meekly follow the sacred text word by word. And, of course, the largest inversion of them all: five Brahmin boys become gods.

For thirty-one days Ramnagar ("Ramatown") is taken over by Ramlila. The streets, back lanes, and courtyards become theaters. Spectators dance themselves into delirium worshipping Rama and Sita. Crowds follow Rama, Sita, and Lakshman into exile; they flood the streets in majestic processions (fig. 5). The characteristic choreography of Ramlila is a procession from one place to another where a scene is performed on a raised stage or within

Fig. 5. The Maharaja of Bandras's Dasahara day procession, from the fort, Ramlila to Ramnagar, 1981. Photo credit: Richard Schechner.

a complex environment of stages, small buildings, and gardens. Spectators take part in the processions then gather in front of the stages or within the theatrical environments. Moving from one place to another is so important that often one day's *lila* (performance) will stop near the end of a scene so that, shortly after the next day's *lila* begins, the whole crowd—actors and spectators alike—move off to another location several kilometers away. In today's Ramlila there is little rebelliousness. Some spectators identify with Ravana, who they regard as heroically resistant to domination by the Brahman caste. Politics were more important at Ramnagar Ramlila's origins in the nineteenth century, when the performance proclaimed Hindu nationalism against both British and Mogul authorities.

New Orleans Mardi Gras descends from European pre-Lenten carnivals, which are the basis for the theorizing of Emile Durkheim, Mikhail Bakhtin, and Victor Turner. By the mid-nineteenth century Mardi Gras had already become what it is today—a mix of fun, sex, commercial exploitation, and hype. As in classic carnivals, inversion of social roles was the order of the day. Whites dressed as African Americans and blacks as whites. And, whatever New Orleans offered by way of sex and fun, there was more of it during Mardi Gras. Mardi Gras remains charged with ludic double negatives. Socially prominent people pretending to be kings, queens, and mythic personages ride on glittering but crummy floats throwing fake jewelry to crowds of "ordinaries" scrambling for souvenirs (and spending

99

Fig. 6. Louis Armstrong as King Zulu, Mardi Gras Day, New Orleans, 1949. Courtesy of William Ransom Hogan Jazz Archive, Tulane University Library. Photo credit: Dan Perry.

like crazy). The Lords of Misrule are not poor people empowered for a day but, rather, the representatives of the ruling class pretending to even greater power and authority. Those in power cannot tolerate even a temporary surrender of their power. Far from giving the poor or oppressed free play, or permitting a charivari-like criticism of established norms, Mardi Gras privileges the already privileged.

Even today the majority of New Orleans African Americans are very poor, and de facto segregation is widely practiced. In Mardi Gras blacks cannot attend white balls (except as servants or sex chattel) or ride on white floats; they walk beside the floats carrying "flambeaux" as slaves did before emancipation. There used to be a critique of official culture in the anticarnival carnival of King Zulu's parade, first organized in 1910 by a few poor and middle-class blacks. Zulu was a parody of the white parades enacted by blacks who parodied white racist attitudes toward blacks. On Mardi Gras day King Zulu followed the final, biggest, and most prestigious white parade, that of Rex, King of Carnival. While white parades had defined routes passing in front of reviewing stands loaded with notables, the Zulus meandered through black neighborhoods or chased on the heels of Rex. Looking at King Zulu's parade as it was in the 1940s (fig. 6), one can see how it functioned in the Bakhtinian sense—as popular culture playing out and mocking race relations, expressing the violent ambivalence with which blacks performed their "place" in New Orleans' society. Even the name *Zulu*—in a New Orleans not familiar with Shaka (not to mention Buthelezi)—carried a racist double message: savage, African, foreign, and dangerous; yet silly, ridiculous, and primitive. King Zulu and his court were dressed in "the traditional costume of the krewe—long black underwear that covered them to wrists and ankles, grass skirts, and wooly wigs. Faces were blackened and eyes and mouths were circled with white."[15] The blackface was like what black minstrel show performers were required to wear: a theatrical reinforcing of the social "blackness" or "negritude" of African Americans.

If Mardi Gras' white elite displaced their identities upwards toward royalty, myth, and godhead, whiter than white, the Zulus' identity was both royal and primitive and blacker than black. King Zulu's court included a garishly overdressed "Big Shot of Africa" and a "royal witch doctor" with "a horned headdress and a golden ring in his nose, carrying a spiked mace." Zulu himself "wore a gold paper crown, dangling earrings, and strings of gleaming beads about his neck. His mantle was dark blue velvet trimmed in gold and edged with white rabbit fur. He carried a jeweled scepter, with which he now and then threatened the small page boy who kept pulling at his mantle. He also wore a leopard-skin vest."[16] More than a little hostility marked the shenanigans of the Zulus. At least into the mid 1960s, when I last saw Mardi Gras, the Zulus acted out the feelings of many New Orleans African Americans regarding race relations in "the city that care forgot." King Zulu and his court did not toss baubles; they hurled coconuts like cannonballs at white spectators.

Today's Zulus are much different than their predecessors. With at least the appearance of improved race relations, King Zulu has been integrated into official Mardi Gras (though still regarded by many as a parody). Zulu's floats are fancier than before, sometimes borrowed from one of the white parades; the costumes are more dignified, the blackface much less common. More of the black community's elite is involved. Tellingly, the coconuts are now handed out rather than pitched. As Zulu became less offensive, it also lost its double-edged bite. Previously, many African Americans disparaged the Zulus, feeling "they satirize their own race and do nothing to uplift it, and many critical Negroes are embarrassed by their antics."[17] Nowadays, the Zulus are "whiter," more peaceful, coopted and stripped of their parodic clarity. Instead of introducing an anticarnival into carnival, the Zulus now participate in the elite masquerade.

An "invented tradition" not at all shy about its consumerist obsession is Daytona Beach Spring Break Weekend.[18] Occurring at the cusp between winter and spring, taking over a strip of Daytona Beach where the rectangular motels meet an undulating beach and ocean, encouraging drinking, carousing, sex, and public display, spring break has the narrative shape of carnival. In 1963, when sixty-five thousand students first descended on Daytona, the event was described as "a wild, drunken orgy."[19] Sex, booze, and sun brings them south, but the narrative action of Spring Break is to compete and consume. Taking 1989 as an example—when four hundred thousand made the Daytona trip—contests included Twentieth Century

Fox's "best buns," Budweiser's "best male body," DeKuyper Schnapps' "DeKuypers DeBody DeLight," Hawaiian Tropic's "Miss Hawaiian Tropic," Playboy Ujena's "summerwear bikini," and Caribe Suntan Lotion's "wet T-shirt," to name just some. Sex, excess, violence, and competition are linked.

All events are sponsored by brand products. "Dozens of banners for Caribe suntan lotion, Roffler hair products and other products are strewn from the balconies, a two-story inflatable Simpatico beer bottle sits near the pool, a giant inflatable Spuds MacKenzie [Budweiser beer mascot] watches over outdoor beer kegs, and hot balloons emblazoned with 'Plymouth Sundance' [car] and 'Karate Kid II' [movie] are anchored everywhere." "In a half-mile stretch along the beach are volleyball games sponsored by Pontiac, Diet Pepsi, Coppertone, Coors Light, and Plymouth. The skies drone with airplanes pulling ads, and the beach—on which cars are allowed—is a parade of mobile billboards." An adman told a reporter that the idea is to "blanket the hotel-bar complex" (like B-52s blanket bombing Vietnam or Iraq?). Joanne Lipman, a company executive, said, "We're not down here for sales, we're down here for image."[20]

According to this executive, college-age youths are "brand conscious but not yet brand loyal." Spring Break is the time to excite them, inebriate them, and burn brand names into their minds. The banners in Tiananmen Square in 1989 and the costumes of King Zulu and his court in the 1940s were made by participants. But in Daytona whatever is on display is made elsewhere by others. The students are there only to receive, cattle to be branded. But do the kids listen? One student told Lipman, "You don't even notice it because it's everywhere you look." The sponsors think otherwise. To them it doesn't matter if a student remembers which brand. The important thing is to learn that the only things worth owning are brand products. Spring Break is a capitalist carnival initiating and training young upscale Americans in their lifelong roles as consumers. The scenography of Spring Break serves its capitalist carnival functions well. The Daytona police make sure that the revels are confined to beachfront motels, the streets immediately adjoining them, and the beach itself. Spring Break is squeezed into "the strip"—a long narrow space, a kind of static parade, easy to police and control. Crowds are not allowed to mass in big circular groups as they did in Tiananmen Square, Washington, Leipzig, or Berlin. Also the beach itself and the airspace above are treated as billboards saturating the youths with brand name messages.

In "direct theatre" large public spaces are transformed into theaters where collective reflexivity is performed, fecund and spectacular excesses displayed. Parades, mass gatherings, street theater, sex, and partying—everything is exaggerated, ritualized, done for show. Masquerading encourages experimenting with behavior and identity slippage. Rulers or ruling ideas are either exalted, as at Mardi Gras, Spring Break, and Ramlila; challenged, as in Washington in 1970 and China in 1989; or overthrown, as in Eastern Europe. Ramlila is complex. Worshipped as gods, the boys are also ordinary people, while the maharaja who witnesses and authorizes their sacred performance is a former king, who, for the month of the festival, acts out a recollected royalty.

Official culture wants its festivals to be entertaining. Mardi Gras and Spring Break are dizzying, drunk, disorderly, and mystifying—mystifying because they present official authorities as fairy-tale royalty, buffoons, clowns, laughing dispensers of free goods, and benign corporate sponsors of drunken erotic contests. It's the old "bread and circuses" trick. People have fun. Less so for obligatory mass turnouts such as those that until now have taken place in Moscow's Red Square marking the anniversary of the Russian Revolution. For whom are these official displays staged? Since the development of television, the audiences are whomever mass media can reach. But there is another audience too. The arrogance of the leaders looking down from reviewing stands is matched by their insecurity (both actual and imagined). They demand reassurance of their popularity and invincibility. Each salute given, each tank rolling by as part of neat and obedient phalanxes, warms the hearts of these leaders, democrats and despots alike.

But when the official leadership is no longer the focus of attention, no longer in control of the means of producing or controlling public celebrations, when the power to produce public fun passes into the hands of ordinary people, events take an unpredictable theatrical turn. Effigies appear, as do homemade banners and posters; street theater flourishes; soapbox orators draw cheering crowds. Official leaders are cut down to size. If they show up, they run the risk of being mocked or chased away as Li, Zhou, Nixon, and members of the GDR politburo were. Officialdom provides scripted fun contained within ritual frames, while unofficial festivity rewrites ritual, dissolving the restrictive frames. The popular street carnival-demonstration is actually a utopian mimesis whose multifocused, idealized, heated, magnified, and transparent clarity of consciousness evaporates once the show is over. Those involved in such festivals of political desire too often deceive themselves into believing their utopian show will run forever. It is not only the tanks of Deng Xiaoping which enviously and with terrible clarity crush the fun but also the longer process, when the revolution is successful, of postrevolutionary jockeying for power. This decay of festival into "dirty politics" is what the Chinese students now underground or in exile have learned, a lesson most American radicals of the 1960s and 1970s never studied. Carnival, more than other forms of theater, can act out a powerful critique of the status quo, but it cannot itself replace the status quo. For the modern world this much was made clear by Robespierre: the carnival indefinitely in power is the Terror.

There are several audiences for direct theater: (1) the participants themselves, (2) journalists, especially television reporters, (3) the mass spectatorship television enjoys, and (4) high-level decision makers in their offices or bunkers. These high-level spectators participate in direct theater for fear of missing the worldwide TV audience. The dramaturgy is further complicated by the fact that the TV apparatus asks for news to be "made," not "found." And the same corporations who underwrite Spring Break sponsor

TV and/or own the networks. This means that all programming—news as well as sports, dramas, sitcoms, talk, and game shows—are actually profit-making entertainments. Television news is not made to be kept and reshown long after the events it records are over. It is a multilayered, throwaway flow of images and words combining on-the-spot action with sophisticated editing and framing procedures to create a narrativized and ritualized product.

Direct theater is raw material for the universally displayed second theater, TV news, which includes often improvised responses to the first theater. Direct theater is reflexive insofar as it is produced for the cameras and designed to force a response. Events are immediate (being there), mediated (taking place on the TV screen), and responsive (reactions to what happens on the screen). Used this way, TV is hot, interactive. The millions of screens function as a collective forum (though not a free forum). Criticism of the direct theater is provided not by aestheticians but by "pundits" and official spokespersons who summarize and explain. Political direct theater is different from the neocarnival direct theater of Mardi Gras or Spring Break. These have been drained of political content, while the made-for-television (or at least highly "media aware") direct theater is mainly political. Or, to put it in a slightly different way, the conservative politics of Mardi Gras and Spring Break are hidden. Therefore, there is no "news" coming from them except a feature story buried near the end of a telecast. Or, if the celebration gets out of hand, an account of how the police handled the rioting. Social order must be restored; the causes of the "disturbance" will be "looked into" (so it won't happen again). On the other hand, the political direct theater of East Europe or China challenges the status quo, wants to overthrow the state.

The more political the direct theater, the more it is staged as, or ends in, swirls, vortexes of activities moving in spirals and circles with not easy to locate centers or heads. Multivocal and multifocal, a popular deconstructing of hierarchy, often blasphemous, irreverent, and obscene, full of small-scale dramas and guerilla theater, the direct theater plays to the roving multiple eyes of many cameras simultaneously ingesting images. The direct theater is not "about" something so much as it is made "of" something. It is actual and symbolic, not referential and representational. Hunger-striking Chinese camped out in Tiananmen Square, Germans climbing on or chipping away at the wall, or young Americans frolicking in the Lincoln Memorial Reflecting Pool are performing more than naked actions. But their symbolic deeds are not imitations played by named characters who exist within copyrighted fictional narratives authored by individuals. Real people—from anonymous players to Wuer Kaixi, Zhao Ziyang, the East German politburo, Berliners, Abbie Hoffman—play their roles in public and pursue not only Stanislavskian objectives and through-lines of action but also historical dialectics.

Television produces and reproduces this popular drama, showing over and over again specific highly theatrical bits (or bytes), what Brecht would call *gests*, creating both *verfremdungseffekt* and a ritual effect. The layering of contending historifications begins with on-the-spot reporters interviewing participants, ordinary people as well as leaders. Many of these "spontaneous" interviews are setups. The material is then laundered through interpretations and editings—"spin controls." Of course, direct theater, with its low impact on global politics, such as Mardi Gras or Ramlila, doesn't need much managing. But, for political direct theater, participants and viewers alike are told what's going on, how to relate to it, and what the future holds. The ultimate layers are hidden from view, taking place in editing rooms and corporate or government offices. TV news gives the impression of—a performance of—"multivocality." But, just as aesthetic drama projects many voices deployed as characters originating from a single voice, the playwright's, so television moves in the opposite direction, knitting the many voices of the streets into a unitary broadcast.

NOTES

1. René Girard, *Violence and the Sacred* (Baltimore: Johns Hopkins University Press, 1977), 119–20; Roger Caillois, *Man and the Sacred* (Glencoe, Ill.: Free Press, 1959), 125.

2. Caillois, *Man and the Sacred*, 123. For such unofficial performances, see Marvin Carlson, *Places of Performance* (Ithaca, N.Y.: Cornell University Press, 1989); and Sally Harrison-Pepper, *Drawing a Circle in the Square: Street Performing in New York's Washington Square Park* (Jackson: University Press of Mississippi, 1990).

3. Jonathan D. Spence, *The Gate of Heavenly Peace* (New York: Viking Penguin, 1981), 17–18.

4. Joseph W. Esherick and Jeffrey N. Wasserstrom, "Acting out Democracy: Political Theater in Modern China," *Journal of Asian Studies* 49, no. 4 (November 1990): 839.

5. Ibid., 841.

6. See Victor Turner, *The Ritual Process* (Chicago: Aldine, 1969); "Liminal to Liminoid, in Play, Flow, Ritual," in *From Ritual to Theatre and Back* (New York: PAJ, 1982), 20–60; and Richard Schechner, "From Ritual to Theatre and Back," *Educational Theatre Journal* 26 (1974): 455–82; and *Performance Theory* (New York: Routledge, 1988).

7. Abbie Hoffman, *Revolution for the Hell of It* (New York: Dial Books, 1968), 30, 183; Jerry Rubin, *Do It!* (New York: Simon and Schuster, 1970), 250. For more detailed expositions of their views, see these sources and Hoffman, *Woodstock Nation* (New York: Vintage Books, 1969); and *Steal This Book* (New York: Pirate Editions, 1971). The term *Yippie* is from the acronym for Youth International Party (YIP) founded by Rubin, Hoffman, and others. YIP never was intended as a "serious" political party but as a gadfly. *Yippy* is taken from *Hippy*, what the "flower children" of the 1960s, inhabitants of the Haight-Ashbury section of San Francisco, were called or called themselves. *Hippie* was soon applied to many of the "tune in, turn on, drop out" generation of American youth. *Hippie* is a diminutive of *hip*, or *hep*, a word from the world of jazz (or crime) first used in the 1910s by African Americans but adopted or adapted by the Beat Generation writers of the 1950s and meaning someone "in the know." All these terms connote alternative life-styles. The 1980s adaptation *Yuppie*—a Young Upwardly Mobile Professional—is a parody of the earlier terms, signaling the very opposite in social status.

8. Ferdinand Protzman, "Thousands Swell Trek to the West by East Germans," *New York Times*, 12 September 1989, A1, A14; Serge Schmemann, "Exodus Galls East Berlin," *New York Times*, 14 September 1989, A14.

9. Serge Schmemann, "Sour German Birthday," *New York Times*, 6 October 1989, A1; "Gorbachev Lends Honecker a Hand," *New York Times*, 7 October 1989, A5.

10. Henry Kamm, "East Berliners March for Democracy," *New York Times*, 22 October 1989, A16.

11. Serge Schmemann, "Another Big Rally in East Germany," *New York Times*, 31 October 1989, A17.

12. Serge Schmemann, "East Germany Opens Frontier to the West," *New York Times*, 10 November 1989, A1.

13. All quoted examples of celebrating are from accounts reported in the *New York Times* on 10–12 November 1989.

14. Craig R. Whitney with David Binder and Serge Schmemann, "Party Coup Turned East German Tide," *New York Times*, 19 November 1989, A27.

15. Robert Tallant, *Mardi Gras* (1948; reprint, Gretna, La.: Pelican Publishing, 1976), 232. See also Samuel Kinser, *Carnival, American Style: Mardi Gras at New Orleans and Mobile* (Chicago: University of Chicago Press, 1990).

16. Tallant, *Mardi Gras*, 232–40.

17. Ibid., 239.

18. See Eric Hobsbawm and Terence Ranger, eds., *The Invention of Tradition* (Cambridge: Cambridge University Press, 1983); and Richard Schechner, "Restoration of Behavior," *Between Theater and Anthropology* (Philadelphia: University of Pennsylvania Press, 1985).

19. C. E. Wright, [Title unknown], *New York Times*, 1964, sec. 10, p. 5.

20. Joanne Lipman, "Spring Break Sponsors in Florida Find Too Much of a Good Thing," *Wall Street Journal*, 21 March 1989, B1, B8.

Semiotics and Deconstruction

Introduction

During the 1980s David Hockney took a series of photographs he called "joiners." These were composite, or collage, photographs made up of a number of separate shots, first taken with a Polaroid and later with a Pentax 120. Many things about these joiners make them illustrative of the critical practices of deconstruction and semiotics. Because so much of the impact of the new theory on theater has involved visual seeing and knowing, I propose to being this section by considering David Hockney's joiner "Noya and Bill Brandt with Self-Portrait."

In this polaroid collage Noya and Bill Brandt sit regarding a group of (polaroid) photos of David Hockney. The Hockney photos are on the floor; the figures gaze down at them. Forty-nine photos make up the whole collage; the spaces in between form a grid that simultaneously overlays and undergirds the whole. Each piece of the composition is assigned meaning in relation to the pieces around it, and, as the eye moves, the composite meanings change—different photos are foregrounded, different ways of seeing come into prominence and recede. Bill has, from one standpoint, two heads; Noya has four feet.[1] They are looking at twelve or thirteen Hockneys. Because of the grid, the edges of the photos are seen as distinct for each individual photo and also as arbitrary in that they do not represent "real" edges. Edges are made or composed, have no transcendent authority. Taken as a whole, the photographs make up a kind of language that can be read, but the units of which are not stable or fixed. The center of the collage seems to move, and the spaces between emphasize the ephemeral unity of the collage. The eye looking seems to slip, to be unable to "fix" on anything—or is it the surface that is slippery?

Hockney offers the viewer a chance to contemplate the problem of the production of meaning. Viewed one way, the meaning of the whole emerges from the relations between the varying units making up the composition, each of which derives its value from its position within the picture-system. Viewed another way, the unsettling autonomy and independence of the various units, and the changing emphases of various aspects, raises questions about the possibility of deciding on any stable meaning whatsoever. The first way of viewing is structuralist, while the second is deconstructive. Both, however, may be said to be semiotic to the extent that they deal with analyzing a system of signs.

While structuralism and semiotics are closely interrelated, they may be understood separately. As Terry Eagleton has pointed out, structuralism is a method, while semiotics is a field. The study of the relations and structures between objects or events comprises the methodology of structuralism; objects or events (or images) treated as signs constitute the semiotic field of inquiry.[2]

Semiotics developed out of linguistics. Early theoreticians of the sign

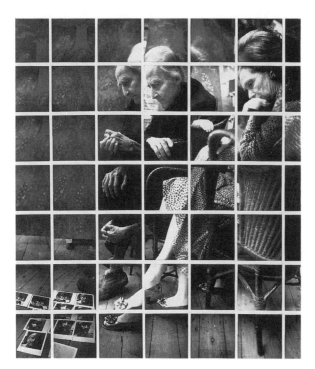

Fig. 1. David Hockney, "Noya and Bill Brandt with Self-Portrait." Photo credit: Rogers, Coleridge and White Ltd.

such as Ferdinand Saussure and Charles Pierce saw that the structure of language was useful for understanding the structure of any sign system. Languages make meaning only differentially; that is, within a given language, words only derive meaning by reference or contrast to other words. The particular language system makes meanings possible through rules, conventions, distinctions. Saussure theorized an important difference between *la langue* (the overall language system) and *la parole* (the particular speech act or utterance).[3] *La parole* only means something because of the enabling system of *la langue*. Since not only language but also human behaviors and customs are signs that operate within the organizing patterns of social systems, Saussure called for a "science of semiology." Claude Lévi-Strauss, doing structuralist anthropology, recognized the affinity between cultural and linguistic analysis and linked his work to semiology and especially to Saussure.[4] In the Hockney joiner the single photos are the meaning-units, which are linked to visual, perceptual, and aesthetic codes and practices, enabling them to produce the overall collage.

Signs, following Saussure, are divided into signifiers and signifieds. The signifier is the sound, or mark, that stands in for the signified, which is the concept, or meaning. Together they point to the referent, which is the actuality referenced. The letters *p e a c h* form a word signifying the concept *peach* and may be used to point to a particular round, yellow piece of fruit. Each of these connections is, however, arbitrary. That is, a different group of markings might just as well serve as signifier for the signified peach. Meaning is therefore conventional. Furthermore, signifiers establish their meaning by reference to what they are not: *peach* is understood as "not apple or perch." Thus, meaning is the functional result of the difference between signs, and always might be otherwise.

As long as the structure of "language" or any other system of signs was thought to be stable and fixed, which Saussure and Pierce believed, the meaning of Hockney's joiner could be derived and established by understanding the various codes and conventions governing that language of the photo-collage. With poststructuralism, however, the certainty and stability of any particular meaning came under radical critique. If meaning is always only present in difference, the stability of any particular sign system overturns. A specific signifier means not only in relation to one other signifier that it is not but to a whole tissue of signifiers, potentially endless, through which meaning moves and slips in an elusive play of signification. From this view meaning is actually always absent, because it never simply "is" present in the sign. As Terry Eagleton puts it, "reading a text is more like tracing this process of constant flickering than it is like counting the beads on a necklace."[5] Furthermore, the reading is not authorized by any stable center of meaning, any structure or system that is not itself implicated in the play of signification. Thus, the faith of structuralists that an analysis of structure would reveal knowledge or truth about reality seemed misplaced. Roland Barthes moved from an early structuralist position to a new theory that posited signification as a free play of signifiers that float, resisting specific associations.

Jacques Derrida, key theorist of deconstruction, also developed a critique of the sign, in which he denied the center, the fixed locus of meaning, the first principle from which other meaning-units could be derived or ranked (sometimes called the "transcendental signifier"). In a famous speech that attacked Lévi-Strauss for a false privileging of nature over culture, Derrida stressed Lévi-Strauss's myopic understanding of the role of writing, and therefore difference, in the formation of culture.[6] Instead, Derrida emphasizes the transmutability of all discourse—that meaning is always deferred, elsewhere, multiple and shifting, and therefore a process but not a product. "One could say," he writes, ". . . that this movement of play, permitted by the lack or absence of a center of origin, is the movement of *supplementarity*. . . . The movement of signification adds something, which results from the fact that there is always more, but this addition is a floating one because it comes to perform a vicarious function, to supplement a lack on the part of the signified."[7] Thus, ironically, there is always a wealth of meaning and a simultaneous absence of meaning in circulation.

Recognizing this limitless plurality of meanings, Derrida developed deconstruction as a method of revealing the illusion of truth, unity, origins, and closure in most ordinary ways of thinking. Christopher Norris begins *What Is Deconstruction?* by explaining, "to 'deconstruct' a text is to draw out conflicting logics of sense and implication, with the object of showing that the text never exactly means what it says or says what it means."[8] Both a philosophical and a rhetorical critique, deconstruction reads against the grain in order to show that it is possible to undo assumed meanings by exposing the play of signification which always occurs in reading texts but which is generally repressed or overlooked. A deconstructive reading of the Hockney joiner would stress how the various pieces of the collage are capable of disrupting or undoing the unity of the whole and how, instead of receiving it as a unified whole, a viewer might unravel the governing logic of the collage.

The concept of "writing" in Derrida is much larger than its commonplace usage. Derrida believes that Western culture has always privileged spoken speech over writing, because of its proximity to the speaker, who authorizes its meaning as natural, or spontaneous, utterance. But this presumes some primacy of individual speaking, some secondariness of writing; it presumes originary meaning at the moment of voice but derivative meaning(s) when writing enters circulation. Derrida contests this model, expanding writing and textuality to include all cultural production and denying as logocentric this search for and faith in the authenticity of origins.

One of the major moves of both poststructuralist semiotics and deconstruction is the redefinition of *subjectivity*. In place of the notion of a free, autonomous self who "speaks" as the origin of meaning, writing itself arises as always already existing, positioning "selves" in a complex network of cultural and linguistic markers, always prior to any particular utterance: thus, the language of écriture, textuality,[9] and writing as something that constructs and marks subjects instead of something they themselves execute. Logos (divine or secular logic),[10] presence, and subjective agency disappear. Subjectivity becomes a site where the process of signification takes place. The self is "written," becomes itself a text to be read. Moreover, any particular text is dissolvable, made up of traces of other meanings, other texts, which undo any received meaning. In place of the old subjective pleasures of authority and mastery (over speech, over writing, over meaning), Roland Barthes describes *jouissance*—the transporting pleasure of being constructed through the play of signification.[11] Because reading gives the reader pleasure, the self receives pleasure through its own multiplicity, even disintegration. "Then perhaps," Barthes writes, "the subject returns, not as illusion, but as *fiction*."[12]

In conflating Derrida and Barthes in this account, I am moving to anticipate the question of the material and historical aspects of the production of meaning. Derrida and certain American deconstructionists are often criticized for their ahistoricity and their erasure of material and historical constraints on the play of signification.[13] One of Derrida's most often quoted pronouncements, "There is nothing outside of the text," seems especially problematic.[14] Deconstruction sees everything as text and, as such, subject to the unraveling play of signification. Thus, history and biography are not authentic; they are texts and therefore unreliable and, so the critique goes, immaterial. However, those semioticians and theorists who, like Michael Ryan, stress deconstruction's radical overturning of hegemonic structures of meaning or, like Barthes, who articulate the sociocultural character of codes and practices, which is always inscribed in texts and on subjects, recuperate a politics for deconstruction.[15] Derrida himself has been understood by some, like Terry Eagleton, as "out to do more than develop new techniques of reading: deconstruction is for him an ultimately *political* practice, an attempt to dismantle the logic by which a particular system of thought, and behind that a whole system of political structures and social institutions, maintains its force."[16]

This issue is important because the political side of deconstruction is necessary in order to understand how semiotics and deconstruction have been most useful to theater critics and practitioners. Semiotics provides a means of articulating the production of meaning-in-performance, while deconstruction provides purpose or motive (the dismantling of usually operative logics of interpretation).

While Saussure and to some extent Pierce imagined a pure language system of correspondence between signifier and signified (Saussure), or sign, interpretant, and object (Pierce), Barthes, following Hjelmslev,[17] introduces a connotative semiotic, which participates in the production of meaning. Thus, history and, more important, ideology enters every text. John Rouse describes the acute level of intertextual connotation in theater practice in his essay: "All the signifying systems used by theatre and drama are always already part of other cultural texts. The codes of these other texts help condition the writing of either dramatic or performance text, just as their meanings pass into the texture of the new text's significations. This is true even, or especially, of the actor's body, which can be examined as a text into which cultural norms for social behavior are written in the guise of stylistic codes for performance behavior."[18]

Theater history is on one level the record of the received and "naturalized" readings of canonical performances. The logos of "fact" has legitimated and enforced traditional scholarship and interpretation. A "fresh" interpretation involves destabilizing the taken-for-grantedness of the production of meaning. Semiotics systematizes a deconstructive effort to dismantle the very language system it describes—reversing its trajectory. Semiotics's taxonomies of icons, indices, and symbols have provided a valuable means of articulating with precision the commonplace of performance theory and criticism: that performance is always more than the text. While setting, costume, or music has always played a role in performance analysis, semiotics has provided a methodology for understanding these elements as sign systems governed by cultural and aesthetic codes, which produce proliferating meanings in addition to the meaning(s) of the written text or of the planned mise-en-scène.

The early work in theater semiotics concentrated on identifying fundamental units for analyses and on forming some typology of theatrical signs.[19] Its greatest practical advantage, however, has been to provide a means of understanding the various relationships between dramatic texts and performance texts (see Rouse), between the social context of the playscript and the social context of the performance (see Patrice Pavis),[20] and between colliding elements, or codes, in the mise-en-scène (see Jim Carmody).

In the essays that make up this section, many of these ideas take on a concrete shape through illustrations of actual performances. John Rouse offers an explanation of how and why the role of the director as the producer of meaning in production has been caught up in issues of authority and forced interpretation instead of being recognized as coproducer of meaning with the audience and the dramatic text. His essay discusses certain post-modern performances that deliberately foreground the pastiche of codes and practices that make it up, providing the audience with an interspace where they can put into question or emphasize their own constitutive powers.

Jim Carmody's essay provides a reading of a production of Molière's *Misanthrope*, which is both deconstructive, insofar as it unravels received meanings and refuses "closure," and semiotic, insofar as it identifies colliding signs in the performance text—colliding in part because of social context and in part because of absence, or *aporia*.[21]

The difference between the two "semiotic" readings of Rouse and Carmody and McDonald's "deconstructive" reading is that, although based in performance, McDonald's reading of *Fanshen* both performs the questioning that is its premise and also turns over the play for viewing-in-motion; that is, the constant mobility of the play is partly visible through the deconstructive moves of the critic and partly visible through the repetitions, reversals, and performed representations of theater itself. When I said that deconstruction is the motive or purpose for reading the semiotics of production, I meant something like what McDonald claims for the play—that to allow any meaning to settle becomes a lie, in fact even a counterrevolutionary one. Like the motion in the Hockney joiner, the play-in-production moves through a series of attempts to "speak justice," fore-grounding the difference between enunciation and reception and also the constitutive action of "acting." It is as if the play will "not stay still," turning itself inside out and its action of questioning over to and for the audience's perception. Especially because the history of the play's original production provides a different connotative semiotic than McDonald's contemporary reading, the flash of motion, like a mote in the eye, renders the invisible trace of *différance* visible.[22]

Semiotics and deconstruction have proved invaluable tools for theater theory and criticism. A wide range of materials on theater semiotics is available, ranging from introductory books by Keir Elam, Marvin Carlson, and Martin Esslin to special journal essays, which have appeared regularly in *Drama Review, Performing Arts Journal, Modern Drama*, and *Theatre Journal*. Deconstruction has also proved increasingly topical in the last decade. Germane to this volume, in the early 1980s David McDonald, then editor of *Theatre Journal*, introduced the terminology and the possibility of deconstructive critical and theatrical practice to a wide readership.[23] A cursory look at regional repertory seasons will turn up many productions that are at least deconstructive of traditional production assumptions, if not more technically deconstructive in design. Avant-garde deconstructive production is ubiquitous: the Wooster Group, Mabou Mines, Split Britches, among many. The following three essays give examples of some of the differing kinds of deconstructive productions.

J. G. R.

NOTES

1. Although, as David Hockney points out about Picasso's work, it isn't really a question of two heads but of two aspects or views of the head: "Even with Picasso, if he puts in two noses, it's the same nose seen twice within one face" (*Hockney on Photography* [New York: Harmony Books, 1988], 61).

2. Terry Eagleton, *Literary Theory: An Introduction* (Minneapolis: University of Minnesota Press, 1983), 99–106.

3. Saussure introduces basic concepts of semiotics in *Course in General Linguistics*, trans. Wade Baskin (New York: McGraw-Hill, 1966). See also Roland Barthes's explication of Saussure, *Elements of Semiology*, trans. Annette Lavers and Colin Smith (New York: Hill and Wang, 1968).

4. See especially "Structural Analysis in Linguistics and in Anthropology," *Structural Anthropology*, trans. Claire Jacobson and Brooke Schoepf (New York: Basic Books, 1963), 31–54.

5. Eagleton, *Literary Theory*, 128.

6. For Derrida's extended critique of Lévi-Strauss, see *Of Grammatology*, trans. Gayatri Chakravorty Spivak (Baltimore: Johns Hopkins University Press, 1976), 97–140.

7. Jacques Derrida, "Structure, Sign, and Play," *Writing and Difference* (Chicago: University of Chicago Press, 1978), 289.

8. Christopher Norris, "Deconstruction, Post-Modernism, and the Visual Arts," *What Is Deconstruction?* ed. Christopher Norris and Andrew Benjamin (London: St. Martin's Press, 1988), 7.

9. For an explication of the meanings of *text*, see Roland Barthes, "From Work to Text," *Image, Music, Text*, trans. Stephen Heath (New York: Hill and Wang, 1977); for a discussion of *écriture*, see especially Susan Sontag's preface to Barthes's *Writing Degree Zero* (New York: Hill and Wang, 1968).

10. "As portrayed by Derrida, the logocentric system always assigns the origin of truth to the *logos*—to the spoken word, to the voice of reason, to the Word of God." This explanation comes from an excellent secondary source: Vincent B. Leitch, *Deconstructive Criticism: An Advanced Introduction* (New York: Columbia University Press, 1983), 25.

11. Sometimes translated as "pleasure," sometimes as "bliss," but always with a sexual connotation of "coming." See Roland Barthes, *The Pleasure of the Text*, trans. Richard Miller (New York: Hill and Wang, 1975).

12. Barthes, *Pleasure of the Text*, 62.

13. The American deconstructionists belonged to what is sometimes called the "Yale school"—never really a school and no longer centered at Yale, in any event—whose seminal book is Harold Bloom et al., *Deconstruction and Criticism* (New York: Seabury Press, 1979).

14. Derrida, *Of Grammatology*, 158.

15. See Michael Ryan, *Marxism and Deconstruction* (Baltimore: Johns Hopkins University Press, 1982).

16. Eagleton, *Literary Theory*, 148.

17. Louis Hjelmslev was a Danish linguist whose *Prolegomena to a Theory of Language* (1969), which put forth the connotative dimensions of signification, influenced Barthes.

18. Rouse, p. 155.

19. See, for example, Keir Elam's *The Semiotics of Theatre and Drama* (London: Methuen, 1980); or the collection of essays in *Poetics Today* 2, no. 3 (1981), under the title "Drama, Theater, Performance: A Semiotic Perspective."

20. For an elegant model of the relationship between text(s), performance, and the role of reception, see Patrice Pavis, "From Text to Performance," *Performing Texts*, ed. Michael Issacharoff and Robin F. Jones (Philadelphia: University of Pennsylvania Press, 1988), 86–100.

21. *Aporia* is a difficult word to define: like a quark, it is a kind of black hole—that point in a text where the string of meaning-units no longer connects and meaning seems to be undone or to drop off. Also, however, it is a place at which a text seems to say that it *cannot* say—a "creative disturbance." Eagleton writes that deconstruction fastens "on the 'symptomatic, points,' the aporia or impasses of meaning, where texts get into trouble, come unstuck, offer to contradict themselves" (*Literary Theory*, 134).

22. Derrida coined this term as a play on two meanings of the French verb *différer*: "to be distinct from, unequal, different"; and "to be delayed, put off, deferred." Thus, adding the dimension of time to the notion of nonidentity, he specifies the elusive play of signification.

23. See, for example, a special issue entitled "Aporia: Revision, Representation and Intertextual Theatre," *Theatre Journal* 35 (March 1983).

Alceste in Hollywood: A Semiotic Reading of *The Misanthrope*

Jim Carmody

> A code cannot be destroyed, only "played off."
> —Roland Barthes, "The Death of the Author"

Alceste, the familiar protagonist of Molière's classic comedy *Le Misanthrope,* is a quintessentially seventeenth-century Parisian creature, the product of a culture far removed in time and space from contemporary Hollywood. Yet Robert Falls's mise-en-scène of this play asks us to accept the proposition that Alceste "belongs" in the Hollywood of 1989.[1] The semiotics of this transplantation, this translation, are the subjects of this essay.

There are, in this essay, at least two semiotic readings of Molière's script in play: Robert Falls's mise-en-scène and my own reconstruction of that mise-en-scène.[2] Furthermore, neither of these readings should be understood as the work of a decontextualized subject. The "Robert Falls mise-en-scène" emerges as the product of a collective effort to engage with the signifying processes of Molière's seventeenth-century theater, the signifying processes of twentieth-century, not-for-profit, American theater, and the ways in which those discursive practices combine dialectically in the variety of subjectivities that constitute any group of artists working on a common project.[3] Similarly, this essay emerges from my own dialectical engagement with the discursive practices already mentioned as well as those of contemporary theater aesthetics and semiotics, not to mention the institution of the American "research" university. Neither this essay nor the Falls mise-en-scène can ultimately be understood semiotically apart from the specific cultural realities in which they are embedded and which they can be seen as embodying.

Although the basic theoretical foundations for the semiotic analysis of mise-en-scène were established many decades ago, actual examples of such analysis are remarkably rare.[4] Indeed, there exists no general agreement among theater semioticians as to how such an analysis ought to proceed or even which kinds of semiotics are likely to produce the most fruitful results. For the purposes of this essay, I have chosen to adopt what has become a characteristic strategy of semiotics (as well as poststructuralism in general) and concentrate on what traditional theater criticism might consider marginal or relatively unessential signifiers of the Falls mise-en-scène: a piece of exercise equipment which remains partially invisible for most of the performance, the final bow taken by the actress playing Célimène, and an excerpt from the subscribers' newsletter at the Goodman Theatre. Readings of these signifiers will, in turn, lead to considerations

Fig. 1. *The Misanthrope*, act 3, La Jolla Playhouse (1989). From left, Arsinoë and Célimène. Photo credit: Jim Carmody.

of the cultural sign "Molière" and the semiotics of restaging classic texts in the American theater.

Throughout the following discussion, it should be understood that I am not arguing for a specific hierarchy of codes or of signs in this mise-en-scène. Falls has systematically refrained from providing a master code (apart from suggesting that the spectator think in terms of analogies, a suggestion I will discuss later); the spectator cannot find an indication of what the "correct" interpretation might be (i.e., what the director wants the spectator to think). Instead, the spectator is confronted by a number of theatrical and cultural codes that continually collide, avoiding the kind of resolution in an aesthetically and ideologically unified "work" which we have been conditioned to anticipate in a classic comedy. Falls refuses to synthesize these disparate codes; instead, he obliges us to read them against each other and through each other. In this, Falls may be following Brecht's advice with respect to the "Separation of the Elements" (which many have recognized as one of the primary semiotic ideas of twentieth-century theater).

From 1666 Paris to 1989 Hollywood

An imposing piece of exercise equipment, a postmodern blending of Universal weight machine and high-tech guillotine, stands close to center stage in George Tsypin's creation of Célimène's Hollywood home. This scenic element, with its wealth of bi-cultural signifieds, offers a provisional entry into the complex semiotics of Robert Falls's 1989 mise-en-scène of Molière's 1666 play, *The Misanthrope*.

Although fully visible to the spectators for at most fifteen minutes, the guillotine blade that "takes the place of" the expected counterweight in the machine makes an unmistakable reference to the French revolution that ended the *ancien régime*, of which the early years of Louis XIV's reign (the 1660s) are the acknowledged cultural highlight. Molière's *Le Misanthrope* is among the celebrated masterworks of that *grand siècle*—indeed, the play is commonly regarded as *the* paradigmatic French classical comedy. Tsypin's visual reference to the French Revolution is reinforced when Arsinoë pulls one of the wires on the machine to send the blade racing dangerously down toward Célimène, who is reclining on the bench.

The guillotine blade can also be read in the context of the cultural codes of "Southern California" or, more specifically, the "Hollywood" community. The oversize weight machine in Célimène's dressing room is no mere decoration. This Célimène works hard to stay in shape and enjoys displaying her well-toned body to Alceste and the others in her circle. Célimène wears a different costume each time she makes an entrance, and in many scenes she appears to move from one consciously adopted pose to another, a behavior that most of the other characters manifest to a lesser degree. These frequent changes of costume and even more frequent changes of pose emphasize the extent to which the sociosexual economies of this microcosm privilege display as the currency of their power exchanges. Célimène enters for her workout dressed in a stretch-nylon, black workout combination with pink trim, carrying a white gym towel and a bottle of Evian mineral water (a sign that invokes both Frenchness and Southern California "health consciousness").[5]

The La Jolla audience usually greeted this first entrance with a laugh of recognition, anticipating the customary satirical comment on the California "fitness life-style." But no such comment is made in this scene. Instead, the presence of the exercise-guillotine machine provides an ironic frame for the bitter dispute between Célimène and Arsinoë by drawing our attention to the ways in which notions of aging and physical attractiveness serve as the axis of dissension between the two "friends." The presence of the guillotine seems to suggest that the physical effort of staying in shape is only one negative aspect of the endless search for attractiveness and of the equally endless competition for attention which characterizes the Hollywood milieu as its codes of conduct emerge in this production.

I begin this discussion of the Falls production by focusing on the exercise-guillotine machine, even though the distinctive contour of the guillotine blade remains invisible to the audience until the machine is moved into place for Célimène's exercise session (Molière's *Misanthrope* 3.4). Following the intermission, which is taken at the end of act 3, the guillotine blade is turned perpendicular to the proscenium line and becomes once again invisible for the final two acts. This very invisibility, however, becomes significant during the coda that Falls stages following the final exit of Philinte and Eliante, which traditionally marks the conclusion of the play. Immediately following that exit, Célimène returns to the stage, once again dressed in workout clothing, carrying a small white towel and a portable tape deck. She lays her towel on the bench, pushes the play button on her tape deck, lies on her back, raises her knees, reaches up for the hand rings, and begins to exercise by raising and lowering the weight/ guillotine blade. She is working hard, and her exhalations are audible over the music. Now that the exercise machine appears only in profile, the spectator can see that the blade of the guillotine is precisely aligned with Célimène's neck. As the lights fade, we watch Célimène work at what appears to be the Sisyphean task of "saving her neck" from the blade.

Falls's mise-en-scène of *The Misanthrope* resolves on Célimène's response to the events of the play. Indeed, the Falls mise-en-scène encourages the spectator to shift focus from Alceste, the title character and the spectator's presumed center of orientation, to Célimène. Falls echoes this emphasis on Célimène in the curtain call when Kim Cattrall (Célimène) steps forward to take a final solo bow. In Molière's text, Philinte has the final line, a line that directs our attention to Alceste, who, we presume, is already en route to the desert refuge of his choice. This focus on Célimène, however, like the image of the guillotine, invites us to reread the mise-en-scène from a perspective that is quite different from that urged on us by Molière's own dramaturgy and the history of its reception.

More than three centuries of accumulated commentary on this play have read *The Misanthrope* as a play about its protagonist, Alceste, the *amoreux atrabilaire* who is named in the play's title. The fact that Molière himself played the part of Alceste and the assumption (dating from the time of the first production) that Célimène was a fictionalized version of his wife, Armande, have been taken as "proof" of the author's intention— that the play should express his (Molière's) criticisms of his contemporaries' (particularly his own wife's) social behavior. Indeed, this titillating blend of the real with the fictional has undoubtedly been a factor in the play's popularity over the centuries and has added a layer to the play's acquired meaning (both the La Jolla Playhouse and Goodman Theatre programs reminded the spectators of the play's autobiographical nature). Of course, all classic texts grow in accumulated significance over time as the endless cycles of interpretation create a complex web of intertexts which all contemporary readings inevitably confront. Robert Falls's reading of *The Misanthrope*, as embodied in his mise-en-scène, must therefore be seen not only as a reading of Molière's script but also as a reading of the traditions of understanding which have become attached to it during three and a half centuries of readings and performances.

Theatrical Coding and Local Semiosis

A consideration of Célimène/Kim Cattrall's final bow offers a particularly useful example of the ways in which Robert Falls stages collisions between a variety of codes as a way of provoking the spectator to work at his or her own reading of the many signifiers deployed in this mise-en-scène.

Indeed, what emerges as the decisive strategy of this mise-en-scène is Falls's insistence on not resolving any tensions that arise from the juxtaposition of theatrical and cultural codes whose differences are more apparent than their similarities. Seen in this light, the Falls mise-en-scène (including the exercise-guillotine machine as well as the final bow of the actress playing Célimène, which I have taken as being emblematic of the production as a whole) can best be understood as the kind of text described by Roland Barthes in his celebrated essay "The Death of the Author":

> A text is not a line of words releasing a single "theological" meaning (the "message" of the Author-God) but a multi-dimensional space in which a variety of writings, none of them original, blend and clash. The text is a tissue of quotations drawn from . . . many cultures and entering into mutual relations of dialogue, parody, contestation, but there is one place where this multiplicity is focused and that place is the reader, not, as was hitherto said, the author.[6]

Thus, the final bow, like the entire text of the mise-en-scène, should be understood as a site of "contestation" where the individual spectator contends with the "tissue of quotations" assembled for these performances of *The Misanthrope*. Only the individual spectator can construct, from this "variety of writings," the final, subjective significance of this theatrical event.

I have pointed out that Kim Cattrall is the only performer who takes a solo bow, which I have interpreted as manifesting the director's desire to position Célimène as the focal figure in his mise-en-scène. But Falls's desire to reconfigure Molière's dramaturgy by decentering Alceste cannot, in itself, account for the way in which the bow itself is performed. Cattrall steps forward in the usual manner from the line of actors to take her solo bow, and the spectator may respond to this movement by reading it as the customary acknowledgment of the "star" performer's special contribution. The bow itself, however, blends a traditional deep curtsy with a flexing of both biceps in a gesture of exultant triumph. The flexing of biceps immediately calls attention to itself by invoking the range of metaphors suggested by the presence of the exercise-guillotine machine throughout the play (the actress takes her curtain call wearing the same workout costume she wears in the coda). Furthermore, this gesture of triumph seems to run counter to the implications of the final sequence in which we see Célimène struggling with the guillotine blade of her exercise machine. Upon further reflection, however, the bow calls to mind an even more complex series of questions: Should the spectator assume that this bow indicates that Célimène emerges unchastened from the multiple rejections she suffers during act 4? If so, how should the spectator understand, in retrospect, Célimène's social behavior throughout acts 1 through 4? If Célimène remains unchastened and unrepentant, should the spectator understand the triumphant bow as a challenge to the traditional reading of the play? Or should the spectator read this final sign as "the-film-actress-from-Hollywood" claiming a victory

Fig. 2. *The Misanthrope,* act 2, La Jolla Playhouse (1989). From left, Célimène and Alceste. Photo credit: Jim Carmody.

for her character when nothing in the rest of the play suggests that one was earned?

The bow invokes a number of theatrical and cultural codes simultaneously: the suggestions of traditional femininity conveyed by the "classical" decorum of the "leading lady's" bow are contested by (but, interestingly enough, not replaced by) a flexing of the biceps, which proposes a contemporary celebration of the athleticized female body. In this final moment of the mise-en-scène, when the code of classical theater (our received notions of how *The Misanthrope* "should" be performed) is subverted for the last time, two representations of the female emerge in/from the body of the same actress. Since spectators' personal ideologies frame their readings of all aspects of a mise-en-scène, each individual will either privilege the "classic" misogynist representation of this character which our culture has inherited from literary and theatrical history or will privilege the representation of a contemporary autonomous woman. To put it more bluntly, the spectator can choose to see Célimène from the perspective of Alceste or to see Alceste from the perspective of Célimène. (It is interesting to note how audiences usually greeted Alceste's final invitation to Célimène to share his desert life with an explosion of derisory laughter.)

Mise-en-Scène and the Classic Text

Questions such as these, however, cannot be considered in isolation, as this mise-en-scène participates in a long tradition of restaging texts that belong to the canon of acknowledged dramatic masterpieces. Like all other such mise-en-scènes, the Falls production of *The Misanthrope* generates much of its significance by responding to that tradition of critical and theatrical interpretation in certain ways. Three hundred and twenty-three years and formidable linguistic and cultural differences separate the first production of *Le Misanthrope* from Robert Falls's adaptation of Neil Bartlett's translation of Molière's play.[7] In the period from 1666 to 1989, the play acquired and shed layer upon layer of accumulated commentary, performance traditions, and translations. Many of these layers remain both accessible and influential. Indeed, from a semiotic perspective, the play known as *The Misanthrope* is, for all practical purposes, absolutely indistinguishable from the many layers of interpretation and ranges of signification which have become attached to it over time, which is another way of saying that the play is what we familiarly term a classic. Robert Falls's adaptation and mise-en-scène of Neil Bartlett's "version" of Molière's *Le Misanthrope* can be read as much as a response to the tradition of restaging classic texts as to the dramaturgy of an individual text by Molière. It can also be read as an exploration of a range of problems which Marvin Carlson has recently discussed in the context of what he calls "local semiosis."[8] Using the theories of Clifford Geertz as a point of departure, Carlson asserts that the creative process "must inevitably be conditioned by the artistic tools of the artist's own culture and by the ways that culture defines and interprets artistic artifacts. . . . Such a view . . . is surely a useful corrective to the naive assumption that such a work makes . . . a specific 'aesthetic' statement, the same for all audiences, whatever their cultural background."[9]

In *Onstage*, the Goodman Theatre's subscriber newsletter, Falls writes about how he approached the problem of local semiosis:

> The world of Alceste and Célimène—the world of the intrigue and backbiting of Louis XIV's court—is a world that's turned up again and again in countless forms in the centuries since. I'd heard of other productions that had set the play just before the French Revolution, in the 1920s, in the 1930s . . . but I knew immediately that I was going to set the play in 1989 in the Hollywood Hills.
>
> I've always had a love-hate relationship with Hollywood. . . . There's no doubt in my mind that the world of agents, actors, screenwriters and producers provides a perfect modern analogue to Molière's world.
>
> From that core idea came . . . the design of the set and costumes (using photos of Madonna's new house in the Hollywood Hills as inspiration), and the discovery of a brilliant new verse translation . . . which we've adapted further for our setting.[10] We're sure that our first show this year will bring our season maxim alive: Then *is* now, the great works of the stage reflect our time just as they reflect times past and future.[11]

In this "director's note" Falls shares with his subscribers some of the ideas that helped shape his semiotic reading of the play. Even though these words

Fig. 3. *The Misanthrope*, act 2, La Jolla Playhouse (1989). From left, Philinte, Clitandre, Acaste, Eliante, Célimène, and Alceste. Photo credit: Jim Carmody.

were not spoken from the stage, contemporary theater semiotics recognizes them as an integral part of the Falls mise-en-scène in that they provide the spectator with information that conditions the spectator's ability to interpret the cultural and theatrical codes deployed on stage. Goodman subscribers came to performances having already read these words. Even those who had not read *Onstage* had almost certainly been exposed to the same ideas in newspaper articles, reviews (many of which quoted or paraphrased the *Onstage* piece), and in the program distributed to spectators at the theater.[12]

Falls describes his perception of Hollywood as "a perfect modern analogue to Molière's world" as the "core idea," the origin of all other artistic choices in the production. Several reviewers, however, criticized the production for its failure to provide a "perfect" analogy, pointing out that Arsinoë's seventeenth-century prudishness, for example, had no counterpart in contemporary Hollywood. But such criticisms fail to appreciate the nature of analogy, which does not pretend to eliminate all differences between the two entities that are being compared. Although he writes "then *is* now" (a rhetorical gesture that has become a commonplace since Jan Kott's *Shakespeare Our Contemporary*), Falls is not suggesting that 1666 Paris and 1989 Hollywood are identical. Indeed, the Falls mise-en-scène succeeds in performance precisely because it continually draws our attention to *both* the similarities and the differences between 1666 and 1989.

As Falls himself points out, setting the play in a period other than the seventeenth century is by now a traditional gambit. But it is difficult to establish an analogy between "then" and "now" if the dialogue refers only to the codes of the culture in which the play was first written and performed. In the case of *The Misanthrope*, the words of Molière in the "standard" translation of Richard Wilbur (a translation that privileges literariness over theatricality and the demands of local semiosis) would sound utterly foreign in the context of George Tsypin's postmodern setting. Neil Bartlett's translation, on the other hand, offers a language that sounds indigenous to the Tsypin scenography and the culture it invokes.

Bartlett's translation (brilliantly) preserves Molière's twelve-syllable rhyming alexandrines, the names of the characters, and Molière's formal mode of address (e.g., Sir, Monsieur, Madame, etc.). Bartlett makes no attempt to employ anything other than contemporary English/American, with the result that the characters speak a language that is not only instantly comprehensible but laden with contemporary cultural resonance (an advantage that the actors enjoyed in Molière's time). At the same time, the poetic texture of Bartlett's language is rich in unexpected rhythm and rhyme, pun and paradox. But Bartlett's translation does more than provide the actors with a contemporary language: it provides them with the language of contemporary Hollywood. Thus, the often wide gap in productions of classic plays between the cultural frame of reference of the classic spoken text and the cultural frame of reference of the contemporary text of the mise-en-scène is, with the exception of character names and French modes of address, almost inconspicuous.

Accustomed to attending foreign plays performed in translation, the spectator may automatically consider the foreign character names insignificant. As a result of the same habit of mind, the spectator may choose to ignore the fact that the characters address each other with a formality that seems strange indeed in the context of the Hollywood Hills. What the spectator cannot fail to notice is that Bartlett has chosen to retain Molière's twelve-syllable line, a verse form that is utterly unfamiliar in the English-speaking theater. The easy accessibility of the contemporary vocabulary is offset by the strangeness of the verse form and the foreignness of certain elements of speech. While Bartlett worked hard and effectively to make the analogy between 1666 Paris and 1989 Hollywood persuasive, he clearly never intended to efface the cultural and temporal divide that separates the two:

> The whole point of translating this play has been to make an elaborate and provocative game out of the collision of the formality of classical French verse and the vivid recognizability of contemporary speech. . . . [*The Misanthrope*] is completely un-English. I wanted the translation to sound foreign, like a foreign work of art, even though the language is comprehensible.[13]

Bartlett never allows the spectator to forget that he or she is dealing with a play from another culture and another time. Indeed, at one point in act 2, Bartlett blatantly reminds the audience of the classic status of *The Misanthrope* when he has Eliante quote two lines from the play in French, the same two lines that Molière gives her to speak at that precise moment: "L'amour pour ordinaire, est peu fait à ces lois, / Et l'on voit les amants vanter toujours les choix." She goes on to translate those lines and the rest of the speech: "Love is blind and not subject to the Laws. / Lovers are used to Love without Good Cause. / No Matter how foolish, the Loved One seems wise.... / *Le Misanthrope*. Act II. It's my own translation."[14]

While Bartlett's citation from *Le Misanthrope* draws attention to the cultural status of Molière's play, it also calls attention to the extraordinary degree to which citation permeates both the Bartlett/Falls text and the mise-en-scène. The first line of the translation/adaptation is an obvious citation: "What's up doc?" Although there are several equally recognizable citations, the unfamiliar verse form in tandem with the often bizarre juxtapositioning of the formal with the vulgar works to make the spoken text sound artificial, as if the entire play were nothing but a tissue of citations. Alceste's final speech provides a good example of this phenomenon:

> I hope you'll be happy, from the depth of my heart
> And that you will be faithful 'til Death Do You Part.
> Crippled by injustice, and spat upon by shits,
> I'll book a one way ticket out of this Abyss
> I'll fly to some city that isn't run by Vice,
> Where a good man can be as honest as he likes.

Similarly, the scenography borrows visual ideas from a variety of periods and cultures, using the visual language of postmodernism to provide a hospitable setting for the intertextualities of Bartlett's and Falls's recreation of Molière's classic text.

Like the translation, the Falls mise-en-scène both advocates and undermines the analogy between Molière's culture and our own. At best, the analogy only partially obscures the foreignness of Molière's play, just as Molière's play only partially illuminates the Hollywood culture. Although Falls and Bartlett succeed in persuading us that the two cultures have much in common, they do not try to persuade us that they are identical. In fact, as I have tried to suggest, they have devoted at least as much creative energy to subverting the proposed similarity as they have to promoting it. Ultimately, the unusual richness of this mise-en-scène results precisely from the many ways in which Falls and Bartlett bring the theatrical and cultural codes of seventeenth-century France and contemporary Southern California to play off each other.

In a brief essay such as this, it is impossible to describe at sufficient length the semiotics of such important elements of mise-en-scène as scenography, costumes, lighting, music, blocking, and acting styles. Each of these topics requires many pages of description before even the most basic analysis can begin. Instead, as I indicated earlier, I have chosen to deal only with the semiotics of selected marginal details, hoping that they will convey the semiotic wealth of this quite extraordinary mise-en-scène.

NOTES

Chapter epigraph from Barthes, "The Death of the Author," in *Image-Music-Text*, trans. Stephen Heath (New York: Hill and Wang, 1977), 144.

1. Robert Falls (director/adapter), Neil Bartlett (translator), George Tsypin (sets), Susan Hilferty (costumes), James F. Ingalls (lighting), Rob Milburn (sound), Walter Bilderback and Richard Pettingill (dramaturges), David Darlow (Alceste), William Brown (Philinte), Del Close (Oronte), Kim Cattrall (Célimène), Christina Haag (Eliante), David Alan Novak (Clitandre), John Douglas Carlile (Acaste), and Peggy Roeder (Arsinoë). The play was first performed at the La Jolla Playhouse in La Jolla, California, on 20 August 1989. After its initial run, the set and costumes were transported to Chicago, where the production opened on 10 October 1989 as the first production of the Goodman Theatre's 1989–90 season.

2. Patrice Pavis provides a detailed discussion of mise-en-scène as a form of semiotic reading in *Languages of the Stage: Essays in the Semiology of the Theatre* (New York: Performing Arts Journal Publications, 1982), 131–61.

3. Throughout the present article, I attribute to "Robert Falls" the authorship of the performance text, which is the subject of this discussion. Such an attribution is, of course, a habitual one in the discussion of production, but it is important to remember that the Robert Falls of this essay is a fictional construct that stands for the real Robert Falls and all those involved in this mise-en-scène.

4. The most thorough presentation in English of these theoretical foundations can be found in Keir Elam, *The Semiotics of Theatre and Drama* (London: Methuen, 1980). Since the 1960s, the theater research group at the Centre National de Recherche Scientifique in Paris has published a number of semiotic readings of various productions in the series *Les voies de la création théâtrale*. The sixth volume of the series includes a particularly impressive analysis by Tadeusz Kowzan of Roger Planchon's influential mise-en-scènes of *Le Tartuffe* in the 1960s and 1970s.

5. This relationship between Frenchness and Southern California "health consciousness" is developed differently in the character of Alceste, who smokes French cigarettes. Alceste is the only smoker in the play. In addition, Alceste's interest in French culture marks him as an outsider in Hollywood. Instead of the "old song" that Molière gives Alceste to sing in act 1, Bartlett has Alceste put Jacques Brel's "Ne Me Quitte Pas" on the turntable and provide a simultaneous translation.

6. Barthes, *Image-Music-Text*, 146–48.

7. Bartlett's "English" version of *The Misanthrope* was first performed at the Edinburgh Festival in 1988 by the Red Shift Theatre Company. The text of this English version can be found in *Bérénice (Racine), Le Misanthrope, The School for Wives (Molière)* (London: Absolute Classics, 1990). All quotations from the "American" version are from *The Misanthrope by Molière*, a new version by Neil Bartlett, further adapted by Robert Falls (Chicago: Goodman Playscripts, 1989). The American version was reprinted in *American Theatre* 7, nos. 4, 5 (July/August, 1990).

8. Marvin Carlson, *Theatre Semiotics: Signs of Life* (Bloomington: Indiana University Press, 1990), 110–21.

9. Carlson, *Theatre Semiotics*, 111.

10. Bartlett's "English" version located the play in London's media world.

11. *Onstage* (Goodman Theatre series) 4, no. 1 (1989): 1.

12. Interestingly enough, the La Jolla Playhouse program included no statement from Robert Falls. The playhouse program included an extract from Bartlett's "A Letter to the Company," twelve citations from the "Maxims of La Rochefoucauld," a brief biography of Molière (which emphasized the autobiographical nature of the

play as well as his difficulties with his wife), and two reproductions of seventeenth-century artworks—an engraving from the 1682 edition of the *Oeuvres de Molière* and the well-known painting of Molière breakfasting with Louis XIV. This last image appeared over the caption: "Power Breakfast: Louis XIV with Molière at Versailles."

13. Neil Bartlett, "A Letter to the Company," *Performing Arts* (San Diego) 2, no. 9 (September 1989): LJP-6. The La Jolla Playhouse program appears as a separately paginated insert after page 20 of *Performing Arts*.

14. Eliante's speech occurs at act 2, scene 4, ll. 711–30. Bartlett's version slightly abridges Molière's text.

Unspeakable Justice:
David Hare's *Fanshen*

David McDonald

J. Hillis Miller describes criticism as "a human activity which depends for its validity on never being at ease with a fixed method. It must constantly put its own grounds in question."[1] In the "Author's Preface" to *Fanshen*, a play about the Chinese Revolution, David Hare informs "those of you who want to mount the work" that "the production of this play must involve you in the continual definition of your objectives and the continual asking of questions."[2] It would seem that criticism, as described by Miller, and the production activity of *Fanshen*, as described by Hare, have an affinity, assuming that they put their own grounds in question. Hare's description of rehearsing *Fanshen* also addresses the problem of adequacy in representation of those lives that are put in question:

> It was the overwhelming priority that we should do these people justice. Although the subject matter was political, the instincts of the company were in essence moral. Everyone sensed an obligation to portray Chinese peasants in a way which was adequate to their suffering.[3]

Questioning the adequacy of the representation of the truth, of doing justice to the subject, justifies the ground of theatrical and critical representation.

Representation has many aspects, but it always has two inseparable sides: one of identity, the other of difference. Representation stressing *identity* (amid differences) is grounded in mimetic fidelity to what it portrays: "The validity of the mimetic copy is established by its truth of correspondence to what it copies."[4] Identification is the generative principle of rational relations and daytime truth. Accuracy, authenticity, and repeatability establish its truth. The master theorist of this side of representation is Plato. Identification "establishes the world as an icon" and a performance based on "genuine participative similarity."[5] In the theory of performance, advocates of Stanislavski recognize the primacy of identity. In *Fanshen* the trial scenes of the villagers display a primary concern for the precise identification of injustice.

The other side of representation stresses *difference* (amid similarities), focusing on a unique truth that appears through a system of differences in which nothing is ever the same. Each representative instance closes in on itself: separate, isolated, and perceived as related only through a grid, grammar, or rhetoric of performative signs. Difference, within identity, generates the awareness of representation as an image that stands apart from the thing it represents, as something other than its referent, or more of the same. Representation through difference is seen as the multiplicity of changing variations, not as iconic participation. Representation turns uncanny: the truth of dreams, nighttime truth. The master theorist of truth as figurative—an "army of metaphors, metonymies and synedoches"—is Nietzsche. The world is read "as if": as phantasm, fiction, simulacra, or in a Platonic derision, as a "copy of copies." In the contemporary performance theory both Brecht and Artaud display variations of the side of difference through systems of "alienation" and the uncanny "cruelty" of the double: the incessant sliding of signified from under the signifier, the schizophrenic duality of any attempt to identify with difference. In *Fanshen* the ironic subversion and catachrestic reversal of each trial scene, and the metaleptic reading of the revolution as a repetition and a consequent fiction, marks this reading of difference as the other hand of identity, an "eternal return of the same."

When pressed into the service of practice or performance the two figures of identity and difference appear as twinned and inseparable as the doubled masks (comic/tragic) of theatrical representation: the schizophrenic twist of the mouth in the doubled configuration of mockery and pain in an attempt to represent the ceaselessly dissatisfied movement of the Other as self. This two-faced dance of undecidability as a ceaseless dissatisfaction recurring in the "empty space" between and within the two masks of mockery and pain repeatedly limes performance as taking place in between the signifiers of self and Other, subject and object, actor and character, fact and fiction, mind and body. The being-caught-in-between, the performance alive between the snap of being there and not-there (*fort/da*)—literally onstage between offstage and out there—living on the borderlines between life and death, a position willy-nilly with its ground in question; a displaced position caught up in the repetition of overturning (*fanshen*) and the metaleptic reversals of equal justice for all. The doubled figure of catachresis represents performative mimesis as a turning over: the literal body turned figurative and the figurative body turned literal. The chinese word *fanshen* means literally "to turn the body."[6]

The turning point of *Fanshen*, a play by David Hare "based on a book by William Hinton" which documents the Communist Revolution in the Chinese village of Long Bow, stages a public address as the summary analysis of the play. The speech, made by the party secretary, defines the action of the Communist Revolution as a mistaken repetition (mere representation) of a revolution that had already happened before they began "turning over" (*fanshen*) the landowners: "Had we not already spontaneously and in advance of the Party undertaken land reform . . . *before* the law was announced?" (emphasis in text, 11.1).[7] The metaleptic *"before,"* as in Derrida's repeated phrase the "always already," turns the conference address, the definitive speech act of the play, into a deconstructive summary, the rereading of a history as fiction. The rhetoric of the summary reverses the "performative opening" (the representation as reality) to an awareness of the reality as representation.[8] The performative "closure of representation" makes the play end, and begin again, as it calls for a new beginning,

Fig. 1. Manami Mitani (Yu-lai), Shelley Booker (Hu Hseuh-Chen, Liu), and Carla Sublett (Chang Ch'uen, Ch'ing lai's wife). Photo credit: Phillip Channing.

a repetition of the revolution, or of its representation.[9] Beginning and end fold into one another as undecidable difference. The new master trope, a chiasmus, deconstruction's "invagination," turns the play inside out. The summary discloses the performative nature of the action, including the speech act of the summary itself. The speech implies that seeing the revolution as a mistake, a performative aberration, serves as a solvent, a part of the solution to the sense of futility, of stasis: turning over what they had already turned over before.[10] The speech concludes that they must begin again, return to overturn. The conclusion that revolution is a mere representation challenges the idea of history as accomplished, progressive action. The summary would substantiate even as it subverts its claim as an "accurate historical record"[11] by challenging the ethical demand to do justice and represent the truth in the only terms that truth and justice can be claimed, as performative representations.

The plot of *Fanshen* progresses by a series of episodes which test an ideal, or moral standard, by the trial of repetition and subversive reversal. *Fanshen* tries to represent justice and ends by subverting that representation. The attempt at the representation and its subversion constitute the movement of the action. The story of *Fanshen*, as allegory, synecdoche, or microcosm, presents the trials of one village as an adequate representation of the Chinese Revolution. The action follows the trials of a village, its cadre and the intervention of party leaders from the initial overthrow of landlord justice through the turns of vigilante, tribunal, and administrative

131

justice. The action at Long Bow village serves as a prototype for the collective struggle to find the answer to Hare's question, "How to structure justice?" or, its corollary, how to adequately represent the truth.[12]

The body of the play consists of judgment scenes in which the villagers and party members confront, judge, and humiliate their peers in public. Dramatic modes of representation vary from the melodrama of justice as vengeance to the farce of justice as bickering and backbiting to the tragedy of justice as sacrificial anarchy and the irony of justice as parable.

The problems of doing justice in casting the play, at least in the Irvine production, carried the motif of revolution into the double, multiple, and effaceable casting of characters.[13] In the Irvine production ten actors, five women and five men, played over thirty roles. In the original production by the Joint Stock Group, seven men played the male parts and two women the female parts.[14] At Irvine actors repeated and reversed roles throughout casting and rehearsals. The initial casting process took a full month of group meetings during which time each actor performed every role. Subsequent casting changes, made to suit the readings and relationships discovered during the rehearsals, continued up until two days before the first public presentation. This created a sense of continuous turmoil—a revolution within the process of representation—and a dependence on ensemble initiative and responsibility. The exchanges created a dialogical interpretation of the text. The dialogue of a "seminar theater" extended the open and close reading of the text to collaborative group direction and design choices. Stage movement, apart from staged violence, was never "fixed," and, although most activity settled into discovered and preferred patterns, those patterns always remained open to discovery and change by any member of the ensemble. Independent actions, made either by chance or by choice, could alter the pattern of group movement, even as group movement influenced independent acts. The "ground plan" was always in question, the movement ceaselessly dissatisfied. A similar freedom of interpretation, apart from memorization, applied to the inflection, tone, coloring, and emphasis in the spoken dialogue. The direction followed the deconstructive premise that the *aporia* of "undecidability" is always already present as the risk and source of vitality in any live theater performance—from the fear of a void at lost cues, lines, and entrances to the sense, as Artaud refers to it, that "the sky can still fall on our heads. And the theater has been created to teach us that first of all."[15] Theater productions, like daily life, have schemes of action, but once in action an awareness that nobody knows what might happen, what role chance might play, creates the urgency of immediate performance.

Undecidability as *aporia*, the figure of speech, attempts to say what cannot be said. It is also a term for "the speechless," for those without a voice, or say, or ability to speak, for "unspeakability," as the impulse of the necessity to speak, to find a voice, to have a say, and a concomitant awareness of the unutterable chaos at the loss of language, sign systems, or the will and ability to speak as a performative act. Deconstruction is simply an awareness that the web of signs, lines, and cues always passes through the undecidability of attempting to say what cannot be said.

Since in the process of casting and rehearsal every actor played every role and so knew the positions of the other, each had a say in the casting that held for the brief, three-day performance run. If the production had run for more than three days, roles would have changed as they did in other productions in this series. Gender, age, ideological and ethnic identity played no decisive part in determining who played the role. Only the authority of a reading, an authority granted by the consensus of group response, assigned a role. Despite the principle of *fanshen*, of repeated reversals and transference of identity, in the end the individual characters remained unique, differentiated, identifiable, and signed by the identity of the actor as the character performing in the scene. Hsien-e, represented by the same actress (Leslie Gray) who portrayed Old Lady Wang, was distinctly different and identifiable as Hsien-e without any change of visual appearance. The script requires a strongly marked identity and difference for both characters. Hsien-e must also change her identity in the course of the action. At the same time the personae of the actors remained distinctly identifiable and separate from the dramatis personae. No attempt was made to mask their self-representation, their own personal identity and difference. All actors played two to four parts, effacing anyone's claim to absolute authority or appropriation of a part. Some were required to be equally convincing in opposite identities. The actress who played the villainous yet cruelly beaten landowner, Kuo Ch'ung-wang (Sarah Dacey), was required to be convincing as the patient, self-effacing, humiliated cadre leader, Hou. The fact that both parts were originally written for males and based on historical (possibly still living) masculine characters was inconsequential to the virtual reality in a performance decentered in the oscillation between identity and difference as determining the representation of a multiple subject. No one questioned the authority of her sexual or ethnic identity to represent two differing Asian males. The actress gave each character a different and unique identity while maintaining without imposing her personal identity. Her personae remained caught between the traces, transferring without transcending those others she represented. Her identity was fictive and self-reflexive without being self-conscious. She was one and many. Any traces of previous identities, or the ironic contrast of positive and negative roles, remained apart, as a trace, from the moment of performance. Discursive perception of likeness in unlike and like was not traced in the gestures and inflection. *Prosopopoeia*, the trope of personification, the figure of a speech act which confers a mask or a face (*prosopon poiein*) and posits "the possibility of the latter's reply," also posits the possibility of a dialogical representation of justice.[16] The unique figurative presence of each character was never sacrificed to abstract theories of the multiple subject.

An important aspect of the staging of the Irvine production was the identity of the performers as students. Instead of attempting to represent Chinese peasants, the student performers represented students attempting to represent Chinese peasants, specifically students at the University of

Fig. 2. Daniel Reinisch (Kuo-Te-Yu, Lai-Tzu, Huan Ch'ao), Leslie Gray (Hsien-e, Old Lady Wang, Ching-Ho), Mason Malone (Tui-Chin, T'ao Yuan, Wen-te), Shelley Booker (Hu Hseuh-Chen, Liu), Manami Mitani (Yu-lai). Photo credit: Phillip Channing.

California, Berkeley (UCB), in the late 1960s staging the play as a protest play. The student performers represented what they were: UCB students representing UCB students. They wore a uniform of their own well-worn denim jeans, jackets, and nondescript shirts that effaced period difference in appearance and even paralleled without repeating in design the ubiquitous blue cotton pants and jackets worn by Chinese peasants. Cultural difference served cultural identity, and vice versa. Asian student riots at UC Berkeley in the spring of 1987, at the time of rehearsals, repeated images of UCB students crashing barricades in the 1960s. Cultural difference repeated as identity. These images of Asian-American student revolutionaries in turn echoed photographic images of student revolutions in Japan and Korea throughout the 1970s and 1980s, or, more pointedly, students leading Mao's Cultural Revolution in China during the 1960s and 1970s, and, most recently, in the postproduction era, the image of a student revolution as the closure of representation for a Chinese Revolution as performed at Tiananmen Square, June 1989. Students performed the part of students performing revolution, a part that students have effectively performed in various cultures and nations during the twentieth century.[17]

The metonymic transfer of student as peasant as revolutionary serves in a Foucauldian archaeology, as an "enunciating subject": a "vacant place," or intersection for producing a representation of revolution and displaying revolution as a discursive formation.[18] The actual, figurative, and functional role of student as student representing students performing revolution developed in the produced image. The rhetorical figure of a student revolution transferred as a metaleptic reversal, a double metonymy, folding over time and space as well as cultural and economic identity. No essential distinction in the visual representation was made between village peasants, cadre workers, party leaders. The indeterminacy and complicity in the exchange of character and functions, although not a prescribed method for doing the play (and not the costuming or imagery chosen by the Joint Stock Group and described by Hare's stage directions) applies to the binary ambiguity of representing revolution in which landlords and peasants, teacher and students, parents and children, male and female reverse roles and repeat their difference as identity seen in each other's eyes. The dramatic increase in the number of Asian students at UC Irvine during the late 1980s was an important consideration in initiating the production. The ethnic difference of the student performers, in contrast to the original British production, reflected the ethnic difference of the audience.

The performance of *Fanshen* begins as nine peasants state their names and how much land they own and give a bit of background on the social and political history of the village and China. Apart from establishing identities and differences, individual and collective, the prologue also establishes the convention of direct address and direct statement ("performative opening") as the representation of a truth. The cumulative effect of the nine unquestioned assertions fictively displaces the dominant position of the audience as the collective authority. This disparity of knowledge between observer and observed, actor and audience, helps to create an illusion of authority and credibility for the performer, and, at the end of the play, an opening for the counter-discursive arising as a response to what has been omitted, condensed, displaced, and revised.

The frenzy at the first outcry against hypocrisy, the accusation of the collaborator, Kuo Te-yu, displays itself as both an improvised and calculated performative. T'ien-ming, the party agitator, uses well-worn tropes and schemes of insistent repetition to provoke a unanimous condemnation. Through repeated accusations he creates a dissatisfied movement, puts their ground in question, and stimulates an echoing figure of sound and fury which shapes their once silent suffering into active violence. A torturous dialogue follows in forcing the landowner Ch'ung-wang to speak, or cry out in a pain that echoes the cause, the original violence. Escalating repetition echoes, and like an echo enlarges the overturning until it exhausts itself when the peasants are left with nothing to overturn but the landowner's ancestral graves, "leaving gaping holes in the countryside" (5.2).

The plea to speak out, "Just to speak it out" (1.1), is the agitator's theme. The drama of speaking out as in itself an action animates the dramatic event of every scene that follows. The drama finds its event in the necessity of representation, "How can we know unless you speak out?" (3.3).

The "classification reviews" show the villagers as a rowdy, petty group more intent on using their new equality and freedom of speech to jab out, mock each other, and have fun than to create a working community. They are stymied by a new language, the party jargon describing rich, poor, and middle-class peasants. Led by Old Lady Wang, the peasants evaluate the village blacksmith, Chang Huan-ch'ao, and fail to classify him because he is nominally not a "peasant." The text of regulations from the central planning committee did not differentiate between the words for a village worker and village peasant, and so they have no word, no name to identify his difference. Peasants work the land; he does not work the land; and, as one peasant correctly points out, "You can't call him something he's not" (7.2). Naming his difference, representing his identity, is deferred. The next peasant they attempt to classify, Wang T'ao-yuan, is the village heroin dealer, who also sells other people's wives and is in misery because his donkey just died from a cold. Three classes are clearly inadequate to represent his situation, and so he receives one vote for each: rich, middle, and poor peasant. He is not deferred: he is simply undecidable. At the end of the classification review the word *peasant* is a synonym for *poor*. Peasants have identified peasants as peasants. Democratic review generates a classless society. They place one another in question, but questioning subverts their differences. They conclude by making a farce of justice, a generic revision of the exhausted, empty-handed leveling reached earlier by melodramatic vengeance.

When the performative accusation turns away from peers to the critical review of leaders in "Passing the Gate," the structure of doing dramatic justice turns tragic. The first revolutionary leader judged, Cheng-k'uan, chairman of the Peasants' Association, fails to pass the gate because he cannot find the words to represent himself. (Their judicial system does not provide "legal representation." The essence of the system is that the accused must represent themselves. Cheng-k'uan does not know how to represent himself with language.) He attempts to repeat the facts, but, since the facts are always doubled by the difference of language, his precision leads him into tragicomic self-contradiction:

> *Hsin-ai:* Being criticized doesn't mean saying yes to everything.
> *Cheng-k'uan:* Yes. No.
> *Hsin-ai:* Be objective and then criticize yourself.
> *Cheng-k'uan:* Yes.
>
> (8.1)

His inability to represent himself as an "objective" truth, to turn his subject into an object, doubles him into the position of using his own voice as evidence against his objectivity. His will to repeat their objective view mocks the performative demand of the play, to "just speak it out." His truth is not their truth; he cannot represent his subject as their object. Representation mocks the demand to just speak objective truth, or speak *just* truth. Cheng-k'uan seems false, divided against himself, when at worst he is clumsy, confused, and honest. He submits to self-abasement, public humiliation, ridicule, loss of office and authority. Mute, tongue-tied honesty, and his servile willingness to respect their authority, proves deadly. Cheng-k'uan's final speech, made later while staring into a bucket containing his dead child, repeats, but with tragic speechlessness, the truth of an inability to find the words, thoughts, or "objects" to justify the loss.

The next peasant leader judged, Hu Hsueh-chen, head of the Woman's Association, once timid and shy, "afraid to speak in public" (4.2), now discovers that her hard-earned confidence, precision, and ability to accurately record her history and represent herself turns others against her. Clear outspoken simplicity provokes outspoken envy. She looks too good to be true: "Because of that look that says she's a leader. That's why the people resent her" (8.1). Her articulate presence makes her superior, therefore not an equal, and so an "injustice" in their midst. Hsueh-chen replies, "I submit to the people. I will try to correct my face" (8.1). Face-saving irony permits her to turn the double play of words in her favor. She has the last word of the scene. Prefiguring the peasant's parable at the end of the play, irony appears as Hare's favored trope for the closure of a scene.

Candidly admitting appearance, the look of a face, as a basis for justice and truth, goodness and beauty, turns the search for the identity of true leaders into a tragifarce. Self-representation, self-personification, the *prosopopoeia* of preserving face and voice for an unseen presence, fails even when it succeeds. In the Irvine production Hsueh-chen was married, as the script directs in a mute tableaux (4.2), to a man silently performed by the same actor who performed Cheng-k'uan. Her present self-effacing and face-saving grace leaves her standing, in tragic closure, alongside a man with her dead child in a bucket.

The collapse of the attempt to establish a democratic structure for justice leads the Party Secretary to single out Comrade Hou, the cadre leader, to account for the failure of party policies in the village. Hou, however, is not given a chance to speak and represent himself or his team. Reversing yet repeating the group failure, the Secretary "speaks over" and so drowns out or fails to listen to the report of his agent. Secretary Ch'en reprimands Hou and orders him to undergo "self-criticism." Hou tries to interrupt, to reply, to let dialogue do justice, but the supervisory voice of the Secretary cuts the story into a pragmatic misrepresentation that serves political purposes.

The order for self-criticism is an oxymoronic *self*-criticism for and by *others*, by his own "comrades." Self-criticism condenses the trial procedures of the village tribunal to the inner circle of voices internalized by common purpose. Close critical reading forces the subject to put his subjective ground in question. The self is treated as a language system: read, edited, and corrected as an ungrounded system of differences suffered through the interpretation of others. Hou is not only denied the right to represent himself but even is challenged on the use of the personal pronoun by Little Li: "I? I? Who is this I? The I who said I don't want my decisions questioned?" (9.2). The privacy of confidential candor is turned against self-confidence. Hou's subject is systematically undermined until "he is at the end of his personality" (9.2). Ch'i-Yun, the most aggressive member of the team, forces Hou to go back and "make specific accusations against yourself. . . . You must trace over everything, every detail, every bad thought" (9.2). She demands that he put his self-effacement, his erasure, into an accurate historical record. He becomes a supplement for the dinner they were to eat.

Michael Coveney's review of the Joint Stock production described this scene of self-criticism as "very funny" and, as a grotesque bridge from the comic to the tragic, it is both very funny and very sad.[19] The scene demands a "close reading" of one character by himself for the others. The Chinese Communist Party (CCP) procedure of "Self Report, Public Appraisal," shows how the close reading of others turns from melodrama to farce to a grotesque theater of cruelty: a dialogue of psychological humiliation, self-righteous hypocrisy, and the systematic erasure of the difference and identity of the narrative subject. The performative speech act extends the mockery of justice. A mockery made all the more perverse by the knowledge of the examiners that the self-accusing victim is innocent.[20] The representation of self-critical truth, disappearing within the suicidal closure of self-negating inspection, puts its own ground in question to the point of exhaustion. Exhausting the subject puts the question in question.

The successive removal of old and new leaders exposes the village to the revival of violence. The attempt at coherent order fragments into three simultaneous yet disparate scenes unified in outcry against the violent intimidation. The triptych shows: (1) Cheng-k'uan staring into the bucket containing his dead infant and asking: "How can we go on? I'm tired. Everyone says I've fanshened, but what's changed?"; (2) the cadre member Chang Ch'eur pleading with old Tui-chin to denounce the violent Yu-lai and being rejected: "You told us to denounce corrupt leaders. And I did. . . . And now he's been released"; and (3) the terror of Hsien-e, attacked by her husband, Wen-te, the son of Yu-lai, and watched by him as "Wen-te thrashes wildly at Hsien-e with his belt" Yu-lai challenges: "Will anyone. Speak" (10.1).

Hsien-e answers his challenge in the following scene when she seeks asylum from the women's association and offers to denounce both her husband and his father. When Hsien-e speaks out in public the play permits the structure of justice to appear without internal contradiction. The moment of Hsien-e's truth is described by Hare as "stunning." The audience plays eyewitness to her truth. When she speaks the audience knows the accuracy of her words; they saw what they signify happen throughout the play. Yet even this scene is put in question. After Yu-lai has been convicted, Secretary Liu questions him:

> *Yu-lai:* I want to die.
> *Liu:* Why?
> *Yu-lai:* There's nothing.
> *Liu:* Nothing?
> *Yu-lai:* Nothing for me."

(10.4)

The party secretary does not question the "for me"—the personal pronoun in question. The credibility of Yu-lai as a representative of despair, rather than its cause, is left unexamined. The questioning of the party secretary puts itself in question. The central party countermands the judgment of the villagers and interprets the achievement of their justice as vengeance. Cloaked in the rhetoric of humane justification, Liu offers a cynical pragmatism, that those with strength and cunning must be rehabilitated to serve the party. Little Li, the passionate and independent voice of the cadre, speaks out and questions the judgment of the secretary. He demands both a consistent policy and one that responds to the will of the people it claims to represent. His criticism puts the authority of fixed party method in question, even as he seeks responsibility. So doing, he represents the playwright's policy for producing the play and displaying the reversible structures of justice through a continuous questioning of objectives.

The climax, or turning point, of the play, its summary speech as stated at the beginning of this essay, places the entire play in question. What the audience has seen, what the characters performed, was not the "true" revolution. The summary speech is critical revision and supplement that presents itself as the true performative act. The Secretary's speech also subverts the structural principles of authority and equality, the "structure of justice" question. Secretary Ch'en appears as a representative for the one transcendental signifier (unutterable referent) whose name is omitted from the play, Chairman Mao. Hare carefully omits any reference to Mao in the entire play. In the summary speech he even performs a slight but telling misrepresentation by omitting a reference to the authority of Mao included in Hinton's record of the speech. Hinton records Ch'en citing Mao along with Lenin, Marx, and Stalin, as icons whose words should be faithfully followed, copied to the letter as sources for the absolute truth.[21] The name of Mao is cited as unquestionable text to support the Secretary's point that the pursuit of justice at the expense of production is extremist and counterrevolutionary. A rhetoric that carefully omits any mention of Mao's name from an entire play permits the play to sustain the fiction of the Chinese Revolution as a pristine return to the *vox populi*, not to the logocentric voice of a supreme subject and a sacred text as the source for legitimacy. By omitting the question of an absolute authority, the image of Mao, the play mystifies the locus of the performative authority. Secretary Ch'en's word, like Mao's, remains absolute and only seems open to question. Party line determines the interpretation of reality for the characters in the play. The principle of dogmatic closure usurps the first principle of the play: "Just to speak it out," with a trace of Yu-lai's "Will anyone. Speak."

The Secretary's speech does not pass without outspoken opposition. Little Li questions the Secretary and gains the nominal point of Ch'en's responsibility, but the interpretation of action and consequences remains unchallenged and unchanged. When Little Li demands accountability from the Secretary, in one of the play's most dramatic scenes of outspoken confrontation, Li echoes the cry for someone to "just speak it out," which initiated the dramatic action and sustained it. His performative courage forces the concession of "primary responsibility." Unfortunately, however, as Li notes of the concession, the Secretary's speech act is "infelicitous":

"You're just saying it" (12.2). Free speech no longer has the force of over-turning monological domination in the play. The Secretary can admit defeat and remain in power, "grounded" in position with the force of authority to shift signifiers and revise the representation of reality. Secretary Ch'en distorts the dramatic sequence of events in order to sustain his argument. The summary speech does not square with the sequence of events presented in the play. No scene shows a redistribution of land prior to Little Li's speech announcing the policy of redistribution. Land redistribution is pre-sented as a separate event from the overthrow of the landowners. The summary conflates the two events, making the second appear to repeat the first. Rhetoric collapses the one into the other as figurative parts of a revolutionary whole transcending mere linear chronology. Rhetoric recon-figures the chronological into an appealing causal explanation for the sense of futility. The unique, discreet authority of the unrepeatable moments of reality (justice momentarily achieved) observed and performed is erased.

The revisionary rhetoric, the mastery of figuration over history, forces the conclusion that they must return and repeat the revolution, the revo-lution they have already repeated. They must unsay what they have said, including the justice and the achieved freedom of speech. Liberty must submit to authority. They must return to the grammar and rule of con-straint, intimidation, and obedient, submissive silence. Questions are per-mitted but only when permitted. The characters have been instructed, and the audience informed, that to make this revolution different from all other Chinese revolutions, where "the blood runs down the gutter and nothing is changed," is to press questions: "The difference is, this time, we think. We ask questions. We analyze" (2.1). When that policy is abandoned the dramatic structure of the play collapses, or turns upon itself in parody, as shown in the denouement.

What the Secretary sees as he gives his explanation to Little Li, and what the Irvine audience saw as he spoke, was the response on the faces reflecting the meaning of his words and his repeated command: "Go back. Tell them" (11.2). When they listen to the Secretary (once the actor of Cheng-ku'an) tell them that they must return they hear both the manipu-lative pretense to an absolute truth and the plain, harsher truth that they have no choice, they have no things, they have not produced enough material. They have only produced action. They must go back, return and repeat, and try to make something work that makes enough things for distributive justice to distribute. The response "written" in the face of the actress who played Hsien-e recorded, if only in the blink of *augenblick*, the recognition that the returning includes not only the sour taste of a life of futility, repeated mistakes, grinding poverty and humiliation, but also the immediate and repeated suffering of violence, pain, and death: being beaten and raped repeatedly, breeding more dead infants in buckets, and obediently not speaking out about injustice.

At the end of the scene when Ch'en repeats the conventional saws, the parting maxims, he concludes with an *abusio:* "They have lived already through many mistakes, but these are just ripples on the surface of the broad yellow river. Go back. Tell them" (12.2). The figure of aberrance, the identity of being a mistake, turns from work to the workers, from the mistakes of the party and the peasants to the mistakes of nature. They become (his) mistakes, the ripples, and the "yellow river."

Ronald Paulson suggests that the representation of revolution has two modes: the first is forward, "producing a rational sequence of events," and the second backward, "merely a regression to earlier stages of being."[22] The final two scenes of *Fanshen* drop the mask of rationality and adopt the "surreal face" of obsessive repetition, deluge, and parabolic grimace. The play turns away from the possibilities of language. Dialogue breaks down and collapses into the hyperreality of propaganda, parody, and parable.

The final scenes of the play reflect the possibility of the two forms of performative representation—one dogmatic, the other dialogical. The cadre returns as ordered to the village, but in their attempt to repeat the old/new order they break off in elliptical, unanswered fragments. At the end of the scene they turn mute, as in a downpour of revolutionary spectacle "they drown in sound and light" (12.1). Multiple, separate, simultaneous dialogues struggled to take place on stage, each one ending in ellipsis, in unspeakable, unutterable *aporia* gesticulating to the effect of how hard, if not impossible, it is to explain: "Yes, it's difficult to explain. Let me explain. Let me try to explain. There are good reasons. . . . It's best to tell you. I'd like to explain . . . let me explain . . . I'd like to explain," and the like (12.1). Unfinished, incomplete, they struggle in anonymity to repeat what they cannot say.

From one point of view this penultimate inability to perform a coherent representation echoes the breakdown into overlapping scenes of dissonant refusal to speak out in the tragic sequence that ended with beatings, bucketed death, and threat: "Will anyone. Speak." The stage directions call for a spectacle of falling red banners and loudspeaker music that drowns out the ability to hear one another; "they mutter on, gesturing" (12.1). The cascading banners may signify playful parody, a recognition of what grotesque absurdity the revolution came to during the Cultural Revolution in the late 1960s, and parody is another mode of subverting, undermining, and overturning the play.

The final scene of the play, the lonely peasant hoeing, returns the play—as William Gaskill, its director, noted—to its beginning. Beginning and end fold together. The Joint Stock Group was criticized for choosing the folding image of revolution as return to repetition.[23] On the other hand, the quiet focus on the solitary image of a peasant is a refreshing contrast to the confused crowd of the previous scene and, curiously, not a mere repetition but the first time any character appears alone on stage. The solitary, anonymous peasant represents all peasants.

Called by Hou to yet another meeting, the peasant turns and recites, or possibly sings, a song that condenses and displaces the performative speech act into a promise and threat:

> There is no Jade Emperor in heaven
> There is no Dragon King on earth

> I am the Jade Emperor
> I am the Dragon King
> Make way for me you hills and mountains
> I'm coming

(12.2)

The meter and syntax of the poem is simple, even pastoral. Sung by an individual, the words could disappear in an innocent, playful, even self-mocking melody. Sung as a chant, however, the text announces the death of god and transfigures the peasant from simplicity itself into a god-horde overturning mountains. The disparity between the two readings may remain undecided. If a reading of the last line, "I'm coming," serves as a response to the call to meeting, then it offers a self-mocking and ironic turn that knows the ambiguity of overturning revolution. Michael Coveney's review indicates that the Joint Stock production undercut the lyric with a comic reading: "The show ends with the comic image of a glum worker being summoned yet again to yet another meeting."[24]

The "I'm coming" becomes messianic terror when read back into historical context. The poem was used as a chant by the student revolutionaries during the Cultural Revolution of 1966. Anyone in the audience, and there were a few, who lived through that revolution and heard the poem as a threat also heard the menacing terror echo even in a shrug. The threat in the final line is enforced by a stage direction that calls for a banner to drop "round the theatre unfurling the words of the poem" (12.2). If the audience missed hearing the meaning of the words, the playwright wants to make certain that we read it. The written text, when dropped, becomes a literal "closure of representation" to surround the reader. Undecidable readings—comic, ironic, or pastoral—would seem to be replaced by the dominance of the threat as prefiguring the truth, the performative closure as a prophetic inscription, the writing on the wall pressed in the face of the audience, if only to provoke a response. In calling for the last words to be dropped in the face of the audience, Hare seems to turn the text toward the prophetic voice as the performative truth: speaking out as echoing the parable of Marxist folklore, the uprising of the masses.

Blessed with a budget that could not afford banners and loudspeakers and with performance space in an art studio that could not accommodate drops, the Irvine production did without swells of music, drapery, and dazzling light at the end of the play. Without the spectacle the presentation of the final scenes echoed the presentational mode of the opening: plain, unchanged, direct address to the audience. The urgency expressed by a Joint Stock actor—"We had to be conscious of what we were trying to say through doing this play"—was still the actor's conscious choice.[25] The final words were not final. They were reflexively framed, turned toward (returned to) or into the context of the style of the play as a whole. The presentation did not opt for parody, pomp, or propaganda. Without a change in spectacle the solo lyric follows as merely a single reply to the litany at the end of the previous scene during which, since the lines were unassigned, each member of the cast spoke a phrase directly to the audience:

> I'd like to know what you think
> What do you think?
> Tell me.
> Let me know what you think.
> What do you think about this?

(12.1)

The absence of any unambiguous answer left a clear opening for the audience. The question "What did you think about this?" anticipates audience reception, the reader's response, as the dialogical end of the play. Every theater performance faces "what did you think about that?" The dialogical response of the audience, the critical action beyond reaction, became the Brechtian aim of the play. In returning to the audience the play once again sought a dialogical structure of judgment, repeating the challenge of each scene to "just speak it out." The production turned upon itself but, in turning upon itself, undid itself in order to begin again. The production repeated the question of speaking out that made the play move or keep turning, "overturning" itself, in order to begin again in the attempt to decide an undecidable, to say what cannot be said, to speak the unspeakable urgency of justice.

NOTES

1. J. Hillis Miller, "The Critic as Host," in *Deconstruction and Criticism* (New York: Seabury Press, 1979), 242.

2. David Hare, "Author's Preface," *Fanshen* (based on a book by William Hinton) (London: Faber and Faber, 1976), 9.

3. David Hare, "Preface," *The Asian Plays* (London: Faber and Faber, 1986), viii.

4. J. Hillis Miller, *Fiction and Repetition: Seven English Novels* (Cambridge: Harvard University Press, 1982), 6.

5. Miller, *Fiction and Repetition*, 6.

6. On the continuous "overturning" of keywords, or fixed positions, in deconstruction, see Jacques Derrida, *Positions*, trans. Alan Bass (Chicago: University of Chicago Press, 1981). *Overturning*, repeated frequently in *Positions*, is another word for *fanshen*, as noted by Hinton and tacitly quoted by Hare in the first line of his adaptation: "Every revolution creates new words. The Chinese Revolution created a whole new vocabulary. A most important word in this vocabulary was *fanshen*. Literally it means 'to turn the body' or 'to turn over.' . . . But it meant much more than this. . . . It meant to enter a new world" (William Hinton, *Fanshen: A Documentary of Revolution in a Chinese Village* [New York: Vintage Books, 1966], vii). A claim that to enter the vocabulary of deconstruction is to enter a "new world" would be farfetched, but then so was the Chinese Revolution.

7. Hare, *Fanshen*. The text of the play is divided into numbered sections and

subsections from 1.1 to 12.2. All subsequent quotations from the dialogue of the play are identified by the section and subsection number following the quotation.

8. Roland Barthes, "The Discourse of History," in *The Rustle of Language*, trans. by Richard Howard (New York: Hill and Wang, 1986), 103. The first line of the play repeats the historian William Hinton's claim that "Fanshen is an accurate record of what once happened in one village four hundred miles south-west of Peking" (1.1). This "performative opening" permits both playwright and historian to conflate in the textual representation the unity of: (1) the time of the event (revolution); (2) the time of writing (textual representation): and (3) performance time (reading). The rhetorical trope that permits this performative opening is *catachresis*, the figure of speech which conflates reality with representation, the event with the speech act that represents its performance.

9. See Jacques Derrida, "The Theater of Cruelty and the Closure of Representation," in *Writing and Difference* (Chicago: University of Chicago Press, 1978), 232–50. Also see Jeffrey Mehlman, *Repetition and Revolution: Marx/Hugo/Balzac* (Berkeley: University of California Press, 1977).

10. Hinton, *Fanshen*, vii.

11. Hare, *Fanshen*, quoting Hinton (*Fanshen*), as cited in note 5.

12. Janelle G. Reinelt, interview with David Hare (25 July 1987).

13. *Fanshen*, directed by David McDonald, produced by the School of Fine Arts and the Critical Theory Program, University of California, Irvine (UCI) (1987). This production was one of a series of nine productions in a ten-year project relating contemporary critical theory to performance sponsored by grants from the School of Criticism and Theory, the Focus Research Program in Critical Theory, the Executive Vice Chancellor, and the School of Fine Arts, UCI (1977–87). The research writing developed while in residence as a fellow at the University of California Humanities Research Institute, 1988–89.

14. Rob Ritchie, ed., *The Joint Stock Book: The Making of a Theatre Collective* (London: Methuen, 1987).

15. Antonin Artaud, *The Theater and Its Double* (New York: Grove Press, 1958), 79.

16. Paul de Man, "Autobiography as De-Facement," in *The Rhetoric of Romanticism* (New York: Columbia University Press, 1984), 76; cited by Jacques Derrida, "Mnemosyne," in *Memories for Paul de Man*, trans. Cecile Lindsay, Wellek Library Lectures at the University of California, Irvine (New York: Columbia University Press, 1986), 27.

17. Timothy Garton Ash, "The Revolution of the Magic Lantern," *New York Review of Books* 36 (February 1990): 42–51. Ash describes the active role that drama students performed in the Czechoslovakian revolution in 1989.

18. Michel Foucault, *The Archaeology of Knowledge (and The Discourse on Language)*, trans. A. M. Sheridan Smith (New York: Pantheon Books, 1972), 92–95.

19. Michael Coveney, "Fanshen: ICA Terrace," *Plays and Players* 22, no. 9, issue 260 (London: Hansom Books, June 1975): 31.

20. Later in the play Little Li tells Ch'en, "Last time we were here you criticized us for arresting Yu-lai. But it was you who approved the arrest in the first place" (11.2). Little Li would know this even at the time he participates in criticizing Hou for arresting Yu-lai (9.2).

21. Hinton, *Fanshen*, 492.

22. Ronald Paulson, *Representations of Revolution (1789–1820)* (New Haven, Conn.: Yale University Press, 1983), 8.

23. Michael Coveney, "Turning Over a New Life," *Plays and Players* 22, no. 9, issue 260 (London: Hansom Books, June 1975): 10–13. For other commentary on the political readings, see William Gaskill, *A Sense of Direction* (New York: Limelight Editions, 1990), 135–36; and Ritchie, *Joint Stock Book*.

24. Coveney, "Fanshen," 31.

25. Coveney, "Turning Over," 11.

Textuality and Authority in Theater and Drama: Some Contemporary Possibilities

John Rouse

The relationship between dramatic text and theatrical performance is, of course, a central element in the Occidental theater. Most productions here continue to be productions "of" a preexisting play text. Exactly what the word *of* means in terms of theories and practices is, however, far from clear. On the one hand, the "of" of theatrical activity is subject to a fair degree of oscillation; on the other, this oscillation takes place only within the authority of cultural norms that condition both theatrical production and audience reception. The relationship between text and performance is, in other words, a question both of the possible and the allowable.

Over the past decade, the ab-normal work of a growing number of playwrights and theater practitioners has exerted increasing pressure on the norm. Theory has yet to engage fully with the challenge of this work, and semiotically oriented theory has proved no exception, as its tendency to resort to marginalizing labels like "performance" or "nondramatic theater" reveals. And yet semiotics offers a theoretical perspective well suited to clarifying both the character of this work and the issues at stake in its challenge, including consequences for semiotics itself. In what follows I hope to identify some of these issues in very broad strokes, in part by discussing some salient characteristics of two rather extreme examples of pressure from the margins which throws them into particularly clear relief.

The Performance Text and the Power of Fiction

Semiotics' possibilities and limitations both begin with its chosen objects of investigation, especially with the now widely accepted notion of the "performance text." This text "is conceived of as a complex network of different types of signs, expressive means, or actions, coming back to the etymology of the word 'text' which implies the idea of texture, of something woven together."[1] By methodological consent, this performance text is strictly separated from the "dramatic" text, at least at first, so that some aspect of the system underlying the production and communication of meaning in either one or the other can then be elaborated analytically. Theater semiotics, then, is concerned with "what takes place between and among performers and spectators, while the epithet 'dramatic' indicates the network of factors relating to the represented fiction."[2]

This methodological separation has empowered theater semiotics' very real accomplishments in describing the internal structures of performance communication. It has also provided a useful model of bi- and intertextuality for retheorizing the relationships of production between the two kinds of texts. This model is particularly suggestive in describing a prominent feature of theatrical modernism, the rise of a "director's theater." Here it begins with two texts and two authors—or, rather, two "author-functions."[3] Foucault's phrase seems particularly well suited to describing the contradictory elaboration of discourse within the performance text: we all know, and usually murmur in passing, that this text is "written" through a collaboration between those who control its various signifying systems (actors, designers, composers, etc.), but we "legitimize" the text's authority by attributing it to the director. And the authority we usually legitimize in this way is not that over the internal constitution of the systems within the performance text but, instead, the relationship between the performance text and the dramatic text, defined as interpretation. /Director/ has become that sign we use to inscribe that connotational consistency and interpretational purpose we propose to glimpse within and behind a "weaving together" of the strands of the dramatic with those of the performance text.

The director's control is less over performance writing than over performance discourse, and this control is shared with the playwright. One thinks immediately of words versus gestures, but words and sentences are taken over as linguistic signs within the performance text and interwoven with other signs according to linguistic but not necessarily dramatic codes: the words, for example, don't control whether an actor laughs or shouts while speaking them (a combination governed by the paralinguistic code), perhaps while turning cartwheels (kinesic code). Directorial discourse is, in fact, usually investigated at this level, the level of the Brechtian *Gestus*— of a "how" that can reveal the "what" in a new light.

At the level of the fiction interpreted by performance, on the other hand, the text's discursive control is considerably more pronounced. Fiction's power has much to do with the theater's historical tendency to privilege iconic signification among its systemic possibilities. Icons, in C. S. Peirce's semiotics, are signs that are "like" the things they represent.[4] Thus, a dramatic character is usually represented by an actor, and that representation usually proceeds through ostension—the actor pretends to be displaying the real thing (the referent) for the spectator to view. But, of course, this referent is not real; the character exists only in the possible world of the fiction, not the real world of the performance. Indeed, in order to "ostend" the character, the theater "de-realizes" the actor, turning him or her into a sign that functions as an element belonging to the same class of concepts as the character, the class "human being."[5] All more precise signification is provided by the fiction, as interpreted by acting and directing.

Interpretation of this kind involves, in turn, a collaboration between play and production with the spectator in what Patrice Pavis calls the "referential illusion": "that we see the *referent* of the sign, when, in fact, what we have before us is only its *signifier*." This, Pavis claims, is the basis for the spectator's "pleasure": "seeing the real world represented before him."[6] But to indulge this pleasure the spectator surrenders authority over signification to the /director/, "who *pretends* (as part of the global fictional discourse) to let us decipher and rewrite the performance."[7]

This point is worth stressing, given a tendency, which I share, to read the dramatic text/performance text binary through poststructuralist notions of textuality such as Roland Barthes's distinction between "work" and "text." For Barthes "the work is a fragment of substance, occupying a part of the space of books (in a library, for example), the Text, is a methodological field." The work can be displayed as an object, but the text can only be demonstrated, *"experienced only in an activity of production."*[8] This distinction seems to capture nicely the difference between the preexisting dramatic text and the same text as it reappears in the concrete situation of enunciation provided by performance interpretation.

The distinction has its dangers, however. "To interpret a text," according to Barthes, "is not to give it a (more or less justified, more or less free) meaning, but on the contrary to appreciate what *plural* constitutes it."[9] Not every critic pursues this goal to such an extreme. But a reader is at least free to compare, to interweave the two clearly separate texts. Modernist directorial interpretation, on the other hand, does not exist in a different time and space from the drama it interprets; rather, it confronts the spectator as iconically already interwoven with the drama. It is one thing to sustain in theory a space for the spectator between the dramatic and performance texts, but directorial practice regularly invades this space, from which it author-itatively recloses the text, performance and performed, into the directorial work.

Intertextual Ostension: The Wooster Group

Theory can suggest that normal interpretational practice is not the only one possible. For alternative examples, however, we must look to the abnormal practices of what we now call "theatrical postmodernism"; the term itself indicates the degree of pressure now building at the margins for a rewriting of norms across the whole text of cultural discourse.

The Wooster Group provides a somewhat extreme example of an intertextual practice that shares the space of interpretation with the spectator. This practice won the Group ironic notoriety at the turn of 1984–85, when threats of legal action by Arthur Miller forced the closing of *L.S.D.* (*...Just the High Points...*). The piece included an adaptation from the final sections of *The Crucible's* four scenes—first in a forty-five minute version, which was then cut to twenty-five minutes, then changed twice more, all to no avail. Miller's action is a reminder that cultural systems develop unevenly: the copyright laws may be a feature of literary modernism, but they ill accord with theatrical modernism, let alone postmodernism.[10]

L.S.D. was performed for the most part at a long table extending across the front of the audience on a raised platform. The piece was divided into four sections. Part 1 collaged a selection of texts by Timothy Leary, William Burroughs, and other gurus of the 1960s drug culture, read spon-

Fig. 1. *Hamletmachine* by Heiner Müller. Directed and designed by Robert Wilson. Thalia Theater, Hamburg (1986). Photo credit: Elisabeth Henrichs.

taneously and at random by male company members wearing 1980s street clothes, against the delivery of set selections from a taped interview with Ann Rower, Leary's babysitter. In Part 2, female and adolescent performers in historical costume joined the men for a rapid passage through "just the high points" of *The Crucible*; the scene ended with a dance. Part 3 set a recreation of the group rehearsing part 2 while on acid against a video that moved from the New England woods (Leary's territory) to locations in Miami (land of G. Gordon Liddy). Part 4 took up the connections introduced geographically by this video; performers at the table recreated part of one of the Liddy-Leary debates. The piece ended with a grotesque dance by the performers, again in costume, this time pseudo-Latino.

Even this summary highlights the irony of Miller's threats concerning copyright law. The selections from his scenes were recognizable and performed in sequence, but *L.S.D.* was not a "normal" production "of" *The Crucible* in any other sense. First of all, the piece did not tell the drama's story; on the contrary, it made dramaturgic use of fragmentation and collage techniques to fracture the narrative spine around which realistic drama organizes its em-bodiment of a possible world, hiding its status as discourse behind a referential illusion—in *The Crucible*'s case, including a historicized reference.

On the semiotic level *L.S.D.* enforced its dramaturgy by minimizing use of iconic signs and by creating a theatrical situation of enunciation in which even iconically selected signs were combined indexically.

The production opened by displaying a literal situation of enunciation—performers sitting at a table "performing" (reading) documents rather than de-realizing themselves to represent fictional roles. The physical setup and

149

Fig. 2. *Hamletmachine* by Heiner Müller. Directed and designed by Robert Wilson. Thalia Theater, Hamburg (1986). Photo credit: Elisabeth Henrichs.

the men's costuming remained unchanged for part 2; *The Crucible* was enunciated from the same place as the collage of 1960s texts and the later Liddy-Leary debate. And the enunciation itself blocked any tendency toward referential illusion. Lines were delivered at a frantic pace, sometimes at high volume. During Miller's scenes of hallucination and hysteria some performers displayed a highly theatricalized mania, some crawled under the table. But the acting made no attempt at psychological realism. The characters were displayed, not embodied. And since the acting avoided iconic interpretation, the women's costume and makeup could function both iconically to signify the historical period of Miller's fiction and as indexes pointing to Miller's drama, which did not "take place" but was conjured into the contiguous space suggested by theory, just beyond the space occupied by the citations actually spoken on the stage.

Considering this activity of citation, it doesn't seem quite accurate to call *L.S.D.* an interpretation of *The Crucible*, but we may well call it a "reading" of the play, a reading staged as an activity of intertextuality. The performance ostended, displayed, a tissue of texts. As it was woven in with documents of dissent from the 1960s, Miller's historicized representation on the hysteria of the McCarthy era as a story about colonial Salem was resituated "as a historical document of the early '50s, as a reminder of both a particular dramatic style and an approach to social and political issues. It becomes an index of ideology, a memento of a particular attitude toward dissent, and a highly equivocal portrait of the counter-cultural hero."[11]

The performance writing commented on the historical limitations of ideology in Miller's text precisely through the process of indexing it. Kate Valk, for example, played Tituba (a "real" black servant in the fiction) in blackface and with an openly fake "darky" accent. The frankly indexical use of the second sign also indexed the potential iconicity of the first (blackface is still routinely used as an element of iconic representation in the German theater, for example) and exposed the ideological overcoding that would condition any attempt to use either sign for iconic passage into the fiction. Valk reinforced this performed insight in the course of part 2 when she switched over to playing the white servant Mary Warren; she dropped the accent but remained in blackface. The formal cause of this interpretation was, in fact, chance; Valk found she didn't have time to remove the makeup. But the interpretive result was to foreground a tradition of theatrical representation now considered ideologically questionable, in America at least, in order to suggest that the tradition of dramatic representation within which Miller could create a black, female, slave character in the first place is at least as dubious.

The blackface itself also cited its own earlier use by the Group itself in *Route 1 & 9* (1981), which caused massive controversy and the temporary loss of one of the Group's grants. The self-citation was thus neither accidental nor incidental; it disclaimed any pretense of objectivity within the performance's situation of enunciation, citing the Group's own experience of persecution, hysteria, and paranoia into the play of signification. Similarly, part 3 staged an example (and a rather private one at that) of the rehearsal activity that always leads to but is normally hidden behind the performance of the resulting interpretation. The performance selected its intertexts from a critical perspective, but it also restlessly surrendered this position of authority to the spectator, to whom it offered its own activity as one of the strands in the developing intertextual discourse. This practice authorized the spectator to close the writing but also encouraged him or her instead to reenact the performance's own movement of self-discovery out into the discourse's material plurality of historical and ideological significations. As Elizabeth LeCompte wrote in a letter to Miller, "I want to put the audience in a position of examining their own relation to this material as 'witnesses'—witnesses to the play itself, as well as witnesses to the 'story' of the play."[12]

Bitextual Ostension: Heiner Müller and Robert Wilson

Speaking of the way in which the Wooster Group writes its performance texts, LeCompte has noted, "I don't ever try to make one part of the play illustrate another. All of the elements of the piece have their own life. They are not supportive or secondary."[13] LeCompte succinctly describes here a key element in postmodern practice. Certainly, the same statement could be made, and has been made, by Robert Wilson. If anything, Wilson's theater has been even more insistent in foregrounding the "separation of the elements" first suggested within modernism by Brechtian theory. Wilson organizes his productions around what he calls a "visual" and an "acoustic score."[14] These are first developed independently, then brought together in rehearsal. But they are not woven together; rather, Wilson's performance texts offer the two scores to the spectator as independent and equal signifying systems.

It isn't hard to understand why audiences took nearly a decade to learn to "make sense" out of Wilson's performance texts. In the first place, he doesn't subordinate the visual score to the acoustic; all of his productions subvert narrative organization, even when they make use of traditional dramatic texts. Wilson also subverts normal rules for the internal structuring of each of his scores. He came to theater from art and architecture and tends to privilege codes from these disciplines when combining the signs of his visual scores. Similarly, his acoustic scores are structured more musically than dramatically. Wilson foregrounds the materiality of language, its rhythms and tones; this tends to block the transitive passage from sound to sense practiced in everyday speech or traditional dramatic dialogue. The result of such combination using the codes of semiotic systems normally subordinated to the referential illusion is that familiarly iconic signs seem incessantly to be divorced from their signifieds and turned into the signifiers of a symbolic system, the conventions governing which we somehow know but seem to have forgotten. This symbolic semiotics combines with the abnormally slow rhythm in which Wilson presents his signs and the evocative beauty of both his scenic elements and lighting to produce the dreamlike quality often noted about Wilson's work.

Wilson's recent work has retained this quality while exploring new discursive possibilities. Wilson tended to limit his earlier work to the structural level, largely (in my possibly logocentric opinion) by creating acoustic scores the linguistic elements of which consisted of selections from a card file collection of found phrases and conversational fragments. Since 1984, however, Wilson frequently has substituted dramatic texts for these selections. He has used texts by Heiner Müller four times in this work, and Müller in turn has praised Wilson's ability to use his language as "material," in contrast to normal German theater practice, where the text is "not accepted as reality but only used to make statements about reality."[15]

Müller has good reasons to appreciate Wilson's theatrical materialism. By 1975 he had come to doubt "that a 'well-made' story (the fable in the classical sense) can adequately deal with reality any more." Instead, he began to develop a dramaturgy of "synthetic fragments."[16] Even at their "most" narrative, these fragments contain only snatches of story, flimsy fictional scaffolds on which Müller fastens unstable images of personal and interpersonal history; in scene 4 of *Hamletmachine*, for example, the figure playing Hamlet, itself perhaps being played by the author, lays aside makeup and costume to describe an uprising that has already happened but not yet taken place, an uprising in which Hamlet meets himself on both sides of the front.

Such metaphors bound the writing, of course, providing the *topoi* of a thematic landscape. But once it has set these limits for discursive play the writing undertakes an "explosion" of its metaphors which dislocates fictional figure and author from the position of authorizing subject.[17] The "I's" that speak their obsessions in the texts and the "I" that writes his obsessions across them hurl themselves into the material body of the discourse and let it carry them toward signification; "the metaphor," Müller notes, "is smarter than the author," and only the "self-movement of the material" maps the thematic landmarks into a field of meaning.[18]

This process of textual construction disperses the authorial center into the tissues of the text. The text is permeable, and interpretable, along these tissues; it invites readers/spectators to engage in its play of metaphoric discourse. But, since there is no longer any kernel of meaning within the material surface, the text resists penetration by a directorial ego looking to pass through to a place from which to "make statements about reality"— as the large number of failed Müller productions would seem to testify.

Wilson's work resists this interpretational temptation, as he demonstrated in an acclaimed production "of" *Hamletmachine*, staged first in the spring of 1986 with students at New York University then remounted at Hamburg's Thalia Theater in the fall. The performance began with a prologue that introduced not Müller's text but Wilson's visual score, together with the nonverbal elements of the acoustic score. The audience found itself forming the fourth wall of a rectangular space; the stage right onstage wall consisted of a startlingly white projection screen, the other three walls were covered by black drapes. Downstage left of center a swivel chair was highlighted in a tight rectangle of light. A table angled diagonally across center stage. Against the drapes upstage of the table stood a tallish, leafless tree.

Lights up discovered a woman sitting on the swivel chair, dressed in sack cloth, her young face framed in frazzled gray-powdered hair; slowly, she turned to face the audience and deliver a silent scream then swiveled back to face the table. Over the course of the next fifteen minutes six other women and seven men took up positions in the space and presented a precisely refined minimal repertory of movements and gestures to the acoustic accompaniment of a one-finger piano version of the melody to "Is that all there is?" Three women, for example, in the costume, hair style, and makeup of the 1940s—including long red fingernails—sat on chairs behind the table, tilting them dangerously to one side. Moving in unison, they turned out to face the audience, smiled, turned back. Or each raised one arm and described a small circle on the top of her head with her index finger, slowly smiling. Periodically, they raked their nails along the table, producing a horrible sound, and smiled. Somewhat later a young man in a white T-shirt carrying a thick book crossed to sit downstage of the table. A rocker in a leather jacket hung with chains crossed with a clumsy, loose-kneed step to sink into the position of Rodin's *Thinker* in a chair behind a young woman in leotard with arms outstretched in a ballet pose. The penultimate figure to enter was a woman in a mid-nineteenth-century red silk dress who crossed to stand silhouetted against the lit scrim, then slowly raised her arms up before her and gazed off into some unknown distance.

Then a man in a black frock coat, black top hat, and blackface entered, crossed to stand behind her, and swiftly brought his hands together a foot in front of her face, as if cutting off her view. Suddenly, these two seemed to become the Hollywood version of a Southern mistress and her slave.

Müller's dramatic, or, more accurately, postdramatic text, is divided into five fragments. Wilson's performance presented scene 3 as a film of its staging in the performance space, projected onto a screen lowered into that space. Before each of the other scenes the entire stage arrangement was turned ninety degrees and a new screen undraped; for scene 4 the audience took the place of the screen, and scene 5 returned to the prologue arrangement. For each scene, live or on film, the gestural repertory introduced in the prologue was restated in the new spatial perspective—repeated, varied, recombined.

As the performers varied their visual text, they spoke Müller's text—all of it, including the stage directions. An exception occurred for scene 3, where the text was written out as subtitles on the film; as it happens, the text to this scene is predominantly stage directions. The Hamlet figure's text was divided between the seven male performers, Ophelia's text among the seven female. The text was not enacted but, rather, put into play spatially. It was clearly delivered but reworked musically. Some lines were repeated by two or more speakers, often contrapuntally. Others were divided between speakers, sometimes in the middle of a sentence. Rhythm disjointed syntax, tonal coloration contrasted emotional content. The text was presented as acoustic material with its own metaphoric content rather than as dramatic dialogue that provides information about the attitudes of its fictional speakers. The audience wove its way through the textures of this acoustic material, and, as it did, it wove this material together with associations awakened by gestural material from a separate visual field.

Wilson's visual text is not a desemanticized field of signifiers; on the contrary, Wilson's text parallels Müller's central European obsessions with a definite range of associations from American culture. But the associations always run parallel; they aren't forced onto the text to explain or delimit its metaphors. Wilson has described the production as a bit like bringing together a silent movie and a radio play; this produces "a different kind of space than when, for example, you take a text and attempt to illustrate it with a movement." Within the space the production ostends two texts and gives the spectator control over writing the intertext. "We make theatre," Wilson notes, "so that the spectator can put it together in his own head."[19]

Regarding the Cultural Intertext

The work of Wilson, Müller, or the Wooster Group allows the spectator to practice intertextuality in the narrower sense, to use specific prior texts in the writing of a new one. But this postmodern practice also reveals a broader understanding of the term, in which it designates a text's "participation in the discursive space of a culture: the relationship between a text and the various languages or signifying practices of a culture and its relation to those texts which articulate for it the possibilities of that culture."[20] In this sense, all the signifying systems used by theater and drama are always already part of other cultural texts. The codes of these other texts help condition the writing of either dramatic or performance text, just as their meanings pass into the texture of the new text's significations. This is true even, or especially, of the actor's body, which can be examined as a text into which cultural norms for social behavior are written in the guise of stylistic codes for performance behavior.[21]

Intertextual relations of this kind can be found between cultural discourse outside the theater and each of the signifying systems in the performance text. The same is true of the dramatic text, although intertextuality here introduces still other codes into the normative mix. The theatrical performance "of" a dramatic text thus involves a far more complex intertextuality than that between two stable and coherent texts. As *L.S.D.*'s indexing use of blackface shows, signification passes cultural connotations into performance at every semiotic seam.

The example also shows, however, that it makes a difference whether these significations pass in unnoticed or whether they can be seized in passage and made available to textualizing activity. Müller's complaint about directors using texts to make statements about reality includes an ideological insight: statements about reality are made, and received, from the place of the norm. The workings of these norms can become textual material only through two different kinds of activity, a different kind of writing and a different kind of reading—a writing like the Wooster Group's, which continually indexes it into the intertext; a writing like Müller's (or the Wooster Group's, in its own way), which restlessly steps away from the signifying positions it temporarily inhabits. Especially, I have tried to show that when coupled with a writing like Wilson's, which so thoroughly defies normal expectations—about how to read the behavioral text of the actor's body, for example—the character of the norm conditioning those expectations on our particular stage of discursive history becomes visible as part of the spectator's intertext, and available to the spectator to rewrite into a new intertext. For the model of reception proposed in all three of these examples from contemporary production is itself a model of production: Do as I do, not as I say.[22]

NOTES

1. Marco De Marinis, "Dramaturgy of the Spectator," trans. Paul Dwyer, *Drama Review* 31, no. 2 (1987): 100.

2. Keir Elam, *The Semiotics of Theatre and Drama* (London: Methuen, 1980), 2.

3. See Michel Foucault, "What Is an Author?" *Language, Counter-Memory, Practice: Selected Essays and Interviews*, ed. Donald F. Bouchard, trans. Donald F. Bouchard and Sherry Simon (Ithaca, N.Y.: Cornell University Press, 1977), 131.

4. Peirce distinguishes the icon from two other classes of signs, indices and symbols. The index is related to its object by factors like causality, as with the bowlegged walk that indicates the cowboy, or physical contiguity, as in the pointing

(index) finger. The relationship between symbols, including linguistic signs, and their objects, on the other hand, is governed strictly by convention.

5. The actor here functions similarly to the jacket and tie one holds up to indicate to a male friend how he should dress for a party. This example, and the concept of ostension, are Umberto Eco's; see "Semiotics of Theatrical Performance," *Drama Review* 21, no. 1 (1977): 110–11.

6. Patrice Pavis, "Production, Reception, and the Social Context," in *On Referring in Literature*, ed. Anne Whiteside and Michael Issacharoff (Bloomington: Indiana University Press, 1987), 122.

7. Patrice Pavis, "Towards a Semiotics of *Mise en Scène?*" trans. Susan Melrose, *Languages of the Stage: Essays on the Semiology of Theatre* (New York: PAJ Publications, 1982), 159.

8. Roland Barthes, "From Work to Text," *Image-Music-Text*, trans. Stephen Heath (London: Fontana, 1977), 156–57.

9. Roland Barthes, *S/Z*, trans. Richard Miller (New York: Hill and Wang, 1974), 5.

10. Gerald Rabkin discusses the theoretical and practical implications of this discongruity in "Is there a Text on this Stage? Theatre/Authorship/Interpretation," *Performing Arts Journal* 9, nos. 2 and 3 (1985): 142–59.

11. David Savran, "The Wooster Group, Arthur Miller and *The Crucible*," *Drama Review* 29, no. 2 (1985): 105. For an extended discussion of *L.S.D.*, see part 3 of Savran's superb *Breaking the Rules: The Wooster Group* (New York: Theatre Communications Group, 1988).

12. Elizabeth LeCompte, quoted in Savran, *Wooster Group*, 102.

13. Elizabeth LeCompte, quoted in Arnold Aronson, "The Wooster Group's *L.S.D.* (. . . Just the High Points . . .)," *Drama Review* 29, no. 2 (1985): 77.

14. Robert Wilson, Heiner Müller, and Wolfgang Wiens, discussants, "*the CIVIL warS*—a Construction in Time and Space," in *the CIVIL warS*, program book for the Cologne production (Frankfurt am Main: Suhrkamp, 1984), 44; my translation, as are all of the following, unless otherwise indicated.

15. Wilson, Müller, and Wiens, "*CIVIL warS*," 49. Müller notes elsewhere that "the first reality of the theatre is the text, not its content" ("Ein Gespräch zwischen Wolfgang Heise und Heiner Müller," in *Brecht 88: Anregungen zum Dialog über die Vernunft am Jahrtausendende*, ed. Wolfgang Heise [Berlin: Henschel, 1989], 201).

16. Heiner Müller, "Ein Brief" (1975), in *Heiner Müller Material: Texte und Kommentare*, ed. Frank Hörnigk (Göttingen: Steidl, 1989), 38, 37. For a fuller discussion, see Carl Weber's foreword to his translations of *Hamletmachine and Other Texts for the Stage* (New York: PAJ Publications, 1984).

17. See Müller's remarks in *Performing Arts Journal* 28, no. 1 (1986): 96.

18. Müller, "Fatzer + Keuner," in *Müller Material*, 31.

19. Robert Wilson, "Be Stupid," interview with Frank Hetschker et al., in *Explosion of a Memory: Heiner Müller DDR, Ein Arbeitsbuch*, ed. Wolfgang Storch (Berlin: Edition Hentrich, 1988), 62–63.

20. Jonathan Culler, *The Pursuit of Signs: Semiotics, Literature, Deconstruction* (Ithaca, N.Y.: Cornell University Press, 1981), 103.

21. For two differing evaluations of this process, see Erika Fischer-Lichte, "Theatre and the Civilizing Process: An Approach to the History of Acting"; and Joseph R. Roach, "Power's Body: The Inscription of Morality as Style," both in *Interpreting the Theatrical Past: Essays in the Historiography of Performance*, ed. Thomas Postlewait and Bruce McConachie (Iowa City: University of Iowa Press, 1989).

22. I reach here the border where study of production hands over to reception

theory and pragmatics, areas in which important work has been done over the past few years. For an introduction and initial bibliography, see Marvin Carlson, "Theatre Audiences and the Reading of Performance," in Postlewait and McConachie, *Interpreting the Theatrical Past*, 82–98; see also Pavis, "Production."

After Marx

Introduction

So too the games we invent
Are unfinished, we hope;
And the things we use in playing
What are they without the dentings from
Many fingers, those places, seemingly damaged
Which produce nobility of form;
And the words too whose
Meaning often changed
With change of users.

—Bertolt Brecht

The history of Marxism can be seen to be in part a history of changed meanings in the hands of many users. This is especially true in matters pertaining to culture. The revisions and reformulations of Marxist ideas in the hands of, for example, Antonio Gramsci, Louis Althusser, Fredric Jameson, Raymond Williams, Theodor Adorno, and Walter Benjamin have provided a rich legacy of theory to contemporary thinkers who are "after" Marx because they follow him as well as because they come after him. In fact, in keeping with contemporary theory's notions of the subject as a contested site of meanings and intertexts, conceiving of Marx as a "self" seems rather quaint. The undecidable questions have to do with how far one can stray afield and still be related to Marxism. Heated debates abound on the relationship of feminism, Foucault, or Derrida to Marxism.[1]

Marxist language can be found all through this book: ideology, hegemony, economism, surplus value, commodification, reification—all these and several other terms have become useful to cultural studies critics, to historians, to psychoanalysts, to feminists. Sue-Ellen Case and Herbert Blau, in the final two essays, assume familiarity with Marxist discourse, even when they critique it. Marxism has been useful for performance interpretation because, as a social event, performances are themselves productive activities that are situated in relation to a particular mode or apparatus of production, representing certain social interests rather than others, and exhibiting the political history of the theater as well as other narratives. Critics may use Marxist tools to analyze the text as ideology, the theater event as political event, or the relation of audience to spectacle in the production of meaning.

Over the last twenty years, Marxism has been engaged in a thoroughgoing and lively reexamination of many of its major theoretical tenets, especially those involving the topics of ideology and cultural production. Four of these issues, pertinent for performance study, are: (1) the definition and constitution of the category of class; (2) the critique of economism and the question of the "last determining instance"; (3) the role of ideology in relation to this elusive "instance"; and (4) questions of history ranging from teleology to periodization.

Marx believed that the fundamental fact of human life was its pro-ductivity and that human beings were defined by their capacity to produce. This primacy of production results in various forms of social organization in various periods. Capitalism arose when goods and services no longer had a use value, that is, an intrinsic value for the producer, but instead acquired an exchange value through circulation in a market. Labor was thus separated from the direct benefit of its toil, and surplus value became the new objective of economic activity. Workers produced for a wage, not a needed object, and owners could alter the relationship between the wage and the established quantity of goods produced. The notion of Marxist alienation is precisely this gap between the maker of something and its direct use or benefit. Because of the understandable antagonism between the owners and the makers (workers), Marx saw an inevitable class struggle in which the interests of these groups were always at odds. For traditional Marxism, economics provides the explanatory principle par excellence. Sometimes called economism, this view holds that political and cultural events can be explained by economics—in other words, that a causal rela-tionship exists between the economic mode of production in a given time and its political, social, and cultural institutions and practices. Of course, the complex and contradictory forces at work in any moment of reality do not neatly conflate into a clear or unified set of economic circumstances; nevertheless, "in the last instance," reality is shaped by an economic determinism.

This economic motor is called the base, and all other aspects of society (law, domestic relations, politics, religion, culture) are considered super-structure. To pursue the spatial aspects of these metaphors, society's insti-tutions are supported by a foundation, which is constituted by the real relations of production at a particular stage of economic development. Of course, as Raymond Williams has pointed out, these metaphors imply a static, unchanging set of relations, which is misleading because this "foun-dation" is neither uniform nor static.[2]

Just as there appeared to be a causal pattern to economic history, so Marx saw a dialectical movement in history which seemed to show progress, through oppositional struggle, toward a utopian communist horizon where each would produce according to ability and receive goods and services according to need. While this teleological notion is bankrupt in our time, other aspects of traditional Marxism have proved resilient and reformulable.

The entire conception of "class" constitutes one of the most important revisionist frontiers in Western Marxism. Chantal Mouffe, for example, offers a socialist feminist attempt to theorize beyond class in light of such new social movements as feminism, the ecological and nuclear struggles, and those around racism and ethnicity, providing a lucid account of the major shift in the rethinking of the concept of class.

Mouffe is opposed to classical Marxism's "class reductionism," in which all social subjects are positioned on the basis of a single economic class membership that determines their various social relations and prac-tices. On the contrary, writes Mouffe, "each social agent is inscribed in a multiplicity of social relations—not only social relations of production but also the social relations, among others, of sex, race, nationality, and vicinity. All these social relations determine positionalities or subject positions, and every social agent is therefore the locus of many subject positions and cannot be reduced to only one."[3] In addition, she rejects the old division between base and superstructure where, in the last instance, a single economic logic resulted in a given social formation, favoring instead a formulation of Gramsci's notion of hegemony in which the locus of power is a social formation produced by diverse articulations among various social relations operating together. Thus, both individuals and social groups are constantly involved in competing and often contradictory positions.

While in capitalism a central part of the hegemonic formation is comprised of the relations of production, the conditions necessary to continually validate capital and its accumulation imply a set of political and cultural practices which are always potential sites of struggle, not reducible to "a last economic instance." For Mouffe, "all social relations can become the locus of antagonism insofar as they are constructed as relations of subordination." The democratic discourse that is our historic legacy in the West conflicts with all existing practices of subordination. "People struggle for equality not because of some ontological postulate but because they have been constructed as subjects in a democratic tradition that puts those values at the center of social life."[4] The economic basis of production shares with political and cultural production the work of constructing the whole of sociality.

This account of the first two issues with which I began, the redefinition of class and the critique of economism, represents a viewpoint that some contemporary Marxists find too radical and others too partial. Fredric Jameson and Perry Anderson, for example, are concerned with keeping operative an explanatory notion of totality and are fearful of the fragmentation into local struggles, which is a possible pitfall of this critical shift and historically evident right now in the problems over ethnicity in Yugoslavia or the former USSR.[5] On the other hand, Jean Baudrillard, in *The Mirror of Production*, attacks the entire Marxist notion of human beings as defined by their ability and need to produce.[6] He, of course, would not even be considered Marxist by many, but I place him within the tradition because he assumes many features of dialectical materialism in order to critique the insufficiently dialectical nature of Marx's view of his own system.

The overturning of classical notions of class and the economy accompanies a reformulation of the meaning and role of ideology in relation to these concepts. Traditional Marxism has had a reflection theory of ideology, which is akin to a reflection theory of representation, wherein the economic base produces certain distortions or myths about the nature of reality, held by subjects as false consciousness. The Frankfurt School of Critical Theory accomplished pioneering work in this area, beginning in the 1930s. Walter Benjamin, Max Horkheimer, Theodor Adorno, and Herbert Marcuse recognized the necessity of theorizing mass culture and cultural production in general as constitutive of social consciousness, mediating and not just reflecting the economic formation.[7]

More recently, Althusser attacked earlier formulations as uncritical empiricism and reinstated ideology as a constitutive practice that produces and reproduces life, freeing it from relegation to the status of superstructure determined by the economic base. The function of ideology is, for Althusser, to position subjects within a specific organization of reality, making available certain fixed relations that pass for the whole of sociality: "In ideology men do indeed express, not the relation between themselves and their conditions of existence, but *the way* they live the relation between them and their conditions of existence. This presupposes both a real relation and an '*imaginary,*' lived relation."[8] Thus, ideology is persuasive as well as coercive; that is, it "hails" subjects into an acceptable position, rather like the operations of psychoanalysis's unconscious. Althusser names this process "interpellation."

Achieving a conception of semiautonomous social practices, however, had the disadvantage of negating history by failing to provide any path for movement and change, since subjects exist wholly *inside* an ideological formation.[9] Combining his ideas with those of psychoanalyst Jacques Lacan, Althusser saw subjects positioned in language and discourse in a once-and-forever interpellation. When May 1968 came along in France, Althusser had no theoretical ground for accounting for this sudden spontaneous upsurge of radical activity. Two British Marxist economists, Barry Hindess and Paul Hirst, showed the idealist underpinnings to Althusser's notion, and, among others, Rosalind Coward and John Ellis identify the psychoanalytic shortcomings of this view: "this Marxist account does not show how the contradictory processes of the individual subject are themselves constituted: this in turn means that it cannot analyse moments of ideological crisis where these subjective processes enter into contradiction with the functioning of ideology itself."[10] Thus, this description leaves subjectivity completely confined within the determinations of an ideological mirror (oedipal, capitalist, white, male).

A number of thinkers have begun to go beyond this theoretical stalemate; Mouffe and Ernesto Laclau through Gramsci emphasize multiple subject positions, opening up the possibility of engaging in ideological struggle. Others like Teresa de Lauretis and Terry Eagleton believe that we exist simultaneously inside and outside ideological formations.[11] Raymond Williams also stressed the dynamic and constitutive status of the cultural in the reproduction of social totality.[12] In the section on cultural studies we have pointed out William's pioneering work on cultural boundaries defined by social class.

Last we come to the matter of rethinking a Marxist notion of history. Most current Marxist scholars recognize that the present social configuration is unlikely to lead to revolution anytime in the near future, if revolution is understood in its Marxist-Leninist sense. The rapid and unexpected changes in Eastern Europe during the last two years have touched off both critique and excitement among those trying to understand the past and the future. While the predictive aspects of Utopian Marxism must be rejected, a concern for theorizing the desired post-Marxist, postcapitalist society is very much a consequence of throwing out the old revolutionary horizon. Fredric Jameson thinks the task of imaging Utopia is "the most urgent task that confronts Marxism today."[13] Perry Anderson describes the task of imagining this future in light of some of the new notions of Marxism: "My presumption . . . is that a socialist society would be a far more complicated one than what we have today. It seems perfectly clear that if you actually had a socialist society in which production, power, and culture were genuinely democratized, you would have an enormous multiplication of different ways of living."[14] The reconception of class, through its critique of difference, contributes to this imperative for imaginative vision. Too often, Marxism has theorized white male experience. Third World revolutionary struggles and feminism require and propel Marxism to accommodate difference. And, while it remains to be seen, after the shopping dust settles in Eastern Europe, "Westernization" may also need to accommodate socialism-after-Marx.

In this part of the book, we have decided to include two essays that are, in some sense, traditionally Marxist. Bruce McConachie's essay looks at the productive apparatus of "producing"; he is particularly cogent in his explanation of the difference it makes to theater history whether or not the economic circumstances of production are part of the explanatory principles of historiography. His methodology is an application of Raymond Williams's strategy of locating and explicating keywords to the term *production*, in both its theatrical and economic meanings. Jim Merod writes both about the politics of producing jazz and also about the politics of doing "theory" itself; he turns analysis back on us as scholars in institutions that produce knowledge to review the implications of our work as scholars and teachers. We chose to include this essay, which is not at all concerned with traditional theater, because it provides an essential intertextual reading of performance and scholarship which makes evident the relationships between the politics of all cultural practices. Although these are not introductory essays, the topic of producing knowledges and performances, with its emphasis on the *mode* of production of culture, is a salient starting point, especially for scholar-practitioners.

Two of the essays in this section are particularly contemporary. British cultural studies has been especially attentive to popular culture, for which it has provided a strong neo-Marxist critique. Philip Auslander positions a popular performance genre, stand-up comedy, within the context of its institutional setting and the social needs of its consumers, who are defined as a self-consciously emergent class. Stand-up acts have moved very rapidly from popular comedy clubs to mass media exposure on cable TV. In Auslander's view, stand-up comedy has offered the perverse comforts of "retro-chic" and "boomer humor" to the children of the 1960s, many of whose hopes for matching the material standard of living attained by their parents waned in the 1980s.

Finally, David Román's essay on gay male subjectivity and politics closes the section on an activist note. Although not laced with Marxist references—indeed, most of these essays do not bear obvious references to Marx—we decided to place this essay together with the others to emphasize that one of the most powerful sites of contemporary political struggle is gay and lesbian sexuality and sexual politics. The essay takes up an activist standpoint and asks key questions about the reception of American gay plays in the era of AIDS. Analyzing the ideological implications of form (bourgeois realism) for counterhegemonic practice, Román has an agenda: how to maximize the "subversive capacity of performance . . . rather than being subsumed by dominant culture." This agenda indirectly links his objectives to those of the Frankfurt School, recalling the Brecht/Lukács debates on the merits of realism. Like other essays in this volume, Román's is part of a network that cuts across section headings. Both Jill Dolan's and Kate Davy's essays are concerned with political struggle and issues of sexuality, and, in part, so is Vivian Patraka's. Read together, they constitute a sexual politics of performance.

Some other uses of Marxism related to theater and performance include Brechtian criticism, which has often provided a site for Marxist aesthetics. Not only Brecht's own theater texts and practice but also exegesis of his theoretical ideas in light of new critical theory have produced a good deal of scholarship, such as *Theatre Journal*'s and Yale/*Theater*'s special issues on Brecht.[15] Feminists have found Brecht useful in conjunction with a materialist analysis. Elin Diamond's essay "Brechtian Theory/Feminist Theory: Toward a Gestic Feminist Criticism" has been very influential.[16] If deconstructing the ideological inscriptions of representation is seen as "after Marx," a great deal of other work is also pertinent. Joseph Roach's "Theatre History and the Ideology of the Aesthetic," Bruce McConachie's recent essay on hegemony, Herbert Blau's "Ideology and Performance," and Mohammed Kowsar's "Althusser on Theatre" all contribute to a fuller understanding of the apparati of performance and its reception.[17]

> How long
> Do works endure? As long
> As they are not completed.
> Since as long as they demand effort
> They do not decay.[18]

J. G. R.

NOTES

Chapter epigraph from "About the Way to Construct Enduring Works," *Bertolt Brecht Poems, 1913–1956,* ed. John Willett and Ralph Manheim (New York: Methuen, 1976), 194.

1. See, for example, *Capitalist Patriarchy and the Case for Socialist Feminism,* ed. Zillah Eisenstein (New York: Monthly Review Press, 1979); Michael Ryan, *Marxism and Deconstruction* (Baltimore: Johns Hopkins University Press, 1982);

Barry Smart, *Foucault, Marxism and Critique* (London: Routledge and Kegan Paul, 1983).

2. See Raymond Williams, "Base and Superstructure in Marxist Cultural Theory," *Problems in Materialism and Culture* (London: Verso, 1980), 31–49.

3. Chantal Mouffe, "Hegemony and New Political Subjects: Toward a New Concept of Democracy," *Marxism and the Interpretation of Culture,* ed. Cary Nelson and Lawrence Grossberg (Urbana and Chicago: University of Illinois Press, 1988), 89–90.

4. Mouffe, "Hegemony and New Political Subjects," 91.

5. See especially Frederic Jameson's *The Political Unconscious* (Ithaca: Cornell University Press, 1981); and Perry Anderson's *In the Tracks of Historical Materialism* (London: Verso, 1983).

6. Trans. Mark Poster (St. Louis: Telos Press, 1975).

7. For an overview of their contribution, see Martin Jay, *The Dialectical Imagination: A History of the Frankfurt School and the Institute of Social Research, 1923-1950* (Boston: Harvard University Press, 1973).

8. Louis Althusser, *For Marx,* trans. Ben Brewster (New York: Pantheon Books, 1969), 233.

9. See Louis Althusser, "Ideology and Ideological State Apparatuses," *Lenin and Philosophy,* trans. Ben Brewster (New York: Monthly Review Press, 1971), 127–86. See also Paul Hirst's explanation and critique of Althusser, *On Law and Ideology* (London: Macmillian, 1979).

10. Rosalind Coward and John Ellis, *Language and Materialism* (London: Routledge and Kegan Paul, 1977), 78.

11. Of particular interest is Ernesto Laclau and Chantal Mouffe, *Hegemony and Socialist Strategy* (London: New Left Books, 1985); and Teresa de Lauretis, *Technologies of Gender* (Bloomington: Indiana University Press, 1987). For a short general introduction, see Terry Eagleton, *Marxism and Literary Criticism* (Berkeley: University of California Press, 1976); but, for an excellent political reading of the history of literary theory and its contemporary manifestations, see *Literary Theory: An Introduction* (Minneapolis: University of Minnesota Press, 1983).

12. For an excellent account of both Althusser and Williams, see John Higgins, "Raymond Williams and the Problem of Ideology," *Postmodernism and Politics,* ed. Jonathan Arac (Minneapolis: University of Minnesota Press, 1986), 112–22.

13. Frederic Jameson, "Cognitive Mapping," in Nelson and Grossberg, *Marxism,* 335.

14. Perry Anderson, "Modernity and Revolution," in Nelson and Grossberg, *Marxism,* 336.

15. December 1987 and spring 1986, respectively. See also Darko Suvin, *To Brecht and Beyond* (New Jersey: Barnes and Noble, 1984).

16. *Drama Review* 32, no. 1 (1988): 82–94. See also my article "Rethinking Brecht: Deconstruction, Feminism and the Politics of Form," *Essays on Brecht, Brecht Yearbook 15,* ed. Marc Silberman et al. (Baltimore: University of Maryland, 1990), 99–110; and "Beyond Brecht: Britain's New Feminist Drama," in *Performing Feminisms: Feminist Critical Theory and Theatre,* ed. Sue-Ellen Case (Baltimore: John Hopkins University Press, 1990), 150–59.

17. Joseph Roach, *Theatre Journal* 41, no. 2 (May 1989): 155–68; Bruce McConachie, "Using the Concept of Cultural Hegemony to Write Theatre History," in *Interpreting the Theatrical Past,* ed. Thomas Postlewait and Bruce A. McConachie (Iowa City: University of Iowa Press, 1989), 37–58; Herbert Blau and Mohammed Kowsar, *Theatre Journal* 35, no. 4 (December 1983): 441–60, 461–74.

18. Brecht, *Bertolt Brecht Poems,* 193.

Historicizing the Relations of Theatrical Production

Bruce A. McConachie

> The producer does what the title says. He or she leads out, leads forth, leads through. The producer is the total organizing human being who generates the impulse from the organization.
>
> —Zelda Fichander

> I never call myself a producer. . . . I'm part of this place. That's all. I'm part of this place, part of the work we do, part of all the people.
>
> —Ellen Stewart

The emergence of the word *production* to mean the process of putting together a stage performance and the event resulting from this process is fairly recent. According to the *Oxford English Dictionary*, this usage dates from 1894 when the *Westminster Gazette* noted that "the production of the Greek play" was "the great event of the past week." Before 1894 English writers termed a theatrical event a *show*, a *presentation*, or a *performance*. These words acquired the general sense of their present theatrical definitions soon after the development of public playhouses in England in the late sixteenth century. From that time until the 1890s, however, English had no single word that encompassed the many processes leading up to stage presentation. During these three hundred years theater artists might "found" companies, "build" costumes and scenery, "cast" plays and "stage" them, but these preperformance activities were not understood as making a total production. Similarly, English writers had no apparent need to introduce the verb *produce* and the noun *producer* in theatrical parlance until the 1890s.[1]

The etymological predecessor of theatrical *production* developed in the discourse of political economy. *Production* in the sense of the manufacture of goods for market exchange began in 1776 in Adam Smith's *The Wealth of Nations*. Several economists elaborated and expanded the term's economic denotations during the nineteenth century. John R. McCulloch spoke of "the production of utility, and consequently of exchangeable value, by appropriating and modifying matter already in existence" in 1825. Henry Fawcett defined *capital* as "wealth which has been appropriated to assist future production." Henry George further expanded the meaning of the term in his statement that "production is always the mother of wages." And the *Manchester Examiner* reported in 1885 that, because the market was glutted, "production has of late been largely going into stock." Although *production* retained earlier, noneconomic meanings, its primary usage by the 1890s referred to the productive processes and results of industrial capitalism.[2] Hence, when the *Westminster Gazette* first termed a theatrical event a production, its readers probably understood that the occasion involved the investment of capital and the hiring of labor to create and sell a product on the entertainment market in the expectation of generating a profit.

Why do *producer* and *production* emerge in theatrical discourse at the end of the last century? In what ways did *production* link artistic and economic activity in the 1890s? And why did it take three hundred years for English writers to denote the process of putting together a show with a single word? The likely answers to these questions have significant implications for the ways in which theater historians construct explanations of past productions. Most immediately, etymological understanding can help the historian to avoid the problem of "presentism," unthinkingly reading current practices back into the past. Further, probing the history of the word can reveal the difficulties historians face in constructing contexts and causalities to explain the relations of theatrical production in the past. It can also suggest a possible strategy for overcoming these difficulties.

Such an investigation is important because theater historians in general have been much more attentive to the means rather than the relations of theatrical production. Scholars know a lot more about the probable stagings of Shakespeare's plays, for instance, than about the company hierarchy within the King's Men and the system of patronage which supported and legitimated the company's existence. While some of this ignorance is due to the paucity of the historical record, the general tendency to focus on means rather than relations has to do with the predeliction of many historians of artistic practice to separate the aesthetic from the practical.[3]

Lack of attention to the social and economic relations of production has been especially deleterious to understanding the sweeping changes that occurred in the Western theater during the nineteenth and early twentieth centuries. In particular, constructions of American theater history could benefit from a fresh look at the productive relations of stock companies before 1870, the similarities between acting stars and nineteenth-century capitalists, and the relations among producers, playwrights, and directors at the turn of the century. Reexamining these institutional social relations on the basis of a neo-Marxist understanding of cultural production constitutes the chief example of this essay. Its primary direction, however, is to historicize theatrical *production*, toward which exploring the etymology of the word is a necessary first step.

As to why theatrical production and its related terms borrowed economic meanings in the 1890s, one explanation might be that the demand for certain kinds of shows and the means of producing them were changing. Artistic and audience desire for aesthetically unified performances and the complexities of staging realistic plays required greater coordination of all the theatrical elements, especially acting, scenery, and lighting, and this led to the emergence of dictatorial, innovative producer-directors. This explanation constructs a causal relation linking changes in demand and productive means to a fundamental alteration in the social relations of theatrical production: aesthetic desires and new technologies cause producers to centralize theater-making under their own control. This is the conventional explanation linking the development of stage realism and institutional changes in the theater at the end of the last century, and it seems to account for the emergence of *production* in theatrical discourse and its ties to economic meanings.[4]

But is this an adequate explanation? To begin with, it's driven mainly by ideas: playwrights, theorists, directors, and others with new concepts and commitments create a theater that fits their aesthetic ideals. Also, this historical construction sidesteps the issue of power relations among the makers of theater, thus calling into question its causal probability. To account for these disparities of power, one alternative explanation might be that capitalists, seeing new opportunities for profit, constituted themselves as producers and rationalized their empowerment on the grounds that they could best offer the public what it wanted. Theater historians have used this explanation too to link the rise of realism with the development of theatrical monopolies.[5]

This alternative construction may gain in credibility, but it simply runs causality in the other direction: the relations of theater production now determine audience demand and the deployment of new technologies. Further, it raises the problem of completeness similar to the "idea-driven" explanation offered above. Why, in other words, should materialistic motives be more central to historical actors than ideational ones? This question begs a larger one: what structural historical forces beyond individual control may have shaped turn-of-the-century Western culture and society—and consequently its theater? This issue, in turn, takes the historian beyond a consideration of causal relations among discrete historical phenomena that are narrowly theatrical and into the broad context of social and economic history. But, once there, how is the theater historian to proceed?

A likely answer to the third question raised above—why it takes the English language so long to come up with one word to denote all the processes of "production"—suggests one promising direction for the historian at sea in contextuality. The usual etymological explanation for all such questions is that writers of English needed several words; one word wouldn't do. Until the 1890s theater making was considered to be a group activity involving several crafts: play writing, acting, scene painting, etc. To be sure, managing was thought necessary to coordinate these crafts for performance, but a manager was not a "producer"; though usually controlling the affairs of a stock company, the manager remained more of a master craftsman than a capitalist, as nineteenth-century writers understood these words.[6] The shift in usage from *manager* to *producer* and the emergence of *production* to denote the producer's actions consequently marked a significant stage in the transformation of dramatic entertainment under capitalism. A parallel transformation in practice and discourse had already occurred in most other crafts. The making of textiles didn't become production, for instance, until capitalists gained control and ownership of the separate crafts of spinning, weaving, cutting, etc. As in the theater, group creation gave way to individual production, the "individual" being either a capitalist or a corporation, the legal extension and enhancement of individual power under capitalism.

This discussion of the possible reasons why language denoting most of the activities of theater-making devolved from several words to one masterterm suggests that theater historians must begin with a general sense of the totality and dynamics of historical cultures to fashion complete explanations of theatrical production. Hermeneutically examining possible interpretations within a notion of totality can generate a more persuasive and complete explanation of the emergence of *production* in the 1890s than constructing causal chains linking such discrete, isolable phenomena as audience demand, business greed, artistic innovation, and new technology. The foregoing discussion also suggests that focusing on the general relations of production within this historical totality can lead the theater scholar to an understanding of productive relations within specific theatrical formations.

The implications of this etymological exploration are consonant with Raymond Williams's approach to historical investigation and explanation. Working out of the traditions of Marxism, Williams fashioned guidelines for exploring the dynamic relations of production within a social-cultural totality, which are especially useful for theater historians. He began by questioning the conventional interpretation of the base-superstructure metaphor, the usual starting point in Marxism for relating the means and relations of production to the culture of any historical period. In the preface to his *Contribution to the Critique of Political Economy*, Marx stated:

> In the social production of their life, men enter into definite relations that are indispensable and independent of their will, relations of production which correspond to a definite stage of development of their material productive forces. The sum total of these relations of production constitutes the economic structure of society, the real foundation, on which rises a legal and political superstructure and to which correspond definite forms of social consciousness. The mode of production of material life conditions the social, political, and intellectual life process in general.[7]

Early Marxists understood from this and similar statements that the productive base determines the cultural superstructure; some even thought that the social relations of material production, such as those found in heavy industry, must control the form and content of cultural practices in any historical era.

Like many neo-Marxists, Williams criticized this reading of the base-superstructure metaphor for its rigidity and reification:

> I would say that each term of the proposition has to be revalued in a particular direction. We have to revalue "determination" towards

the setting of limits and the exertion of pressure, and away from a predicted, prefigured and controlled content. We have to revalue "superstructure" towards a related range of cultural practices, and away from a reflected, reproduced or specifically dependent content. And, crucially, we have to revalue "the base" away from the notion of a fixed economic or technological abstraction, and towards the specific activities of men in real social and economic relationships, containing fundamental contradictions and variations and therefore always in a state of dynamic process.[8]

For Williams "the base" must be seen as the social and economic activities of a totality that also includes specific cultural practices, not as foundational relations that somehow reproduce themselves in a separate cultural sphere.

Williams's synthesis of base and superstructure within a social-cultural totality plays upon ambiguities in Marx's writings concerning the nature of production. In his introduction to the *Grundrisse* Marx, focusing on how society reproduces itself, concluded: "Not that production, distribution, exchange and consumption are identical, but that they all form the members of a totality, distinctions within a unity." Marx made a similar point in the next section of his introduction on distribution: while "a definite production thus determines a definite consumption, distribution and exchange as well as definite relations between these differing moments . . . , production is itself determined by other moments." As Marxist critic Ben Fine concludes, "There is no simple relation between production and the rest of the economy, mode of production, or social formation. Indeed, even what constitutes an object of production is ambiguous [in the writings of Marx]." Fine adds that "it would be a mistake to see Marx's or Marxism's understanding of production as being exclusively preoccupied with material production. At a general level it is concerned with the reproduction of the social formation as well as of the economy."[9]

Williams would agree. To understand the social relations of production broadly conceived he turns to Gramsci's notion of hegemony. "For hegemony supposes the existence of something which is truly total, which is not merely secondary or superstructural," states Williams, "but is lived at such a depth, which saturates the society to such an extent . . . that it corresponds to the reality of social experience very much more clearly than any notions derived from the formula of base and superstructure." For Williams hegemony centers on a "system of practices, meanings, and values" which legitimates the interests of historically dominant social groups.[10] The social relations resulting from the complex and dynamic interplay among groups within hegemonic systems are the prime movers of history for Williams, producing both material goods and nonmaterial meanings and values.

Williams's shift from a base-superstructure model to a concept of hegemonic totality emphasizing productive relations allows him to develop procedures for the historical analysis of culture which are both encompassing and revealing. He defines culture as "a signifying system through which . . . a social order is communicated, reproduced, experienced, and explored."[11] Culture, then, includes material and nonmaterial phenomena, both of which are central to the process of affirming and reproducing (as well as challenging) hegemonic social relations. These historical formations produce cultural products much as they produce automobiles and race relations, but, insists Williams, art, literature, and theatrical performances are not consummable goods like some of the other products of hegemony. Williams enjoins critics and historians to shift their definition of a "work of art" from an object to a practice. Rather than attempting to isolate the art object and, in Kantian fashion, separate out its inherent components, the historian should investigate the nature and conditions of its historical practice. For the theater historian this means close attention to the social relations and means of producing the material realities of historical theaters (scripts, acting companies, playhouses, scenery, etc.) as well as to the nonmaterial response of situated audiences in historical periods.

In *The Sociology of Culture* Williams outlines methods and concepts for analyzing cultural production. His insights in chapter 2, "Institutions," are particularly useful for theater historians. Assuming that his theoretical constructs are no more than a "set of working hypotheses," Williams considers the variety of productive relations which have existed historically in cultural institutions, including the theater.[12] Some early societies, notes Williams, provided directly for what he terms "instituted artists"; the Celtic bards, for instance, were officially recognized as a part of the ruling structure of Celtic society. Williams distinguishes between "instituted artists" and artists supported by patronage, noting, however, that some overlap between the types has occurred. The craftsmen of Dionysus in ancient Greece exemplify such an overlap, since both the polis and wealthy patrons supported their theatrical productions. Regarding patronage production itself, Williams lists several types.[13] For the historian concerned with distinguishing between the social relations that sustained and constrained much of Molière's theater (retainer and commission patronage) and Shakespeare's public productions (protection and support patronage), this typology is vital. It also speaks to the structural tensions inherent in state funding of the arts (the public as patron).

Williams devotes most of this chapter to artistic production for the market, the last distinctive kind of social relationship to develop historically in the production of culture. Within this form Williams distinguishes among several types of market production: (1) artisanal; (2) post-artisanal, which includes a further distinction between the producer selling his work to (a) a distributive intermediary or (b) a productive intermediary; (3) market professional; and (4) corporate professional.[14]

This last set of distinctions for artistic production within institutions provides a particularly helpful set of coordinates for mapping the changes in productive relations which occurred in the American theater during the nineteenth and early twentieth centuries. Using Williams's ideas to examine what is conventionally called "stock company production," for instance, it is apparent that this term is too general to encompass the variety of social relations involved in making and presenting theater during most of the century. Insofar as company managers were independent makers of theater who offered their troupe's work for direct sale on the local market, these managers and their craftspeople were "artisans." While the success of managers and their companies depended primarily on the market, it was also linked to a lingering form of "sponsorship patronage," most evident in the yearly benefits taken by each actor. Stock company managers also engaged in "post-artisanal" theatrical production, specifically as "distributive intermediaries," when they jobbed in stars or contracted with entire companies to perform on their stages. Warren and Wood, managers of the Chestnut Street Theatre Company, for instance, gave half of their seasons over to stars, ballet, and opera companies in the early 1820s, and they prided themselves on their conservative management.[15] In short, stock company production involved three significantly different kinds of social relations: sponsorship patronage, artisanal market, and post-artisanal market production.

Had the contributors to *American Theatre Companies, 1749–1887* distinguished among these relations of production, they would have written a very different book. As it is, most of these scholars focus on the artisanal productions of the companies themselves and largely ignore their managers' attempts to cultivate the patronage of the elite or bring national stars to their local theaters. The preface to *American Theatre Companies* even muddies a clear focus on artisanal market production by announcing that "theatre is a communal art, arising out of the coordinated efforts of the members of a group." Such statements mystify relations of superordination and subordination within theater companies and between companies and the market.[16]

Like stock company production, the "star system" must be broken down into its component parts to see the different productive relations operating within it. Unless these distinctions are made, theater historians run the risk of assuming that most stars were not entrepreneurs. One American theater historian, for instance, waits until his narrative reaches the 1890s to label a section of his book "Enter the Businessman."[17] On the contrary, when stars such as Edwin Forrest and Charlotte Cushman temporarily worked with a local stock company to present their repertoire, the star and the manager of the company functioned, through contractual agreement, as distributive intermediaries of the star's talent. Like their counterparts among energetic artisans in the mid-nineteenth century, the major American stars elevated themselves from craftsperson to capitalist by taking control of their own careers and charging what the market would bear for their services. This change in productive relations led to altered social relations within the theater. Actor Otis Skinner recalled that "caste distinctions were observed" whenever a star rehearsed with a stock company.[18]

The star system benefited other capitalists besides the stars themselves. A few company managers, such as Thomas Hamblin at the Bowery Theatre in New York, created minor stars who remained contractually committed to them and earned their distributive intermediaries handsome profits through their appearances with other companies. Other businessmen made money in the star system by controlling the distribution circuit through which the stars traveled. E. A. Marshall, for instance, established a touring circuit in the early 1850s which began at his enormous Broadway Theatre in New York (seating capacity 4,500), included his own theaters in Boston, Philadelphia, Baltimore, and Washington, and extended to allied theaters in Cincinnati, Louisville, St. Louis, and New Orleans. The emergence of "combination" companies after the Civil War streamlined the distributive system of relations but did not alter its fundamentals. Stars, now "in combination" with a full company of actors, continued to work with other capitalists to profit from the distribution of their theatrical products.[19]

The monopolistic power exerted by the Theatrical Syndicate and later by the Shuberts did, however, change the fundamentals of show business from distributive to productive intermediary relations. Williams notes that the main distinction between the two types of post-artisanal relations is that, in the second, the maker of the artwork (or performance, in this case) no longer profits directly from the sale of his or her product. Rather, the productive intermediary "invests in the purchase of a work for the purpose of profit; it is now his relations with the market which are direct." The initial maker is typically reduced to "offering his labour to produce works of a certain known type."[20] The Shuberts acted as productive intermediaries, for instance, not only when they produced a show themselves but also when they leased one of their many playhouses to a non-Schubert producer, since contracts typically specified that theater owners would share in the profits of Broadway hits. In both cases the Shuberts hired actors, musicians, and scenic artists for their known abilities to create successful shows and marketed the product of the labor of those creative others.

Early twentieth-century producers like the Shuberts did not directly hire playwrights, however. Playwrights had become *market professionals,* Williams's term to denote "a participant in the direct market process of the sale of his work." The International Copyright Agreement of 1886, by recognizing the products of writing as transferrable private property, effectively constituted, notes Williams, "a specific kind of social relationship which can be defined as a form of professional independence within integrated and dominant market relations."[21] Although this copyright agreement gave playwrights more leverage with producers, it bound their work more closely to the market. Plays simply became the land upon which producers could build shows by hiring labor and investing capital. This sense of the economic utility of scripts survives in the lingo of Broadway and Hollywood today: producers buy "options" on "properties" they are considering for future "development." The playscript, like real estate, is necessary to the process of capitalist production in the entertainment industry.[22]

Unlike playwrights, play directors did not become market professionals. Williams's discussion of the relations of artistic production in market capitalism implicitly contradicts the conventional historical wisdom regarding the "rise of the director." According to Helen Krich Chinoy in *Directors on Directing,* the late nineteenth-century director "filled so pressing a need that he quickly pre-empted the hegemony that had rested for centuries with playwrights and actors. . . . The appearance of the director ushered in a new theatrical epoch. His experiments, his failures, and his triumphs set and sustained the stage."[23] In truth, directors had and continue to exercise less independence than playwrights and far less power than producers in the modern theater. Most early directors in the United States, like Augustin Daly and David Belasco, should rather be called producers, since their artistic control depended fundamentally on their economic hegemony over the relations of production within their companies. Indeed, directors who were not primarily producers did not emerge in the American theater until 1900. A 1906 article in the magazine *The Theatre* paragraphed the leading directors of the decade. Among the more than thirty listed were William Seymour ("heads the Charles Frohman stage department . . . a firm disciplinarian, yet suave, kindly in manner"), Ned Wayburn (works for Klaw and Erlanger, "his specialty is the management of chorus girls"), and George W. Marion (directs musicals for producer Henry W. Savage, "handles his forces with a firm hand"). Hired by the Syndicate, the Shuberts, and other producers to stage their shows and keep order in their casts, these functionaries were more like factory foremen turning out formulaic products than artistic innovators.[24]

In Williams's terminology play directors were (and substantially remain) "corporate professionals," salaried employees akin to newspaper writers in publishing since neither can copyright their work. Significantly, one of the directors noted in the 1906 article accused another of stealing a piece of stage business which he had invented. Lacking copyright protection, he could only advocate the formation of an association among directors to adjudicate such matters.[25] Unlike most other theater artists "effectively or wholly employed within the new corporate structures," however, play directors did retain a small measure of individual economic power. Whereas unions now bargain with producers over the wages of scenic artists, musicians, costumers, and actors, directors negotiate individually on the basis of a minimum contract set by the Society of Stage Directors and Choreographers, which is not a union.[26]

Historicizing the relations of theatrical production opens up the possibility of a more complete historical sociology of the theater, a subdiscipline still in its infancy in theater studies. Were such a sociology to follow in the pathbreaking tradition of Raymond Williams, it would require extensive empirical and theoretical investigations into the sociohistorical conditions necessary for the emergence of various kinds of theater, the relations between historical forms of theatrical expression and the dominant ideology of a historical period, and the functions of theater in reproducing, modifying, or contradicting hegemonic relations of production. Such studies could transform the discourse of theater history as it is presently taught and written in the United States.

NOTES

Chapter epigraphs from Zelda Fichandler, "The Arena Stage"; and Ellen Stewart, "La Mama Experimental Theatre Club," in *Producers on Producing*, ed. Stephen Langley (New York: Drama Books, 1976), 78, 138.

1. *Oxford English Dictionary (O.E.D.)*, 2d ed. (Oxford: Clarendon, 1989), 12:564–68. The verb *produce* was used as early as 1836 to mean "introduce," in the sense of a manager producing an actor or play to the public. This meaning of the word, however, did not carry with it the actions associated with preperformance preparation.

2. *O.E.D.*, 12:566.

3. See Joseph R. Roach, "Theatre History and the Ideology of the Aesthetic," *Theatre Journal* 41, no. 2 (1989): 155–68. Roach discusses "the widely shared historiographical assumption of theatre scholars, derived from German idealist philosophy and eighteenth-century theories of art, that the aesthetic exists as an autonomous category, transcending the sublunary sphere of power relations and ideologies" (155).

4. See, for example, the first four chapters of Oscar G. Brockett and Robert Findlay's *Century of Innovation: A History of European and American Drama since 1870* (Englewood Cliffs, N.J.: Prentice-Hall, 1973), 1–119. Brockett and Findlay discuss the emergence of the director but have little to say about other changes in the productive relations of the theater.

5. See Garff B. Wilson, *Three Hundred Years of American Drama and Theatre* (Englewood Cliffs, N.J.: Prentice-Hall, 1982), 149–62. Wilson relies on Jack Poggi, *Theater in America: The Impact of Economic Forces, 1870–1967* (Ithaca, N.Y.: Cornell University Press, 1968).

6. According to the *O.E.D.*, a *master craftsman* is "a workman who is qualified by training and experience to teach apprentices and to carry on his trade on his own account" (9:443). A *capitalist*, on the other hand, is "one who has accumulated capital; one who has capital available for employment in financial or industrial enterprises" (2:863). Typically, theatrical managers had little accumulated capital and did not own their means of production. The actor-managers of the late nineteenth century, such as Henry Irving and William Gillette, however, were transitional figures, as I explain below.

7. Karl Marx, Preface, *Contribution to the Critique of Political Economy* (New York: International, 1970), 1.

8. Raymond Williams, "Base and Superstructure in Marxist Cultural Theory," *Problems in Materialism and Culture* (London: NLB, 1980), 34.

9. *Grundrisse*, quoted by Ben Fine in "Production," in *A Dictionary of Marxist Thought*, ed. Tom Bottomore (Cambridge: Harvard University Press, 1983), 396, 397; see also "Base and Superstructure," "Forces and Relations of Production," and "Reproduction" in the *Dictionary*.

10. Raymond Williams, *Problems in Materialism and Culture*, 37, 38. For more on hegemony and its uses in scholarship, see my article "Using the Concept of Cultural Hegemony to Write Theatre History," in *Interpreting the Theatrical Past*, ed. Thomas Postlewait and Bruce A. McConachie (Iowa City: University of Iowa Press, 1989), 37–58. Williams's notion of a hegemonic totality goes beyond the sense of the concept of hegemony as deployed by Gramsci, who retained a base-superstructure explanation for the production of culture.

11. Raymond Williams, *Towards a Sociology of Culture* (New York: Schocken Books, 1982), 13.

12. Ibid., 35.

13. Ibid., 36–44.

14. Ibid., 44–56.

15. Regarding Warren and Wood, see my article "William B. Wood and the 'Pathos of Paternalism,'" *Theatre Survey* 28, no. 1 (1987): 1–14. For an overview of changes in productive relations in the American theater during the nineteenth century, see my article "Pacifying American Theatrical Audiences, 1820–1900," in *For Fun and Profit: The Transformation of Leisure in the United States*, ed. Richard Butsch (Philadelphia: Temple University Press, 1990), 47–70.

16. *American Theatre Companies*, ed. Weldon B. Durham (Westport, Conn.: Greenwood Press, 1986), vii.

17. Wilson, *Three Hundred Years*, 160.

18. *Footlights and Spotlights: Recollections of My Life on the Stage* (1923; reprint, Westport, Conn.: Greenwood Press, 1972), 58.

19. See the 1881 obituary on Marshall in the *New York Clipper*, included in Joseph Ireland's *Extra-Illustrated Records of the New York Stage*, Harvard Theatre Collection, vol. 2, pt. 13, 35. On combination companies, see Poggi, *Theater in America*, 3–8.

20. Williams, *Towards a Sociology*, 45.

21. Ibid., 47, 48.

22. Stephen Langley, *Theatre Management in America: Principle and Practice*, rev. ed. (New York: Drama Book Publishers, 1980), 96–101.

23. Helen Krich Chinoy, "The Emergence of the Director," in *Directors on Directing: A Source Book of the Modern Theatre*, ed. Toby Cole and Helen Krich Chinoy, rev. ed. (Indianapolis: Bobbs-Merrill, 1963), 3.

24. Edward Fales Coward, "The Men Who Direct the Destinies of the Stage," *The Theatre: Illustrated Magazine of Dramatic and Musical Art* 6 (July 1906): 188, 189.

25. Frank Smithson accused Ben Teal of stealing an S formation involving members of a chorus line. See the "Ben Teal File," Robinson Locke Collection, New York Public Library, Lincoln Center.

26. Williams, *Towards a Sociology*, 51; on current theatrical unions and societies, see Langley, *Theatre Management*, 109–23.

Resistance to Theory: The Contradictions of Post–Cold War Criticism (with an Interlude on the Politics of Jazz)

Jim Merod

The contradictions of post–Cold War criticism in North America take place not only in classrooms and department meetings across the continent but also in the surprise that attends the confrontation of more than one million soldiers in the Saudi desert. That surprise can be found in the curious lack of preparation for the sudden reemergence of well-entrenched Cold War attitudes, policies, and rhetoric celebrated within the major news media as George Bush marshals a new Middle East military order. Like the contradictions of the forty-plus-year post–Second World War era in which "freedom" was assured by the intellectual's license to roam among treasured classical texts along essentially formalistic interpretive lines, the continuation of American military hegemony links traditional national ideals with reworked slogans that tolerate dissent at a respectful distance from serious collective action. As 1990 gave way to 1991, the Bush post–Cold War strategists moved with haste to reverse Saddam Hussein's invasion of Kuwait. Despite the mountainous Reagan deficit that casts each movement of the capitalistic state in shadows, the surge of United States forces across the Iraqi border promises a quick but uncertain victory. The uncertainty resides with both political and economic interests. What lasting repercussion will the bombing of Baghdad have as negotiation and rebuilding replace armed conflict? What costs of "peacekeeping" will follow the costs of war making?

None of these issues erase the scenes and reports of Kuwaiti citizens murdered, raped, held hostage, tortured. They do not justify, either, innocent Iraqi people being mutilated by stray bombs. One remembers, nonetheless, those brief weeks in 1990 when Soviet and American cooperation portended, for many, the "end of history" and the emergence of geopolitical sanity. Even then a guerilla war was in progress daily—in cities across North America, on the streets of the underclass working population.

The surprise that one discovers among American intellectuals and academics is not astonishment sparked by the incongruity of soldiers sent to armed confrontation for poorly defined capitalistic internationalism. The surprise that rippled across North American campuses in the fall of 1990 was the consternation of the duped liberal optimist who thought, for a few months after the Berlin Wall became a jumble of souvenir rocks, that world peace was about to break out. Instead, the post–Cold War era begins in earnest with a United States assault force nearly one-half million men and women strong, composed of "volunteer" conscripts drawn massively from the laboring, the undereducated, and unprofessionalized classes, and boasting a disproportionate number of Black and other minority soldiers, sailors, and marines. The air force, in an age of supertechnological weaponry, remains mostly white—a branch of service without grunts.

The contradictions of the emerging post–Cold War era—contradictions that inhabit literary theory and cultural criticism—perpetuate those of the ready-alert militarized era they survive. One way to frame the tenacity of such contradictoriness, of the peculiarly North American form of encouraging intellectual conformity while celebrating dissent and democratic openness, is to trace the career of American pragmatism in the way that Cornel West has. Pragmatism, West writes, "is a diverse and heterogenous tradition" that spans a century and a half, from Ralph Waldo Emerson to Richard Rorty, and it

> emerges with profound insights and myopic blindnesses, enabling strengths and debilitating weaknesses, all resulting from distinctive features of American civilization: its revolutionary beginning combined with a slave-based economy; its elastic liberal rule of law combined with an entrenched business-dominated status quo; its hybrid culture in combination with a collective self-definition as homogeneously Anglo-American; its obsession with mobility, contingency, and pecuniary liquidity combined with a deep moralistic impulse; and its impatience with theories and philosophies alongside ingenious technological innovation, political strategies of compromise, and personal devices for comfort and convenience.[1]

On one hand, West is aware of the regenerative energy that drives capitalistic institutions while being distressed by the culture of crisis and pseudoredemption that North America's contradictory cultural logic spawns. In particular, he is "disturbed by the transformation of highly intelligent liberal intellectuals into tendentious neoconservatives owing to crude ethnic identity-based allegiances and vulgar neonationalist sentiments." On the other hand, West may underestimate (or merely understate) the perpetual transformative energy of the North American military apparatus to draw, both first and last, upon "a continuous cultural commentary or set of interpretations that attempt to explain America to itself at a particular historical moment."[2] That self-defining commentary is the job of the North American intellectual class—a class of word workers and image makers which includes journalists and media executives as well as academics.

As I write these words, the ground war in Kuwait has just begun. North American television coverage of the air war has been closely directed by government and military restrictions. The widespread assumption that such censorship is necessary and reasonable governs the calm acceptance of press restrictions by the press itself. One might have expected debate about the scope of the restrictions, the totality of censorship. One would have believed, perhaps, that newspaper and television journalists might find some antagonism between the military's wish to keep Iraq ignorant of coalition troop movements and its absolute control of all access to battlefield information.

The stifled debate about fundamental issues of press coverage of battlefield maneuvers reflects the terms in which this war has been formed from its outset. The simple binarism of Western virtues against an Arab dictator's evil has come to supersede any debate about access to information, political complexities, or historical facts. The simplistic imagery of "America at War," framed in the pathos of fearful wives and children and mothers, dominates all memory or retrieval of the circumstances that created this crisis in an area where Western political and economic interests first stimulate and then respond to a sequence of crises. The drama of incompletely interpreted, widely televised geopolitical upheaval will not cease with the suspension of this conflict. A fundamental logic of capitulation to state-manufactured definitions of Western interests, of patriotism, of the Arab world, and of history itself governs the way "popular opinion" is molded by the consciousness industry.

The term *consciousness industry*, crafted by Hans Magnus Enzensberger during the Indochina War, identifies the hegemonic unity of outlook at work within the administrators and managers who control giant media corporations such as the *Los Angeles Times*, the National Broadcasting Corporation, and the entire gamut of television and print journalism. Not so often noticed in the use of a term like *consciousness industry*, which denotes the creative manipulation of public dialogue concerning important national and international events, is the ambivalent mixture of admiration and scorn with which the world of journalism regards the academic world.

On one side, both print and visual media journalists have drawn their legitimacy from academic training and from their own "expertise" with words and information. Journalists are, in a very ill-defined and also somewhat constricted way, intellectuals. Just that blurred self-image and its qualified partiality drives the majority of journalistic workers to disavow the notion of an intellectual identity. Instead, they imagine themselves as independent writers and reporters, people hedged by policies and forces running at them from every sector. Their "independence" is a matter of professional tradition that offers some room to craft sentences that may survive an editor's revisions. Their professional identity is gained against other professional occupations and identities with equal claims to prestige and independence, one of them the role of the academic intellectual.

This rivalry for an independent professional identity, for a clarity of truth telling that makes sense and has a use in the public world of ordinary activity, constructs the other side on which the journalist's ambivalence takes place. The print journalist sees the work of newspaper or magazine reportage to be free of the obfuscating protocols of academic rigor. No footnotes need burden the directness of the print journalist's writing. A sort of luminous immediacy lights the way of the newspaper writer. The journalist in each sector recognizes that a much more detailed account of the story printed or narrated in the news resides with the historian and the scholar. But the historian and the scholar have the advantage of days and weeks to tell about things that the journalist has hours, and sometimes only minutes, to report. Virtually every journalist takes considerable pride in the ability to put several layers of information, partial leads, contradictory accounts, and just plain reportorial instinct into a cogent, persuasive piece of writing crafted against the pressure of unbreakable deadlines. The journalist's independent professional identity, therefore, carries a good measure of detachment, even distrust bordering on scorn, generated against the isolated, leisurely pontification of the academic writer, who has no deadlines so pressing, no clear prose so necessary, and no audience waiting in the wings.

I point to the rivalry between these two kinds of intellectual work because, despite the disavowal that marks each from the other by a mostly unconscious but nonetheless mutually affirmed agreement, journalists and academic writers share common professional habits and outlooks. Each sector operates largely in terms of standards that are self-made, self-revised, and nearly universally imposed throughout the activities of their professional work. The journalist and the academic share a generic professional independence from outside policing or surveillance.

A larger pattern of shared interests between journalists and academics can be found in the ambivalent admiration granted each by the other. Journalism (especially, recently, television journalism) draws heavily from academic writers, who construct stories about the "meaning" of dramatic world events. Professor Stephen Cohen has become a media star as *glasnost* works its way through a variety of television reports and commentaries. An articulate Princeton "Sovietologist" commands respect in proportion to his ability to lend star quality to Ted Koppel's late night talking news show or to any other "in-depth" report about Mikhail Gorbachev's regime. Before that principal story dominated the airwaves, Professor Alan Dershowitz from Harvard gained media ascendancy as a commentator about two dramatic issues: emerging Supreme Court judicial rulings and the ongoing controversy concerning the Israeli treatment of Palestinians. With the Persian Gulf War, new momentary academic "experts" have risen to stardom. The lesson to be drawn is the covert relationship of exploitation and publicity hidden within the media journalist's expression of professional interest for the academic viewpoint.

One might ask why the simplifications and easy binarisms by which the Persian Gulf War has been staged do not come under withering criticism by intellectuals. The answer is that enough academics are brought within the admiring glow of print and television attention to blur the media as a target for analysis. Newspaper, magazine, and television attention can single out those academic writers who have risen from the pack, who need not count themselves as drones in the disregarded fields of intellectual production. In some ways not difficult to calculate, journalistic attention has become a separate coin by which the academic career has gained its highest prestige and gratification. Despite the uneasy alliance between academics and journalists, the world of journalism, with its egregious simplicities, does not appear as a viable object of concentrated public criticism for mainstream academics. That task is left to more radical critics.

In fact, the underlying professional independence that each of these two sectors enjoys may contribute to their tacit agreement not to probe too far beneath reigning public (and governmental) opinion. Their professional identities joined in mutual suspicion about the ultimate worth of the other's labor, a muffled solidarity of tolerance bonds the academic and journalistic realms. The essential stamp of professional merit in both worlds is granted to those who act on the commonsense rule not to violate professional common sense.

I preface my discussion of that genuinely performative academic space now called "theory" by looking at the hegemonic conformity that underlies the shared identity of academic and journalist alike because their shared outlook is precisely the tolerant attitude of intolerance for those who seek to explore professional and cultural contradictions. An attitude of professional scorn or surprise or amazement masks a deeper intolerance for anyone who looks too closely at habits that bond professionals within their circle— habits that sometimes reinforce larger social patterns of conduct and allow the very object of one's intellectual analysis to escape beneath amazed, surprised, or scornful eyes.

I recognize in all of this that the student of theory and of academic critical debate may feel a form of submersion in the tidal wave of critics and positions and publications that now make up a much contested academic field called "critical theory." Such submersion is not unusual in one's years of graduate study. It sometimes feels like intellectual vertigo, a kind of temporary cognitive drowning. That condition, or its threat at least, goes with the territory. One does not become a rigorous critical intellectual without several kinds of trauma, challenge, uncertainty, (but also) triumph. One's triumph as a beginning student of critical theory may well be a form of intellectual stubbornness.

The issue at stake in my prefatory remarks here is not the "rightness" of the struggle in the Persian Gulf. I am concerned that the best-trained critical readers and writers that our educational system offers the world of public debate too often neglect the uncommon sense of looking contradictory values, habits, and policies square in the center of their double logics. The student of academic criticism, and all that we proudly designate as Theory, may be tempted to bog down in the sand of densely populated domestic deserts.

Seven or eight years ago, in a happier time, when the White House was filled with magical plans for heaven-born nuclear dragons and the sky began to fill more brightly with surveillance, a somewhat enigmatic writer named Paul de Man noted, with cryptic candor, that "nothing can overcome the resistance to theory since theory is itself this resistance." In the years since that tantalizing, altogether engaging statement was written Paul de Man's star has dimmed and even collapsed in upon itself.[3] De Man's career may reflect the trajectory of Theory as de Man imagined Theory's own self-resistance. Resistance *to* theory and the resistance *of* theory are not the same thing, although in de Man's teasing statement the identity is asserted by inadvertent insinuation.

I do not want to take up the case of Paul de Man's career, so celebrated across the past two years in the leading intellectual journals. I will note that I have written, skeptically and at some length, about de Man;[4] I have found him always to be one of the most provocative critical writers of our time. I invoke de Man here, no doubt problematically, because any course of study in or about Theory cannot avoid seminal utterances provided by that cagey, now battered, writer. The student and the professor confront the entanglements of criticism and Theory at the moment they encounter their own personal and publically induced resistances to the abstractions that academic writing breeds. Such resistances—experienced as scorn, revulsion, nausea, or cynical discontent—are part of the growth of intellectual ability in university settings. An older generation of college teachers, raised to expect referential clarity and stylistic elegance, clawed its way toward self-certainties impossible to circulate professionally in an era of anti-representational warfare.

Teachers have always faced resistances to one or another piece of doctrinaire wisdom. But, at some point in one's commitment as a teacher, the work of reading and writing as a *public* and not merely private (professionalized, career-driven) act becomes burdensome. It can seem difficult to imagine and impossible to attain: an anachronistic ideal. If irony was de Man's perennial delight, the unironic surplus of confusion when irony is pushed too far was in part his undoing as a theorist and as an overly defended critic. Resistance *to* theory often betrays the mind stretched to its limit. The resistances *of* theory are the unavoidable conflicts of competing arguments at work on texts, positions, notions, and their relations in the world.

My title may promise to deliver a word toward a completed, well-made "theory of resistance"—with everything at stake that the concept of resistance, among the world's political networks, can be imagined to entail. The de Manian figure of the teacher's resistance to theory, taken in close proximity to a politically alert theory of social and institutional resistance, beguiles an unwary glance into foreign territory. Here's what I have in mind.

For some time the acts of reading and writing with critical scrutiny have been framed by two mutually affirming, mutually antagonistic intellectual commitments. In a harshly reductive frame the affirming antagonism can be seen in the cooperating divergence of academic writing, on one hand, and everything that the less theoretical, more politically aroused writer who aims to engage public consciousness represents, on the other hand.[5] Without academic writing and its historical memory, we have little need for theory and no ground for much of the social and political energy on which active intellectual resistance to real world circumstances draws. In one sense it is not difficult to understand the fears expressed by many traditional academic writers. Intellectual work in the years since the Indochina War has become, in North America, more aware of its institutional settings. That awareness can only provoke varying degrees of conscience, a variety of concerns with the ways that knowledge circulates within the academy and, through the academy, into the world.

In short, any neat separation of academic from extra-academic writing misses the imbrication of knowledge within the professional and institutional networks that cross the academy and the economy on a worldwide reach. Any neat connection that asserts the affirming mutuality of academic theory and of writing in its range of ambitions, however, misses the difference between the resistances of theory and theories of resistance. That difference can be partly accounted for by the simple fact that academic writers usually imagine themselves writing for academic readers, which is to say specialists like themselves, people who intend to master a fairly circumscribed body of knowledge. A writer who intends to foster public conscience, who writes to enable concrete political resistance to things as they are, reaches toward everyone.

Let me be more direct. The activist writer working from a basis of conscience and political savvy does not fail to promote admiration from more cautious, less activist intellectuals. But such a writer can be targeted as someone who separates the act of intellectual or political resistance from professional protocols that more wary, world-weary writers defend as the academic community's last (or next) best hope in an otherwise hopeless age. The time is always dark and the temptation of a certain (all too prevalent) cast of mind is to gauge the academic enclosure as a bastion of clarity in an increasingly barbaric environment. The truly iconoclastic writer, regardless of intellectual persuasion, will always arouse the intellectual community. But the issue for students of critical theory in the United States near the close of the century is not how to adore uniqueness; instead, the student needs to examine inducements to commonplace certainties and mind-numbing professional routines. The accommodation to what has been put in place, accommodation to things that prevail and thus seduce or dominate imagination, remains the nearest temptation for any active mind.

If, therefore, the most blatant image of intellectual resistance to the largely unconscious subtext of postmodern capitalistic state culture continues to be the committed eloquence of a writer such as Noam Chomsky or the recently deceased I. F. Stone—i.e., someone whose general interests in the common public good somehow are brought without distortion within the orbit of professional concerns—the alternative, more theoretically competent image of resistance available to the cautious student is an academically housed critic seeking intellectual solidarity within the margins of established positions and identities.

I have in mind here a writer of a restless interrogative urgency that is rare, rarely found, but found nonetheless in the work of Gayatri Chakravorty Spivak. Spivak calls notice to the dignity of work traditionally demeaned, "the endless labor of work that gets regularly undone . . . the sort of work that is defined away because it is repetitive."[6] She means, of course, the critical stitching and unstitching of texts, figures, concepts, notions, arguments, positions, and the like, all of which make up the unending task of standing guard within shifting, sometimes seemingly bottomless circumstances.

At one end of the evaluative spectrum we find "man's work," the so-called progressive, masculine force of institution-bearing "social engineering" (the phrase finds its way to Spivak from Richard Rorty). At the other end, we come across what R. P. Blackmur called "the critic's job of work," which is a ceaseless vigilance without rewards except for the sheer awareness, sometimes shared, of recommitting energy to the indecipherable (at any rate, inextricable) knots of social and cultural bonding.

When I choose writers like Chomsky and Stone as examples of a traditional intellectual resistance less dependent on Theory than on a rational, altogether positioned yet functionally general assault on common cultural understandings, I could as easily have chosen Edward Said, who writes with an awareness of both intellectual and more massively international, geopolitical forces. I might have pointed, as well, to André Brink, the South African novelist and critical essayist, who speaks with enormous authority about the inhuman state of siege at work in his country. Brink clarifies our notion of culture when he insists that, for us, in circumstances routinely ignored, "understanding violence may well be the first step toward an understanding of culture."[7]

The virtue of Spivak's understanding of culture's violence, and the insidious permutations of a "culture of violence" (culture and violence sewn together in a perpetually redoubled set of bindings), is the clarity that it offers about the limits of academic theory. Spivak is remarkably unsentimental about the commerce of academic commodification, "the buying and selling of big [academic] names in all kinds of disciplines, all of [it] substituting for careful, slow, attentive, classroom teaching."[8] Whatever force of intellectual or cultural or political resistance the theorist may accomplish surely circles through the dialogue that transpires with students. Spivak is, among prominent and persistently challenging theorists, more committed to test the interchange between theory and teaching than most.

In one sense theory is essentially a product of the academy and, as such, the "property" of expert readers who boost and demote interpretive frameworks. Theory, in this light, is bought and sold not so much in (or as) the sale of books—total volumes distributed, consumed, circulated, etc.—but within the salable inventory of an academic career, an intellectual persona, a packaged and marketed if, also, somewhat probingly self-reflective professional identity.

In another sense Theory produces the engine of interpretation which drives classroom exercises. It may be that the vast majority of high school and, for that matter, college teachers take little advantage of the sexy dialectics of advanced theory mongering (which Stanley Fish has dubbed, with characteristic aggressive sobriety, "theory talk"—a designation meant to maim the slow but seemingly inexorable drift to the Left among theorists). Yet, any teacher anywhere who is hip enough to entertain herself while also gearing up for the best of the few still breathing at an advanced point in the educational regime will confess that a little Foucault on carceral networks and a little more Derrida on textual indeterminacy opens up a whole menagerie of unsuspected interactions.

I spoof the reigning curricular mechanics of the past twenty years because few teachers working these fields have found a fully active, pedagogically productive use for theory except in the highly mediated form that it takes as the utmost metareflection on all things intellectual. Theory produces theory, just as one poem motivates another poem. Perhaps the question that politically engaged teachers need to ask is how the most elegant and tough-minded ways of reading both texts and the institutional world can now contribute to teaching practices that arm students to read with pride in their own capacities to think, speak, argue, and eventually make decisions that are capable of intervening within specific worksites where knowledge counts for something.

Spivak offers us a glimpse at the limit (one limit) of academic theory production and also at the self-disturbing resistance of theory when it confronts its own intervention within relationships of power. One of Spivak's most provocative moves is to offer herself—her own ideals, scorn, intellectual gymnastics, multiple identities, fetishized as well as lionized authorial persona, and more. Spivak puts her range of attitudes and analytic maneuvers on display as instances of theory in motion—theory activated in the flesh-and-blood interactions of ordinary (and, sometimes, not so ordinary) events. In this, she has successfully assumed a position of considerable authority and persuasion in the critical profession. But the disarming quality of her gesture to put herself forward as an example of someone who is at once "representative" of several identities, somewhat at odds with one another, while seeking out the self-discrediting, self-undermining character of the uses to which representations are put is the flexibility and mobility that gesture grants the writer.

Spivak is ruthless to trace what she calls "the textuality of value," what I'll call the instituted violence of value. Part of the logic of the text and the violence of value everywhere we read and work is the unconscious assertion of the need to generate what Marx called "surplus value," which means the creation of something for nothing, the exploitation of those who have little or no authority and power by everyone who gets leverage in the marketplace. The textuality of value in the region of academic theory can be found in the idealizing of significant writers who become "big names," large presences on the intellectual horizon. In our era universities recruit academic stars the way corporations in the Reagan years learned to raid vulnerable enterprises by junk bond–inflated buyouts. The subtext in that realm of value is the violence it institutes to the interdisciplinary ambition of recent curricular configurations. How do you initiate and sustain the group dynamics of shared learning, and of interactive teaching, focused both on student development and on the subtlety of intellectual positions, when a high-powered, extremely visible department or school within a major university is constantly seeking the advantage of building its star-studded intellectual stable? I point here to the task of converting freshmen and sophomores at thousands of colleges and universities—converting them to the excitement, viability, and courage needed to make active critical thinking part of their emerging intellectual maturity. For this task the representative status of the academic luminary in North America is boxed, packaged, and marketed for its dubious worth.

I pose this problem in part as a consequence of the limitation of academic theory as it stands, but the problem is equally a source of the refusal by theoreticians at high levels of conceptual agility to imagine the central role of their own teaching in the world of intellectual productivity. The problem as I pose it cannot be assigned to capitalistic patterns of surplus value pure and direct. Without question capitalistic habits own too much hold on the thinking and behavior of universities in each segment of their operations. But that is the nature of a game that universities did not invent but have enabled historically, and with which they now cooperate. Yet to seek a theoretical or polemical origin for commodifying high-profile professors, for marginalizing teaching at its most powerfully and actively instructive (which is to say, when teaching animates surprising surpluses not of value but of joy and outrage and curiosity), to fob off the professional inclination on the part of theorists, scholars, and intellectuals in the academy to commandeer their own workspace as a symptom of capitalistic mindsets turns out, always, to miss the point of an ongoing critique like the one Spivak offers.

Reading, she suggests, must be strategic. It is strategic when it works against whatever grain it is asked to follow. The mode of opposition may be of nearly infinite variety. The point of pedagogical and theoretical resistance, of strategic opposition to reigning truths and norms, is not deviance for its own sake. It is to prepare for both individual and collective assertions of noncompliance with coercions that allow domination to exist with guiltless, sometimes invisible abandon. An unending debate can go forward about the logic and mechanics of domination. Michel Foucault's writing has advanced a complex understanding of the microtechnologies of control and restraint. Edward Said has furthered our sense of the specific historical density of knowledge and of our insertion in cultures that both impede and construct everything that knowledge fosters. Said has been concerned with the relentless denial of secular agencies and energies in a clerically driven idealizing of culture. That antisecular habit supplants human solidarity with religious orthodoxy. One of Said's targets has been the no less relentless inclination to textualize everything historical and solidly institutional, concretely political, stubbornly resistant to merely (or fundamentally) analytical operations.

Academic theory finds a limit, for Said, in its own complicity with jargons and ideologies that obscure the human costs of intellectual and institutional action. Theory, for him, after counting its evaporating commitments to human protest and political struggle, must become more "life-enhancing and constitutively opposed to every form of tyranny, domination, and abuse; its social goals are noncoercive knowledge produced in the interests of human freedom."[9] Note the agreement between Said and Spivak (despite a certain amount of dissonance otherwise). In his statement from "Secular Criticism," Said has substituted the word *criticism* for the term *theory*. That shift is not accidental. It marks a slight polemical thrust away from conceptual and analytical rarefaction toward greater degrees of concrete, at any extent, overt intervention within the region called textuality. Said favors essay writing over theory construction. In this he shares with Nietzsche and Foucault an antisystematic, even countertheoretical inclination. Each of those three writers prefers the specific interrogation of a discretely bounded examination—of a term, a concept, a text, or an event—to the multiple exfoliations of complicated, deeply nuanced systematic thought. In this they lean toward what Spivak has called a "wild" practice: i.e., a somewhat gymnastic, explosively mobile concentration of verbal and interrogative energy on objects of interest which, inevitably, entangle the critical reader/theorist in a transferential relationship of some kind. Spivak looks at the necessary mobility of her own critical writing as an outcome of the explicit and overt political immersions that define every act of writing. Therefore, she writes, "the political subject distances itself from the analyst-in-transference by declaring an 'interest' by way of a 'wild' rather than theoretically-grounded practice."[10]

It is important to note that Foucault tried for the majority of his writing career to avoid declaring "interest" except in the most objective way possible. One could think of this habit as "scholastically political." Such interest, of course, was always constructed by Foucault to undermine fraudulent authority—which sometimes for him seemed to appear ubiquitously as *all* authority. (We need to notice here that Said's writing has appeared to Spivak as potentially "a certain kind of glib access to globality . . . a sort of pretentious transnationalism" which may box the critical theorist into old fashioned "strategic" discourses.)[11]

In all of this shifting between positions, academic theory declares an interest in becoming a more responsible and actively political part of cultural reality. Provocative teaching often stages itself as active, as disruptive, as capable of inducing curiosity. Such teaching frequently stages itself as in touch with not just texts but with texts as tools and weapons, texts as windows on lost or obscured or even close and familiar (though sometimes unnoticed) worlds. These texts may not be, in the intellectual exchange between active minds, so much "things" as "sites" of history and of interpretation. I take, therefore, a somewhat sardonic distance from the idealizing notion of the teacher: the teacher as enabler, conserver, facilitator, etc. None of those is inappropriate, but the displacement or estrangement that Spivak is reaching for in her writing on theory and its pitfalls, on teaching and its delusions, suggests a need to retrace our steps through our classrooms and across the sublime or demoted self-image we carry as responsible inciters of riotous classroom energy.

Recently, in a column for the *San Diego Union* I referred to a local saxophonist as a "jazz provocateur." The term was accurate because this particular musician grew up in the home of New Orleans trombonist Kid Ory,

Fig. 1. From left to right, Albert "Tootie" Heath (drums), Jimmie Noone, Jr. (tenor sax), John Leitham (bass), Nick Brignola (baritone sax), and Frank Strazzeli (piano). San Diego (1990). Photo credit: Michael Oletta.

as the orphaned son of clarinetist Jimmie Noone, Sr. His outlook on the world has been shaped by experiences that put a high value on stirring up maximum musical energy. The man I was writing about, Jimmie Noone, Jr., is a cheerful musician and a charismatic entertainer. His notion of ordinary human interaction is an evening when everyone with musical ability of any kind collaborates to make the greatest possible lyrical high jinks. The notion of jazz "provocation," which carries a somewhat euphoric pedagogical urgency, is a concept appropriate to the younger Noone's musicianship. It is, for the purpose of understanding a great deal of what is left out, overlooked, and just plain unimagined in the world of critical theory and its teaching practices, a useful notion.

The world of critical theory may appear to be a universe distant from the high-spirited environment of the jazz musician. Jazz is a unique North American cultural energy that, nonetheless, for all the technical sophistication it has evolved in its ninety-year lifetime, reflects both the cultural opportunities and the social traumas of this century; the very interests and circumstances addressed by critical discourses are no less addressed by the jazz musician's stylistic changes. The world of artistic performance is subject to economic and political pressures that define the entire cultural ensemble, including the work of writers, teachers, and critical theorists. What is most remarkable about this common ground is not the shared social and institutional circumstances but the exclusion that continues to separate the activity of the jazz musician from the work of the critical teacher.

Of course, intellectual effort is routinely thought to be distinct from the world of entertainment. The critical theorist and the teacher operate in the realm of "high" culture; the jazz musician, perhaps the jazz critic too, operates in a lower cultural orbit. The separation between "high" theoretical discourse and "low" jazz entertainment reinforces a political stratification built not only on racial and professional lines of exclusion but also on a less visible inability to imagine the common circumstances that they share.

Jimmie Noone, Jr., points out the altered landscape that greeted young musicians in the Second World War era. Big bands were flourishing from coast to coast, and dance halls all the way from Catalina Island's Avalon Ballroom to the fancy vacation retreats on Cape Cod were filled with moonlight serenaders. Despite the improved climate for work, most of those bands were segregated. White bands received the largest share of the high-paying jobs. At the same time those bands frequently stole material from more talented Black arrangers, composers, and band leaders. The cultural climate was ripe for the Black jazz musician to rebuke artistic styles so easily coopted. As a result, the most innovative young musicians found a way to move beyond "danceable" lyrics. An experimental fury called Be Bop, pioneered by Thelonious Monk, Charlie Parker, Dizzy Gillespie, and Bud Powell, complicated expected approaches to standard material. A well-known song like "I Got Rhythm" became a vehicle for literally hundreds of magnificently contorted, complex harmonic variations. The musical consequence was a more demarcated musical environment. An alert jazz musician was now at work on extremely fast improvisational logics based on a closely held understanding of chord changes developed specifically for individual compositions. Jazz, born in the dark gin halls and brothels of New Orleans, Chicago, and Kansas City, later transported to the concert hall and upper-middle-class speakeasy, once again became an indelibly Black art form with rules and codes of its own communal bonding.

Noone, himself devoted to the earliest origins of jazz in New Orleans, looks upon the Second World War "break" with that older heritage as an exciting yet risk-taking enterprise. The Black musician regained artistic identity and cultural solidarity at the expense of losing a large part of the jazz audience, both Black and white. Ironically, as jazz began to reemerge from the internal struggle of its own artistic evolution—a transit into greater popularity in the 1950s and 1960s—the combined traumas that divested North American culture of its idealistic innocence (assassinations, civil rights protests, and a disastrous war in Indochina) assaulted the world of the jazz musician too. The remarkable jazz renaissance of the late 1950s, which can be documented by hundreds of important recordings and dozens of artistically challenging jazz groups, gave way to increasingly strident sounds that replaced acoustic instruments with electronic circuitry. Many Black jazz musicians moved to Europe. Record companies turned from harmonic intricacy to histrionic intensity. Warm-hearted musical excitement seemed inappropriate in an era of cultural upheaval.

The political impact of this marginalizing set of occurrences is subtle. In the late 1960s and throughout the two decades that followed, jazz became an arena for competing artistic preferences and styles—a mélange of under-supported musical outlooks that, together, relegated the art form as a whole to a somewhat rarefied status. Jazz became in those years, as never before, an "art" music rather than a popular music. Only recently, within the last three years perhaps, record companies and several filmmakers have seen that the final members of the Be Bop founding fathers (Dizzy Gillespie and Max Roach) and even more senior survivors (Doc Cheatham and Benny Carter) are still alive and playing vigorously, fully deserving of attention and commercial marketing. Nostalgia, profit, and a vague sense of cultural history have swirled together to give jazz revived interest. Most important of all for this revival has been the potential for sales created by the com-bination of the compact disc reproduction format and out-of-print master recordings that attract new buyers.

Once an art form becomes detached from the organic network that initiates its impulse, the twilight patronage of museum coteries or of aca-demic rescue relegates its purpose to historical memory and potentially elitist pleasure. In the case of jazz something far more vital, far less certain is at work. First, a large group of talented young musicians has been developed in high school and university jazz programs. These musicians seem to be in the process of enriching the highly sophisticated harmonic and lyric complexities developed in the opening phases of the Be Bop movement (from the early 1940s through the late 1950s). At the same moment they are rediscovering songs, instruments, and arrangements pop-ular in the earliest decades of the century. These young musicians are dedicated to preserving the major jazz traditions even as they advance new musical possibilities. The fact that the most glamorous and/or professionally alert among them have been signed to lucrative recording contracts suggests that a new phase in the development of jazz as a popular art may be taking hold, an era that can produce a hybrid "organic" enclave of distinctly well-trained musicians whose connection to jazz history and its communal roots is mediated by professional learning and also commercial savvy. The polit-ical result of this generational revival, headed in some degree by popular "stars" (such as Wynton and Branford Marsalis, Marcus Roberts, Roy Hargrove, Philip Harper, Chris Potter, and others), can be imagined partly in terms of (1) crossing age lines by putting older and younger musicians into artistic interaction (in concerts, clubs, and television settings); (2) crossing racial lines by bringing Black and white and Asian audiences into contact with one another; (3) reawakening interest among Black commu-nities in a body of music created, nurtured, and developed into a permanent cultural significance by Black artists; and (4) slowly, but with some signs of promise, eliminating the long-standing sexist subordination of talented female musicians. Stacy Rowles, trumpeter and flugelhornist; Terri Lynn Carrington, drummer; Gerri Allen, pianist; Jane Ira Bloom, soprano sax-ophonist; Holly Hofmann, jazz flutist: all of these women have gained professional recognition and, collectively, indicate the enormity of a poten-tial that once again cannot be allowed to go unnoticed.

The most profound political consequence that may be able to emerge from the repopularizing retrenchment of jazz from within its own self-animation rests with the consciousness of North American commercial culture. I look at jazz as a cultural archive of the Black community which has marked the entire social logic of twentieth-century life in North America and, to a lesser extent, in Europe and Japan. It may be that music is the lingua franca of all people and all cultures and that jazz is its most common discourse.

Regardless of the entertainment pleasure that jazz brings to Japan and Europe, its legacy in the United States is to remind its citizens of oppression and survival, of justice obliterated and justice demanded. One cannot hear the lyrical beauty of Art Farmer's flugelhorn and not somehow know—or be under the obligation to discover—that the calm intensity of his playing carries an obscure, altogether palpable energy from his Black heritage and his heritage as a part Blackfoot native American. The mixed racial and cultural legacy of Black and Indian songfulness inhabited the music of this century's greatest North American composer, Edward Kennedy ("Duke") Ellington.

I digress a moment from critical theory to share an "interlude" about jazz and its political reach because, as a theorist and as a jazz critic, I cannot *hear* the words of Michel Foucault or Paul de Man without hearing also Louis Armstrong and Charlie Parker. I cannot hear Pops and Bird, in turn, without recognizing the liberating hope and self-eviscerating vigilance at work in theoretical lyricists as forceful as Gayatri Spivak and that stubborn refuser of the great jazz tradition, Edward Said.

Said, of course, scorns music so vulgar and rough with energy as Parker's and Armstrong's and Monk's. To which one notes that even sensitive, well-ventilated minds have their own tonal deafness. The burden of accounting for hope in the political ramifications of a musical art so demoted, misunderstood, and, finally, misrepresented (even by admirers like Stanley Crouch) derives from the unaddressed weight of this nation's malign neglect of its Black heritage, of its Black creativity, of its Black youth left to die in the waste of inner-city squalor, drugs, and violence. As George Bush and the one hundred and first Congress of the United States address Saddam Hussein's annexation of Kuwait—an annexation in part prompted by Bush's State Department's assurance to Hussein, in the summer of 1990, that the United States viewed Iraq's dispute with Kuwait as "an internal Arab matter"—the lives of people of color within our own borders remain unnoticed, unverified.

Observing the unregenerate constancy of that legacy of aggression and disavowal, a critic of jazz and a critic of texts and ideologies has slim reason to be optimistic. My reflection on the political efficacy of a regenerate jazz vanguard comes merely to this. Whatever dignity Black culture may receive in the revisions of hegemonic academic work, it is more likely to gain leverage from its musical than its still ignored literary achievements.

Critical theory at its most interesting constructs a set of "riffs" on problematics rehearsed by other theoretically imaginative improvisationalists. Critics like Spivak and Said and their brooding band of sometimes hostile lovers make possible readings of writers (and painters and actors and musicians, no less) who may be in sympathy with radical political and cultural objectives while being out-of-sync with the verbal world of argumentative dexterity. In such confused territory André Brink's apparently simultaneous resistance to theory and to fascism may offer a form of resistance which rejuvenates the purposes of critical intellect. Brink provides an older, now slightly tattered image of the writer and intellect as rebel. That is an image assaulted, even demoted, in our fancy professionalized era of postmodern hipness. It is demoted because, on one side, the writer and the intellectual are housed for the most part within the very institutions (i.e., universities and publishing enterprises) where contemporary distributions of knowledge gain their force, focus, and authority. The writer-as-rebel, in short, is drastically contradicted by the writer-as-employed. Institutional authority, so discredited and compromised by affiliations with commerce, government, image making, and all the apparatus of credibility and stability, washes over the writer—conferring authority on the writer but de-idealizing the purity of the writer's consciousness and privilege.

Some useful concept of the writer and the teacher as besieged interrogators still can be garnered from the rubble of our suspicious age. Not everyone and everything are fractured all of the time by institutional compromises and by the self-centeredness of personal interests. I cannot resurrect an image of neutrality, objectivity, or phenomenological "bracketing" to alleviate the writer's insertion in the fractious network of human values. But I will assert, along with Brink, a hopeful belief that, after analysis and deconstructive suspicion have done their best or worst, a remainder staggers on to witness and to argue, to comprehend and to subvert. It is not a detached majesterial consciousness that remains. It is not a remnant of Whitmanic self-reflection staggering down the shoreline after songful likeness and the sea's final word. Writers, like teachers, do carry into each act of assertive and interrogative discourse something akin to "awareness, and courage, and humility. And a sense of loyalty to the truth, and to the imperative need to speak it fearlessly."[12]

The role of consciousness heightening, of carving out "representative space" for the careful inspection of codes and images that allow state power to thrive alongside (and within) corporate power: that role is not self-evident in our schools and colleges. No one arrives fresh from graduate school to teach an initial class in rhetoric or on Melville prepared to disrupt conventional understandings about texts, authors, and pedagogical routines. Whatever challenge to school and student expectations any teacher creates from the mix of experience and theory surely relies upon awareness and courage and humility. Thus, the teacher's obligation, like the writer's, is to have a burdened future ever in sight without evasion. Confronted by heroic trivia, commercial glut, we take refuge in texts and theory with the resistances they bring and the resistances they prompt. One resistance is the refuge our profession's romance with Theory offers the critical writer. This refuge is, in fact, a retreat when it becomes a self-performing display of academic knowledge. Despite the self-authorizations at work in opposing that romance, despite the need to succumb to Theory's weight even at the moment of tactical differentiation, I find André Brink's statement of courage and humility to be a step toward alert and collective resistance within the institutional logic of intellectual work. Such resistance is not directed at Theory as an institution but to Theory's inadvert disablement in the cause of letting people who are seldom heard speak.

In the work of that ambition this essay is dedicated to my friend and colleague Benny Golson, and to the memory of the late Jimmie Noone, Jr. (1938–91).

NOTES

1. Cornell West, *The American Evasion of Philosophy: A Genealogy of Pragmatism* (Madison: University of Wisconsin Press, 1988), 5.

2. Ibid., 5.

3. The bright career and dim aftermath of Paul de Man's position in the world of academic criticism are summarized by David Lehman in *Signs of the Times: Deconstruction and the Fall of Paul de Man* (New York: Poseidon Press, 1991). The issue of contention is the anti-Semitic journal articles that de Man wrote as a young writer for *Le Soir* newspaper in Brussels during the Nazi occupation.

4. Jim Merod, *The Political Responsibility of the Critic* (Ithaca, N.Y.: Cornell University Press, 1987).

5. As an "assignment" for the committed student of theory who wishes to plot differences between more and less politically engaged uses of theory, I might point toward the journal *Representations* (based at the University of California–Berkeley) and a considerably more interrogative, institutionally directed Foucauldian critique to be found in the writing of Paul Bové and the writers associated with the journal *boundary 2* (based at the University of Pittsburgh).

6. "Naming," interview, with Gayatri Chakravorty Spivak and Maria Koundara, *Stanford Humanities Review* 1 (1989): 88–89.

7. André Brink, *Writing in a State of Siege* (New York: Summit Books, 1983), 228.

8. Gayatri Chakravorty Spivak, *In Other Worlds: Essays in Cultural Politics* (New York: Methuen, 1987), 14.

9. Edward Said, *The World, the Text, and the Critic* (Cambridge: Harvard University Press, 1983), 29.

10. Spivak, "Naming," 97.

11. Spivak, *In Other Worlds*, 268.

12. Brink, *Writing*, 13.

Comedy about the Failure of Comedy: Stand-up Comedy and Postmodernism

Philip Auslander

One of the cultural phenomena of the 1980s has been the rebirth of stand-up comedy as a popular form of performance. *Variety*, with typical alacrity, observes that "Wags Wax Weightier in Show World."[1] The appearance of films, plays, novels, and television programs about stand-up comedians and their milieux, as well as the all-comedy cable television services on the horizon, are indices to the current power of the stand-up comedian as a cultural icon. This phenomenon can be traced to several causes. The Los Angeles comedians' strike of 1979 against nonpaying "showcase" clubs, which resulted in stand-up comedy's becoming a paying profession beyond the limited opportunities offered by Las Vegas, elegant nightclubs interested only in big-name entertainers, and television talk and variety shows, ushered in the current boom in comedy clubs. Whereas in the 1950s and 1960s the primary venues available to stand-up comics were music clubs and strip bars, where they were always relegated to "opening act" status, the comedy club purveys comedy itself as its primary commodity. In 1964 there were two comedy clubs in the United States, both in New York City. By the mid 1970s New York and Los Angeles both provided homes to showcase comedy clubs. In 1980 there were ten paying clubs across the United States; today there is a circuit of over three hundred clubs nationally, with about two thousand working comedians filling their nightly bills.[2]

Another central cause of the renaissance in stand-up comedy is cable television. Network television has traditionally offered stand-up comedians very few opportunities to ply their primary trade: comedians have usually appeared as performers in sketches or as actors in situation comedies. The few openings available for the actual performance of stand-up comedy were (and still are) largely limited to brief spots on variety and talk shows (*The Tonight Show* with Johnny Carson and *Late Night with David Letterman* are the major venues of this sort currently). Cable television networks, beginning with the Home Box Office channel (HBO) in 1975, have been willing and able to offer stand-up comics places in programs which duplicate the conditions under which they perform in clubs (e.g., a series of comedians, each doing a ten-minute set), or even their own hour-long specials. Such specials are inexpensive to produce (compared with made-for-cable movies, for example) and have helped to make watching stand-up comedy a regular practice for many viewers, who are then more inclined than ever before to seek out comedy in clubs. Like the clubs outside of New York and Los Angeles, comedy programs on smaller cable networks have become career stepping stones for some comics, who eventually get major national exposure on Carson or Letterman, television or film acting roles, even television commercials or positions as the hosts of game shows.[3] Robin Williams, Michael Keaton, and Roseanne Barr are among the stand-up comics who have launched successful film and television acting careers. Judy Tenuta, who has had relatively little network television exposure, was nevertheless chosen to do a series of commercials for Dr Pepper based on her stand-up act.

Current stand-up comedy is a distinctive, perhaps distinctly post-modern, performance mode, which must be understood in terms of its relation to other postmodern performance discourses and to a specific, culturally and generationally defined audience. Stand-up comedy is no longer confined to the cultural ghetto that stretched from burlesque houses to the Borscht Belt but has become a primary source of entertainment for a middle-class, cable-viewing, club-going audience.[4] The comedians themselves are mostly, like their audiences, of the baby boom generation, middle-class and suburban in origin. This is a new development in stand-up comedy, which has been historically a medium dominated by performers who stressed their urban, immigrant origins.[5] Such comedy was implicitly the response of a relative outsider to a hostile environment. Today's stand-up comedy, by contrast, is for and by the socially and culturally enfranchised: white, middle-class professionals of the baby boom generation.[6] Stand-up comedy currently occupies an ambiguous position on a smooth cultural continuum with two other performance modes also chiefly supported by the same audience: performance art and rock music. I will argue here that the cultural positioning of current stand-up comedy reflects the postmodern breakdown of distinctions among cultural discourses but also that the present form of stand-up comedy is largely shaped and limited by its relation to that most determining of postmodern cultural forces, the mass media. In these respects it is comparable to rock music as a cultural discourse that appeals to and can be used to exploit the particular desires and anxieties of the baby boom generation.

One of the hallmarks of postmodern culture is the breakdown of distinctions between "high" and "mass," or "popular," culture. Traditionally, art world performance might fall into the former category, and rock music and stand-up comedy would surely fall into the latter. Today, however, the work of specific practitioners of any of these performance modes can occupy liminal positions between categories, or, more precisely, they can occupy different categories simultaneously. Laurie Anderson is a performance artist whose work blurs the distinction between performance art and rock music. The videotape of performance artist Spalding Gray's monologue *Terrors of Pleasure* appears in a tape series called "Comedy Club." (While many of the performances in this series were in fact recorded in clubs, the Gray tape was recorded at Lincoln Center, which, in another blurring of cultural realms, may now perhaps be regarded as the nation's largest comedy club.) The printed versions of his monologues can be found in the Humor section of many bookstores, alongside collections by the likes of Art Buchwald and Erma Bombeck (and most books by stand-up comedians) and at some distance from the Fine Arts section, where books containing records of the work of other performance artists may be found. Conversely, Whoopi Goldberg was often described as a performance artist early in her career; she, along with stand-up comics as diverse as Lily Tomlin and Jackie Mason, has performed an extended stand-up act as a Broadway production. Stand-up comic Sandra Bernhard occupies this ambiguous cultural territory self-consciously: although she appears on television as a stand-up comic, she describes herself in a program note as a "rock and roll performance artist" and appeared at the head of a rock band in her otherwise solo off-Broadway show, *Without You, I'm Nothing*.

One result of this blurring is that both performance artists and stand-up comics currently enjoy enormous cultural mobility, eliding distinctions between forms of performance, high art and popular culture, and the traditional distinctions among audiences which go along with them. Thus, Spalding Gray, to cite but one example, has access to the audience for downtown New York performance but also to the cable television and home videotape audiences in the guise of a stand-up comic. His recent performance on the New York stage in Thornton Wilder's *Our Town*, which was stylistically of a piece with his other performances, made him available to yet another audience. That his work has succeeded in these different (though overlapping) cultural realms presumably enhances his marketability as an actor in films and on television. The point here is that Gray is not unique in this respect: a number of performers from both the high and mass cultural ends of the continuum are enjoying similar mobility (e.g., stand-up comics-cum-actors Steve Martin and Robin Williams in Beckett's *Waiting for Godot*; rock musician Sting acting in films and on stage in Brecht's *Threepenny Opera*).[7]

If the distinctions between stand-up comedy and performance art are blurry at the level of their dissemination through cultural categories, media, and institutions, they are no less so at the formal level. Just as monologic performance art like Gray's has wandered into the stand-up comedy category, some of the more extravagant, self-reflexive, and extreme versions of stand-up comedy—the work of Steve Martin, Andy Kaufman, "Bobcat" Goldthwait, and Sam Kinison, for example—could easily be called performance art if presented in art venues instead of in comedy clubs or on television, as could the multiple-character comedy of Lily Tomlin and Whoopi Goldberg. Similarly, some performance art, notably Eric Bogosian's early pieces, reflects the influence of post–Lenny Bruce stand-up comedy; Bogosian's multiple-character style is formally close to Tomlin and Goldberg as well. Goldthwait, who is openly hostile to performance art and to calling stand-up comedy "art," both of which he considers pretentious, nevertheless tacitly acknowledges the lack of formal distinction between them in the following, typically acerbic, comment: "Last night there was a lull in my act, and I said, 'Jesus, one more lull and I'm going to be a performance artist.'"[8]

If stand-up comedy's shading into performance art is a relatively recent phenomenon, its relation to rock music has a longer history. It has become virtually a commonplace among culture watchers that stand-up comics have supplanted rock stars as the cultural icons of the baby boom generation. Stephen Holden, a popular music critic for the *New York Times*, has formalized this relation by equating comic styles with musical styles: Roseanne Barr's comedy with "country-pop," Steven Wright's with new wave music, Sam Kinison's with hard rock, etc.[9] Although these equations are fairly arbitrary, the idea that stand-up comedy is a fellow traveler of rock music is a valuable insight into stand-up comedy's cultural positioning. During the 1970s the practice of referring to full-length performances by stand-up comics as "concerts" evolved. Rock musicians and stand-up comedians also pioneered the college campus entertainment circuit. In the absence of other opportunities prior to the current renaissance, many comedians followed the musicians' practice of touring campuses. Because these comedians would frequently open for rock groups, they had to develop styles of comedy which would appeal to the rock audience.

Since the 1960s the record has been a central medium for stand-up comics. The popularity of Bill Cosby and George Carlin, in particular, derives to a very great extent from their successful recordings of the 1960s and 1970s. Their admirers would frequently treat comedy bits from the records as if they were popular songs, memorizing and repeating them. The ability of cable television to promote stand-up comedy depends in large part on the audience's willingness to treat comedy routines like popular songs, as performances they are willing to experience verbatim over and over again. The conventional wisdom has long been that television destroys comics by devouring material that may have taken years to develop in a few minutes' broadcast to a huge, nationwide audience. In fact, however, the cable networks have discovered that audiences *will* go to see the same comedy routines performed "live" that they have already seen on television, that they *want* to see the comic perform his or her "greatest hits."[10]

Richard Fields, owner of the New York showcase comedy club Catch a Rising Star, sees a link between the increased popularity of stand-up comedy and a decline of interest in rock music. In his view the stand-up comic has become a substitute for the countercultural rock star. In Fields's opinion rock itself became too overtly commodified:

> What happned is that rock and roll became the way to sell Pepsi and blue jeans—it became a multi-million dollar business, and people got fed up; they were looking for something else. As a result of this, a new, unaffected form of entertainment came up—a thing called comedy. The comic comes in with a little manilla envelope, no heavy equipment.[11]

Both the appeal of stand-up comedy and its commodity status are considerably more complex than Fields suggests, however. Stand-up comedy is a fundamentally old-fashioned, labor-intensive, low-tech performance mode. The circuit of clubs the comedian must travel, frequently by car, is reminiscent of nothing so much as the vaudeville circuits of the nineteenth and early twentieth centuries. The microphone and spotlight are the only necessary technologies; the human presence remains paramount. While these features distinguish stand-up comedy from the many technologically oriented, decentering postmodern performance modes, I would argue that they are consonant with another aspect of the postmodern sensibility. Like much of postmodern culture, stand-up comedy purveys "the shock of the old," the sense of the eternal return of cultural forms.[12] Fredric Jameson identifies "the nostalgia mode" as an essential constituent of the postmodern sensibility.[13] Indeed, there is a kind of retro chic in going to a club to see a comedian, an activity that seems to belong to an earlier period yet, paradoxically, is very much a product of the cable television revolution.

The appeal of this retro chic is not lost on the largely yuppie audience that patronizes comedy clubs. Neither is it lost on the owners and designers of the clubs: the bare brick wall is the central icon of comedy club decoration, whether or not the club is in a building that is so constructed. (The bare brick wall has also been recreated in the sets for television programs, which are meant to suggest the ambience of a comedy club.) Presumably, the image of the comedian performing before that bare brick wall is meant to evoke the cultural memory of Lenny Bruce performing in those celebrated "toilets," the strip clubs, and that of the Greenwich Village folk music clubs where the stand-up comedians of the next generation got their start. (Despite their lack of success, the Smothers Brothers' recent return to television is another example of nostalgia for the latter cultural moment.)

It is important to note in this context the association of stand-up comedy with the counterculture of the 1960s. Tony Hendra, formerly an editor of the *National Lampoon*, analyzes what he calls "boomer humor," which he sees as an essentially anarchic, countercultural response to the complacency of the postwar period paralleling the countercultural moment in rock music.[14] For Hendra the neoconservatism of the Reagan years spelled the end for this anarchic impulse.[15] Other observers of comedy agree: comedian George Carlin, for example, describes the social attitude of the typical American comedy audience today as "Play the game, make some money, get a nice house, try to keep the kids out of jail and fucking retire." Betsy Borns, who quotes this statement, suggests that perhaps the baby boomers seek to allay some of their guilt at having abandoned their idealism through vicarious experience, by watching comedians who, simply by virtue of being comedians, adopt nonconformist postures.[16]

Taken together, then, the old-fashionedness of stand-up comedy as a performance practice, its self-conscious association with the protest song movement and counterculture of the 1960s, and the sense that it continues to offer a kind of immediacy and accessibility that rock music, in its current corporate guise, has lost, enable its audience to feel that it has not abandoned its own earlier (or, by now, its parents') activist idealism and cultural landmarks. But this comforting feeling is the product of vicarious experience within an ahistorical environment that in fact has little to do with the eras and impulses it evokes. Paradoxically, the current audience for stand-up comedy wants to be reassured of its 1960s credentials but does not want its relatively conservative and conformist values challenged.[17] Many young comedians, members of the same generation as their audiences, are happy to oblige by referring primarily to the popular culture of the early and mid 1960s, the songs, television programs, and cartoons their audiences enjoyed as youngsters. Carol Leifer, for example, does a funny routine in which she mocks popular songs like Petula Clark's "Don't Sleep in the Subway" and Richard Harris's "MacArthur's Park" as if they were of immediate, current concern. The point is that, to her comedy club audiences, many of whom probably switched off "oldies" or "classic rock" radio stations before entering the club, they are. A specific version of the 1960s is reified in current stand-up comedy: the stereotypical early 1960s of comfortable, suburban living, not the political 1960s, the Vietnam 1960s, the civil rights 1960s. Where those years and issues are evoked they are evoked in terms of pleasant cultural memories, focusing particularly on the music. This phenomenon would seem to justify Jameson's fear that postmodern culture is a "pathological symptom of a society that has become incapable of dealing with time and history" and is therefore "condemned to seek the historical past through our own pop images and stereotypes about that past."[18] At stake here is a kind of willed amnesia; as Tom Shales puts it, "When baby boomers became yuppies, they were anxious to forget the disillusion that had set in when the Sixties fizzled and the Seventies congealed. They want comedy now that reminds them of safer, saner times, not Vietnam and Watergate and political assassinations."[19] It comes as no surprise to find that there are very few comedians around who do topical, political material. Most of those comedians whose work retains a political edge generally belong, like Carlin, to the previous generation of comedians.

Current stand-up comedy, then, typically assuages baby boomer/yuppie guilt at having abandoned the ideals of the 1960s by depoliticizing the 1960s, rewriting that era nostalgically as a simpler time when it was possible to have the idyllic childhood that baby boomers fear their own children are not having. The comedy club has become a refuge for a generation caught in a popular cultural vacuum, too old for stadium rock, too young for Las Vegas. Going to a nightclub (as opposed to a rock concert or disco) is a leisure-time activity that, until recently, would have been associated with the generation preceding that of the baby boomers. Discos are passé, however, and adult baby boomers seldom go to rock concerts, except as a self-consciously nostalgic act, unless accompanying their children. The comedy club thus permits the baby boomers a limited identification with their parents, which may serve to reassure them of their own upward mobility at a time when many people their age have no hope of even matching their parents' standard of living, while simultaneously stressing their origins as children of the 1960s.

Despite Fields's characterization of stand-up comedy as an alternative to overly commodified rock music, the institutional contexts of stand-up comedy (e.g., the comedy club, cable television) raise questions about how genuine or long-standing such (relative) noncommodity status can be. Borns observes that the cable companies' initial decision to feature stand-up comedy was a demographic one: "cable programmers targeted their product to a particular audience they felt was most likely to pay for television."[20] Stand-up comedy seems to be already well on its way to the same commodity status that Fields believes ruined rock music, as comedians are called upon to host game shows, those monuments to consumerism, and to use their stand-up personae and routines to promote products directly (e.g., Jay Leno's Doritos commercials, Judy Tenuta's ads for Dr Pepper). Simon Frith's account of the use of rock music in advertising is applicable to stand-up comedy as well. Frith emphasizes that rock music of the 1960s, especially, has become a valuable tool for advertisers because

> the aging rock audience already believes it has lost its hold on the rock secret, which is why the advertisers' smooth promises touch us. Nostalgia and authenticity provide salespeople with such effective patter because we do believe that rock's aim was once true, our desires once unequivocal.[21]

As I have tried to show, it is this same nostalgic desire for authenticity (in the sense of "authentic," as opposed to cynical, commodified, popular culture) which underlies the appeal of stand-up comedy to the baby boomer audience, the desire to believe either that one has not altogether lost touch with the "rock secret" (in the broadest cultural sense of that phrase) after all or that one can at least project oneself back to an earlier time when one clearly was in possession of it. For this reason a stand-up comic can lend his or her sales pitch the same appearance of authenticity that a Beatles song can give a Nike running shoe commercial and thus deliver "the elusive upwardly mobile baby boom audience" to the advertiser.[22]

Frith further describes what he calls "the rock version of the postmodern condition: a media complex in which music only has meaning as long as it keeps circulating, [and] 'authentic' sounds are only recognized by their place in a system of signs."[23] Stand-up comedy seems to be taking its place within this same circulation: as with rock musicians, the comedians' personae, as much as their work, become the "authentic" elements exploited for their commercial potential. Such exploitation, in turn, creates the conditions for the production of ever more exploitable comedy. Topical comedy is deemphasized because it does not circulate easily through the media complex; since its references become dated, it cannot be used profitably over and over again. This would also account for the success of comedy that is based largely on the past, which remains fixed, rather than the ever-shifting present. Also, as Hendra observes, comedy, which used to take the media complex itself as its object of commentary, seems now to want to replicate the very thing it formerly critiqued.[24] Not only do current comedians use television programs as the subjects of much of their humor, the form of their work replicates that of television programs themselves. Shales points out that Robin Williams, for example, not only draws his material from television but "is television incarnate, a frantic dervish of flash images offered up for our recognition if not precisely our delectation."

He goes on to observe that most stand-up comedy now, unlike Williams's, is "delivered in a conversational style that is synchronized with the talk-show rhythms of television."[25] David Marc, in a discussion of television situation comedy, distinguishes stand-up comedy from television comedy by arguing that, whereas the situation comedy is "the technology of the assembly-line brought to art," "stand-up comedy is a surviving bastion of individual expression."[26] In fact, however, this distinction too is eroding as stand-up comedy recreates the experience of television, even in live performance. The absence of topical comedy and the degree to which stand-up comedy, in both conversational and more overtly performative styles, has come to resemble television itself are symptomatic of the cultural conditions described by Frith in his account of the current state of rock music.

Clearly, these conditions militate against the production of comedy as a substantial discourse. The nostalgic nature of current stand-up comedy is symptomatic not just of the baby boomers' ambiguous relation to their own history but also of a more widespread cultural malaise. Shales calls it "the comedy of anomie," "the comedy of not being precisely sure what's funny" in a world that may not even exist tomorrow.[27] Marc sees "a heroic quality" in stand-up comedy: "If the threat of atomic doom has reduced us to powerless resentful children awaiting punishment, it is difficult to resist the bigmouth who can spit in the eye of civilization with a bit of grace."[28] While Marc may have identified one aspect of stand-up comedy's current appeal, he does not take into sufficient account the cultural and institutional contexts in which stand-up comedy is presented. As my analysis shows, stand-up comedy as a discourse is so caught up in and dependent upon the circulation system of postmodern consumer culture that it can hardly be said to be in a position to spit. What one might refer to as "early postmodern stand-up comedy," the comedy of the late 1970s, seemed to acknowledge both the impotence of comedy to address the nuclear age and its inevitable complicity with the media complex. This work qualifies as postmodern "pastiche" in Jameson's sense:

> Pastiche is, like parody, the imitation of a peculiar or unique style, the wearing of a stylistic mask, speech in a dead language: but it is a neutral practice of such mimicry without parody's ulterior motive, without the satirical impulse, without laughter, without that still latent feeling that there exists something *normal* compared to which what is being imitated is rather comic.[29]

Steve Martin's stand-up comedy exemplifies this tendency perfectly: Martin adopts the gestures, tone, and manner of the traditional stand-up comedian, of a rather desperate comedian, in fact, who will resort to wearing rabbit ears or a fake arrow through his head to get a laugh. But Martin's pastiche of stand-up comedy is void of content; his persona is likewise blank and cynical, obviously only going through the motions of seeming to want the audience's attention and affection. An even more extreme case is that of the late Andy Kaufman, whose comic personae seemed designed to mock the cult of show business personalities. Kaufman's work derived its force, however, from the fact that it became harder and harder to tell if Kaufman really was a satirist or if he was metamorphosing schizophrenically into the very thing he was satirizing. As his televised publicity stunts became more and more extreme (e.g., offering to wrestle with women on various programs), the possibility that he was not so much parodying the excesses encouraged by the media's promise of celebrity as simply *enacting* them became more and more distinct.

I do not want to say that this performance work was anything less than conceptually brilliant or that it elicited no laughter. The laughter, however, was frequently either a sort of conditioned response (i.e., in the presence of something that looks like comedy, we laugh) or the nearest possible approximation to an appropriate response to a discomfiting situation. Comedy writer Anne Beatts has described Martin's work, in particular, as "comedy about the failure of comedy."[30] She means that such comedy seems to have given up on the possibility that comedy could function as a significant critical discourse on the model of classical satire and settles for the mannerisms of comedy as a dead language. In fact, all postmodern stand-up comedy is comedy about the failure of comedy. The early postmodern comedy of the late 1970s takes the failure of comedy, the impossibility of being a comedian, as its premise. The more recent comedy of the comedy club boom retreats from that premise to the more traditional notion that comedy can have content but demonstrates the failure of comedy as a critical discourse through its appeal to nostalgia and complicity with consumerism.

We can align these two moments of postmodern stand-up comedy with the two kinds of laughter described by Herbert Blau in his trenchant essay "Comedy since the Absurd." Early postmodern stand-up comedy gives rise to a laughter whose origin is unclear: "we may be laughing anyhow, not knowing what else to do or unable to control it or—isn't that the living end—we may be laughing intolerably at ourselves, not knowing where the laughter comes from, or if the spastic noise we're making is really a laugh." The alternative to this grim laughter that may not be laughter is "the pallid laughter of amnesia," to which so much current nostalgic stand-up comedy surely gives rise.[31]

Our evaluation of current stand-up comedy, however, need not be exclusively negative. Perhaps the single most significant development of the current stand-up comedy boom is the fact that more women comics than ever before are finding audiences. Although the cultural positioning of stand-up comedy makes its potential as a critical practice questionable regardless of the comic's gender, women comics are in the best position to restore a critical edge to stand-up comedy, and many of the best are doing just that. I have treated this issue at length elsewhere;[32] for my purpose here, I will only note that throughout its history stand-up comedy has been a male-dominated form. Even the performance dynamic of stand-up comedy, in which the comic seeks to dominate and control the audience and its responses with the phallic microphone, seems to make it an unlikely candidate as a women's performance practice.

Our society sees joke telling as an unacceptably aggressive behavior for women, and stigmatizes the funny woman. Joke telling is a male preserve because humor is linked with power; women are supposed to be the objects of jokes, not joking subjects. In this context the disruption of norms for what (and who) is funny, which Jameson cites as a feature of postmodern culture, is not at all a bad thing. The frequent appearance of women on the stand-up comedy stage is a breakthrough with genuine social implications which may highlight a realignment of gender roles within our society. Female comics bring previously unrepresented perspectives, and a host of new ideas and sensibilities, to the stand-up comedy stage. For a woman to do stand-up comedy at all, given its traditional identification with male dominance, may be a political act in itself.

NOTES

1. Joe Cohen, "Wags Wax Weightier in Show World," *Variety* 24 (August 1987): 69.

2. This background information derives from Betsy Borns, *Comic Lives: Inside the World of American Stand-up Comedy* (New York: Simon and Schuster, 1987), 30–45. Borns provides a thorough account of current stand-up comedy in the United States, its practitioners and milieux. For useful discussions of the recent history of stand-up comedy in the United States, see David Marc, *Comic Visions: Television Comedy and American Culture* (Boston: Unwin Hyman, 1989), 12–19, 33–40; and Tony Hendra, *Going Too Far* (New York: Doubleday, 1987), pt. 1. Hendra generally provides a useful critical context for contemporary stand-up and television comedy. For general journalistic accounts of stand-up comedy's newfound popularity, see Jim Geoghan, "Waiter, There's a Joke in My Soup," *New York Times*, 20 August 1989, sec. 2, 1+; Alvin P. Sanoff, "Climbing the Ladder of Laughs," *U.S. News & World Report* (12 September 1988): 56–58; and Richard Zoglin, "Stand-up Comedy on a Roll: A Thriving Club Scene Primes Stars of the Future," *Time* (24 August 1987): 56–57. Tom Shales provides a more acute, culturally critical journalistic account in "Is Comedy Making a Comeback or What? America Laughs Again!" *Esquire* (October 1987): 118–29. Geoghan cites an estimate that suggests that, currently, there may be as many as ten thousand practicing stand-up comedians in the United States.

3. See Borns, *Comic Lives*, 45–52.

4. It may be provocative in this context to observe that in 1989 there were exactly as many comedy clubs in the United States as there were regional theaters.

5. See Geoghan, "Waiter," 36; Marc, *Comic Visions*, 38–43.

6. I am not suggesting, of course, that all comedians or audience members are white, middle-class professionals, although Black comedians, for example, frequently note how few Blacks there are in the typical comedy club audience. To achieve large-scale success, any comic, regardless of gender, class, or ethnic identity, must find a way of addressing the audience I have described, though there are also specific venues in which other audiences can enjoy comedy.

7. I have discussed this cultural phenomenon and its implications in greater detail in my article "Going With the Flow: Performance Art and Mass Culture," *Drama Review* 33, no. 2 (1989): 119–36.

8. As quoted in Borns, *Comic Lives*, 287.

9. Stephen Holden, "Comic Pedigrees," *New York Times*, 20 August 1989, sec. 2, 37.

10. Borns, *Comic Lives*, 50.

11. As quoted in Ibid., 54.

12. Charles Jencks, *What Is Postmodernism?* (New York: St. Martin's Press, 1986), 43.

13. Fredric Jameson, "Postmodernism and Consumer Society," in *Postmodernism and Its Discontents: Theories, Practices*, ed. E. Ann Kaplan (London and New York: Verso, 1988), 18–20.

14. Of particular interest is Hendra's discussion of the simultaneous evolution of psychedelic rock and the brand of social and political satire represented by The Committee, an improvisational comedy group in San Francisco during the 1960s (*Going Too Far*, chaps. 7,8).

15. Ibid., 452. One particularly disturbing manifestation of cultural neoconservatism is the racist and misogynist material with which some comics, notably Sam Kinison and Andrew Dice Clay, have found success. Jon Pareles has pointed out parallels between this development and similar expressions in recent popular music, especially heavy metal and rap ("There's a New Sound in Pop Music: Bigotry," *New York Times*, 10 September 1989, sec. 2, 1+). This is not a simple issue. As David Marc reminds us, stand-up comics do not appear before us as themselves but as fictive personae (*Comic Visions*, 17–18). Just as we would not necessarily censure a playwright whose characters express such attitudes, we should hesitate to censure a stand-up comic whose persona expresses them. Tom Shales even suggests that such comedy may be "an antidote to complacent Reaganism instead of just another exploitation of 'the mood of the country' " precisely because of its lack of restraint and decorum, its outrageousness ("Is Comedy Making a Comeback," 126). In the final analysis, what may be most disturbing about this development is not that a small number of performers undertake to display such personae but, rather, that their audiences have responded by making them stars.

16. Borns, *Comic Lives*, 52–53.

17. This combination of conflicting desires is illustrated perfectly in an episode of the current incarnation of "The Twilight Zone" television series, itself a revival of a series popular when the baby boomers were children. Entitled "The Girl That I Married," this episode depicts the travails of a burnt-out yuppie lawyer who is beginning to feel angst at having abandoned his youthful idealism (he's a corporate attorney instead of a public defender, etc.). He enters into an affair with his own wife's eighteen-year-old hippie self, brought to life from a photograph. Through her, he rediscovers some of his old passion; she also compels him to try to explain how the 1960s became the 1980s. Eventually, she persuades him to leave her own older self. He resolves to do so, only to discover that his wife has been carrying on an affair with *his* own younger self, a bearded idealist (the dead giveaway is that she's been rereading *Siddhartha*). The two acknowledge that they admire the passion and fire of their younger selves but also admit that they were beginning to find their arrogance and naïveté tedious. They console themselves by affirming that their lives are not over, that they can still act in a socially conscious fashion. The lawyer resolves to "put in some time" at the local legal aid clinic, while his wife suggests that they have a baby. This story, with its self-serving, sentimental, and complacent resolution, is a telling dramatization of the mood I have been describing.

18. Jameson, "Postmodernism," 20.

19. Shales, "Is Comedy Making a Comeback," 120.

20. Borns, *Comic Lives*, 49–50.

21. Simon Frith, "Picking Up the Pieces," in *Facing the Music*, ed. Simon Frith (New York: Pantheon Books, 1988), 90–91.

22. Borns, *Comic Lives*, 52.

23. Frith, "Picking Up the Pieces," 91.

24. Hendra, *Going Too Far*, 426–47.

25. Shales, "Is Comedy Making a Comeback," 120.

26. Marc, *Comic Visions*, 13, 12.

27. Shales, "Is Comedy Making a Comeback," 118.

28. Marc, *Comic Visions*, 13.

29. Jameson, "Postmodernism," 16.

30. From an interview with Anne Beatts published in Denise Collier and Kathleen Beckett, *Spare Ribs: Women in the Humor Biz* (New York: St. Martin's Press, 1980), 34.

31. Herbert Blau, "Comedy since the Absurd," *The Eye of Prey: Subversions of the Postmodern* (Bloomington: Indiana University Press, 1987), 35, 39–40.

32. I have discussed the issues specific to women's stand-up comedy in my article "'Brought to You by Fem Rage': Stand-up Comedy and the Politics of Gender," forthcoming in *Feminism and Performance: Text and Theory*, ed. Lynda Hart and Peggy Phelan (Ann Arbor: University of Michigan Press).

Performing All Our Lives: AIDS, Performance, Community

David Román

Felix, Jack, Bert, Chet, Andre, Johnny—these are but a few of the names of the recent dead. All of these men died of complications due to AIDS. But what distinguishes these gay men from countless others is that their deaths have all been performed in contemporary theaters, both national and regional, in plays written by contemporary American gay male play-wrights.[1] My interest is to contextualize these deaths within a larger canvas of current gay male performative practices as well as to critically interrogate the ramifications of these recent cultural representations of gay men, AIDS, and the dead. My aim here is twofold. First, I am interested in the politics of representation and reception of the rather recent phenomenon of main-stream American gay plays and the formal designs of realist drama from which these works often borrow. And, second, I look for alternative/oppositional models of representation in gay male culture which address, from an activist standpoint, the interrelated issues of AIDS, performance, and community.

Performing All Our Lives: AIDS

> AIDS activists know that silence equals death, but we also know that this cannot be *said*, it must be *performed* in an anarchistic politics that sometimes coincides with and supports the political action of our allies working within the unitary power system, but sometimes contradicts it, or seems simply mad in the traditional public realm.
>
> —Cindy Patton, *Inventing AIDS*

Recent queries into cultural responses to AIDS have been critical of domi-nant discourses—from the media, the law, science, for example—that dictate a monolithic presentation of a so-called reality of AIDS, one in which conservative mainstays of "family" and "nation" are threatened.[2] Yet cul-tural critics of the arts have gone further by implicating those, including gay people, who abide by the liberal perspective that there is a scientific reality of AIDS which posits a rational and, thus, acceptable response to the epidemic. Douglas Crimp explains the ramifications of this type of thinking in relation to the arts: "Within the arts, the scientific explanation and management of AIDS is largely taken for granted, and it therefore largely assumed that cultural producers can respond to the epidemic in only two ways: by raising money for scientific research and service organi-zations or by creating works that express the human suffering and loss."[3]

For Crimp and many others what is needed most to combat the misrepresentations of AIDS are cultural practices that intervene into dominant cultural discourses and representations in order to destabilize the fictions constructed by an ideology that posits such fictions as essential truths about AIDS.[4] Furthermore, instead of simply accepting an aesthetic idealist notion of art as transcendent, artists should recognize the capacity of art to critically engage in the historical moment that constructs AIDS. The role of the gay-identified artist is especially critical in such a project, particularly in order to challenge the anxiety-prone and fantasy-laden heterosexist depictions of gay men equated *as* AIDS.

While cultural critics, artists, and AIDS activists have since been successful in scrutinizing the politics of representation within the media and popular culture at large, the theater has been surprisingly dislocated from such discussions and projects.[5] This is not to say, of course, that the theater has not given birth to a vital cultural response to AIDS. What I suggest instead is that the theater's cultural response to AIDS has not engendered the type of discussion actively debated within the other arts. A quick perusal of a handful of recent AIDS plays and their cultural reception may establish my point. Many of these plays by gay men which deal directly with AIDS have been celebrated by both mainstream and gay audiences for their compassionate portrayal of people with AIDS and their loved ones. From Larry Kramer's *The Normal Heart* (1985) up through William Finn's *Falsettoland* (1990) gay men have been heroicly maneuvered from a previously marginalized space on the peripherals of the plot to center stage. If early mainstream American plays depicted gay men as degenerates who threaten the morality of the family and the country, the new American plays written by gay-identified playwrights present "ordinary" gay men who struggle valiantly against all odds in the catastrophe of AIDS. Kramer's *The Normal Heart* best exemplifies these early AIDS plays that attempt to normalize gay behavior within the context of a larger humanity. Ned, the play's protagonist, speaks the ethos of this sentiment: "I don't want to be considered different."[6] In fact, Kramer has the characters of *The Normal Heart* go to great lengths to demonstrate just how conventional they are in terms of how they live their lives. They just happen to be gay, happen to be dying of AIDS.

The Normal Heart can be seen as a play that participates in a double mission: on the one hand, Kramer is urgent in his demand to disseminate to a large, mainstream audience necessary information about AIDS. The theater becomes the arena in which social issues are offered for discussion, speculation, debate. On the other hand, Kramer seems equally committed to dramatizing what his protagonist claims is a "culture that isn't just sexual." Indeed, Kramer goes so far as to have Ned Weeks and his lover marry, offering the traditional closure of conventional narratives of heterosexual love.[7] Kramer's choice to use theater as the medium successfully engaged its mainstream audiences to feel for its protagonists by universalizing such issues as love, sexuality, and death. Furthermore, Kramer's choice of realist techniques of engagement and empathy secure such a response.

Douglas Crimp, one of the few critics to challenge the play, finds most disturbing precisely Kramer's employment of these elements of nineteenth-century realist theater: "The genre employed by Kramer will dictate a reactionary content of a different kind: because the play is written within the most traditional conventions of bourgeois theater, its politics are the politics of bourgeois individualism."[8] What's striking, however, is not so much the complaint against Kramer but, rather, how gay-identified theater chooses at this point to assimilate within the confines of mainstream production. Just as feminist theater in its early phases attempted to stage positive representations of women, Kramer, like many of his contemporaries, holds a belief in the attributes of realist theater to postulate positive images of gay men without considering the effects of the realist form.[9] Furthermore, to complicate the issue Kramer's play offers yet a second traditional closure typical of realist theater: death. Realist drama is so imbedded in the prevailing ideology of naturalized heterosexuality in dominant culture that it offers no representational position for gay men or lesbians which is not marginal or a site of defeat.

Still, my point here is neither to contest Kramer's choice of genre nor disclaim its activist base. At its historical moment it was politically necessary to stage AIDS in order to educate mainstream audiences as well as to document and initiate discussion about AIDS from a gay male outlook. From this perspective *The Normal Heart* succeeded in its mission, having been staged almost continuously at the Public Theater in New York City from 1985 to 1988 and thus reaching a wide population. Nonetheless, one of the ramifications of this style of play—the "way we live now" syndrome—is that the representation of gay people with AIDS only solidifies dominant images of gay men. As Stuart Marshall writes on the images of gay men within television and printed media, "Death and homosexuality are now inseparably linked in public consciousness." The new convention of the "AIDS victim" housed within the limits of realist drama where he meets inevitable death contributes to what Marshall describes as a form of demoralization: "This representation [of the "AIDS victim"] is too close—it taps our most profound fears in this terrible health crisis and its calculated effect is demoralization."[10]

Kramer's play is but one of many plays that promote this "demoralization" through realism.[11] Such a reliance on the power of realist drama to enable change seems utopian in scope and does not take into account other modes of representation beginning to circulate, which reject empathy and its resulting cathartic release. While plays that elicit identification and emotion from their audience may be the more dominant means of current representation, other less traditional forms of performance have emerged to contest and intervene in the production of the "AIDS victim" within conventional drama. Rather than attempting to imitate life in order for us to "reflect back on it," as Michael Feingold suggests, these alternative modes insist on more direct, even confrontational approaches that destabilize the givens of realist forms—the essential subject, narrative plot lines that suppose a mimetic trajectory, resolution through closure, and, finally, traditional theater structures that impose a formalized relationship between performance practice and spectator reception.[12]

Performing All Our Lives: Performance

> As marginal as it might be, performance art makes me feel alive
> sometimes, and that can't be bad.
> —Linda Frye Burnham

Perhaps because of its enigmatic, slippery status within the arts, as well as its politicized history as a counterhegemonic practice, it shouldn't be too surprising that strategies to usurp dominant modes of representation of gay men and AIDS in contemporary American culture are being offered by performance artists. Since performance art has so eluded critical definitions it may be useful to provide a brief overview of the way in which performance art has been described historically, its relationship with theater, and its position within mass cultural politics and trends. In short, performance art is "live art by artists," and, according to Roselee Goldberg: "the history of performance art in the twentieth century is the history of a permissive, open-ended medium with endless variables, executed by artists impatient with the limitations of more established art forms, and determined to take art directly to the public." Given the flexibility within such an art form, performance art has often been a successful medium for artists to directly engage in a critical commentary on established social practices as well a widely accepted artistic conventions.[13] Furthermore, the long complicated and unresolved relationship between performance and the theater posits a necessary critique of theatrical practices upheld as models of and for representation. If performance art is more visually and conceptually based than the theater, then it stands to reason that what's at issue in performance art is the very notion of representation.[14] While some of the earlier advocates and producers of performance art viewed the medium as radically outside of theatrical conventions and more in dialogue with the visual arts, more recent critics have seen the possible intersections between the visual arts and the theater that blur any separationist categorical tendencies.[15] Moreover, recent critics have further argued that performance art, although not theater proper, holds the capacity to provide a radical critique of precisely the issues of representation, subject position, and performer-audience dynamics which are staged in the theater. Since these issues are central to understanding the alternative/oppositional images provided by gay-identified performance artists, further explication seems necessary.

Central to the debate concerning performance and theater is the fundamental question of performance art as an oppositional strategy and its own implication within the commodification of all art forms. For Josette Féral performance, unlike theater, demystifies the subject on stage. She argues that performance can "therefore be seen as an art-form whose primary aim is to undo 'competencies' (which are primarily theatrical)" and, thus, "poses a challenge to the theatre and to any reflection that theatre may make upon itself. Performance reorients such reflections by forcing them to open up and by compelling them to explore the margins of theatre."[16] Performance, then, according to this account, rejects formal confines and furthermore destabilizes conventions associated with the theater. Representations in performance defy specific symbolic structures that characterize theatrical practice. Or, in other words, performance, due to its *discontinuity*, offers neither a fixed subject position nor an essential representation of the "real." Féral's essay offers important insights into the question of peformance art and its relation to representation as it pertains to gay men and AIDS. If performance art stages the discontinuity of the subject and, recalling Crimp, if an anti-idealist notion of art is in order to challenge demoralized representations of gay men and AIDS, then it becomes apparent that any activist aesthetic out to dismantle received premonitions about gay men and AIDS could find expression through performance. Cultural critics concerned with representations of gay men and AIDS must continue to examine mainstream productions but need also to identify the degrees of opposition staged in conventional and alternative theaters, performance spaces, and nontraditional performance locations in order to explicate the possibilities of resistance offered by gay activist–identified artists.

Yet it is important to note that performance art is not itself outside of the problems of the theater. The current commodification process of much performance art suggests that any subversive potential inherent in the art form loses its capacity to engage in any radical critique once it enters more mainstream mass culture venues and spectatorships.[17] In a much quoted passage Jeanie Forte asks:

> Just how much does the work retain any potentially subversive impact once it has achieved commercial viability? . . . Yet if performance artists are doomed to relative obscurity, playing only to audiences of "the converted," how will societal consciousness be raised (or abrased) on a larger scale? Should this even be a conscious goal?[18]

Although Forte questions exclusively the politics of women's performance, her concerns about commodification are central for any oppositional strategy "entrapped" within the dynamics of mass culture. Gay men need only be reminded how earlier stagings of the subversive capacity of camp and drag were appropriated into mass culture as mere entertainments by mainstream national theaters.[19] Furthermore, commodification doesn't necessarily refute subversion but, rather, repositions performance within a context that at once recognizes the medium's own implication within mass cultural systems of representation and reception. It's not as if performance can be placed outside the inspection by which it holds traditional art accountable, nor can performance be placed outside of the operative tensions of popular culture. Instead, it becomes necessary to consider the degrees of opposition performance offers within cultural practices at large and, as Philip Auslander comments, recognize how performance "*problematizes*, but does not *reject*, the representational means it shares with other cultural practices."[20]

These are vital considerations for gay-identified performers who address sexuality and AIDS in their work. It becomes necessary then to identify the pitfalls of oppositional strategies of representation in order to comment on the processes of complicity in the circulation of representations. The short history of gay drama in the age of AIDS has already demonstrated how one type of drama intended as political intervention—the humanist depiction of suffering and loss—can have problematic ramifications when mainstreamed. It is on such points that gay male critics as well as performers and activists must look at lesbian feminist criticism on performance in order to fully contextualize their work.

Lesbian feminist criticism focused on performance has already initiated a necessary investigation of the performative ramifications of lesbian representation in both mainstream and alternative theaters. Questioning the politics of representation and reception in a diverse field of performances, these critics eloquently argue that alternative venues, such as the WOW Cafe, rather than ghettoizing lesbian issues within an enclosed lesbian community, offer a critical practice that begins to articulate the diversity encoded by such problematic terms as *lesbian sexuality* and *lesbian desire* and even the term *lesbian* itself.[21] Recognizing the importance of difference within any notion of a lesbian subject position, Jill Dolan argues against an essentialist reading of the lesbian subject imposing constructed truths:

> The remaining, complex, different [lesbian] referent, without truth, remains dependent on the materiality of actual lesbians who move in and out of dominant discourse in very different ways because of their positions within race, class, and variant expressions of their sexuality—dragging at the margins of structure and ideology.[22]

This same type of scrutiny is necessary for any critique of the representations of gay men and/or gay men with AIDS as well as in order to explore, reclaim, indeed *perform* what we mean by gay male sexuality, identity, and living with AIDS.

While such projects hold the hints of positing an essential truth about these issues, their capacity to provide a radical critique of dominant modes of representing gay male sexuality and AIDS are what strikes me as most immediate. A gay and/or AIDS activist performance aesthetic sets out to offer new images of gay men and people with AIDS which challenge dominant modes of (mis)understanding gay men and AIDS. If, for the moment at least, traditional theater widely associates gay men with AIDS, and if such stagings offer only a universalizing identification that obliterates difference and, furthermore, demand a formal closure that can only be presented through the death of the gay male, even if it is staged as a humanist tragedy, then we should seek out performances in other venues which may offer alternative and oppositional representations. This, of course, is by no means a new agenda. Gay men and lesbians have long produced a variety of alternatives to conventional theater spaces both in order to explore sexuality and to fight discrimination.[23] Furthermore, current gay, lesbian,

Fig. 1. Tim Miller. Photo credit: Chuck Stallard.

and AIDS activist movements (Queer Nation and ACT UP) have adopted performative measures in order to engage a wide spectrum of reactions toward their public demonstrations.[24]

Performing All Our Lives: Community

> It is the inaccurate way in which happenings between human beings
> are represented that restricts our pleasure in the theatre. The reason:
> we and our forebears have a different relationship to what is shown.
> —Bertolt Brecht, *Brecht on Theatre*

Many of the various communities left out of the privileges of dominant culture, including but not limited to gays and lesbians, people with AIDS, and people of color (and all of the intersections of these subject positions), have found in performance a means to explore such issues as identity and representation. The revitalization of performance by political artists outside of dominant culture indicates the emerging recognition of performance *as* a political tool, effective for its immediacy, stripped-down cost effectiveness and transportability.[25] Tim Miller is one gay-identified artist who works with performance as a political tool to combat homophobia, AIDS, and censorship and who uses performance to mobilize people into action. In all of his work Miller questions what it means to be gay in a thoroughly complicated, postmodern world and, more urgently, in a world that needs to cope with the omnipresence of AIDS. Miller's work exemplifies the type of performance which sets as its goal an activist's intervention in both the crisis of the AIDS epidemic and its subsequent crisis in representation. In his most recent piece *SEX/LOVE/STORIES* (1991) Miller chronicles his experiences as a gay man, dismantling any sense of mimetic transference by offering the following prefatory disclaimer: "I remember so many things, some of them even happened."[26] Thus, what's at stake is not so much a recording of his life but, rather, a deliberate displacement of this life through performance. Miller's main technique—storytelling interspersed with music, movement, screen projections, and dance—is reminiscent of Brechtian devices employed to allow the spectator to maintain a critical eye on the performative process at hand. In this sense the spectator is obliged to engage in the political and social commentary within the performance.

Although Miller's narrative catapults him from coast to coast, pointing to the instability of any attempt to foreground a reality of place, I'd like to focus on two especially relevant moments in his performance which point to the type of oppositional potential I've been alluding to throughout my discussion. The first concerns a literally "stripped-down" interrogation of gay male sexuality in the midst of AIDS, while the second offers a utopian possibility emerging from such a necessary radical self-critique of the body.

In the section that follows the powerful *ubi sunt* component, by now standard in autobiographical gay male expressions, where Miller questions his own survival amid a litany of the dead, Miller returns from the wanderings of urban sexual explorations to the most local of all geographies, that of the naked body. In a dialogue with his flaccid penis Miller details the price that gay men have paid in light of AIDS and its cultural representations. Initially, what is striking in this scene is how the demoralization of gay men faced with the contemporary realities of AIDS sets up a seemingly irreconcilable distance between sexual desire and sexual possibility. Miller's penis refuses to "get hard" despite the encouragement offered by Miller's reasonings. Yet, for a mainly gay audience offered the voyeuristic moment of surveying Miller's attractive physique, what occurs here is an immediate "stimulation," which results from the gay gaze toward the naked male body.[27] Miller seems to manipulate this response by beckoning the spectator to at once notice his penis—"will he get hard, and if so what then?"—and not notice his penis, the "embarrassment" of impotence. While the spectator is implicated in the physicality of this moment, the narrative that accompanies Miller's nakedness disturbs this objectification of the gay male body. In Miller's piece gay male desire is repositioned from the "demoralization" typical of traditional representation by the gradual shift from the personal landscape of the body into the social arena of the gay body politic. Rather than focusing on the impotence of any gay sexuality and the resulting low self-esteem of the desiring gay subject, Miller reminds the spectator of the potency of gay sexuality as a direct expression of the gay body politic. The flaccid penis represents this gay body politic and its need to reinvigorate a sex-positive attitude:

> Get hard, because it still feels good to be touched . . .
> get hard because there is so much that is gone . . .

> get hard, because you can remember you are alive . . .
>
> get hard because every time I come I think of the men I've loved who are dead . . .
>
> get hard because I am a queer and it is good and I am good and I don't just mean in bed . . .

Miller recuperates the sexual without apology and returns to his audience the repoliticization of the body that has been appropriated and reinscribed by dominant discourse as diseased. If Kramer's Ned posits the gay body politic as demanding "a recognition of a culture that isn't just sexual" and points to history for his evidence, Miller reinscribes the sexual and demands a recognition of a culture that isn't just transhistorical.[28] He uses his body to at once arouse our desire and politicize that desire in the process. By the end of the section performer and spectator shift from the physical demoralization of desire in the age of AIDS to its important role in reinscribing a sex-positive and life-affirming gay sexuality that can counter the debilitations offered by dominant representations of gay male sexuality.

While the "get hard" segment of *SEX/LOVE/STORIES* reclaims for gay sexuality an enabling capacity for self-determination, the "Civil Disobedience Weekend" section, which ends the performance proper, offers a utopian rendering of what happens when gay men who celebrate their sexuality meet. At its root "Civil Disobedience Weekend" suggests the powerful and transformative ramifications of men loving men, or at least of men having sex. The piece begins with the retelling of the incarceration of a group of gay activists and artists; jailed for demonstrating in front of the Los Angeles Federal Building on issues ranging from AIDS negligence to government censorship of the arts. Men are separated from women and sent to their separate cells. Despite the authorities' attempts to stifle the erotic and the political, the gay men left in the holding cell engage in a wild orgy of safer sexual expression that ends not only with the collective orgasm of the group but also the spilling of the seed for a new world order where AIDS activists and artists gain political stature and rule. AIDS activists, gay artists, even gay professors, "bring each other off," giving new meaning to the chant of ACTION = LIFE. With an impromptu gathering of the Los Angeles Philharmonic providing the soundtrack for a complete global restructuring (Beethoven's Ninth Symphony), Miller euphorically describes the results of their demonstration. Thousands of people, speaking dozens of languages, are dancing in the streets; the federal police have resigned and joined ACT UP; Gorbachev and Yeltsin have sent a memo to the activists with the hopes of establishing an international democracy led by artists and activists; George Bush, on the other hand, has fled the White House, and what's left of the U.S. government has decided to place AIDS and other domestic issues as the top budget priorities. Even national monuments across the country have been transformed, now honoring those who fought for social justice and an end to the AIDS epidemic.

Undoubtedly, much of this piece plays humorously—indeed, can be viewed as satire at its most provocative—and this seems to be the point. Miller effectively distances the viewer through campiness, self-effacement, and direct narrative undercutting. Thus, while the spectator may find direct identification in the fantasies (both the sexual and utopian), Miller refuses to allow any cathartic release. This is, after all, an imaginative retelling of an event that can only possibly be rendered as "real" from the perspective of the future. What is important in terms of the politics of representation is how Miller refuses assimilation as an option and posits direct usurpation as *the* fantasy or the not *yet* real.[29] This is a remarkable departure from the current assimilationist positions of gay-identified culture.

It's no wonder then that such performances have fueled conservative fires across the country and have unfortunately resulted in Miller's recent defunding from the National Endowment for the Arts (NEA). While plays that offer demoralized depictions of gay men, associating gay sexuality with AIDS and AIDS with death, are championed by liberal and conservative critics alike, Miller's performances challenging these dominant representations are censored or, at best, "unauthorized." Instead of slipping into the commodifications of mass culture, current gay, lesbian, and even "feminist" performance art has been ostracized by the most recent emergence of anti-theatrical sentiment, a sentiment that historically is anxious of both the homoerotics and the transgressive capacity of the theater.

The subversive capacity of performance—to challenge dominant ideologies, address the crisis of representation, and reject the confines of conventional art practices—rather than being subsumed by dominant culture pushes those on the vanguard of artistic expression back to an immediate "locality." Tim Miller remains a case in point. At Highways in Santa Monica, California, the performance space he cofounded and codirects, Miller offers free performance workshops—one workshop for gay men to explore identity issues and another workshop open to anyone interested in group performance projects and strategies that create a cultural response to the role of AIDS in all our lives.[30] Individuals from both groups have "performed" their experiences in various capacities not only at Highways but also throughout Los Angeles. The groups have also participated in such community projects as World AIDS Day/Day without Art (1 December 1990) where over forty people held an all-night AIDS vigil, which included various performances, stories, and songs; retreats with ACT UP–LA; and, more recently, a collective performance in response to issues of censorship and homophobia. Participants in the workshops reflect, to a large degree, the diversity of the Los Angeles population and together interact to form a community that utilizes performance to express differences and a self-determined agency in order to engage in the necessary dialogues that may effect social change. If nothing more, these local performative practices powerfully articulate not so much the voice *of* an activist aesthetic but, rather, the richness of voices *from* such a position. The resulting continual proliferation of subjective responses to AIDS and gay and lesbian sexuality and identity only calls attention to the socially heterogeneous representations that are being *performed* in these local venues.[31] For critics who argue that gay and lesbian performance only preaches to the "choir," it is important to recognize that such a choir does not exist unless one presupposes (which Miller does not) that there is only possible a singular monolithic community of activists which reflect the "ideal spectator." In any event conversion entails more than simply rhetoric; it demands a conversion of ideas and belief systems into direct action, a possibility only beginning to come into fruition.[32]

With 130,000 dead in the United States alone, art is still not enough. And the theater, in the broader gay and/or AIDS activist agenda, is only one of many sites of struggle. I have attempted to argue, however, that direct action can result from performance, as Tim Miller's work begins to demonstrate, and thereby positions performance as a medium to be taken seriously—as seriously by critics interested in gay sexuality, AIDS, and the politics of representation as it is by its most abhorrent dismissers. It is by performing all our lives that we produce a chaotic multiplicity of representations, representations that displace, by the very process of proliferation, the authority of a conservative ideology of sexual hegemony, AIDS myths, and aesthetic practices. These endless multiplications and proliferations of difference and confrontation engendered through performance deconstruct oppressive systems of representation and demonstrate the radical capacity of political art in a reactionary, conservative age to both articulate resistance and generate necessary social change.[33]

NOTES

1. Felix in Larry Kramer, *The Normal Heart* (1985), Jack in David Greenspan, *Jack* (1990), Bert in Robert Chesley, *Jerker* (1985), Chet in William M. Hoffman, *As Is* (1985), Andre in Terrence McNally, *Andre's Mother* (1988), Johnny in Lanford Wilson, *A Poster of the Cosmos* (1988).

2. See, for starters, the important writings of the following: Cindy Patton, *Inventing AIDS* (New York: Routledge, 1990); Simon Watney, *Policing Desire: Pornography, AIDS, and the Media*, 2d ed. (Minneapolis: University of Minnesota Press, 1989); and the special issue of *October* 43 (1987), reissued as *AIDS: Cultural Analysis/Cultural Activism*, ed. Douglas Crimp (Cambridge: MIT Press, 1989).

3. Crimp, Introduction, *AIDS*, 3.

4. Misrepresentations include such popular contentions that depict the person with AIDS as "victim," gay men as inherently "diseased," women as "carriers," people of color as "dirty," etc. For a detailed analysis of such representations, see the following essays in *October* 43 (1987): Sander Gilman, "AIDS and Syphilis: The Iconography of Disease," 87–108; Max Navarre, "Fighting the Victim Label"; and "PWA Coalition Portfolio," 143–68; as well as essays in *Ecstatic Antibodies: Resisting the AIDS Mythology*, ed. Tessa Boffin and Sunil Gupta (London: Rivers Oram Press, 1990).

5. See the extensive critiques of the arts, media, and popular culture in the texts by Watney, Crimp, and Patton, cited in note 2; Boffin and Gupta, *Ecstatic Antibodies*; *Taking Liberties: AIDS and Cultural Politics*, ed. Erica Carter and Simon Watney (London: Serpent's Tail, 1989); *differences* (special issue entitled "Life and Death in Sexuality: Reproductive Technologies and AIDS") 1 (1989); and *Personal*

Dispatches: Writers Confront AIDS, ed. John Preston (New York: St. Martin's Press, 1989). Patton's Inventing AIDS, an indispensable study, provides excellent documentation for those interested in a more thorough bibliography.

6. Larry Kramer, The Normal Heart (New York: New American Library, 1985), 57.

7. See Joseph Allen Boone, Tradition Counter Tradition: Love and the Form of Fiction (Chicago: University of Chicago Press, 1987).

8. In "How to Have Promiscuity in an Epidemic," (AIDS, 248), Douglas Crimp takes Kramer to task for writing a pièce à clef: "a form adopted for the very purpose of presenting the author's experience and views in dramatic form" (248). For further critiques of the play, see Sue Ellis and Paul Heritage, "AIDS and the Cultural Response: The Normal Heart and We All Fall Down," in Coming on Strong: Gay Politics and Culture, ed. Simon Shepherd and Mick Wallis (London: Unwin Hyman, 1989), 39–53; Simon Watney, "Common Knowledge," High Performance 36 (1986): 44–47. Finally, see Kramer's own response to critiques of the play from the gay Left in Reports from the Holocaust: The Making of an AIDS Activist (New York: St. Martin's Press, 1989).

9. For a discussion of feminist theater and realism, see Janelle G. Reinelt, "Feminist Theory and the Problem of Performance," Modern Drama 32 (1989): 48–57; as it concerns lesbian representation, see Jill Dolan, "Lesbian Subjectivity in Realism: Dragging at the Margins of Structure and Ideology," in Performing Feminisms: Feminist Critical Theory and Theatre, ed. Sue-Ellen Case (Baltimore: Johns Hopkins University Press, 1990), 40–53.

10. Stuart Marshall, "Picturing Deviancy," in Boffin and Gupta, Ecstatic Antibodies, 21.

11. In the important anthology of AIDS plays The Way We Live Now: American Plays and the AIDS Crisis (New York: Theater Communications Group, 1990) Michael Feingold prefaces the anthology and writes: "Plays are first models of behavior, imitations of life which reflect back on it. They give us patterns to follow or reject, motives and meanings for action, consequences to hope for or to avoid; in their ambiguities they offer alternatives" (xv).

12. Sue-Ellen Case offers an excellent overview of these issues as they pertain to feminist theater. While her insights focus on the practices of women in the theater, many of her ideas are useful in considering the ramifications of the subject position in contemporary gay, male-identified theater. See her essay "From Split Subject to Split Britches," in Feminine Focus: The New Women Playwrights, ed. Enoch Brater (New York: Oxford University Press, 1989), 126–46.

13. RoseLee Goldberg, Performance Art: From Futurism to Present, rev. ed. (New York: Harry N. Abrams, 1988), 9. See Goldberg's documentation of early performance artists and their social commentary as well as Sue-Ellen Case's survey of women and performance art in chapter 3 of Feminism and Theatre (New York: Methuen, 1988), 56–61.

14. Linda Frye Burnham, "High Performance," Performance Art, and Me, / TDR: A Journal of Performance Studies 30, no. 2 (1986): 15–51.

15. This departure from a strict compliance arguing for performance arts' "location" as a visual art is especially evident in the 1980s. See Burnham, "High Performance," for the history of the performance art movement and its continual contradictions and internal debates.

16. Josette Féral, "Performance and Theatricality: The Subject Demystified," Modern Drama 25 (1982): 179.

17. Jeanie Forte raises many of these concerns in her article "Women's Performance

Art: Feminism and Post-Modernism," in Case, *Performing Feminisms*, 251–69; see especially her discussion of Karen Finley (268).

18. Ibid., 268.

19. I borrow this insight from Mark Gevisser's provocative account of this phenomenon on Broadway in such plays as *Torch Song Trilogy, La Cage aux Folles,* and *M. Butterfly* ("Gay Theater Today," *Theater* 21 [1990]: 46–51). Gevisser suggests that these plays inevitably present drag queens as entertainers: "just as black culture has been presented to mainstream white America as a minstrel show, gay culture is presented to mainstream, heterosexual America as a drag show" (48).

20. Philip Auslander, "Going with the Flow: Performance Art and Mass Culture," *TDR: A Journal of Performance Studies* 33, no. 2 (1989): 119–36. See also Jon Erickson, "Appropriation and Transgression in Contemporary American Performance: The Wooster Group, Holly Hughes, and Karen Finley," *Theatre Journal* 42 (1990): 225–36.

21. See Jill Dolan's important essay "Breaking the Code: Musings on Lesbian Sexuality and the Performer," *Modern Drama* (1989): 146–58; as well as Teresa de Lauretis, "Sexual Indifference and Lesbian Representation," in Case, *Performing Feminisms*; and Judith Butler, *Gender Trouble: Feminism and the Subversion of Identity* (New York: Routledge, 1990).

22. Dolan, "Lesbian Subjectivity in Realism," 53.

23. See Gevisser, "Gay Theater Today." Although Gevisser provides a glimpse into some alternative venues in New York City alone, many of his examples are found throughout gay and lesbian communities in the United States.

24. For a more detailed account of ACT UP, see Douglas Crimp with Adam Rolston, *AIDS Demo Graphics* (Seattle: Bay Press, 1990).

25. See, for instance, Linda Frye Burnham "Getting on the Highways: Taking Responsibility for the Culture in the '90s," *Journal of Dramatic Theory and Criticism* 5, no. 1 (Fall 1990): 264–77; and Guillermo Gomez-Peña, "The Multi-Cultural Paradigm," *High Performance* 12, no. 3 (1989).

26. All quotations from *SEX/LOVE/STORIES* are from the author's performance text.

27. I am reminded here of Richard Dyer's observations on gay male pornography, specifically his claim that the narratives of conventional gay pornography position the viewer to anticipate orgasm. See "Coming to Terms," in *Out There: Marginalization and Contemporary Cultures*, ed. Russell Ferguson et al. (Cambridge: MIT Press, 1990), 289–98. My reading of Miller's "get hard" segment does not by any means imply the piece is "pornographic," but, rather, suggests that Miller manipulates the spectator into the narrative of gay porn only to reposition the spectator from orgasmic anticipation to political action. Furthermore, I'm not suggesting that all gay male spectators share this same arousal but, following Dyer's lead, allow for the powerful culturally determined configurations of gay male sexual desire which permeate much of contemporary urban gay culture. On this issue, see Leo Bersani, "Is the Rectum a Grave?" *October* 43 (1987): 197–222.

28. In this sense Miller's performances celebrate the sexual in the manner urged by John Clum in his call for work that allows for theatricality, play, and pleasure ("'A Culture That Isn't Just Sexual': Dramatizing Gay Male History," *Theatre Journal* 41 [1989]: 169–89).

29. Here Miller seems to undertake what Judith Butler advocates in her brilliant reading of the Helms amendment and its own implication as a site of homosexual pornography. In "The Force of Fantasy: Feminism, Mapplethorpe, and Discursive Excess," *differences* 2 (1990): 105–25, she writes: "My recommendation is not to

solve this crisis of identity politics [who and what wields the power to define the homosexual real] but to proliferate and intensify this crisis . . . the task is to affirm identity categories as a site of inevitable rifting, in which the phantasmatic fails to preempt the linguistic perogative of the real" (121).

30. See Jordan Peimer's short but telling article "Professor Tim's Gay 101," *Frontiers* (15 March 1991): 45.

31. I should add that Miller is only one of many performers who engage social commentary and activism through their work. For the documentation of gay performers' response to AIDS, see the special issue of *High Performance*, "Art and Crisis: AIDS and the Gay Politic," *High Performance* 36 (1986), and the exhibition catalog for *AIDS: The Artists' Response*, curator Jan Zita Grover (Columbus: Ohio State University: 1989). Furthermore, there is a growing movement of performance and AIDS activism in communities of color by gay and nongay artists. In Los Angeles alone Keith Antar Mason, who leads AIDS workshops at Highways and works closely with African-American communities, is also concerned with issues of representation in his performances; Luis Alfaro, who works as an AIDS crisis manager, AIDS educator, and performance artist, documents the diverse responses of the Latino/a community.

32. Further evidence in the direct action intervention that characterizes contemporary performance is the collaborative efforts of Tim Miller and Holly Hughes to establish the National Fund for Lesbian and Gay Artists (1991) in response to the NEA defunding of Miller, Hughes, John Fleck, and Karen Finley and to encourage emerging gay and lesbian talent.

33. A version of this paper was presented at the 1991 "Unauthorized Sexual Behavior Conference" at the University of California–Riverside. I'd like to thank George Haggerty, Sue-Ellen Case, and Joe Boone for their encouragement; Dorinne Kondo and Douglas Swenson for letting me talk these issues out; and Tim Miller for sharing his work—this essay is for him.

Feminism(s)

Introduction

> You do not have to be me in order for us to fight alongside each
> other. I do not have to be you to recognize that our wars are the
> same. What we must do is commit ourselves to some future that can
> include each other and to work toward that future with the
> particular strengths of our individual identities. And in order to do
> this, we must allow each other our differences at the same time as
> we recognize our sameness.
>
> —Audre Lorde

Feminism as a critical theory has had an extremely important impact on theater studies over the past twenty years, perhaps because, like film (for which it has also been theoretically transforming), feminism is especially suited to address the specularity of stage and screen. Making distinctions between material circumstances or effects and the immaterial, between the power relations that inscribe "looking" and those of being looked at, between the body as a resource of subjects and as an intertextual site of cultural production, between Woman as a generalized cultural category and individual, particular women, feminism has engaged performance in every aspect of its history, its representations, its reception. It is simultaneously theory and practice; to be a feminist scholar is to practice political resistance to tradition, to dominance, to patriarchy.

The results of the serious practice of feminism can be seen in terms of performance practices in which new women playwrights, artists, directors, producers, and designers have organized and fought for the means of production and also in terms of the articles, essays, and books that have appeared which revise theater history and provide critical and theoretical perspectives on performances. While, on the one hand, the gains have been significant, establishing feminism as a force to be reckoned with in any contemporary account of performance, on the other hand, it is still an embattled position. Money and resources are severely limited for most feminist artists, and the National Endowment for the Arts (NEA) can always make resources even scarcer for a Holly Hughes or a Karen Finley. The academy still looks dubiously at women's studies programs and faculty, and the new national debate over "politically correct" thinking registers the latest rearguard action against feminist theoretical and critical agendas.

Feminism must be defined with a political edge; its application to performance is and must be a political act. Jill Dolan writes that "feminism begins with a keen awareness of exclusion from male cultural, social, sexual, political and intellectual discourse,"[1] to which I would add, "and ends with a resolve to radically change these circumstances." Whether one seeks parity and inclusion with males, an alternative women's culture, or some combination, the realization of women's historical oppression leads to direct action, where scholarship is itself a form of action and struggle. Under-

225

standing that this struggle belongs to women, it is a matter of some debate whether or not men can *be* feminists; certainly they can be sympathetic and supportive of feminism and can use feminist methodology to inform their own work, as a number of men in theater studies have done. Their role is comparable to the supportive but not primary role played by many whites in the civil rights movement.

The use of the term *feminism* is misleading, and for this reason it does not appear in the title to this section. "Feminism(s)" refers both to the differences in ideology and program among women who are feminists and also to the different kinds of scholarly activity engaged in by performance scholars. It acknowledges the race, class, age, sexual preference, location, and many other attributes marking the positions of women engaged in feminist activity, both scholarly and artistic.

Usually, three types of feminism are described, but they do not form an adequate typology and are frequently augmented with at least two more. I think they still offer useful distinctions for those beginning the study of feminism, and so I repeat them here in a succinct shorthand formation suggested by Gayle Austin:[2]

Liberal
    1. Minimizes differences between men and women
    2. Works for success within system; reform, not revolt
    3. Individual more important than the group
Radical
    1. Stresses superiority of female attributes and difference between male and female modes
    2. Favors separate female systems
    3. Individual more important than the group
Materialist
    1. Minimizes biological differences between men and women
    2. Stresses material conditions of production such as history, race, class, gender
    3. Group more important than the individual[3]

Particularly useful is Austin's emphasis, in the first two typologies, on individual rather than group practices. Coming out of the strong attention to female experience at the heart of consciousness raising (CR) groups in North America and the emphasis on female speech and writing in French feminist discourse, there remains a tendency to privilege individual freedom, especially in liberal feminism. On the contrary, materialist feminism "describes and understands women as members of groups or classes, and is more concerned with liberation of the group." Although this characterization is too schematic, it helps illuminate the difference between a playwright like Beth Henley and a playwright like Caryl Churchill, between Wendy Wasserstein's *Uncommon Women and Others* and Ntozake Shange's *for colored girls who have considered suicide when the rainbow is enuf.*

The unique struggles of women of color and of lesbian women have made it imperative to recognize the hazard of homogenizing women within the three "types" of feminism. Lesbians have long struggled with "compulsory heterosexuality,"[4] while women of color face such specific issues as how to or even whether to form an identity politics with white women on some issues and with black men (for example) on other issues across often competing practices.[5] Because recognizing and respecting the diversity of women's positions is critical to any feminist discourse, it is important to continually call attention to the multifaceted nature of the feminist critique.

The questions that feminists have brought to representation have profoundly affected many areas of performance theory and criticism. All major types of feminism have made important contributions to the field. Furthermore, the essays in this section could also have been placed in other sections (Ellen Donkin's in "History and Historiography," Jeanie Forte's in "Cultural Studies"), while essays located in other places also fit here (Tracy Davis's could move from "History and Historiography," Elin Diamond's from "Psychoanalysis"). This mobility is due, in part, to the nature of the feminist critique: since it is political and also deeply personal, it cannot be put on and taken off again like a critical coat every time the scholar goes calling on a new topic; it is rather more like a second skin, which goes everywhere. Thus, Vivian Patraka's topic is not ostensibly a feminist one, but her feminism is palpable in her argument.

The essays collected here are, in some ways, "in house," by which I mean that they assume a commitment to the feminist critique and a familiarity with the basic terrain of the arguments. They all push, in some way, on the limits of the various debates or engage in rethinking certain central issues (like essentialism). To go back and reconstruct the path leading to this research is no small task because a good deal of important work has appeared in the last decade. Only a beginning road map is provided here.

Early books like Helen Krich Chinoy and Linda Walsh Jenkins's *Women in American Theatre* and Michelene Wandor's British *Understudies* (both published in 1981) are now in second editions. They introduced feminist topics and women artists and, especially in the case of Wandor, provided a historical narrative for the rise of second-wave feminism's performances. They were joined recently by *Notable Women in American Theatre*, which is a kind of encyclopedia of "notable" writers, performers, directors, and other women associated with theater.[6] These works provide beginning subject matter resources, especially for historical research. Sue-Ellen Case has been extremely instrumental in setting a feminist agenda for performance studies. Her concise book *Feminism and Theatre* is the best single introduction to the theoretical and critical issues under discussion here. Her editorship of *Theatre Journal* also provided a forum for many important feminist essays and several special issues. A selection of that work has been published in the collection *Performing Feminisms*, some of whose contributors also appear in this volume.[7] Since 1984 *Women and Performance* has established itself as a journal of theory, publishing many ground-breaking essays, including Jill Dolan's on the nature of representation, "Gender Impersonation Onstage: Destroying or Maintaining the

Mirror of Gender Roles" (1985). But in addition to these citations there are many others of note: Helene Keyssar's *Feminist Theatre*, Lynda Hart's collection of essays *Making a Spectacle*,[8] a special issue of *Modern Drama* on "women in the theatre" (March 1989), and Jill Dolan's and Gayle Austin's books previously cited above. The Women and Theatre Program (WTP) of the American Theatre in Higher Education association (ATHE) has brought a great deal of productive vitality to the organization. In 1990 over one hundred women attended the preconvention programs, and the central convention panels sponsored by WTP were similarly well attended by a wide constituency.

Of course, since feminism is completely interdisciplinary, much of the seminal work underpinning performance theory comes from anthropology, political science, philosophy, psychology, and film studies. Although there is not room to cite that work within these brief pages, it does seem necessary to point out the basic and crucial work on representations of women, subject positioning, the male gaze, and the notion of "suture" appearing in film theory. E. Ann Kaplan on the male gaze, Teresa de Lauretis on the oedipal character of all narrative, Laura Mulvey on visual pleasure and spectatorship—these contributions to film discourse have been immensely fruitful for live performance theory as well.[9]

The essays that appear here under the "Feminism(s)" rubric mark the latest developments in several different types of feminist performance research. Ellen Donkin's essay on Sara Siddons is, on the one hand, a contribution to writing "herstory"; the task of reinserting information and emphases on historical women, in this case an actress, who are either left out of canonical history or who, as with Siddons, are understood through patriarchal narratives and self-narratives complicit with patriarchal assumptions. On the other hand, Donkin is engaged in theorizing how, in the moment of reception, Siddons was able to assert her autonomy and subjectivity and resist the usual closure of representation. To do so, Donkin must both reexamine the "evidence," such as first-person accounts of the event, and also reason her way through to a possible theoretical construction of her own. Her essay traverses the border of history and theory, illustrating the way feminism has recently expanded the customary definitions of both.

Jeanie Forte's essay "Focus on the Body" brings with it three important issues for feminist performance criticism. Women performance artists have been particularly concerned with representations of female experience. The solo work of many women has introduced new subject matter and also new representational strategies. Second, Forte also locates one of the most difficult problematics of feminist work: how to theorize a specific female experience without reconstructing and reaffirming an essential bipolar opposition between men and women, which leads to little more than biological determinism. The body is the source of much female experience, but what, if any part of it, is "essential"? Where does gender construction confront biology? If the body is represented as the source of knowledge, or subjectivity, does it not also reappear as a gender prison? Forte attempts to work with the body without succumbing to an essentialist position. The third issue in the essay is the way women can profitably use male theoreticians for feminist purposes. In her use of Michel Foucault, Forte both claims and transforms his terms, pointing out the gender blindness of his analyses while developing a specifically feminist notion of the deployment of sexuality for purposes of manipulation and control of women's bodies.[10]

Jill Dolan's essay puts the necessity of political resistance at the center of her concern. It moves beyond the first-wave politics of representing lesbian and gay male sexuality to interrogate what truly constitutes disruption in this historical moment and in light of current dominant theater practices. The essay takes for granted the earlier insistence on feminist critical practice as committed to radical change and instead investigates how to maximize disruption, how to insist on struggle. It speaks to the "already committed" about making good on the commitment. It also articulates a lesbian feminist critique of homosexual and heterosexual representations. Like Kate Davy's article, this article is closely related to David Román's essay on gay male subjectivity and representation, which can be found in "After Marx."

Kate Davy's examination of the theater of Charles Ludlum is an example of feminist analysis of male work, a contribution to gay studies, and also a demonstration of an extremely important critical practice: rethinking and reassessing analyses and judgments in light of new ideas and events. One of the tasks of feminists scholars in this time is to historicize our own work as well as the work we study. Davy is reconsidering some previous ideas in light of "new news." In so doing, she illuminates Ludlum's contribution and also its historical reception and institutional appropriation. She writes as a lesbian feminist, showing both the intersection between her position and that of gay males and also its contradistinction.

Traces of the feminist project can be found in every section of this book, even when the essays were written by men. It has had an enormous impact on the field. Turn over a theatrical paving stone—you'll surely find a feminist or two.

'

J. G. R.

NOTES

Chapter epigraph from Audre Lorde, *Sister Outsider* (Trumansburg, N.Y.: Crossing Press, 1984), 142.

1. Jill Dolan, *The Feminist Spectator as Critic* (1988; reprint, Ann Arbor: University of Michigan Press, 1991), 3.

2. Both Sue-Ellen Case in *Feminism and Theatre* (New York: Methuen, 1988) and Jill Dolan in *Feminist Spectator* provide discussions of these categories, their exclusions and shortcomings, and use them to organize their own analyses. For a full philosophical discussion of these and other matters, see Alison M. Jagger, *Feminist Politics and Human Nature* (Totowa, N.J.: Rowman and Allanheld, 1983).

3. Gayle Austin, *Feminist Theories for Dramatic Criticism* (Ann Arbor: University of Michigan Press, 1990), 6.

4. Adrienne Rich's term from an influential essay, "Compulsory Heterosexuality and Lesbian Existence," *Signs: Journal of Women in Culture and Society* 5 (Summer 1980): 631–60.

5. See, for example, Barbara Smith, "Toward a Black Feminist Criticism," *The New Feminist Criticism: Essays on Women, Literature, and Theory*, ed. by Elaine Showalter (New York: Pantheon Books, 1985), 168–85. See also Hazel V. Carby, "'Woman's Era': Rethinking Black Feminist Theory," *Reconstructing Womanhood: The Emergence of the Afro-American Woman Novelist* (Oxford: Oxford University Press, 1987), 3–19.

6. Ed. Alice M. Robinson et al. (Greenwood Press, 1989).

7. Sue-Ellen Case, ed., *Performing Feminisms: Critical Theory and Theatre* (Baltimore: Johns Hopkins University Press, 1990).

8. Helene Keyssar, *Feminist Theatre* (London: Macmillan, 1984); *Making a Spectacle: Feminist Perspectives on Contemporary Women's Drama* (Ann Arbor: University of Michigan Press, 1989).

9. See E. Ann Kaplan, *Women and Film* (New York and London: Methuen, 1983); Teresa de Lauretis, *Alice Doesn't: Feminism, Semiotics, Cinema* (Bloomington: Indiana University Press, 1984); Laura Mulvey, "Visual Pleasure and Narrative Cinema," *Screen* 16, no. 13 (Autumn 1975).

10. Michel Foucault cuts across multiple sections of this book and has been useful to many performance theorists. Some of his most important works, in addition to the work on sexuality cited by Jeanie Forte, include *Discipline and Punish*, *The Order of Things*, *The Archaeology of Knowledge*, and *Madness and Civilization*.

Fe/male Impersonation: The Discourse of Camp

Kate Davy

In the course of what is still a relatively brief history of feminist criticism in theater, much has been written about work that originated in a woman-run performance space in New York called the WOW Cafe.[1] As a collective endeavor, WOW (Women's One World) has no single artistic vision guiding its productions; at base it is a producing organization that allows members of its collective to showcase work. The result is a wide range of offerings each season representing enormously disparate production types and performance styles. WOW is as much a community as it is a theater, and because any member of the collective can produce and perform—including women with no previous training or experience in theater—shows at WOW vary as much in quality as they do in approach. WOW might be considered a kind of preeminent community theater, which is not to suggest that its importance lies primarily in its sociology. Some of the most significant feminist theater of the last decade was created by women who started out at WOW, and most of those women continue to work there.

Despite vastly different artistic abilities and sensibilities, however, a common and compelling feature of WOW performances can be identified, one that distinguishes WOW work from that of other theaters. WOW productions represent lesbian sexualities on the stage and presume lesbians as the audience. Lisa Kron, a professionally trained actress and longtime WOW director and performer, admits, "Sometimes our theatre is really rough. But the audience we play for needs us. Lesbians never see themselves represented. And seeing yourself represented is what makes you feel you have a place in the world."[2]

The world as constituted by lesbians and inhabited by lesbians is the premise from which most WOW productions proceed, a premise whose consequences radically shift the nature of the performative address. These are not "coming out" plays addressed to straight audiences in a bid for understanding and acceptance. Nor are they plays about lesbian relationships within separatist communities. Instead, parody is the staple of WOW productions, parodies that take on a wide range of forms from reworkings of classical texts to spoofs on genres such as the detective film, the romance novel, and the television talk show, soap opera, or sitcom. Some WOW artists employ avant-garde strategies to make essentially non-narrative work, pieces structured more like a poem than a plot. Performance pieces that construct lesbian spectatorial communities tend to drop from the performative address the heterosexuality that underpins hegemonic representations, what Monique Wittig might describe as the cultural products of "the straight mind."[3] For spectators whose sole experience with dominant

231

culture is one of either being erased entirely or foregrounded as tragically "Other" against a (hetero)sexuality inscribed as fiercely normative, the experience of being addressed as if inhabiting a discursive space, an elsewhere eked out in the gaps of hegemonic representations, is both profound and exhilarating.

Traditionally, regardless of genre, what has marked WOW productions is that they are peopled entirely with lesbian characters. In *Heart of the Scorpion*, for instance, Alice Forrester's 1984 parody of the romance novel—a form that can scarcely be imagined outside of heterosexual dating and mating—all the couples were lesbian couples. There was only one man in the play, and "he" was represented by a life-size, homemade-looking stuffed dummy with a somewhat piglike face. He had no lines. Using a television talk show format for her nightclub act entitled *Carmelita Tropicana Chats*, Carmelita addressed her "studio audience" and, by extension, her entire television viewing audience as if all were lesbians.[4] The cast of Lisa Kron's 1988 production *Paradykes Lost*, which loosely followed a conventional murder mystery formula, included a detective, an ingenue and her grande dame aunt, a couple (one of whom had a history, in the form of a liaison, with the detective), a butler, and an assortment of eccentric singles. Kron used butch-femme as a cultural paradigm for lesbian sexuality to build a play in which all the characters had women's names, all were played by women, and all were explicitly identified as lesbian in the dialogue. None of these productions constructs a world "out there" of heterosexual culture which the world of the play and its characters are up against. As a result, the operations of heterosexuality as an institution are made visible by the unrelenting and rather jolting presumption that heterosexuals do not exist.

Configuring plays peopled almost exclusively with lesbian characters represents one strategy for making work that insists on a lesbian worldview. Of course, it is not the only way to create a theater *for* lesbians, a theater that responds to lesbian subjectivities. But until recently it has been a central and crucial strategy for WOW, one that has distinguished it from its gay male counterpart, that is, camp, or Ridiculous Theater, in which men impersonate women in narratives peopled for the most part by heterosexual characters. In 1988 a group of WOW artists began to experiment with representing heterosexual couples during their improvisational rehearsal process. Although the idea was abandoned before the piece opened, the notion of cross-dressing was in the air and hotly debated among WOW practitioners.

Within the year the idea was played out in a production of Sheridan's *School for Scandal*, directed by Alice Forrester and Heidi Griffiths. All the roles were played by women including the male characters, which were played by women in drag. In his review of the production for the *Village Voice* Robert Massa bemoaned the fact that the production inadequately commented on the play's sexism "as if the point of women's theater were simply to cast, not to recast."[5] He said that, as a spectator, "you soon forget all the roles are played by women." And in the final line of the review he maintained that "even the ones playing female characters appear to be in drag." In other words, it was possible to read this *School for Scandal* as

Fig. 1. Claire Moed as Sir Oliver Surface and Babs Davy as Sir Peter Teazle in *School for Scandal*. Photo credit: Dona Ann McAdams.

cast entirely with men. How can agency for women be realized representationally in a theatrical configuration that once again, like all hegemonic discourses, privileges the male voice and erases women as speaking subjects?

Massa's gloss on *School for Scandal* is, of course, particular and, as such, a matter of reception. Like all spectators, Massa brings to every encounter with any performance his own relationships with discourses and practices in society, relationships that influence in significant ways how meaning is produced and how a performance is read. It is through institutions and their attendant discourses and practices that readers learn how to read cultural artifacts. Spectators who believe that lesbian women are gender-reversed inverts, for example, might read WOW's *School for Scandal* as exemplary lesbian theater in which the female characters are played by mannish lesbians in drag. But I think not. Women are effaced in *School for Scandal* because there is no institutionalized paradigm for reading male impersonation. Female impersonation, on the other hand, has a long, rich history, from classical theater and film to television (Jack Benny, Milton Berle, Jamie Farr, Red Skelton, Flip Wilson, Jonathan Winters), in which men are not subsumed. On the contrary, female impersonation, while it certainly says something about women, is primarily about men, addressed to men, and for men.[6] Male impersonation has no such familiar institutionalized history in which women impersonating men say something about women.[7] Both female and male impersonation foreground the male voice, and, either way, women are erased. Moreover, it is in the discourse of camp humor that female impersonation is firmly embedded.

Camp has been a central descriptor of Theater of the Ridiculous since its beginnings in the work of John Vaccaro, Ronald Tavel, and Charles Ludlam in the mid 1960s. The same has not been true for lesbian theater. While reviewers might deem a particular piece "campy," camp has not been a central identifying feature of WOW work, nor has it been a standard part of the collective's rhetoric. WOW performances have been compared to Theater of the Ridiculous as having a certain affinity in their farcical style and the use of irony and double entendre, two core characteristics of camp. Like Theater of the Ridiculous, WOW artists borrow scenarios from classical and popular performance forms as sources for their work. But until 1988 WOW performers did not adopt the heterosexual imperative that drives these narratives. They did not impersonate women and men in heterosexual couplings. Impersonation is the arena in which camp falls short as a definitive characteristic of most WOW work. The butch of butch-femme gender play is engaged in lesbian representation, not male impersonation. I contend that, as the notion of camp has circulated among WOW practitioners in recent years, it has garnered a certain currency that has noticably influenced the work.

As 1990 began, *Anniversary Waltz*, a production by WOW's cofounders Lois Weaver and Peggy Shaw, used a wedding conceit as the frame of reference for a piece about their ten-year relationship as theater artists and lovers. Weaver donned a traditional white wedding dress and veil and clutched a bridal bouquet for the opening scene of the piece during which they talked about being "married" without really foregrounding the fact that, as lesbians, this is not one of their civil rights. As 1990 came to a close, the Five Lesbian Brothers (Maureen Angelos, Babs Davy, Dominique Dibbell, Peg Healey, and Lisa Kron) staged *Voyage to Lesbos (II)*, a narrative that focused on the wedding day of an on-again, off-again lesbian. While her future husband remained in the wings, his "dick" and its pleasures were pivotal.[8]

The reasons why WOW work is changing are many, and not all have to do with the issues surrounding impersonation. From an economic perspective the desire to move out of the fourth-floor walk-up loft space that currently houses WOW and seats only fifty spectators is understandable. Some WOW artists are weary of scratching out an existence in what they think is becoming a ghetto for lesbian theater. Shaw once commented with pointed irony that, "when lesbians make it to Off Broadway, it's the boys who are doing it."[9] She was referring to drag performer Charles Busch's long-running off-Broadway show *Lesbian Vampires of Sodom*. In emulating "the boys'" success at moving into mainstream venues there is perhaps the inclination to think that one must adopt the boys' performative strategies. *Lesbian Vampires of Sodom* is generally heralded as the epitome of camp.

In her ground-breaking book *Mother Camp: Female Impersonators in America*, Esther Newton defines *camp* as a system of humor and states that "the drag queen is its natural exponent."[10] Explicating this assertion is, in essence, the project of her book, a work that includes, as a footnote, the following:

> There are also women who perform as men: male impersonators ("drag butches"). They are a recognized part of the profession, but there are very few of them. . . . The relative scarcity of male impersonation presents important theoretical problems. (5 n. 13)

My argument focuses on the fact of this "scarcity of male impersonation" and posits that it has something to do with the inability of camp to serve lesbian women engaged in theatrical endeavors in the same ways it serves gay men. In her definition of *camp* Newton states that it "depends on the perception or creation of *incongruous juxtapositions*" (106). She explains that, while any very incongruous contrast can be campy, "masculine-feminine juxtapositions are, of course, the most characteristic kind of camp" (107). It could be said that WOW's project has been to sidestep the fierce binarism that drives masculine-feminine heterogendering, a binarism that, by its very nature, subsumes and erases women. My project is twofold: (1) to investigate the subversive potential of cross-dressing for gay male theater as it is embedded in the discourse of camp; and (2) to delineate the dangers of this same discourse for articulating a feminist subject position vis-à-vis the dynamics of butch-femme gender play in lesbian theater.

When asked to explain the significance of the title of her book Newton writes "'Mother Camp' as an honorific implies something about the relationship of the female impersonator to his gay audience. A female impersonator will sometimes refer to himself as 'mother,' as in 'Your mother's gonna explain all these dirty words to you'" (xx). She then describes the drag queen as "a *magical dream figure*: the fusion of mother and son" (xx; my emphasis). Here Newton makes a gesture toward reception, that is, the hold and effect the drag queen has on his audience. The preponderance of female impersonation—across representational forms and addressed to very different spectatorial communities—suggests that in the intersection of representation and response there is something both magical and compelling about a cross-dressed male.

Of the cross-dressed female's relationship to her counterpart in popular nineteenth-century theater, Peter Ackroyd writes:

> The male impersonator, the actress in trousers, seems . . . to lack depth and resonance . . . [and] is never anything more than what she pretends to be; a feminine, noble mind in a boy's body. It is a peculiarly sentimental, and therefore harmless reversal. The female impersonator, on the other hand, has more dramatic presence—the idea of a male mind and body underneath a female costume evokes memories and fears to which laughter is perhaps the best reaction.[11]

In 1928 Jean Cocteau wrote an essay on "a magical dream figure," an American acrobat named Vander Clyde who performed an enormously effective and popular drag act in Parisian music halls under the name "Barbette." Ostensibly writing about the virtues of skill and concentration using Barbette as a model of professionalism, Cocteau produced instead a brief treatise on reception vis-à-vis female impersonation. What Cocteau finds so compelling about Barbette's turn is his ability to seduce the eye of the beholder into believing he is a woman when the empirical evidence suggests otherwise. He describes how Barbette's gown, with its tulle shoulder straps, does not conceal the absence of breasts and how his acrobatic act demands he use his body and muscles in such a way that "he doesn't look very feminine."[12]

Cocteau invites the reader to join him in the audience and then explains that, "When Barbette comes on, he throws dust in our eyes. He throws it all at once, so violently that he can then concentrate only on his work as an acrobat. From then on his male movements will serve him instead of giving him away" (223). This metaphor of dust blinding the audience to the "truth" about Barbette suggests that it is not only what Barbette himself does to enact the gender role of the "Other" but that the mystifications of the entire theatrical apparatus support the illusion as well. It is also clear from Cocteau's description of his own spectatorial response that the duplicitous nature of this "illusion of woman," this absent presence, is the source of his fascination. He writes: "Barbette moves in silence. In spite of the orchestra which accompanies his act, his graceful poses and perilous exploits, his turn seems to be far away, taking place in the streets of dream, in a place where sounds cannot be heard, it seems to be summoned by the telescope or by sleep" (224).

Here Cocteau describes his spectatorial intervention in terms of fantasy, a fantasy evoked by the distance between himself and Barbette, who he describes as being faraway, unreachable, dreamlike, unavailable to consciousness. Fantasy is also evoked by the condition of absence constitutive of the experience of watching film. Indeed, Cocteau relates the effect of Barbette's turn to film: "The cinema has supplanted realistic sculpture. Its marble figures, its large pallid heads, its shapes and shadows with splendid lighting replace what the eye previously demanded from statues. Barbette derives from these moving statues. Even when one knows him, he cannot lose his mystery" (224).

Cocteau is not so much blinded by the dust Barbette throws in his eyes as he is transfixed by it, suspended by the duplicity of the image Barbette constructs. Cocteau contends that Barbette retains his status as enigma even for spectators who have already witnessed his turn and know he will pull off his wig at the finish of his act to reveal his masculine self. Cocteau would attribute Barbette's mystery to his ability to send mixed, incongruous signals of masculine and feminine in the guise of a single gender, seducing even those spectators who know better into once again believing he is a woman.

But I think it also has to do with the ways in which the image of woman circulates in the representational economies of dominant culture, especially since Cocteau identifies the experience of watching film as the source from which Barbette's sense of mystery is derived. The absence of live objects and bodies constitutive of film resonates profoundly with the absence of woman as speaking subject in the construction of woman as presence, as body. The appropriation of this construction by male performers marks a kind of cultural neologism in the form of an image that resists definition and at the same time generates an excess of meanings. The strict polarization of man/woman in heterogendering precludes the possibility of reading men in drag "wholistically." Female impersonation provides, in short, a seemingly endless source of fascination because, unlike male impersonation, the man who appropriates his "opposite" is not simultaneously effaced by it.

The intensely felt sense of mystery Cocteau describes as invoked by Barbette's act is an apt description of the effect Charles Ludlam creates when he plays women's roles in his Ridiculous Theatrical Company productions—an effect he places in the service of very different ends. In his extraordinary 1973 production of *Camille* Ludlam played Alexandre Dumas fils' Marguerite, the Lady of the Camillias, as well as Greta Garbo's version of the character from the 1937 film to Bill Vehr's Armand Duval in full period costume.[13] Unlike the narrative construction of Barbette's act—his supposed simulation of a woman and subsequent transformation into a man—Ludlam's hairy chest was clearly visible above the cut of his gown, signaling his status as male from his first entrance. Hence, in the process of enacting the passionate and doomed love affair between Marguerite and Armand which dominates the *Camille* narrative, Ludlam and Vehr made manifest the desire of two men for each other. At the same time, like Barbette, Ludlam conjured a credible representation of a woman despite clearly visible evidence to the contrary. In his review for *Women's Wear Daily* Martin Gottfried wrote that "Ludlam becomes quite believable as Camille." Writing for the *New York Times*, Clive Barnes called Ludlam "a completely convincing Camille."[14]

In playing Marguerite, Ludlam negotiated a position somewhere between a Brechtian presentation of the character and an illusionistic portrayal, a position between the parameters Barthes articulates when he writes that "the Oriental transvestite [actor] does not copy Woman but signifies her; not bogged down in the model, but detached from its signified; Femininity is presented to read, not to see: translation, not transgression."[15] Although Ludlam mostly played the role for comic effect, he also played it earnestly in moments where he milked the pathos of a scene, hushing the audience, to seduce them into "seeing" a woman as a kind of "set up" for moments when he dropped the character altogether to deliver a line or two as his actor/playwright/gay-male self.

In the final act, for instance, Marguerite on her death bed—her penniless, consumptive state played earnestly by Ludlam—calls to her faithful maid, "I'm cold. Nanine, throw another faggot on the fire!" Nanine replies, "There are no more faggots in the house." Dropping the character, Ludlam sits bolt upright, surveys the audience skeptically, and says plain-

Fig. 2. Charles Ludlam as Marguerite Gautier and Bill Vehr as Armand Duval in *Camille*. Photo credit: John Stern.

tively, "No faggots in the house?" Then he throws his dust, returns the character to her deathbed, and says, "Open the window, Nanine. See if there are any in the street."[16]

In a piece entitled "Reading Past the Heterosexual Imperative" I argued that male drag emphasizes the illusionistic qualities of impersonation in that the actor attempts to simulate that which he is not, the Other. Instead of foregrounding dominant culture's fiercely polarized gender roles, men's camp assumes them and plays them out. I concluded that male camp tends to reinscribe, rather than undermine, the dominant culture paradigms it appropriates for its farce and means to parody.[17] In this characterization of gay male theater I was thinking specifically of Ludlam's Ridiculous Theatrical Company on the west side of Greenwich Village, using it as a means for clarifying what lesbian performance at WOW in the East Village is not. Since then, the torturous experience of the Milwaukee Repertory Theater's heterosexist production of Ludlam's play *Irma Vep* has jolted me into a reconsideration of what Ludlam's theater is not.

Subtitled "A Penny Dreadful," Ludlam's *The Mystery of Irma Vep* is a pastiche of popular, sensationalistic Victorian plots to which he adds recognizable touches from *Dracula*, the Sherlock Holmes's tale *Hound of the Baskervilles*, and Hollywood films. The action takes place at Manda-crest, a mansion on the English Moors, where a new wife has come to replace the enigmatic and recently deceased woman whose portrait dominates the living room—clearly, a reference to Hitchcock's *Rebecca*. The

238

Fig. 3. Richard Halverson as Lady Enid and Jim Cunningham as her maid in *The Mystery of Irma Vep*, Milwaukee Repertory Theatre. Photo credit: Mark Avery.

play's four male characters and four female characters are all played by the same two male actors in a tour de force of disguise, impersonation, and breathtakingly rapid costume changes.

The palpable desire of two men for each other, which permeated *Camille* and drove the original production of *Irma Vep* in which Ludlam played Lady Enid to Everett Quinton's Lord Edgar, was utterly absent from the Milwaukee Repertory Theater's production.[18] Instead, the actors maintained their status as traditionally masculine men foregrounding their ability as actors in a kind of competitive duel of caricature constructions. They never touched at all suggestively, and the stage kiss called for in the script was not executed. The intelligent, lovelorn Lady Enid came across as a dithering frump. The touch of disdain these manly men projected at having to play women's parts (a touch required in order to maintain enough distance from gay male performance) cast a misogynous pall over the entire event. In the production's final gesture, one meant to confirm and punctuate the heterosexuality that inscribed this homophobic rendering of Ludlam's work, the actors took their bows then turned squarely to each other and shook hands.

Ironically, but accurately, two of the four reviews of the production use the word *straight* to describe the acting style. The critic for Milwaukee's major morning newspaper wrote, "They play their absolutely ridiculous (that is, in the famed Ridiculous Theatrical Company sense of the word) roles absolutely straight."[19]

The homoerotic potential of the script—after all, the roles could have been cast with a woman and a man—was manifest through the performative strategies of camp in the performance text of the original production. Wayne R. Dynes writes in the *Encyclopedia of Homosexuality* that "camp is not grounded in speech or writing as much as it is in gesture, performance, and public display. When it is verbal it is expressed less through direct statement than through implication, innuendo, and intonation."[20] Gay audiences for Ludlam's production of *Vep* laughed delightedly at double entendres, such as the line "How do you take it?" delivered pointedly by the maid (Everett Quinton) as "she" served tea to Lady Enid (Ludlam). Taken aback, Lady Enid replies, "I beg your pardon?" The maid, tongue in cheek, explains, "Your tea, miss." When Lady Enid insists that she takes it plain, the maid says both caustically and knowingly, "That's queer." To which Lady Enid replies, in a moment of camaraderie and with a conspiratorial tone, "Queer?" (770). Even in the absence of such innuendo it is possible for particular readers to understand the text as homoerotic. Following the publication of Ludlam's collected works, for instance, Neil Bartlett—who had never seen an original Ridiculous Theatrical Company production—wrote in his review of the collected plays that *Irma Vep* is "an alarmingly true metaphor of the love between two men."[21]

Ludlam does not represent homosexuality by writing plays about gay couples. Ludlam's male actors flaunt their sexuality, their desire for each other, in texts he constructs out of pieces of classical and popular narratives. They play the heterosexual couples that people these scenarios, flaunting and thereby presenting the gay male under, alongside, and outside of the straight male and female characters valorized in these canonized texts. Ludlam opens a window in representation, takes the faggots he sees in the street and puts them on the stage, making their desire for each other visible.

More important, perhaps, homosexual practice is implicit in this presentation of homoerotic desire. Earl Jackson, Jr., argues that male homosexuality both promises and threatens to disestablish "the transcendence of the phallus from the penis, disinvesting male genitalia (and hence biological identity) of their former privilege to universal principles of order and signification."[22] In a cogent explication of the ways in which male homosexuality opposes, by not participating in, the Oedipal triangle, Jackson states, "Male homosexual desire for the penis does not require the penis to be hypostatized into a universal principle, embracing female subjectivity and sexuality as well" (471). Ludlam's making visible of homoerotic desire signals homosexual practice, the subversive site of all that phallocratic culture attempts to suppress, contain, and eradicate.

That a dominant culture venue such as a regional theater could so effortlessly erase, render invisible in its (re)production, any representation of the marginalized group that generated the original cultural product, raises a plethora of thorny issues related to appropriation, context, and address. But it also raises questions about the nature of Ludlam's texts as destabilizing forces, questions about his theater's potential to subvert and disrupt dominant culture's system of representation.

In an interview I conducted with Ludlam during a subsequent run of *Camille* in 1974 he argued emphatically two seemingly contradictory positions for the production. He maintained that his rendering of *Camille* is not an expression of homosexuality and, at the same time, that it represents a form of coming out. In the space of these contradictions lies the operating principle of camp. In his comedies Ludlam adheres to a set of aesthetic universals, one of which he identifies as the theatrical convention of men impersonating women both historically and across cultures.

Ludlum casts his portrayals of women in the great tradition of transvestism in the classical theaters of the Greeks, Elizabethans, and Japanese. Of his form of impersonation he says, "This is nothing new. It has nothing to do with homosexuality. I use it as a theatrical device. It distances the performer from the role. It takes more art to play a role that is very unlike yourself. You must use everything; you must use your imagination to the utmost to create the impression."[23] And the impression he creates undeniably works for "mixed audiences." "It is not a gay audience," he explains. "Although a lot of gay people do see it, an enormous number of straight people also come—couples clutching each other and weeping at the death scene, hugging each other all the closer." He thinks this is true because *Camille* "transcends gay. It's a love story. It's the story of Adam and Eve. It's the romantic ideal questioned and rethought."

Ludlam locates the "homosexual overtones" of his *Camille* in the narrative's dynamics of forbidden love. But his rethinking of the romantic ideal is manifest in his (re)casting; if *Camille* is the story of Adam and Eve, Ludlam's version has two Adams. Of his casting choices he says, "I think it's presenting a positive image. I think it's coming out on a certain level. But I don't think it's gay. It's a matter of being able to see the story freshly, without prejudice. It's a matter of giving the audience a new vision instead of reinforcing fixed habits of thought." In other words the play is not gay inasmuch as its address is not exclusively homosexual, but within the dynamics of the production the machinations of homosexuality surface, "come out," and are rendered visible in the pockets, gaps, and fissures of an ultimately less-than-monolithic heterosexual configuration. This is Ludlam's way of dismantling prejudice, of gesturing toward a new vision, of negotiating a partially closeted, partially out-of-the closet artistic and political stance, a stance played out in the contradiction of camp.

Dynes writes, "Undeniably, camp is subversive, but not too much so, for it depends for its survival on the patronage of high society, the entertainment world, advertising, and the media" (189). This may help to explain why lesbian theater work produced on the other side of the Village has not moved, as Ludlam's work has, into mainstream venues. The Milwaukee Rep is unlikely to present plays with titles like *The Lady Dick, The Well of Horniness,* or *Paradykes Lost.*

In her essay "Toward a Butch-Femme Aesthetic" Sue-Ellen Case delineates a strategy within lesbian discourse and performance practice aimed precisely at challenging dominant culture and the violence of its attendant discourses.[24] Camp is a central player in an argument that picks up where

Teresa de Lauretis ends in her essay entitled "The Technology of Gender."[25] In this essay de Lauretis makes an important critical move in distinguishing and moving away from the ideologically bound female subject position to a more promising and, therefore, more encouraging feminist subject. She locates the subject of feminism in the micropolitical practices and cultural productions of feminism and characterizes it as existing both inside and outside of gender as ideological representation in that this subject moves between two contradictory spaces. De Lauretis explains:

> It is a movement between the (represented) discursive space of the positions made available by hegemonic discourses and the space-off, the elsewhere, of those discourses: those other spaces both discursive and social that exist, since feminist practices have (re)constructed them, in the margins (or "between the lines," or "against the grain") of hegemonic discourses and in the interstices of institutions, in counter-practices and new forms of community. (26)

De Lauretis locates the feminist subject in this "elsewhere," engendered there in the tension created by the condition of inhabiting the two kinds of spaces at once, conscious of the pull in contrary directions.

The female subject, on the other hand, is trapped in hegemonic discourses as "woman," the always already spoken for construction that replaces women as speaking subjects in representation. This construction is anathema to women as historical beings and social subjects because it signifies a (feminine) essence intrinsic to all women, thereby reducing them to "nature," "mother," and, ultimately, the object of (male) desire. "Woman" replaces women and marks their absence. In this configuration the lesbian is doubly missing in that even her absence is not inscribed. This is both her oppression and her promise as a destabilizing force.

De Lauretis not only distinguishes between the female subject and the subject of feminism, she also identifies the female subject position as inescapably trapped in the phallocratic contract of heterosexuality. Borrowing Irigaray's notion of "hom(m)osexuality" as the term of sexual (in)difference, that is, the term that signifies a single practice and representation of the sexual—male—de Lauretis identifies hom(m)osexuality as in fact the term of heterosexuality.[26] So that when she states that, in order to begin the process of change, "we must walk out of the male-centered frame of reference in which gender and sexuality are (re)produced by the discourse of male sexuality" ("Technology," 17), she means that, at the level of discourse, we must walk out of the hom(m)osexual frame and its phallocratic contract, the heterosexual contract.

In a brilliant theoretical maneuver Case recuperates the lesbian butch suppressed historically by the feminist movement, reassimilates recent feminist theoretical strategies, and maps the butch-femme subject position—one that provides, in her words, "a ground that could resolve the project of constructing the feminist subject position" (289). In other words, a position outside the heterosexual contract.

In her project Case employs camp as a strategy in combination with the discourse of the butch-femme couple "to provide the liberation of the feminist subject" (286). My only quarrel with her project, a project that has been enormously influential in constructing an alternative to the female subject, is her use of camp. Because she invokes camp as a "discourse," instead of merely using its salient elements, the baggage of camp discourse is imbricated in her argument. The result is that the subject position she constructs does not walk out of the hom(m)osexual frame of reference as effectively as it could, for camp as a discourse is both ironically and paradoxically the discourse of hom(m)osexuality, that is, male sexuality.

In Case's scheme camp is a neutral, non-ideologically bound discourse in that it is produced by both gay men and lesbians out of the condition of being closeted. Furthermore, it is available as a strategy for other marginalized groups in much the same way that "coming out" is available for assimilation as a euphemism for heterosexuals coming out of whatever it is they come out of, except, of course, the closet of homosexuality. In using *camp* generically, Case falls into the same trap de Lauretis identifies when the word *homosexual* is used to refer to both gay men and lesbians "sliding inexorably, it seems, into its uncanny hommo-sexual double" ("Sexual Indifference," 163). The tools that camp provides—artifice, wit, irony, exaggeration—are available to butch-femme gender play separate from the ways in which they are inscribed by camp as a historically marked phenomenon.

Equally significant to camp as a discourse, as a system of signs, is the cross-dressed male, who is not merely an element or an instance but a central figure. Cocteau's Barbette and Ludlam's Marguerite are figures that incorporate and subsume the sexuality of the Other, of woman. Like the construction "woman," the cross-dressed male specularizes the phallus, providing a screen on which anxieties of castration and loss of the privileged phallus are projected and compensated for through the dynamics of fantasy. The cross-dressed male plays the absence of women from phallocratic discourse; woman as signifier is profoundly empty.

In theorizing the subversive potential of gay male discourses and practices Jackson notes:

> Throughout history, for various reasons, male homoerotic practices have been supportive of, rather than subversive to, hegemonic conceptions of masculinity. Even in the postmodern, late capitalist societies of the twentieth century, male homoerotic discourses are often reinscribed within the very patriarchy they would seem to countermand. (459)

As a discourse with a historical specificity, camp undermines the attempt to construct a subject position that hopes to resonate with what Audre Lorde describes as a "house of difference." Lorde's house filled with difference(s) suggests for de Lauretis "a more complex image of the psycho-socio-sexual subject . . . which does not deny gender or sex but transcends them" ("Sexual Indifference," 164). This is the challenge Case takes on and meets in theorizing her "dynamic duo," as she refers to the butch-femme couple, out of and within recent feminist theories of the psychoanalytic notion of "womanliness as masquerade." Case's dynamic duo "play on the phallic economy rather than to it" (291), foregrounding its fictions as fiction by negotiating its "realities" between two lesbian women.

I have argued that the iconography of butch-femme culture present in performances at WOW is not about cross-dressing ("Reading Past," 156). Wearing the gender of the "other" sex is not the point. Nor is it about drag in the sense of simulation. No attempt is made to hide the lesbian beneath a mask of male or female gender identity; to fool the audience, even momentarily, is not the objective. As a dimension of erotic identity, butch-femme is about sexuality and its myriad nuances. It is also about gender in that it appropriates gender in its social articulation and representational construction. In butch-femme iconograpy attributes that in dominant culture are associated with strict gender roles are not sex-class specific. Worn by lesbians, these attributes have meanings for lesbians in a same-sex, lesbian culture that do not necessarily symbolize conformity to rules of gender behavior and the oppositional dynamics of polarized gender roles.

The articulation of desire in the dynamics of butch-femme gender play in lesbian performance positions this performance outside heterosexuality both as a social institution and as a representational model, by realigning what Jill Dolan describes as the "dynamics of desire" between performance and its spectators. Dolan writes, "When the locus of desire changes, the demonstration of sexuality and gender roles also changes."[27] Butch-femme as a signifying practice in lesbian theater differs from male drag performance in that it dismantles the construction "woman" and challenges male sexuality as the universal norm. It challenges the heterosexual contract that de Lauretis identifies as "the very site in which the social relations of gender and thus gender ideology are re-produced in everyday life" (17).

Case's butch-femme subject position is successfully articulated outside the hom(m)osexual frame of reference, where it could have broader play if it were not encumbered by camp. Positioned inside a lesbian discourse that is every bit as artificial as camp in its gender play of phallocratic fictions, the butch-femme subject position, like its original referent in the butch-femme couple, is more lethal to hegemonic discourses than Charles Ludlam's Marguerite and Charles Busch's "lesbians of sodom."

Butch-femme gender roles played in the streets and on the stage signify, through lesbian desire, Irigaray's "goods that refuse to go to market" and Wittig's lesbian subject who is not man/not woman.[28] As such, butch-femme artifice is so much more a part of lesbian discourse than camp discourse that it not only resists assimilation, because it is too dangerous, but it allows for the play of other differences as well.

Dynes emphasizes that "camp is always presented with an invisible wink" (190). But, instead of realizing the promise and threat of its subversive potential for imagining and inscribing an "elsewhere" for alternative social and sexual realities, the wink of camp (re)assures its audience of the ultimate harmlessness of its play, its palatability for bourgeois sensibilities. When the butch-femme subject winks phallocratic culture is not reassured.

Camp is neither good nor bad; it is just more or less effectively deployed. In the context of gay male theater and its venues camp is indeed a means of signaling through the flames, while in lesbian performance it tends to fuel and fan the fire. How gay and lesbian theater as cultural production might effect social change outside of gay and lesbian contexts demands an examination of how its subversive meanings can be articulated and sustained in a hegemonic culture "bent" on benign assimilation or discursive and political eradication.[29] This seems to me the most crucial project for the future if change is the goal. Change is not possible, as de Lauretis so graphically puts it, "without altering the existing social relations and the heterosexual structures to which our society, and most others, are securely screwed" ("Technology," 21).

NOTES

1. See, among others, my article "Constructing the Spectator: Reception, Context, and Address in Lesbian Performance," *Performing Arts Journal* 10 (1986): 43–52; Jill Dolan, *The Feminist Spectator as Critic* (1988; reprint, Ann Arbor: University of Michigan Press, 1991); and Alisa Solomon, "The WOW Cafe," *Drama Review* 29, no. 1 (1985): 92–101.

2. Lisa Kron, as quoted by Dorothy Chansky, in "WOW Cafe: A Stage of Their Own," *Theatre Week* (24–30 September 1990): 39–41.

3. Monique Wittig, "The Straight Mind," *Feminist Issues* 1 (1980): 103–11.

4. See my piece "Heart of the Scorpion at the WOW Cafe"; and Jill Dolan, "Carmelita Tropicana Chats at the Club Chandalier"; both in *Drama Review* 29, no. 1 (1985): 52–56 and 26–32.

5. Robert Massa, "Comedy of Womanners," the *Village Voice* 33 (10 January 1989): 97.

6. In the chapter entitled "Lesbian Feminism and the Gay Rights Movement: Another View of Male Supremacy, Another Separatism," in her book *The Politics of Reality: Essays in Feminist Theory* (Trumansburg, N.Y.: Crossing Press, 1983), 128–51, Marilyn Frye links effeminacy, as a style, with what she calls the "gay institution of the impersonation of women" and writes: "What gay male affectation of femininity seems to me to be is a kind of serious sport in which men may exercise their power and control over the feminine. . . . Some gay men achieve, indeed, prodigious mastery of the feminine. . . . But the mastery of the feminine is not feminine. It is masculine" (137). In the text she asserts that female impersonation is a "mockery of women"; in a footnote, however, she amends her position with "the realization that gay effeminacy has so little to do with women that it is not even primarily the mockery of women I had thought it was" (151 n. 3).

7. This is not to suggest that male impersonation was uncommon in certain periods. See Laurence Senelick, "The Evolution of the Male Impersonator on the Nineteenth-Century Popular Stage," *Essays in Theatre* 1 (1982): 29–44. See also Sue-Ellen Case's discussion of the salon of Natalie Barney as a form of "personal theatre" in which women performed for all-women audiences (*Feminism and Theatre* [New York: Methuen, 1988], 50–53).

Homer Dickens's book *What a Drag: Men as Women and Women as Men in the Movies* features a surprisingly large number of women in drag. But with the exception of Marlene Dietrich, Greta Garbo in *Queen Christina,* and Julie Andrews in *Victor/Victoria,* few are memorable. This is the point: there is a familiarity about many of the men in drag that denotes, I think, a certain convention inscribed in the popular imagination. Given the relatively forgettable nature of much male impersonation, it is ironic when, in her book *Hollywood Androgyny* (New York: Columbia University Press, 1985), Rebecca Bell-Metereau points out that "in distinct contrast to the relative rarity and negative connotations of female impersonation before 1960, females dressed in male clothing appear frequently in American film" (66).

8. While I juxtapose these two productions to indicate a certain shift in perspective, the differences between them are paramount. *Anniversary Waltz* employs a number of heterosexual tropes but is not subsumed by them; it maintains its lesbian stance. Shaw and Weaver work through some extraordinary nonheterogendered positionalities within a butch-femme representational economy. *Voyage to Lesbos,* on the other hand, is obsessively concerned with heterosexuality in a failed attempt to critique it. Without much of a leap, it could be read as a play about lesbian "penis envy."

9. Personal interview with Peggy Shaw and Lois Weaver, New York City, Spring 1985.

10. Esther Newton, *Mother Camp: Female Impersonators in America* (Chicago: University of Chicago Press, 1972), xx; hereafter page numbers will be cited in the text.

11. Peter Ackroyd, *Dressing Up: Transvestism and Drag: The History of an Obsession* (New York: Simon and Schuster, 1979), 102.

12. *Cocteau's World: An Anthology of Writings by Jean Cocteau,* ed. Margaret Crosland (New York: Dodd, Mead, 1972), 224; hereafter page numbers will be cited in the text.

13. I saw the original production in the spring of 1973 at the 13th Street Theatre in New York City as well as every subsequent revival of it. Readers familiar with the experimental theater scene in those days will appreciate the following anecdote: When I interviewed Ludlam in the fall of 1974, I mentioned to him that the Living Theatre's Julian Beck and Judith Malina were in the audience the first time I saw *Camille* and that I was struck by their stoicism in the face of such high comedy. Ludlam responded, "Oh, but they came back stage afterwards and said that they *loved* it; they just thought it was irrelevant, that it had nothing to do with reality."

For a reading of Ludlam's *Camille* which is quite different from mine, see Stefan Brecht, *Queer Theatre* (Frankfurt: Suhrkamp, 1978), 88–93.

14. Martin Gottfried, "The Theatre: *Camille,*" *Women's Wear Daily,* 15 May 1974; Clive Barnes, "Stage: An Oddly Touching 'Camille,'" *New York Times,* 14 May 1974. These reviews are from the first revival of *Camille* in the spring of 1974. The original production opened in the spring of 1973. Both reviews were obtained from the files of the Ridiculous Theatrical Company, New York.

15. Roland Barthes, *Empire of Signs* (New York: Hill and Wang, 1982), 53. I am grateful to Laurence Senelick for bringing this cite to my attention.

16. *The Complete Plays of Charles Ludlam,* ed. Steven Samuels and Everett Quinton (New York: Harper and Row, 1989), 246. All subsequent references to Ludlam's plays are taken from this collection and are cited in the text.

17. See my essay entitled "Reading Past the Heterosexual Imperative: *Dress Suits to Hire,*" *Drama Review* 33: no. 1 (1989): 153–70; hereafter page numbers will be cited in the text.

18. I attended the Milwaukee Repertory Theater's production in the Stiemke Theater in September 1989 as well as Ludlam's original production in his theater at One Sheridan Square in New York in November 1984.

19. Jay Joslyn, "Rep's Spoof 'Irma Vep' Smashingly Successful," *Milwaukee Sentinel*, 18 September 1989. A review also appeared on the same day in the evening paper, the *Milwaukee Journal*, by Damien Jaques, in which he conflated *camp* with *drag* then used "camp," "campiness," and "high camp" to describe what he saw.

20. Wayne R. Dynes, "Camp," *Encyclopedia of Homosexuality*, ed. Wayne R. Dynes (New York: Garland, 1990), 189; hereafter page numbers will be cited in the text.

21. Neil Bartlett, "Just Ridiculous," *American Theatre* (April 1990): 50–51.

22. Earl Jackson, Jr., "Kabuki Narratives of Male Homoerotic Desire in Saikaku and Mishima," *Theatre Journal* 41 (1989): 470; hereafter page numbers will be cited in the text.

23. Personal interview with Charles Ludlam, New York City, 13 October 1974. Before beginning the interview, I asked Ludlam to say something to be sure the recorder was picking up his voice. Hence, the first words on the tape are "This is Charles Ludlam speaking for posterity." He died of AIDS on 28 May 1987. All subsequent quotations are from this interview and do not carry page number references.

24. Sue-Ellen Case, "Toward a Butch-Femme Aesthetic," in *Making a Spectacle: Feminist Essays on Contemporary Women's Theatre*, ed. Lynda Hart (Ann Arbor: University of Michigan Press, 1989), 282–99; hereafter page numbers will be cited in the text.

25. Teresa de Lauretis, "The Technology of Gender," *Technologies of Gender: Essays on Theory, Film, and Fiction* (Bloomington: Indiana University Press, 1987), 1–30; hereafter page numbers will be cited in the text.

26. Teresa de Lauretis, "Sexual Indifference and Lesbian Representation," *Theatre Journal* 40 (1988): 156; hereafter page numbers will be cited in the text.

27. Jill Dolan, "The Dynamics of Desire: Sexuality and Gender in Pornography and Performance," *Theatre Journal* 39 (1987): 173.

28. Luce Irigaray, "When the Goods Get Together," in *New French Feminisms: An Anthology*, ed. Elaine Marks and Isabelle de Courtivron (New York: Schocken Books, 1981), 110; Monique Wittig, "One is Not Born a Woman," *Feminist Issues* 1, no. 2 (1981): 47–54.

29. Susan Sontag's enormously influential "Notes on 'Camp,'" in her collected essays *Against Interpretation* (New York: Dell, 1966), 275–92, strikes me as exemplary of benign assimilation. She nearly edits homosexuals out of camp and deems it a fundamentally apolitical phenomenon.

Focus on the Body: Pain, Praxis, and Pleasure in Feminist Performance

Jeanie Forte

"Some days I'm denim. Some days I'm cashmere. But underneath it all I'm a woman, every day."

"You make me feel—you make me feel—you make me feel like a natural woman."

In both of these quotations from mass cultural forms, there is a reference to something perceived to be real, something presumed concretely knowable as the state of being woman which is found/located in the body—the natural qualities of femininity that exist "underneath" everything else. This "essentialist" belief, embedded within a humanist, Cartesian view of the world, persists in most Western cultural systems, despite the heady success of a postmodernist perspective in the academic arena. The postmodernist view exposes the impossibility of such knowability, deconstructing the "real" as a fiction that serves a particular ideology. For feminists postmodernist theory enables an understanding of gender within culture and in relation to the supposed referentiality of the female body and shifts focus to the body in representational systems. It has also become next to impossible, however, to discuss the female body without having to discursively "skirt" around it, as it were, and field charges of essentialism. As one theorist recently said to another, we can't theorize the body because "the body has no apparatus." And, as Jane Gallop notes, talking about the body raises the specter of referentiality, the threat of slipping into a thematics of the body, as if there were a "body itself," unmediated by textuality. "Belief in simple referentiality is not only unpoetic but also ultimately politically conservative, because it cannot recognize that the reality to which it appeals is a traditional ideological construction, whether one terms it phallomorphic, or metaphysical, or bourgeois, or something else."[1] In this way, talking about a differentiated body produces the threat of essentialism and the fear that claiming the body will only reinforce the structures of oppression which naturalize gender construction.

Yet investigating a politics of the body has always been paramount for feminists in addressing the category "women" and the ways in which that category is constitutive of an oppressed class in patriarchy. As de Beauvoir and Wittig demonstrated, one is not born a Woman (with capital *W*), but the corollary to their observations is that being born in a female body has immediate determining ramifications of one's cultural experience. For Adrienne Rich this is the starting point of a "politics of location," in what she calls the most intimate of geographies:

> Here at least I know I exist, that living human individual whom the young Marx called "the first premise of all human history".... But

it was not as a Marxist that I turned to this place, back from philosophy and literature and science and theology in which I had looked
for myself in vain. It was as a radical feminist.

The politics of pregnability and motherhood. The politics of
orgasm. The politics of rape and incest, of abortion, birth control,
forcible sterilization. Of prostitution and marital sex. Of what had
been named sexual liberation. Of prescriptive heterosexuality. Of lesbian existence.

And Marxist feminists were often pioneers in this work. But for
many women I knew, the need to begin with the female body—our
own—was understood not as applying a Marxist principle to women
but as locating the grounds from which to speak with authority as
women. Not to transcend this body but to reclaim it. To re-connect
our thinking and speaking with the body of this particular living
human individual, a woman.[2]

But what is the body? queries Alison Jaggar, articulating the difficulties
of theorizing something corporeal.[3] In our dominant philosophical tradition
body is only in opposition to the mind, the "biologically given, the material,
the immanent . . . that which marks the boundaries between the 'inner' self
and the 'external' world." Rather than allowing that tradition to circumscribe
discussion of the body or to define physical experience, feminists such as
Rich and Jaggar are insisting on an awareness of the complex set of social
and historical systems which shape our lives (and literally our bodies) as
women; not in simply "acted-upon" fashion but in the interactive process
of the construction of subjectivity. Or, as Susan Bordo so succinctly puts
it; "the body . . . is a medium of culture."[4]

For some this may seem ludicrously obvious, or at best a dated
revelation, one that apparently comes late to this author. But there are
reasons why I think it is crucial for Anglo-American feminism, and particularly feminist performance theory, to focus on the body at this historical
juncture. For one, it contains the possibility of a reconsideration of so-
called practical aspects of body politics, as a much-needed rebalancing of
abstraction in relation to materiality. As Bordo notes, "Among feminist
theorists in this country, the study of cultural 'representations' of the female
body has flourished, and it has often been brilliantly illuminating and
instrumental to a feminist rereading of culture. But the study of cultural
representations alone, divorced from consideration of their relation to the
practical lives of bodies, can obscure and mislead."[5] Our increased understanding of this relationship, between the "material" body and the body
in representation, contains the possibility for new strategies in feminist
performance.

This does not necessarily signal a turn to biology or nature as something unmediated but to a different "register" other than the symbolic
dimension, to use a Foucauldian term—the register of the "useful" body
rather than the "intelligible" body. Our cultural conceptions of the body,
norms, etc., including scientific, philosophic, and aesthetic representations,

construct the intelligible body. Those same representations also help to shape the structures by which the living body is adapted into a useful body. This is a helpful theoretical model for feminists, in making attempts to understand the complex interaction of body and culture and the apparent collusion with dominant systems: the body "is not *only* a text of culture. It is also . . . a practical, direct locus of social control. Banally, through table manners and toilet habits, through seemingly trivial routines, rules, and practices, culture is 'made body,' . . . As such it is put 'beyond the grasp of consciousness . . . [untouchable] by voluntary, deliberate transformation.' Our conscious politics, social commitments, strivings for change may be undermined and betrayed by the life of our bodies."[6] Similarly, Elaine Scarry warns that it is almost impossible to assess the myriad ways in which the nation-state "penetrates the deepest layers of consciousness, and manifests itself in the body itself. . . . The political identity of the body is usually learned unconsciously, effortlessly, and very early."[7]

Thus, an investigation of the practical rules and regulations through which the body (in this case, specifically female) is trained (to become useful) enables a material exploration of feminine praxis, of the cultural forms that enforce and support an aesthetic norm of femininity.[8] By approaching the body in representation from the perspective of this other register, such an investigation promises to unveil new strategies of resistance or make visible already operating strategies within the performance mode. Granted that the performance arena entails a special set of considerations in relation to sociocultural processes in general, being a specific site of representational custom, but my focus in this essay is on female performance artists who purport to be "themselves" in the act of performing—thus, they are themselves provoking a blurring of distinctions between reality and representation and inviting their audiences to "read" their actions in the wider context of their lives outside of performance. It is not my intention to construct a "sociology" of this performance but, rather, to attempt an initial inquiry into certain theoretical modes that might provide a different understanding of our encounters with the female body in feminist performance art.

The Performing Body in Pain

Gayatri Chakravorty Spivak, in more than one recent essay, charts a path of resistance through an analysis of material oppressions of the female body. In her otherwise skeptical examination of French feminism she finds in the focus on women's pleasure the possibility for "re-affirming the historically discontinuous yet common 'object'-ification of the sexed subject as woman." She furthermore sees this as a corrective for Western feminism's unremitting, albeit unintentional, colonialism in relation to Third World women. Institutional changes in the United States, however large or slight, do not change the focus of Western feminism, which is defined by the feminist investigator as subject; Spivak chides that "there has to be a simultaneous other focus: not merely who am I? but who is the other woman?"[9]

In Spivak's view the most promising investigation that works to shift feminist focus into an international frame concerns the effacement of the clitoris. Insofar as the clitoris embodies, literally and symbolically, women's pleasure outside of reproductive functions, it is not useful to (and in fact must be suppressed in) a "uterine" social organization; advanced capitalism, for example, dependent on home buying and, therefore, the sanctity of the nuclear family, must negate any but the uterine norm of motherhood. Spivak further notes that "it is this ideologico-material repression of the clitoris as the signifier of the sexed subject that operates the specific oppression of women." An investigation of the clitoris' effacement would not merely aim to substitute a clitoral social organization but also to dernormalize the uterine organization in all the ways that it operates to directly and indirectly subjugate women. She cautions that this work cannot alone eliminate problems of race and class or necessarily escape the colonialism of First World feminism toward the Third.

> [But] it might, one hopes, promote a sense of our common yet history-specific lot. It ties together the terrified child held down by her grandmother as the blood runs down her groin and the "liberated" heterosexual woman who . . . confronts . . . the "shame" of admitting to the "abnormality" of her orgasm [or] the acceptance of such a "special" need; and the radical feminist who, setting herself apart from the circle of reproduction, systematically discloses the beauty of the lesbian body; the dowried bride—a body for burning—and the female wage-slave—a body for maximum exploitation.[10]

The list of such manifestations of the effacement of the clitoris could obviously be much longer.

Spivak's suggestion also brings to mind the work of Elaine Scarry on the body in pain, an intersection that echoes some of my earliest musings on this topic: in my initial interest in the apparent limits of theory (which I now perceive also as the limits of language), the inability of theory to manifest the material, or useful body, I searched for those circumstances in which the body is undeniable, when the body's material presence is a condition of the circumstance. Interestingly, one is that of pain, and another is that of live performance: two cases when the body must be acknowledged, when it becomes visible/palpable through inhabiting temporally a process that depends fundamentally on its presence. This led me to Scarry's work on the discursive problematics regarding pain, in which I found immediate analogies to the problems I was experiencing in theorizing the performing body.

Scarry notes that pain is "that which cannot be denied and that which cannot be confirmed" and, as such, is always subject to doubt when claimed by someone other than oneself. It shows a persistent resistance to language, in fact actively destroying language, in that it reduces its subject to a state anterior to language and this is essential to what pain is. It resists language because it has no object, no referential content. It is not of or for anything.

Nevertheless, the language of pain is first and foremost an attempt to communicate to the person who is not in pain, in order to move them into action; "verbally expressing pain is a necessary prelude to the collective task of diminishing pain."[11] Scarry cites, for example, the literature of Amnesty International and its firsthand accounts of torture, the purpose of which is to get the reader to identify with the tortured, to be moved to end that suffering, as if it were her or his own.

One crucial aspect of contemporary feminism is the expression of pain, the pain of a female body in patriarchal culture (and I refer back to Rich's litany of body politics quoted earlier as well as Spivak's list). One may be tempted to add that this is not talking about "just" psychological suffering, only to realize that this discourse necessarily reinscribes Cartesian categories of mind and body and removes the discussion from the context of ideology. Scarry's point is that the discourse of pain crucially depends on getting others to listen and secondarily on eliminating the tendency to doubt the reports. A glaring case in point where the feminist movement seems to be miserably failing in this attempt would be in the recent pro-choice struggles.[12]

One perhaps surprising venue for such communication, however, is in feminist performance. Like Amnesty International, the feminist performer aims to communicate her experience of the female body, of her pain and what meanings it carries, within a specific cultural context. Angelika Festa's performance Untitled Dance with Fish and Others (1987), for example, both embodied the actual pain of being awkwardly suspended from a pole for twenty-four hours and referred in imagery to "women tied to white hospital beds in the name of 'curing hysteria,' force-feeding anorexia, or tending to the various medical conditions by which women have been painfully dominated and with which we continue to be perversely enthralled." The communication of pain in this performance is "uncompromising," unescapable, contingent upon an "intense process of physical and mental labor . . . registered through the body of a woman in pain."[13] Festa's reference is to the entrapment of representation, but her medium is the communication of pain.

Using Scarry's model, the pain women experience because they are female in a patriarchal culture would seem to resemble torture; that is, the bodies do not "consent" to their being used. The "torture" is a fact of political power through covert systems, however, and not an overt act of war, perhaps partially explaining how it is possible for many women to participate in or support the activities that result in the torture of other women, or even of themselves. I recall Spivak's image of the grandmother, holding the child for clitoridectomy. Such collusion, I believe, does not make it any less torture but heightens the need for an analysis of feminine praxis. Susan Bordo records the apparent "collusion" of women in the protest pathologies of hysteria, agoraphobia, and anorexia, noting that such symptoms arise in unconscious protest against feminine praxis yet perversely destroy the protester; resistance, for women, proves extremely difficult and complex, inevitably involving some degree of identity crisis. Bordo

Fig. 1. "The Empress with bound feet." From Genny Lim's *XX*, featuring (left to right) Koichi Tamano and Brenda Aoki, The Lab, San Francisco (1987). Photo credit: Lily Hall.

also points out that women of the twentieth century are in fact faring worse now than in the nineteenth in terms of the increase of these pathologies and enjoins contemporary feminism to focus on feminine praxis and its undoing in order to reverse this trend.[14]

Genny Lim's performance piece *XX* (1987) combines spoken texts about the practice of foot binding, generally enforced by women, with visuals of female performers in native dress crawling or hobbling across stage. The torture of foot binding is graphic and palpable in the piece, enlisting horror and amazement that so many women would willingly impose this torture on their daughters. The habituation of the useful body to oppression enables the cycle of torture to continue, until perhaps the collective expression of pain successfully intervenes to end it—or, more commonly, power structures that deploy and arbitrate bodily norms, functions, aesthetics, no longer require this particular usage. That is, when it becomes more useful to the state for women *not* to bind their feet, then the practice is discouraged, through ethical or legal arguments.

In Lim's piece the foot binding is juxtaposed with a contemporary Asian-American woman describing the oppressive weight of her cultural heritage and its rigid gender codes, along with scenes from an abusive relationship. The piece thus makes clear the analogous and interrelated structures of oppression of both the useful and intelligible body. Although the practice of foot binding has abated, the ideology that conditions women to abuse continues, in more subtle, covert systems.

In Vanalyne Green's *Trick or Drink* (1983–85) she reports the material pains of bulimia through a variety of images and media, citing the deterioration of her teeth, the weakening of her esophagus, and threat of cancer, the convulsive and overly sensitive stomach, the damage to her heart and other organs from roller coaster weight changes. In the context of discussing her parents' alcoholism and her own struggle with addictive behaviors she vividly communicates her pain, making visible a particular complex of cultural structures that specifically oppress women.

In each of the performances cited above the focus is on the body and its pain, situated within cultural practices that both mark the body's gender and derive from its gendered oppression. Festa's performance is notably different from the others in that the performance itself resonates with the actual presence of pain—certainly nothing new in the world of performance art, echoing earlier "body art" pieces by Stellarc, Burden, Valie Export, and others. The imagery of Festa's piece, however, specifically invokes feminine praxis and women's oppression: e.g., instead of hanging by fish hooks, emblems of male ritual, she hangs by yards of white fabric, associated with centuries of women's culture, handiwork, and orientation to service and sacrifice.

(C)litoral Performance

While there are many other performances I could cite in the context of pain, I would rather reach back to Spivak's comment concerning the exploration/ expression of women's pleasure—embodied in the clitoris—as a strategy for resistance, named but not fulfilled in the writings of French feminists. It is somewhat surprising that, in the context of extolling the French focus on women's body/pleasure as a potential arena for subversion of masculist ideology, Spivak moves into a discussion of women's commonality in the oppressive effacement of the physical emblem of that pleasure, thus speaking of women's pain. Are we only able to speak of the clitoris in its effacement, only in the pain of women's bodies? Does speaking of pleasure remove the discussion from the register of the useful body and threaten to trap us, once again, in essentialism?

The French strain of feminism of which Spivak speaks has frequently been branded essentialist, in its locating the possibility of women's discourse (écriture féminine) in the female body. As Hélène Cixous asserts: "Women are body. More body, hence more writing." Marguerite Duras declares, "The rhetoric of women [as] one that is anchored in the organism, in the body."[15] Granted that such statements court essentialism, there is still the material aspect broached, of uncovering the body's relationship to power, of making the female body visible in contradistinction to its patriarchal invention.

In articulating the female body's relationship to power a more specific focus on sexuality in the network of power relations seems required, and once again Foucault is useful. *The History of Sexuality* details the "deployment of sexuality" since the eighteenth century as a system of power, a strategy of dominant ideology in the manipulation and control of bodies. Sexuality, "an especially dense transfer point for relations of power," is deployed through "specific mechanisms of knowledge and power centering

on sex," including the hysterization of women's bodies. Through the operation of these mechanisms, sexuality emerges as the name of a historical
construct, "a great surface network in which the stimulation of bodies, the
intensification of pleasures, the incitement to discourse, the formation of
special knowledges, the strengthening of controls and resistances, are linked
to one another, in accordance with a few major strategies of knowledge
and power."[16]

The deployment of sexuality is linked to the economy through the
body, the body that "produces and consumes"—a perspective shared by
Bordo and Scarry, among others. But for Foucault this deployment has
produced an intensification of the body, with its increased exploitation in
the movement of power to consolidate and protect its position. As part of
this deployment, "sex" has emerged as something "other than bodies,
organs, somatic localizations, functions, anatomo-physiological systems,
sensations and pleasures." Indeed, sex is made to appear the opposite of
power, taking on the character of taboo as "that agency which appears to
dominate us and that secret which seems to underlie all that we are"; quite
the contrary, Foucault's analysis of the complex interweave of biology and
history reveals that sex is *not* an autonomous agency but, rather, "the most
speculative, most ideal, and most internal element in a deployment of
sexuality organized by power in its grip on bodies and their materiality,
their forces, energies, sensations and pleasures." By creating this imaginary
element, the deployment of sexuality established the *desire* for sex, a desire
that makes us think that we, too, are autonomous beings, with some
"essential" ingredient untouched by power—when in fact we are, by elab-
orating and treasuring this desire, this secret and mysterious inner "urge,"
inextricably "fastened" to the deployment of sexuality, "the constitutive
movement of power."[17]

I have taken the time here to elaborate Foucault's theories because
they are key in the necessary shift from a focus on female desire to a focus
on the female body in feminine praxis, pain, and pleasure. While noting
that Foucault himself strangely avoids or overlooks the particular gender
economy inherent in his model, I nevertheless feel that this perspective
contains enormous potential for feminist inquiry, especially in the liberation
from the fixation on desire endemic to recent theory.[18] In the past I have
written that the articulation of female desire in performance has the capacity
to produce the most powerful subversion of ideology. My reconsideration
at this time involves increased dissatisfaction with the term *desire* and its
ground in the psychoanalytic paradigm, a theoretical model that has yet
to construct woman as speaking subject, as something other than object
to male desire.[19] The further difficulty in establishing desire as a material,
historical referent provides another clue as to its inefficiency for feminism;
one is always "tracing" desire, following its footprints in the snow of the
imaginary. Foucault's historical account of the deployment of sexuality, by
contrast, squarely locates the emergence of desire as an element of that
deployment, revealing it as a figment of individual power which gives the
illusion of autonomy. Our obsession with and focus on desire in part

prevents us from examining the nature of power as it wields sexuality and commands bodies. Close to the end of his book, Foucault produces something of a manifesto:

> [One] must not think that by saying yes to sex, one says no to power; on the contrary, . . . [it] is the agency of sex that we must break away from, if we aim . . . to counter the grips of power with the claims of bodies, pleasures, and knowledges, in their multiplicity and their possibility of resistance. The rallying point for the counterattack against the deployment of sexuality ought not to be sex-desire, but bodies and pleasures.[20]

Of course, Foucault does not detail strategies, leaving us to ponder the question of how this goal is to be achieved. The other theoretical models for body-pleasure subversion are equally short on specific strategy: Cixous's mandate to "write the body" is notoriously imprecise; and Luce Irigaray, under the heading "Women out of the bedroom," merely exhorts women to "do what comes to mind, do what you like; without 'reasons,' without 'valid motives,' without 'justification.'"[21] Hardly clear maps for action.

So, what, specifically in the context of feminist performance, would constitute this particular political move? How might it be possible for a feminist performer to express "female" pleasure, especially in terms of the female body, without resorting to essentialist categories?[22] I believe that at least a partial answer resides in a concept of erotic agency; that women artists, manipulating imagery in order to inscribe themselves in discourse as erotic agents or to create an erotic sensibility, may transgress the limits of representation and construct a different viewing space wherein both the spectator and performer become differentiated subjects.[23] This transgressive erotic agency may come in a variety of representations that on surface might not appear "sexual," in the common understanding of that term, and that is precisely the point of this perspective.

In this regard I find Eileen O'Neill's definitions of *pornography* and *erotica* useful: in her lexicon *pornography* refers to sexually explicit representations that have arousal as their aim; *erotica*, by contrast, expresses sexual arousal and pleasure rather than causing it—"It is what suggests it, puts me in touch with its possibility, by making me aware of myself as a physical, sexual being. The erotic reminds me, as it were, of *my very fleshiness* and of my capacity for sexual pleasure. Erotica may cause sexual excitement, but . . . this . . . is not essential to it" (my emphasis).[24] She further draws a necessary distinction between these first two categories and a third, which includes material that aims at sexual arousal via presented harm to another person, naming it "noxious," from the Latin *nocere*, meaning "to harm."

The centuries-old conventions surrounding the figuration of the female body and sexuality, those covert systems discussed earlier, would seem to negate the possibility of political efficacy within an erotic agenda, but, on the contrary, such a focus can foreground those conventions and divest them of at least some of their deployed power. In one of the most infamous and problematic of Barbara Smith's works (*Feed Me* [1973]) she partitioned a small space in a gallery, filled it with a mattress, rug, pillows, incense, massage oils, candles, and other trappings of pleasure and comfort, including food and wine. During the twenty-four hours of the installation, Smith sat nude in this space, with a notice at the entrance inviting spectators to join her and interact with her for short periods of time. Many feminists have criticized this work for reinscribing structures of voyeurism and fetishism, when in fact it defied them. Agreed, sexually explicit material in a woman's performance can often invoke representational processes that consume the female body as a sexualized object; but here the construction and communication of the artist as erotic agent intervenes to break down her cultural construction as fantasy object and replace it with something not previously perceived—the subject-performer. Jessica Benjamin outlines this process as a moment of recognition between self and Other, "of really recognizing the other as existing outside the self and not just as a bundle of my own projections, . . . [which is] the decisive aspect of differentiation." In a performance such as Smith's the recognition is commanded, conversely perpetrated as a condition of the spectator's involvement, so that Smith is no longer an object for consumption, "a bundle of projections," but an erotic subject, one who expresses her own pleasure. In Benjamin's elaboration "the clarity of such a moment, the heightened awareness of both self and other, the reciprocal recognition that intensifies the self's freedom of expression, is actually the goal of erotic union."[25] Smith's performance, knowingly called "Feed Me" (not "let me feed you"), created a heightened body awareness and erotic sensibility while asserting the pleasure-ability of her own body. Smith has said of this piece that she would not have allowed an interaction that was not positive toward her: "I would prevent any action which I did not consider food"; and further articulated her erotic agency in regard to her artwork in general: "For me my art accomplishes my own liberation. It makes me stronger. For others it acts as any art does, a confrontation that they must face on their own terms."[26]

The artist as erotic agent can also operate to dismantle the appearance of sexual offering, as in Karen Finley's transgressive performances. In *The Constant State of Desire* (1987) the very title promises a protracted stimulation of our innermost urges, a furtive titillation of that mysterious state, when instead we are bombarded with horrific descriptions of noxious sexual acts, incest, suicides, degradation, torture, and male castration for revenge.[27] While Finley sometimes disrobes in her work, her body is not the passive nude of classical representation, as she covers herself with food, candy, ashes, or feathers, curiously evoking both self-abuse and sensual self-pleasuring. The myriad, usually perverse forms of sexuality are described in first person but from different personae, including male teenagers, small girls, old men, etc.—the effect of which is to put "Karen Finley" under erasure, deconstructing the problematics of representation and throwing into question the spectator's relationship to desire.[28] Here her erotic agency is expressed through refusal, a defiance of consumption as object by aggressively

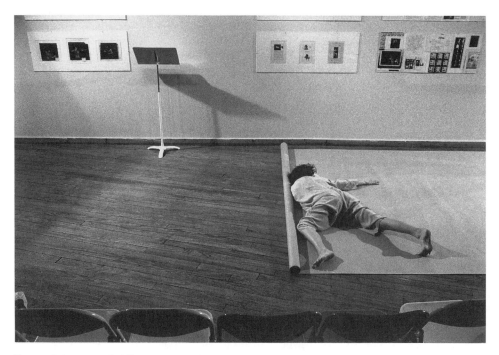

Fig. 2. Marianne Goldberg in *The Body Word Series*. Photo credit: Robert Tobey.

destroying both the object of fantasy and the potential alternative: in O'Neill's terms Finley proffers pornography, only to transform it.

Marianne Goldberg's dance-text performances (what she calls her Body-Word Series), in marked contrast, provide another mode of erotic agency, in her sensual exploration of her body's impulses and pleasures. Whether speaking a text herself or working with voice-over, Goldberg uses her body to intervene with unrehearsed movement, breaking the illusion of cohesive narrative through the assertion of bodily pleasure in gesture. In one performance of *Hudson Rover* (1989) she rolls on the floor, slowly wrapping and then unwrapping her (clothed) body in blue fabric, seemingly oblivious to anything other than the feel of hard and soft surfaces. A videocamera is passed among the audience members, as each is invited to tape a portion of the performance—a move that foregrounds the act of spectatorship, also serving to exaggerate Goldberg's representational status as performing body. By constantly interrupting the text with various forms of "body," she further counteracts the gazing process, creating an erotic atmosphere of body awareness, breaking the audience's identification with the abstraction of language. Rather than invoking sex or sexual desire, Goldberg's work focuses on her subjective pleasure in her own body and its possibilities for movement, a focus that nevertheless generates a kind of tension some spectators apparently find disturbing. I feel it is her ability to demonstrate pleasure, her refusal of objectification in her articulation of body as artist-agent, which disturbs; which confronts the masculist ideology embedded in conventions of representation.[29]

258   While I could continue to cite many other performances, my hope is that

Fig. 3. Marianne Goldberg in *The Body Word Series*. Photo credit: Robert Tobey.

the few mentioned begin to point up a variety of subversive modes of performance which call upon an erotic sensibility already in use by feminist performers, a collection of differences which nevertheless have the similar effect of intervention into representational systems that objectify the female body. I am interested in suggesting avenues of inquiry in our attempts to avoid both the distancing tendency of theory and the threat of essentialism in addressing the female body in performance. At this point in history it is politically imperative that feminists construct the language, the theoretical models, that will enable analysis of feminine praxis and the oppressions of the female body. The theories and methodologies outlined herein may provide further possibilities for the articulation of the problematics concerning the female body in performance and inspire new strategies based on an exploration of feminist representations of pain, feminine praxis, and pleasure.

NOTES

1. Jane Gallop, *Thinking through the Body* (New York: Columbia University Press, 1988), 93, 98.

2. Adrienne Rich, "Notes on a Politics of Location," in *Women, Feminist Identity and Society in the 1980s*, ed. Myriam Diaz-Diocaretz and Iris Zavala (Amsterdam: John Benjamins, 1985), 9.

3. Alison M. Jaggar, "Introduction," in *Gender/Body/Knowledge: Feminist Reconstructions of Being and Knowing*, ed. Alison M. Jaggar and Susan R. Bordo (New Brunswick, N.J.: Rutgers University Press, 1989), 4.

4. See Susan R. Bordo, "The Body and the Reproduction of Femininity: A Feminist Appropriation of Foucault," in Jaggar and Bordo, *Gender/Body/Knowledge*,

13; Teresa de Lauretis, "Semiotics and Experience," in *Alice Doesn't: Feminism, Semiotics, Cinema* (Bloomington: Indiana University Press, 1984), 158–86.

5. Bordo, "Body and the Reproduction of Femininity," 27.

6. Ibid., 25–26, 13. In a related but notably different context, Catherine Clément defends the persistence of class struggle by noting "a considerable shift between the reality of class struggle and the way that it is lived mythically, especially by intellectuals who have difficulty being able to size up the reality of struggles directly, because they are in a position where work on language and the Imaginary have fundamental importance and can put blinders on them" (Hélène Cixous and Catherine Clément, *The Newly Born Woman*, trans. Betsy Wing [Minneapolis: University of Minnesota Press, 1986], 159). To quote Sheila Rowbotham: "There are enormous and serious difficulties in the relationship between groups of people who have been subordinated and theory. A movement helps you to overcome some of the oppressive distancing of theory and this has been a . . . continuing creative endeavour of women's liberation" (quoted in Rich, *Notes on a Politics of Location*, 17).

7. Elaine Scarry, *The Body in Pain: The Making and Unmaking of the World* (New York: Oxford University Press, 1985), 109.

8. Bordo, "Body and the Reproduction of Femininity," 26.

9. Gayatri Chakravorty Spivak, "French Feminism in an International Frame," *In Other Worlds: Essays in Cultural Politics* (New York: Routledge, 1988), 150.

10. Ibid., 153.

11. Scarry, *Body in Pain*, 4, 9.

12. This particular struggle seems marked not only by the inability to communicate the pain of crisis pregnancy and illegal abortion but also by a failure to locate the female body in the structures of power referred to by Bordo and others earlier; such a strategy might prove to have a significant coalescing effect among women from opposing sides of the abortion debate rather than pitting them continually at odds in a red herring argument of ethics or morality. Also see Faye Ginsburg, "The Body Politic," in *Pleasure and Danger: Exploring Female Sexuality*, ed. Carole Vance (New York and London: Routledge and Kegan Paul, 1984). "In writing off the pro-life response as simply reactionary or 'anti-sex,' pro-choice activists fail to recognize the degree to which women in this country—by choice and by circumstance—are still invested in a system which connects their sexuality to heterosexuality, childbearing, and the support of a husband" (186). And in a similar vein, Irene Diamond and Lee Quinby write that to polarize the abortion debate over ethics versus reproductive rights situates the argument in the language of control characteristic of a technology of sex, which then cannot recognize the problem within the context of the deployment of sexuality ("American Feminism and the Language of Control," in *Feminism and Foucault: Reflections on Resistance*, ed. Diamond and Quinby [Boston: Northeastern University Press, 1988], 197).

13. Peggy Phelan, "Feminist Theory, Poststructuralism, and Performance," *TDR: A Journal of Performance Studies* 32, no. 1 (1988): 122, 123.

14. See Sandra Lee Bartky, "Foucault, Femininity, and the Modernization of Patriarchal Power"; Susan R. Bordo, "Anorexia Nervosa: Psychopathology as the Crystallization of Culture," both in Diamond and Quinby, *Feminism and Foucault*, 61–86 and 87–118; and Bordo, "Body and the Reproduction of Femininity," 28.

15. Hélène Cixous, "The Laugh of the Medusa"; Marguerite Duras, quoted in "Utopias," both in *New French Feminisms: An Anthology*, ed. Elaine Marks and Isabelle de Courtivron (1980; reprint, New York: Shocken Books, 1981), 244–64 and 238.

16. Michel Foucault, *The History of Sexuality* (New York: Vintage Books, 1980), 1:103, 104, 105–6.

17. Foucault, *History of Sexuality*, 1:152–53, 155, 157.

18. For a more extended and interdisciplinary discussion of the possibilities for feminism within Foucauldian thought, see Diamond and Quinby, *Feminism and Foucault*. Especially see Sandra Lee Bartky, who notes:

> Foucault treats the body throughout as if it were one, as if the bodily experiences of men and women did not differ and as if men and women bore the same relationship to the characteristic institutions of modern life. . . . he is blind to those disciplines that produce a modality of embodiment that is peculiarly feminine. . . . his analysis as whole reproduces that sexism which is endemic throughout Western political theory. ("Foucault, Feminism, and the Modernization of Patriarchal Power," 63–64)

19. See Jessica Benjamin, "A Desire of One's Own: Psychoanalytic Feminism and Intersubjective Space," in *Feminist Studies / Critical Studies*, ed. Teresa de Lauretis (Bloomington: Indiana University Press, 1986). Her struggle to create a model for the identification of female desire is marked by its deferment into the future, wholly dependent on the construction of a feminist mode of parenting which seems unrealistic at best and unremittingly utopian at worst. The strength of the essay lies in her clear description of the problematics of this project and the various attempts that have been made heretofore.

20. Foucault, *History of Sexuality*, 1:157.

21. Luce Irigaray, *This Sex Which Is Not One* (New York: Cornell University Press, 1985), 204.

22. Another concomitant argument, too lengthy and complex to include in this paper, concerns our present inability to theoretically explore and assess the political efficacy of a particular performance beyond individual spectator response without rejecting the postmodern frame. The notion that each "reader" of text constructs her/his own text does not account for the potential shared experience of an audience, who presumably may construct even remotely similar performance "texts" when simultaneously witnessing the same event. Put another way, is it necessary that everyone be "reading" the body the same way before "writing" the body can be effective? That there are bound to be responsive differences is a given, but the degree to which a shift in consciousness can be obtained, observed, and even predicted is some measure of the success of a feminist agenda, which aims to effect change. The tension generated by the conflict between a political need, such as feminism's, and the postmodern refusal of a collective response has yet to be examined.

23. This resonates with Jessica Benjamin's conception of the "intersubjective" mode, an organizing model for woman's desire which is an alternative to the phallic, or intrapsychic, mode: "The intrapsychic mode operates at the level of subject-object experience, where the other's actual independent subjectivity is not relevant. . . . the intersubjective mode, where two subjects meet, where both woman and man can be subject, may point to a locus for woman's independent desire, a relationship to desire that is not represented by the phallus" ("Desire of One's Own," 92–93).

24. Eileen O'Neill, "(Re)presentations of Eros: Exploring Female Sexual Agency," in Jaggar and Bordo, *Gender/Body/Knowledge*, 69.

25. Benjamin, "Desire of One's Own," 93.

26. "Interview with Barbara Smith by Moira Roth," excerpted in *Performance Anthology*, ed. Carl E. Loeffler and Darlene Tong (San Francisco: Contemporary Arts Press, 1980), 118.

27. See *TDR: A Journal of Performance Studies* 32, no. 1 (1988): 152–58, for a text of this piece, along with an interview of Finley.

28. See Eileen O'Neill for a similar discussion of Cindy Sherman's self-portrait film stills, which "do not represent a particular woman but the problematics of representation itself" ("(Re)presentations of Eros," 75).

29. Goldberg herself has spoken of a "moire" pattern (borrowing from the jargon of print) generated by her intersections of body and text, an unpredictable blurring of communication which throws both spectator and performer into uncertainty, which she now deliberately courts in her work. Although Goldberg does not specifically attribute the moire pattern to an erotic sensibility in her work, clearly it is the body element of the performance, the intervention and sudden emergence of the body into/over text, that creates this tension—which I would name "erotic." (See Goldberg, "The Non-Essentialist Body" [Paper presented at ATHE, August 1989].)

Practicing Cultural Disruptions: Gay and Lesbian Representation and Sexuality

Jill Dolan

Consider these scenarios:

1. At an art gallery and performance space in downtown Milwaukee, a long table at the entryway is set with colorful mints and peanuts and pink napkins decorated with black-lined hearts and flowers which announce "Happy Anniversary Peggy and Lois." The festive tone announces a real anniversary framed as a performance called *Anniversary Waltz*, which celebrates the ten-year relationship of Peggy Shaw and Lois Weaver, cofounders with Deborah Margolin of the lesbian feminist performance troupe Split Britches. *Anniversary Waltz* combines bits of "classic" Split Britches performances with a smattering of new material, held together with vaudevillian patter about relationships. The piece purports to offer a look at lesbian longevity; instead, although it shifts through the lesbian-specific iconography of butch-femme relationships, it constructs an innocuous glimpse into a more generic notion of coupleness.
2. Theatre X, also in Milwaukee, mounts a production of Robert Chesley's *Jerker, or the Helping Hand* (1986), a play whose structuring device is pornographic phone sex between two gay men, one of whom eventually dies of AIDS. The text describes scenes of nonconventional sexual fantasy that inspire both men to masturbate. But the performers never enact the sexual fantasies or the masturbation indicated by the text. Their bodies remain clothed and untouched, as their encounters move from completely anonymous, graphically sexual calls to a relational intimacy based on knowledge of each others' voices and yearnings.
3. The fourth annual Lesbian Variety Show in Madison, Wisconsin, is disrupted by two acts that employ butch-femme and sadomasochistic iconography. In the context of a mostly lesbian cultural feminist celebration of femaleness, actions that represent taboo sexual practice intrude on the Variety Show's worship of gender difference.[1] The transgressive performances are decried in the local feminist press as representations of violence against women, and guidelines are drawn up to guard against the inclusion of such images in next year's show.

In the cultural and political climate of the 1990s what do gay and

lesbian representations like these mean? Do their meanings read as assimilative or transgressive, now that dominant regimes of power and knowledge
are once again branding homosexual representations as pornographic and
obscene? The National Endowment for the Arts' (NEA) recently released
guidelines to artists seeking to receive or keep their funding relies on the
Supreme Court's 1973 definition of obscenity in the *Miller v. California*
decision. Obscenity is defined as work that: (1) the "average person, applying contemporary community standards, would find appeals to the prurient
interest"; (2) "depicts or describes sexual conduct in a patently offensive
way," particularly—according to the NEA—homoerotic and sadomasochistic activities; and (3) "lacks serious literary, artistic, political, or scientific value."[2]

This definition relies on the commonsense knowledge of a generic
viewer to determine obscenity. Historically, this viewer most resembles the
white, heterosexual, male senator from North Carolina, Jesse Helms, whose
outcry over the Robert Mapplethorpe and Andres Serrano exhibits
prompted that the new language of censorship be attached to all of the
NEA's funding awards.[3] The determination of behavior considered "patently
offensive" is based on the standards of his dominant cultural community.
If gay or lesbian community standards were applied to test obscenity and
if the assumed spectator of artistic work were a lesbian or gay man, commonsense connotations of prurience would certainly shift.[4]

But as the feminist antipornography movement exemplifies, the radicality of such a shift cannot always be assumed. Some commentators even
point to "the complicity of the anti-pornography movement in the larger
moral panic," which, in part, has prompted the renewed vigilantism over
obscenity.[5] As Daphne Read notes presciently, "It seems reasonable to fear
that new legislation [developed by Catharine A. MacKinnon and Andrea
Dworkin] aimed at censoring or regulating pornography might be used
more broadly to repress gays and lesbians, artists, and others . . . in spite
of a feminist presence in the political process."[6]

Foucault suggests that throughout history what appears to be the
repression of sexuality actually proliferates different ways in which it enters
discourse, some of which resist hegemonic power.[7] Perhaps the regressive
outlawing of gay and lesbian images as prurient and obscene will prompt
the reradicalization of their meaning effects in the 1990s. Perhaps representations of gay and lesbian sexuality will regain their potential to disrupt
hegemonic meanings by invoking the excess of sexual practice, after a brief
period of neutralizing assimilation into the dominant discourse on sexuality
as alternative life-styles and identities.

The furious discussion promoted by the congressional compromise
measure to Helms's proposed amendment to the NEA appropriations bill
is focused on representations of bodies, desire, and spectatorial pleasure
which transgress the boundaries of white heterosexual propriety. For
instance, Mapplethorpe's pleasurable citing/sighting of black male bodies
in classically sculpted poses, often with penises erect, implies sexual practices anathema to the virulently racist and homophobic likes of Senator

Helms. By offering homosexual and cross-racial visual pleasure in flesh, they visually flaunt a rejection of compulsory heterosexual practice.[8] Exhibited in galleries and museums, the photographs take public representational space to image eroticized organs, which simply by virtue of being seen, contest dominant cultural regimes of knowledge and power about sexuality and race.

The possibility for transgression in such representations lies in the hint of sexual practice and seduction they envision, not in the gay life-style to which they refer, which superficially has come to resemble the quotidian routines of heterosexual relationships. Teresa de Lauretis, writing on lesbian representation, cautions that it is exceedingly difficult to alter the "standard of vision, the frame of reference of visibility, of *what can be seen*," since "the conventions of seeing, and the relations of desire and meaning in spectatorship, [remain] partially anchored or contained by a frame of visibility that is still heterosexual."[9] As a result, most representations of lesbian and gay sexuality remain mired in realist images of life-style and identity which fail to exceed the heterosexual frame.

The representation of sex politics as life-style, prompted partly by the Personal is Political slogan of the early white feminist movement, has limited efficacy in a culture in which life-styles are so easily assimilated, commodified, and neutralized by dominant ideology. Black feminist theorist bell hooks suggests that the emphasis on identity and life-style in white feminism, for example, has contributed to the movement's elitism and defused its ability to move social discourse. hooks says, "To emphasize . . . engagement with feminist struggle as political commitment, we could avoid using the phrase 'I am a feminist' (a linguistic structure designed to refer to some personal aspect of identity and self-definition) and could state 'I advocate feminism.'"[10]

Saying "I am a lesbian" has been validated in cultural feminist discourse as speech that breaks the silence of lesbian existence under heterosexual hegemony. But in the 1970s and 1980s lesbianism's too rigid attachment to an identity politics of gender by terms such as *woman-identification* recloseted active sexual practice.[11] Cultural feminism reified same-sex female relationships as a new and better version of the heterosexual family, a claim that has limited potential for changing the dominant discourse on how sexuality organizes culture and experience.[12] *Anniversary Waltz*, for example, is ultimately an assimilationist lesbian text because of its emphasis on romance and familial relations rather than sexual ones.[13]

A somewhat idealized lesbian family anchors the text's narrative of the vicissitudes of Weaver and Shaw's relationship—their partnership is inscribed as a marriage, from the pink table napkins on display in the lobby to textual references to the now twenty-year-old daughter the couple raised. Although Weaver and Shaw mock the conventions of heterosexual marriage by "lesbianizing" the familiar, deprecatory popular cultural patter about such relationships, their own partnership, though played as camp, remains the somewhat romanticized center of the text.

When they began performing together in the early 1980s Weaver's and Shaw's personal and performative butch-femme role-playing lent the couple a certain notoriety.[14] The antisex rhetoric of cultural feminism made their butch-femme display of sexual possibilities and practice—informed by what appeared to be an appropriation of heterosexual and male/female gender roles—a transgressive representation in feminist and mainstream contexts.[15] Early productions at the WOW Cafe, where Split Britches primarily performed, were often decried in feminist media as politically regressive because they employed butch-femme iconography and role playing.

But in *Anniversary Waltz* Weaver and Shaw play with butch-femme iconography and roles only by trading the costumes of gender evenly between them. As the piece progresses through bits of the couple's performative and personal history, they peel off layers of costuming to reveal the signs of the opposite role underneath. Their manipulation of butch-femme solely as clothing moves it away from the transgressions of its historical signification. Rather than referring to sexual practice, like the Mapplethorpe photographs, the images that comprise *Anniversary Waltz* focus resolutely on lesbian life-styles. Under the rubric of a long-term relationship the transgressive difference of alternative forms of lesbian sexuality once represented by the complexity of butch-femme drops out. Its costumes become empty sets of gendered clothing without referents to sexual practice or more than the most polite, nostalgic evidence of desire.

Extending hooks's analogy to "I practice lesbian sex" (in all its varieties), rather than "I am a lesbian," would initiate a discourse that might displace the emphasis on life-styles and relationships and break open the sanctimonious strictures of politically correct lesbian identifications. A renewed focus on marginalized sex acts, instead of romantic, familial relationships, might reassert the transgressive quality of lesbians who enter the public sphere as representations. De Lauretis's cautionary analysis ends by apparently suggesting that only butch-femme lesbians can enter, together, the heterosexual frame of vision.[16] Making sexual practice blatantly visible on gendered bodies that wear this deconstruction of compulsory heterosexuality might still be a productively alienating act.[17]

Such a move might indicate a return to historical definitions of "deviant" sexuality as acts, rather than people. Eve Kosofsky Sedgwick, for instance, writes that in histories of sexual taxonomy "the proscription of particular *acts* called 'sodomy' (acts that might be performed by anybody), [were] displaced after the late nineteenth century by the definition of particular kinds of *persons*, specifically 'homosexuals.'"[18] Emphasizing the individual person over sexual acts or practice available for performance by *any body* inscribes homosexuality and lesbianism as biologically essentialized problems of life-styles, rather than as social practices that comprise sex acts accomplished with agency differently through history.[19]

The choice of sex acts are what mark gay and lesbian bodies as different agents within history. Judith Butler proposes, "As an intentionally organized materiality, the body is always an embodying *of* possibilities both conditioned and circumscribed by historical convention. . . . the body *is* a historical situation . . . a manner of doing, dramatizing, and *reproducing* a historical situation."[20] In the 1950s, for example, lesbian bodies coded with butch-femme iconography represented a transgressive accomplishment—the naming and practice of lesbian desire in a violently heterosexist climate. Lesbians who represented themselves as butch-femme in the 1970s bore traces of its courageous history, as they refused to retreat to the closet built by feminism. Even lesbian bodies of the 1980s and 1990s, when visible in representation, retain traces of the history of butch-femme resistance to dominant ideology which can still be accessed as transgressive. The disruption it symbolized can be realized by actively representing the desire and sexual practice to which butch-femme once referred. As Joan Nestle remarks, "For gay people, history is a place where the body carries its own story."[21]

The Mapplethorpe debacle indicates that speaking homo or lesbian sex, as opposed to identity, in public forums is still transgressive enough to activate the machinery of state power. Even if, as Foucault cautions, such transgressions do not exceed the discourse on sexuality but only set the poles of one extreme, the sex practice to which they refer contests the hegemonic principles of sexual difference which heterosexuality reifies. Representations of sexual practice which deviate from heterosexual acts threaten pornographic excess at sites accustomed to inscribing sex only as erotic, romantic love according to a heterosexual model.

In her book on hard-core film pornography Linda Williams offers a useful working definition of pornography as "the visual (and sometimes aural) representation of living, moving bodies engaged in explicit, usually unfaked, sexual acts with a primary intent of arousing viewers."[22] Making visible gay male or lesbian bodies in motion, engaged in sex acts, is perhaps one most radical way to disrupt dominant cultural discourse on sexuality and gender. The "primary intent of arousing viewers" might inaugurate a theory of reception based very materially—instead of psychoanalytically— on an invitation to participate in the seduction of alternative locations of desire.

It could be argued, then, that representing any sex act publically is transgressive. Williams, in fact, argues that explicitness will demystify what Foucault calls the transcendent secret of sex. I agree and intend to suggest that imaging gay and lesbian sex in the public sphere, rather than imagining it in the private, moves toward Foucault's notion of a different economy of bodies and pleasure.[23]

Some performance forms and contexts, however, seem more capable than others of accomplishing the "making seen" of such sexual practice. Homosexuality's assertion of the same can hardly be accommodated in bourgeois realism, for example, which asserts moral and sexual bipolarity— right/wrong, good/bad, and male/female—and maintains heterosexual difference as its organizing principle.[24] In his article on dramatizing gay male history John Clum organizes his textual explications by designating certain plays as either "outside/heterosexual" or "inside/homosexual" perspectives on gay subject matter.[25] But the "inside" gay male texts in Clum's analysis which use realism to inscribe their heroic lovers into discourse exemplify the dominant culture's inability to see or to image the marginalized sexual practice that at least partly girds a definition of homosexual identity. Clum's discomfort with defining homosexual identity solely as sexual practice, signaled by his article's title ("A Culture That Isn't Just Sexual"), leads him to argue in favor of the representation of gay life-styles rather than gay sex.

Nestle suggests the reverse, insisting that, for gay men and lesbians, "being a sexual people is our gift to the world."[26] But traditional theatrical forms tend to work structurally to keep the sexual gifts of gay and lesbian subjects invisible. Even in the texts Clum examines as favorably exploring gay male identity, realism approves the male lovers' sexuality as moral and right because it is romantic, not physical, and usually rewards their celibacy with death. There's a move in these inside texts toward the "outside" perspective, which legislates that sexuality be heterosexuality or not be imaged at all.

In the incipient realism, for example, of Martin Sherman's *Bent* (1979) and Chesley's *Jerker,* both of which Clum discusses in his article, sex is exiled to a nonphysical plane.[27] *Bent* opens on the day-after, postcarnal denouement of Max's one-night stand with a leatherclad Gestapo flunky. Their evening of anonymous sex, replete with intimations of sadomasochistic (s/m) play, is implicitly punished when *Schutzstaffel* (SS) troops storm Max's apartment. The wilder side of gay male sex is tinged with amorality by its quick equation with Nazi terror.

The physicality of sex at least referred to in the first scene is then elided situationally by the play's content. Once Max is interred in a camp, he and Horst, the gay man he meets there, are constrained to verbal sex, the possibility of physical union eternally deferred by the watchful eyes of the guards. The men's surreptitious exchanges serve as a trope for the way realism operates on marginalized sexuality. Under the eyes of the dominant culture gay male sex must be expressed furtively, described but not performed, and must culminate in orgasms of affirming emotional love rather than physical transport—that is, erotics rather than pornography.

Williams suggests that the distinction between erotics and pornography—often posed by both dominant culture executors like the Meese Commission, as well as by antiporn feminists, who too frequently travel similar ideological terrain—is loaded with moralizing that stifles a more productive inquiry into the representation of sex:

> The very notion of erotica as "good," clean, non-explicit representations of sexual pleasure in opposition to dirty, explicit pornographic ones is false.... The one emphasizes desire, the other satisfaction. Depending on who is looking, both can appear dirty, perverse, or too explicit.... We need to see pornography in all its naked explicitness if we are to speak frankly about sexual power and pleasure and if we are to demystify sex.[28]

Privileging erotica over pornography is particularly troubling in gay and lesbian representations, since the nonexplicitness of erotica continues to mask the difference of gay and lesbian sex. Likewise, realism helps formally to repress references to active sex, cloaking bodies and pleasure under a domestic guise of romantic propriety. Pornography exceeds realism by lifting the cloak to reveal the action; its explicitness offers material investigations into the discourses of power, as well as pleasure.

Chesley's *Jerker*, since it is less realist than *Bent* at the outset and marks itself as explicitly pornographic, at first holds out potential to represent transgressive sexual practice in a radical way. *Jerker, or the Helping Hand*, is subtitled, "A Pornographic Elegy with Redeeming Social Value and a Hymn to the Queer Men of San Francisco in Twenty Telephone Calls, Many of Them Dirty." First performed in 1986, the text is marked by the constrained sexuality of a community plagued with AIDS. The play confines its graphic descriptions of sexual practice to literally disembodied phone sex between two gay men, never performing their fantasies to set in motion the pornography of desiring, visible, moving homosexual bodies. Although they never meet, Bert and J. R. fall in love over the phone shortly before Bert dies of AIDS. The move toward an ill-fated romance disqualifies *Jerker* as pornography because, as Williams says, paraphrasing Susan Sontag, porn is never primarily about the formation of a couple.[29]

Jerker's subversive potential lies in the ten or so phone calls before its descent into empathy for the loving and the dead. The phone calls begin as completely anonymous and aggressively sexual, almost clinical descriptions of sometimes sadomasochistic sex play. But the calls progress to an intimacy that makes the sex scenes they describe emotional, erotic, and relational, rather than pornographic. The fantasies culminate in J. R.'s fairy tale about three men who simply sleep together and don't have sex at all.

Theatre X's 1989 production of *Jerker* chose several Brechtian techniques to resist the text's pull toward theatrical and ideological convention. A male narrator was placed at a table behind the bifurcated set, from which he read aloud the stage directions. The directions throughout the published text indicate that the men literally "jerk off," although their erections, given realism's politesse, are carefully hidden under their bedclothes or their underwear. The two actors playing J. R. and Bert for Theatre X were fully clothed through the entire play, and, although they verbally announced their orgasms, they never touched their bodies. Often the performers' actions resisted the instructions read from the text.

Such a Brechtian intervention worked on the representation of gay male sexual practice in several ways. First, it quite literally refused to embody it by maintaining the distance of intellectual description. The fantasies related by J. R. and Bert were relegated even farther from physical inscription in representation because they remained narrative, and even their orgasmic effects went unimaged. The inversion of the Brechtian *gestus* to nonshowing, nonaction, perhaps exemplified gay male social relations in the age of AIDS—sex relegated to telephone technology and history, imagination and nostalgia, and exiled, still, from representation.

Secondly, while gay male sex was verbalized in the Theatre X production, by choosing not to visualize it, the production suppressed the trangressions of pornography in favor of erotics and failed to actualize pornography's disruptive potential. Enacting the culminating masturbatory orgasms of *Jerker*'s sex fantasies might have been a more radical transgression of the ethical bourgeois performance space, less aesthetic than the critical distance imposed by even the Brechtian frame. The noninteraction of the performers would have adequately maintained the commentary on the isolation of sex bound by AIDS.

Because of its ideological and formal movement away from pornography into erotic realism, *Jerker* fails as a truly radical explication of gay male representations of sexual practice. But few lesbian texts come to mind that at least match *Jerker*'s frank descriptions of sex. The characters in Jane Chambers's and Sarah Dreher's realist plays, for instance, fall in and out of romantic love, but they rarely engage in anything more sexual than a hug or a kiss.[30]

Lesbian sexual practice remains repressed in these plays by the exigencies of propriety—both of the dominant culture and of the lesbian cultural feminist discourse on sexuality. The distinction in lesbian cultural feminism between erotics and pornography is marked by the iconographic representation of power on female bodies. Hegemonic antiporn feminism has so successfully infiltrated lesbian discourse in the 1980s that even erotica has been flattened out and carefully monitored for any evidence of politically incorrect sex practice. As Foucault might observe, however, such regimes of power seem inevitably to breed resistance. The 1980s also saw the "implantation of perversions" within lesbian communities.[31] The new visibility of sadomasochistic practices and representational styles seemed to replace butch-femme as the location of cultural feminist anxiety over imagining or imaging sexual practice between women.

But while "avant-garde" lesbians begin to textualize practices that cultural feminism still decries as pornographic, representing s/m as sexual style is still read as a violent invasion of lesbian cultural feminist erotic images. The fourth annual Lesbian Variety Show in Madison, Wisconsin, exemplified the friction between these opposing discourses. The Variety Show is a product of the city's lesbian cultural feminist community, whose demography is best generalized as young, middle-class, and white. In 1989 the show's preferred representations of the eroticized feminine body were disrupted by the intrusion of representations of gender, power, and sex which its context could only inscribe as pornographic.[32]

The first half of the Variety Show presented poets and musicians who crooned lesbian love verse in repetitive rhythms and equally repetitive chords. The cultural feminist-inspired ethos of "woman spirit" hung in the air like a musky mist, and spectators generally applauded the acts of empowering verbalization and sometimes interpretive movement which celebrated the erotics of femininity.[33]

Two back-to-back acts in the second half of the show broke the aura. In the first two women performed a lip sync and dance routine to the rock song "Push It" by a group called Salt 'n Peppa. As the song began, one woman entered wearing a black leather vest, jeans, boots, and handcuffs at her waist, lip-syncing and snapping her fingers to the beat. The lip syncing liberated this act from the naturalized cultural feminist representational economy in which the variety show had been trading into a gay male performance tradition in which dressing up in gender roles and impersonating singers has a long subcultural history.[34] Suddenly, the Variety Show's feminine aesthetic was disrupted by a large gay woman in butch clothing, furiously moving her lips to a male musician's rock song.

Rather than Weaver and Shaw's innocuous trading of gendered clothing, this act used its leather and lace to tease out the seduction of butch-femme as sexual roles. When the first woman's partner entered the stage, the butch-femme dynamic and all of its class connotations were secured. The second woman wore high-heeled black shoes, fishnet stockings, and only pasties on her breasts. She danced into the space to seduce the first woman, and the two acted out the song in a way that referred to sexual practice as it had not been before during the long evening. The sheer display of their bodies, layered with butch-femme and vaguely s/m iconography, inscribed the act within bar dyke culture, outside the hegemonic meanings of middle-class white feminism.

The next act outdid the transgressions of the first. In a much more stylized performance that quoted the conventions of body-building contests as well as gay lip-sync spectacles, two women power lifters performed an interpretation of Barbra Streisand's song "Prisoner." The pun was intended, since the act's content included relatively explicit references to s/m.

As in the first act, bodies were present here in full force, clearly sexualized and also genderized, an admission of difference that the staunchly feminine show could not contain. At the play's open one woman stood facing the spectators with her arms crossed over her bare chest, wearing black jeans, black boots, a black watchcap, and mirror sunglasses. As the Streisand song began, she flexed her quite well-defined muscles in a display that flattered her V-shaped body. Uncrossing her arms revealed her breasts as small flaps of skin; the practiced, constructed power of her body seemed to have tampered even with her biology. Femininity was startlingly absent.

Her partner, wearing a white tank T-shirt, cut-off jean shorts, and the ubiquitous black boots, knelt at her feet in apparent supplication. The two began a dance of sorts in which they posed and manipulated the power dynamic their bodies described. When the woman in shorts produced a studded collar, which she offered to the woman in the mirrored sunglasses, indicating she would like to wear it, the audience booed loudly, and the performers broke their severe demeanor and laughed. Once the collar was fastened around the kneeling woman's neck, the one in mirrored sunglasses pulled her into sexualized positions of dominance and submission.

At the song's end, however, the power dynamic abruptly shifted as the kneeling woman rose to her feet and picked up in her arms the woman with mirrored sunglasses, who waved coyly to the audience and was carried off. The abrupt shift seemed to intend parody and also, for those willing to read it, offered a political meaning about the fluidity of power positions in sex and perhaps in gendered relationships and representation as well.

This act proved a radical disruption of a safely eroticized female space, by transgressors who performed sexual seduction through a complex assumption and deconstruction of gender roles inflected with power. For some lesbian spectators, myself included, the scene was clever and seductive, a reference to the "variety" of lesbian sexual practice. The performers' obvious self-consciousness seemed to intend the kind of playful discussion about lesbian sexual potential launched by proponents like Susie Bright. But the scene has been described in the Madison radical feminist press as a pornographic act of violence against women. Newspapers for months after the event carried emotional outpourings that testified to the suffering this act caused. Relying on what Williams calls "naive realism," spectators claimed the images of so-called violence actually caused violence to be inflicted.[35]

As Williams suggests, after Walter Kendrick, pornography is really only defined by its censorship.[36] While Jesse Helms legislates against publicly funded displays of gay male sexuality in representation, the lesbian cultural feminist community perpetrates its own censorship by legislating the correct representations of lesbian sex. Imaging the explicit relationship between power, gender, and sex offends cultural feminist propriety.

Writing about sadomasochistic heterosexual pornography, Williams comments that in art "real sex, like real death, is unaesthetic and therefore out of place."[37] Because gay male or lesbian sex is completely out of place—unimaged, unimagined, invisible—in traditional aesthetic contexts, the most transgressive act at this historical moment would be representing it to excess, in dominant and marginalized reception communities. The explicitness of pornography seems the most constructive choice for practicing cultural disruptions.[38]

NOTES

1. By "cultural feminism" I mean to indicate a strain of feminist ideology and politics sometimes called "radical" or "essentialist," which reifies gender differences and privileges female values as inherently, innately superior to male ones. Although some commentators feel the designation "cultural" is inappropriate because it allows this brand of feminism apparently to corner the market on culture, Alice Echols's distinction between this more recent strain of feminism and the radical feminism that preceded it in the late 1960s and early 1970s is most persuasive. See Echols, *Daring to be Bad: Radical Feminism in America, 1967–1975* (Minneapolis: University of Minnesota Press, 1989).

2. See William H. Honan, "Endowment Tightens Obscenity Rule," *New York Times*, 11 July 1990, B3.

3. For an excellent discussion of the political issues raised by the Mapplethorpe and Serrano exhibits and a chronology of the events surrounding the NEA censorship debates, see Peggy Phelan, "Serrano, Mapplethorpe, the NEA, and You: 'Money Talks,' October 1989," *TDR: A Journal of Performance Studies* 34, no. 1 (Spring 1990): 4–15. *American Theatre* has also detailed the controversy in its government coverage over the past year.

4. For a cogent, poststructuralist feminist explication of the ideological implications of commonsense knowledge, see Chris Weedon, *Feminist Practice and Post-Structuralist Theory* (London and New York: Basil Blackwell, 1987), 75–80.

5. Daphne Read, "(De)Constructing Pornography: Feminisms in Conflict," in *Passion and Power: Sexuality in History*, ed. Kathy Peiss and Christina Simmons, with Robert A. Padgug (Philadelphia: Temple University Press, 1989), 282.

6. Read, "(De)Constructing Pornography," 281.

7. See Michel Foucault, *The History of Sexuality*, vol. 1 (New York: Vintage Books, 1980).

8. See, for example, Robert Mapplethorpe, *Black Book* (New York: St. Martin's Press, 1980).

9. Teresa de Lauretis, "Sexual Indifference and Lesbian Representation," in *Performing Feminisms: Feminist Critical Theory and Theatre*, ed. Sue-Ellen Case (Baltimore: Johns Hopkins University Press, 1990), 33, 35.

10. bell hooks, *From Margin to Center* (Boston: Beacon Press, 1984), 29.

11. This history of lesbian suppression under both radical and cultural feminism is now well documented. See, for example, Sue-Ellen Case, "Toward a Butch-Femme Aesthetic," in *Making a Spectacle: Feminist Essays on Contemporary Women's Theatre*, ed. Lynda Hart (Ann Arbor: University of Michigan Press, 1989), 282–99; and Echols, *Daring to be Bad*. See Adrienne Rich, "Compulsory Heterosexuality and Lesbian Existence," in *Powers of Desire; The Politics of Sexuality*, ed. Ann Snitow, Christine Stansell, and Sharon Thompson (New York: Monthly Review Press, 1983), 177–205, for the quintessential text on "women-identified women."

12. See Jan Clausen, "My Interesting Condition," *Out/Look* 2, no. 3 (Winter 1990): 11–21, for a painfully honest discussion of the political and emotional strictures of life in a "new" lesbian family.

13. I attended the performance discussed below on 29 June 1990 at the Walker Point Art Center in Milwaukee, Wisconsin.

14. See Sue-Ellen Case, "From Split Subject to Split Britches," in *Feminine Focus: The New Women Playwrights*, ed. Enoch Brater (New York: Oxford University Press, 1989), 126–46; "Toward a Butch-Femme Aesthetic"; and Jill Dolan, *The Feminist Spectator as Critic* (1988; reprint, Ann Arbor: University of Michigan Press, 1991), esp. chap. 4, "The Dynamics of Desire," 59–81, for explications of Weaver's and Shaw's personal and performative roles.

15. For theoretical work on butch-femme role playing as politically and culturally transgressive, see, for example, Case, "Toward a Butch-Femme Aesthetic"; Madeline Davis and Elizabeth Lapovsky Kennedy, "Oral History and the Study of Sexuality in the Lesbian Community: Buffalo, New York, 1940–1960," in *Hidden from History: Reclaiming the Gay and Lesbian Past*, ed. Martin Baume Duberman, Martha Vicinus, and George Chauncey (New York: New American Library, 1989), 426–40; Davis and Kennedy, "The Reproduction of Butch-Fem Roles: A Social Constructionist Approach," in Peiss and Simmons, *Passion and Power*, 241–56; and Joan Nestle, *A Restricted Country* (Ithaca: Firebrand Books, 1987).

16. de Lauretis, "Sexual Indifference," 39.

17. See Elaine Marks, "Lesbian Intertextuality," in *Homosexualities and French Literature*, ed. George Stambolian and Elaine Marks (Ithaca: Cornell University Press, 1979), in which, referring to Monique Wittig's *Le corps lesbien*, she suggests that images "sufficiently blatant . . . withstand reabsorption into male literary culture" (375). The analogy might hold here.

18. Eve Kosofsky Sedgwick, "Across Gender, across Sexuality: Willa Cather and Others," in *Displacing Homophobia: Gay Male Perspectives in Literature and Cul-*

ture, ed. Ronald R. Butters, John M. Clum, and Michael Moon (Durham: Duke University Press, 1989), 59.

19. See Davis and Kennedy, "Reproduction of Butch-Fem Roles," for further discussion of essentializing versus more historical, social constructionist definitions of lesbian and homosexual identity.

20. Judith Butler, "Performative Acts and Gender Constitution: An Essay in Phenomenology and Feminist Theory," in Case, *Performing Feminisms*, 272, emphasis in original.

21. Nestle, *Restricted Country*, 9.

22. Linda Williams, *Hard Core: Power, Pleasure, and the "Frenzy of the Visible"* (Berkeley: University of California Press, 1989), 30.

23. See Foucault, *History of Sexuality*, 1:156–59.

24. For an explication of lesbian subjectivities marginalized by realism's ethical and heterosexual codes, see Jill Dolan, "'Lesbian' Subjectivity in Realism: Dragging at the Margins of Structure and Ideology," in Case, *Performing Feminisms*, 40–53.

25. John Clum, "'A Culture That Isn't Just Sexual': Dramatizing Gay Male History," *Theatre Journal* 41 (1989): 169–89.

26. Nestle, *Restricted Country*, 10.

27. Martin Sherman, *Bent*; Robert Chesley, *Jerker, or the Helping Hand*, in both *Out Front: Contemporary Gay and Lesbian Plays*, ed. Don Shewey (New York: Grove Press, 1988), 79–148, 449–92.

28. Williams, *Hard Core*, 227. Unfortunately, Williams's own text ends by describing newer porn films, created either by women or for heterosexual couples, which, although they explore options among a range of sexual practices, retain the monogamous ideal of the heterosexual couple as their textual and spectatorial standard; see, in particular, 229–79.

29. Ibid., 151.

30. See, for example, Jane Chambers, *Last Summer at Bluefish Cove* (New York: JH Press, 1982); and Sarah Dreher's *8×10 Glossy* and *Ruby Christmas*, in *Places, Please! The First Anthology of Lesbian Plays*, ed. Kate McDermott (Iowa City: Aunt Lute, 1985), 41–92 and 137–92. Holly Hughes's raucous play *The Well of Horniness* (in Shewey, *Out Front*, 221–52) is reminiscent of *Jerker* in its use of language to break the taboo of homosexual discourse, but its transgressions remain verbal and cloaked in subcultural references. *The Well's* radio play genesis also works to repress the pornographic effects of bodies in motion to the margins of the text.

31. See Foucault, *History of Sexuality*, 1:36–49. He writes, "The implantation of perversions is an instrument-effect: it is through the isolation, intensification, and consolidation of peripheral sexualities that relations of power to sex and pleasure branched out and multiplied, measured the body, and penetrated modes of conduct" (48). Cultural feminism's isolation of lesbian "deviant" sexualities saw porn magazines like *On Our Backs* and *Bad Attitude* wrest their own piece of public discourse to transgress the law of politically correct sex developed by cultural feminist ideology. Pat Califia, s/m advocate and founder of the s/m support group Samois, published *Sapphistry*, a sex manual and disquisition on lesbian sexual variation, which was in its third edition by 1988 (Naiad Press, 1988). Susie Bright, editor of *On Our Backs* and author of its Susie Sexpert columns, published a flamboyantly frank compilation of her essays in 1990, all of which describe and celebrate a loosening of lesbian sexual mores (*Susie Sexpert's Lesbian Sex World* [Pittsburgh and San Francisco: Cleis Press 1990]).

32. I attended the performance discussed below on 18 November 1989 at the Barrymore Theatre in Madison, Wisconsin.

33. I don't mean to be facetious here, but I do mean to evoke the self-righteousness of these performances and the sanctimonious response they evoked.

34. The disjuncture between gay male and lesbian subcultures prompted by cultural feminism has recently been documented, in an effort to forge new alliances between the two groups as sexually stigmatized communities. Borrowing from gay male subculture, therefore, is a transgressive act in a cultural feminist setting. See Rich, "Compulsory Heterosexuality," for a historical example of feminism's betrayal of gay men. For work on the new alliances, see Nestle, *Restricted Country;* and Gayle Rubin, "Thinking Sex: Notes for a Radical Theory of the Politics of Sexuality," in *Pleasure and Danger,* ed. Carol Vance (Boston: Routledge, 1984), 267–318.

35. See, for example, *Feminist Voices* (15 December–8 February 1990, Madison, Wis.), 4, 6; (9 February–8 March 1990, Madison, Wis.), 11–13; *Wisconsin Light* (11–24 January 1990, Milwaukee, Wis.), 5, 11. On "naive realism," see Williams, *Hard Core,* esp. 184–228.

36. Ibid., 12.

37. Ibid., 38.

38. I would like to thank Stacy Wolf for her insightful comments in discussion around the issues in this article and for her thoughtful responses to preliminary drafts.

Mrs. Siddons Looks Back in Anger: Feminist Historiography for Eighteenth-Century British Theater

Ellen Donkin

Theater history is full of accounts of women performers in conflicts of various kinds. Some occur in relation to audiences, others with playwrights or managers, and some among the women performers themselves. The history of women's performance has been shaped by these disparate incidents. Gathered up and taken as a whole, they tell a larger story. One such story is this: that in all areas of theater, but particularly in performance, women have made repeated efforts to establish a point of view that is distinct from that of men. In performance these efforts usually took the form of subverting dramatic texts that failed to reflect the reality of women's lives. Some of these attempts to subvert were conscious; many were not. In theoretical terms we can formulate as follows: that the history of women's performance is the history of a struggle for a subject, rather than an object, position in representation. In Britain women performers have attempted to undermine this positioning ever since they were legally allowed onstage. Among the most interesting of these attempts was a night in October 1784 on which the actress Sarah Siddons (1755–1831) came into sharp conflict with her audience and subsequently forced them to look at women onstage in a completely different way.

This positioning of women as object on stage has a distinct moment of inception in British history. When Charles II returned from France in 1660 and decreed that actresses might appear on the legitimate stage, it marked the beginning of a shift in British consciousness. The appearance of women on stage constituted not only an aesthetic development for the theater but also a change in society at large. By occupying the stage women now routinely occupied public space, not just on the stage but also in the public imagination. This change touched off some deep anxieties and initiated a series of tacit negotiations about the conditions under which women would be allowed to occupy public space. The theater became a venue for negotiating gender roles.[1]

The initial contract was straightforward. Women in the British theater might occupy space on stage, but only as an object of desire or ridicule. There was no place on the stage for a woman's own assessment of the world she lived in. She might have opinions of that world offstage, and she might even voice them in private life, but not in a public theatrical event. It wasn't just that the plays provided her with limiting stereotypes of female behavior but that her very body on the stage implicated her in a certain relationship with the viewing audience. The notion of the actress as prostitute was an expression of this relationship. It had little to do with her private conduct offstage and everything to do with the projected desires of the viewing audience.

The career of Nell Gwyn points up some of the larger problems faced by actresses throughout theater history. Nell Gwyn was in fact a prostitute, but contemporary commentators siezed upon her work as an actress and her activities as a prostitute as somehow intrinsically related, as this bit of verse spells out:

> Next in the Playhouse she took her degree
> As men commence at University.
> No doctors, till they've masters been before;
> So she no player was till first a whore.[2]

Moreover, by 1668 Nell Gwyn had become a mistress to Charles II.[3] Charles was an enthusiastic theatergoer, and his presence in the theater, amid the common knowledge that he was sleeping with Nell, reinforced the audience's disposition to view any woman onstage carnally. The theater itself was shaped in such a way that for most of the audience it was possible to watch Charles watching Nell. In fact, it was difficult to do anything else.[4]

Theoreticians have called this kind of carnal looking "the gaze" and have asserted that the gaze in our culture is male.[5] In other words, the way events and characters unfold in representation tends to reward the eye of the heterosexual male subject. The woman in representation functions as object to this subject gaze; she is the one looked at rather than the one who does the looking. The Restoration gaze, with Charles and the audience as a collectively male-identified subject and Nell Gwyn as female object, constituted a paradigmatic contract, a "technology of gender," which reinforced an old set of power relations even as it *appeared* to give women a new place in representation.[6]

It was not until much later, in 1899, that the notion of a *female* subject had been sufficiently formulated for one actress to speak about it. The turn-of-the-century American actress Mary Shaw wrote that "the woman's point of view was usually not respected by manager, producer or actor." This failing resulted in the appearance on stage of heroines who "talk and act not as real women would, but as men think that women ought to talk and act."[7] Shaw's analysis suggests that a strong subject position for women is one that is necessarily grounded in women's experience rather than on men's fantasies about that experience. She concluded that there was an urgent need for a different kind of drama, one that included believable women characters in believable circumstances.

But in eighteenth-century Britain there was no such drama, and the obstacles for actresses in mainstream theater seeking a strong subject position were considerable. Even as mainstream theater offered employment and a certain provisional membership in the power structure, it placed women in roles that reified their position as object, not just in the world of the play but also, by extension, in the world at large. Theorists have made a useful distinction between "women" and "Woman." By performing these roles the actress publicly reinforced a notion of Woman. That notion of Woman had a positioning effect on real women, on the way they lived their lives, on what men expected from them, and on what they expected from themselves.[8] As she performed Woman, these cultural expectations of women *circled back* to the actress in performance through the demands of a very vocal audience. This circling back created a potential closure in the system that made change difficult to accomplish or even to conceive.

Two factors, however, made possible the disruption of this relatively closed system. The first has to do with the nature of performance. One of the most important lessons of semiotics for the theater has been the idea that performance and text constitute two distinct sets of signs which are more or less equally weighted in the way an audience assigns them importance. The text of a play in performance is not privileged as "truer" than the actions of actors on stage or any other component of production.[9] This idea has important bearing on the female subject in performance history. It suggests that, in spite of texts that reinforced an existing ideology about Woman, actual performances by women could maintain a certain degree of autonomy from that text and create a very different set of messages for the audience.

So, although the popular drama of the eighteenth century is full of roles in which heroines (to quote Mary Shaw again) talk and act only "as men think women ought to talk and act," gifted actresses found ways to perform powerfully inside these texts all the time. They had to. The irony of their position was that, although audiences demanded from the text the comfort and familiarity of the norms of Womanhood, *what in fact they responded to in performance was something that potentially ruptured that comfort and familiarity.* That something was female subjectivity, which registered the contradictions, the anger, the desire, the humor, the powerlessness, and the perspective of the female subject in history. For the audience this kind of performance was a form of voyeurism. Under no circumstances were they interested in seeing this unpredictable and powerful presence work itself free of the constraints of the narrative. But they were captivated nonetheless by the potential for danger, the ripple of excitement, the spectacle of agony, as the actress gave them a glimpse of the power inside.[10]

As a general rule, the play texts themselves cooperated. Most popular plays provided at least one scene in which the actress could explode into a vitality and power that were absent from the rest of her role. These were the scenes in which she made her "hits," or "points," as they were called. Necessarily, any such scene was carefully contained and rationalized by the plot. But to judge from various memoirs and reviews, in spite of this containment, these scenes resonated in memory long after the details of the plot were forgotten. These scenes functioned as pry bars; they penetrated the ideological closure of representation and created a space in which women, not Woman, could be heard onstage, if only momentarily. They did not solve the problem of a fully developed female subject onstage, but they kept something alive.

The second factor that challenged this closed system was audience reception. In the eighteenth century reception played a complex role in this destabilization process. Keir Elam writes: "In sponsoring the performance, the audience issues, as it were, a collective 'directive' to the performers, instructing them to provide in return a bona fide product (or production) of a certain kind—hence the outrage of certain spectators whose expectations are openly flouted, as was the case with various 1960s experiments. The audience's relative passivity as 'receiver' is in fact an active choice which imposes certain obligations on the elected 'senders.'"[11] Elam's observations are useful because they remind us of the way in which audience expectation shapes performance, especially around the way women are represented onstage. What needs revising for our purposes, however, is his characterization of the audience as passive, even as he argues against that passivity. Indeed, eighteenth-century audiences can in no sense be thought of as passive. They had the power to determine the survival of both plays and performers. They were far more powerful than the press. Based on audience response, a theater manager would decide from night to night whether to run the show or rotate it out of the repertory. These audiences were unconstrained in registering their approval or disapproval of any aspect of performance. I call them "shouting" audiences.[12] One contemporary analogy is the parliamentary institution in which the prime minister makes herself or himself available once a week for questions and answers in the House of Commons. Depending on the volatility of the issue, a barely contained multiplicity of shouting voices are heard, both singly and in chorus, alternating with the (rehearsed) statements of the prime minister.

This legitimated parley between audience and performers meant that the "reception loop" of performer to audience back to performer again was an extremely tight one. If innovation was introduced successfully onstage, it could be ratified by audience response instantaneously. The press participated in this process, but only after the fact. When a breathing, murmuring, commenting, laughing audience responded positively to something new in a performer's work, it cemented that change on the spot, and the performer was given permission to continue and build on it. This was not the leisurely process of reader-response; it had more in common with deals being made in the pit of a commodities exchange. So, although it can be argued that production and performance as a whole tended to reinforce dominant ideology, that process was by no means monolithic. In a single evening the "horizon of expectations" for an audience could change; what had been unacceptable in the Wednesday evening performance by one actress could be found plausible and moving on Thursday in the performance of another actress, opening up new possibilities for playwrights and actresses alike.[13] The playhouse, as we have noted, functioned as a liminal space in which gender roles were negotiated and renegotiated. In this process the audience was a wild card. Innovation did not happen often, but when it happened, it happened fast.

These two factors, the autonomous nature of performance and the power of audience reception, were to play important parts in the story that follows. During this evening in the career of Sarah Siddons "the balance of forces maintaining a particular hegemony" became unstable, and the audience accepted the terms of a new "contract" for women on the stage.[14] This contract marked an important change for women in performance; it opened the way for a more complete female presence on the English stage.

5 October 1784 was Mrs. Siddons's opening night at Drury Lane for the 1784–85 season. She had just returned from a summer season of work in Dublin, during which she had been accused (unjustly, as it turned out) by two fellow actors, West Digges and William Brereton, of first refusing to perform in their benefits and then of charging an exorbitant sum for appearing. On this particular evening, as Mrs. Siddons came onstage for the first scene of the play, she was greeted by an audience so hostile that it was impossible to perform. The auditorium was filled with derisive calls of "Off! Off!"

It was no happenstance that hostilities broke out on this particular evening. Mrs. Siddons was moving into the zenith of her career; no woman performer in memory had so captivated the British public. The spring before she had been painted by Joshua Reynolds as the Tragic Muse. She was joining a hall of fame which included celebrities like David Garrick. This outbreak was an overt challenge to her membership in that power structure.

The background to this incident is supplied by at least three different accounts, one of them by Wally Oulton, a contemporary chronicler of the theater; the second by James Boaden, Mrs. Siddons's first major biographer; and the third by Mrs. Siddons herself. It is not certain that Oulton's is an eyewitness account, but Boaden was present on the evening in question, and Mrs. Siddons was the unwilling principal in the event. I will quote Oulton's account first, in full:

> On Mrs. Siddons's first appearance this season, in the part of Mrs. Beverley in *The Gamester,* she met with strong opposition, on account of some malicious reports concerning her conduct, during her last visit to Dublin; where, as insinuated, she refused to perform for the benefits of Messrs. Digges and Brereton, who were then dangerously ill. Mrs. Siddons did agree to perform for the first gentleman without any gratuity, and for Mr. Brereton on very moderate terms; but when the benefits were commencing she was *in reality* taken ill, being confined to her bed for a fortnight. On Mrs. Siddons's appearance this season, her applauders had the majority; she repeatedly court-seyed [sic] to the audience, and seemed as if she wished to exculpate herself from the charges brought against her in the Public Papers: the tumult however encreasing [sic] Mr. Kemble came on, bowed respectfully to the audience, and took his sister by the hand, and as the noise continued, both retired. In about six minutes after, Mrs. Siddons came on again, and addressed the audience, declaring that everything should be explain'ed [sic] to the satisfaction of the public, and that

she had been most unjustly traduced. The theatre still continuing in an uproar, she retired again; and Mr. King came forward; he said Mrs. Siddons's reception had discomposed her so much, she prayed the Indulgence of the House for a short time, and the Performance should go on: upwards of forty minutes elapsed before the curtain rose for the play, when Mrs. Siddons's friends having obtained silence, she went through her character with astonishing firmness, and she was announced for the part of Lady Randolph on a succeeding night. The malice of Mrs. Siddons's enemies became soon apparent, and all terminated to her credit.[15]

There are three things about Oulton's account which are worth reflection. The first is that the disruptions that took place that night were apparently much more compelling than the actual production itself. In any event, they take up far more space than his comments on the performance of the actual text. The second is that the furor over her alleged failure to perform in the benefits described was disproportionate to the size of the infraction and should probably make us suspicious. In point of fact, Mrs. Siddons *had* performed a benefit for Digges, at considerable personal expense and trouble, and her failure to perform for Brereton was the result of legitimate illness and conflicting contractual obligations. In any case, Digges was a member of the Daly company in Dublin where Mrs. Siddons had been working during the summer and was hardly known to London audiences. Brereton was much better known, but only because he had costarred with Mrs. Siddons as Jaffier to her Belvidera in Otway's *Venice Preserv'd*. His claim to fame depended upon her choice of costar. It is interesting to note that by the fall of 1784 Mrs. Siddons was increasingly turning to her brother, John Philip Kemble, to play roles of this kind, and Brereton (correctly) felt himself in danger of being replaced.[16] Brereton's resentment was vented publicly through a series of newspaper columns and found a ready response in the audience at large. The furor, then, which allegedly was *about* Digges and Brereton, is more likely to have been produced *by* them.

The third arresting aspect of Oulton's report is the term *astonishing firmness*. What exactly does Oulton mean? Is he expressing admiration for the actress's composure under pressure? Is it astonishing firmness in the context of a stereotypically compliant character for whom firmness is a peculiar but interesting acting choice? Is it some combination of his awareness of her composure under pressure *inside the context* of the character? Why is this firmness "astonishing"?

We learn more from Boaden, whose account includes a detailed description of the event and of the letters to the newspaper leading up to it (2:105–18). He reports that Brereton, who was to play Lewson in *The Gamester* that evening, was *backstage* the entire time of this uproar in the theater and that his failure to appear onstage to quell the angry crowds by vindicating Mrs. Siddons was highly incriminating. "How keenly envy follows great success," comments Boaden dryly (2:81). Boaden reiterates Oulton's description of Kemble leading Mrs. Siddons offstage, in a kind of "masquerade of womanliness," a deliberate attempt to create a scenario of rescue and maidenly distress.[17] Boaden then reconstructs Mrs. Siddons's address to the audience when she subsequently came out alone, after the six-minute interlude described by Oulton above.[18] He writes:

> After some interval, calls for her became less mixed with opposition and she came again onstage, but *alone* and thus addressed the audience: "Ladies and Gentlemen: The kind and flattering partiality which I have uniformly experienced in this place would make the present interruption distressing to me indeed, were I in the slightest degree conscious of having deserved your censure. I feel no such consciousness. The stories which have been circulated against me are calumnies. When they shall be proved to be true, my aspersers will be justified: but till then, my respect for the public leads me to be confident that I shall be protected from unmerited insult." (2:115)

Boaden comments:

> It was not very usual to hear a *lady* on such occasions; the delicacy of the sex, while it becomes accustomed to repeat the sentiments of others, shrinks from the seeming boldness of publicly uttering their own. But there was a *male dignity* [my emphasis] in the understanding of Mrs. Siddons that raised her above the helpless timidity of other women; and it was certainly without surprise, and evidently with profound admiration, that they heard this NOBLE BEING assert her innocence and demand protection . . . if I were to mark the moment, which I should think she most frequently revolved, as affording her the greatest *satisfaction*, the fortitude of this night and its enthusiastic reception by all who heard and saw it, seem most worthily to claim so happy a distinction. (2:116)

Boaden's conjecture that these events were pivotal in Mrs. Siddons's career is borne out in her own memoirs (although with one complicated twist, as we shall see.)[19] In this tiny volume of thirty-three pages, written in the last year of her life, the events leading up to and including 5 October 1784 occupy fully seven pages at the end. The remaining several decades of her career are compressed into a handful of paragraphs on the final page. Contemporary commentary reinforces Boaden's conjecture; one publication reported the event as a "very aweful [sic] trial—a trial which, in great measure, determined her future fame—perhaps her residence in this metropolis."[20]

Boaden's account has two important claims on our attention. The first is that his report of the events clearly suggests that Mrs. Siddons, by dint of personal conviction and courage, routed the opposition single-handedly. The second is his use of the term *male dignity* to describe her self-presentation during this climactic moment. The term *male* applied to Mrs. Siddons suggests that some aspect of gender construction had gotten muddy in this moment of confrontation.

We turn finally to Mrs. Siddons's own account of the events of 5 October. We hardly recognize it as the same set of events. First of all, she makes no mention of Brereton at all and instead places the blame squarely on the Irish manager Daly, her employer during the summer of 1784, and accuses him of having engineered the entire confrontation long distance. Daly was a womanizer and a notorious nuisance,[21] but in this instance Mrs. Siddons is also closing family ranks. Brereton, who died in 1787 in a madhouse at Hoxton, left a widow named Priscilla who subsequently married Mrs. Siddons's brother and costar, John Philip Kemble. This same Priscilla was an actress in *The Gamester* company the night of the disturbance, a fact that is not recorded either by Boaden or Oulton, playing Charlotte to Mrs. Siddons's Mrs. Beverley in the opening scene of the play. "Mrs. B. [Brereton] was mean enough to sneak off the stage and leave her [Mrs. Siddons] to stand the insults of a malicious party tho' she knew the whole disturbance was on her account and that her husband had at least been obliged to contradict the reports that concern'd him."[22] Out of respect for her brother's memory Mrs. Siddons avoids casting aspersions on either of the Breretons, and the intriguing reference to the disturbance being on Mrs. Brereton's account is not illuminated, although there were rumors circulating at the time that Brereton was in love with Mrs. Siddons.[23] The uproar in the theater perhaps suited both the Breretons, Mrs. Brereton for reasons of personal jealousy and Mr. Brereton for reasons of professional jealousy.

Second and most important, Mrs. Siddons's narrative of the events makes *no mention whatever* of her speech to the audience, the speech that Boaden is at such pains to reconstruct. Instead, she states that after her brother rescued her from the stage she went offstage and fainted. According to her, it was only the combined efforts of Mr. Siddons, John Philip Kemble, and Mr. Sheridan (Richard Brinsley), together with the prospect of her children living in want, which enabled her to go back onstage and face her audience. All this in six minutes, if we are to believe Oulton's account. "I fainted . . . I was besought by husband, my brother, and Mr. Sheridan to present myself again before that audience by whom I had been so cruelly and unjustly degraded, and where, but in consideration of my children, I never would have appeared again" (31).

Then, suddenly, the crisis is over, and she is in the midst of the first act. She makes no mention whatever of her speech of self-defense to the audience. It is as if it never took place. "But what was my astonishment to find [myself], on the rising of the curtain, recieved [sic] with a *silence so profound* that I was absolutely awe-struck and *never yet have been able to account for this surprising contrast,* for I really think the falling of a pin might have been heard upon the stage" (31; my emphasis). But both Boaden and Oulton report that she did address the audience directly, and Boaden, if not always unbiased, can certainly be trusted as a reliable reporter of events as he saw them.

What then are we to make of the fact that these reports do not tally? How is it that, at the very moment in which Boaden observes with obvious admiration a "male dignity" in Mrs. Siddons, her own memory fails her completely? How are we to reconcile Oulton's observation of "astonishing firmness" with a woman who has just fainted and can only be persuaded onto the stage again by the manly intervention of husband and brother? Sheridan's sister Betsy, who visited with Mrs. Siddons a few days afterward, noted that "she seems hurt to the soul, but her feelings seem to be more of the indignant kind than any other."[24] One wonders where the indignation is to be found in her own account.

Some of the answers to these discrepancies are suggested by a more careful look at the text of the play.[25] *The Gamester,* by Edward Moore, is a moral fable about the evils of gambling and has as its central character a Mr. Beverley, who, in spite of a devoted wife (Mrs. Siddons's role) and an infant son, gambles away their considerable livelihood and reduces them to desperate poverty. Mrs. Beverley, however, can only exclaim her continuing devotion and need for him. Her lines read like a litany of disclaimers to the subject position. She says to her sister-in-law: "I live but to oblige him," and to her desperate and obsessed husband, "I have no wants when you are present, nor wishes in your absence but to be blessed with your return." This devotion reaches a ludicrous climax when she hands over to Beverley her remaining handful of jewels, even though this remnant of family fortune is all that protects her and her son from utter destitution. Elizabeth Inchbald's trenchant remarks on the play in her 1808 anthology suggest that, from a woman's point of view, the play stretched credibility. She describes Mrs. Beverley as "egregiously impassioned by conjugal love."[26]

It is tempting to equate a strong subject postion with strong emotional display in performance, but a careful distinction must be made. The role of Mrs. Beverley, although it had no claim to a strong female subject position, had several opportunities for an actress to display strong emotions. In one key scene Mrs. Beverley is approached by the sordid Stukely, who hopes to seduce her in a moment of weakness and desperation. The rejection of Stukely was a potential "hit" for the actress playing Mrs. Beverley. In a blaze of righteous fury she says to Stukely: "Would that these eyes had Heaven's own lightening [sic], that, with a look, thus I might blast thee! Am I then fallen so low? Has poverty so humbled me, that I should listen to a hellish offer, and sell my soul for bread? Oh, villain! villain!"[27] It was one of those moments in which the performance of the text gave the actress an opportunity to *hint* at a powerful subjectivity within the confines of a recuperative plot, affording the audience excitement without serious risk to ideological expectations. Mrs. Beverley's "egregious" loyalty to Mr. Beverley flew in the face of logic and even of survival itself. But it was precisely designed to reinforce the intrinsic rightness of laws that prevented women from having any legal or financial identity apart from their husbands. In plays like *The Gamester* these laws were seen to reflect a preexisting condition of nature. As the play demonstrated, Woman herself would not have wanted things any other way.

But on the night of 5 October something happened which dislodged expectations in a more substantive way. If we can believe Oulton and

Boaden, Mrs. Siddons, an actress whose reputation had been built upon never breaking character, stepped outside of both character and dramatic narrative, turned in righteous anger, and *looked back* at her audience. In that moment she registered what she thought of them. She forced her audience to deal with her, not as object but as speaking subject. She expressed personal indignation and disdain, without the benefit of a recuperative plot. In other words, she reversed the direction of the gaze. The audience now had the experience of being the object of a female gaze in the theater, and it created a shift in power relations.

That power shift was, as Boaden and Oulton confirm, collectively ratified by audience reception. In the intervening forty minutes Mrs. Siddons's terms for appearing onstage without harrassment were unconditionally accepted. When she reappeared, the impact of that power shift continued to resonate inside the performance of Mrs. Beverley, to such an extent that Oulton records an "astonishing firmness." It was impossible that night for the audience to view Mrs. Siddons as Mrs. Beverley without the memory of the earlier outburst. This must have been particularly true during the scene in which she spurned Mr. Stukely. The confrontation forty minutes before had created a springboard into a performance of Mrs. Beverley which oscillated at high frequency between actress as subject and character as object.

Mrs. Siddons had destabilized the Restoration contract. She had opportunistically grasped a hostile audience by the throat and renegotiated the terms under which she would appear. It was by no means a conscious effort to establish herself as "female subject" (even if the category had existed); it was simply a gritty determination to survive. But its consequences were important: it opened up a space in representation which had not been there before, and the audience at that historical moment registered its willingness to accept the change.[28]

One may argue that this assertion of the female subject was a wobbly imposition on a play that made no real room for the female subject within. Nevertheless, it was an important start. It had the effect of putting Mrs. Siddons's performance as Mrs. Beverley in quotation marks; the acting was seen to be a production of the actress and not coextensive with the actress.[29] This distinction made possible a different complexity of female presence both on the stage and in the audience. The price of being able to fantasize about or identify with Mrs. Beverley was the concomitant awareness of Mrs. Siddons herself as a subject. In some sense, the audience had been put on notice. Even as they watched her, they were aware that she was also watching them. They no longer occupied a safe space in the house from which to survey the body of the actress, as they had in 1660. The actress was now in a position to look back.

The distinction between the female subject *inside* representation and the female subject *outside* representation is an important one.[30] The moment in which Mrs. Siddons established herself as a female subject was without question outside of the text of this play. She spoke in her own words and delivered her indignation not to a culturally approved target (Mr. Stukely) but to the immediate source of the trouble, the audience. Her voices as outraged actress and outraged character need to be carefully distinguished. She could not yet claim a full subject position *inside* of dramatic narrative, but clearly something had taken place. Perhaps one way to distinguish between a female subject inside and a female subject outside representation might be to make a distinction between subject *voice* and subject *position*. When we speak of Mrs. Siddons playing Mrs. Beverley, for example, she is a subject voice. In spite of the ideologically sanitized role she plays, certain moments of the play allow for displays of power and rage that gesture in the direction of female subjectivity. When, however, we speak of Mrs. Siddons confronting her audience directly with her indignation about their outrageous behavior, we describe a subject position, because her presence has not been neutralized by an ideologically sanitizing plot and character. In a different kind of play, and in a different century, Mrs. Siddons theoretically could have occupied a subject position inside of a play text. But it was eighteenth-century London, and the play was *The Gamester*. In order to fully occupy a subject position Mrs. Siddons had to step outside of the play. In a broad sense her indignant address to the audience was structurally necessitated by the failure of representation itself to find adequate space for her subjectivity within the play. In speaking to the audience directly, however, she empowered the existing subject voice within the play and opened up certain possibilities for the future in play-writing and in women's performance.

When Boaden speaks of Mrs. Siddons's having a "male dignity," it may be his way of describing the taking of a subject position. He under-stands the subject position, in this case speaking for oneself, as a male activity: "the delicacy of the [female] sex shrinks ... from the seeming boldness of publicly uttering their own [sentiments]" (2:116). In his efforts to describe what he sees her doing that night he falls back on the only terminology he has at hand. In doing so he exposes the inadequacy of the analysis. Mrs. Siddons becomes the locus in which assumptions about femaleness and maleness lose meaning. Maleness, in this instance, reveals itself as a constructed social position and not as a biological statement of fact.

The remaining mystery is Mrs. Siddons's own failure to record this moment of confrontation in her memoirs. One wonders if the omission was a conscious or an unconscious one. Certainly it would appear that she had little to lose by telling the truth as she remembered it; her career was long since over, and she was in the last year of her life. I suspect her recorded amazement at confronting a suddenly quiet audience is not simply a coy invention. *It is as if someone else had quieted the audience.*[31] This experience of claiming a strong subject position constituted such an aber-ration that it was difficult to incorporate into consciousness. How was she to think of herself at once as the embodiment of Womanhood and as having a "male dignity"? Her unprecedented position of power in the theater was contingent upon her persuasiveness as Woman, both in public and in private life. In the grid of her consciousness, which had been so powerfully shaped and informed by the roles she played, there was no precedent for aberrant "male" behavior.[32] Without a place to lodge, the memory of this incident split off and drifted away.

We see in this drifting away the consequences of a lifetime of work in mainstream theater. Mrs. Siddons was someone who could operate defensively and powerfully in her own behalf but could not consciously remember having done so.[33] She was, in effect, a split subject.[34] It is a chronic temptation in feminist revisions of theater history to imagine that oppression created a group of women who were not allowed to speak about what they knew. In fact it appears that the situation was more complicated: that they didn't know what they knew.[35] Mrs. Siddons's participation in this moment of change had guaranteed neither her recognition of that change nor her ability to build on it. She was, like her audiences, caught up in the fluxes of history, a history in which she participated without control or consciousness.

Nonetheless, there had been change. Mrs. Siddons continued to work, and audiences continued to be more or less disruptive, but never again did she face just another noisy crowd. The neutralized claims of that 1784 opening night audience would ever after be present in the audiences that followed. It was a modest legacy but an important one.

Fredric Jameson has written that a careful analysis of incidents in mainstream culture like this one will uncover traces of other cultural voices, opposing voices that have been marginalized and muffled. This multiplicity of clear and muffled voices is in some instances the only record left to us of an underlying social struggle, one that history books are usually at pains to simplify or eliminate.[36] In this case both the hegemonic and the oppositional voices belonged to Mrs. Siddons. The contradictory voices of Mrs. Beverley, of the memoirs, and of the indignant speech to the audience were all generated by the same person. In this sense Mrs. Siddons's career is paradigmatic. Any woman whose survival and financial independence rest upon her ability to represent herself as Other, in ways that are deeply at odds with her experience, is likely to show these curious signs of conflict and struggle.

Without gender as a category of inquiry, the significance of these multiple voices is lost, and the political implications of anecdotes like this one become, to use Jameson's term, unconscious. The feminist theater historian must identify material like this as a form of politically unconscious theater history and begin the work of extricating the female performer from the ideological apparatus in which she worked. The story lies in the gaps and contradictions between the voices—not in what they tell us but in what they avoid or do not remember.

NOTES

1. See Victor Turner, *From Ritual to Theatre: The Human Seriousness of Play* (New York: Performing Arts Journal Publications, 1982), 11, in which Turner suggests theater as a means to scrutinize sociocultural systems.

2. Roy MacGregor-Hastie, *Nell Gwyn* (London: Robert Hale, 1987), 35. This bit of verse was written by Rochester.

3. Ibid., 82.

4. Feminist film theorists have called this process of watching as if through someone else's eyes "suture." See Kaja Silverman, *The Subject of Semiotics* (New York: Oxford University Press, 1983), 194–236.

5. Laura Mulvey's essay "Visual Pleasure and Narrative Cinema," in *Screen* 16 (1975): 6–18, has been extremely influential. See also Silverman's discussion of this article in *The Subject of Semiotics*, 222–25; and E. Ann Kaplan, in *Women and Film: Both Sides of the Camera* (New York: Methuen, 1983), 14. This theoretical work has had far-reaching implications for our discipline. The gaze of the theater historian, which has held a position of lofty ungendered neutrality for decades, may now be seen to be male.

6. See Teresa de Lauretis, *Technologies of Gender: Essays on Theory, Film, and Fiction* (Bloomington: Indiana University Press, 1987), ix.

7. Alice M. Robinson, Vera Mowry Roberts, and Milly S. Barranger, eds., *Notable Women in the American Theatre* (New York: Greenwood Press, 1989), 786–87.

8. Sue-Ellen Case, *Feminism and Theatre* (New York: Methuen, 1988), 7. For a wonderful case in point, see also James Boaden, *Memoirs of Mrs. Siddons* (London: Henry Colburn, 1827), 1:301, who describes fashionable women of the day imitating the actress Sarah Siddons in "deportment . . . utterance . . . and dress". Hereafter page numbers will be cited in the text.

9. See Susan Bassnett-McGuire, "An Introduction to Theatre Semiotics," *Theatre Quarterly* 10 (1980): 47–53.

10. My thanks to Michael Wilson for pointing out to me that Mrs. Siddons was always at her best in scenes in which she spurned an immoral lover.

11. Keir Elam, *The Semiotics of Theatre and Drama* (London and New York: Methuen, 1980), 96.

12. I have borrowed the term from African-American culture, in which "shouting" or "calling" are approved ways for audiences to respond at certain public events.

13. For a discussion of the term *horizon of expectations*, see Robert Holub, *Reception Theory* (London and New York: Methuen, 1984), 42–44.

14. Janelle Reinelt, "Speculations on Spectatorship: Dominant Hegemony and the Historical Moment," *Proceedings of the International Federation for Theatre Research* (Stockholm: Nordic Theatre Studies, 1990): 128–31. Reinelt here is developing ideas from Antonio Gramsci's "Analysis of Situations: Relations of Force," in *Selections from the Prison Notebooks*, ed. and trans. Quintin Hoare and Geoffrey Nowell Smith (London: Laurence and Wishout, 1977).

15. Wally Chamberlain Oulton, *The History of the Theatres of London* (1771–1795; reprint, London: Martin and Bain, 1796), 1:134; hereafter page numbers will be cited in the text.

16. Brereton's career only lasted another year, to November 1785, after which he disappeared from the Drury Lane roster permanently. Reports were that he declined rapidly into mental illness and died at Hoxton Asylum in 1787. After November of 1785, Kemble did in fact take over many of Brereton's former roles. See Charles Beecher Hogan, ed., *The London Stage, 1660–1800*, pt. 5 vol. 2, (Carbondale: Southern Illinois University Press, 1968), for night-by-night records of performances at Drury Lane.

17. See Sue-Ellen Case, "Toward a Butch-Femme Aesthetic," *Making a Spectacle*, ed. Lynda Hart (Ann Arbor: University of Michigan Press, 1989). She cites Joan

Riviere's discussion of "the masquerade of womanliness" as a way to understand how heterosexual women in positions of power will perform a certain coquettishness or helplessness in order to "avert anxiety and the retribution feared from men" (291).

18. Roger Manvell states that this was a prepared speech; unfortunately, he does not cite his source. See Manvell, *Sarah Siddons: Portrait of an Actress* (London: William Heinemann, 1970), 113.

19. *The Reminiscences of Sarah Kemble Siddons, 1773-1785*, ed. William Van Lennep (Cambridge: Widener Library, 1942). These memoirs also cite the appearance in the pit of a man who speaks out in Mrs. Siddons's behalf, "impelled by benevolence and a manly feeling for the oppressed," and helping to create an aura of heroic rescue from persecution in her account (30). Hereafter page numbers will be cited in the text.

20. *Town and Country Magazine* (October 1784), 510.

21. He had made a pest of himself to many others, including Mrs. Siddons's good friend, the actress and playwright Elizabeth Inchbald, during the 1782-83 Dublin season.

22. *Betsy Sheridan's Journal: Letters from Sheridan's Sister 1784-1786 and 1788-1790*, ed. William Le Fanu (New Brunswick, N.J.: Rutgers University Press, 1960), 32. Betsy Sheridan was unable to attend opening night because her father was ill, so this information comes to us second-hand, probably through her brother.

23. See Mrs. Clement Parsons, *The Incomparable Siddons* (1909; reprint, New York: Benjamin Blom, 1969), 101. Parsons mentions an infatuation but does not give her source.

24. LeFanu, *Betsy Sheridan's Journal*, 32.

25. The play is printed in *The British Theatre*, ed. Elizabeth Inchbald, vol. 14 (London: Longman, Hurst, Rees and Orme, 1808), together with an introduction to the play by Mrs. Inchbald.

26. Ibid., 37, 30, 4.

27. Ibid., 46.

28. Janelle Reinelt, "Feminist Theory and Performance," *Modern Drama* 31 (1989): 55. "Novelty on a historical scale, finally, emerges when a specific historic moment, a confluence of events and forces converge which makes radical change possible. Subjects are able to grasp the new social formation as it coalesces and to position themselves in relationship to it."

29. Elin Diamond, "Brechtian Theory, Feminist Theory," *Drama Review* 32 (1988): 90. "Looking at the character, the spectator is constantly intercepted by the actor/subject, and the latter, heeding no fourth wall, *is theoretically free to look back* . . . no one side signifies authority, knowledge, or the law" (my emphasis).

30. See de Lauretis, *Technologies of Gender*, 10: "Women are both inside and outside gender, at once within and without representation."

31. See Thomas Postlewait's "Autobiography and Theatre History," in *Interpreting the Theatrical Past*, ed. Thomas Postlewait and Bruce McConachie (Iowa City: University of Iowa Press, 1989), 268: "These actresses . . . go out of their way, with few exceptions, to offer a life story that credits to others key aspects of their strength, their purpose, their identity." It is also true that contemporary biographers tend to cooperate in that process. Manvell's account of Mrs. Siddons frequently assigns agency to the men in her life; see his *Sarah Siddons*, 115.

32. See Silverman, *Subject of Semiotics*, which for our purposes suggests that unconscious and cultural determinants play a strong role in omissions of this kind: "The concept of subjectivity, as we shall see, marks a radical departure from this

philosophical tradition [of individualism] by giving a more central place to the *unconscious and to cultural overdetermination* than it does to consciousness" [emphasis mine] (126).

33. See Carolyn Heilbrun, *Writing a Woman's Life* (New York and London: W. W. Norton, 1988). It is interesting to consider Heilbrun's argument from the perspective of this article. She and Postlewait both argue that women writing their autobiographies omit their own agency in their lives, crediting others with having inspired or educated or guided them (see note 31 above). One of the implications of this study is that these omissions may be unconscious because representation in the culture offered a woman no models for assigning agency to herself.

34. Sue-Ellen Case, "From Split Subject to Split Britches," in *Feminine Focus: The New Women Playwrights,* ed. Enoch Brater (New York: Oxford University, 1989), 127–34, gives a helpful analysis of the way the split subject manifests itself in dramatic literature.

35. See Christopher Bollas, *The Shadow of the Object* (New York: Columbia University Press, 1987), 73, in which Bollas describes these unconscious contents as "the unthought known" and suggests that, under certain kinds of pressure, they will "split off" from the subject. He cites a clinical example of a patient whose rage at and need for his parents split off so that he could present to them the affability that he knew they would reward. These feelings reemerged much later in analysis.

36. See Fredric Jameson, *The Political Unconscious* (Ithaca: Cornell University Press, 1981), 85–86.

Theater History and Historiography

Introduction

Historians often begin the history of the discipline of theater history with an anecdote of irretrievable loss. The seventeen-volume compilation of sources on the ancient theater, assembled in the reign of Augustus by Juba II of the African province of Mauretania, disappeared. Only fragments of its mouth-watering table of contents could be reconstructed from other sources. This parable of disinheritance articulates a wistful sense of incompletion, which seems to haunt theater historians generally, even when documents do survive intact, because of the evanescence of performance itself. Some profess to find themselves "in the unenviable position of the art historian who plans to evaluate the lost paintings of Polygnotus and Zeuxis."[1]

This self-consciousness about the perceived contradiction of writing the history of so notoriously transient a form as theater suggests a point of entrance for critical theory. As they reflect on the fragility of their subject, theater historians struggle with problems of historiography—theories of writing about history. Not the least of these problems is the absence of the transcendental signified (call it performance) from the linguistic or pictorial residue of what historians optimistically call "sources," a word that holds out the false promise of authentic origin. In this sense no document can survive intact, and even the particularly Western preoccupation with trying to write everything down—ethnography, biography, historiography, and the rest—cannot put Juba back together again. Perpetually reminded of irretrievable loss, then, theater historians should be among the most receptive to the theoretical problems of interpretation and representation.

Like other varieties of historical inquiry, however, the history of theater has struggled with its own oedipal ambivalence toward positivism. In its vulgar sense, which is often associated with the nineteenth-century social philosopher Auguste Comte, positivism reckons that empirical science is the supreme form of knowledge and that facts are its only useful objects. In response to the advancement of Western technoscience, Comte organized the history of knowledge into a master narrative of progress, from "primitive" theology, propagating myths, to "civilized" science, discovering natural laws in the facts of nature. The durable imprint of this teleology in the collective historical consciousness of theater scholars might be measured in the number of texts and survey courses that tell a story of progress from the origins of theater in the sympathetic magic of "primitive peoples" before the beginning of history to the Pisgah sights of European modernism at its end.

Perhaps the more instrumental impact of positivism has been in its methodological assumptions, which stress the objective reconstruction of truths based on the facts. Few contemporary historians succumb to vulgar positivism, but some remain more alert than others to its more subtle reappearances—such as in the masking of ideologies as impartial conclusions or the passing off of contested events as historical facts. That Columbus discovered America in 1492 was once presented in schools as a positive historical "fact," verified by multiple documentary sources. A number of difficulties quickly emerge from any such facts as these, however, not the least of which (in this example) is the Eurocentricity of the word *discover*, which suggests the original revelation of a previously uninhabited continent. If schools would teach that Columbus *encountered* America in 1492 (and many more of them now do), the indigenous peoples and cultures of the continent that came to be called America would at least not be automatically erased by the facts. But that indigenous peoples and cultures existed in the pre-Columbian era is itself a factual claim, a claim of the sort that historians do tend to insist upon. It is not the insistence that facts exist that makes positivism vulgar but, rather, the insistence that facts can remain neutral. A number of contemporary theater historians, skeptical of claims to impartiality, have adopted the critical approaches to the historical record suggested by other sections in this book, including feminism, Marxism, semiotics, and cultural studies. The kind of thinking which examines all factual claims (and everything else) in relationship to social, cultural, and ideological forces has been called "postpositivist."[2]

The position of theater history as a contemporary academic discipline is nevertheless still influenced by its early links to *Theaterwissenschaft* in Germany. The original projectors of this "theater science" (or, more appetizingly, "theater studies") focused on the nonliterary aspects of theater, which entailed the reconstruction of the conditions of historic performances, including theater architecture, staging, and acting style. Here the influence of positivism was more subtle and more long lasting. *Theaterwissenschaft* separated the study of historical documents, the supposed repository of objective facts, from the study of the works of dramatic literature, the supposed domain of the subjective imagination. In this division of labor historians were to reconstruct the past from the solid documentary record, while literary critics were left to interpret the mysteries of dramatic form. This dichotomy has to some extent endured in theater history, even in otherwise postpositivist work. It has had important consequences for the continuing development of the field, including its sometimes vexed relationship with literature departments and its general reluctance to embrace "literary" theory.[3]

Theory has challenged the assumption that there is a fundamental difference between literary texts and other kinds of texts. It has proposed alternatively that all forms of writing are as distanced from the real world as literature was once thought to be (see "Semiotics and Deconstruction"). This challenge takes a number of different forms, but for the present purpose five are the most pertinent: the "intertextuality" defined by New Historicism and/or cultural poetics; the theories of reciprocal interaction between literature, speech, and popular culture in Mikhail Bakhtin; the metahistorical critique of Hayden White; the hermeneutics of narrativity of Paul Ricoeur; and the theory of discourse of Michel Foucault.

New Historicists interpret historical documents such as laws, treatises, and chronicles as if they were literary texts, and they tend to read plays as if they were official documents. They attempt to discern instances of intertextuality, erasing the line that scholars once drew between literature and its cultural background. In reading *King Lear* and an Elizabethan treatise on exorcism intertextually, for example, Stephen Greenblatt explains: "history cannot simply be set against literary texts as either stable antithesis or stable background, and the protective isolation of those texts gives way to a sense of their interaction with other texts and hence the permeability of their boundaries."[4] In setting forth the term *cultural poetics* (as an improved alternative to *New Historicism*), Greenblatt reads as literary texts both the trail markers directing hikers in Yosemite National Park and the anecdotal lore, including *People* magazine, surrounding Norman Mailer's association with Gary Gilmore and Jack Abbott.[5] Cultural poetics can make a claim to anti-elitism, and it foregrounds popular culture with a flourish that ought to attract the attention of historians of performance.[6]

Intertextuality need not be limited to scripted works and documents. The notions of "text" and "event" overlap as they enlarge. On the margins of literacy and orality, performance events (or the anecdotes through which they most often survive in memory) may enter into the reconstruction of historic cultural configurations with no less authority than other texts. This is especially important in establishing the history of groups whose members have been in some way marginalized or silenced. In the section called "Feminism(s)," for instance, Ellen Donkin's historical article on Sarah Siddons is devoted to one of those anecdotes that provide very rich texts indeed, a stimulus to what Clifford Geertz calls "thick description": by reading the anecdote closely Donkin is able to suggest how relationships between gender and authority produced and were produced by the interplay of an actress, a scripted role, and an eighteenth-century English audience. In this section Tracy Davis interprets the sharpshooting career of Annie Oakley within the cultural configuration of marriage in late nineteenth-century America. In the arguments of both Donkin and Davis, popular performance concentrates the social values of a culture with clarifying force.

For the Russian linguist and social theorist Mikhail Bakhtin, performance plays an important, if not immediately obvious role. His study of Rabelais illuminates the pervasiveness of the carnivalesque in popular culture and in literature.[7] More important for Marvin Carlson's purposes, Bakhtin's interactive concepts of "dialogism" and "heteroglossia" converge in his key notion of "utterance," the socially instrumental speech act. Although Bakhtin developed his theories to address the novel principally, they suggest to Carlson new ways of opening up the interactions between playtexts and performers (and between playtexts and playgoers). Carlson, like Rosemarie Bank and Vivian Patraka, deals with dramatic texts as cultural artifacts, the residue of transactions between artists and spectators. An application of Bakhtin's social theories of language to postpositivist reconstructions of nonscripted performance events, for example, might feature gunfire as gendered utterance, as in Davis's account of Annie Oakley, or expressive silence as dialogue, as in Donkin's account of Sarah Siddons.

Tracy Davis takes aim at the American historian and metahistorian Hayden White's *Tropics of Discourse: Essays in Cultural Criticism.* White blurs the boundaries of history and literature by arguing that historians arrange their materials according to narrative and rhetorical designs, plots and tropes, made available to them by works of literature. For White the function of such tropes is not ornamental but constitutive of narrative history. Davis receives this pronouncement with telling irony, but it is interesting to compare as romances the story she tells about Oakley, as a strong-willed female performer with a partially invisible male helpmate (or repressed double), to the story Donkin tells about Siddons, in which the men appear in time to disappear. Confronting in depth the question of narrative and history, the philosopher Paul Ricoeur examines hermeneutics, or methodologies of interpretation, as a fundamental historiographic problem. In a later section Thomas Postlewait explores this issue in specific relationship to theater history: "In telling our stories," he concludes, "we have become self-conscious of our strategies of understanding" (see "Hermeneutics and Phenomenology").

One formidable component of the current self-consciousness about knowledge, its production and replication, is the antihumanist theory of discourse of Michel Foucault. In setting aside the venerable literary-humanist category of "author" in favor of something called the "author function," Foucault advances a theory of historical knowledge which organizes all writing into categories of discursive regularity—the rules that govern what statements can or cannot be made within different institutional contexts and structures.[8] These include medicine and hospitals, penology and prisons, sexuality and psychoanalysis. Knowledge is constituted and regulated discursively within institutional power relations, and the "human subject" (call it "man"), like the author, is the invention of an obsolete discourse. Since the field of theater history has long been dominated by biographical approaches—the theatrical counterpart of the literary "life and works"— Foucault offers a challenge to historians. In an analysis shaped in part by Foucauldian ideas, Rosemarie Bank shows the limitations of binary discursive thinking—say, avant-garde versus mainstream—in explaining the work of the New Playwrights Theatre in the 1920s. She proposes instead a more complicated array of juxtaposed discourses analogous to the spatiotemporal discontinuities then being articulated by quantum physics. She suggests that the way critics and historians talk about institutions, even the way artists think about the institutions in which they participate, emerges from a very limited menu of discursive choices.

Foucault has also been instrumental in encouraging, particularly among New Historicists, what Paul Ricoeur has called in another context a "hermeneutics of suspicion."[9] By interpreting all knowledge as constituted in and by relations of power, Foucault seeks to disclose the subliminal existence of vast coercive networks operating as "micropolitics" diffused at the "capillary" level of human activity. They are not part of a centralized conspiracy, nor do they proceed according to a moral plan, though they render their effects most clearly visible in bodies—incarcerated bodies, hospitalized bodies, educated bodies, that is, generally docile bodies.[10] Jeanie Forte takes up these issues in "Feminism(s)," though feminists and others have found Foucault's political commitments more elusive than his trenchant description of modern social technologies. For Foucault, following Nietzsche, the genealogies of power and knowledge seem to remain beyond good and evil.

The Marxist theorist Walter Benjamin offered a more overtly moralized anticipation of Foucault's vision of social order when he wrote: "There is no document of civilization, which is not at the same time a document of barbarism."[11] Benjamin spoke out against fascism, and in particular against its proclivity for aesthetizing politics, making states and people media in the hands of tyrant-creators. Vivian Patraka confronts the theatrical history of fascism in her account of recent plays, some of them documentary dramas, on the subject of the Holocaust. Her subject forces historians to face the facts—their undeniability as well as their refusal of innocence. The desolating inadequacy of either a review of documents or a narrative account to represent the reality of such events, before which the serene mask of objectivity must dissolve, refers the historian to the hallucinatory images of fiction, the historic archive of lies like truth.

J. R. R.

NOTES

1. A. M. Nagler, *A Source Book in Theatrical History* (New York: Dover, 1959), ix. For an introduction to the issues of the discipline of theater history, see Thomas Postlewait and Bruce A. McConachie, eds., *Interpreting the Theatrical Past: Essays in the Historiography of Performance* (Iowa City: University of Iowa Press, 1989).

2. Bruce A. McConachie, "Towards a Postpositivist Theatre History," *Theatre Journal* 37 (1985): 465–86. For an example of the impact of theoretical revision on traditional theater-historical materials, see Marvin Carlson, *Places of Performance: The Semiotics of Theatre Architecture* (Ithaca and London: Cornell University Press, 1989).

3. See Michael Booth, "Theatre History and the Literary Critic," *Yearbook of English Studies* 9 (1979): 15–27. This impasse is, of course, negotiable; see, for example: Nina Auerbach, *Private Theatricals: The Lives of Victorians* (Cambridge: Harvard University Press, 1990); Terry Castle, *Carnival and Civilization: The Carnivalesque in Eighteenth-Century English Culture and Civilization* (Stanford: Stanford University Press, 1986); and Martin Meisel, *Realizations: Narrative, Pictorial, and Theatrical Arts in Nineteenth-Century England* (Princeton, N.J.: Princeton University Press, 1983). For a sympathetic account of the pioneers of theater history, see Michael Quinn, "*Theatrewissenschaft* in the History of Theatre Study," *Theatre Survey* 32 (1991): 123–36.

4. Stephen Greenblatt, *Shakespearean Negotiations: The Circulation of Social Energy in Renaissance England* (Berkeley and Los Angeles: University of California Press, 1988), 95.

5. Greenblatt, "Towards a Poetics of Culture," in *The New Historicism*, ed. H. Aram Veeser (New York and London: Routledge, 1989), 1–14.

6. See, for example, Peter Stallybrass and Allon White, *The Politics and Poetics of Transgression* (Ithaca: Cornell University Press, 1986).

7. See, in this volume, Marvin Carlson, "Theatre and Dialogism," n. 2, 4–8; and Samuel Kinser, *Rabelais' Carnival: Text, Context, Metatext* (Berkeley: University of California Press, 1990).

8. See, in this volume, Rosemarie Bank, "The Doubled Subject and the New Playwrights Theatre, 1927–1929," n. 6; and Michel Foucault, *The Archaeology of Knowledge [and] The Discourse on Language*, trans. A. M. Sheridan Smith (New York: Pantheon Books, 1972); and *The Order of Things: An Archaeology of the Human Sciences* (New York: Vintage Books, 1973).

9. Paul Ricoeur, *Freud and Philosophy: An Essay on Interpretation*, trans. Dennis Savage (New Haven and London: Yale University Press, 1970), 32–36.

10. Michel Foucault, *Discipline and Punish: The Birth of the Prison*, trans. Alan Sheridan (New York: Vintage Books, 1979); and *The History of Sexuality*, vol. 1, trans. Robert Hurley (New York: Vintage Books, 1980).

11. Walter Benjamin, "Theses on the Philosophy of History," in *Illuminations*, trans. Harry Zohn (New York: Shocken Books, 1969), 256.

Annie Oakley and Her Ideal Husband of No Importance

Tracy C. Davis

In *Tropics of Discourse*, Hayden White asserts that all histories invariably schematize events in one of four plotting patterns: comedy, tragedy, romance, or satire. The use of these genre typologies, he argues, is imperative both for the configuring of a sensible narrative and in order to communicate the sense to a reader. Theater scholars may be ecstatic to see a familiar taxonomy showing up so prominently in the philosophy of history, but before emotion overwhelms judgment the corollary should be closely examined. A few grammatical glosses economically placed within the following passage provide the fuse for its implosion:

> And when he [the universal reader] has perceived the class or type to which the story that he is reading belongs, he [the opposite of she] experiences the effect of having the events in the story explained to him. He has at this point not only successfully *followed* the story; he has grasped the point of it, *understood* it, as well [in terms to which he relates]. The original strangeness, mystery, or exoticism of the events is dispelled. . . . They are familiarized, not only because the reader now has more *information* about the events, but also because he has been shown how the data conform to an *icon* of a comprehensible finished process, a plot structure with which he is familiar as a part of his cultural endowment.[1]

In recent decades feminist scholars have intensely examined the classical cultures that spurred these discursive conventions and the literary traditions that perpetuated them as preeminent classifications. Consequently, genres are now more often seen as philosophical reflections of ideology rather than absolute a priori categorizations.[2] Religious, social, and economic patriarchies privileged genres into normative aesthetic concepts without regard for the experience or traditions of women or other suppressed classes. By unquestioningly accepting the patriarchal base of the generic terminology of literature and historiography, the "cultural endowment" that White presumes readers to share with historians is exclusively male on both sides of the exchange. Historiographic genre theory erroneously presumes universality; if literary theory is equipped to offer any unique ammunition to feminist historiography, perhaps this is it.

Material on Annie Oakley demonstrates the point. Both biographical accounts and descriptions of the performances of the most famous female crack shot associated with William F. Cody's Wild West shows are invariably structured in the manner of romance narratives.[3] What they include (and exclude) and the terms in which events are relayed conceptualizes who Oakley was to herself and to her contemporaries and how she related to the performance traditions in which she took part. The chivalric narrative of feats at arms and exploits in love dominates descriptions of Oakley, but there are moments both historically and biographically when the ideology that defines romance is incompatible with details of her life. At such points narratives either swerve to the alternate romantic strain (i.e., from shooting exploits to love, or vice versa) or omit significant details. The results reveal the limitations of genre for relating history and mark the optimal entry points for feminist analyses.

The basic events of Oakley's early life are easily paraphrased, while still retaining the typical emphasis on successive victorious turns with adversity acted out in unusual locations. Oakley was born and raised in western Ohio (hardly an outpost of civilization in 1860), yet this detail is exoticized in biographical accounts by spicy metaphors of the frontier. Her large Quaker family was destabilized by the death of her father then of her first stepfather. Poverty forced Oakley from her "log cabin" origins into the county workhouse, whereupon she was fostered out as a servant with people who cruelly treated her and kept education and kin at bay. This period with what she calls "wolf" captors who imposed on her the drudgery of feminized and servile labor is the low point of her life, her greatest struggle with adversity, a metaphoric descent into hell, and a savage rite of passage requiring stamina to endure and ingenuity to escape. She reemerged, back in the idyllic "woodlands" of western Ohio, turned her precocious ability for hunting and shooting to commercial purposes, augmented the family's meager resources in the recession of the mid 1870s, and before long had paid off the mortgage. At the age of sixteen, while on a family visit in Cincinnati, a contest was arranged against Frank Butler, a touring actor, who routinely accepted such challenges as a profitable sideline to entr'acte sharpshooting demonstrations. This was the man she married and ultimately worked with for the rest of her life.

Most biographies credit this contest as a clear victory for Oakley, who on her first meeting with Butler shot forty-nine targets to his forty-eight. In the 1946 musical comedy version of the story (*Annie Get Your Gun*) Oakley's skill takes a holiday when she has this first shooting contest with a man—a timely lesson for wives of returning veterans. Thirty years later *Ms.* magazine argued that the musical was chiefly to blame for Annie Oakley being "not so much buried in history as character-assassinated by the feminine mystique."[4] Yet other accounts also deliberatley attempt to disrupt the romance-at-arms narrative by downplaying the significance of the extraordinary behavior on the part of a woman and accentuating instead a romance-of-love narrative of female subservience. In such cases, particularly when the historian balks at the details of a woman's iconoclasm, the romance genre accommodates Oakley's feminized persona in lieu of a narrative of female accomplishment.

The popular magazine *Guns*, for example, summarizes Oakley's and Butler's legacy to the world as showing "the fun and companionship that

Fig. 1. From Annie Oakley's Scrapbooks: "Champion Woman Rifle Shot of the World Shows Women of Cincinnati How to Protect Themselves"

awaited a man and wife who shared their guns together."[5] The article's juxtaposition of Oakley's story with tales of 1950s female shooting champions (also described as "blondes" and beauty queens appended to men) and a retraction of Calamity Jane's claims to celebrity illuminates with halogen clarity *Guns'* ideological perspective. Interestingly, the article makes a blatant attempt to negate individualism and accomplishment in women rifle shots of two eras: the active years of the female suffrage movement and the boom years following World War II. The article concludes with a tale of seventeenth-century German shooting contests for virgin female prizes; these, it argues, were "as moral as any 'arranged' marriage. At least the girl knew that her future husband would be among the best shooters, with a sure path to distinction and wealth ... an ideal husband, in fact."[6] In other words the contested woman would have the protection of guns without knowing how to handle them, a circumstance indivisible with total economic dependence. Like these historicized virgins and marksmen, Oakley and Butler also met at a *schützenverein*, but their situation had significant inversions, which are acknowledged in variations written in periods when fewer restrictions were made on women's economic liberation. In such versions the romance-at-arms adventure is more apparent.

In Courtney Riley Cooper's 1927 biography, Oakley's first meeting with Butler is described in terms of a medieval challenge at arms between a known champion and a young female underdog. Modernized only by the weapons, the contest was silently governed by a chivalric code of honor in which both parties participated earnestly, and the vanquished was implicitly obligated to acknowledge the superior skill and honor of the victor. Apparently, Butler was governed by the contest's outcome for he devoted his life to glorifying Oakley's superior skill. Butler's lifelong obeisance in the shooting arena seems to represent the attainment of a classless society— one of the implications of romance narratives—in a marriage of congruous individuals. Taken in the historical perspective of late nineteenth-century politics, Butler's role suggests suffragist wish fulfillment, for he conforms to a feminized pattern by sacrificing his ego for love. But this is only accomplished through a chronological lacuna in the narrative. The couple was married a year after the contest (possibly bigamously at first, for Butler's divorce may not have been final), but biographies are silent on the years

301

between 1876 and 1882. In all likelihood, Oakley stayed close to her family while Butler toured, anticipating the birth of children; this is not the stuff of adventure narratives, and neither the activities in the first years of their marriage nor their childless state is ever mentioned.

As soon as possible, biographers rush on to 1882 and details of Oakley's first appearance—as a last minute stand-in for John Graham—in Butler's shooting act. Her career shapes the narratives from this point, going from melodrama to the Sells Brothers' Circus then in 1885 to Cody's Wild West, though it is curious that the deflection of focus onto Oakley is diametrically opposite to cultural norms privileging male agency. As Joyce Warren, a literary critic, argues:

> Despite the emphasis on individualism in nineteenth-century America, women in all walks of life were seen not as individuals but as secondary characters in the drama of the [male] American individualist.... Women and the home represented stability in a rapidly changing society, and women were forced into a more circumscribed position to facilitate the transition to an industrial society.[7]

For biographers the unusual qualities of Oakley's and Butler's marriage are overshadowed by Oakley's international fame. Some contemporaries recognized that Butler quietly maintained his own stature as a professional shot by participating in rifle club contests and representing arms and ammunition manufacturers, but for the vast theatrical public of the nineteenth century he was the love-struck facilitator of his famous wife's act. It is as if Butler's "unimportance" in the public realm is offset by these more private competitions and his shooting is reduced to a hobby; meanwhile, Oakley's iconoclasm in the public realm is offset by details emphasizing her conventional domesticity. Thus, the marriage is "normalized."

Biographies rely heavily on contemporaneous newspaper accounts,[8] and pick up on their consistent emphasis of Oakley's petite stature, unpretentious yet genteel social graces, and home-centered life. These are standard ploys in publicity, interviews, and features about women but are neither incidental to the public construction of Oakley's identity nor extraneous to the narrative plotting. Her accomplishments in gardening and needlecraft and the joy she allegedly derived from being able to "broil a steak or cook a roast as well as anyone,"[9] seem to have complemented her extraordinary facility with firearms and created a hybrid of the wilderness-hunter and the hunter-cultivator (classic American mythoi of the period):[10]

> Making tea and toasting muffins was the occupation of the best lady rifle shot in the world when a *World* reporter called to see her yesterday afternoon at her cosy apartments opposite Madison Square Garden. The sitting-room was littered with breech-loading shotguns, rifles and revolvers, while the mantel-piece and tables were resplendent with gold and silver trophies brought back from Europe by this slender yet muscular Diana of the Northwest.[11]

This 1888 account, like so many others from both Europe and North America, goes on to detail the romantic exoticism of Oakley's associates in the Wild West show and the royalty she socialized with on adventurous foreign tours. Emphasizing the hearthside, Vestia tempers Diana—or perhaps an Amazonian potential. Butler, an "ideal" husband, consistently wins whenever a rival suitor vies for her attention.

The episodic plots of affliction and redemption, so evident in Oakley's childhood, resume in 1901 when she suffered the first of a series of accidents and physical setbacks. She always emerges shooting as straight and true as ever, so her heroism is intact, but her significant exploits and all original permutations of love and feats of arms are in the past. Oakley's and Butler's remaining years were spent in unsuccessful forays into management, competitive shooting, and demonstrations for military trainees, yet are merely glosses in biographies such as *Missie*. Biographers chronicle this period rather than writing history proper.[12] This switch in narrative technique signals historians' discomfort with a new sedentary phase in Oakley's life when in many respects Butler (supposedly a squire, not a knight) is more professionally active. When the exotic adventure ceases (and can no longer play against the domestic idyll, as in the 1880s and 1890s) the romance plot terminates. All that remains after the chronicle is a sentimental conclusion of mutual illness, death, and burial in 1926. Traditional historians fail to recognize any romance plot in the last quarter century of their subjects' lives. Feminists, however, might disagree.

In 1915, finally relinquishing theatrical obligations, Butler and Oakley took up winter residence at a North Carolina resort, where, instead of retiring, he took charge of the skeet range (his competitive forte) while she specialized in giving shooting lessons to women.[13] She claimed in a letter "that is my pleasure, for which there is no charge or compensation on my part."[14] Apparently, Oakley was committed to advocating women's self-defense; a pamphlet she wrote on the topic in the early years of the century was frequently reproduced in the press but is entirely absent from romance narratives. Oakley states:

> Probably no weapon of defense . . . is so adapted for a woman's use against an attack of the "Jack the Ripper" sort as a 32- caliber revolver of a good make. I would advise every woman who has to go out at night and expects to travel some dangerous locality to learn the correct use of a good 32-caliber revolver.

Her identification, as a world-renowned sharpshooter, with women of all types and conditions is unequivocal:

> For the woman living in the lonely farmhouse, and for the business woman returning home late at night from work, the knowledge of how to use a pistol is a Godsend. . . . I would say to a woman "never make a bluff at using a revolver for defense. Always if the weapon

is drawn, be ready to shoot, and be ready to shoot before the enemy shoots."[15]

The "enemy," as Fifth Amendment defenders would recognize, is not a squirrel, buffalo, or Axis soldier but American males. The purpose in reproducing this information is not to claim a past member in the feminist sisterhood—serving theory rather than history—but rather to signal what Oakley thought important and to point out one instance where self-definition is absent from romantic plots. There are also significant omissions in the metaphoric readings of Oakley's and Butler's performance work which the contextualizing terms of feminist theory can uncover.

Oakley's success as a petite white female sharpshooter who rose to fame in the 1880s is an enticing story. Her professional partnership with her husband, who prepared her guns and propelled and propped the targets for her to shoot at, is a delicious contradiction of domestic power acted out ritualistically in the public arena. Her friendship with Sitting Bull, the Sioux nemesis of Yankee military machismo, makes the problem even richer. The mentalité that sustained Oakley through her career despite these seeming heresies has been entirely unexplored by biographers, yet it is crucial for a meaningful theater history. Explaining the past may inevitably lead to mythic modes of representation inseparable from a historian's ideological perspective: the plotting and the contextualizing of data alike reflect cultural endowments but need not present interpretation as one-dimensionally as the romance genre or the sieve of white patriarchy. Socialist feminists such as Cora Kaplan insist on the necessity of studying relations between the sexes as changeable processes of social construction;[16] this is a sound historiographic position. In practice it allows room for considering how a figure such as Annie Oakley reflects culture, intervenes with culture, generates culture, and opposes culture. What follows is an attempt to live up to this potential by modeling an application on a small scale.

Oakley never swooned, fainted, or averred; her hand was absolutely steady and her bullets, like her gaze, always pierced the mark. Like her marriage, the normalization of these traits—ideologically incompatible in eastern American culture of the time—into a single highly revered feminine figure was a complex achievement. Sarah Blackstone contends that in sharpshooting acts "it did not matter if the performer was male or female, big or small, old or young, as long as he or she could shoot with great accuracy."[17] This is a hasty conclusion, judging by the press's fascination with feminized details about Annie Oakley. Despite its fictionalization of frontier life, Cody's show ritualized western work of various kinds. In pioneer culture, with its agricultural base, divisions of power did not usually arise out of individuals' predilections toward types of labor but, rather, out of absolutes like sex and race. Oakley's glaring divergence from the norm is significant.

Every aspect of the Wild West show was permeated with gendered meaning, including the casting of mimed plays, equestrian demonstrations, and sharpshooting. It is not just noteworthy that women appeared in the bill: what they did and with whom is also significant. Although Oakley starred in Cody's show and Butler never received billing of any kind, their performance was actually a duo act in every sense. The family basis of the act may have been a major factor in the neutralization of Oakley's masculinized pursuits and abilities, even though its dynamic placed the husband in a weak, secondary role. Oakley always had focus, as her niece's description of the components of the 1887 Command Performance before Queen Victoria shows:

> As the driver of the Prairie Schooner whipped up the lazy oxen with the long rawhide whip to hurry them along as they approached the exit, in rode Annie Oakley, alone a picture as she rode around the arena. . . . She ended her race around the arena by riding up in front of the Queen's Box, and her spirited horse made a low bow to the audience. Annie's long brown hair flying in the breeze as she turned to ride to the center of the arena, was typical of the Western cowgirl. Then in rode Frank Butler.

Oakley and Butler were the only company members widely known as spouses. She and her ideal husband stood apart from American literary and social traditions associated with the western frontier. From the time they joined Cody's outfit Butler ceased to be a Daniel Boone leading his family from one place to another, motivated by his perpetual self-interest. At the same time Oakley ceased to be a Rebecca Boone waiting patiently at her mother's fireside or trailing along faithfully out of affectionate devotion.[18] She was the star whose career determined her husband's peregrinations both globally and in the arena. After establishing Oakley within a western context, the act properly began. Butler's participation was indispensable and probably involved inapparent precision:

> He carried a basket of glass balls, and a gun for Annie. As they rode around the arena at breakneck speed, he threw the glass balls into the air, and she shot, breaking the balls, sometimes two, and even more, at a time. Then Annie stood upon the horse's back, and finished breaking the balls by shooting them as Frank threw them while he rode along by her side. They then dismounted.

The performance closely conforms to the steps Paul Bouissac identifies in circus acts which, he asserts, derive from folktales of transformation.[19] The equestrian section warms up the performers and the audience and functions as a qualifying test. The main test—actually a series of similar tests on two themes—follows. The variations all involve either precision shooting that somewhat imperils Butler as he holds targets away from his body or shots aimed at moving targets.

> Now came the remainder of the act: Frank stood about fifty feet from Annie and held a small, two by five inch card. . . . With a twenty-

Fig. 2. F. E. Butler. Courtesy of the
Buffalo Bill Historical Center.

two rifle Annie shot through the small red heart as many as fifty
times in succession. Next Frank held the cards with the edge toward
her, and she, using a pistol, would cut the cards in two. . . . She broke
clay-pigeons thrown from the traps, not only one at a time, but as
many as four. Frank would swing a cord around his body, at the end
of which was a glass ball; Annie would lie backwards over a chair,
and with the gun upside down, would break the ball. Another clever
stunt she performed, was to hold a pistol backward over her shoulder,
and using a silver knife for a mirror, would break a ball that Frank
whirled around his body which was tied on the end of the string.
When the arena grounds were level enough, Annie would ride around
on a bicycle without holding to the handlebars, and shoot objects
thrown [by Frank] into the air.

Next came what Bouissac terms the "glorifying test" that demonstrates
unusual skill on the part of Oakley and extraordinary nerve on the part
of Butler.

She said by this time she was in good practice, and would prove it
by shooting the ashes from a cigarette which Frank held in his mouth.
Next he held a dime between his first and second fingers, with the
edge toward her, and with a twenty-two rifle she hit it, sending it
whizzing through the air.[20]

This description includes the typical exercises of their act. An alternative
glorifying test consisted of a William Tell stunt with other family members—
their dogs—sitting still while Oakley's unfailing aim blasted away apples
rather than their heads. This, like the cigarette and dime exercises with

Butler, is an additional performed testimonial of fidelity and trust within the family unit.

In most accounts of Oakley's act Butler is unidentified or completely absent from the narrative. Like a midwife Butler had no allure, presence, or productive role, but he possessed technical expertise, and he facilitated. Oakley once described how, as a child, her precocity with firearms was checked by a brother who "crammed the barrel of the gun full of powder and shot, and put it into my hands, not knowing how dangerous it might be" to try to dissuade her from shooting. "My face was torn and bleeding and my brother was greatly alarmed. But he had set out to teach me a lesson and he said to me, 'Now, will you quit shooting?' I was scarcely able to speak, but I stamped my foot and cried out, 'No, never!'"[21] As an adult performer, in contrast to a child rebel, her gender-atypical pursuits were nurtured rather than hindered by a masculinized figure of authority. His "invisibility" makes him both ideal and of no importance. Nevertheless, his participation is symbolically and functionally crucial. The stage act showed a woman taking up the machines most symbolic of patriarchy and the phallus and reversing the conventional simulacrum of oppression by turning the instruments against her husband. This represented danger but not violence, and skill at arms but not combat, which made the performance exciting but not discomfiting.[22] Between a marriage of equals the reversal was relatively apolitical.

By shooting at her husband, pets, and (during European tours) male heads of state, Oakley demonstrated the wilderness's ability (as Nature, or the feminine) to strike out dangerously (though controlled, under influence of the masculine) at Civilization in patriarchal and domestically tamed personae. As a perpetually youthful child of the eastern Midwest, Oakley's geopolitical heritage was considerably more tame and peaceful than the image of performers who were actually from the West; her costumes showed femaleness but not femininity, which signaled compliance with the gender-differentiated codes of personal display while proclaiming strict sexual propriety.

Like countless circus turns over the ages, theirs was a family act. Its rituals had ideological meaning relating gender to geography, work, and law. Oakley's partnership with an Irish immigrant underlined the old-world civility practiced in their profusely embroidered and immaculately gardened muffin-scented homes. This is essential to the public interpretation of the private woman through the window of her performance. Other members of Cody's retinue had distinct ideological identities. Lillian Smith, another female sharpshooter, was billed as "The California Huntress" and followed the "Primeval Forest" first act of The History of American Civilization, whereas Oakley followed the "Cattle Ranch" third act, which consisted of vignettes of natives' attacks on a western settlement.[23] Lillian Smith was contextualized with the untamed precivilized era of experience. Similarly, the exiled Gabriel Dumont, who appeared in the earliest Wild West season, appealed because of his role in the Riel Rebellion of Northwest Canada. "Buffalo Bill" Cody himself represented hunting and the West before law.

Fig. 3. "Annie Oakley Receiving Their Royal Highnesses the Prince and Princess of Wales in Her Tent"

ANNIE OAKLEY

Receiving T.R.H. Prince & Princess of Wales in her tent

They were exotic, dangerous, and primal in ways that Oakley was not. It is no wonder that Oakley was singled out for an audience with Queen Victoria: one domestic female with sovereign power within a civilized family "show" recognized another.

Race, ethnicity, and gender also combined in the Wild West show in a multitude of permutations replete with cultural significance. Oakley made her first appearance on horseback, and, as Blackstone points out, the combination of equipment, costume, and rider served to support prevalent beliefs about social groups' positions in the nature/civilization dichotomy.

> The Indian rode bareback (an almost wild horse ridden by an equally wild person), the cowboy rode in the Western saddle (a working man with his most valuable piece of equipment), the Western girls rode astride (unrefined women showing their rough upbringing), and the English gentleman rode an English jumping saddle (a highly sophisticated man in complete control of his animal with almost no equipment).[24]

The Cody Museum preserves a western saddle tooled with Oakley's insignia, but her knee-length stage dresses would have required her to ride sidesaddle in performance (a quasi-pioneer in an aristocratic seat). The equestrian messages were refined by the performative roles of the participants. In part of Cody's all-round shooting demonstration, like Oakley's, he required an assistant to ride alongside him and throw targets as he galloped around the arena. These assistants varied over the years but included a nine-year-old white girl, a native American man, and a Mexican man:[25] all members of groups oppressed and degraded in the rapidly industrializing East and colonizing West and Southwest of the United States.[26] Though Cody shot over their heads, the gunfire was still aimed in the direction of specific social groups' delegates. In the equestrian segment of Oakley's act, therefore, the mature, mustached, Irish-American Butler may seem to be the antithesis of Cody's assistants but was typed by association with their emasculated, conquered status.

In addition to demonstrating snap shooting, Cody also enacted the hunt of game, incidents of frontier life, and segments of the Indian Wars. The explicit point of scenarios like *The Deadwood Stage, The Attack on the Settler's Cabin, A Prairie Emigrant Train Crossing the Plains,* and of buffalo runs (billed as "the last of the only known Native Herd")[27] is contained in the enactment of direct genocide of aboriginal plains tribes and indirect genocide through the extermination of their principal food source. Shooting in the Wild West show did, therefore, take on iconic meaning of lethal and specific significant political conflicts. Cody fired blank cartridges in these segments, whereas in Oakley's act the ammunition was live, but while his shooting at a particular race and species was malevolent in implication because it supported racial prerogatives of expansionist ambition, her bullets were released with benign intent toward a member of the patriarchy to whom she was personally devoted. Despite Butler's enlightened political attitudes and feminized position within the performance, this contains a hint of misrule and inversion of the social order in contrast to Cody's enforcement and amplification of white preferences.

As her shooting partner, Butler took on a brotherly role; as her stage manager and munitions expert, he took a husband's part in the danger; and, as her manager and booking agent, he functioned paternally. Walter Havinghurst notes in his biography: "He was ten years older, and all his life he called her his little girl. . . . She had never had a father; now she had father, brother, husband, in one changing man."[28] Another paternal figure is also significant in Oakley's story. As with Butler, the gender dynamic of this relationship has passed without examination.

When Sitting Bull (Te Toncka Ua Tocka) was asked if he regretted the Little Big Horn massacre, he is cited as saying: "I have answered to my people for the Indians slain in that fight. The chief that sent Custer must answer to his people."[29] As Richard Slotkin argues, the American mythos derived from James Fenimore Cooper's Leatherstocking novels attributes natives with unique racial gifts and responses to ethical questions.[30] In the foregoing comment and in his unorthodox relationship with Oakley, Sitting Bull demonstrates that social peace is not achieved through conflict, annihilation, or the vindication of a "just" cause, but through understanding and mutual respect between honorable parties. As a female and a native—outsiders from privileged Americanism—Oakley and Sitting Bull bonded as if in blood and recognized individualism in each other which was denied as a matter of course to their social groups. The reciprocal admiration between Sitting Bull and Annie Oakley is a facet of their life stories often reiterated in contemporaneous press accounts, for the status marked her uniqueness among the Wild West company. The Euro-American mythos of the frontier reflects deep fears of natives abducting and sexually attacking white women (a racist phobia entwined in pretexts for the catastrophic Washita slaughter of 1868, which established Custer's reputation);[31] this had a bearing on Oakley's act when, as in the 1895–96 seasons, it followed a scenario involving natives' attack on a settlers' cabin, a massacre, fight, and rescue of white female hostages. Sitting Bull's gesture of adopting Oakley peacefully and renaming her Watanya Cicilia (Little Sure Shot) subverts the existing white mythos, as she was delighted to be designated a daughter of the so-called inferior race.

Her ready acceptance of an honorary place in Sitting Bull's nuclear family and of a name in the language of a people that Cody and the Seventh Cavalry conspired to exterminate makes her distinct from prevailing white values and the dramatic thrust of the Wild West show. Though billed as "Foes in '76—Friends in '85" Cody and Sitting Bull's camaraderie was erroneous, for their interests remained diametrically opposed. Audiences recognized this by booing Sitting Bull's entrances, so Oakley's dedication allied her with a cultural villain. Nevertheless, part of her unblemished public image may deserve to be due to this moral, familial, and political iconoclasm marking an ethic almost unique among American Caucasians of her time.

As mass entertainment, the Wild West show pleased millions. No wonder. But it is worthwhile for modern historians to reflect that the Wild West show's representations of gender and race complied with hegemonic ideology and that Oakley and her husband "of no importance" stood apart from this in several distinctive respects. It was in the interests of the press to laud the "American tradition" fostered by the Wild West, just as it was in the interests of celebratory biographies to comply with romantic structures to construe Oakley historically.

This is not intended to suggest that Oakley was perceived as a traitor because of her sympathies with Sitting Bull any more than she was perceived as a virago because of the feminized position in which her sharpshooting act placed Butler. The fact that in her time she was revered as feminine, faithful, and superb at her specialty suggests the public saw what they wanted to see and that journalists' and readers' imaginations found ways to mitigate her "anti-cultural" traits.

Applying contemporary theories of race and gender to history writing reveals complications in what was formerly a rather straightforward image. Lawrence Levine admits that with the incorporation of different methodologies "historians find themselves again and again complicating simple pictures, finding intricacies where before we had certainties, turning unity into multiplicity, clarity into ambiguity."[32] This is not necessarily a disadvantage. One of the drawbacks of much critical theory is that it tends to propose universal truths, insufficiently recognizing that few people apart from critical theorists find experience as clear-cut as theory; even fewer devote mental energy to puzzling out the ideological context of the inter-active discourses of anyone or anything. Yet it is arguable that the exercise of critical analysis on a historical figure can usefully model the information that contemporaries synthesized effortlessly and thoughtlessly.

Historical revisions spurred by late twentieth-century consciousness bear out Nietzsche's dictum "you can explain the past only by what is most powerful in the present"[33] and with a tenet of gender studies which asserts that the coexistent categories of gender, class, and race continually modify each other in experience and should be negotiated in critical writing.[34] There are fashions in everything, including historiography, literary theory, and feminism, but the practice of conjoining each field's analytical tradition and textual materials is especially promising for theater studies. Not all con-junctions are fruitful for historical practice, but at the very least theory can empower history with the means to interpret social ideology.

NOTES

1. Hayden White, *Tropics of Discourse* (Baltimore and London: Johns Hopkins University Press, 1978), 86.

2. Most of such work focuses on the novel. White does not distinguish between dramatic and novelistic genres, which for the broad purposes of his argument is forgivable. For applications in dramatic criticism, see Sue-Ellen Case, *Feminism and Theatre* (Baskingstoke: Macmillan, 1988); Carol W. Gelderman, "The Male Nature of Tragedy," *Prairie Schooner* (Fall 1975): 220–36; and Leonard Tennenhouse, *Power on Display: The Politics of Shakespeare's Genres* (New York and London: Methuen, 1986).

3. Oakley has not been the subject of true scholarly study, though it is hoped that Shirl Kasper's forthcoming biography will improve the picture considerably; a myth-dispelling biography of the quality of Donald Bert Russell's *Lives and Legends of Buffalo Bill* (Norman: University of Oklahoma Press, 1960), and an in-depth performance study along the lines of Craig Francis Nieuwenhuyse, "Six-Guns on the Stage: Buffalo Bill Cody's First Celebration of the Conquest of the American Frontier" (Ph.D., University of California–Berkeley, 1981), are long overdue. Among nonjuvenile full-length biographies, one may be considered official: Annie Fern Swartwout, *Missie: An Historical Biography of Annie Oakley* (Blanchester, Ohio: Brown, 1947). Three more are ranked as standard works: Courtney Riley Cooper, *Annie Oakley, Woman at Arms* (New York: Duffield, 1927); Walter Havinghurst, *Annie Oakley of the Wild West* (New York: Macmillan, 1954); and Isabelle E. Sayers, *Annie Oakley and Buffalo Bill's Wild West* (New York: Dover, 1981).

4. Bonnie Kreps, "Annie Oakley's Untold Love Story," *Ms.* 5, no. 7 (January 1977): 8.

5. K. D. Curtis, "Can Women Outshoot Men?" *Guns* (July 1955): 53.

6. Ibid., 54.

7. Joyce W. Warren, *The American Narcissus: Individualism and Women in Nineteenth-Century American Fiction* (New Brunswick, N.J.: Rutgers University Press, 1984), 8.

8. Annie Oakley's scrapbooks, held at the Buffalo Bill Historical Center (Cody, Wyo.), are the principal source.

9. Amy Leslie, "Play and Players," ca. 1905; and "Women and Society," *Ohio*

State Journal, 28 August 1906. Both clippings are from Oakley's scrapbooks.

10. Annette Kolodny, *The Land before Her: Fantasy and Experience of the American Frontiers, 1630–1860* (Chapel Hill and London: University of North Carolina Press, 1984), 67.

11. "The Woman Rifle Expert," *World*, 8 January 1888; from Oakley's scrapbooks.

12. Hayden White, *The Content of the Form: Narrative Discourse and Historical Representation* (Baltimore and London: Johns Hopkins University Press, 1987), 1–25.

13. Sayers, *Annie Oakley*, 82–83.

14. Letter to the *Tribune*, dated 2 February 1917; from Oakley's scrapbooks.

15. "Rifle Expert Talks of Women and Firearms," *Cincinnati Times-Star*, ca. 1904; from Oakley's scrapbooks. This was not, as Curtis suggests, strictly intended as advice to husbands teaching their wives ("Can Women Outshoot," 53).

16. Cora Kaplan, *Sea Changes: Culture and Feminism* (London: Verso, 1986).

17. Sarah J. Blackstone, *Buckskins, Bullets,and Business: A History of Buffalo Bill's Wild West* (Westport, Conn.: Greenwood Press, 1986), 111.

18. Kolodny, *Land before Her*, 84. This assessment is based on Timothy Flint's *Biographical Memoir of Daniel Boone, the First Settler of Kentucky* (Cincinnati: N. and G. Gilford, 1833).

19. Paul Bouissac, *Circus and Culture: A Semiotic Approach* (Bloomington: Indiana University Press, 1976), 25.

20. Swartwout, *Missie*, 127–29.

21. "Annie Oakley, Crack Shot, Likes Housework," *Ohio State Journal*, 28 August 1906; from Oakley's scrapbooks.

22. It could be turned to combat use, as Oakley and Butler showed in their firearms demonstrations for military trainees in World War I. This, though a performance of equality, retained the domestic element in a dog target.

23. A detailed description of *The Drama of Civilization* is provided by William Brasmer in "The Wild West and the Drama of Civilization," *Western Popular Theatre*, ed. David Mayer and Kenneth Richards (London: Methuen, 1977), 133–56.

24. Blackstone, *Buckskins*, 110.

25. Ibid., 60, 84.

26. Richard Slotkin, *The Fatal Environment: The Myth of the Frontier in the Age of Industrialization, 1800–1890* (New York: Atheneum, 1985), 139.

27. Programs for 1896–97, Harvard Theatre Collection.

28. Havinghurst, *Annie Oakley*, 21–22.

29. W. Fletcher Johnson, *The Life of Sitting Bull and the Indian War*; cited in Sayers, *Annie Oakley*, 22.

30. Slotkin, *Fatal Environment*, 88.

31. Ibid., 403–4.

32. Lawrence W. Levine, "The Unpredictable Past: Reflections on Recent American Historiography," *American Historical Review* 94, no. 3 (June 1989): 679.

33. Friedrich Nietzsche, *The Use and Abuse of History*; cited in Linda Hutcheon, *The Poetics of Postmodernism: History, Theory, Fiction* (London: Routledge, 1988), 99.

34. Demonstrations can be found in Elaine Showalter, ed., *Speaking of Gender* (New York and London: Routledge, 1989).

Theater and Dialogism

Marvin Carlson

The writings of Mikhail Bakhtin have in recent years become increasingly influential in a wide variety of intellectual fields, including psychology, anthropology, sociology, linguistics, communication theory, semiotics, and literary theory. Although some of Bakhtin's central concepts, such as dialogism, the subject of this study, have distinctly dramatic overtones, Bakhtin's own central interest in the novel and his relatively few and relatively undeveloped comments on drama have discouraged commentators, until very recently, from considering how the concerns of this highly original writer, which have proven so illuminating in the study of the novel, might be applied to other genres.

The writings of Bakhtin form a large and complex body of work, written over a lengthy career and published under a variety of names. Although a central group of concerns forms the foundation of all of these works,[1] different emphases in different works have attracted the attention of different subsequent theorists. Theater theorists attracted to Bakhtin have been particularly interested in his book on Rabelais,[2] with its concept of carnivalization and the challenge posed by carnival to social hierarchies and structures of authority. Doubtless this attraction may in part be explained by the congruence of Bakhtin's "carnivalesque" with certain ideas in the extremely influential writings of such anthropologists as Arnold Van Gennep and Victor Turner. The concept of the "liminal," an in-between stage where normal societal organization disappears, closely analogous to Bakhtin's "carnival," was first applied to the study of rites of passage by such theorists but subsequently, especially by Turner, to a similarly open ground for the creation of art in general and theater in particular.[3] The carnivalesque has become a very helpful concept for the many theorists today who from a variety of perspectives seek to resist the totalizing tendencies of traditional social and literary analysis. Like the anthropological liminal, the Bakhtinian carnivalesque directs our attention to models of transformation and counterproduction, to centers of parody and excess both within the heart of any social system and at its margins. This approach has been particularly popular among theorists of Renaissance English drama,[4] but it has also been applied to subjects as varied as Ludvig Holberg's popular *Jeppe of the Hill*,[5] feminist performance,[6] medieval drama,[7] and contemporary theater in Quebec.[8]

In his more recently translated studies of Dostoevsky, of the novel, and in certain other writings that have been less considered by drama theorists than the work on Rabelais, Bakhtin focuses upon a related but somewhat different set of concerns, having to do with the authorial voice.[9] I should like to explore here some of the implications of these for dramatic

313

theory. The central concepts of "dialogism" in the first of these two books and "heteroglossia" in the second are closely related and are presented by Bakhtin not only as distinguishing marks of novelization but, indeed, the source of the novel's superiority over other literary endeavors. Both work against regularizing and canonizing forces in literature and language (monologism and monoglossia) producing the expression of multiple perspectives through contrasting voices. Often in Bakhtin's description of these concepts the drama seems a more apt example than the novel. Heteroglossia, for example, is described in one passage as "another's speech in another's language. . . . It serves two speakers at the same time and expresses simultaneously two different intentions: the direct intention of the character who is speaking, and the refracted intention of the author."[10] In explaining what makes a Dostoevsky novel dialogic, Bakhtin explains that "it is constructed not as a whole of a single consciousness, absorbing other consciousnesses as objects into itself, but as a whole formed by the interaction of several consciousnesses, none of which entirely becomes an object for the other."[11]

When one encounters such dramatically flavored observations as these one is tempted to share the frustration and puzzlement of Todorov, who notes that one waits in vain for an extended comparison of the novel and drama in Bakhtin, parallel to the frequent comparison of the novel and the epic.[12] Nevertheless it is clear from the references to drama, general and specific, scattered through Bakhtin's writings that, whatever the impressions his comments on dialogism and heteroglossia might give, he considered the drama in essence a monologic genre, opposed by its nature to the flexibility essential to the novel. One of the clearest expressions of this conviction is found in Bakhtin's comments on dialogue in Dostoevsky, where he specifically rejects the view of Leonid Grossman, an earlier Dostoevsky scholar, that Dostoevsky's dialogues could be thought of as dramatic, precisely on the grounds that dialogue in drama is actually in Bakhtin's terms monological:

> In drama, of course, this monologic framework does not find direct verbal expression, but precisely in drama is it especially monolithic. The rejoinders in a dramatic dialogue do not rip apart the represented world, do not make it multi-leveled; on the contrary, if they are to be authentically dramatic, these rejoinders necessitate the utmost monolithic unity of that world. In drama the world must be made from a single piece. Any weakening of this monolithic quality leads to a weakening of dramatic effect. The characters come together dialogically in the unified field of vision of author, director, and audience, against the clearly defined background of a single-tiered world.[13]

It is surely significant that when Bakhtin speaks of the monologism of drama he refers almost invariably to tragedy, and especially to classic tragedy, noting such phenomena as the regularizing poetic form, the focus on the hero, with other characters merely reflecting his concerns, and the drive of tragedy toward the resolution of differences, in which Bakhtin seems to be looking back to Hegel and the tradition of German romantic theory on tragedy. Yet, even if one concludes that high tragedy is a mono-logic form, by no means as certain as Bakhtin suggests, there is clearly a vast range of drama that falls outside this genre, much of it as disruptive of the represented world as anything in the novelistic tradition. The whole tradition of comedy, from Aristophanes onward, opens itself in this direction, and the drama has been one of the cultural centers of parody, which Bakhtin advances as one of the most ancient forms of dialogism, the representing of the language of another.[14] Not only does parody function as a generic focus in itself, but perhaps even more striking, and more directly relevant to Bakhtin's concern, it can even subvert the dramatic world from within by direct challenge to the unity of its dominant voice. Renaissance drama is full of examples, a single famous one being the speech of the clown Clarín in the final act of Calderón's *Life is a Dream*, eulogizing his horse and beginning:

> Mounted on a fire-eating steed
> (excuse me if I touch things up
> a bit in telling you this story),
> on whose hide a map is finely drawn,
> for of course his body is the earth,
> and his heart the fire locked up
> in his breast, his froth the sea,
> his breath the wind and in
> this sweltering chaos I stand
> agape . . . [15]

Not only is this speech a general parody of the *gongorist* descriptions of the leading characters, but it parodies specifically the famous flamboyant opening speech by Rosaura, which begins:

> Where have you thrown me, mad horse,
> half griffin? You rage like the storm,
> then flicker like lightning
> outspeeding light, off in a flash
> like a fish without scales,
> or a white featherless bird
> in headlong flight.[16]

Of course, a central function of clown figures like Clarín is often to provide just this sort of alternative voice within the structure of the drama. Another obvious example is Falstaff, perhaps most clearly in his scene with Hal parodying a royal audience. Bakhtin does speak of the appearance in the Middle Ages of the rogue, the clown, and the fool, who provided "Otherness" to the "low genres,"[17] though he does not mention that prominent among these low genres was the popular theater.

The modern drama, from realism onward, receives even less attention in Bakhtin's writings, yet it is particularly in the modern drama where a variety of forces have worked to increase the plurality of voices and to encourage what a number of twentieth-century German critics have called open forms. At best Bakhtin only hints at this development when he remarks that during the late nineteenth century in such writers as Ibsen and Hauptmann the drama became "novelized"—that is, involved with "an indeterminacy, a certain semantic open-endedness, a living contact with unfinished, still-evolving contemporary reality (the open-ended present)," which in Bakhtin's view characterized the novel.[18] What Bakhtin seems to be suggesting in this brief passage is the departure of the realistic dramatists of that period from the calculated structures of the well-made play, where the manipulations of the dramatist were so clear that all voices indeed seemed echoes of his voice and all actions controlled by a single intellect.

With dramatists like Ibsen and Hauptmann, as Bakhtin realized, and perhaps even more strikingly with Chekhov, a very different sort of dynamic is at work. The reality they sought to depict was shifting, ambiguous, evanescent. Its developments were surprising and often unpredictable, its events and situations often unclear, its values contradictory, with no obvious voice of authority to resolve these confusions. English critics, accustomed to clear moral positions, raged against Ibsen's obscenity. French critics, willing to be more casual on moral questions but devoted to unambiguous structure and motivation, complained of Nordic fogs and mysticism and confessed themselves quite unable to deal with something so elusive and multifaceted as Ibsen's symbolic wild duck. Certainly the lack of (or sometimes, as in *A Doll House, Candida,* or *The Cherry Orchard,* subversion of) a traditional dramatic structure was an important feature of late nineteenth-century realistic drama, but other related features also suggest Bakhtin's novelistic concerns. One of the most important of these is the disappearance of a voice within the play or an implied social structure outside the play that provides a single authenticating position against which the various voices in the play can be measured.

Bakhtin remarks on many occasions that, although dialogism and the development of self through dialogue with others is an essential characteristic of humanity, it is found only on occasion and in varying degrees even in his favored genre, the novel. Indeed, even if, as Bakhtin argues, the tendency of the novel as a genre is toward heteroglossia, the tradition of the genre provides a wide variety of approaches to this matter, ranging from novels of almost unalloyed monologism to those of Dostoevsky, who perhaps alone seems fully to have fulfilled Bakhtin's idea of true polyphonic discourse in literature. Certainly it may also be readily observed that in the field of drama the consciousness of the author is in certain works the obvious controlling element and in others is clearly subordinated to the dynamics of the interpersonal forces of the created characters. Nevertheless, the modern drama, especially since the advent of realism, has favored the latter course; indeed, for the past hundred years or so a dramatic author could expect to invite criticism if his or her characters seemed mere mouthpieces or puppets for their creator. Even so polemic a dramatist as Shaw has been widely praised for allowing characters in his plays with whom he clearly disagreed personally to argue their positions with the same authority and conviction as those whom the real Shaw was more likely to support. One can surely claim of such characters what Bakhtin claims for those of Dostoevsky, that they are not "voiceless slaves" but "*free* people, capable of standing *alongside* their creator, capable of not agreeing with him and even of rebelling against him."[19]

The author-god in Bakhtin's polyphonic novel is not, as Katerina Clark and Michael Holquist perceptively observe, an actively participating Old Testament Jehovah but, rather, a Christ like that in *The Brothers Karamazov*, who is silent so that others may speak. "In the best kenotic tradition, Dostoevsky gives up the privilege of a distinct and higher being to descend into his text, to be among his creatures."[20] Determined to stress the innovativeness of Dostoevsky, Bakhtin finds this quality limited or absent in earlier authors, both novelistic and dramatic. Of Shakespeare, for example, he makes the rather surprising claim that "in essence each play contains only one fully valid voice, the voice of the hero."[21] Few students or producers of Shakespeare would, I imagine, find this claim convincing.

The variety of voices in Shakespearian texts, and specifically the independence of many characters from the boundaries of that text, has been an important theme in Shakespearian criticism, at least since the famous essay on Falstaff by Maurice Morgann.[22] When we come to the theater of Ibsen or, even more strikingly, of Chekhov, this phenomenon is even more clearly observable. In one of his rare pronouncements on his own work Ibsen warned potential translators of *The Wild Duck* that "one must be extremely familiar with the Norwegian language to be able to understand how thoroughly each separate character in the play has his own individual and idiosyncratic mode of expression."[23] Such extreme care with the individual speech traits of the characters was only a symptom of Ibsen's more basic concern with suggesting that the reality seen by each character and expressed through each idiolect was unique, personal, and seeking to assert its own position amid the competing voices offered within the play. So striking has this multifaceted reality become in Chekhov that glancing and oblique discourse becomes almost a distinguishing mark of his dramatic universe.

Thus, it seems clear that the concepts of dialogism and heteroglossia, like that of carnivalization, may be useful in discussing the operations of works beyond the specific examples adduced by Bakhtin. One of the most important results of an author relinquishing monologistic control over a text is that the text, like life itself, becomes much more clearly open-ended, a point that Bakhtin stresses in many passages, and which clearly has implications for much of modern art. Novelization for him means "above all, an indeterminacy, a certain semantic open-endedness, a living contact with the unfinished, still-evolving contemporary reality (the open-ended present)."[24] In the Dostoevskian novel this open-endedness arises directly from the author's refusal to circumscribe or confine the dialogic relations within his work. These dialogues, between characters and between characters and author, thus remain internally unresolved, free and open, in a relationship of unending refraction.[25]

The basic building block of Bakhtin's system is the utterance, the meeting point of a wide variety of different concerns. It is where the speaking subject attempts to wrest a new and personal meaning from a language system already long established by other usages, where a new context provides an inevitable fresh perspective on an inherited expression, where the speaker speaks in anticipation of and in response to the perceived or presumed actives of another person, and finally where that other, the recipient, must participate in all these activities from another perspective. It is in the utterance that the restrictive and systematizing forces of canonization are placed in perpetual conflict with the unique and situation-oriented forces of heteroglossia.[26]

Since the novel itself (or the drama) may be considered a particularly complex type of utterance by its author, containing (as all complex utterances do) heteroglossic elements within itself, then the receiver of this utterance, both real and presumed, shares the responsibility for the creation of its meaning. Like C. S. Peirce, Bakhtin placed particular emphasis both upon the uniqueness of the communication event and the equal responsibility of the sender and the receiver for creating its "meaning." Indeed, there is a very close correspondence between Bakhtin's utterance and Peirce's "dynamic interpretant," which Peirce defines as "that which is experienced in each act of Interpretation and is different in each from that of any other."[27] The desire of Bakhtin to situate his utterance in a unique historical context leads him to anticipate the concerns of modern reader-response and reception theorists.

All of these concerns—the self-effacing author, the dialogic principal, the historical placement of the utterance, and the creative contribution of recipients who may be chronologically far removed from the creation of the original text—may in fact be applied to the written drama, which is phenomenologically close to the novel and thus the object of Bakhtin's relatively few observations on this genre. But they have a particular interest and a rather different significance when we apply them to the realization of that drama on the stage. Not surprisingly, Bakhtin, whose interest is the history and development of the novel, does not at all consider enactment, though this process provides even richer possibilities for the elaboration of his theoretical concerns than does the direct relationship of reader and text. This major area is suggested only, I believe, in a single fleeting but insightful note. In Bakhtin's discussion of the "chronotope"—the spatial and temporal situation of the work of art—he remarks that the text is in fact created by a "real, unitary and as yet incomplete historical world" set off by that text and including the author, "the performers of the text (if they exist) and finally the listeners or readers who recreate and in so doing renew the text."[28]

Certainly if we focus upon the drama as a text created with performance in mind, then this introduces a new kind of openness into that text not at all available to the novel. However freely Dostoevsky allows his characters to speak for themselves, they are still necessarily bound within his own imagination and the chronotope of that imagination. A dramatic author, on the other hand, must recognize that his characters are in a much more radical sense only partly his own, since in the theater they will be embodied by persons whose views of reality will be necessarily different, even if these are actors of his own time and culture, and when the play is recreated in another chronotope its discourse will necessarily move even further from his own. In addition, the whole production apparatus, including the director and potentially a whole range of contributing artists working on scenery, lighting, sound, costumes, and so on, will provide yet other views of reality and fresh "voices" in the articulation of the produced play. Certain authors attempt through stage directions, external pronouncements, or the authorization of "official" productions to control this process more than others, but the production history of any major playwright shows clearly that individual performance utterances are inevitably going to differ very widely one from another. Those "novelistic" dramatists mentioned by Bakhtin seem to have been particularly aware of this. A play like *The Wild Duck* or the dramas of Chekhov seem to be designed to elicit a variety of emotional responses upon different readings or stagings. Like the Ekdal attic, these works look different in daylight than in moonlight, in mornings and in afternoons, in rainy or pleasant weather. Hence the inability of the performance tradition to decide even on so basic a matter as the overall emotional tonality of these works.

Whether dramatic authors seem significantly concerned with the matter or not, a disjuncture between author and enactors is obviously impossible to eliminate. Bakhtin speaks in some of his early writings of a "surplus" of meaning, which is what the individual adds to that perceptive universe he shares with others. By the same token, an actor in a play brings an inevitable surplus to his role, simply by virtue of the fact that he is a living human being, even when the playwright has not been particularly conscious of this concern.

It may seem, as we consider theatrical production in modern times, that the theater's inevitable heteroglossia has been to an important extent controlled and qualified by the emergence of the director, whose monologism in production may replace that of the author in the written text. Theatrical enactment, as something shown rather than recounted, is closest to those novels in which the narrative voice is most hidden, the authorial presence being manifested rather in the control and arrangement of other voices and of incidents. Even so, one clearly may speak of directors who are essentially monologic, subordinating the entire production to their own voice and often accused of turning their actors into puppets, and those who are dialogic, allowing the voices of others to enter into full conversation with each other and with themselves.

Yet even in the work of the most monologic of stage directors the theatrical situation itself involves dialogic elements not present in novelization, since the director is in normal theatrical production necessarily involved in dialogue on the one hand with the written text and on the other with the actors who will embody it, each with voices of their own. When Edward Gordon Craig at the beginning of this century set out his theoretical defense of the monologistic director, he was clearly well aware of these dialogic challenges. As a result, to develop a true art of the theater he would both turn away from the production of "literary" drama such as Shakespeare to such forms as the masque and attempt to silence the independent human voice of the actor by replacing him with the perfectly controllable "über-marionette."[29]

Within the body of his writings, even to some extent within these same essays, Craig drew back from the extreme position suggested by these statements. Although certain of the great directors of his era such as Max Reinhardt and Vsevolod Meyerhold were from time to time accused of usurping the voice of the dramatic author or of turning their actors into puppets, even these most monologistic of directors were unable to repress totally the dialogism built into the very nature of theatrical enactment.

Craig's suggestion that the modern director declare a kind of independence from the literary text by turning to something more like the masque has never been seriously pursued except, it might be argued, in certain parts of the modern experimental theater. On the contrary, the major directors of this century, from Meyerhold and Reinhardt onward, have normally built their reputations, and even their notoriety, upon their dialogues and, many would say, their confrontations with classic texts. Bahktin's concept of utterance takes on new and fascinating implications when we look at both the original written script and the subsequent performances of that script as utterances. The director as a speaking subject also attempts to wrest a new and personal meaning from a language system already long established by other usages, where a new context provides an inevitable fresh perspective on an inherited expression, the play and its performance tradition. In the performed play, as in the utterance, the restrictive and systematizing forces of canonization confront the unique and situation-oriented force of heteroglossia.[30] This inevitable dialogue of playwright and director in modern production is widely acknowledged, even when it is disguised under the frequent debate concerning the director's responsibility to being "faithful" to the text. And too the central role of the theatrical enactment in which the work of the director is included might be spoken of precisely as the placement of the partly canonized text in the unique and situation-oriented domain of the individual utterance, the performance.[31]

Even more evident phenomenologically in the theater is the heteroglossia created by the physical presence of a group of actors. This sense of multiple individual psyches, each bringing its own surplus to the dialogic process, is an inevitable part of the performance experience, though it also has been qualified and conditioned by historical circumstances. In periods and theaters that emphasized the star, a single character might in fact come close to being the "single valid voice" Bahktin speaks of as typical for the drama, though even then the physical and psychic presence of other actors would to some extent subvert this effect. In part this is due to the fact that minor characters can remain essentially unrealized in a novel, while on stage, if they appear at all, they must appear as real human beings whose presence is phenomenologically no less than that of any other human presence on the same stage.

The rise of realism and the emphasis on the ensemble rather than the star has naturally encouraged this process. Even Stanislavski, whose emphasis on the "super-objective" and the through-line of action, established by the dramatist and faithfully followed by director and actors, has a distinctly monologist orientation; he recognizes the power and the necessity of encouraging each actor to bring the surplus of the individual voice to this process, as we see in the striking passage in which his fictional director Tortsov interrogates an actor who is playing a gondolier in *Othello*. Although this actor appears only as part of the crowd aroused by Iago and Roderigo at the opening of the play, Tortsov expects him to know his position in the household, his duties, his relation to his fellows and his master, so that when he appears on stage it will not be merely as a part of a manipulated background but as an independent voice with its own perspective on the world of the drama and entering into a full dialogue with other voices.[32]

Such an encouragement of individual stage voices, present throughout theater history but perhaps particularly obvious on the modern stage, not only produces dialogism in the performance itself but also allows the audience to focus upon and relate to different elements in the dialogue with a freedom impossible in the novel. According to their own desire, they may relate not only to the hero but to any of the independent psychic presences existing as independent voices on the stage. There is a "Far Side" cartoon that shows a city in flames under atomic attack and citizens fleeing on foot and in cars. In one of the cars is a dog, who in the midst of this chaos is looking at another dog on the curb. The caption says, "And then Jake saw something that grabbed his attention." The Jakes in a theater audience always have this power. A butler watching a play may follow with close attention the stage butler so long as the butler remains physically present in a way he would be quite unable to do in a novel. The common expressions in the theater of "upstaging," or "fly-catching," can have no equivalence in the novel since the multiple voices there are not truly as free as they are on stage, where they can resist and even actually subvert both the voice and the overall plan of the author.

Of course, the novel and other literary forms, as the reader-response theorists have noted, continue to generate new dialogues with new readers as cultural constellations change. In Bakhtin's words "the work and the world represented in it enter the real world and enrich it, and the real world enters the work and its world as part of the process of its creation, as well as part of its subsequent life, in a continual renewing of the work through the creative perception of listeners and readers."[33] The theater, through the particularly open-ended process of performance reinterpretation and the heteroglossia provided by the multiple voices of enactment, provides an utterance, in Bakhtin's sense, of particular complexity. Because of this complexity, the heteroglossia and dialogism of the theatrical experience, perhaps even more than Bahktin's favored genre, should provide a rich area for the study of the creation of meanings and of psychic relationships.

NOTES

1. The best introduction to Bakhtin's life and thought in English is Katerina Clark and Michael Holquist, *Mikhail Bakhtin* (Cambridge: Harvard University Press, 1984). Also very helpful is Tsvetan Todorov, *Mikhail Bakhtin: The Dialogical Principle*, trans. Wlad Godzich (Minneapolis: University of Minnesota Press, 1984).

2. Mikhail Bakhtin, *Rabelais and His World*, trans. Helen Iswolsky (Cambridge: MIT Press, 1965).

3. Victor Turner, *From Ritual to Theater: The Human Seriousness of Play* (New York: Performing Arts Publications, 1982).

4. The approach has been examined most extensively by Michael D. Bristol in *Carnival and Theater* (New York: Methuen, 1985); but see also Jonathan Haynes, "Festivity and the Dramatic Economy of Jonson's *Bartholomew Fair*," *ELH* 51 (Winter 1984): 645–68; and Manfred Pfister, "Comic Subversion: A Bakhtinian View of the Comic in Shakespeare," *Deutsche Shakespeare-Gesellschaft West: Jahrbuch 1987* (Bochum: Kamp, 1987), 27–43.

5. Jostein Bortnes, "*Jeppe paa Bjerget*: En Karnevalisert virkelghetsvisjon," *Edda* (1987): 13–23.

6. Mary Russo, "Female Grotesques: Carnival and Theory," *Feminist Studies/Critical Studies*, ed. Teresa de Lauretis (Milwaukee: University of Wisconsin, 1986), 213–29.

7. Anthony Gash, "Carnival against Lent: The Ambivalence of Medieval Drama," *Medieval Literature: Criticism, Ideology, and History*, ed. David Aers (New York: St. Martin's Press, 1986), 74–98.

8. Jane Moss, "Giants and Fat Ladies: Carnival Themes in Contemporary Québec Theatre," *Québec Studies* 3 (1985): 160–68.

9. Bakhtin, *Problems of Dostoevsky's Poetics*, ed. and trans. Caryl Emerson (Minneapolis: University of Minnesota Press, 1984); *The Dialogic Imagination*, ed. Michael Holquist, trans. Caryl Emerson and Michael Holquist (Austin: University of Texas Press, 1981).

10. Ibid., 324.

11. Bakhtin, *Problems*, 18.

12. Tzvetan Todorov, *Mikhail Bakhtin: The Dialogical Principle*, trans. Wlad Godzich (Minneapolis: University of Minnesota Press, 1984), 90.

13. Bakhtin, *Problems*, 17.

14. Bakhtin, *Dialogic*, 51.

15. Pedro Calderón de la Barca, *Life is a Dream*, trans. Edwin Honig (New York: Hill and Wang, 1970), 96.

16. Ibid., 3.

17. Bakhtin, *Dialogic*, 159.

18. Ibid., 5–7.

19. Bakhtin, *Problems*, 6.

20. Clark and Holquist, *Bakhtin*, 249.

21. Bakhtin, *Problems*, 34.

22. Maurice Morgann, "An Essay on the Dramatic Character of Sir John Falstaff," in *Shakespeare Criticism 1623–1840*, ed. D. Nichol Smith (London: Oxford University Press, 1916), 153–89.

23. Notes to *The Wild Duck*, trans. James Walter McFarlane (New York: Oxford, 1961), 440.

24. Bakhtin, *Dialogic*, 7.

25. Ibid., 349.

26. Ibid., 272.

27. C. S. Peirce, *Semiotics and Significs*, ed. C. S. Hardwick (Bloomington: Indiana University Press, 1977), 111.

28. Bakhtin, *Dialogic*, 253.

29. Edward Gordon Craig, *On the Art of the Theatre* (Chicago: Browne's, 1911), 138; "The Actor and the Über-Marionette," *Mask* 1, no. 3 (May 1908): 11.

30. Bakhtin, *Dialogic*, 272.

31. For a further exploration of this concern, see "Local Semiosis and Theatrical Interpretation," in my book *Theatre Semiotics: Signs of Life* (Bloomington: Indiana University Press, 1990), 110–22.

32. Constantin Stanislavski, *Creating a Role*, trans. E. R. Hapgood (Theatre Arts: New York, 1961), 8.

33. Bakhtin, *Dialogic*, 254.

The Doubled Subject and the New Playwrights Theatre, 1927–1929

Rosemarie K. Bank

That many of our attempts to organize the field of theater history have resulted in a binary strategy of negation (that is, definition by positing an opposing term or concept) is now a common subject at professional meetings and in scholarly writing. Accounts of the New Playwrights Theatre of the 1920s reflect such a strategy, since its history has been read largely in terms of two positionings: first, as an experimental theater in opposition to commerical American theater values and practices, and, second, as an art theater whose largely "expressionistic style" of dramaturgy and production prevented it from effectively presenting the sociopolitical values to which its founders—John Howard Lawson, Em Jo Basshe, Michael Gold, Francis Faragoh, and John Dos Passos—were dedicated.[1]

Much of contemporary theory and criticism in recent years has pointed out the limitations of bipolar juxtapositions articulated in the 1960s and 1970s, with their concentrations upon displacements of Self and Other, and argued for analyses that escape binary strategies of negation.[2] The emergence of the doubled (multiple) view, what I have elsewhere called the theater historian in the mirror,[3] may be clearer at the moment in relation to dramatic theory and theater historiography than in relation to specific theater historical operations. Accordingly, the New Playwrights Theatre provides a working example of how an event may be lifted from the binary matrix in which it has been embedded as a subject for historical investigation and freed from the "truth value" ascribed to it.[4] As Foucault observes, "It's not a matter of emancipating truth from every system of power (which would be a chimera, for truth is already power) but of detaching the power of truth from the forms of hegemony, social, economic and cultural, within which it operates at the present time."[5] Important here is not the power play of verification, for there is no truth to serve as the focus for a battle for interpretative supremacy. Rather, the approach focuses upon the onset of multiple discontinuities that signal the presence of a systems-wide transformation, shifts of power which occur when cognitive authority—what truth is and who gets to decide—is challenged.[6] The process of detaching the power of truth from a reading of the New Playwrights as a theater in conflict between art and politics reflects an overarching question: why does the perception of an opposition between artistic expression and sociopolitical criticism in the theater become a subject for discourse in the United States in the 1920s and in subsequent times?

The genealogy of the New Playwrights Theatre suggests a number of relationships bespeaking the discontinuity of American theater in the 1920s.

All the founders of the group had abandoned the mainstream theater for experimental organizations where their early works were produced: Basshe's *Adam Solitaire* was presented by the Provincetown Players in 1925; better known as a novelist than a dramatist, Dos Passos's *The Moon is a Gong* (*The Garbage Man*) was produced at the Cherry Lane Theatre in 1926; Faragoh, who had been drama editor of *Pearson's Magazine*, translated Ferenc Molnár's *The Glass Slipper* for the Theatre Guild's 1925 production, and the Neighborhood Playhouse presented his *Pinwheel* in 1927; Gold, co-editor and editor of the *New Masses*, had three one-act plays produced by Provincetown between 1917 and 1920; best established among the five as a playwright, Lawson's *Roger Bloomer* was produced by the Equity Players in 1923, his *Processional* by the Guild in 1925, and his *Nirvana* by the Provincetown in 1926.[7] The Theatre Guild, Provincetown, and Neighborhood Playhouse had all been established to secure various artistic functions the commercial theater was perceived not to encourage. The New Playwrights Theatre joined this rebellion in 1927 but sought escape as well from the bourgeois and commercial values it thought drove the other experimental theaters toward musical reviews, classics, and revivals of the standard repertory and away from dramatizations of a progressive sociopolitical bent.[8]

Simultaneous with displacements of power in theatrical production in the 1920s, evident in the manifestos and practices of these groups, were aesthetic transformations on a wide scale. Dos Passos and Lawson had witnessed these firsthand in Paris after the armistice:

> We were hardly out of uniform before we were hearing the music of Stravinsky, looking at the paintings of Picasso and Juan Gris, standing in line for opening nights of Diaghilev's Ballet Russe. *Ulysses* had just been printed by Shakespeare and Company. Performances like "Noces" and "Sacre du Printemps" or Cocteau's *Mariés de la Tour Eiffel* were giving us a fresh notion of what might go on the stage. We saw photographs of productions by Meyerhold and Piscator. In the motion pictures we were enormously stimulated by Eisenstein's "Cruiser Potemkin."[9]

Though other members of the New Playwrights Theatre also traveled (Gold to Moscow and Germany), American print sources in the decade publicized, critically empowered, and made readily available to anyone both popular culture and the connection between avant-garde art and avant-garde theater.[10] The theatrical "event" in this confluence of discontinuities was the International Theatre Exposition of February–March 1926, held in New York City: "Organized primarily by the de Stijl architect Frederick Kiesler, the exhibition included the Dutch modernists, the Germans, the Russians and others, with examples of new stage sets based on Constructivist and de Stijl principles. The exposition included 2000 models from sixteen countries."[11] Displayed in Steinway Hall rather than tucked into an art gallery, the International Theatre Exposition contained exhibits relating to productions by Vsevolod Meyerhold and Alexander Yakovlevich Taïrov, plays by Ernst Toller and Georg Kaiser, and scene designs by Americans Boris Aronson, Mordecai Gorelik, Robert Edmond Jones, Donald Oenslager, and Cleon Throckmorton.[12] The intersection of non-resemblance-based art and theater was mapped by the topographist of the new American theater, Sheldon Cheney, who observed of the exhibition:

> A group of European artists in league with the Expressionists, Constructivists and Dadaists of the other arts, have abandoned representation and created new and strikingly theatrical backgrounds for acted plays. One is no longer "modern" over there unless one "constructs," unless one's creativeness is informed by the spirit of the machine age. Engineering, mechanics, planes, volumes, these are the materials with which the mind of the newest stage decorator composes—in a time when the talk is all "anti-decorative," and "composition" is to be understood in a non-pictorial but nonetheless symphonic sense.[13]

It seems reasonable for theater scholars to assume that these transformations in theatrical production were as familiar to theater people and audiences in the 1920s as they are to us, for, as Marvin Carlson has observed, audiences as well as theater historians and practitioners have "strategies for organizing and interpreting their involvement with the theatre event."[14] Indeed, semiotic flags signing the New Playwrights' reading of the event they were about to launch were raised prior to their first production in several newspapers and in Lawson's playbill note "The New Showmanship" accompanying the Neighborhood Playhouse's 3 February 1927 production of Francis Faragoh's *Pinwheel*.[15] Lawson's equation of commercial with bad and nonresemblance with good theater signaled relationships Em Jo Basshe addressed in his 27 February manifesto in the *New York Times*, which appeared a few days before the 2 March 1927 opening of the New Playwrights' first production, Lawson's *Loud Speaker*. Basshe evoked "a theatre where the spirit, the movement, the music of the age is carried on, accentuated, amplified, crystalized. A theatre which shocks, terrifies, matches wits with the audience. . . . In all, a theatre which is as drunken, as barbaric, as clangerous as our age."[16] Throughout its brief life the New Playwrights Theatre utilized the pages of newspapers and journals to keep its artistic and social goals before the theater public.

The New Playwrights Theatre produced eight plays. Beginning with a half-season of two plays, Lawson's *Loud Speaker* and Basshe's *Earth*, in March–April of 1927, the theater's first full season began in October of 1927 and included Paul Sifton's *The Belt*, Basshe's *The Centuries*, Lawson's *International*, and concluded with Gold's *Hoboken Blues* in February 1928. No additional plays were produced until Upton Sinclair's *Singing Jailbirds* in December of 1928, but its relative success was not sustained by Dos Passos's *Airways, Inc.*, which ran for four weeks in the spring of 1929 and marked the end of the New Playwrights Theatre.[17] The gaps in the production schedule—March to October 1927, February to December 1928—

suggest the kinds of managerial problems that often plagued noncommercial theaters during the 1920s, chiefly small audiences, short runs, and insufficient capital.[18]

The perception of an opposition between artistic expression and sociopolitical criticism in the New Playwrights Theatre is thrown into clear relief by the group's productions. Among its founders, John Howard Lawson, Michael Gold, and John Dos Passos came to the theater in 1927 with established political credentials, Lawson's via his plays and frequent articles, Gold through his connection with the *New Masses,* and Dos Passos as a well known novelist and social critic. Their plays bear out commitments to popular forms (jazz, blues, machine noise, dance), a non-resemblance-based mise-en-scène (variously described as futuristic, expressionistic, and surrealistic), and criticism of capitalism as an exploitative and dehumanizing system. Lawson's *Loud Speaker* set the tone with a Meyerhold-inspired set of slides and ladders and use of the auditorium by actors to satirize American politics via a corrupt governor and his somnolent electorate.[19] Lawson's *International* carried the blend of artistic experiment, popular culture, and political criticism further by interweaving a petroleum capitalist, Marxist revolutionaries, world war, and fascism into a free-flowing collage of scenes set around the world.[20] Gold's *Hoboken Blues* (subtitled "the Black Rip van Winkle" and intended to be played by black actors in black-and-white face) employed circus ads, African masks, Harlem locales, a sunflower field, dollar signs, and a jungle setting to carry its central figure through time and space, exposing racism in the process and pleading for classless brotherhood.[21] Dos Passos's *Airways, Inc.,* perhaps the most resemblance-based of the New Playwrights Theatre productions, set two houses before a looming factory that controls the lives of the workers near it, who are crushed by its antilabor tactics and values and ultimately strike it.[22]

The New Playwrights Theatre did not produce a work by one of its founders, Francis Faragoh, whose *Pinwheel* had already been optioned by the Neighborhood Playhouse. In its blend of social criticism and non-resemblance-based mise-en-scène, *Pinwheel* is kindred to other New Playwrights Theatre plays, shifting kinetically from New York City to Coney Island, dance hall to office, movie palace or set, street, tenement, park, and other locations, and through sound and special effects suggesting a pinwheel-like spiral of imprisonment in harsh economic realities and the endless motion of city life.[23] Em Jo Basshe's *Earth,* centering on a rural black community in the 1880s beset by racism, poverty, and mysticism, seems less clearly political in its dramaturgy than primitive, yet the potential of poetic language and non-resemblance-based scenic effects to suggest universal human suffering was captured both in it and in Basshe's *The Centuries,* which focuses upon the oppression of Jewish urban poverty through several generations of economic exploitation, unionization, repression by tradition, gangsterism, and suburban flight.[24]

Playwright Paul Sifton was added to the theater's board in its second season. His play *The Belt* is a pro-labor depiction of auto workers who are dehumanized by an assembly line (the continuously humming belt, visible behind an upstage scrim) that controls the workers' lives as clearly as its economic byproducts cheapen and enslave them, until they find the courage to revolt.[25] Upton Sinclair's *Singing Jailbirds*, the only play by a non–board member the group presented and its longest-running production, brought the New Playwrights Theatre Sinclair's established reformist credentials and his status as a prominent political theorist and major American novelist. In addition, while all New Playwrights Theatre productions used music, some quite extensively, this revival of Sinclair's 1924 play was the theater's only musical. The mise-en-scène juxtaposed various locations— prison scenes, a hobo jungle, home, courtroom, ranch, restaurant—between which the actors freely circulated, including crossovers by characters, alive or dead, into each other's scenes. The central story is that of a Wobbly (member of the Industrial Workers of the World [I.W.W.]) longshoreman arrested for organizing, whose life is reviewed while the imprisoned organizer slowly dies from starvation, cold, beating, and isolation.[26] "Solidarity Forever" and other I.W.W. songs, which the audience sings as a chorus, augmented the New Playwrights Theatre's usual offerings of popular music.

All of these plays are spatially or temporally fragmented, pieces for the stage rather than the library. Even the brief description here may suggest that the New Playwrights forged a theater language on every level intentionally stripped, broken, distorted, and energized, a practical application of the discontinuities, of which Foucault speaks, that signal the contesting of a definition of rationality.[27] The New Playwrights Theatre's practice counterpositioned the political subject, not in the one universe of industrial capitalism most clearly implicated in Marxist theory in the 1920s and often in the essays written by Lawson and Gold, but in the multiuniverses of a displaced subject—social, political, psychological, cultural—evident in the wide-scale discontinuities of the postwar decade. In this the New Playwrights Theatre made provisional use of dualism—worker against boss and human against dehumanizing structures—which they displaced in turn in production so as to make clearer that there are more than two sides (as, for example, in the repression of worker by worker).[28] Historical accounts may debate the degree of success ascribable to the New Playwrights' escape from binary strategies of negation, but we can appropriately attend here to the perpetuation of a dualistic reading that ignores "artistic expression vs. socio-political criticism" as a created issue serving various attempts to assign the power of truth to strategies of cultural appropriation.

The experimental theater experience of the New Playwrights' founders and their fascination with the International Theatre Exhibition of 1926—Gorelik and Throckmorton were to design for the theater, Oenslager to do *Pinwheel*—draws attention to the extent to which prewar theatrical traditions had been displaced. Indeed, it is suggested that "the art critics lagged behind the theatre critics such as Cheney and Macgowan" in understanding and supporting new work.[29] In theater, that support was not universal, since for every Cheney there might be an Alexander Woollcott ready to dismiss writers like Lawson, Gold, Dos Passos, Sifton, and Sinclair as "revolting playwrights."[30] Such contemptuous readings of theater work sometimes sought to associate innovation with bolshevism, to paint art red and thereby impugn its value as art to a capitalist society.[31] Marxist views of art, for example those of G. V. Plekhanov, Anatoly Lunacharsky, and Leon Trotsky, were not unknown in the United States in the 1920s and stood against institutionalized "new criticism" and its jettisoning of historical concerns.[32] Significant to theater, literary criticism in the 1920s could be antiperformative, suggesting that theatrical, cultural, and social conditions were unrelated to dramatic art, and indeed the proponents of such views had enjoyed more than two decades of academic influence at institutions that often trained New York's arbiters of theatrical practice.[33]

Proponents of new criticism, even when theater critics, might be expected to privilege the text, to prefer a linear narrative, resemblance-based characters acting in causal ways, and language that preserved the continuity of both the story line and characterization. The New Playwrights Theatre rarely provided any of these. Marxist critics, who took history and social context as fundamental to any artistic enterprise, were not necessarily more sympathetic to the experimental enterprise in the 1920s. Indeed, the Fifteenth Party Congress of 1927 passed a resolution emphasizing the need for theater to reflect class warfare and to reject bourgeois ideologies and artistic techniques hostile to the proletariat.[34] American Marxist theatrical criticism engaged the tension between proletarian art as of necessity resemblance based versus the view prevalent earlier in the decade and in the New Playwrights Theatre that theatrical experimentation liberated class conflict from the bonds of bourgeois artistic traditions that contained and obscured it.[35]

Removing the power of truth from either the new critical or the resemblance-oriented Marxist critical perspectives, neither of which enjoyed uncontested cognitive authority within their own cultural formations, allows us to consider the New Playwrights Theatre not as a failed attempt at political theater nor as a failed attempt at literary theater, but as an attempt at non-resemblance-based experimental theater reflecting the quantum universe Albert Einstein, Werner Heisenberg, and others were in the process of articulating at the fifth Solvey physics conference in Brussels in 1927, the year the New Playwrights Theatre was born.[36] This analogy is not implicated as causal, though the 1919 eclipse experiment confirming Einstein's theory of the curvature of space was widely publicized in the United States.[37] Rather, modern physics, taken in tandem with Foucault's spatial historiography, provides an analytical strategy that does not push the activities of this theater to opposing poles but begins instead to open up the New Playwrights Theatre as part of a systems-wide transformation underway in the 1920s.

Visible in Foucault's work is the joining of matter and energy (things and processes) in modern physics' indeterminate universe. In this universe difference is necessary for definition, prohibitions are legitimized as important forms of information, and conventional temporal and spatial sequencing is replaced "with systematic relations in which the subject is merely a variable function, objects have no fixed substance, space and time interact, and change is discontinuous."[38] Like the quantum universe, there are no boundaries to Foucault's history, no authorized readings, no deterministic causality, no privileging of information accumulated over time, no observer authorized "correct" history; instead, as Stanley Aronowitz observes, "relations, not things, [are] the true objects of inquiry."[39]

In a more detailed analysis of New Playwrights Theatre productions than will be possible here, a historian would note multiple discontinuous relationships (and that these have often been read as dramaturgical and performative faults). In *Loudspeaker*, for example, Lawson utilizes a jazz orchestra, on view above the multiple setting, to play "when the occasion demands it" and in counterpoint to choreographed movement.[40] *Hoboken Blues* calls for a setting that is "an orderly chaos of color and fantasy" and scenes that "overlap slightly [giving] en effect of simultaneous planes of action—as in some futurist paintings."[41] In *International* Lawson calls for a women's chorus combining "jazz treatment with the dignified narrative strophe and antistrophe of Greek drama"; indeed, he saw the play as a symphony.[42] The discontinuity of the plot, with its many temporal and spatial shifts, promotes social analysis via juxtaposition, for example of sexual colonization and imperialism. As a machine-age ballet, Sifton's *The Belt* can continuously contrast by simultaneously representing the "ordinary" home of a worker, the hypnotic hum of the assembly line, and the larger world represented by the scrim masking the assembly line (described as a "splotched orange or impressionist portrait of the whole system of straight line production—a composite of machinery, middle class luxury, a family group in a car on the 'open road,' à la Satevepost, show and movie posters, corner of a bankbook, gin bottles, church, dollarsign, flag, organized charity, movie star, Mother, and the Holy Grail").[43]

A focus on discontinuous relationships in Sinclair's *Singing Jailbirds* exposes a dynamic among dream scenes, "real" scenes, and recalled scenes in which time is folded back on itself by moving the hero, "Red" Adams, toward a future death that is already in the past. One readily notices the play's favorable portrayal of the I.W.W. and a hostility toward shipping bosses, the wealthy, law, and the legal system. Freed from reduction to agitprop, however, it is possible to see the play as creating and critiquing the creation of proletarian heroes, legends separated from the personal and political relationships of human life in order to create authorized "true" histories that are both more and less than what they historicize.[44] Dos Passos's *Airways, Inc.*, and Basshe's two New Playwrights Theatre plays, *Earth* and *The Centuries*, also provide opportunities to approach characters as variable functions, as events charted by the observer/dramatist in terms alternatively of their position (status as social objects at given moments) or their energy (the processes of change they exemplify). As Faragoh observed of *Pinwheel*, with its Everywoman "Jane," her "Guy," and her "Sugar Daddy," the characters are experimental exemplars, illustrations of civilizations and their philosophies, "a focusing, a tangible presentation" of universes in which a movie, a myth, or a dream has truth value as great as lived experience, since (as in the "new" physics) discontinuous change is characteristic of experience and no state is immutably "truer" than another.[45]

Binary readings of the New Playwrights Theatre have intensified rather than diminished in the years since 1929. Though reviewers in the 1920s like Stark Young and Brooks Atkinson were not unsympathetic toward the New Playwrights Theatre's efforts, Depression and post-1930s readings have been less so. As binary positions hardened after 1929, the Left followed the Fifteenth Party Congress in turning away from non-resemblance-based theater forms. Theater groups of the 1930s castigated earlier experiments; as Clurman said of the New Playwrights, "Their productions were undisciplined, amateurish, lyrical, frivolous."[46] A general reading of the 1920s as escapist, not "serious," light-minded in its theatrical tastes no less than its political sensitivity gained force.[47] Even where there is interest in the political stage, preferences for a more continuous drama in the traditions of new criticism can follow Dos Passos's 1931 assessment of the New Playwrights Theatre's efforts as "crude," "heavyhanded," condemning its "raucous style," "frenzied theatricalism," seeing its "unwillingness to conciliate the audience" as a search for "new ways to baffle and distress the public," its "haphazard dramatics" employing muddles of styles simultaneously sentimental and "forbiddingly disputatious," when they did not fall into "melodrama," "lofty rhetoric," "bathos," and other faults occasioned by a "lack of control" or "the thinness of their ideas."[48]

Binary strategies of negation seem to encourage qualitative readings. These were not without precedent in the 1920s; Don Passos, for example, implicated both radicals and reactionaries in the failure of the New Playwrights Theatre, citing an unwillingness to support departures from proscenium staging or the abandonment of "realism."[49] In succeeding decades historical accounts have positioned the New Playwrights Theatre between artistic expression and sociopolitical criticism, a polarization intensified in the cold war when the political agendas of interwar theater were reread to suggest subversion by Marxists (this is a position Dos Passos assumes in his 1954 fictionalized account of the New Playwrights Theatre, his 1966 memoir, and in a 1959 recollection of his "feeling of the hopelessness of the struggle with organized communists [in the New Playwrights Theatre]— with whom I still sympathized in some things—who were busy boring from within").[50]

The 1920s offers a rich matrix of systems-wide transformations encouraging analytical strategies that will carry scholarship beyond a view of theater in the decade as either experimental or commercial, artistically innovative or socially committed. The pursuit of continuity in theater history has extended strategies of negation beyond the New Playwrights Theatre to all the "little theater" groups of the 1910s and 1920s, indeed beyond 1929. Viewed as a discontinuous phenomenon, however, non-resemblance-based art gains a reading in terms of itself. Instead of dismissable liabilities, its dynamics become visible: how are bodies positioned in space; how many temporal levels are being experienced; does the action move horizontally or vertically; how is sound imbricated; how is gender encoded, identity sited, antinomy utilized? In the discontinous universe, the political functions as a form of power/energy, not as a resemblance requiring explanation or justification in terms of an external, real world.

Finally, we may ask ourselves as historians why we give cognitive authority to strategies of negation. We may, of course, satisfy ourselves that, like the Newtonians, we have fixed an object in time and space. If, however, we displace this notion, as quantum relativity displaced Newton's universe, we can ask ourselves (among very many questions) why we "want" to see a conflict between art and politics in American theater. What is empowered in the instances when this binary is evoked in theater history, in colonial times, in the Jacksonian era, the Progressive age, the 1920s, or in our own day? Who attaches the power of truth to this discourse and for what reasons? As Foucault observes, dualism can be provisionally useful in helping us displace ourselves and our subject, but such positionings must themselves be displaced in order to dissolve the illusion that we and the events we study are immune from the effects of the truths we empower.

NOTES

1. The New Playwrights Theatre forms a subject in: Malcolm Goldstein, *The Political Stage: American Drama and Theatre of the Great Depression* (New York: Oxford University Press, 1974); Mardi Valgemae, *Accelerated Grimace: Expressionism in the American Drama of the 1920s* (Carbondale: Southern Illinois University Press, 1972); and Jay Williams, *Stage Left* (New York: Charles Scribner's Sons, 1974).

2. Feminist scholarship has in particular addressed bipolarity and may be considered exemplary. In theater, see: Sue-Ellen Case, *Feminism and Theatre* (London: Macmillan, 1988); Case, ed., *Performing Feminisms: Feminist Critical Theory and Theatre* (Baltimore: Johns Hopkins University Press, 1990); Jill Dolan, *The Feminist Spectator as Critic* (1988; reprint, Ann Arbor: University of Michigan Press, 1988); and Lynda Hart, ed., *Making a Spectacle: Feminist Essays on Contemporary Women's Theatre* (Ann Arbor: University of Michigan Press, 1989). In general, see: Gayatri Chakravorty Spivak, esp. "Feminism and Critical Theory," *In Other Worlds* (New York: Methuen, 1987), 77–92 and 277–280; and "The New Historicism: Political Commitment and the Postmodern Critic," in *The New Historicism*, ed. Aram Veeser (New York: Routledge, 1989), 277–92. Also see Seyla Benhabib and Drucilla Cornell, eds., *Feminism as Critique* (Minneapolis: University of Minnesota Press, 1987).

3. See "The Theatre Historian in the Mirror: Transformation in the Space of Representation," *Journal of Dramatic Theory and Criticism* 3, no. 2 (Spring 1989): 219–28.

4. Definitions of a few terms may be useful. I read the word *event* after modern physics: something observed *and* an observer. The intersection of the two in physics and theater history/historiography is traced in my article "Time, Space, Timespace, Spacetime: Theatre History in Simultaneous Universes," *JDT&C* 5, no. 2 (1991): 65–84. The word *lifted* I think of in the senses of *aufhebung* juxtaposed in Spivak's "Speculation on Reading Marx after Reading Derrida," in *Post-structuralism and*

the Question of History, ed. Derek Attridge et al. (Cambridge: Cambridge University Press, 1987), 30–62, a useful shorthand to remind the historian that the process of lifting up an event phenomenon for examination always submerges others. Finally, the term *non-resemblance-based* in this essay follows Foucault (see his discussion of the painting "Las Meninas" in *The Order of Things* and of Magritte in *This Is Not a Pipe*) in signaling an artwork that is not trying to "imitate" "nature" in any of those ways to which we traditionally afix the words *representational* or *realistic.*

5. Michel Foucault, "Truth and Power," in *Power/Knowledge,* ed. Colin Gordon (New York: Pantheon Books, 1980), 133.

6. See, for example, Foucault's "What Is an Author?," *Language, Counter-Memory, Practice,* tran. Donald F. Bouchard (Ithaca: Cornell University Press, 1977), 113–38, in which he discusses the forces that contest for authority to determine what is "true," an issue also engaged in his "Truth and Power," 112.

7. See the sources cited in note 1 for the histories of these authors' early theater works.

8. Lawson, Gold, and Dos Passos had helped form the Workers' Theatre in 1926, an amateur organization concerned with labor issues. In moving, as other experimental theaters in the 1910s and 1920s had done, toward professionalism, the New Playwrights Theatre sought a higher caliber acting company and a seasonal repertory of plays wherein popular works could help unpopular or controversial ones gain a hearing. For accounts, see Goldstein, *Political Stage,* 13, 16; and Williams, *Stage Left,* 19.

9. John Dos Passos, *The Theme Is Freedom* (New York: Dodd, Mead, 1956), 41.

10. Among sources giving critical status to popular culture were Gilbert Seldes's *The Seven Lively Arts* (New York: Harper, 1924). The connection between avant-garde art and avant-garde theater is explored in Huntly Carter's *The New Theatre and Cinema of Soviet Russia* (London: Chapman and Dodd, 1924) and *The New Spirit in the Russian Theatre* (London and New York: Bretano's, 1929); Sheldon Cheney's *The Art Theatre* (1917; reprint, New York: Alfred A. Knopf, 1925); and Oliver M. Sayler's *The Russian Theatre under the Revolution* (Boston: Little, Brown, 1920).

11. Susan N. Platt, *Modernism in the 1920s: Interpretation of Modern Art in New York from Expressionism to Constructivism* (Ann Arbor: UMI Press, 1985), 124.

12. Valgemae, *Accelerated Grimace,* 85–86.

13. Sheldon Cheney, "The International Theatre Exhibition," *Theatre Arts Monthly* (March 1926): 203. In the November 1927 issue Cheney described the constructivist settings shown at the exhibition as characteristically nonpictorial and lacking the details of nature (857).

14. Marvin Carlson, "Theatre Audiences and the Reading of Performance," in *Interpreting the Theatrical Past,* ed. Thomas Postlewait and Bruce McConachie (Iowa City: University of Iowa Press, 1989), 86. Carlson evokes a number of reader-response strategies potentially useful to theater research.

15. Lawson's article is in playbill no. 4 for the 1926–27 Neighborhood Playhouse season, parts of which are reprinted in Valgemae, *Accelerated Grimace,* 84–85.

16. Em Jo Basshe, "The Revolt on Fifty-second Street," *New York Times,* 27 February 1927, sec. 7, p. 4.

17. The New Playwrights Theatre productions were:

Loud Speaker (2 March 1927)
Earth (9 March 1927)
The Belt (19 October 1927)

The Centuries (29 November 1927)
International (12 January 1928)
Hoboken Blues (17 February 1928)
Singing Jailbirds (4 December 1928)
Airways, Inc. (Spring 1929)

Opening dates have been verified from the *New York Times*, except for Dos Passos's play, for which I could not locate the premiere (see *Three Plays* [New York: Harcourt and Brace, 1934], for Dos Passos's dating). Listings in Burns Mantle are frequently incorrect both for opening dates and lengths of run of New Playwrights Theatre productions.

18. The New Playwrights Theatre relied heavily upon one backer, financier Otto Kahn, rather than securing broad-based support. Grants from Kahn totaled $53,600 by the time the group stopped producing (see Kahn's papers at Princeton University and Goldstein, *Political Stage*, 24).

19. See John Howard Lawson, *Loud Speaker* (New York: Macaulay, 1927).

20. See John Howard Lawson, *International* (New York: Macaulay, 1928).

21. See Michael Gold, *Hoboken Blues*, in *The American Caravan*, ed. Van Wyck Brooks et al. (New York: Literary Guild of America, 1927).

22. See John Dos Passos, *Airways, Inc.*, in *Three Plays*.

23. See Francis Faragoh, *Pinwheel* (New York: John Day, 1927).

24. See Em Jo Basshe, *Earth* and *The Centuries* (New York: Macaulay, 1927).

25. See Paul Sifton, *The Belt* (New York: Macaulay, 1927).

26. See Upton Sinclair, *Singing Jailbirds* (Long Beach, Calif.: by the author, 1924), in Special Collections, Kent State University Library.

27. Michel Foucault, "Politics and Reason," in *Michel Foucault: Politics, Philosophy, Culture*, ed. Lawrence Kritzman (New York: Routledge, 1988), 84.

28. The provisional usefulness of conceiving a subject in terms of pro and contra and, in turn, the need to displace such binaries is discussed in Foucault's "Power and Sex," in Kritzman, *Michel Foucault*, 120–21.

29. Platt, *Modernism*, 127.

30. This often repeated assessment (e.g., see Goldstein, *Political Stage*) is traced to Harold Clurman's *The Fervent Years* (New York: Hill and Wang, 1945), 18. I have been unable to trace it to Woollcott.

31. See, for example, Murdock Pemberton, "The Art Galleries," in *New Yorker* (11 December 1926): 98–100: "Here is something that the artless city editor goes wild about; chances for all sorts of sneering, funny stories about Bolshevik art."

32. See, for example, Anatoly Lunacharsky, "Art and Marxism," *Modern Quarterly* 5 (1928); or G. V. Plekhanov, "Materialism and Art," *Modern Quarterly* 1 (1924); or Leon Trotsky, *Literature and Revolution*, tran. Rose Strunsky (1925; reprint, New York: Russell and Russell, 1957).

33. Marvin Carlson discusses this tendency in new criticism in his *Theories of the Theatre* (Ithaca: Cornell University Press, 1984), 368.

34. See Carlson's account (Ibid., 361) of the avant-garde Russian group Oberiu as one of the last attempts to contest the tightening bonds of socialist realism. Their 1928 manifesto might have been written by the New Playwrights Theatre and certainly describes its use of non-resemblance-based techniques.

35. See, for example, Michael Gold's argument that all the New Playwrights Theatre's plays "are mass plays. All of them convey the spirit of workers revolt," though his own *New Masses* staffers could not always see proletarian orientations in New Playwrights Theatre productions (for Gold, see "A New Masses Theatre," *New Masses* [November 1927], 23).

36. See Jonathan Culler, "Criticism and Institutions," in *Post-Structuralism and the Question of History*, 85, for Culler's reading of how the U.S. literary critical institution appropriates new ideas, a discourse relevant to the new critical–new Marxist intersection in the 1930s. For my reading of the physics-theater connection, see the *JDT&C* article mentioned in note 4.

37. The popularization of relativity and non-Euclidian geometry in reference to art is the subject of Linda D. Henderson, *The Fourth Dimension and Non-Euclidean Geometry in Modern Art* (Princeton: Princeton University Press, 1983), in which she discusses the difference in the spread of the new physics in the United States, which had many popular science magazines, and France, which did not.

38. Pamela Major-Poetzl, *Michel Foucault's Archaeology of Western Culture* (Chapel Hill: University of North Carolina Press, 1983), 104.

39. See, among many works by Foucault, "Language to Infinity," *Language, Counter-Memory, Practice*. For Aronowitz, see *Science as Power* (Minneapolis: University of Minnesota Press, 1988), 250.

40. Lawson, *Loud Speaker*, 16.

41. Gold, *Hoboken Blues*, 548.

42. Lawson, *International*, 7.

43. Sifton, *The Belt*, 67.

44. *Singing Jailbirds* was the only New Playwrights Theatre play dealing with a personified history, labor leader Joe Hill's.

45. Francis Faragoh, "Letter," *New York Evening Post*, 19 February 1927; cited by Valgemae, *Accelerated Grimace*, 94–95.

46. Clurman, *Fervent Years*, 18.

47. Valgemae's sympathetic assessment of the New Playwrights Theatre suggests its failure was due to audiences in the 1920s preferring "entertainment" (*Accelerated Grimace*, 96). Goldstein observes, "in 1927 the revolution seemed not so much a threat as a vague, impractical, and somewhat naive notion" (*Political Stage*, 15–16).

48. Dos Passos, "The American Theatre: 1930–31," *New Republic* (1 April 1931): 171. For other descriptors, see Goldstein, *Political Stage*, 12, 16, 18, 19, 20, 21, 25.

49. Dos Passos, "Did the New Playwrights Theatre Fail?" *New Masses* (August 1929): 13.

50. The novel *Most Likely to Succeed* recounts a "Craftsmen's Theatre" with loosely disguised New Playwrights Theatre members at work on a production. Dos Passos's memoir is *The Best of Times: An Informal Memoir* (New York: New American Library, 1966). The recollection cited preceded a Broadway dramatization of Dos Passos's novel; see "Looking Back on *USA*," *New York Times*, 25 October 1959, sec. 2, p. 5. Undermining by communists in the New Playwrights Theatre is a reading against Gold and Lawson, who were or became party members. See, for example, Goldstein, *Political Stage:* "The assignment of leadership to Gold created a barrier at the very start because his perfervid faith in communism put him out of touch with things as they were. Inclined always, as his journalism never failed to show, to overestimate the power of the Party and the intellectuals close to it, he could not realize the difficulty involved in conquering a stage whose favorite philosopher was not Marx, but Freud" (25).

Fascist Ideology and Theatricalization

Vivian M. Patraka

Writing about contemporary drama, fascism, and the Holocaust in a previous article, I explored tropes about language in relationship to the process of re-presenting history. What is the appropriate response to the historical practice of fascism and to the way language is used to construct and to resist it? At the end of the article I noted how the plays under analysis suggested areas for further exploration. In particular I wanted to elaborate an ideological practice operative in fascism which produces simultaneous, contradictory lies that act to obscure events rather than to raise questions.[1]

To explore this concept in relation to the theatricalization of fascist ideology and its operations I examined three contemporary works, each of which uncovers the logic of a contradictory and obscuring dualistic discourse in fascist ideological practice: Saul Friedlander's 1984 book *Reflections of Nazism*, Eve Kosofsky Sedgwick's 1988 article in *Genders*, "Privilege of Unknowing: Lesbianism and Epistemology in Diderot," and, finally, Alice Yaeger Kaplan's theorizing on fascism in her 1986 book *Reproductions of Banality: Fascism, Literature, and French Intellectual Life*. Friedlander identifies the juxtaposition of aestheticized political dualities, especially that of "the kitsch aesthetic and the themes of death," as critical to the operations of fascist ideology.[2] Sedgwick asserts that

> a defining feature of twentieth-century fascism . . . will prove to have been a double ideological thrust along the axis of same-sex bonding or desire. . . . In a knowledge-regime that pushes toward the homosexual heightening of homosocial bonds, it is the twinning with that push of an equally powerful homophobia, and most of all the enforcement of cognitive impermeability between the two, that will represent the access of fascism.[3]

Kaplan investigates how fascism

> works by binding doubles, a process that leads to persistent blindness to the fascist machinery in theories that insist on deciding between two parts of fascism. . . . Splitting and binding in fascism empty its language of the kind of content or consistency that usually helps explain political doctrines.[4]

Thus, all three theorists describe what Kaplan calls the totalizing "polarity machine" of fascist ideology—a machine that would, in Klaus Theweleit's words, fuel "the fascist process of appropriating and transmuting reality."[5]

In this essay I will examine some contemporary plays in light of these bipolar mechanisms in the fascist imagination, raise some questions about representations of fascism in the theater, and explore the ways in which these plays do or do not construct what might be called a "dangerous history" for their contemporary spectators.[6] By staging dangerous history I mean the use of history in theater to create a political critique of the present by revealing repeating or resonant structures in the past. Such a critique need not be a direct assault upon spectators to challenge their conceptions of "how to respond." But the representation needs to challenge the safety of local conditions and structures in an unfacile way—one that in this case might reveal present or potential fascistic structures or suggest ways in which they might be mutated or recycled by the slippery operations of a fascist machinery in a postmodern context.

Such works refuse to make the either/or choices about fascism which Kaplan describes—choices allowing fascist ideology to "pass" under a certain limited rubric, e.g., fascism as exclusively antimodernist or as exclusively right wing, that safely contains/explains it. Nor do they, in Friedlander's terms, offer interpretations that easily turn "into a rationalization that normalizes, smoothes, and neutralizes our vision of the past" and so cancels the threat of history. Those that do so Friedlander calls "voluntary or involuntary modalities of exorcism," which replicate the Nazi's maneuvers to "neutralize their own actions" (59). Friedlander also identifies what I would call another, opposite kind of dangerous history, which he connects especially to 1970s films about fascism. While intending to interrogate and subvert fascism, the underlying logic of these films actually reproduces fascism's aestheticized dualities uncritically. This aesthetic reproduction is especially dangerous in light of Kaplan's insistence on fascism's own aestheticization of politics and domination.[7]

To clarify this "new discourse that replicates fascist ideology" it is necessary to explore Friedlander's contention that Nazi aesthetics and the power of its appeal lay in the coexistence and juxtaposition of two contradictory series. The effect of these series was to create a contradictory response: fascination, terror, ecstasy, and the "simultaneous desire for absolute submission and total freedom" (xv). These effects were accomplished by yoking together, on the one hand, love of death ("a ritualized, stylized, and aestheticized death" [15]), nihilism, pessimism, primordial myth, blind destiny that leads to inevitable destruction, apocalypse and universal conflagration, the leader as superhuman object of desire, and pseudospirituality exploiting esotericism and mystery, with, on the other hand, kitsch emotion ("a simplified, degraded, insipid but all the more insinuating romanticism," [12]), including nostalgia, sentimentality, the everyday invested with legend, and the leader as Everyman representing petit bourgeois codes of respecting "the established order."

Austrian playwright Thomas Bernhard's *On the Eve of Retirement*[8] (in German, 1979) manifests the way this aestheticized discourse, as expressed in the theater, reproduces rather than exposes fascist ideology. The play depicts a claustrophobic, perverse, incestuous familial conspiracy of two sisters and their *Schutzstaffel* (SS) brother—former concentration camp overseer and currently chief justice, now about to retire. Instead of presenting the ideological aspects of the fascist brother's relation to his sisters, Bernhard literalizes it sexually in a way that detracts from our understanding of the "sister" as Theweleit describes her in *Male Fantasies:*

> The "sister," viewed as a love object, serves to define the *limits* of possible object choices. Anything beyond her name is uncharted, dangerous territory, yet she herself is taboo. What this all comes down to, again, is that no object seems attainable and no object relations seem capable of being formed. (125)

Thus, Bernhard's literalness reinscribes Nazi rhetoric into the rhetoric of a sick family. The trio's obsessive interest in and desire for death and chaos intersects with compulsively repeated clichés, especially those about nature. Nostalgia for a romanticized German past and ideals of heroism and destiny intermingle with a ritualized fixation on purity versus filth, on poison, putrefication, degeneration, corrosion, depravity, and decay. The intersection of kitsch and horrific destruction is exemplified by the photo album over which they pore, which alternates pictures of family holidays with images of the concentration camps and those killed in them. Finally, there is a paranoid aestheticizing in their frequent references to ghastly atmosphere, horrible house, abominable pit, crushing monsters, insanity, and fanaticism—all of which functions to screen and transform their past into a Gothic narrative (as if something "happened" to them).

Their mutually guilt-ridden accusations revolve around certain words: *infected, disgusting, perverted, abominable, vicious, brutal, violated, despicable,* and *dangerous.* This creates a language so overloaded that it devours the parameters for judgment and positions spectators, like the sister Clara, whose role it is to ritually judge her siblings, as silent and paralyzed. About *Eve of Retirement* Denis Calandra asserts that "the thematic material of the play could be the substance of any number of Post–World War II German plays; but whereas someone like Heiner Müller forces the audience to face the brutalities of German history and its continuing present influence, Bernhard's satirical thrust leads to a general misanthropy" (149). He even attributes Bernhard's relative success with theater audiences in Germany to "the middle class German's perchant for self-criticism to the point of self-hatred," as well as to this theatergoing public's "latent masochism"[9]—an attribute Friedlander took note of in delineating his aestheticized dualities. But, even if spectators reject the brother's claim that "there is a criminal in each of us" or that "we are all victims of the war," they are liable to sink into a fascinated revulsion for a miasma of theatricalized fascism in which theater becomes the characters' own self-conscious aesthetic system for endlessly reproducing their obsessions. Hence the peril of a theatricalized version of fascist ideology which unintentionally accedes to fascism's own theatricalizing instead of framing it by an informing context.

I contrast *Eve of Retirement* with a 1984 semidocumentary German film, *The Wannsee Conference.* The film neither "familializes" fascism nor frames it within eroticized perversity but, instead, portrays with chilling banality an eighty-five minute conference attended by third-tier Nazi civilian and military governors from throughout Europe and presided over by Reinhard Heydrich, head of the Nazi security police. In the comfortable Berlin suburb of Wannsee, on 20 January 1942, the "Jewish Question" has become purely a question of logistics—of implementing the "Final Solution" as efficiently as possible. The audience for the film is at risk because the film refuses to locate fascism in a demonized, charismatic, manipulating figure who hypnotizes his followers. Instead, we are faced with "ordinary," competitive, rather jovial bureaucrats, none of whom wants to be saddled with "all the work" of implementing genocide.

The actual function of this documented meeting, according to the film's producer Manfred Korytowski, rests upon the desire of the SS for "the approval of the ministries so that everything would be legal and they would all be in it together. Nobody wanted to make the decision themselves. Heydrich wanted them all gathered together at this conference . . . making it legally binding."[10] The audience faces a historical demonstration of the unlimited amount of state violence that can legally be put at a state's disposal. The deliberate, seemingly neutral precision of the film's realism itself serves to underscore the horrific nature of the event. One might suppose that such a tableau—mostly "talking heads" around a table—would be appropriate for theater. But it is the circling of the camera among the faces, creating a narrative of complicity, that gives the work much of its power. Thus, my preference for *Wannsee* may be the result of trying to impose on drama a semidocumentary form more appropriate to film.

Friedlander identifies the aesthetic perils in representations based on "Nazism as an unlimited field for a surge of the imagination, for a use of aesthetic effects, for a demonstration of literary brilliance" (xvi). In *The Darkness We Carry: Drama of the Holocaust*, Robert Skloot also identifies a kind of exploitation in which there is more enjoyment by the playwright of "grim speculations" and more desire "to provoke theatrical excitement" than there should be.[11] This certainly suggests a specifically theatrical, dangerous way of presenting history. One example Skloot gives of such a work is Joan Schenkar's 1982 play, *The Last of Hitler*.[12] Perhaps at times the play does radiate a sense of fascination for its own willed villainies, even if it resolutely attempts to deconstruct the mystifying demonic associated with them. Still, having written about this play before, I would like to suggest some contexts for understanding what Schenkar is trying to do.

Kaplan speaks of the way fascist ideology mutates according to the political tensions of the moment and the way fascist language appeals "at different emotional registers at different moments of fascism's history" (24). She describes a process of recycling old and new human reflexes to serve a politics of destruction (32). If Schenkar's work is a kind of circus of sliding metaphor, it is this mutating, flexible, recycling reproducibility of fascist ideology in language that her work is trying to capture and subvert. In *The Last of Hitler* Schenkar undercuts both the way metaphor continually reinscribes itself and the conserving structure of metaphoric equivalences,

CRITICAL THEORY AND PERFORMANCE

340

hence its addictiveness. She accomplishes this by using metaphors parodically and by slightly altering and skewing them in the course of their repetitions to create a theatricalized endgame for the metaphors that fuel fascist ideology. This technique opposes, in Friedlander's terms, fascism's use of the language of "accumulation, repetition, redundancy," and "the circular language of invocation" to create a kind of hypnosis (21).

Moreover, Schenkar's central metaphors of emplotment are, I think, more pointed and effective than those of, say, James Schevill's *Cathedral of Ice* (1975),[13] another "circus of metaphor" piece that, like Schenkar's, is vengefully iconoclastic and suggests, as hers does, the United States as a ground for fascist ideology and anti-Semitism. *Ice* is metaphorically emplotted in a "Dream Machine" that creates eerie comic and serious dream images relating to contemporary themes of power in the context of the history of the Third Reich. The Hitler/Narrator tries to control its images but cannot. The dream machine, however, is a somewhat vague, ambiguous conceit; by contrast, Schenkar stages her piece within a giant brainlike 1940s radio. On stage the huge radio console is framed by a radio proscenium; embedded in the radio are the two miked broadcasters who are contemporary and therefore self-consciously present "The Last of Hitler" radio show. The radio speaker hangs over the top of the stage like an immense, malignant mushroom, and the giant radio tubes glow with fluorescent pink light as if organic and growing. From this radio emerge all sorts of broadcasts with a fascist potential.

Thus, Schenkar's central conceit locates her work among the specific, historical shifts in representation created by radio along with silent film at the beginning of the twentieth century (and the way these two, taken together, separated hearing from seeing for the first time, as Kaplan notes). Russell Berman's foreword to *Reproductions of Banality* describes "the radio [as] the field in which the fascist demagogue . . . appropriates the modern mass media as part of the resistance to modernity."[14] Kaplan further elaborates the historical function of radio:

> With the advent of radio and the transformation of all the political figures into disembodied "speakers," wooing the public on microphone, the 1930s became a veritable festival of oral gratification. Fascist regimes weren't the only ones that "used" voice . . . not . . . all disembodied political voices were fascist but . . . the machinery of the media gave birth to a new kind of ideological vulnerability. (23)

This machinery offered intense possibilities for oral slogans and the cult of the recorded, amplified voice. Kaplan goes on to assert that

> what fascism transforms is not the means of production or distribution of wealth in the state, but the technical means by which the state reproduces its own legitimacy before individuals. When fascism took power, it took charge of the imaginary, using the most advanced sophisticated agents of representation available . . . new elements in

the "design" of everyday life that few knew to take seriously as political forces. (34)

Schenkar's use of radio evokes this historical moment of disembodied voice and intertwines it with the effects of radio on 1940s America. In doing so the play theatricalizes the creation of subjectivity by newer media forms. Investigating radio's potential to become, in Schenkar's words, "a vast circulatory system transmitting poisons to infected cells," she empha- sizes the power of broadcasting, of the voice in the dark, to convey language undiluted by visual imagery penetrating within our domestic spaces. Since we need not stop our everyday activities to hear it, what is heard insinuates itself into the fabric of our lives. Throughout the play characters who obsessively listen to radio repeat the phrase "I heard it on the radio" as a kind of validation of any popular sentiment they express, a direct trans- mission from the cultural brain to theirs. It is as if the voices on the radio become a single, coherent, authoritative Voice: outside the Voice lurks the terrifying landscape of infectious difference, "the impure" of fascist ideol- ogy. The *Last of Hitler* puts spectators at risk because it historicizes the fascist potential in twentieth-century media technology and because it in- sists on breaking down the borders between twentieth-century American colloquial culture and Fascist practice. Schenkar's use of the paradox of staged radio theater exposes something fundamental about the nature of the medium of radio which could not be exposed through this medium itself. Thus, I want to raise a more general question, given fascism's use of twentieth-century media innovations: how well can the much older form, drama, represent this use, or is it precisely this older form that can frame and interrogate the effects of mass culture and our complicity in responding to them?

Indeed, earlier in the century Walter Benjamin, considering the rela- tionship of theater to newer media, asserted that only commercial theater's position is usurped by newer technological media. Such forms as epic theater can use these media strategically to both learn from them (appropriate such techniques as montage) and "enter into debate with them."[15] But despite Benjamin's (and my own) preference for works that use Brechtian techniques, there are conditions under which the traditional techniques of realistic identification may be useful. Responding to the powerful impact of the American television series "Holocaust" for West German viewers, Andreas Huyssen states:

> In post-war German drama, the socio-psychological need for identifi- cation with the Jews as victims clashed to varying degrees with the dramaturgic and narrative strategies of avant-garde and/or docu- mentary theater. The historic evolution of dramatic form and the canon of political educators emphasizing document, rational explanation, and social theory had bypassed the specific needs of spectators.[16]

He opens debate on the notion that a "cognitive rational understanding of

German anti-Semitism under National Socialism is per se incompatible with an emotional melodramatic representation of history" (95). Where there is audience resistance to applying realism's normalizing concepts of what it means to be "human" to a particular "category" of humans, the form can assimilate a group that the audience resists acknowledging. But the group is inevitably assimilated from the point of view of the group's victimization and the suffering entailed in an intense desire to be "just like us," where "us" is hegemonic. The politics of identification in such as case involve a deliberate reinscribing of the dominant order to extend to the marginal group.

Martin Sherman's 1979 play, *Bent*,[17] which focuses on a particularly horrific historical moment in gay oppression,[18] fits this rubric. The play responds to two resistances from heterosexual audiences: one, that of acknowledging the humanness (i.e., lack of difference from themselves) of male homosexuals; and, two, that of their historical unwillingness to admit homosexuals to the canonical list of those who "count" as victims of Nazi genocide.[19] To respond to the first resistance, to quote John Clum, Sherman's *Bent* reveals "a culture that isn't just sexual" and "affirms 'traditional family values' with only one minor difference: it validates homosexual love within the framework of heterosexual marriage" (178). To respond to the second, Sherman portrays both the excruciatingly cruel and murderous treatment of homosexuals by the Nazis and acts defying the Nazis by gay men. But to drive home its point the play creates an unfortunate hierarchy of suffering among the various groups within the camp (Max connives for a Yellow Star so he will be treated better than if he is wearing a Pink Triangle),[20] and, since this hierarchy is the grounds for the obligatory realist narrative of moral growth (Max puts on the dead Horst's jacket with its Pink Triangle at the play's end), it is unhelpful for Sherman's project, even though it is central to the play's structure.

The most dangerous history *Bent* creates for its resistant spectators occurs in the play's second half, which constructs homosexual love and its passionate expression in language as not only unrelated to fascist homosocial practices but resistant *to* fascism. But in *Bent's* earlier scenes a problematic effect occurs resulting from the play's many agendas (some, no doubt, a direct result of the dearth of plays on this subject). These scenes portray an image of the central character, Max, as drunk, stoned, promiscuous, brawling, and attracted to homosexual fascists, one of whom he calls "my own little storm trooper." Although this storm trooper is almost immediately victimized himself by being shot by Nazis in Max's apartment, the portrayal still leaves room for an interpretation Eve Sedgwick identifies as

> the dangerously homophobic folk-widsom now endemic in both high- and middle-brow culture that . . . sees a sexualized "decadence" from whose image the supposedly answering image of fascism is seen as inseparable [thereby encouraging the hallucination, and here she cites Richard Plant (16)] "that the incomprehensible Nazi crimes could be

easily explained: the Nazis were simply homosexual perverts." (123)

This move allows us to distance fascism from our (heterosexual) selves as well as reinforce "this culture's distaste, not for fascism, but for homosexuality itself" (124). Separate from outright homophobia, this confusion of the homosexual with the violent homosocial is partly engendered by what Theweleit refers to as fascist "filiarchy, in which fascists secure their patriarchal dominance as sons, not fathers."[21] But it is also the text's twinning of two different homosexual historical moments, as part of the play's agenda for its gay audience, which may accidentally contribute to this impression. As John Clum notes:

> The Holocaust provides a background of brutal oppression. But the real issue of the play is self-oppression manifested in behavior that would be considered typical for an urban gay man in 1979. . . . The opening of *Bent* . . . is purposely ambiguous as to the time period [in order to comment on] some of the more common elements of the gay world, circa 1979. Fashionable S&M is interpreted as cruelty, a result of one's own self-hatred; promiscuity is presented as an evasion of intimacy; sex is seen as a stage in the progress toward emotional intimacy. (175, 176, 178)

Thus, despite *Bent*'s painful detailing of the violence and terror to which Max and other homosexuals were subject under the Third Reich, I wonder if the play actually provides spectators with what Sedgwick refers to as an "availability across the society of values or language or worldviews that would explicitly allow these strong [sexual] charges [of homosexuality] to be respected, felt through, legitimated, and inhabited, not to say loved" (121). As Clum suggests, despite the theatrically electrifying "talking sex" scenes between Max and Horst, the "availability" to spectators is constructed on a desexualized liberal defense of individual rights in tandem with the appeal of the motif of doomed love rather than on any challenge by specific sexual practice to the sex/gender system as presently constructed. Which is only to say, especially in light of the publication of Plant's *Pink Triangle*, that we need more plays about homosexuals, the Holocaust, and fascist ideology—a project that seems especially urgent in light of, for example, William F. Buckley's demand for the tattooing of AIDS victims.[22]

I would like to see a play that explores Sedgwick's version of binding and splitting in relationship to fascism and homosexuality. She describes this as

> a very heightened foregrounding of same-sex bonding (especially male) to the individual and societal mind: heightened in its visibility, in its perceived problematicalness, and not least importantly in its investment with a charge specifically of "sexuality" [which combines with extreme homophobia] . . . to produce the cognitive and ideological *apartheid* around homosexuality that will provide the undergirding

of any new fascism. . . . Fascism is distinctive in this century not for the intensity of its homoerotic charge, but rather for the virulence of the homophobic prohibiton by which that charge, once crystallized as an object of knowledge, is then denied *to* knowledge and hence most manipulably mobilized. (121)

If the polarity machine of fascist ideology underscores the difference of homosexuality from heterosexuality, fixates on them in tandem with a violent homophobia, then realist works that create human identity through the erasure of difference would be the least likely to be able to dramatize these operations. My own desire for a drama that articulates Sedgwick's ideas raises another question: to what degree is theory, in this case theory about fascist ideology and practice, performable, theatricalizable? Certainly, plays themselves express ideological structures in their content and form, whether deliberately or not, and certainly scholars have traced expressions of theories in plays. But am I reversing the process by wanting dramatists to self-consciously dramatize theoretical ideas?

One play that powerfully theatricalizes recent theorizing about fascism is the "Auschwitz" section of Peter Barnes's *Laughter* (1978). When Kaplan explores one aspect of the polarity machine in fascism's abstract/literal dichotomy she states:

> Just as the regime of art practiced by the established fascist state is cloyingly unimaginative, consolidated fascist ideology relies more and more on literal characterization and representations of its chosen negativity. Nazism partakes in the actual extermination of its projected negative fantasy in the concentration camps. Postpone . . . argues that the work of the camps was to render Jewish people—the threatening and the abstract—into a non-people, into abstracted shadows (skeletons) of humanity. Camp administration "proved" that Jews were "reducible" by ritually wresting from the masses of exterminated bodies all that remained on them of use-value, such as clothes, gold fillings, hair, and so on. (31)

This reductive literalizing and its horrific results are the repressed visual text of "Auschwitz." Barnes's drama is set in 1942 in an office where ordinary civil servants administer the concentration camps while denying the literalness of what they do through the abstract, distancing language of writing, numbering, and jesting. But at a critical point late in the play the file cabinets crack open and slide away to reveal "a vast mound of filthy, wet straw dummies. . . . They spill forward to show all are painted light blue, have no faces, and numbers tattooed on their left arms. . . . Two monstrous figures appear . . . [and] hit the dummies with thick wood clubs." Each uses a "large iron hook, knife, pincers and a small sack" to tear at the corpses to recover gold teeth, false eyes, and jewelry from the corpses.[23]

Thus, this scene is poised on the horrific moment of "reducibility" which Kaplan describes. And the denial, then, by the office workers of what they see suggests not the evil banality of Arendt's imaginationless Eichman but, rather, the willed refusal to imagine at any cost, in order to construct the facade of the everyday. Instead of limiting the expression of fascism to political events, Barnes, with his "ordinary" office in "Auschwitz," dramatizes the fascist ideology implicit in their culture of everyday, in the characters' relationship to a lived experience they perceive as expressing their private, apolitical selves. The dangerous history of this play marks the cumulative historical ability of the everyday to create the institutionalized, bureaucratic organization of incarceration and murder.

And "Auschwitz" is also dangerous in the way it delineates the changing sociohistorical context of fascist practice by theatricalizing how a more established, seemingly "civilized" fascist bourgeois culture feeds off an earlier, more visibly violent populist form, making it into a kind of covert, respectable industry. Many plays dramatize the beginning phases of fascism; some dramatize fascism in a kind of eternal present despite frequent historical references. But, as Kaplan notes, fascism's "history corresponds to a topological shift":

> After an initial, rallying period, during which a left-sounding movement appeals to a populist petty bourgeois, the movement's power is consolidated in formal bureaucracy; populist ties are severed or dissolved into party ties and economic power passes back into the hands of the traditional capitalist channels. . . . The populist ideal mutates toward an elitist one. (33)

Barnes locates his play at the historical moment of that "topological shift," depicting a centralized, bureaucratic state based on solid middle-class values. He historicizes this shift of power in the opposing presence of the character Gottleb, a vicious "old-style" Nazi SS officer who evokes the earlier, dramatically violent "gathering" stages of fascism and who at the end of the play is defeated by the bureaucrats. They close "Auschwitz" with a macabre singing of "This Is a Brotherhood of Man" from *How to Succeed in Business without Really Trying*.

Barnes's vision in *Laughter* was not reassuring to his audience and "unsafe" by comparison with some of his other works, such as *The Ruling Class* (which took aim at that class and not the middle class). In an interview with Mark Bly and Doug Wagner in 1981, Barnes described the response to *Laughter:*

> When we did *Laughter* at the Royal Court, I used to go into performances, and I felt waves of hate coming out of the audience. They actively loathed it. Actively. It came out like steam. The actors used to say: "God we could feel it up on the stage." The British want a theatre of reassurance, one of affirmation. They do not want a theatre of disturbance.[24]

Joan Schenkar, too, wants to give her audience a theater of disturbance. When I interviewed her about *The Last of Hitler* she told me:

> I'm interested in no escape, in really imprisoning the audience in a way—yes, taking prisoners . . . and in a way forcing them to enter these nightmares. . . . So what I'm always trying to do . . . is make two things happen at once, at least, which is to keep this humor going so people are laughing and underneath it keep this dreadful subtext going in which the thing at which people are laughing at is too awful for words. . . . I mean in the best of all possible productions I've made you laugh at something dreadful, just dreadful.

I watched the play several times, and there were always some people who fled the theater. Both Schenkar and Barnes insinuate terrific challenges to their audiences by means of a very disturbing and even savage comedy. Both in their own ways ask audiences to inhabit fascist ideology and its operations, to be implicated by being caught by surprise in something we might want to condemn but not to understand quite that well.

To review this exploration, in terms of the polarities of fascist ideological practice I noted at the outset, Bernhard's *Eve of Retirement* obscures the field between the two contradictory series and risks reproducing fascist ideology. The realistic structure of Sherman's *Bent* may prevent it from theatricalizing the complexity of fascist ideology, but it certainly dramatizes the grotesque effects of the polarity machine as expressed in the splitting off of homosexuality in a murderous discourse of Otherness. Schenkar's *Last of Hitler* "works over," mutates, the polarities to finally disintegrate them, historically portraying one mass medium and its production and transmission of these polarities as well as underscoring the way the production of fascist ideology is embedded in its modes of representation. Barnes's *Laughter* succeeds in theatricalizing the mutating use, appealing to different needs, different constituencies, and different emotional registers at different historical moments of fascist ideology. His employment of a group configuration within comedy allows him to avoid the single-person-as-protagonist configuration common to "serious drama" and so to theatricalize the drama of fascist ideology in relationship to lived experience among a range of individuals.

The Last of Hitler and *Laughter,* one in its surreal comic form, the other in its Brechtian comedy, serve as ways to theatricalize and so to frame by their forms the relationship of the everyday to fascist ideology— a relationship that realism, though ostensibly providing details of both history and everyday life, obscures, even if ideology and its effects are the play's ostensible subject. Schenkar and Barnes eschew the faulty proposition that making contact with the most ugly, horrifying, and bizarre nightmares within the representation of fascism as operatic *Götterdämmerung* will in itself lead to an understanding of fascism and of "the mind of Hitler" without these metaphors being yoked to the most banal compliances and back turnings, to everyday self-deceptions in the service of fascist ideology.

Representing fascism calls for intolerance without facile condemnation and for the acknowledgment of complicity in the structures that can create it, for the negation of individual rights pursued in practicing fascism, rather than a carefully balanced system of liberal ethics as a frame that must reduce fascist ideology to mass manipulation and the obliteration of the individual. Ideally, a theatricalization of fascist ideology not only must mark the fluidity of the fascist dichotomies and highlight their construction within representation, but it also must ask for what purpose and to what effect.

NOTES

1. Vivian M. Patraka, "Contemporary Drama, Fascism, and the Holocaust," *Theatre Journal* 39 (1987): 65–77. The research for two earlier versions of this paper, one presented at the New Languages for the Stage conference, University of Kansas, 1988, and one at New Directions in Theatre Research, the Eleventh World Congress of the International Federation for Theatre Research, Stockholm, 1989, was made possible by a Summer Faculty Research Grant from Bowling Green State University in 1988. I wish to thank my colleague at Bowling Green, Ellen Berry, for her advice and editorial help.

2. Saul Friedlander, *Reflections of Nazism: An Essay on Kitsch and Death*, trans. Thomas Weyr (New York: Avon Books, 1984), 1. Further references will be made parenthetically in the text.

3. Eve Kosofsky Sedgwick, "Privilege of Knowing: Lesbianism and Epistemology in Diderot," *Genders* 1 (Spring 1988): 121. Further references will be made parenthetically in the text.

4. Kaplan goes on to ask:

Is fascism modern or antimodern? Is it revolutionary or conservative, left or right? [Or is this an] attempt to reduce fascism's power by intellectually stopping its binding mechanism [?] . . . [And] splitting, after all, is really much the same activity as binding done in reverse. . . . The fascist anti-Semite was also a "splitter," separating what he feared from what he desired by projecting all he didn't understand in modern life onto the Jews, and all that he wished to recuperate in modern life onto the fascist state. (Alice Yaeger Kaplan, *Reproductions of Banality: Fascism, Literature, and French Intellectual Life* [Minneapolis: University of Minnesota, 1986], 24)

Further references will be made parenthetically in the text.

5. Klaus Theweleit, *Male Fantasies*, vol. 1: *Women, Floods, Bodies, History*, trans. Stephen Conway in collaboration with Erica Carter and Chris Turner (Minneapolis: University of Minnesota Press, 1987), 89. Further references will be made parenthetically in the text.

6. Cf. Helene Keyssar, "Doing Dangerous History: Caryl Churchill and a Mouthful of Birds," in *Caryl Churchill: A Casebook*, ed. Phyllis R. Randall (New York: Garland, 1988).

7. The theorizing of aestheticization and of its effects by Kaplan and Friedlander, with its contemporary emphasis on obscuring binaries, builds on the earlier theorizing of fascist aestheticization by Walter Benjamin. Benjamin wrote:

The growing proletarianization of modern man and the increasing formation of masses are two aspects of the same process. Fascism attempts to organize the newly created proletarian masses without affecting the property structure which the masses strive to eliminate. Fascism sees its salvation in giving these masses not their right, but instead a chance to express themselves. The masses have a right to change property relations: fascism seeks to give them an expression while preserving property. The logical result of fascism is the introduction of aesthetics into political life. . . . All efforts to render politics aesthetic culminate in one thing: war. War and war only can set a goal for mass movements on the largest scale while respecting traditional property system. This is the political formula for the situation. ("The Work of Art in the Age of Mechanical Reproduction," *Illuminations*, ed. Hannah Arendt, trans. Harry Zohn [New York: Schocken Books, 1969], 243)

8. Thomas Bernhard, *The President* and *Eve of Retirement*, trans. Gitta Honegger (New York: Performing Art Journal Publications, 1982).

9. Denis Calandra, *New German Dramatists: A Study of Peter Handke, Franz Xaver Kroetz, Rainer Werner Fassbinder, Heiner Müller, Thomas Brasch, Thomas Bernhard and Botho Strauss* (New York: Grove Press, 1983), 149, 140. Further references will be made parenthetically within the text.

10. Korytowski is quoted in Desmond Ryan, "The day the Nazis plotted genocide," *Philadelphia Inquirer*, 6 December 1987, sec. 16, p. A13.

11. Robert Skloot, *The Darkness We Carry: The Drama of the Holocaust* (Madison: University of Wisconsin Press, 1988), 70.

12. Joan Schenkar, *The Last of Hitler* (unpub. play, 1982).

13. James Shevill, *Cathedral of Ice*, in *Plays of the Holocaust*, ed. Elinor Fuchs (New York: Theatre Communications Group, 1987), 231–301.

14. Russell Berman, foreword to Kaplan, *Reproductions of Banality*, xxii.

15. Benjamin wrote:

This [mainstream, illusionist] theatre, with its complicated machinery, its gigantic supporting staff, its sophisticated effects, has become a "means against the producers" not least in seeking to enlist them in the hopeless competitive struggle in which film and radio have enmeshed it. This theatre—whether in its educating or its entertaining role; the two are complementary—is that of a sated class for which everything it touches becomes a stimulant. Its position is lost. Not so that of a theatre that, instead of competing with newer instruments of publication, seeks to use and learn from them, in short, to enter into debate with them. This debate the epic theatre has made its own affair. ("The Author as Producer," in *Art after Modernism: Rethinking Representation*, ed. Brian Wallis [New York: The New Museum of Contemporary Art, 1984], 306)

16. Andreas Huyssen, *After the Great Divide: Modernism, Mass Culture, Postmodernism* (Bloomington: Indiana University Press, 1986), 114. Further references will be made parenthetically in the text.

17. Martin Sherman, *Bent* (New York: Avon Books, 1979).

18. John Clum identifies this historical impulse as a central genre of gay male drama: "Oppression and resistance and survival and heroic making are the stuff of gay history, much of what can be called gay drama is an expression of what might be called 'historical impulse' in gay literature—depicting and defining the collective past of gay men to affirm a sense of identity and solidarity, and to educate

the dominant culture about the brutality of its homophobia" (John M. Clum, "'A Culture That Isn't Just Sexual': Dramatizing Gay Male History," *Theatre Journal* 41 [1989]: 169). Further references will be made parenthetically in the text.

19. For an important discussion of the relationship of realism to lesbian representation in theater, see Jill Dolan, "'Lesbian' Subjectivity in Realism: Dragging at the Margins of Structure and Ideology," in *Performing Feminisms: The Critical Act*, ed. Sue-Ellen Case (Baltimore: Johns Hopkins University Press, 1990), 40–53.

20. Richard Plant does note, however, that "the mortality rate for homosexuals incarcerated by the Nazis was, it appears, relatively higher, in the camps and after their release, than that of other persecuted groups. Researchers learned that the gays, marked by pink triangles, were a relatively small minority in the camps but had a proportionately higher mortality rate than, for example, the more numerous political prisoners, who wore red patches" (*The Pink Triangle: The Nazi War against Homosexuals* [New York: Henry Holt, 1986], 14). Further references will be made parenthetically in the text.

21. Theweleit writes:

Whether heroes or chief opponents, fathers are categorically denied a voice. . . . To a remarkable extent, they are simply dispensed with. Even the generals whose reports appear here . . . write as *sons*. . . . They write as the sons who have survived the disgraceful abdication of their father, Wilhelm II, and who now intend to make up for his errors. . . . Patriarchy secures its dominance under fascism in the form of a "filiarchy"—that much is clear. Nothing but sons as far as the eye can see—Hitler too is one of their number. (*Male Fantasies*, 108)

22. In fact, the historical event of AIDS twinned with the denial of funds to work supporting homosexuality in the Thatcher period affected the site and circumstance of production when *Bent* was repeated in 1990 at the National Theatre. Gerard Raymond notes in "Ch-Ch-Ch-Changing at the National," *Theatre Week* (30 April–6 May 1990): "This current production began its life as a single benefit performance on June 25, 1989, celebrating the tenth anniversary of the play. It was held at the Adelphi Theatre, in the West End, to fund-raise for The Stonewall Group, which lobbies for gay rights. Leading actors were cast in every role, including the late Ian Charleson (who died from AIDS this year)" (21).

23. Peter Barnes, *Laughter* (London: Heinemann, 1978), 64–65.

24. Mark Bly and Doug Wagner, "Theater of the Extreme: An Interview with Peter Barnes," *Theater* 12 (1981): 45.

Hermeneutics and Phenomenology

Introduction

Neither hermeneutics nor phenomenology claims to have a set of doctrines of its own. Each is rather understood by its practitioners as a method of interpretation, of understanding. Each has its separate history, yet each term has traversed the other in the usages of twentieth-century European philosophy and critical theory. *Hermeneutics* derives from the Greek verb meaning "to interpret," cognate to Hermes, the messenger god, discoverer of language and writing, who translated what lay beyond human experience into comprehensible terms. Hermeneutics is most often associated with the interpretation of texts, and it can refer to the specific practices of Biblical exegesis as well as to more general textual interpretation. In practical terms it means a way of interpreting interpretations. *Phenomenology* makes more fundamental claims. It derives from the Greek word meaning "that which shows itself"—in the sense of the revealed, the visible, the manifest—prior to interpretation. The intuitive apprehension and penetrating description of such first-order phenomena constitute the agenda of phenomenologists. Both hermeneutics and phenomenology claim to operate as mental disciplines—of reading, of perceiving, of imagining.

Key to the discipline of reading is the "hermeneutic circle," a process so named by the nineteenth-century German philosopher Wilhelm Dilthey. The act of reading a whole sentence (such as the one you are reading now) depends upon your understanding of its individual words, yet you cannot determine the meaning of the individual words until you have grasped the meaning of the sentence as a whole—apparently a vicious circle. The actual experience of disciplined reading, however, reconstitutes that apparent dilemma into a positive process: the hermeneutic circle consists of an alternation of anticipation and retrospection as your understanding grows through the reciprocal interplay of the words and the sentence, the sentences and the text as a whole. From the standpoint of performance, the concept of hermeneutics has deep roots in oral expression, which by its nature intensifies the interpretive experience of the work. That may be one important reason why the ancients read aloud, even when they read alone, and to this day it underlies the idea of a singer's "interpretation" of a song.[1] In other words performance itself may be viewed as a hermeneutic process.

Key to the discipline of perception and imagination in phenomenological understanding is Edmund Husserl's concept of *epoche*, which suggests a pause, a moment of suspension of all presuppositions about the nature of experience. In this moment belief in the actual existence of the perceived phenomenon is suspended, "bracketed," so that its essential qualities may be apprehended. Phenomenology, unlike most of the theories discussed in this volume, relies upon "essences," a set of necessary and sufficient conditions for the existence of an entity, the fundamental supposition of essentialism (see the introduction to "Feminism[s]"). Phenomenological essences are not to be fully apprehended by the direct, empirical inspection of objects but, rather, by the imaginative intuition of them. It is helpful to recall that Husserl, the founder of phenomenology as a way of doing philosophy, was a mathematician, who, like Descartes, could "see" geometric figures vividly with his mind's eye. Phenomenologists like to pick objects up with their minds, so to speak, and turn them around, examining them from all sides. This cannot be accomplished by viewing them frontally as they are embedded in the rest of the experiential world—hence bracketing. Aspects of Husserl's thought have been variously developed and transformed in the philosophies of Martin Heidegger and Maurice Merleau-Ponty (see Elin Diamond's essay "The Violence of 'We': Politicizing Identification," in this volume).

Phenomenology, which abounds with theatrical metaphors, has proved useful in the theoretical study of drama and particularly of theatrical performance. Beginning with Husserl's student Max Scheler, who wrote on the phenomenology of tragedy, literary theorists such as Roman Ingarden have examined the ways in which drama is experienced differently from other works of literature because of the implied contingencies of performance invested in its language and its structure.[2] More recently, Bruce Wilshire in *Role Playing and Identity: The Limits of Theatre as Metaphor* has proposed that phenomenology can "disclose the essential characteristics of theatre art." Stressing role playing and surrogation particularly, he brackets "standing in" and "authorization" of the actor in the part as a fundamental characteristic without which the performance event would not be theater.[3]

In his suggestive book on phenomenology and theater, Bert O. States explains his purpose as "a form of critical description that is phenomenological in the sense that it focuses on the activity of theatre *making itself* out of its essential materials: speech, sound, movement, scenery, text, etc."[4] In his article for this volume, "The Phenomenological Attitude," States enlarges his discussion of the complementary effect of phenomenology and semiotics. Working together they provide a kind of binocular vision: phenomenology sees the stage as direct experience ("everything is nothing but itself"); semiotics sees it as wholly significative ("everything is something else"). States calls upon the concept of "defamiliarization" developed by the leader of Russian formalism, Victor Shklovsky, to assert that the "phenomenological attitude" enables the theorist to experience familiar objects in new ways. States's title is apt: the word *attitude* suggests the orientation of a body relative to a steady reference line or plane such as the horizon. In this case the horizon is the phenomenological essence of the theater.

In the title of his article, "History, Hermeneutics, and Narrativity," Thomas Postlewait frames the word *hermeneutics* with *history* on one side and *narrativity* on the other. Postlewait conceives of hermeneutics as Hans-Georg Gadamer does (following Heidegger) as the phenomenology of reading.[5] Gadamer's account of the hermeneutic circle includes the idea of "fore-structure of understanding," an acknowledgment that readers come to texts with what reader-response theorists have called "a horizon of expectation" which prepares and shapes their reception of the work.[6] This reopens the question of historical understanding and prejudice (see the introduction to "Theater History and Historiography") but with another layer of complication—the phenomenologically problematic status of all interpretations. In approaching this question Postlewait brackets "narrativity," the essential quality of story-ness, as the condition of historical writing and reading. Drawing upon Paul Ricoeur's monumental *Time and Narrative*, he argues that narrative is the inevitable response to "our consciousness of time, our consciousness of history," and, consequently, that a hermeneutics, a theory of interpreting interpretations, is the inevitable burden of a disciplined process of historical reading.

J. R. R.

NOTES

1. In *Hermeneutics: Interpretation Theory in Schleiermacher, Dilthey, Heidegger, and Gadamer* (Evanston, Ill.: Northwestern University Press, 1969) (see Thomas Postlewait, "History, Hermeneutics, and Narrativity," in this volume, n. 1), Richard Palmer elaborates on the implicit contest of orality and literacy in the historic meaning of hermeneutics (12–32). The basic ethnocentricity of philosophical claims to methodological neutrality has been examined by Jacques Derrida, "White Mythology: Metaphor in the Text of Philosophy," *Margins of Philosophy* (Chicago: University of Chicago Press, 1982), 207–71. See also Judith Butler, "Performative Acts and Gender Constitution: An Essay in Phenomenology and Feminist Theory," in *Performing Feminisms: Feminist Critical Theory and the Theatre*, ed. Sue-Ellen Case (Baltimore and London: Johns Hopkins University Press, 1990), 270–82.

2. Roman Ingarden, *The Literary Work of Art: An Investigation of the Borderlines of Ontology, Logic and Theory of Literature. With an Appendix on the Function of Language in the Theatre*, trans. George Grabowicz (Evanston, Ill.: Northwestern University Press, 1973). See also Marvin Carlson, *Theories of the Theatre: A Historical and Critical Survey, from the Greeks to the Present* (Ithaca and London: Cornell University Press, 1984), 334–35, 442–43.

3. See Bert O. States, "The Phenomenological Attitude," in this volume, n. 13.

4. Bert O. States, *Great Reckonings in Little Rooms: On the Phenomenology of Theatre* (Berkeley and London: University of California Press, 1985), 1.

5. Hans-Georg Gadamer, *Truth and Method* (New York: Seabury Press, 1975).

6. See Hans Robert Jauss, "Literary History as a Challenge to Literary Theory," in *Critical Theory since 1965*, ed. Hazard Adams and Leroy Searle (Tallahassee: Florida State University Press, 1986), 163–83.

History, Hermeneutics, and Narrativity

Thomas Postlewait

> Soon as
> you stop
> having trouble
> getting down
> to earth
> you start
> having trouble
> getting off
> the ground

—A. R. Ammons, "Cleavage"

Historical scholarship, in its two-part mission of research and writing, is primarily a hermeneutical enterprise of interpretation—of understanding and explaining textual, iconographic, and material records.[1] The first part of the task, historical research, requires the skill to locate and decipher the remaining traces of past events. Because the past itself is beyond reach, the historian is always reading the shadowy remains, the images on the cave wall. The second part of the task, historical writing, requires the talent to create a new explanatory order for those past events, a written record that describes and interprets what possibly happened in the past. Or, to be more exact, the historian redescribes and reinterprets what the traces from the past delineated, illustrated, exhibited, described, and interpreted.[2]

In the process of writing, of giving possible shape to what went before, the historian uses certain formal and rhetorical strategies, certain methods of configuration. What is absent is made textually present, but not without transformational consequences because of the methods of selection, the techniques of writing, and the retrospective nature of the historian's understanding. This textual evocation of the past, an intellectual movement from absence to presence, is the basic topic I wish to consider here. I want to outline, from the point of view of hermeneutics, a debate on the uses of narrative in historical writing. And I want to suggest that it is surely time, after two centuries, to move beyond this debate, to see that the key issue is not whether narrative should or should not be used in historical writing but, rather, how it contributes—at several levels of articulation and in several modes of representation—to the interpretive processes of research and writing.[3]

Most historians grant that there is no single, exclusive way that our historical understanding must be applied and expressed. It can follow numerous organizational strategies, depending upon not only the specific methodology each historian uses for research and reporting but also the assumptions, categories, codes, and purposes that define and shape historical scholarship at any particular time. Many attempts have been made during the last two hundred years to establish professional procedures, but there has been little agreement among historians upon a systematic mode of inquiry, analysis, and reporting. At best historians have had to content themselves with guides and practical rules. Neither rationalism nor empiricism, the two major shaping forces on historical scholarship, has been able to ground the profession in procedural laws of judgment and expression.

Nonetheless, many historians have assumed that, whatever the approach used, the fundamental purpose of historical study is to tell the story of human activities, endeavors, and accomplishments. In his widely used guide *History: Its Purpose and Method*, for example, G. J. Renier argues: "History is the story of human beings, and nothing else."[4] Or, as Peter Munz states, history is the study of change, of the succession of events: "For this reason, narrative history is history par excellence."[5] This formal report, or "story," more than a mere chronology, reveals how and why specific past events occurred, one after another, and were possibly linked. The narrative provides coherence.

Not surprisingly, then, *history* and *story* are often used as corresponding, even interchangeable, terms and concepts. This practice is reinforced by the fact that *history* and *story* are often yoked lexically in many languages. In various Germanic and Romance languages, for example, one word can often carry the double meaning of history and story (e.g., *die Geschichte, l'histoire*). The Latin root of "story" is *historia*, hence old French *estoire* and modern French *histoire*. This etymological condition may well suggest more than mere ambiguity or confusion, as Paul Ricoeur argues: "Our languages most probably preserve (and indicate) by means of this overdetermination of words . . . a certain mutual belonging between acts of narrating (or writing) history and the fact of being in history, between *doing* history and *being* historical. In other words, *the form of life to which narrative discourse belongs is our historical condition itself*."[6]

But this common usage is not without problems in the discipline of history, which has aspired to the status of a science or social science. Ever since the Enlightenment the field of history has aligned itself with scientific procedures, values, and aims. Thus, in the nineteenth century historians organized archives and developed objective, analytical methods for the study of "primary" sources. And in the modern age many historians have attempted to merge historical study with one or another of the fields in the social sciences, especially economics, geography, statistics, demographics, sociology, ethnology, and symbolic anthropology.[7] Yet despite—or probably because of—these developments, historians have continued to debate whether their profession is essentially a science or an art. And at the center of this debate is the problem of narrativity in historical writing.[8]

In this regard various attempts were made in the nineteenth century to develop scientific models for historical research, from August Comte's positivism to Leopold von Ranke's critical methods for analyzing documents.[9] This commitment to objective and empirical procedures in research did not, however, rule out an equally strong commitment to narrative reporting, to telling either the grand, sweeping story of the evolution of human life and civilization or the more specific story of the motives and aims of political agents and national governments. In both cases the narrative celebrated the triumphant development of European culture and ideology, ordained by either science or God.

In Germany this development of a historical science (*Geschichtswissenschaft*) was grounded in hermeneutics, as Georg Iggers points out:

> The hermeneutic method as conceived by Ranke was inseparable from certain basic philosophic assumptions. What made historical knowledge possible for Ranke, as it did for the German tradition of hermeneutics for over a century from Wilhelm von Humboldt and Friedrich Schleiermacher to J. G. Droysen, Wilhelm Dilthey, and Friedrich Meinecke, was the notion that history was the realm of "spirit," but of spirit conceived very differently from the way it was understood in Hegel's philosophy. If Hegel had stressed the unity of world history and had seen in history a process in which spirit through continuous self-negation translated itself into increasingly rational institutions, the hermeneutic tradition . . . stressed that spirit manifested itself in individualized forms. History was made up of "individualities," each possessing their [*sic*] internal structure and a meaning and purpose unique to them alone. Not only persons possessed the qualities of individuality but in an even more profound sense so did the great collective bodies which had grown in the course of history— states, nations, cultures, mankind.[10]

The historian, trained to delineate this historical "spirit" (which Ranke believed to be implicitly expressed in the sources), achieves a sympathetic understanding of the past.[11]

In historical writing this understanding takes the form of a narrative that reveals what Ranke called the "inner connection" of human history, a relatedness among events. He assumed that the continuity and direction of history derived from individual leadership and national character (or *Volksgeist*) rather than from social or economic forces. So the historian's mission, based upon a reading of documents in state archives, was to spell out the nature of human decisions and actions, as they contributed to the development of national policies. The story to be told should center on the actions of historical agents, those key figures who gave meaning and direction to institutions, nations, and epochs.

Despite the success of Ranke's research methodology, his historical model, with its emphasis upon national policy decisions, was soon challenged by such people as Karl Marx, H. T. Buckle, Hippolyte Taine, Emile Durkheim, and Max Weber, who developed alternative interpretive models for explaining historical processes. Systems, patterns, regularities, and uniformities rather than "individualities" became the focus of research and analysis. The hermeneutical task of deciphering documents for the motives and intentions of individuals was rejected. Also, the search for a historical spirit (either Hegelian or Rankean) was dismissed as hopelessly idealistic. Geography, economics, race, social codes, and institutions would now provide the basis of analysis. For those historians, the individual, even the leader, no longer made things happen. History, and its meanings, must reside in the material world.

Accordingly, there was an attempt to deny Ranke's narrative approach to the writing of history. But, even though a history of individual actions and motives was set aside (at least partially), the grand history of evolutionary and progressive change usually asserted itself. A narrative of the complex development of Western civilization, capitalism, bureaucracies, institutions, and social classes still held sway—with division and conflict (and sometimes the hope or promise of reunification) serving as the dominant action. In other words, the narrative of struggle still dominated, even though new explanations for conflict and order were put forward. And, even in the case of those historians who attempted to refute progressive thinking (e.g., Jacob Burckhardt), a narrative model, such as the dissolution of civilizations, was no less central to the analysis.[12]

In the twentieth century the strongest criticism of the uses (or misuses) of narrative form in the writing of history has continued to come from those historians and philosophers who have attempted to establish historical study upon a scientific foundation. Fernand Braudel of the Annales school in France, for example, has looked with disdain at the old narrative histories that focused on major figures and political events because these histories gave too much credence, it was felt, to the motivations and values of individuals. Such histories, tied too exclusively to the documents produced by these figures (and to outdated assumptions about human intentionality and causality), have provided a narrative of human events and actions which fails to reveal the larger economic, social, and geographical forces shaping material culture and civilization. Scientific history, Braudel argues, should provide data and analysis, not storytelling.

It is a mistake, however, to assume that Braudel and other members of the Annales school dismissed the old narrative history simply because of its emphasis upon specific individuals and events.[13] Their critique developed out of their commitment to a synchronic rather than diachronic history. Also, they no longer accepted the evolutionary and progressive (or Whig) view of history. In the Annales models of history sequential development is delayed or denied or perhaps we should say that it is displaced while a structural matrix, such as Braudel's *"longue durée"* (long time span or duration) is established for containing and explaining human actions. "The *longue durée*," Braudel writes,

> is the endless, inexhaustible history of structures and groups of structures. For the historian a structure is not just a thing built, put together; it also means permanence, something for more than centuries (time too is a structure). This great structure travels through vast tracts of time without changing; if it deteriorates during the long

journey, it simply restores itself as it goes along and regains its health, and in the final analysis its characteristics alter only very slowly.[14]

In this synchronic web the individual is caught like an insignificant insect and soon dispatched by the all-consuming historical processes.

Does this structuralist approach to history rule out narrative? Not really, even though it may put in question (if not always throw out of court) historical stories that privilege an individual's motives and self-understanding. As several commentators on Braudel's works have noted, narrative modes of figuration and emplotment still operate in this basically materialist worldview.[15] From metaphoric tropes (e.g., the tendency to personify historical forces and movements) to generic models (e.g., satire), Braudel draws upon narrative modes of configuration. (Note, for example, the journey and organic metaphors in Braudel's statement quoted above.) Although the Annales historians may disperse an individual's motives and actions into the historical cosmos of material conditions (which find expression in a cultural *mentalité*), they still have a human story to tell of structural formations and transformations. In the process, a grand—if dark—morality tale is articulated, worthy of the totalizing reach of the allegorical imagination.[16]

One other thing needs to be noted here: the structuralist idea of the *longue durée*, which conceptually operates as a formative or constitutive category for ordering history, may have been developed as a description of materialist culture, but its use as a boundary concept—a formal idea for historical knowledge—often serves a hermeneutical function not so unlike the concept of *Geist* in Rankean or Hegelian history. Both concepts operate as methodological principles of interpretation. Although Braudel's structuralist idea no longer locates the underlying forces of history in individualities or "Reason," it still acts as the historian's own mentalist construct for identifying the forces that organize and shape history. Once taken up, it becomes a categorical assumption that arranges and produces the historian's thought about history. Codified in this manner, it serves as an objectification of a historical process that the historian reads into—rather than simply discovers within—the past (or, more exactly, the evidence from the past). To note this is not to imply that the concept of the *longue durée* lacks historical significance. But we need to see that structuralist formulations, though developed to describe and reconstruct a "collectivity" in the past, become, in their usage, the collective *mentalité* of the historian, the mode of thought which engenders and then reifies an order and meaning for history.[17]

So, the idea of *longue durée*—like other popular concepts such as *mentalité, episteme, zeitgeist, gestalt,* paradigm, discourse, ideology, hegemony, civilizing process, discursive formations—serves as an interpretive model for identifying and explaining historical conditions, social practices, epochs. More to the point, a narrative of social thought, behavior, power, and control emerges from these concepts. Of course, there are sundry differences in *interpretive meaning* between such concepts as Ranke's his-

torical spirit of power, Marx's ideology, Burckhardt's culture, Weber's Protestant ethic, Talcott Parson's functionalism, Jacques Le Goff's *mentalité*,
Jurgen Habermas's modernity, and Michel Foucault's discursive formations.
But in terms of *interpretive strategy*, a process of constituting and framing
history by means of ideas that function as models of explanation, these
concepts reveal striking similarities.[18] Moreover, each concept produces a
narrative, an organized representation (*mimesis*) and emplotment (*mythos*)
of how and why events and actions occur. That is the whole point.

Instead of attempting to deny narrative a place in history, historians and
philosophers of history might better examine how narrative operates in
historical scholarship, from the original constitution of documents to the
processes of writing. This in fact has been the aim of a number of people,
including R. G. Collingwood, Raymond Aron, Kenneth Burke, William
Dray, Arthur Danto, W. B. Gallie, Louis O. Mink, Nancy Struever, Hayden
White, Peter Munz, Paul Veyne, and Paul Ricoeur. While not defending
the old narrative histories and biographies that have been prevalent in
historical study, they have argued against attempts to ground history exclusively in the methods and theories of the social sciences and the sciences.
They wish to show how narrative form and narrative consciousness contribute to the processes of historical understanding.

   This investigation has entailed a shift away from a debate that has
depended upon the false dichotomy between scientific method and narrative
art in historical writing. Increasingly, contemporary historians have acknowledged that scientific and narrative methods are necessarily interrelated—
that the specific and the general, the objective and the subjective, the material
and the mental, the real and the known, the testimony and the judgment are
all joined by the historian's own methods of designation, apportionment,
coordination, figuration, and construction. Whatever the approach, narrative assumptions, techniques, and strategies serve the historian's method of
constituting the past.[19]

   The relationship between history and narrative is, as Ricoeur notes,
"extraordinarily complex."[20] Still, the fundamental assumption, briefly
stated, is that this relation centers on the methods and functions of explanation and interpretation in history. Historical explanations must take up the
dynamic linkage between events—a correlation that explains the processes
of historical change, processes that are understood in terms of the actions of
human beings (represented variously as individuals, groups, classes, races,
nations, or civilizations). The representation of these actions takes the form
of some kind of narrative order because the actions are not simply chronological or sequential. They are joined. In other words, the task of describing
and explaining what happened also includes the need to interpret how and
why human events occurred. Narrative provides coherence, a process of
emplotment which configures these actions into a meaningful, comprehensible interpretation.

   As historians—and as readers of history—we shape (and reshape) past
events into meanings that take the holistic order of narratives, not just the

sequential order of chronological conjunctions. Narrative form, Mink argues, is a "cognitive instrument" for understanding history, "an ensemble of interrelationships of many different kinds as a single whole." The meanings of history are thus realized in the discursive order of historical narratives. Our configurational—and categorical—modes of comprehension generate narrative discourses that shape both the historical record and our historical consciousness of that record. Despite our neat distinctions between history and fiction, narrative form brings the two "closer together than common sense could well accept."[21]

This concord rests, in turn, on what Paul Ricoeur calls "a reciprocity between narrativity and temporality" in historical understanding. That is, we make sense of the infinite flow of time by means of narrative configurations of events and actions. Ricoeur argues that there is "the closest parallel between the epistemology of historical explanation and that of narrative grammar."[22] Human temporality, our uneasy consciousnsess of being in time (and our ability to think of ourselves in terms of beginnings and ends), provides the condition and the need for articulating this experience in some kind of narrative order. We provide meaning for time. This process of ordering is done by means of a coherent plot that shapes historical events into probable human actions, configured by meaningful beginnings, middles, and ends. We provide, in other words, a poetics for historical occurrences. Events are not significant in and of themselves; their possible meanings, always in excess of a simple, chronological description, derive from the symbolic order that we provide through narrativity. From Ricoeur's viewpoint, then, narrative is the artifice, the model, that historians adapt for ordering the past. We use this model, which can take many forms, as a project of appropriation and disclosure, an innovation that gives to the discordance, or aporia of temporality, the concordance, or causal order of narrativity.

One of the definitive features of this concordance is the way narrative serves as a mode of retrospective organization, a method for producing a followable story. Of course, the totality of what happened in the past cannot be perceived or reported. What the historian has access to are certain traces of events, sources that already interpret the past. The historian, examining some of these traces, selects and organizes a number of events into a meaningful order. Thus, as Louis O. Mink notes, history writing provides a "retrospective intelligibility" for the representation of human actions.[23] The process of selecting and ordering historical information into a comprehensive whole typically follows the form of a narrative structure, in part because the historian knows how things worked out. The historical report fulfills (i.e., illustrates, organizes, embodies, and completes) this way of knowing. All historical narratives, in this sense, are teleological; they all give shape to time, which in itself has no shape. Also, our historical understanding, as Hans-Georg Gadamer argues, is from a specific perspective: history is seen and understood through a consciousness in the present.[24] This consciousness, which Ricoeur calls "historical intentionality," functions like point of view in narrative: it is a filter, a perspective, a mediator. We reflect backwards, giving to successive events an order, a selective process of alignment by means of our retrospective judgment.

The key question, then, is whether narrativity is intrinsic to human consciousness. Ricoeur, Mink, and Hayden White seem to hold back from this argument (or at least waver in their analysis), but David Carr argues that "narrative structure pervades our very experience of time and social existence, independently of our contemplating the past as historians." In other words, Carr is prepared to argue for the necessity of narrative in the perception and representation of reality. "Narrative form is not a dress which covers something else but the structure inherent in human experience and action."[25] As individuals and as social groups, we constitute our being, our experience, and the world by means of a "temporal grasp" of consciousness. Coherence is achieved through narrative configurations, mental acts of retrospective and prospective engagement with existence. We narrate our lives as we experience them. Historians, therefore, are doing what comes naturally; they are understanding the past the same way we understand all of life. The events and actions of history are configured by the historian just as the events and actions of daily life are configured by each individual. Or as Paul Veyne states: "History is made of the same substance as the lives of each of us."[26]

Some theorists would claim that the historical use of narrative is an imposition upon the world, a distortion of reality (but this argument assumes that somehow, in an *a priori* manner, we have direct access to the real, that we first perceive and know what happened then reshape it to fit a narrative structure). Other theorists, such as Carr, Munz, and Veyne, argue that the perception of reality, however defined and constituted, depends upon narrative understanding. This ontological (and phenomenological) proposition is no doubt crucial to philosophical analysis, but for historians, who are focused on the pragmatic issue of historical writing, it is not a necessary argument. Whether or not narrativity is central to human consciousness, it is central to historical understanding, as Aron, Mink, Ricoeur, White, Veyne, and Carr agree.

The challenge for historians, then, is to understand better how the models and discourses of narrativity organize the writing process. The immediate problem, however, is that there are various modes of emplotment and figuration, and this abundance is what worries some historians. With so many choices, does the discipline of history offer, in the final analysis, little more than a series of competing tales, each following its own rules of order, yet none having sufficient hold on truth and reality? If we are imprisoned in controlling languages (*mentalités*, discursive formations, hegemonies, ideologies, narratives), what is the justification for history? And, if each narrative sets its own agenda, does this mean that the model determines, before the fact, the meaning of the events? Does the historian always find, to the exclusion of all other relevant sources, only the evidence that produces this narrative? Is the study of history then condemned to circular arguments, to generating arbitrary laws of order in the very process of making order?

It would seem that the modernist conceit is true: the center does not hold. Understanding in the modern world, lacking any single point of order and certainty, drifts through the hermeneutical attitudes, a condition of endlessly shifting perspectives and values. Or in the words of A. R. Ammons:

> a center's absolute, if relative: but every point in
>   spacetimematter's
>
> a center: reality is abob with centers: indeed, there is
> nothing but centers: centers of galaxies, systems,
>   planets, asteroids,
> moons, drifts, atoms, electrons: and the center, as of the
>
> earth, where all turns and pressures meet, is
>   inexpressibly light,
> still, and empty . . . [27]

This apparent condition of relativity (defined often as arbitrariness and chaos) troubles those who oppose the use of narrative in history. Whether the topic is narrative, rhetoric, discourse, tropes, symbols, or myths, many historians continue to feel uneasy and sometimes angered by these supposedly extraneous matters of textuality.[28] To a certain extent this uneasiness with the foregrounding of narrative and discourse is understandable, but the desire to ignore, dismiss, or deny narrativity serves no worthy purpose. The issue of narrativity in history is going to remain a problem. Perhaps, however, we can begin to focus on the real problem: not how to remove narrative from history but, rather, how to understand its operations. This is why the middle term in my title, *hermeneutics*, is the key issue before us. If we are to comprehend the relation between history and narrativity, we will need to accept the challenges of interpretation theory.

The study of history provides us with ideas of order and meaning of the past, interpretations offered from different perspectives. That there are many perspectives, many centers of order, should not unnerve us, unless of course we are determined to believe that the choices for understanding are between either a singular order or a threatening chaos. This proposition is a familiar one today (e.g., the arguments over education: curricula, the canon), but why should multiplicity be defined as chaos? And in turn why should a new alternative be taken as the new truth? There are many truths to be told about the past, not simply one ordained story.

In telling our stories we have become self-conscious of our strategies of understanding. We recognize that each strategy tends to privilege a certain perspective and explanation. This does not mean, however, that any explanation is as good as any other. Most of us realize that some stories are better than others, some storytellers make us see more than we had seen before: more in the details, more in the shapes of history.

Whatever our perspective, the task before us is not to return to some Edenic position (a positivist paradise), before the fall into narrative consciousness. The temptations of nostalgia should be resisted. We are condemned not simply to time but, much more interestingly, to making sense in various ways of our consciousness of time, our consciousness of being in history. Narrative gives shape to our understanding, it offers a way of regarding the events of the past.

Each viewpoint provides a vital perspective, a possible but not exclusive center for organizing our understanding. In the words, once again, of Ammons: "I am conscious that the / landscape is fixed at the same time that I can move around in it: / a poem is the same way."[29] We might say something similar about the writing of history, which organizes the landscape of our personal and collective memories, distributed in the traces. In a sense the past is fixed: having already happened, it cannot be changed; it is what it has become (which is nothing now). But we cannot comprehend or represent it fully, in its totality, not even in a master narrative of necessity (though Hegel, Marx, Freud, and others have attempted to tell this story). Only by moving around, shifting our perspectives, can we see the heterogeneous aspects of it. The motion of our thoughts gives it meaning. We create a presence to represent an absence. Accordingly, the past—or the meaning of the past—is simultaneously fixed and unstable, full and empty. It is both within language and without. Only narratives, with their centers "absolute if relative," can do justice to this essential paradox.

NOTES

1. Hermeneutics, which I define broadly as the theory of interpretation, provides the basis for analysis in this essay but is not, I want to insist, an essential, foundational, or systematic method for discovering and expressing truth. Historical scholarship, though diligent in its search for what happened in the past, is not a discipline that discovers final truths. Its problems, as I conceive them, are primarily epistemological rather than ontological. Historical reports are representations, perhaps supreme fictions, of the past, but not incarnations. I thus wish to distinguish my use of the concept from that of the exegetical tradition that developed hermeneutics as a means of bringing forth the buried, hidden, or secret meanings of sacred texts, a process of uncovering and revealing an ultimate truth. For an analysis of this hermeneutical tradition as it developed from Biblical exegesis to modern philosophy, see Richard Palmer, *Hermeneutics: Interpretation Theory in Schleiermacher, Dilthey, Heidegger, and Gadamer* (Evanston, Ill.: Northwestern University Press, 1969).

One other point: as I hope will become clear in this essay, I see no need to spell out the long argument on the supposed distinctions between understanding (*verstehen*) and explanation (*erklären*) which runs through hermeneutical theory. See, however, Paul Ricoeur, *Time and Narrative*, 3 vols. (Chicago: University of Chicago Press, 1984–88), for the history of this argument and its displacement as a key issue in modern historiography, Also see chap. 4, "Explanation and Understanding," in Ricoeur's *Interpretation Theory: Discourse and the Surplus of Meaning* (Fort Worth: Texas Christian University Press, 1976). And of equal importance is Ricoeur's essay "What Is a Text?: Explanation and Understanding," in *Hermeneutics and the Human Sciences*, ed. and trans. John B. Thompson (Cambridge: Cambridge University Press; and Paris: Editions de la Maison de Sciences de l'Homme, 1981).

2. Even "primary" evidence expresses, within its possible modes of collocation and representation, a historical set of values, assumptions, beliefs, and viewpoints. Every denotation has its connotations, which is to say that signs occur within a cultural milieu.

3. I first took up the topic of this essay in a book review I wrote for *Theatre Journal* (December 1989) on David Carr, *Time, Narrative, and History* (Bloomington: Indiana University Press, 1986); Louis O. Mink's *Historical Understanding* (Ithaca, N.Y.: Cornell University Press, 1987); and Paul Ricoeur's *Time and Narrative*. Some of the ideas in this essay were developed originally in that review.

4. G. J. Renier, *History: Its Purpose and Method* (New York: Harper and Row, 1965), 32.

5. Peter Munz, *The Shapes of Time: A New Look at the Philosophy of History* (Middletown, Conn.: Wesleyan University Press, 1977), 22.

6. Paul Ricoeur, "The Narrative Function," in Thompson, *Hermeneutics*, 288; emphasis in original.

7. In many American universities, for instance, history has moved from the humanities to the social sciences. Accordingly, those historians who do cultural or intellectual history have often found themselves rather isolated within their own discipline, as if they had failed to move forward with the times. For a current illustration of the conditions and concerns of the cultural historian, see Dominick LaCapra, *Rethinking Intellectual History: Texts, Contexts, Language* (Ithaca: Cornell University Press, 1983); Dominick LaCapra and Steven L. Kaplan, eds., *Modern European Intellectual History: Reappraisals and New Perspectives* (Ithaca: Cornell University Press, 1982).

8. For instance, over one-half of *The Philosophy of History in Our time* (ed. Hans Meyerhoff [Garden City, N.Y.: Doubleday, 1959]), a popular collection of essays by leading historians and philosophers, is given over to the central problem: "Clio—Science or Muse?"

9. It is noteworthy that, despite the differences between Comte's positivism (e.g., the emphasis upon empirical observation) and Ranke's idealism (e.g., the emphasis upon *Volksgeist*), both approaches to history were justified as being scientific.

10. Georg G. Iggers, *New Directions in European Historiography*, rev. ed. (Middletown, Conn.: Wesleyan University Press, 1984), 19–20.

11. More specifically, this "spirit" was identified by Ranke as the operation of "power," which nations manifest in their dealings with one another, as he noted in a fragment from the 1830s:

In power itself there appears a spiritual substance, an original genius, which has a life of its own, fulfills conditions more or less peculiar to itself, and creates for itself its own domain. The task of history is the observation of this life which cannot be characterized through One thought or One word; the spirit which manifests itself in the world is not so confined; its presence suffuses the bounds of its existence; nothing is accidental in it, its appearance has its grounds in everything. (Quoted in *The Varieties of History: From Voltaire to the Present*, ed. Fritz Stern [New York: Random House, 1973], 60)

12. Moreover, narrative plots and tropes controlled the writing of history, as Hayden White has shown in his major study of the "poetics" of nineteenth-century historians, *Metahistory: The Historical Imagination in Nineteenth-Century Europe* (Baltimore: Johns Hopkins University Press, 1973). See also Stephen Bann, *The Clothing of Clio: A Study of the Representation of History in Nineteenth-Century Britain and France* (Cambridge: Cambridge University Press, 1984).

13. We should keep in mind that some of the Annales historians continued to do biographical study, although they attempted to place the individual within the social culture and *mentalité* of the time. Lucien Febvre, for example, wrote separate case studies of Martin Luther, François Rabelais, and Marguerite de Navarre.

14. Fernand Braudel, *On History*, trans. Sarah Matthews (Chicago: University of Chicago Press, 1980), 75.

15. See, for instance, Hans Kellner's *Language and Historical Representation: Getting the Story Crooked* (Madison: University of Wisconsin Press, 1989), esp. chap. 7, "Disorderly Conduct: Braudel's Mediterranean Satire." Also see Paul Ricoeur, *Time and Narrative*, trans. Kathleen McLaughlin and David Pellauer (Chicago: University of Chicago Press, 1984), 1:96–111, 208–25.

16. Perhaps the grandest morality tale of all is presented by Philippe Aries in *The Hour of Our Death*, trans. Helen Weaver (New York: Random House, 1981). It is a magnificent history of attitudes and representations of death in Western Christian cultures from the medieval age to the present. Its four models of death, as Paul Ricoeur notes in *Time and Narrative*, tell the story of how death was perceived and accommodated in different eras.

17. Part of the issue here is the way generalizations operate in historical study. For commentary on this problem, see books by the following people, listed in sec. 3 of the bibliography in *Interpreting the Theatrical Past*, ed. Thomas Postlewait and Bruce McConachie (Iowa City: Iowa University Press, 1989): William Dray, David Hackett Fischer, W. B. Gallie, Louis Gottschalk, Christopher Lloyd, Louis O. Mink, Peter Munz, Stephen Pepper, Frederick Suppe, and Paul Veyne.

18. This possibility of a shared heritage, from Kant and Hegel to Habermas and Foucault, is exactly what Foucault himself contemplated toward the end of his life. See the essay "What Is Enlightenment?" in *The Foucault Reader*, ed. Paul Rabinow (New York: Pantheon Books, 1984). Also see the essays by Habermas, David Couzens Hoy, and Hubert L. Dreyfus and Paul Rabinow, in *Foucault: A Critical Reader*, ed. David Couzens Hoy (Oxford: Basil Blackwell, 1986).

19. See, for example, Martha Banta's *Imaging American Women: Idea and Ideals in Cultural History* (1987); Robert Darnton's *The Great Cat Massacre and Other Episodes in French Cultural History* (1984); Natalie Zemon Davis's *The Return of Martin Guerre* (1985); Carlo Ginsberg's *The Cheese and the Worms: The Cosmos of a Sixteenth-Century Miller* (1980); E. J. Hobsbawm, *Primitive Rebels* (1959); Emmanuel Le Roy Ladurie's *Montaillou: The Promised Land of Error* (1978); Keith Thomas's *Religion and the Decline of Magic: Studies in Popular Beliefs in Sixteenth and Seventeenth-Century England* (1971); and E. P. Thompson's *The Making of the English Working Class* (1963).

20. Ricoeur, *Time and Narrative*, 1:227.

21. Louis O. Mink, *Historical Understanding*, ed. Brian Fay, Eugene O. Golob, and Richard T. Vann (Ithaca: Cornell University Press, 1987), 198, 203.

22. Ricoeur, *Time and Narrative*, 1:3, 2:158.

23. Mink, *Historical Understanding*, 116.

24. Palmer, *Hermeneutics*, 176.

25. Carr, *Time, Narrative, and History*, 9, 65.

26. Paul Veyne, *Writing History: Essay on Epistemology*, trans. Mina Moore-Rinvolucri (Middletown, Conn.: Wesleyan University Press, 1984), 31.

27. A. R. Ammons, "Essay on Poetics," in *Collected Poems, 1951–1971* (New York: W. W. Norton, 1972), 299. All the poems quoted in this essay are in this collection.

28. For an overview on the resistance in the historical profession to the study

of narrativity, rhetoric, and discourse, see Hans Kellner, "Triangular Anxieties: The Present State of European Intellectual History," in LaCapra and Kaplan, *Modern European Intellectual History*, 111–36; reprinted in Kellner, *Language and Historical Representation*.

29. Ammons, "Essay on Poetics," 310.

The Phenomenological Attitude

Bert O. States

> All things exist as they are perceived: at least in relation to the
> percipient.... But poetry defeats the curse which binds us to be
> subjected to the accident of surrounding impressions. And whether it
> spreads its own figured curtain, or withdraws life's dark veil from
> before the scene of things, it equally creates for us a being within
> our being. It makes us the inhabitants of a world to which the
> familiar world is a chaos. It reproduces the common universe of
> which we are portions and percipients, and it purges from our
> inward sight the film of familiarity which obscures from us the
> wonder of our being. It compels us to feel that which we perceive,
> and to imagine that which we know. It creates anew the universe,
> after it has been annihilated in our minds by the recurrence of
> impressions blunted by reiteration.
>
> —Percy Bysshe Shelley, *A Defense of Poetry*

This passage becomes less dated when you consider that it was written
nearly a century before Victor Shklovsky's attempt to align the method of
criticism and the function of art in the now famous concept of perceptual
"defamiliarization."[1] If anything, Shelley's language is even more "phenomenological" than Shklovsky's, but what we learn from Shelley is that a
phenomenological attitude toward the world (or what Husserl calls the
"phenomenological Standpoint") does not depend on knowing the "science"
of phenomenology. It is rather an ability to see through "the film of familiarity" which blunts "the scene of things" through its reiteration. Those in
whom this attitude "exists to excess," Shelley goes on, are called poets; but
they might also be called critics. Indeed, they could be any "inhabitants"
of the world who have a natural gift for the *epoche*, or the capacity to
put into perceptual brackets "the accident of surrounding impressions" and
to see what phenomenologists call "the things themselves." So right off,
when we speak of criticism in the phenomenological mode, we are referring
less to a relentless methodology or a deep philosophical concern for the
nature of consciousness than to an attitude that manifests itself with varying
degrees of purity and one that may come and go in a given exercise as
critical objectives change. It would be nice if we had a less pretentious (or
at least *shorter*) term for this kind of commentary, if only to avoid hints
of "scientific" aspiration, but the best I have been able to manage is neo-
impressionism, and that opens even more embarrassing risks in an age that
seems bent on exposing the myth of a reliable self.

Nevertheless, phenomenological criticism is a form of impressionism—
or, as Maurice Natanson calls it, "methodological solipsism."[2] It is some
comfort to add, however, that the Impressionists were very good painters
of *phenomena*, in the strict sense of that word. In their own way they were

369

painting a perceptual critique of the real world, much as the critic of theater might try to show that the world of a play is opaque, geometrical, primordial, dense, sparse, and so on. To close the circle criticism derived from the phenomenological attitude is highly *mimetic* in its methodology. That is, owing to the nature of its project, phenomenological criticism—like phenomenology itself—tends to rely strongly on some variation of figural description, or "proof" by metaphor. On this account it is probably the most personal form of critical commentary and hence is a useful counterbalance to the increasingly impersonal methodology in so much of today's criticism.

I am not implying that we should all run out and buy a pair of philosopher's brackets; but if one were looking for an alternative to the radical skepticism of deconstruction and postmodernism—its "uninhibited questioning of everything," as Eugene Goodheart puts it[3]—one can find it most readily in the phenomenological attitude that uninhibitedly *accepts* everything it sees. Indeed, the aim of phenomenological criticism seems to be the reverse of the aim of deconstruction in that it seeks, as Mikel Dufrenne puts it, "the-being-at-the-end-of-oppositions in which idea and thing, subject and object, noesis and noema, are dialectically united."[4] It is no contradiction of this claim to add that deconstructive philosophy is intimately connected with the phenomenological movement (especially with Heidegger and Husserl) as to basic questions of being, meaning, and consciousness. I am referring mainly to the practice of deconstruction as it descends from philosophy *into* criticism—the species we encounter regularly in our journals (sometimes without a single mention of the *D*-word) where the aim is to show the paradox of presumed identity, the retreat of meaning before the finger of definition, or to demonstrate how a text "has already dismantled itself" before the critic arrives.[5] Phenomenological criticism, however, posits a stopping place, as it were, *at* the starting place, not of all possible meanings but of meaning and feeling as they arise in a direct encounter with the art object. A phenomenological approach offers a critique of what cosmological physics might call "the first four seconds" of the perceptual explosion. It is beside the point to claim that the first four seconds are always tainted by a lifetime of perceptual habit within a narrow cultural frame. It is only the moment of absorption that counts; what conditions the moment and what follows it are somebody else's business.

I am not using the expression "first four seconds" in a strict durational sense, as the physicist might speak, however literally or loosely, of the first four seconds of the "Big Bang." I intend it as referring to the "moment"— soon or late—in which an object or an image establishes itself in our perception as something, as Shelley puts it, that "creates for us a being within our being [and] compels us to feel that which we perceive." Such an experience is commonly delayed or prevented by all sorts of everyday significations that attend the appearance of any object or image. Moreover, it is one thing to *have* such an experience (when one has it), another to know what to do with it from an analytical standpoint. It turns out to be an immensely complex problem.

Adolf Reinach, for example, a student of Husserl, is said to have devoted an entire semester studying the ways in which one experiences a mailbox.[6] This makes a nice joke on the philosopher, but there is more to a mailbox than meets the eye. No matter how much you fondle it, study it, turn it this way or that, or walk around it, a mailbox will always look you straight in the face, like a cat that won't let you get behind it. Most people aren't bothered by this problem, but the fact that you can never see *all* of a mailbox raises the imponderable question of the frontality of everything in the world before the eye of consciousness. This is the foundational problem of phenomenology. For this frontal quality of all experience, as Husserl says, is what keeps the world from being *all me*:[7] if I could see all sides of a mailbox at once, if I could perceive its interior, its composition, its angles and curves, its materiality, its field of world relationships, its functions, its vicissitudes, its history, and its deterioration in one grand cubistic glance, in what sense can it be said to be exterior to me, of the world rather than of myself? Such "vision" could only occur at what we may safely call the "Divine Standpoint." Moreover, if inside the mailbox we should discover a letter written by God containing a definitive description of all that a phenomenologist could possibly—ideally—want to know about a mailbox, we would be no better off because language itself contains an even more virulent form of frontality. In this frontality we perceive one word or phrase at a time and the rest hides or slides into a "backside" along with the mailbox we are ignoring as we read the divine description of what a mailbox is.

In one way or another this problem takes us to the base of all our concerns with the problematics of meaning: the central terms of our critical discourse—*presence, representation, repetition, deferral, difference, aporia, supplementation, referentiality, indetermination*—can be treated as variations on the principle of frontality. For frontality is not simply the perception of the surface facing us; it carries with it what Husserl calls the "apperception" of the rest of the object which is, in "a kind of" way, "co-present" even though unseen: "what is there perceptually motivates [belief in] something else being there too."[8]

It is easy to see why phenomenologists are drawn to the theater metaphor so often. In what other art form is the frontality of experience more amply demonstrated? In what other art form do we *apperceive* so much rotundity in what we merely *perceive* ("the vasty fields of France," etc.)? Before the world, Sartre says, we are as spectators at a play.[9] Moreover, theater is the paradigmatic place for the display of the drama of presence and absence; for theater, unlike the mailbox, produces its effect precisely through a deliberate collaboration between its frontside ("on" stage) and its backside ("off") whereby anticipation is created through acts of entrance and exit (the recoil of the world beyond), and finally between the frontside illusion (character and scene) and the backside reality (the actor, the unseen stage brace that "props" up the illusion). Beyond all this, theatergoing in itself is a kind of bracketing, or *epoche*, in which we willingly, if not involuntarily, suspend our belief in the empirical world and attend to a half-reality already "reduced" by the premeditations and manipulations of a series of prior and present artists. As a consequence, phenomenology cannot look at a theater stage in the way that it looks at the simple mailbox, which has no such illusionary pretentions (unless it is placed on a stage). What is required, then, is still another suspension that does not cancel the first or throw us altogether out of the illusion into reality, or throw reality altogether out of the illusion, but brackets what each would convey exclusively and retains as "co-present" both what we have consented to disbelieve (reality) and the belief we have temporarily "willed" in its place (the illusion). Merleau-Ponty suggests that the modern phenomenologist/painter strives to show "how the world becomes world";[10] the phenomenological critic strives to show how theater becomes theater—that is, how theater throws up the pretense that it is another kind of reality than the one constituting the ground on which its pretense is based.

We see this most clearly in stage scenery. If one looks at the stage setting in the spell of the *epoche,* one sees that it is the means of creating the illusion that there is no scenery there but only a world, a reality (of sorts). Scenery comes into existence in order to deny that it exists—a duplicity at the heart of carpentry. You may ask: isn't this really a description of naturalistic scenery? What about stylized scenery? obvious scenery? scenery in which trees and chairs are played by actors? It really makes no difference. Even in these forms, in calling attention to itself, in seeming to say "I exist. I am nothing but scenery!" scenery is lying, or speaking with the permission of the mimesis. Even in Brecht's tacky world where scenery deliberately remains scenery ("built to last three hours"), it is nevertheless fabricated in such a way that its fabrication constitutes the illusion. "It must be clear that the play is taking place in a theater," the designer may have said to the carpenters. "Make the scenery look like badly designed scenery." Whereupon the carpenters labor skillfully to bring about this slapdash failure, this nondisguise of bad art, this backside become frontside, this absence become presence, of which the newspaper critic (with luck) will write, "Y's settings are brilliantly conceived to produce the illusion that the play is taking place in a theater."

The *epoche* (roughly synonymous with *bracketing* and *reduction*) bears some resemblance to Michelangelo's notion that the sculptor releases the statue from the stone in which it is imprisoned. That is, in order to appear as an essence that has its "being within our being," as Shelley says, the phenomenon must be released from its perceptual bondage in the "natural" world—or, indeed, from its collaboration with other phenomena in the same theatrical illusion. Since the case of stage scenery is a relatively simple one, let us apply the idea to one of the most immaterial, yet fundamental, phenomena in the theater experience: our perception of *character.* Is it possible to isolate an entity called character, the behavioral essence that characters in a play are said to possess? Immediately, we are faced with a perceptual problem expressed most succinctly in Henry James's famous definition of character and incident: "What is character but the determination of incident? What is incident but the illustration of character?"[11] So there is character, seemingly linked to incident (action) as indissolubly as Escher's swimming fish are linked to the birds flying "through" them. And the problem is complicated still further by the fact that the character is being played by an actor who is not the character but who forms the entire perceptual ground from which any such essence as character can appear.

So, if we are supposedly perceiving character as a persistent essence in individual behavior in what way can we say that it is distinct from the person of the actor? How can we know it? How do we feel its being? Is its persistence not the simple persistence of, say, Olivier playing Othello? Finally, there is the problem that any character seems to undergo changes as the incidents lead to different moods and the display of different traits. As we say, character "develops." So what is it in the character phenomenon which persists? If character changes with every scene, or within single scenes, or even constantly, where do the eye and ear get the notion that something called character is iterating itself, always being itself, in this chaos of different and differing phenomena in the stage world?

I set up these resistances in the spirit of the *epoche* itself, for they are the kinds of things that must be chiseled away, or bracketed, before we can release the "figure" of character from the overall illusion and determine that there is, indeed, an aspect of Othello that cannot be charged exclusively to Olivier's personal persistence and something that is phenomenally distinct from incident and survives all changes and so-called development.

Othello's character is not my topic here, but, if one were pursuing an essense of Othello, it would be found through Husserl's principle of copresence. Or, to paraphrase another phenomenologist, the presence of one "side" of Othello in a given scene, and the absence of all the other "sides" of the Othello of previous scenes, *are what becomes present.*"[12] If Othello's character accumulates ("changing" as it goes), it is accumulating according to an Othello "law" determined, in the first place, by Shakespeare's sense of consistency in his creation and, in the second place, by Olivier's interpretation of that consistency. As for Olivier lending his visible "weight" to Othello's invisible character, this is obviously a strong factor: Othello's character would be very different were John Gielgud playing him. But then Olivier's actor-character would be very different if he were playing Hamlet rather than Othello. In any event there is an essence of Othello on the stage at all times which never changes or at least never violates an invisibly circumscribed field of behavioral potentiality. (Othello, for example, would never—like Hamlet—wonder how long a man might lie in the earth ere he rot; nor would Othello "scan" his vengeance so scrupulously.) Othello is always a formation of presence and absence; his character is never absent or present in the way that one of his traits (say, anger) is present or absent. Othello's character may be likened to a sphere revolving in space: it may reveal different sides or features as it turns, but it always remains the same sphere, it always continues around "the backside."

You may well ask what one can *do* with such information. Isn't it finally rather obvious? Indeed it is. Phenomenology, as Bruce Wilshire says, "is the systematic attempt to unmask the obvious."[13] Like Shelley's idea of poetry, phenomenology is an effort to recover what in our experience has been "annihilated . . . by reiteration." In order to gain a systematic idea of how theater affects us, we need (among other things) an awareness of character essence and the contribution of its persistence to the stream of radically changing events we call a plot. This is one of the basic tensions through which theater becomes theater. Still, it is only one kind of phenomenological problem. Another might involve an examination of character as a perceptual locus of "hidden" cultural assumptions. It would be interesting, for example, to conduct a comparative phenomenology of different kinds of character essense (Greek, Shakespearean, Restoration, "psychological," naturalistic); or, to put it another way, what were playwrights in a given period making character *of* (what is its DNA?) which may have been beneath their own awareness? Such findings might serve very well in the context of new historical criticism, which itself involves a seeing of what absences may be co-present in artifacts we have heretofore regarded as things that are entirely *present* to the eye.

I want to turn now to the question of how one recognizes a phenomenological description. Earlier I said that the phenomenological attitude might be present in almost any critical exercise. Reader-response criticism, for example, has a heavily phenomenological bent insofar as it is concerned with the transaction between consciousness and text. I detect it less often in semiotic discourse, but this may be a judgment based on my sampling of semiotic literature. In any case Umberto Eco's description of the complementarity of semiotic and phenomenological practice offers a useful way of sorting the differences:

> A rereading . . . of Husserl's discussions might induce us to state that semiotic meaning is simply the socialized codification of a perceptual experience which the phenomenological *epoche* should restore to us in its original form. . . . Phenomenology undertakes to rebuild from the beginning the conditions necessary for the formation of cultural units which semiotics instead accepts as data because communication functions on the basis of them. The phenomenological *epoche* would therefore refer perception back to a stage where referents are no longer confronted as explicit messages but as extremely ambiguous texts akin to aesthetic ones.[14]

This is hardly a denial that semiotics may adopt the phenomenological attitude for its own purposes. Indeed, Keir Elam argues that "any semiotics worthy of the name . . . is eminently phenomenological, and the reverse may well also be true."[15] The degree of truth in this statement would depend on where one draws the line between semiotics and phenomenology. It is my sense that as long as semiotics holds the notion that all things (on a stage, for example) can be fully treated as *signs*—that is, as transparent codes of socialized meaning—it cannot adopt the phenomenological attitude in any "eminent" way. Husserl is quite plain on this point: "The spatial thing which we see is . . . perceived, we are consciously aware of it as given in its *embodied form*. We are not given an image or a sign *in its place*. We must not substitute the consciousness of a sign or an image for a perception."[16] Of course, Husserl is not talking here about perception as it occurs in the theater where we *are* confronted by images and signs. But in the theater something is *also itself* as well; we can always (if we choose) see an object on a stage as we see, say, a bird in a feeder, and, though the bird in the feeder may be a sign of spring, it is not the sign of a bird. More complexly, however, in the theater we see an object in its "embodied form" as having a double aspect, one of which is significative, the other (like the bird) self-given; and when we treat one of these aspects to the exclusion of the other—it doesn't matter which—we are not taking a phenomenological attitude toward what has been intentionally set before us on the stage. At a play Dufrenne says, "I do not posit the real as real, because there is also the unreal which this real designates; I do not posit the unreal and unreal, because there is also the real which promotes and supports this unreal."[17] Phenomenology occurs in the "seam" between these two faces of the object.

Still, in principle, Elan is right. There is no reason that the phenomenological and the semiotic attitudes cannot compatibly blend into each other. Let me cite a passage from Patrice Pavis's *Languages of the Stage* which will illustrate what I take to be a fusion of semiotic—in this case, semiological—and phenomenological interests. Here is Pavis explaining why the mime's "universe of gesture is [only] contaminated" by the spoken word:

> When the body tries to say too much, and with too much wit, the body is "talkative," overstated by an overly precise story and discourse.
>
> The mime should therefore be left alone, and his only dialogue should be the one established between what he does and what he does not do, between normative gestures and their poetic deviation: the comparison between two universes of differing coherence and modality, between our immobility and the limits of our body, and his movements and original mode of existence creates the dialogue in the spectator.
>
> But this dialogue is only initiated—with Amiel as with all mimes—when the body begins to unfold, tears itself from inert matter and sketches in a narrative.[18]

The topic here is "the discourse of the mime" and how we "read" the sequence of mime gestures. Hence we find words like *modality, gestural narrativity, framing, segmentations of gesture, codification*, and so on, which belong to "the discourse" of semiotics and semiology. But it seems to me that descriptive methods of semiology and phenomenology are almost equally in evidence in this passage: *discourse* could easily be replaced by *presence* or *appearance*, or, in Pavis's own words, the "original mode of existence" of the mime—the essence of the mime, to invoke the classical phenomenological term. Here the body of the mime appears before me in all of the economy and purity of gesture which results from the mime's self-deprivation of an audible voice. Through Pavis's description I sense exactly why the power of the mime rests in the "dialogue between what he does and what he does not do"—in brief, between what is present and what is absent.

I suspect I knew all this already, and it is certainly "obvious" to me now. The point is that I didn't *know* I knew it, and there is all the value of such a description. What is obvious is also what is transparent and therefore unseen—like a dead metaphor or, to invoke Brecht's example, like the face of the watch on your wrist. And the peculiar effect of the phenomenological statement is that of discovering something in the backyard of your memory that has somehow bypassed awareness—"Sight," Bachelard says, "says too many things at one time"[19]—or has got there without being consciously processed as a "datum" of experience. It is at once forgotten and remembered. I take the passage, then, to be (whatever else it is) an example of phenomenological reduction because it puts on hold all codes of communication, all referentiality in the *content* of the mime's narrative, in order to "rebuild from the beginning," as Eco says, the primordial *form* of the mime's body. The mime has not yet become a "sign" or a "cultural unit"; he or she is simply the realization of a certain potential in human expressiveness.

Roland Barthes's project in *Mythologies* is to write a semiology of the bourgeois world by analyzing the language of its myths. Myth is a "pure ideographic system" that steals its meanings from one order of signification and plants them surreptitiously in another. The delicacy of Barthes's semiological problem in these essays—tracing a myth back to its origins in a "first language"—requires that the invisible be made visible, since the myth (plastic, steak and chips, ornamental cooking) is exactly what we cannot see because we are too busy living it. Here is where he calls upon the phenomenological eye. Barthes has always been a closet phenomenologist.[20] He cannot resist the lure of the "absolute," the pursuit of the essence of the culturally disguised thing, until he corners it and it turns and faces him openly. Here he is—semiologist, phenomenologist (who could possibly sort out the voices?)—tracking the essence of Greta Garbo's face in order to tell us why we have "deified" it:

> It is indeed an admirable face-object. In *Queen Christina*, . . . the make-up has the snowy thickness of a mask: it is not a painted face, but one set in plaster, protected by the surface of the colour, not by its lineaments. Amid all this snow at once fragile and compact, the eyes alone, black like strange soft flesh, but not in the least expressive, are two faintly tremulous wounds. In spite of its extreme beauty, this face, not drawn but sculpted in something smooth and friable, that is, at once perfect and ephemeral, comes to resemble the flour-white

complexion of Charlie Chaplin, the dark vegetation of his eyes, his totem-like countenance.[21]

For me the most striking image in this passage is "the dark vegetation of his eyes." This is its *punctum,* as Barthes would say, or the element "which rises from the scene, shoots out of it like an arrow, and pierces me"[22] (just as the puntcum of the Pavis passage is: "the body begins to unfold, tears itself from inert matter and sketches in a narrative"). Who has ever thought of Chaplin's eyes in this way, yet who does not instantly see "the connection"? Who does not a moment later see the connection between Chaplin and Garbo as this dark vegetation drains, like intertextual makeup, out of Chaplin's face into hers and thence into the whole granular black white world of "early" film? But for a split second, before the image begins giving in to these significations, one sees only something absolutely new, and the response, as Baudelaire might say, is instantaneous laughter in the soul. For on one of its levels this is a kind of pure joke, an adventure in grotesque. And what is grotesque but the creation of a new phenomenon, something without a history of signification or, rather (in this case), something with two histories—*eyes* and *vegetation*—that have been fused and abbreviated in a bridge of recognition, something both arbitrary and right: arbitrary because it is an unanticipated confusion of realms, right because the old Chaplin eyes that one has always *over*seen in the ensemble of the famous face suddenly shoot out of the scene and pierce you.

To claim these felicities of expression as the property of phenomenology would be rather like claiming that a bird was yours because it flew into your feeder. If anything, phenomenology and semiology borrow them from the poet and the artist, and this is really the sense of my discussion. The larger frame of Shelley's remark that poets possess a certain attitude "in excess" is that poets are those who are able to observe "a certain rhythm and order [in] natural objects," or "[that] relation subsisting, first between existence and perception, and secondly between perception and expression." The poet's language, therefore, is "vitally metaphorical [in that] it marks the before unapprehended relations of things and perpetuates their apprehension." This sentiment can be found over and over in the literature of phenomenology. Consider the simple statement that the phenomenological attitude "is admittedly a difficult process to describe, so Husserl used many different metaphors"[23]—beginning, incidentally, with the three key metaphors (bracketing, reduction, and the *epoche*) that form the basis of phenomenological method. Or again:

> what usually happens is that the [phenomenologist] will project a single imaginative variant, but one that is strategic, crucial, and usually colorful, one that brings out a certain necessity in the thing we wish to examine. It is not easy to capture the right imaginative variant, to pick out the dramatic, vivid example that shows a necessity. We

need fantasy to do so. Thus we need imagination to be good at philosophical analysis.[24]

In view of our interests here the term *phenomenological* can be thought of as pertaining not to a subfield of philosophy or a scientific movement but, instead, to the mode of thought and expression the mind naturally adopts when questions relating to our awareness of being and appearance arise. Thus defined, the mission of any form of phenomenological critique is to describe what Cezanne called "the world's instant," by which we mean not simply a paintable instant but also any instant that is perceptually "apprehended" as carrying, or leading to, an intuition about what it *is* and what it is *doing* before our eyes. Thus phenomenology is forced, through the sheer poverty of scientific language in the face of subjective experience, to say (to itself and to its reader), "It is *like* this: the eyes are [like] dark vegetation," or "The mime's body tears itself from inert matter." For there is no other way to trap an essence in "frontal" expression, since essence is not a kind of information or a "fact" of matter (like valence or specific gravity) but, rather, a transaction between consciousness and the thickness of existence, something that keeps on going around the back but is also here as well. In the phenomenological sense essence, one may say, is founded in a personification through which the world is invested with a human consciousness: perception and object become synonymous. Thus the impulse toward mimesis in phenomenological commentary, so noticeable in Heidegger, Husserl, Merleau-Ponty, Sartre, and Bachelard, would seem to be an attempt to forestall the retreat of the object into signification (understood as its infinite cultural referentiality), to arrest it in a radical defamiliarization that names without defining and pictures without limiting. The essence is at once caught and freed, as it is in experience itself.

NOTES

1. See Victor Shklovsky, "Art as Technique," *Russian Formalist Criticism: Four Essays*, trans. Lee T. Lemon and Marion J. Reis (Lincoln and London: University of Nebraska Press, 1965), 3–24. Robert Scholes calls attention to the similarity between the Shelley passage and Shkolvsky's concept of defamiliarization in *Structuralism in Literature: An Introduction* (New Haven and London: Yale University Press, 1976), 174–75. Scholes is interested in the structuralist parallel between Shelley and Shklovsky, whereas my own interest is strictly phenomenological, though I trust it is apparent that I have no desire to label either Shelley or Shklovsky as phenomenologists.

2. Maurice Natanson, "Solipsism and Sociality," *New Literature History* 5 (1974): 243.

3. Eugene Goodheart, *The Failure of Criticism* (Cambridge: Harvard University Press, 1978), 14.

4. Mikel Dufrenne, *The Phenomenology of Aesthetic Experience*, trans. Edward S. Casey, Albert A. Anderson, Willis Domingo, Leon Jacobson (Evanston, Ill.: Northwestern University Press, 1973), xlix.

5. J. Hillis Miller, "Stevens' Rock and Criticism as Cure, II," *Georgia Review* 30 (1976): 341.

6. Hans-Georg Gadamer, *Philosophical Hermeneutics*, trans. David E. Linge (Berkeley, Los Angeles, and London: University of California Press, 1977), 133.

7. Edmund Husserl, *Cartesian Meditations: An Introduction to Phenomenology*, trans. Dorion Cairns (The Hague: Martinus Nijhoff, 1960), 109.

8. Husserl, *Cartesian Meditations*, 109–10.

9. Jean-Paul Sartre, *The Psychology of Imagination*, trans. Bernard Frechtman (New York: Washington Square Press, 1968), 82.

10. Maurice Merleau-Ponty, *The Primacy of Perception and Other Essays on Phenomenological Psychology, the Philosophy of Art, History and Politics*, ed. James M. Edie (Evanston, Ill.: Northwestern University Press, 1964), 181.

11. Henry James, *The Art of Fiction* (New York: Oxford University Press, 1948), 13.

12. Robert Sokolowski, "The Theory of Phenomenological Description," *Descriptions*, ed. Don Ihde and Hugh J. Silverman (Albany: State University of New York Press, 1985), 17. Sokolowski's statement reads: "If we focus on the present and the absent as such, a new dimension becomes thematic for us. It is not the case that this side is present and the other dies are absent, but rather [the present of this side and the absence of those sides] are what becomes 'present.'"

13. Bruce Wilshire, *Role Playing and Identity: The Limits of Theatre as Metaphor* (Bloomington: Indiana University Press, 1982), 11. Wilshire's book is a basic text in the phenomenology of theater.

14. Umberto Eco, *A Theory of Semiotics* (Bloomington: Indiana University Press, 1979), 167.

15. Keir Elam, review of my *Great Reckonings in Little Rooms*, in *Times Literary Supplement* (7 March 1986): 250.

16. Edmund Husserl, *Ideas: General Introduction to Pure Phenomenology*, trans. W. R. Boyce Gibson (London: George Allen and Unwin, 1952), 136.

17. Dufrenne, *Phenomenology*, 10.

18. Patrice Pavis, *Languages of the Stage: Essays in the Semiology of Theatre* (New York: Performing Arts Journal Publications, 1983), 56.

19. Gaston Bachelard, *The Poetics of Space*, trans. Maria Jolas (Boston: Beacon Press, 1969), 215.

20. "I am too much of a phenomenologist to like anything but appearances to my own measure" (Roland Barthes, *Camera Lucida: Reflections on Photography*, trans. Richard Howard [New York: Hill and Wang, 1981], 33).

21. Roland Barthes, *Mythologies*, trans. Annette Lavers (New York: Hill and Wang, 1972), 56.

22. Barthes, *Camera Lucida*, 26.

23. David Stewart and Algis Mickunas, *Exploring Phenomenology: A Guide to the Field and its Literature* (Chicago: American Library Association, 1974), 26.

24. Sokolowski, "Theory of Phenomenological Description," 23. For an excellent overview of the role of metaphor in phenomenological description, see David Levin's "The Poetic Function of Phenomenological Discourse," *Phenomenology in a Pluralistic Context*, ed. William L. McBride and Calvin O. Schrag (Albany: State University of New York Press, 1983), 216–34. On the question of metaphor as description, see George E. Yoos, "A Phenomenological Look at Metaphor," *Philosophy and Phenomenological Research* 32 (1971): 78–88. On the more general matter of metaphor as an aspect of philosophical language, see James M. Edie, *Speaking and Meaning: The Phenomenology of Language* (Bloomington and London: Indiana University Press, 1976), 151–94.

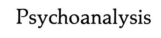

Psychoanalysis

Introduction

Contemporary critical theory has been very "critical" of the notion of a unified, autonomous subject—which has presided as the reigning conception of the self since Descartes first proclaimed that fundamental knowledge was knowledge of the conscious self reflecting on itself reflecting. For performance studies this destabilization of the self, or devaluation (rather like currency), has been extremely fruitful, raising a number of pressing questions about texts, characters, actors, and spectatorship. Perhaps because performance directly involves corporeal individuals breathing, thinking, speaking, moving in front of other similar organisms, the intimate questions of human behavior have always been central to performance. This "intimate geography" of the self concerns interior private experience—conscious and unconscious desires, expressions, significations. The attempt to get outside of the ongoing process of this interior living in order to see and understand how it happens constitutes a metatheatrics of everyday life: trying to see the invisible, to make present what seems to be eternal absence, to affirm what may be undecidable.

Sigmund Freud is, of course, the foundational theorist of psychoanalysis.[1] Freud viewed human life as a materially grounded struggle to ensure survival. The pleasure principle, in dialectical relationship with the reality principle, determines individuals to forgo personal gratification in order to obtain other goals, ultimately connected with survival. If one denies or delays gratification too often or too systematically, neurosis ensues. Sometimes, however, a creative tension comes from this displacement of psychic energy—a creative tension that may produce works of art, knowledge, civilization itself.

In many ways human beings are divided within themselves. Freud divides the subject into unconscious and preconscious in *The Interpretation of Dreams* (1900) and into id, ego, and superego in his later work (e.g., *New Introductory Lectures* [1933]). For the earlier Freud the unconscious was the seat of primary processes seeking gratification in the most direct way possible, while the secondary processes of the preconscious mediated and delayed gratification, responding to cultural determinants by insisting on circuitous ways of achieving pleasure. Since the two reacted to one another, the unconscious as well as the preconscious (and of course the conscious) was materially grounded in culture. In his later work Freud tended to stress the overlap between conscious and preconscious and to describe the id as pure drive for pleasure, uncontrolled by cultural prohibition. The ego is the seat of adjustment to the reality principle, and the superego is a kind of bank of repressions and taboos which also functions as an image of the ideal other, usually based on the father. The preconscious and the ego (and in earlier Freud the unconscious) are engaged in producing symbolic activities such as sublimation, displacement, and dreamwork, all aimed at synthetic pleasures when direct pleasures are forbidden.

We have certain basic needs that are mediated by our dependence on a "family" who meets these needs in infancy; enter the oedipal crisis. Since children are learning language at about the same time that they discover sexual difference, sexuality and language become intertwined. The child must learn how to negotiate the desire for the mother (source of direct pleasure, e.g., the breast) over and against the authority of the father. Simultaneously, he or she must learn the symbolic order, the determinate network of social roles that are legitimated by society and authorized by the father. Repression of desire is thus the price for successful socialization.

While this semiotization of the psyche was only implicit in Freud, Jacques Lacan significantly modified the intimate geography under discussion through his insistence that the unconscious is structured like a language.[2] Bringing a semiotic and an anthropological analysis to traditional Freudian categories, he saw that sublimation, transference, and dreamwork were all aspects of signification. In addition, Lacan also brings to bear the marks of the existential thinkers in France who wrote so prolifically about human alienation. Freud, while explaining that human beings did not have access to all parts of their "selves," was still not given to ruminating on the dark night of the alienated soul who wished to recover and become congruent with its *en soi* but who was condemned to the positioning knowledge only of the *pour soi*. I am referring to Jean-Paul Sartre's distinction between the in-itself, that essence of self which is inert, unknowable, only definitive at death, and the for-itself, which is basically consciousness, a transparent contentless self that seeks to "know" the in-itself in order to be whole. This notion from *Being and Nothingness* seems to brood over certain aspects of the psychoanalytic project as configured by Lacan, intensifying the aspects of loneliness and loss.[3]

Psychoanalysis provides a dramatic scenario for the subject, and both Freud and Lacan figure it as a journey that leads to differentiation: first of self from other, then of male from female; finally the self joins sociality, becoming again connected to a social body while at the same time retaining a fundamental difference from it.

In a way all psychoanalytic narratives are romantic; they are based on nostalgia for a prior state of bliss—connectedness, wholeness, undifferentiation—which birth inevitably interrupts. The path of human life is toward ever more acute detachment from this primordial experience of unity. The infant first feels connected to the mother's body and to all objects in its environment then gradually comes to recognize the difference between itself and Other, while also having its body colonized into territories or zones of various (cultural) functions; pleasure zones, to be sure, but here, not there, and thus already within a regulating economy, which will also teach "so much," not more, and now, not then. Achieving consciousness is itself possible only when accompanied by a loss of fundamental self-knowledge. One enters language and conceptual categories only by forfeiting direct contact with internal needs and drives. Self-knowledge is bartered for social knowledge, and social knowledge is always coercive.

For Lacan, transcending Freud, the oedipal crisis is not just a crisis of the body; it is refigured as a social crisis of language acquisition. The fear of castration is not just the fear of losing or lacking the male appendage; it is the fear of not having the power to participate in the male-determined logic of signification. The phallus, symbol of this ruling order rather than of the physical penis, is the sign of the paternal realm of agential activity, which conforms to the law of the Name of the Father, to use Luce Irigaray's terminology.[4] Thus, the biological and familial relations of the child to its world become intimately tied to the sociality of which he or she is an inevitable effect. The conflation of physical and familial with social and juridical produces the intimate geography of the self, a geography of inner splintering and outer alienation.

For female subjects this narrative is obviously especially distressing. Since the Symbolic Order into which human beings are inducted is a phallocratic one, women cannot really enter discourse. Irigaray, one of Lacan's students and an important feminist critic, writes that "the feminine occurs only within models and laws devised by male subjects. Which implies that there are not really two sexes, but only one. A single practice and representation of the sexual . . . this model, a *phallic* one, shares the values promulgated by patriarchal society and culture, values inscribed in the philosophical corpus: property, production, order, form, unity, visibility . . . and erection."[5] For male subjects there is some sorrow in the separation of internal knowledge from social knowledge at the stage of language acquisition/oedipalization, but for female subjects there seems to be only exclusion from the symbolic order: castration comes home with new meaning—what is lacked is the means to signify. We will come back to this dilemma after examining a particularly suggestive aspect of Lacan's psychoanalytic account of the subject.

The "mirror stage" might be seen as one of the Lacanian enhancements of Freud which is especially useful for performance theory. Here the individual child first "sees" his image (always "his" with Lacan) outside of himself and identifies this "picture" of a unified self as itself. It is, however, utterly Other, an ideal self, a culturally constituted self (since by now perception too has been conditioned). The child will henceforward desire to recapture and to be congruent with this image of self, will also mourn for the lost self, which is forever absent. While this "loss" is not the primordial loss (which is the moment of sexual differentiation in the womb, when the child is unable to "be" both female and male), it is a central experience of self-alienation and also of desire for the Other, even at the same time that this Other is a version of the self.

This notion of the mirror stage has been especially useful for performance studies because of the analogy between it and the mimetic mirror of the stage, which reflects representations of the self and its world. The social construction of the representations leaves no doubt that the reflection in the stage mirror is also Other, not identical to any viewing selves, and not "accurate" about any so-called human nature but, rather, a sociocultural construct of ideal images. Besides demystifying the nature of such representation, however, Lacan provides an explanation of why spectators are in thrall to these representations, why their desiring apparatus is set in motion each time a stage mirror simulates this experience. Many of the basic theoretical questions of dramatic theory touch on this psychological process: the role and purpose of aesthetic experience, the Aristotelian notion of catharsis (what happens to spectators when they view), the Platonic/Aristotelian debates about the danger/good of mimesis, the question of presence in acting theory (or, more historically, the association between the character of the actor and the character of the play), the modern discourse on the role of empathy, and the benefits of alienation in receiving representation. All these topics can be seen as intimately linked to the paradigm of the mirror stage, and, while psychoanalysis provides other pertinent areas of investigation for performance theory, this section concentrates its major focus on the issue of identification and its role for the subject.

Specifically with reference to performance, a number of feminist theorists have drawn on psychoanalytic ideas. Sue-Ellen Case, Jeannette Savona, and Rosette Lamont, in addition to Elin Diamond, have all contributed to this discourse.[6] Barbara Freedman, attempting a recuperation of theater for disruptive feminist activity, recently writes, "The performative side of theatre emerges here as a process of staging the disturbance and reversal of the gaze. . . . A theatrical model is thus ideally suited to the project of decentering and subverting fields of representation that face postmodern theory."[7]

Male performance scholars have also contributed to psychoanalytic discourse. Herb Blau maintains much the same relationship to psychoanalysis as he does to Marxism: simultaneous engagement and distance.[8] Timothy Murray recently delivered the keynote address "Drama Trauma: Psychoanalysis and the Epistemology of Tragedy" at the Twelfth Annual Themes in Drama Conference in Riverside, California. (Madness in drama was the theme.)[9] Mohammad Kowsar has provided an application of Deleuze/Guattari's "schizoanalysis" to Danton's Death and Marat/Sade.[10]

The two essays included here respond to the Freudian/Lacanian account of identification in opposite ways. Seeing tragedy as a genre caught up with the condemned-to-fail desire for the desire of another, Kowsar provides a gloss on Lacan's reading of Antigone, which stresses the beauty of the deliberate choice to pursue such desire beyond the laws of man and god. Ethical, perhaps because finally disinterested, this choice is figured in Antigone as noble and sad. To desire the desire of another is to move beyond good and evil to encounter the attraction/repulsion of "the thing"—the always-other that is simultaneously threat and supreme object of desire—and to see the self positioned as object in another's subjective narrative. Kowsar's central question, answered through Lacan's reading of Freud and Sophocles, is: "How, then, can a subject's desire, so unmindful to mere pleasure, so overwhelmingly self-destructive, nevertheless appear so beautiful, as it does when it converges on Antigone?"

For Diamond, however, concerned to rescue something constructive from a narrative of desire which has been destructive for women, the process of identification can be liberatory and productive of social change to the extent that the subject processes new possibilities and redefines its own positionality through multiple identifications, each of which has a different potential within a given historical context. In her essay Freud is revisited to critique Lacan for his insufficient historicity. Lacan's lugubrious lingering on lack is replaced by an emphasis on multiplicity and appropriation: the self becomes richer through its identifications, the subject position more varied. Noncongruency is a positive effect of the split subject, rather than a negative; desire leads the way to the experience of more, not less— abundance, not lack. Diamond here returns to the psychoanalytic narrative for a reconsideration of the process of signification. Her account offers an escape from the tyranny of the symbolic. In this she joins Julia Kristeva, among others, who theorize alternative modes of signification. (I do not mean that Diamond embraces Kristeva's particular theory because, in her emphasis on the "maternal" aspects of the semiotic, Kristeva's theory is dangerously essentialistic, something Diamond eschews.)[11]

Kristeva describes a dual signifying process, semiotic and symbolic, as constitutive of the human subject. The symbolic is the paternal order, recognized in signification by such attributes as consciousness, rationality, closure, fixity. The semiotic is the maternal flow of possibilities, resting on the play of the repressed contents of the unconscious through drive charges or impulses that retain within the signifying process the earlier prelinguistic stage of connection to the mother. While signifying practice requires "thetic" activity (Kristeva uses Husserl's term for the predictive judgment endemic to the signifying process), this activity is countered or matched by a hetero- geneity that is always in excess, disruptive, wandering, a kind of blurring or fuzziness. The activity of the semiotic disposition unsettles meanings, is finally a questioning moment that unseats the settled subject and con- stitutes a subject-in-process/on trial. Kristeva thus opens up a role for the feminine in signification—the feminine reenters discourse through its hetero- geneity, its negativity, its deconstruction of the thetic.[12] Psychoanalytic theory here intersects semiotics and deconstruction (compare the section entitled "Semiotics and Deconstruction" in this book).

Both Kristeva and Diamond essentially redefine the meaning of the subject's encounter with Otherness; for both it is part of a productive dissonance as well as a potential source of alienation. Quite apart from assigning male and female "dispositions" to the subject, as Kristeva does, what is important here is to recognize the difference in emphasis, value, and meaning placed by feminist theorists on the experience of differenti- ation, identification, and otherness—as opposed to traditional male inter- pretations of these experiences. In this regard Kowsar and Diamond offer essays that illustrate the gendered differences typical of psychoanalytic approaches.

J. G. R.

NOTES

1. For a review of Freud and subsequent treatments of psychoanalysis, see Terry Eagleton, *Literary Theory: An Introduction* (Minneapolis: University of Minnesota Press, 1983), chap. 5. Kaja Silverman is especially helpful in contrasting and comparing Freud with Lacan in *The Subject of Semiotics* (Oxford: Oxford University Press, 1983). See also *The Language of Psychoanalysis*, ed. J. Laplanche and J. B. Pontalis, trans. Donald Nicholson-Smith (New York: W. W. Norton, 1973). To begin reading Freud, one might start with *A General Introduction to Psychoanalysis*, trans. J. Riviere (London: Liveright Pub. Corp., 1953); or *Civilization and Its Discontents*, trans. J. Riviere (London: Hogarth Press, 1930).

2. Lacan himself is somewhat difficult to read because his major work comes in the form of a series of lectures, some of which are translated and published, although Lacan was deliberately unsystematic. *Ecrits: A Selection* (trans. Alan Sheridan [New York: W. W. Norton, 1977]) is the most available text; *Feminine Sexuality* (ed. Juliet Mitchell and Jacqueline Rose, trans. Jacqueline Rose [New York: W. W. Norton, 1982]) provides another source, with excellent introductions by Juliet Mitchell and Jacqueline Rose.

Gilles Deleuze and Felix Guattari have also made an important theoretical contribution with *Anti-Oedipus*, which is their critique of Freudian categories, or rather an attempt to read political, economic, and social "economics" in terms of the flow of desire produced through "desiring-machines." I regret the absence of an exemplary essay in this secton (*Anti-Oedipus*, trans. Robert Hurley, Mark Seem, and Helen R. Lane [Minneapolis: University of Minnesota Press, 1983]).

3. Trans. Hazel E. Barnes (New York: Simon and Schuster, 1956).

4. Luce Irigaray and Julia Kristeva, both of whom have been previously cited, join Hélène Cixous and Catherine Clément to constitute the major French feminists who respond to Lacan. An important secondary source is Alice A. Jardine's *Gynesis* (Ithaca: Cornell University Press, 1985).

5. Luce Irigaray, *This Sex Which Is Not One* (New York: Cornell University Press, 1985), 86.

6. See recent essays by these women in *Feminine Focus*, ed. Enoch Brater (New York: Oxford University Press, 1989).

7. Barbara Freedman, "Frame-Up: Feminism, Psychoanalysis, Theatre," *Theatre Journal* 40, no. 3 (October 1988): 393–94.

8. In addition to his contribution to this volume, see his two most recent books, *The Eye of Prey* (Bloomington: Press of Indiana University Press, 1987); and *The Audience* (Baltimore: Johns Hopkins University Press, 1990); see also "The Audition of Dream and Events," *Drama Review* 31, no. 3 (Fall 1987): 59–73.

9. 16 February 1990.

10. Mohamad Kowsar, "Analytics of Schizophrenia: A Deleuze-Guattarian Consideration of Buchner's *Danton's Death* and Weiss's *Marat/Sade*," *Modern Drama* 27, no. 3 (September 1984): 361–81.

11. For an account of some of the possibilities and problems with Kristeva's theory, see Drucilla Cornell and Adam Thurschwell, "Feminism, Negativity, Intersubjectivity," in *Feminism as Critique*, ed. Seyla Benhabib and Drucilla Cornell (Minneapolis: University of Minnesota Press, 1987), 143–62. In the context of feminist performance theory, see my article "Feminist Theory and the Problems of Performance," *Modern Drama* 32, no. 1 (1989): 48–57.

12. In the signifying economy of poetic language, according to Kristeva, "the semiotic is not only a constraint as is the symbolic, but it tends to gain the upper

hand at the expense of the thetic and predicative constraints of the ego's judging consciousness." Thus, the artistic text become an especially privileged site of struggle where the social code is destroyed and renewed (*Desire in Language* [New York: Columbia University Press, 1980], 137).

The Violence of "We": Politicizing Identification

Elin Diamond

In "Sorties" of *La Jeune Née* (*The Newly Born Woman*) Hélène Cixous takes a brief moment to describe the dangerous pleasures of identification. She strategically takes up the hysteric's position, presenting her own history as a random series of passionate identifications: She is Penthesileia, Achilles, an eagle, a vulture as well as all of Freud's hysterics and their narrative counterparts: "I have been all the characters Dora played, the ones who killed her, the ones who got shivers when she ran through them, and in the end I got away, having been Freud one day, Mrs. Freud another, also Mr. K . . . , Mrs. K . . . and the wound Dora inflicted on them." Cixous's gender crossings are of course intentional: she is performing the originary bisexuality Freud attributed to all hysterics. In a later section, speaking as it were in her own voice, Cixous recapitulates the delights of the process: "One never reads except by identification. But what kind? When I say identification, I do not say loss of self. I become, I inhabit. I enter. Inhabiting someone at that moment I can feel myself traversed by that person's initiatives and actions."[1] With her usual metaphoric accuracy Cixous is describing the mimetic pleasure of identification—becoming or inhabiting the other on stage or in spectatorial fantasy, I stand in for her, act in his place. Such acts are distinctly imperialistic and narcissistic: I lose nothing—there is no loss of self—rather I appropriate you, amplifying my "I" into an authoritative "we."

The link between identification and the authoritative "we" figures into reception theory since Plato and Aristotle, although students of drama and performance, are more familiar with the unrigorous "we" of the traditional critic who projects her/his subjective impressions and analyses on all members of a theater audience—as in "we feel [Hamlet's] remorse" or "we understand [Hedda's] frustration." One of the effects of such rhetoric (in which the emotions and thoughts of others are assumed to follow our model) is a factitious but powerful sense of community which buttresses but also conceals the narcissistic claims of the critic. Interweaving discussions of Plato and Aristotle with psychoanalytic theory, I will suggest that the dominance of dramatic realism (mid-nineteenth century to the present) has promoted this preemptory "we" and that phenomenological criticism, while it offers invaluable insights into theatrical consciousness, heightens the problem by eliminating historical contradiction. I will end by suggesting that psychoanalysis, read through a feminist materialist lens, might suggest a different kind of reception. Though identification seems to promote the annihilation of difference—and thus violence to the other—it may also suggest the problematizing of models that support such violence. Rather than upholding a strong unitary subject that constrains others to become copies of ourselves, identification might be understood as a psychic activity that destabilizes the subject. Rather than upholding a social status quo, identification might be seen as producing historical contradiction. Because it bridges the psychic and the social, identification has political effects, which leads me to suggest that perhaps we (feminists and others involved in cultural critique) might begin to politicize our identifications.

Let's return briefly to Cixous's statement: "One never reads except by identification. But what kind? When I say identification, I do not say loss of self. I become, I inhabit. I enter. Inhabiting someone at that moment I can feel myself traversed by that person's initiatives and actions." A deconstructive writer, Cixous characteristically both affirms and unravels her pleasure. On the one hand, she presents the terroristic thrill of standing in for the other; on the other hand, the terror of "feel[ing] traversed" by her. Throughout Freud's many discussions of identification this doubleness reigns. Identification never loses the horrific aspect of introjection—the primitive incorporation of the rivalrous other as with the Ur-father of the Mosaic tribe. Even in his more schematic formulations in, for example, *The Ego and the Id* (to which we will return), the little boy who wants "to be his father and take his place everywhere"—especially in the mother's bed— is eventually haunted by imagined bodily violence: castration. Cixous herself links identification to violation. In a parenthetical aside following the above citation she writes: "Actually that feeling of being traversed by the other disturbed me. When I was younger I was afraid because I realized I was capable of mimicry." Being the other, feeling the other traversing her, abolishes distance and difference, that which is necessary to establishing the boundaries of the self. To identify is apparently not only to incorporate but to be incorporated. To be radically destabilized.

Plato's loathing of the theater begins here: not only is the drama a third-order copy of Ideal Forms, but the mimetic performer and the spectator who vicariously participates in such imitations also produce the instability of unitary identity which constitutes membership in the Republic. What is refreshing about reading the sections of *The Republic* which deal with recitation and performance is that Plato never underestimates desire, both its inaccessibility to consciousness and its relationship to power. Giving himself up to the performance, identifying with the pain of the tragic hero, the male spectator risks loss of control when he leaves the theater. "Womanish" or clownish activity at performances might lead to a breakdown in gender roles or disciplined behavior in society. "Few," says Socrates, "are capable of reflecting that to enter into another's feelings must have an effect on our own: the emotions of pity our sympathy has strengthened will not be easy to restrain when we are suffering ourselves."[2]

Plato would understand the definition of *identification* offered by J. Laplanche and J. B. Pontalis in *The Language of Psychoanalysis* because it confirms his worst fears: "The psychological process whereby a subject assimilates an aspect, property, or attribute of the other and is transformed, wholly or partially, after the model the other provides. It is by means of a series of identifications that the personality is constituted and specified."[3] Identification, then, is psychological, that is, partially unconscious and not immediately accessible to rational scrutiny; this alone makes it something to be feared. More troubling, the subject takes on, takes *in*, features of the other and is "transformed," wholly or partially, in conformity to that model. This implies that the subject has no prior identity; rather, identity is formed in the crucible of identifications; the subject is "specified," distinguished from all other subjects not by his immortal soul but by his identifications, and these identifications stem not from disciplined reason but from desire, what Plato calls a "weakness in our nature" or a "trick of illusion."

Aristotle tamed such fears, making imitation the central and enabling heuristic of the developing human. As he writes in chapter 4 of *The Poetics*, we learn by imitation. At the theater of the great tragedians who offer us exemplary characters and emplotments of their suffering, we spectators become uplifted through the purgative actions of catharsis. We identify with the ideal and universal referents the performers embody. I use *we* advisedly. Ironically, Plato's wish for spectatorial discipline in spite of mimesis becomes possible in Artistotle *because of* mimesis. Pity and fear may appear to be private emotions, but they are registered collectively, as the final effect of spectatorial identification with the heroes of tragedy—those, as Aristotle is at pains to tell us, who are good but flawed, whose actions are probable if horrific, in other words, who invite an edifying identification from the audience. These constructive models of human behavior are good for communal health, offering heroic Olympian images (as Nietzsche said of this Apollonian art) in which Greek male spectators would find reflected back to them the superiority of their culture. (Of course, women and slaves would not appear in these heroic mirrors; as Aristotle notes in chapter 15 of *The Poetics*, their cultural referents—actual women and slaves—were too inferior for stage life.) For Aristotle, then, identification combines catharsis with social discipline: built on the universally upheld virtues of consistency and causality, catharsis adjusts its spectators to accept the truth and rightness of the hero's destiny and the play's action. In such acceptance the spectator reaffirms his place—his role—in the polis.

It is the universalizing model of truth, the reinscription of a social status quo, the enforcing of cultural discipline, which has brought mimesis under critical scrutiny in this century. For self-reflexive modernists and contemporary culture critics mimesis was/is not merely a morphological issue, proposing likenesses between made objects and their real or natural counterparts, between characters and real performers. Mimesis is profoundly epistemological, a way of knowing and judging the truth. It sets up normative rules of inclusion and exclusion by which a text, be it the text of a play or the text of someone's behavior, may be judged. Not surprisingly, mimetic discourse, when it emanates from spectators and critics, tends to enlist such comforting abstractions as nature, truth, reality, humanity, human nature, and common sense in its "analyses." Such abstractions tend to mystify the critic's identifactory investments in her objects of study—that is, the appropriation of authors and texts to her perspective so that they become extensions of her own desires and ideologies. (Isn't this precisely what black feminists have correctly found wanting in the texts of some white feminists? Because she was identifying with her own whiteness—and by extension identifying whiteness with female sexuality— Judy Chicago did not see that of all the plates in her Dinner Party creation the Sojourner Truth plate lacked a vagina. Because she was identifying with Eurocentric models of literary authority, Ellen Moers did not see that she had excluded women of color—except Lorraine Hansberry—in her *Literary Women*, a foundational text of Anglo-American feminism. What is revealing in both cases is that, as feminists, Chicago and Moers thought they were producing new sites of "we"—a we that empowered women, but in fact excluded many women.)[4]

Dramatic realism produces precisely those conditions that allow for the creation of a smugly self-identifying spectator/critic and the creation in the late nineteenth century of an aggressively bourgeois we. Not only does realism tirelessly play out the oedipal family drama, it also follows the curve of Plato's condemnation of mimesis but inverts the valuation. The lifelike stage sign reinforces the epistemology of an objective world, for the referent is not simply implied; it is reaffirmed in the activity of reception. Which is to say, realism is more than an interpretation of reality passing as reality; it produces "reality" by positioning its spectators to recognize and verify its truths. Naturalizing the relation between character and actor, setting and world, realism's project is always ideological, drawing spectators into identifications with its coherent fictions. It is through such identifications that realism surreptitiously reinforces (even if it argues with) the social arrangements of the society it claims to mirror. My favorite example—a deceptively simple example—comes from an account of the reception of Hedda Gabler in London in 1891. In her memoir, *Ibsen and the Actress*, Elizabeth Robins, who premiered the role of Hedda and other Ibsen heroines, quotes one of her female spectators: "How should men understand Hedda on the stage when they didn't understand her in the person of their wives, their daughters, their woman friends? One lady of our acquaintance, married and not noticeably unhappy, said laughing, Hedda is all of us."[5] Here identification creates "we" with a vengeance. Not only does the spectator see and reproduce a real relation between sign and referent, she achieves through her identification a satisfying group identity; through Hedda the spectator becomes "all of us." By her capture in this illusory mirror she eliminates difference between herself and others and, at least on the surface, any sense of historical contingency.

A phenomenological account of reception would applaud the woman spectator's rapt involvement with Hedda as the essence of theatrical consciousness. Post-Husserlian phenomenology concerns itself with acts of perception which comprise both the particularity of a subject's perspective as well as the essence of the object perceived. The dramatic image—in this case, Robin's bringing to presence the fiction that is Hedda—allows the spectator to bracket empirical considerations and to see Hedda whole, as an "all" that expresses the truth of "us." That theater should be particularly receptive to phenomenological description is not surprising. Like Kant, Husserl understood phenomena as that which "appears to consciousness," but for the latter there was no "unknowable world behind the appearances"; what matters is what appears "in person"[6]—the performance, one might say, not the play. Husserl's famous reduction—wherein a transcendent subject suspends belief in a causally related, empirically organized world in order to focus on the specific ontology of the object—is analogous to the bracketed otherness of the theater space where, as Bert O. States puts it, "There is no ontological difference between the object and the image." Rather "theater ingests the world of objects and signs only to bring images to life. In the image, a defamiliarized and desymbolized object is 'uplifted to the view' where we see it as being phenomenally heavy with itself."[7] States's emphasis on perspective ("where we see it") and the beingness of the object-turned-image rehearses Husserl's famous dictum: philosophy must return "to the things themselves," beginning with a description of things as they appear to a particular consciousness.

Merleau-Ponty adds another element to phenomenological consciousness which is of particular importance to theater reception, and that is the lived presence of the body: "the word 'here' applied to my body does not refer to a determinate position in relation to other positions or to external co-ordinates, but the laying down of the first co-ordinates."[8] Rather than being an object *of*, the body anchors us *to* consciousness, and it is that particular embodied relation that brings to light the essence of the play's action and characters. The body-turned-image has, as Gaston Bachelard puts it, "an entity and a dynamism of its own . . . a direct ontology"; or, as States puts it, "philosophy in the theater must unfold itself, literally, as the thinking of a body."[9]

But suppose we turn down the intensity of the phenomenological spotlight and wonder what body is in view, what body is viewing? Can bodies either perform or perceive outside of the material markings of gender, race, or ethnicity? And can the mode of seeing which is called "phenomenological" be devoid of desire? Interestingly, when phenomenological methods are used to discuss theatrical identification both the desire and the material specificity of perceiving subjects tend to drop out.

Bruce Wilshire, for example, understands identification as a strong heuristic whereby spectators and actors explore the mimetic structure of all human relations: "Through the actor's deliberate identifications with and standings in we discover our largely undeliberate identifications-with and standings-in." In a nice turn of phrase he continues, "The actor models modeling, enacts enactment," which "reveals" to the audience "our involvements." For Wilshire, then, the spectator's identification with Hedda reveals her continuing identification with others, which the theater and its actors enact for her. She learns from Hedda that "my fellow human beings are a picture of *myself.*" Wilshire would not view this response as narcissistic or appropriative but, rather, as a means of achieving a transcendent wholeness. In this respect the phenomenological account of reception reinscribes the effects of dramatic realism, leaving in place the coherent subject/spectator while asserting "universal and enduring" conditions that undergird the humanity of the object (character). More problematic, the phenomenologist's perceptions denude both subject and object of historical specificity: "Great variability in their [the objects'] manifestation and intensity from culture to culture and age to age does not undermine but just the reverse, it undergirds their generality."[10] Similarly, Austin Quigley seeks a generalized universal enlightenment for his spectators, eliding any notion of gendered representation or reception, of power hierarchies within the apparatus of representation or within the historical context. He assumes instead that the spectators' "shared culture" and "shared humanity" will help them move from "temporary disorientation" to "subsequent reorientation," another way perhaps of linking identification with conventional models and cultural discipline. Of the contemporary theater phenomenologists, only States refers (though only once) to identification in the more problematic relation to subjective desire: "the actor is someone like us who consents to serve as the channel through which the poet's art can be brought out of the realm of imitation and briefly detained, *for our narcissistic pleasure*, in the realm of being."[11]

Would a psychoanalytic account permit the material specificity we hunger for? We might separate Lacanian and Freudian views of identification by proposing two distinct readings of the Hedda Gabler example. For Lacanians the married woman's capture by the image of Hedda would be explained by the narcissistic lures of the mirror stage which carry over from early infancy, through childhood, and into adulthood. Lacking controlled motor development, the infant sees its image in the mirror as a coherent whole, thus misrecognizes himself (the *hommelette*, or little man, is usually privileged here) as a complete autonomous Other. Introjecting this mirror image as an ideal ego, or identificatory model, he spends the rest of his life desiring versions of it—at, for example, Hollywood movies.[12] In Lacan identification, always in the register of the imaginary, is always narcissistic; the perceived other is always a version of me. Difference, contradiction are all occluded in the subject's initial and continuing capture in the mimetic mirror.

In Freud identification is also narcissistic but complicated by the very thing that Lacanian identification wants to leave out—namely, historical contradiction. Let me briefly review a number of relevant texts. In *The Interpretation of Dreams* (1900) identification is still linked to hysterical mimicry; it enables his patients "not only to express their own symptoms, but those of a large number of other people."[13] The hysteric—and this is surely Cixous's pose in *The Newly Born Woman*—will enter, become, inhabit because she wants to "play all the parts." In "On Narcissism" (1914) mimicry is replaced by the idea of substitution. This troubling and in many ways confused essay has drawn fire for its outrageous acts of naming: homosexuals are demonized because their love objects are not true others but only versions of themselves; women are denigrated because, like children and cats, they are incapable of forming attachments to others. What is crucial to this discussion is that here Freud associates identification with a decathexis of the object, a turning inward instead of outward toward the other.

In *Mourning and Melancholia* (1917) this turning inward is replaced by the notion that identification substitutes for losing the other. The ego introjects a lost object, which is then set up inside the ego and becomes a model of identification, thereby changing the ego. By the time he writes *Group Psychology and the Analysis of the Ego* in 1921 Freud will say that the ego is transformed by such identifications. In fact, in this essay he decides that identification occurs not only to compensate for loss, as in *Mourning and Melancholia*, but continually, throughout psychic life. We are continually taking in objects we desire, continually identifying with or imitating these objects, and *continually being transformed by them*. In other words, identification in Freud always works both ways: it is an assimilative or appropriative act, making the other the same as me or me the same as the other, but at the same time it causes the I/ego to be transformed by the other. What this suggests is that the borders of identity, the wholeness and consistency of identity, is transgressed by every act of identification.

The Ego and the Id is the famous 1923 text in which Freud remaps the topography of the psyche—the unruly id, the ego equated with "reason and common sense," and the proscriptive and disciplinary superego are all given their local habitations. Yet in this essay Freud affirms that identification is a constitutive part of psychic life: the process, he says, occurs in all phases of development, and "it makes it possible to suppose that the character of the ego is a precipitate of abandoned object choices and that it contains the history of those object choices."[14]

In other words, it would be impossible to conceptualize a subject in the process of identification who would not be engaged, however unconsciously, with the history of her identifications, which is at least partly the history of her psychic life with others. Moreover, the ego, which Freud uses interchangeably with the "self," is here conceived as an effect of continued transformation. He even writes an amusing dialogue between the ever-accommodating ego and the insatiable libido: "When the ego assumes the features of the other it is trying to make good the id's loss by saying 'Look you can love me too, I am so like the object.'"[15] And in this imitation of the Other the ego transforms and transforms again. Identification, says Freud, builds the character of the ego. Like all Freud's theatrical metaphors, this one emphasizes construction over essence. The ego, this representative of reason and common sense, is a theatrical fiction, permeable, transformable, a precipitate of the subject's psychic history with others. The humanist notion of identity as a model that the self enacts over time—that is unique, unified, coherent, and consistent—is belied precisely by the temporality, the specific historicity of the identification process.

Might we *situate* Elizabeth Robins's spectator, however, provisionally, in an identification process, not by reconstructing her imaginary, but by reimagining the highly gendered cultural context in which her identifications took place? In male Victorian accounts of spectatorship at Ibsen's plays women were accused of behaving like hysterics—not only entering into the passion and morbidity of fictional characters but, in fact, imitating them, passionately weeping into their handkerchiefs. Interestingly, in her own testimony of identification the woman spectator is laughing.[16]

For the governesses, schoolteachers, and married women who sat in these matinee audiences, aware of, if not contributing to, the contemporary scandal of women's suffrage, perhaps the destruction and suicide of Hedda Gabler validated their antipatriarchal tendencies. The Married Woman's Property Act of 1882 (nine years before the play's London debut) gave women the right to their own property after marriage, but these and earlier reforms hardly introduced social and sexual equality between genders. (Is this why she was laughing?) Thinking of Ibsen's 1891 spectators as historical subjects, as bourgeois consumers yet not full citizens, complicates the coherence of a spectatorial we. Is it possible to think of the spectator's self-affirming "all of us" as an empowering social fantasy? Might we think of her identifications as having a distinctly political edge? With her laughing reference to "all of us" the spectator is perhaps suggesting a new social arrangement, one that transforms *her* more than it defines or circumscribes Hedda. Viewed this way, she does not reinforce a social status quo but, arguably, describes a new if temporary social space—a space occupied by women in matinee performances of Ibsen's plays. It seems ridiculous from our vantage point to see realism in the service of revolution, yet cultural subjects, entering into and inhabiting powerful roles, are conceivably capable of transformation.

Only by attending to the projections, the narcissistic, self-transforming fantasies of historical subjects can we begin to imagine a politics of identification—a politics that dismantles the phenomenological universals of transcendent subjects and objects, that places identity in an unstable and contingent relation to identification, and that works close to the nerves that divide/connect the psychic and the social.

NOTES

1. Hélène Cixous and Cathérine Clément, *The Newly Born Woman*, trans. Betsy Wing (Minneapolis: University of Minnesota Press, 1975), 99, 148.

2. Plato, *The Republic*, trans. Francis Cornford (New York: Oxford University Press, 1966), 338 (X-605).

3. J. Laplanche and J. B. Pontalis, *The Language of Psychoanalysis*, trans. Donald Nicholson-Smith (New York: W. W. Norton, 1973), 205.

4. See Alice Walker, "One Child of One's Own: A Meaningful Digression within the Work(s)—An Excerpt," in *All the Women Are White, All the Blacks Are Men, but some of Us Are Brave*, ed. Gloria T. Hull, Patricia Bell Scott, and Barbara Smith (New York: The Feminist Press, 1982), 37–44.

5. Elizabeth Robins, *Ibsen and the Actress* (London: Hogarth Press, 1928), 18.

6. John F. Bannan, *The Philosophy of Merleau-Ponty* (New York: Harcourt Brace Jovanovich, 1967), 8.

7. Bert O. States, *Great Reckonings in Little Rooms: On the Phenomenology of Theater* (Berkeley: University of California Press, 1985), 35, 37.

8. Maurice Merleau-Ponty, *The Phenomenology of Perception*, trans. Colin Smith (London: Routledge and Kegan Paul, 1962), 100.

9. Gaston Bachelard, *The Poetics of Space*, trans. Maria Jolas (Boston: Beacon Press, 1958), xii; States, *Great Reckonings*, 133.

10. Bruce Wilshire, *Role-Playing and Identity* (Bloomington: Indiana University Press, 1982), 14, 16, 26, 69.

11. Austin Quigley, *The Modern Stage and Other Worlds* (New York: Methuen, 1985), 63. States, *Great Reckonings*, 128, my emphasis.

12. Cf. Laura Mulvey, "Visual Pleasure and Narrative Cinema," *Screen* 16, no. 3 (Autumn 1975): 6–18.

13. Sigmund Freud, *The Interpretation of Dreams*, trans. James Strachey (New York: Avon), 183.

14. Sigmund Freud, *Standard Edition of the Complete Psychological Works* (London: Hogarth Press, 1971), 29:29.

15. Ibid., 29:30.

16. Robins, *Ibsen*, xx.

Lacan's *Antigone:* A Case Study in Psychoanalytical Ethics

Mohammad Kowsar

What is an ethics of psychoanalysis? Where in the province of meta-psychological investigation should an avowed Freudian reside to conduct ethical interrogations that are in keeping with the canonical assertions but also demonstrative of sufficient alterity to justify a claim to novel ethical findings? In league with such inquiries, the analysis of Sophocles' *Antigone* by Jacques Lacan clearly professes a complex mission, to explore an ethical territory commensurate with the interests of psychoanalysis—a close scrutiny that entails scanning the entire field from a philosophical and onto-logical perspective—and to show with conclusive evidence that the Freudian project, when put to a rigorous test, will always identify human action, in its relationship to desire, as something that will invariably shelter a veiled meaning.[1] Pursuing Lacan's subtle thoughts on *Antigone* is to glean uncommon aesthetic insights germane to those characteristics that authorize the appearance of the tragic hero and to the peculiarities that shape tragic action. It is in fact quite astonishing to observe how far Lacan's ethical inquest manages to penetrate beyond the age-old controversies surrounding the problem of tragedy. Lacan's astute appraisal of the Sophoclean text is indebted to his particular methodology, one that has received extensive recognition from scholars who are active in numerous interdisciplinary studies. Concomitant with his psychoanalytical practice, Lacan's procedure upholds the primacy of "language" in conformity with the linguistic theories of Ferdinand de Saussure. The seminar on *Antigone* exposes the reader not only to an unprecedented interpretation of the classical text but also to a set of theoretical formulations that test and expand Freud's own ethical and aesthetic principles.

In the comparative examination conducted by Lacan the thematic concerns of Sophocles' *Antigone* seem to keep covenant with Freud's terse declarations in *Beyond the Pleasure Principle:*

> It may be difficult, too, for many of us, to abandon the belief that there is an instinct towards perfection at work in human beings, which has brought them to their present high level of intellectual achievement and ethical sublimation and which may be expected to watch over their development into supermen. I have no faith, however, in the existence of any such internal instinct and I cannot see how this benevolent illusion is to be preserved.[2]

This text signals a definite parting of company with the positive and constructive characteristics of libidinal economy. As an ontic declaration, its anti-telic stance is unmistakable. With a firm voice Freud describes the human experience as something aimless, thereby revoking any claim to transcendent vitalism, confirming the irrationality of instincts, and challenging the immanence of "humanist" ethics.

Lacan's study of *Antigone* (under the rubric of an ethical consideration) corroborates the truth of this passage and proceeds to redefine the nature and functions of ethics. But what remains hidden in Freud's discourse, what Lacan wants to add to render Freud comprehensible, is the central role of language in an irrational universe. The truths asserted by Freud cannot reach the light of day if somehow the facticity of language (including the very important ambiguity lodged at the foundation of all words) is to be left out of psychoanalytical investigations. Furthermore, this kind of neglect will engender further miscalculations at the level of ontological and meta-psychological considerations. Lacan observes that Freud is fundamentally aware of aporia, but, since the original model for the aporetic condition exists in the signifier-signified dyad applicable to all words, and because Freud does not interrogate the structure of the unconscious according to a Saussurian formula, it remains the French psychoanalyst's task to illuminate the meaning of the Freudian texts and to remain loyal to the truths of those texts at the same time.

Lacan draws our attention to the fact that Freud has left numerous clues discouraging a reading that would endow his works with the attributes of "humanism." According to Lacan, psychoanalysis is decidedly not a humanism. If anything, psychoanalysis is about language, and it is in the famous song of the Chorus in *Antigone*, the celebrated first stasimon,[3] generally regarded as the great eulogy to man, that Lacan will point out an aggregate misreading, both at the level of word interpretation and at the level of content. The chief instances of misunderstanding issue from insensitivity to the actual words of the text, a general tendency to embrace simple explanations whenever the Sophoclean text chooses to remain intentionally ambiguous. It is obvious that Greek words and phrases, in Lacan's translation, follow an unexpected logic, yielding a radically different perspective on the tragic context.

An initial glance at what Lacan locates in the Chorus's statements can serve to confirm the radicality of Lacan's interpretation. The Chorus, Lacan insists, informs us that man is far from being unequivocally artful and resourceful: that his universally acknowledged impotence in face of death—an insuperable limit—gives rise to the "creation" of new "maladies" (S VII.321), a fact that negates the more generally accepted interpretation, which celebrates his ability to discover cures to illnesses; that his craft and contrivance is a mandate that drives him only sometimes toward good but just as often toward evil; and, finally, that man's best interest lies in making an absolute distinction when it comes to the advocacy of the laws. The laws of the land are separate from *dike*, the law ordained by god, and, in fact, mixing these laws entails a serious risk (S VII.322). Sophocles has organized things in such a way that Antigone, in any case, will have to play her fate not against *dike*, which Lacan assures us she understands only too well, but against the chthonian dictum of *ate*,[4] yet another order quite distinct from terrestrial laws and the separate justice of the gods.

A closer observation of Lacan's detailed analysis of the first stasimon proves that his reading parts company with the normative studies of this text at every turn. Initial contention is raised with the statement that expresses: "man faces no future helpless." Lacan points out that here Sophocles is employing an oxymoron—a figurative usage that he often repeats in the text—with the combination of the contradictory words, *pandaporos aporos* (meaning "of many resources" and "resourceless," respectively). Such a syntactic operation generates enough ambiguity within this particular statement to jettison the implied notion of man's all-encompassing ingenuity before life's trials (S VII.320). Furthermore, the Chorus is quite clearly indicating in the same statement that man's contact with the future is characterized by a detour implicating *ouden* (nothing). Sophocles, in other words, associates "nothing" with that which crosses the path of man in the course of time; this is not at all the same as supposing that there are "no future" obstacles that will remain unchallenged by the skillful man. According to Lacan, the Chorus is saying that sometimes artfully and sometimes artlessly this man "goes toward nothing that might befall him" (S VII.321). More precisely, "he goes *pandaporos*, cunningly, and *aporos*, always screwed. He always misses the point. He manages to have all of his cleverness backfire on him" (S VII.321).

Lacan persists in showing us that Sophocles is neither a humanist nor a rationalist. In fact, the Sophoclean genius is most evident whenever he depicts human destiny as a phenomenon that is wholly guided by the aporetic rules that govern the unconscious. And to acknowledge aporia is not only to maintain a healthy respect for death but also to adopt a "creative" attitude toward somatic and psychic illnesses. Accordingly, the Chorus in *Antigone* indicates very clearly that man has not really found cures to incurable maladies but, instead, "created" a science of maladies with which he can establish a structural relationship between aporia and death. "He has found no resolution for death, but he finds formidable devices, the maladies he has created" (S VII.321). This is a "heck of a device," argues Lacan, particularly when it becomes clear that the Chorus is actually stating that man "escapes into *impossible maladies*," rather than "*escaping from maladies*" (S VII.321).

The Chorus also informs us that it is true that invention and creation are the handmaidens of a certain cleverness, but aporia is not to be subjugated by craft, nor can there be a hope of canceling the unknown. To the extent that the unknown is ubiquitous, the sagacious, hence the clever, man, must accede to a law that will direct ethical human aspiration, not with hope, nor hopelessly, but "beyond all hope" toward both good and evil (S VII.321).

Lacan believes that in the universe of *Antigone* there is only one law that functions this way: it is neither a social law nor a divine law but the law of *ate*. The law of *ate* designates a borderline dimension, a space that is radically free of all material and worldly attachments. It is the beyond-the-pale sphere of a living death. From this position the subject can tell the difference between the laws of the state and those associated with the gods with absolute clarity. It is as if the subject located in this space is endowed with a penetration of vision which is supremely tragic, which is also to say that it is tantamount to ethical lucidity. The subject positioned here is illuminated but cannot be gazed upon for too long, for the radiance, the very truth that the subject evokes, even though it emanates from a place of beauty, is so overpowering that it causes the beholder to blink, to turn away, registering, paradoxically enough, beauty's other effect— pain. Thus, the famous first stasimon provides distinct juridical definitions and consigns (to human action) unavoidable ethical consequences.

Tragedy, ethics, and death—these are the topics that interest Lacan in *Antigone*. There is, nevertheless, a moment in the proceedings which strikes Lacan as pivotal for understanding the coordinate of desire, that is the role of eros as it structures the tragic thrust of the play. Eros is evoked during an entire choral ode (the third stasimon), but it is the startled reaction of the Theban elders to Antigone, who has now become the embodiment of love—even at this very crucial point when her death sentence is presented to us as something irrevocable—which is (for Lacan) the most telling incident of the play. The Chorus will say that "desire is made visible" (*imeros emarghes*) in the eyes of the young bride.[5] Antigone, without any doubt, is the agent by which desire is made so apparent, with such overwhelming brilliance. Antigone, Lacan insists, occupies a "place of desire inasmuch as it is the desire for nothing, the relationship of man with his lack of being" (S VII.345). At this place she appears as a "mirage," but impossibly and transcendentally lovely; here she dazzles.

The scope of Lacan's argument is really very vast. Undaunted, he mixes ethical and aesthetic categories and proceeds to prove to us that he is following Freud himself, who had already established that beauty and pleasure can never enter an agreement innocently, that whatever accord drawn up between them must perforce pay lip service to the laws of good and proper conduct, on the one hand, and respond to the radical demands of death's reality, on the other. Freud's seminal study in neurology, *The Project for a Scientific Psychology*, in 1895 had alluded to the complex ethical questions raised by psychoanalysis in some detail.[6] Lacan is convinced that the explication of the *Project*, wherein Freud had claimed that the "initial helplessness of human beings is the *primal source* of all *moral motives*" (318), is imperative, if the ethical implications of a literary masterpiece such as *Antigone* (and its relationship to psychoanalysis) is to be fully appreciated.

The values of good and bad, never intended by Freud to be judged on some ideal plane, first appear problematic for humans at the level of sentience, that is, in that prethinking, pre-articulating state when pleasure and unpleasure tend to navigate between perception and consciousness, a psychic activity effected in response to external and internal stimuli. Part of the aim of the neurological project was to study the impact of the environment upon the organism, the drawing of a relationship between the activity of object phenomena upon a subject that must find some manner of receiving external stimuli without being swamped, overwhelmed, obliterated. It is no secret that the organism, for Freud, must always negotiate within an economy of pleasure and unpleasure, that its survival depends upon shielding and protecting itself against the onslaught of too powerful excitations. It is precisely the surplus excitation directed toward the organism (although endogenous stimuli also exercise considerable coercion within the cellular and intercellular sphere) which must be controlled and ultimately derouted. What "neurones" manage to implicate in the process of defense and control is an entire operation involving the actions of "stimulus, substitution, conversion and discharge" (295); these are sentientious categories that are implicit in all human perceptions. The quantity of energy displayed by the nervous system in discharge moves toward a homeostasis, conforming to the "principle of neuronal inertia"; this is none other than the choice of a path of least resistance, *a flight from the stimulus*" (296); but total adherence to this kind of "neuronal inertia" is abandoned when "endogenous stimuli," which "have their origin in the cells of the body," such as "hunger, respiration, sexuality," press upon the organism to discharge (297). To deal with these demands the nervous system cannot withdraw but must preserve enough energy at the level of the secondary process for what Lacan calls "the conservation of life" (S VII.58).

Part of Freud's general hypothesis delineating the neurological field attests to the presence of "perceptual neurones," which are fundamental to consciousness and to thought. Gròsso módo, perceptual neurones, in relationship to the primary process, produce fantasy and hallucination, and in relation to the secondary process they activate thought and speech. Lacan's reading of Freud, one that is always responding to the role of speech and language in psychoanalysis, would inform us that a connecting chain exists between perception and consciousness which extends from "the most archaic unconscious to the articulated form of the word by the subject," that is, something that "passes between *Wahrnehmung* (perception) and *Bewusstsein* (consciousness), or "between skin and flesh" as it were (S VII.64). The mediating unconscious provides a structural opposition that is in itself a sign-making apparatus, intimately involved in processes engaged in the accumulation and discharge of psychic energy. The process that Freud designated as *Bahnung* (facilitation) is for Lacan none other than a release unto reality and "something that is . . . very close to language," or its "articulation" (S VII.46–47, 50).[7]

Thought production lodges itself firmly at the site where the unconscious exercises its influence over the ego (*Ich*), an ego that must define itself in relationship to the exterior world. In *Project* Freud is succinct on this matter: "The aim and end of all thought-processes is thus to bring about a *state of identity*, the conveying of a cathexis . . . emanating from outside, into a neurone cathected from the ego" (332). Furthermore, Freud's neurological definition of the ego corroborates its mediative and structural role: the ego can be identified as "a group of neurones which is constantly cathected and thus corresponds to the *vehicle of the store* required by the

secondary function" (323). In this respect the ego acts as a regulative apparatus, exercising "inhibition," that is, "influencing the repetition of experiences of pain and of affects" (323). Lacan acknowledges that the ego
deploys a system of checks and balances comparable to the secondary
function activity, but he insists that the ego itself is "for a great part
unconscious" (S VII.62).

The unconscious is intimately involved in the process of cognition—
that which connects perceptual identity with thought identity. Achieving
identity for a subject can be approximated through a circuitous and divided
path known as reality testing, which is none other than the subject's attempt
at cognition of real objects. At this point Lacan can suggest that that which
connects perceptual identity and thought identity, that which suffers substitution, undergoes conversion, and is released with discharge is *das Ding*
(The Thing). For Freud the thing had appeared in the realm of perception
as *Sachvorstellung* (Thing-Presentation); in the domain of thought as *Wort-
vorstellung* (Word Presentation). Lacan, however, is conscious of a third
coordinate for *das Ding*, which is related to both modes of presentation
but also stands autonomous and apart—in a position best described as the
"absolute Other of the subject that must be recovered" (S VII.65). It is in
fact Freud's endeavor to define the process of cognition with the example
of the *Nebenmensch* (a fellow human being) which will allow Lacan the
occasion to locate his own and what he considers Freud's central intended
distinction, the category of *das Ding*:

> Let us suppose that the object which furnishes the perception resembles
> the subject—a *fellow human-being*. If so, the theoretical interest [taken
> in it] is also explained by the fact that an object *like this* was simul-
> taneously the [subject's] first satisfying object and further his first
> hostile object, as well as his sole helping power. For this reason, it is
> in relation to a fellow human-being that a human-being learns to
> cognize. Then the perceptual complexes proceeding from this fellow
> human-being will in part be new and non-comparable—his *features*,
> for instance, in the visual sphere; but other visual perceptions—e.g.
> those of the movements of his hands—will coincide in the subject
> with memories of quite similar visual impressions of his own, of his
> own body, [memories] which are associated with memories of move-
> ments experienced by himself. Other perceptions of the object too—
> if, for instance, he screams—will awaken the memory of his [the
> subject's] own screaming and at the same time of his own experiences
> of pain. Thus the complex of the fellow human-being falls apart into
> two components, of which one makes an impression by its constant
> structure and stays together as a *thing*, while the other can be *under-
> stood* by the activity of memory—that is, can be traced back to infor-
> mation from [the subject's] own body. This dissection of a perceptual
> complex is described as *cognizing* it; it involves a *judgement* and when
> this last aim has been attained it comes to an end. (*Project*, 331)

This text retains for Lacan the force of axiomatic truth. He endorses Freud's accentuation of the dual nature of the object as something that presents itself as both satisfying and hostile. This is to say that, when an object is perceived by a subject through the intermediary of a fellow human being, it guarantees not only the provisions for potential satisfaction but also an occasion for the subject to realize that his fellow human being is "other," situated on the outside, a stranger (*Fremde*), and, by definition, hostile.

Now Freud indicates with some clarity that the pleasure principle harbors in itself the energetic combination of pleasure and unpleasure. And in terms of the argument we have followed thus far this means that, whenever a subject's inclination toward an object is erotically charged, at a certain level of investment (cathexis) a second impulse, just as persistent, will appear to curtail hypertension and quantitative increase of excitement—one that exercises avoidance and recoil when anticipating the kind of overflow of psychic energy which can result in pain. Lacan wants us to realize that the conditions that breed hostility in the perceptions of the subject do not define themselves primarily by the rules of pleasure and unpleasure. In fact the split that accompanies the realization of the fellow human being as stranger is only asymptotic to the pleasure-unpleasure dyad; more to the point, it is found where a radical cleavage exists at the primordial level, where the self discovers himself to be other to the "Other," precisely where the Other appears to the subject as thing. And if the thing never appears independent of the primordial alienation that structures the relationship of the subject with the Other, any manner of ascertaining the facticity of the separation is conceivable solely by the articulated signs of language. In this sense the thing speaks, and quite often "it speaks"—in Lacan's evocation of Freud—"where it is least expected, namely, where there is pain."[8]

The thing acts as the signifying coordinate for the pain of separation, standing in the place of the lost object—the object of desire. It is incorrect to take the thing for a lost sign, because an affective relationship with it is always established. A subject projects and "conserves distance" with it (S VII.68), relating to its articulated expression of being from the place of the "prehistoric Other" (S VII.87). We are in the presence of a subject, as it were, that is standing disoriented between an I (as lack) and a Thou (overdetermined), seeking not so much a lost object, for the object is never really lost, but one that needs to be found again.[9] What is always sought by the subject, guided by unconscious desire, is the duplication of an original experience of satisfaction. Refinding, in this case, is tantamount to an impossible attempt at relocating desire at the original site of integration with the object. Desire's aim is to repeat itself, and repetition by its very nature introduces a condition that can never be exactly the same. Alterity and difference accompany the irretrievable nature of the original condition.

Still, a desiring subject will demand, as Joël Dor has succinctly pointed out, that desire be heard.[10] This demand is projected to the Other by language, desire's messenger. But between the original substance of the demand and the formal message—that is, the mediating factor—a separation occurs born of naming the "unnameable."[11] Demand's entity appears only as the lack of coincidence between desire's essence and what must perforce be named. But this structure of incommensurability is the chief measure of the Other's real inaccessibility to the subject's desire. This is why the Other, forever lost and essentially unavailable to him, will be seen by the subject as a thing, an entity whose articulated desire (twice removed from his own) he will emulate. Progressively, the subject's demands for recognition, conditioned by the Other's desire, received and acted upon by way of a language that is always representative of the Other's desire, will find itself in a necessary relationship with the thing but also conserving greater and greater distance from it. A subject's desire, thus, is defined by this distance (gap) that separates it from the thing. The thing, following this logic, exists as lack, or as absence. The ontological status of the thing is a being-in-lack (*manque à être*), and as such it appears both as object of desire and the object that causes desire.[12]

For Lacan the thing negotiates with the real (that is, the real in its entire structural complexity, including the ever-present reality of a displaced object that must be recovered). For the thing to enter any kind of relationship with the real it must enter the signifying chain of language as part of an arrangement supervised by the pleasure principle. Here language is entrusted with the task of deploying patterns of communication by way of metaphor and metonymy. But the thing, being essentially aporetic, a "no thing," will present itself always as something else or "Other thing" (S VII.143). Hence the condition of the thing's detachment (being split) from the objects that represent it. Through language, therefore, the subject will enter a relationship of desire with a fellow human being, but it is not through a fellow human being that desire will confer to the subject a basic understanding of his alienated condition. If anything, the fellow human being will project image models and impose rules of conduct which are anathema to desire's objectives. The fellow human being, wearing the many guises of reason, common sense, and Christian charity, will always conduct himself with preternatural cruelty; it is normal for the fellow human being to inflict pain, a pain that harks back to that initial cleavage within the subject's psyche when it first reached out to assume an identity through the mediation of the primordial Other and was thwarted forever, but introduced, instead, to the order of the thing.

Consequently, of all dictums, none is more nefarious than the law of "love thy neighbor," none more misleading, more enmeshing in the coils of servitude than the recommendation to love another as oneself. Lacan insists that Freud was "literally horrified by love of one's neighbor" (S VII.219). Because it was obvious to Freud (in Lacan's view) that what the Other is obstacling at every turn is the royal road to desire's satisfaction, perpetually denying any share of happiness that the subject might consider attaining. In this respect the Other's arsenal is replete with persuasive moral arguments, none deadlier, in fact, than the notion of the "good," which serves as a discourse that can contain, interrogate, organize, and structure the entire dynamics of pleasure and unpleasure. In this sense the good will always appear as the juridical right to "deprive others," and it is from this position that the Other will erect a "powerful wall before the path of our desire" (S VII.270).

For Lacan ethics and aesthetics are linked by the common denominator of desire and share analogous correspondences. The function of the good consigns to pleasure a limit and a beyond; the function of the "beautiful" is that which appears beyond the limit set by the good. In the person of Antigone, Lacan can identify for us the dialectics of beauty and desire, in the sense that desire manifests itself in its purest expression as something that is projected beyond human laws. Thus, Lacan reevaluates tragedy by identifying the central conflict of tragic action as "the effect of beauty on desire" (S VII.291).

This novel discourse does not cancel the technical terms associated with tragedy; in fact, pity and fear still play a role in the dialectics of desire, as does that particular notion of catharsis which is linked to the Dionysian *sparagmos*. But tragedy, for Lacan, is first and foremost a function of desire, and any kind of epiphany, with its concomitant pleasure, can be understood in relationship to a crisis that desire undergoes when faced with the challenge of crossing over "into another dimension" (S VII.288). Pleasure is located, according to Lacan, on this side (*deçà*) of "the fearful center of desire's aspiration," death—and Freud had said as much—on the other side, beyond (*au-delà*) (S VII.288). Between this side (where pleasure resides) and beyond (the place of certain death) there lies pity and fear. As passions, the functions of pity and fear are to fold back on the central image of desire and to modify the subject's psychic status with a single representation, which is the effect of beauty. Reverberating from Antigone, this sudden effect of beauty designates a "place" of "limits" (S VII.291). Furthermore, by marking a place of limits, Antigone's beauty will structure a relationship between this side and beyond. Beyond lies death; but this side, having experienced the effect of beauty, is no longer here, a place of the living, but a place for a life that not only anticipates death but also partakes in death. As such, the place of pure desire (associated with Antigone) is a zone that is circumscribed by two deaths: "death encroaching on the domain of life, life encroaching on death" (S VII.291).

In the text of Sophocles, Antigone is the unique tragic personality. Creon also suffers; but his suffering originates in a realm that is foreign to Antigone. The Chorus is probably alluding to Creon only when it advises against confusing the law of the land "with the *dike* of the gods" (S VII.322). To do so puts a character at fault. Creon is guilty in the sense that his judgment fails him; he is in error, and "hamartia" is applicable solely to him. But his hamartia cannot fuel a tragic experience. It is Antigone, and only she, who catapults the dynamics of this play into the realm of tragedy.

Hamartia has no real place in Antigone's personal project, nor is it, Aristotle's view notwithstanding, the central condition of tragedy. Antigone suffers neither pity nor fear, but she does distinguish between gods' laws, on the one hand, and civic laws, on the other. She realizes perfectly how Creon is paralyzed by the confounding mixture of two sets of laws. Her own choice to bury Polynices has nothing to do with *dike*, however. In fact, she can fully appreciate that *dike* would be offended by Polynices' shameful betrayal of Thebes, but she herself is not in any manner guided

CRITICAL THEORY AND PERFORMANCE

408

by the will of Zeus. This is to say that she is quite aware that gods do issue dictums that are sometimes comparable to and in the spirit of rituals and ceremonies conceived to uphold human respect for death and the dying, but in the matter of Polynices' burial the separate realms of civic and divine laws hold no power over her. What she must do is to cover the obscenity of an exposed corpse, that of her brother, precisely "for her brother" who has "passed on to the underworld," and "it is in the name of the most chthonian blood ties that she is opposed to the commandments of Creon" (S VII.322). Antigone's reasoning, Lacan admits, is at first glance somewhat cockeyed. She claims that a woman has absolutely no power over the conditions that provide her with brothers; when brothers die they cannot be replaced. On the other hand, chance puts no limits on the number of lovers, husbands, and children that a woman can acquire in a lifetime. Therefore, loyalty to a brother has the highest priority.

Lacan finds hidden sense in Antigone's strange argument. He shows that the key to her reasoning is in reference to "the matrix," the bond that connects her brothers born from an identical mother to "the same father, the criminal father," who is Oedipus (S VII.324). What is at stake is the "name" of a brother who is blood related. Specifically, it is a question of asserting his "being," now on the wane, his corpse having been left in the open, unburied. She cannot allow wild beasts (creatures without names) to desecrate the fallen body of Polynices. In other words, Polynices is her brother; he has had a name, and for her he is "unique." And to assert the integrity of his being is to recover her own being.

Lacan establishes that Antigone's seemingly inexplicable behavior emanates from the ambiguity that rests at the heart of desire itself. Desire can be expressed as a state of tension which supports, at its core, the problematics of being, or death-as-limit: this is the ontic issue that gives substance to being in the first place. Desire expresses itself primarily through flirtation with death. How, then, can a subject's desire, so unmindful to mere pleasure and so overwhelmingly self-destructive, nevertheless, appear so beautiful, as it does when it converges on Antigone? Through the resonance, brilliance, and "splendor" (éclat), says Lacan, of the "image" that Antigone projects at the crossroads of desire's interplay (S VII.291). Here, following a dialectics of libidinal investment, a desiring subject—one who is already operating within the symbolic field of language, one whose desires are ipso facto structured by language, and, finally, one who makes an elementary distinction between the self as subject and others as the Other—will always desire someone else's desire. In its simplest formulation the law of desire claims that what a subject most desires is to be recognized as "being" desirable by the Other.

The Chorus in Antigone, of course, does not understand all this. But looking at Antigone, catching the light of her resplendent eyes, it observes an image at once fascinating and "blinding" (S VII.327). Lacan imagines that the Chorus blinks. In that blinking of the eyes it is ascertained that Antigone, or rather her splendor, is not of this world. This is equivalent to saying that Antigone's desire is not of this world and, because she is at this moment, more than ever, the very incarnation of her desire, she too is elsewhere, at "the limit," at the very place where the Other finds legitimacy, that is, at the site of an originary metaphoric ordinance. In fact, this is the place of *ate*, or that zone where life and death encroach upon each other's dominions. Hence the chthonic nature of *ate*. Antigone's journey in life can be appreciated only with respect to the exigencies of *ate*. In its most specific manifestation *ate* (which, according to Lacan, is mentioned some twenty times in the Sophoclean text) is "part of a beginning and a linkage, an adversity of the Labdacides" (S VII.306). *Ate*, for Lacan, has a wider application than sorrow and misfortune. Antigone is bound to her family by *mereemna* (concern) and *mneema* (memory): it is "the *mereemna* of the Labdacides that pushes Antigone to the frontiers of *ate*" (S VII.307).

Responding as she does to *ate*, Antigone is forced to appear in a position that has the semblance of criminality, particularly vis-à-vis the laws of Creon. But a superficial distinction between good and evil, one that would relegate correct ethical behavior only to the beleaguered tyrant, is to consider only the sphere of "practical good." This is conceivable and adequate only in the limited universe of human laws. The fact remains that the good practiced by Creon will always malfunction where the stakes are "inhuman." Conversely, because Antigone can no longer stay in the world of common good, because her beauty is not a common beauty, because her desire is not normal, and, finally, because she harbors very little concern for life among the living, she "goes beyond human limits." Her desire "aims at a point . . . beyond *ate*" (S VII.306). Following the trajectory of Antigone's desire in this manner, Lacan takes us beyond the good, beyond pleasure itself, and introduces us to a transgression, which the Chorus at a crucial point of the play finds fascinating. We have already witnessed that beyond pleasure Lacan has also delineated the order of the thing as that painful truth that fascinates, even as it promotes a pure desire for death and nothingness.

The final component of Lacan's argument, the part that incorporates an ethical concern, revolves around a consequential assertion, to wit: psychoanalytical ethics acknowledges only one moral error, and that is when a subject withdraws before the claims of his desire (S VII.362). Antigone does not; she incorporates her desire. As noted, the Chorus is dazzled by *imeros emarghes* (desire made visible) and blinks. Lacan sees Antigone's overpowering beauty as a structuring phenomenon: "the function of the beautiful being precisely that which indicates the place of the relationship of man to his own death, and to indicate it to us in a dazzlement" (S VII.342).

Explaining tragedy as a consequence of the dialectics of desire, a kind of agonic relationship between Eros and Thanatos, is clearly a discourse in keeping with basic Freudian assumptions. Lacan's contribution to this familiar discourse is to raise the stakes of the dispute. He does it by compounding ethical and aesthetic considerations; by introducing ontological suppositions; by insisting on the primacy of language; and by analyzing the social being in terms of a unique process of acculturation.

Lacan is in agreement with Claude Lévi-Strauss when he asserts that cultures are founded on the basis of a fundamental, primordial law—the "interdiction of incest" between the child and the mother (S VII.83). The desire for the mother (the original most intimate other that the child will perceive as "friend"), forbidden as it is, is structured by the "relationship of the unconscious with The Thing" (S VII.83). In life Antigone is separated from her mother by this death-offering thing. More than any other character of fiction, Antigone identifies with the desire of her mother (the Other). "The desire of the mother is at once the founder of the entire structure, that which has brought to the light of day the unique offsprings, Eteocles, Polynices, Antigone, Ismene, but it is at the same time a criminal desire" (S VII.329). Of the two brothers one is clearly a criminal, a transgressor who occupies an integral role in the familial structure. The fabric of the entire lineage is, in fact, woven through the warps and woofs of incestuous desire. The Labdacides are time immemorially a criminal lot. As individuals they are pawns to a structural scheme that brands each family member guilty; each destiny is tied inextricably to the destiny of the other; and all are controlled by *ate*. Antigone recognizes this and assumes a terrible responsibility, that of deciding "to be the pure and simple guardian of the criminal as such" (S VII.329).

Death, the Chorus informs us, is the permanent mystery that will not be explained by man. Death establishes limits, and it is in response to its ubiquitous presence that human culture will establish a morality, an aesthetic, and an erotics. *Ate* is not, strictly speaking, death, but a primordial signifier that preexists in an articulated form like an arc of nothingness over the paranthetical moment of life. The good and desire find their dialectical counterparts in excess and crime; the beautiful finds its most resonant and startling image in its identification with death. Lacan believes that a chain of signifying associations leads from excess to crime and to death, key experiential categories prefigured in the overreaching arc of *ate*. Psychoanalytical ethics shows that beyond human laws a desire—which is unavoidably the desire of the Other—can break certain limits, and that beyond "morality" and "erotics" a desire can hope to aim at a point beyond *ate* (S VII.101).

Antigone sets herself very squarely in relationship to that which aspires to a point beyond *ate*. Decidedly, human life cannot long support such an aspiration; nonetheless, Antigone's tragic triumph is to "perpetuate, eternalize, immortalize this *ate*" (S VII.329). And in the end, within the dark Theban tomb, when Antigone has finally hung herself, the act of suicide itself appears merely as an inconsequential epilogue to an already completed tragic itinerary.

NOTES

1. Lacan's extended examination of the Sophoclean text appears in chapters 19 through 21 of *Le séminaire de Jacques Lacan, Livre VII: L'éthique de la psychoanalyse* (1959–60), text established by Jacques-Alain Miller (Paris: Editions du Seuil, 1986).

Henceforth, all citations from this book will appear as S VII, followed by page number in the text. All references to this work are my own translation.

2. Sigmund Freud, *Beyond the Pleasure Principle*, (1920) in *The Standard Edition of the Complete Psychological Works of Sigmund Freud* (London: Hogarth Press, 1955), 18:42.

3. See Sophocles, *Antigone*, trans. Elizabeth Wyckoff, in *Complete Greek Tragedies*, vol. 1, ed. David Grene and Richmond Lattimore (Chicago: University of Chicago Press, 1954). Wyckoff's rendering of the song is fairly representative of the typical reading of this text by English translators. The passages relevant to Lacan's argument are as follows:

Many the wonders but nothing walks stranger than man.
. . . this clever man.
He controls with craft the beasts of the open air,
walker on hills. . . .
Language, and thought like the wind
and the feelings that make the town,
he has taught himself, and shelter against the cold,
refuge from rain. He can always help himself.
He faces no future helpless. There's only death
that he cannot escape from. He has contrived
refuge from illnesses once beyond all cure.
. . . Clever beyond all dreams
the inventive craft that he has
which may drive him one time or another to well or ill.
When he honors the laws of the land and the gods' sworn right
high indeed is his city; but stateless the man
who dares to dwell with dishonor. Not by my fire,
never to share my thoughts, who does these things. (170–71)

Lacan, who translates directly from the Greek, also cites the French translation of Robert Pignarre; see Sophocles, *Théâtre Complet* (Paris: Flammarion, 1964), 77. Wyckoff and Pignarre show great similarities in their renderings of the Greek text.

4. That *dike* is translatable to such concepts as "compensation, legal proceedings, justice" leaves little room for contention; see F. E. Peters, *Greek Philosophical Terms* (New York: New York University Press, 1967), 38. The meaning of *ate* sustains greater ambiguity; in his *Myth and Thought among the Greeks* (Boston: Routledge and Kegan Paul, 1983), Jean Pierre Vernant provides a range of possible interpretations, including the following: *ate* is the grandchild of "Nux" (Night) and child of the evil aspect of "Eris," that is "Strife" (94); it is also associated with "aberrations of the mind" (75); moreover, it is "related to Darkness, Scotos . . . an image of the darkness which enshrouds the human spirit suddenly, enfolding it in shadows" (115); finally, *ate* appears as "oblivion and the spirit of error" and also as "criminal waywardness" that leads to "defilement, punishment, and death which result from this" (115).

5. In Wyckoff's translation, the sentence reads as follows: "Desire looks clear from the eyes of a lovely bride: / power as strong as the founded world" (*Antigone*, 187).

6. Sigmund Freud, *Project for a Scientific Psychology*, in *Standard Edition* (1966), 1:283–347; hereafter cited by page number in the text.

7. "Term used by Freud at a time when he was putting forward a neurological

model of the functioning of the psychic apparatus (1895): the excitation, in passing from one neurone to another, runs into a certain resistance; where its passage results in a permanent reduction in this resistance, there is said to be facilitation; excitation will opt for a facilitated pathway in preference to one where no facilitation has occurred" (J. Laplanche and J. B. Pontalis, *The Language of Psycho-Analysis*, trans. Donald Nicholson-Smith [New York: W. W. Norton, 1973], 157). Lacan suggests that *Bahnung* is misrepresented by the English *facilitation. Bahnung* should evoke the "constitution of a path of continuity, a chain . . . it can even be drawn to a signifying chain" (S VII, 49–50).

8. Jacques Lacan, *Ecrits: A Selection*, trans. Alan Sheridan (New York: W. W. Norton, 1977), 125.

9. Freud had written: "The first and immediate aim, therefore, of reality-testing is, not to *find* an object in real perception which corresponds to the one presented, but to *refind* such an object, to convince oneself that it is still there" (*Negation, Standard Edition* 19 (1961): 237–38.

10. Joël Dor, *Introduction à la lecture de Lacan: 1. L'inconscient structuré comme un language* (Paris: Editions Denoël, 1985), 116–17.

11. Ibid., 189.

12. Ibid., 188–89.

Critical Convergences

Introduction

In a volume such as this we can only begin to do justice to the wide variety of critical practices that have enriched the understanding of performance in recent years. Yet two essays in this section sum up the concerns of the book by demonstrating the interdependence of the various critical theories on one another and also by situating the practice of critical theory within its disciplinary and sociohistorical contexts. Sue-Ellen Case and Herbert Blau seem particularly appropriate to speak to the critical convergences that this volume has attempted to chart. As Case recounts in her introduction, she and Blau have shared part of the concrete history of this movement toward theory, and together they represent two generations of theater scholars whose work shapes and is shaped by critical theory. In his National Endowment for the Humanities (NEH) seminars for younger scholars and in her work as editor of *Theatre Journal*, Herbert Blau and Sue-Ellen Case have disseminated the information, the methodologies, and the attitudes of the new theory, making it possible for others to learn and to use it. Both reflect on their personal histories within the field—Case on her position as editor and executive within an academic professional organization, Blau on his role as a director within the structure of expectations of the rehearsal process.

They also bring together the dual foci of this book: the role of theory in performance analysis and the role of the theorist in the construction of performance meanings. Blau looks at the relationship between theatrical practice (acting, rehearsing, directing, watching) and the production of culture. Case looks at the relationship between the production of knowledge in the academy (writing, speaking, representing, advocating) and the production of culture. Both expand performance to its widest definitional limit: where, as Blau says, it gives the "lie to life." Underlying the two summary essays of "critical convergences," three common principles operate: (1) an assumed obligation on the part of theorists to historicize the ideological contexts of their arguments; (2) an even more rigorous responsibility (that they openly accept and acknowledge) to mark clearly their own positions in relationship to those contexts; and (3) the consequent necessity of a wide reading in—and a scrupulous but broadly conceived range of allusions to—diverse critical schools and approaches. These three principles may be said to characterize not only the two essays printed here but also the best work of many of the theorists thinking and writing about performance today.

This is not to say that different theorists apply the same principles in exactly the same ways. Whereas Sue-Ellen Case explores the historical antecedents to her own position within the institutional structure of theater studies today, Herbert Blau projects what Foucault has called a "history of the present" into the future. Both examine the moral or political implications of their positions and actions—Blau questioning the directorial invasion of the actor's unconscious, Case the placement of her work at a press with a colonialist history. Both want to share what they have learned, but neither will rest comfortably for long in an uncriticized position. Though they overlap at several points, the theoretical perspectives that Blau and Case hold emerge from contrasting discursive networks.

Blau alludes most frequently to the texts of the literary canon and particularly to those of high modernism, irradiated by psychoanalytic, Marxist, and Gramscian analyses, to question their premises and yet to draw sustenance from their energies. His brand of skepticism recalls that of Samuel Beckett, the undiscouraged fatalist who makes an appearance toward the end of his essay. Case most frequently alludes to the radical cultural critiques of postcolonial discourse, the New Historicism, and cultural studies, informed but not solely limited by Lacanian psychoanalytic, deconstructive, or feminist strategies of reading. Both Blau and Case move freely through diverse theoretical schools, but they also reject the unselective pluralism to which such freedom might succumb.

If Case and Blau exemplify the new theorists, they are also "threshholders," those who straddle the debates between modernism and postmodernism, participating by training, instinct, and politics in an eloborate shifting of positions. For politically committed scholars such as Case, the problem with postmodernism involves the absence of a "she," "this position [which] is unaccounted for in the Freudian paradigm of the primal scene, the Symbolic in Lacan, and 'writing' in Derrida." Elsewhere Case has written about the difficulty of using the new theory (particularly psychoanalysis) without getting caught in its apparatus—being chased, as she puts it, by the hellhounds of theory while trying to make a getaway with some useful tools. Completely aware of the patriarchal structure of narrativity and of the history of modernism as stories about (male) heroes in which women are relegated to the status of "Other," Case has little truck either with modernism's disguised teleology or with its colonial markings.

If Case is positioned in the postmodern with a nuanced respect for what is recuperable in the modern, Blau is firmly situated in modernism with a visionary command of the postmodern in its varied manifestations. Conversely, while he often uses Marx and Marxist categories to probe performance and the wider production of culture, he roundly critiques Marxist positioning, considering the Marxist *idea* to be so rife with contradictions that it has "soiled or invalidated whatever truth there was in the idea . . . almost everywhere in the world." And, while he cogently identifies the emptying out of meanings and signifiers, the commodification of all subjects, especially actors, and the mesmerizing simulacra of spectacle, these observations come from a voice resonant with a desire that it might be otherwise and a resilience about the struggle to ascertain what remains to be done, even if "no idea can be stable for very long, without contradiction, no less ideologically certified with an extended life expectancy."

Thus, in ending, Case and Blau bring us face to face with the original terms of this book: critical theory. Theory here is *critical* in the sense that it is crucial to performance: it offers the critiques that should always accompany human reflection and action, particularly under the conditions of crisis which mark the postmodern world. *Theory*, in this phrase, acts out its cognate relationship to *theater*: both derive from the Greek word for seeing and sight, and both suggest a continuous possibility to envision and to re-envision the world.

J. G. R. and J. R. R.

Theory/History/Revolution

Sue-Ellen Case

This essay began as a paper written to be delivered before the Association for Theatre in Higher Education (ATHE). Since the basis of my argument rests upon the notion that knowledge is material and social, produced within institutional alliances, I would like to retain that context in order to situate these ideas more literally within their specific alliances and conditions. The paper was part of a two-panel structure entitled "History/Theory/Revolution: The New Convergence." In a sense, the dynamics between those two factors—i.e., the intellectual project of a revolutionary convergence of history and theory vis-à-vis the institution of the academy—is the fulcrum for these ideas. To begin with, the very topic of the panels, the confluence of theory and history, was designed to address a competitive debate between the camps of traditional historians and contemporary theorists which has been raging in the various theater departments and within the ATHE itself for over a decade. The rhetorical use of the panel title was to persuade those warring camps that their scholarly methods and projects actually intertwine. The first panel was designed to address that convergence on its own terms, and the second panel was contructed to serve as critical applications of such a convergence to specific material. Within that overall construction, my project was to discuss the use of history within critical theory.[1] My discussion sets out to write within the new tradition, in the style of writing, as well as to address its strategies.

"Suddenly, An Age of Theory"

Elizabeth Bruss coined the subtitle of this section at the turn of the decade into the 1980s.[2] I think her phrase accurately represents the radical move to theory in the two decades of the 1970s and 1980s. The relatively minor part of her argument which serves as the base of my own is in the ac- knowledgment that the historical and material conditions of the late 1960s changed the workings of the academy and thus its theory:

> the decade in which these changes occurred was certainly one in which knowledge and the institutions responsible for gathering and dissem- inating it were faced with unwonted skepticism and even open attack, both for the uses to which research had been put and for those to which it had not. Charges of irrelevance on the one hand, and of ideological contamination or even wholesale appropriation for corrupt and inhuman ends, on the other, were hardly to be met by the usual appeal to disciplinary purity and technical efficiency. . . . One can pick out easily enough the factors that promoted this condition . . . coop-

eration between the academy and the military in covert military operations and an overtly unpopular war . . . and the problem of a new
heterogeneity of ethnic heritage and race and class erupting into what
had been the small and traditionally restricted world of higher
education.[3]

In other words the political activism on the streets and the campuses
in the late 1960s slowly bored its way down into the methodology and
epistemology of the disciplines themselves. That activism brought new disciplines on campus, such as ethnic studies and women's studies. It also
produced a generation of graduate students who divided their time between
demonstrating on the streets and studying for graduate seminars, which
met in the homes of striking professors who refused (for draft registration
reasons, among others) to teach on campus. I was learning a combination
of new criticism and traditional scholarship in the living room of Ruby
Cohn by night and joining her on the strike line by day. At the same time
I was living in the notorious Haight/Ashbury. Soon after that, I joined
Cohn, Robert Corrigan, and Herbert Blau for the founding years of California Institute for the Arts. Thus, in my twenties, I participated in the
integrated spectacle of the close reading of avant-garde texts (Beckett), the
performance of experimental theater, student strikes, LSD trips, and the
simultaneous (for me) founding of a counterculture and of a new school
designed to integrate the arts. The chair of my former department, Barry
Witham, has similar memories, as does my feminist theory colleague, Elin
Diamond. I am not merely reminiscing here, but illustrating that there is
a material, historical foundation for the change in the disciplines—not only
in the sense of the official history of the institutions but also within the
experiences of a generation of graduate students, for whom scholarship and
political activism were necessarily intertwined. These people are now associate professors, department chairs, editors, officers in the national organizations, etc. Their history is inscribed in their work. It is through this
history that the word *revolution* became appended, in the title of the panels,
to theory and history. The change in theory and history is linked to the
recent period of activism on and about university campuses.[4] This is not
to imply that the convergence of theory and history is necessarily generational, nor determined solely by history. I would simply suggest that this
revolutionary dynamic from the 1960s is at play within the radical alteration
of scholarly structures.

The rise of contemporary critical theory, then, began in response to
a historical and social challenge to epistemology and notions of ontology
as they had been produced in the academy. Ultimately, these events challenged liberal humanism itself—the residence of value in the arts. Critically,
the rise of feminist and ethnic critiques of the universal subject of humanism
disrupted its hegemonic voice. Historically, humanism began to be perceived
within its own historical alliances with imperial practices—specifically,
within its role in British colonial practices.[5] Thus, its own history of colonial
collusion began to mark its claim to "eternal, universal" values. Together,

the historical and critical critiques challenged concepts of aesthetic value to include the subjects that had been excluded and to investigate inclusionary/exclusionary principles. In this way the material critique of the academy as the site of production of knowledge spread to include the material productions of aesthetic value and history. Beyond the academy and the crisis of the 1960s the national and political uses of history—the history of history—marked its operational principles. The "revolution" in history and theory, then, began with a similar historical challenge, and the nature of this challenge tied those scholarly pursuits to actual production practices both within institutions and within the operating assumptions of the disciplines themselves. The sense of social uprising in the streets carried over into the changes in the academy, mandating a "sudden" change—the revolutionary dynamic that broke violently with traditional assumptions and energetically produced a new basis for reading and writing.

In a sense this forging of intellectual and institutional practice around these issues of federal intervention, ethnicity, and gender continues to redefine areas of study and the academy. A recent cover of the *New York Times Magazine* (1 April 1990) featured a portrait of Henry Louis Gates, Jr., billed as "Black Studies New Star." Along with Gates's accomplishments in publishing, the article within attends to his hiring requirements, his salary, and other material consequences of his scholarship. Gates represents the simultaneous radicalization of studies and institutional practices which began in the 1960s. His success rests on the radical break and the forging of a new kind of discipline, along with his precise understanding of how hiring practices coincide with epistemology. What conservatives brand as "entrepeneurial" in the successful manipulation of the academy by women and, in this case, an African American is really the refinement of revolutionary convergence that began in the 1960s.

Meanwhile, Back at the ATHE

To return now to the institutional site for the production of these thoughts on convergence, I want to recall here the title of the panel for which these ideas were gathered, "History/Theory/Revolution: The New Convergence," as inscribed with the history of the 1960s and the changing demographic student population, and as addressed to the ATHE. Perhaps the most significant aspect of the ATHE, as a production site, is its drive to become a representative organization of the discipline of theater in colleges and universities. Rising from the ashes of the erstwhile American Theatre Association (ATA), this newly reconfigured organization must (re)construct its claim that its members, its panels, its standards, its awards, and its guidelines somehow represent the profession. Moreover, this association is organized along liberal democratic lines that construct a representative governmental structure. This type of organization and its goal have a trickle-down effect, casting panelists within its conventions in a kind of representative role as well. Theoretically, I could tease out the implications of this kind of representation in discourse, using Gayatri Chakravorty Spivak's notion of *vertreten* from Marx—that is, how a representative is part of a chain of substitutions culminating in the executive force.[6] In other words I could trace how the executive functions in this organization for which my talk is written actually impel theoretical displacements in my text.

One literal illustration of this bridge from the executive to the representative panel member would certainly be my own membership on the board of the ATHE at the time of the panel—a position contingent upon my role as editor of its official journal—*Theatre Journal*. The journal had been under attack from the vice president of publications and a certain contingent of traditional theater historians for its seemingly exclusionary theoretical bias. Answering the charge that we did not publish history, I had repeatedly argued that we did indeed publish historical articles but perhaps not what they considered history. Thus, I was quite aware of representing my own executive position on the panel. I was also aware of how representational politics played out through the composition of the panel, as I read along with Marvin Carlson and Thomas Postlewait, respected members of the history contingent. In fact, the composition of the panel seemed itself a rhetorical image that signified executive force through national organizations (American Society for Theatre Research [ASTR]) and, in the case of Carlson and Postlewait, their own home institutions. In speaking, I noted this executive element, along with the represented ratio of men to women (2:1) and historians to theorist.

To move on to the hermeneutic question raised by this representative position, it might be formulated: what kinds of displacements in the text of the talk were occasioned by this representative site of its delivery? First, the point of attack for the historical/critical convergence did not spring from my labors in the feminist fields—ordinarily my methodology and area of research; rather, my identity in the ATHE, my institutional identity, displaced my scholarly and overall political position. Further, this effect, known in new historicism and critical theory as the institutionalization of knowledge, became the discourse of configuring the convergence.

By this point in this article I realize this process of foregrounding the institutionalization of knowledge is a bit like Rebecca's letter in *Our Town*, which is addressed to Grover's Corners; Sutton County; New Hampshire; United States of America; Continent of North America; Western Hemisphere; the Earth; the Solar System; the Universe; the Mind of God. I suppose the operation of situating discourse reads something like that, but without naturalizing the hierarchies as Rebecca's taxonomy does. Yet, at this point in the scholarship there is no longer the sense that knowing is promiscuous and can float, like Ivory soap, 99.01 percent pure of its material circumstances, nor that its critical assumptions and structures are at any time free from these concerns. In feminist critical theory these kinds of considerations arise within the politics of location.[7] The critiques by women of color and Third World women have forced critical discourse to admit heterogeneity at its base and to find operating principles that are inclusionary.[8] The politics of location at all times, then, foreground differences and accommodate them into the theory-making process. In practice, this leads the critic to note, simultaneously, the representative message in the site of representation (the composition of the panels, for example, in ethnicity and gender) and in the structures of theorizing. The politics of location also operate simultaneously within the foregrounding of the critic's own personal situation and the social codes, practices, and institutions that intersect her personal situation.

My executive position as an editor of a journal extended out into the critical traditions reflected in the convergent articles the journal had sought to publish: the critical application of the theories of Derrida, Althusser, Foucault, Lacan, Raymond Williams, Terry Eagleton, de Lauretis, Silverman, Hortense Spillers, Bakhtin, and Gramsci, and others. Institutionally, these theories became executive in the changes they wrought in the market of publication. They occasioned the founding of new journals with names and directions such as *Sub-stance, Semiotexte, Praxis, Telos, New German Critique, Women and Theatre, Genders;* special issues such as "'Race,' Writing, and Difference," "Displacing Homophobia," "Body/Masquerade," and my own "Theatre and Hegemony"; and new series in the presses such as *Theories of Representation and Difference* (Indiana University Press), *Gay and Lesbian Theory* (Columbia University Press), and *New Accents* (in the erstwhile Methuen Press).

A new readership was formed with a new expertise in the contemporary shifts in scholarship. This market, in turn, created a new sense of what an editor was looking for, what could get published, and, finally, what looked good to college councils and other tenuring bodies. New publication practices were not necessarily genre specific; did not necessarily distinguish between pop culture and so-called art; mixed historical strategies and critical ones; published authors and topics that crossed disciplines; and encouraged the discourse of topics and identities that were hitherto banned from "polite" academic scholarship. In other words the institution of publication and its consequent retrofitting of tenuring values also marks the material production of this convergence. Thus, the generation of New Historicists and critical theorists emerged. These are today's Foucauldian archaeologists, or Geertzian ethnologists of culture, with a feminist and ethnic critique impacting on their applications.

Looping back into the writing of this paper, this critical/publishing apparatus has so altered the sense of representation, and thereby performance, that this paper on "theater," in an anthology claiming a more traditional sense of genre, can focus on the production of knowledge at the site of the academy as performance. The "fourth wall" of critical language has become the opaque mesh of social practices—a performance in and of itself. The inclusive flow of the politics of representation can no longer be successfully contained by fourth walls, stages, or theaters themselves. The site of the Symbolic, the mirror of art, begins in infancy (Lacan) and plays on the body and within the individual's performance in discourse—moving from the three-act structure to the Primal Scene.

At Last, the Primal Scene

I have become aware that something like a narrative keeps haunting my discussion of this convergence. It's as if something happened in the 1960s and is marching through time. In spite of the deconstructive mode, operating here through the politics of location (when Lenin wrote "two steps forward and one step back" he did not realize he was also describing the new writing style), remnants of the tracing of influence and a developmental strategy seem "loose" in the discourse. When I seek to discover what fosters this impulse to narrativize I keep returning to the formulation of "convergence" itself. I can only imagine the convergence of critical theory and history as something like a scholarly primal scene. In other words it's like watching your parents "do it."

The primal scene is not a bad metaphor for this convergence in that it marks the social gendering of the types of knowledge, and here I mean the feminization of theory and the masculinization of history. Theory, in its proximity to the shifting strategies of interpretation, is cast in a role of "soft" and feminized knowing, whereas traditional history, in its proximity to "hard" fact, is masculinized within patriarchal funding and tenuring considerations. The metaphor of the primal scene also configures seduction into the scholarly enterprise, that is, the Lacanian dynamic of desire/split subjectivity in the Symbolic. And, finally, this metaphor foregrounds the bipolar, and heterosexist, imprint on the notion of convergence itself—that I must understand how "opposites attract." I am not sure that I personally take much pleasure in that text.

The primal scene, however, is not about my pleasure, in that sense, but positions me as one who watches. As a critic, watching this convergence of theory and history, I am infantalized before coupling structures of authority, both excited and afraid, while displacing like mad. The authority invested in history and theory always infantalizes the one who dares to manipulate them, while also investing in her some of their authority. But in this convergence the metaphor lifts the critic out of the onanistic pleasures of the single discipline to witness their coming together, marking in this writing the workings of the unconscious and thus destabilizing that which pretends to know. In this way the traditional notion of critical writing— that it moves by rational development—gives way to writing as an itinerary of displacements.

The "I" of the author, then, is both brought into the critical writing and banished into the unconscious. While the Freudian/Lacanian psycho-analytic critique controls much of this understanding of how theory/history convergence works as a primal scene, the notion of writing depends greatly on Derrida.[9] What I am glossing over, however, in order to utilize Derrida and Lacan here, is their configuration of this process exclusively within the father-son dyad. While I have gleefully inserted the feminine pronoun, making my authorial identity operable in the paradigm as a "she," this position is unaccounted for in the Freudian paradigm of the primal scene, the Symbolic in Lacan, and "writing" in Derrida. Accustomed, as I am, to operating in drag, I won't stop here, though this really is a stopping point. My institutional alliances have committed me to discussing this convergence as a positive coupling that is fruitful. I will attend to its progeny soon. But this institutional commitment once more overcomes my feminist critique, which at this point would disallow continuing to valorize the convergence because the structures beneath it are patriarchal.

On the bright side of things let me, then, while still claiming the feminine pronoun but operating in drag, celebrate the deployment of a metaphor itself. When Heiner Müller privileged Kafka's metaphors over Brecht's distanciated truths he asserted that it was because metaphors register a proximity: one does not deploy a metaphor until one can see the whites of their eyes. Metaphors are not like Brechtian Enlightened, transparent knowing that betokens an objective distance from the object of study, and from the movement of history. Rather, metaphors register the complicated, compacted truth of the moment. Metaphors, instances of convergence themselves, attest to complication and the potential of contradiction.[10]

Deploying a metaphor of the coupling of history / critical theory as the primal scene does not move the former term into the realm of the latter. Although in the past terms of literary discourse resided solely within the realm of the critical, within the new convergence it is the reassessment of history as discourse which "weds" the two fields. Foucault described history as an archive of discourse, "that is to say, the accumulated existence of discourse," thereby constituting the making of history as "the analysis of discourse in its modality of archive."[11] This acute awareness of the operations of discourse in the constitution of critical theory and history has created numerous strategies and reflexivities in confronting or even defining the cultural artifact which are characteristic of these new convergences. The use of metaphor is one; the theorizing of narrativity is another.

While the metaphor of the primal scene enables a postmodern description of the convergence, it is the deconstructive critique of narrativity which enabled the metaphor. I don't mean to suggest here that the honeymoon is over but, rather, that it is both present and deferred. The metaphor of convergence is enabled by the dismanteling of the narrative assumption that produced it in the first place. One abandons narrativity for the metaphor only after the deconstruction of narrativity; yet the notion of convergence depends on narrativity. After all, in most plays that convergence, that *komos*, provides the pleasurable end of the story, while here the *komos* and its unraveling proceed alongside one another. So, while holding the Ur-coupling of theory and history in mind, I want to proceed to the deconstruction of narrative strategies.

The critique of narrativity operates on both critical and historical discourses. On the one hand, there is a critique of narrativity which operates directly on the object of critical theory, as in Alice Rayner's article "Harold Pinter: Narrative and Presence."[12] On the other hand, there is the critique of how narrative structures have formed the writing of history, as in Daniel Brewer's article "Stages of the Enlightened Sublime: Narrating Sublimation" on the historicizing of eighteenth-century France as "narrating the sublime."[13] Both historical pursuits and literary theory have been informed by the kinds of questions this critique raises. What happens when history becomes a story? What happens when the drama becomes a story? What happens when the scholar narrativizes her own knowing? Narrative structures affect the constitution of events and their interrelationships. They organize the construction of human agency through the model of hero-as-subject and structure his-story as the pursuit and subsequent domination of the object (be that object women, other cultures, or nature).[14]

Employing this critique of narrative, I can return to the earlier notion of the "masculinization of history," casting it in the role of father in this primal scene of convergence through its collusion with narrative form. Narrative history constructs heroes and all that they imply in its subject/object construction. In fact, narrative history itself has accrued thereby some of the status of such heroes and their stories of successful domination through its constant construction of them. Now, the consequence of such subjects, such heroes, as mentioned above, and their masculinization in the patriarchy is the relegation of women to the status of Other in the narrative. In a sense women have been exiled to a realm "outside of history."

The object status that narrative history has "awarded" women has been reclaimed by some feminist historians as an effective agency—what Phyllis Rackin has called "Anti-Historians."[15] Enabled by the bipolar opposition inherent in the social gendering of knowledge, Rackin turns its exclusionary practice back on itself. In reading *I Henry VI* Rackin contrasts the history making of an imposing tower of names which Sir William Lucy constructs against what she terms as St. Joan's reductive, nominalistic, historical sense. She asserts that, within such heroic, narrative historical projects as Lucy's, the lives of women and their priorities operate as a threat to the project of writing English history.[16] Rackin posits the border of traditional history at the feminine.

Rackin's procedure—in theorizing about history from within a Shakespearean playtext, while cross-referencing the text with material, historical conditions—rests on the common base of discourse for both history and theory. She employs both literary and historical critiques, practicing a feminist version of what Raymond Williams termed "cultural materialism"—the historicizing of literary production and its reception and the theorizing of history at the same time.[17] Rackin transgresses what used to be considered the differences among art and life: dramatic texts and historical evidence. Discourse, or the operations of representation in language, renders literary and historical writings as literature. As Myra Jehlen suggests in "Patrolling the Borders: Feminist Historiography and the New Historicism," "literature qualifies and renders contingent upon language what passes for historical fact."[18] This traversal of text and historical documents is a key operation in New Historicism and what once was called the Renaissance.

The Progeny of the Convergence

Assuming, finally, the fraught convergence of history/theory/revolution, some examples of its operations might serve to animate the primal tableau. The practice of Renaissance new historicism, for example, offers an illustration of how literary and historical strategies converge. In the case of Shakespeare, Stephen Greenblatt has suggested (as in Rackin) that the object of such study is no longer constituted as a playtext but, instead, as a "cultural artifact." Using this notion, Greenblatt weaves the colonial practices of England into textual practices and, likewise, illustrates ways in which the stage colluded in creating a colonial mentality. Greenblatt employs the Foucauldian model of power to reveal both modes of subversion and their containment in Shakespearean texts and, homologously, in Renaissance political practice.[19]

While Greenblatt's new historicism opens up the text to social projects and vice versa, Carolyn Porter in her article "Are We Being Historical Yet?" further problematizes the remnants of idealism in Greenblatt's moves. Porter's critique illustrates the way in which the materialist dialectic proceeds through the writing of the new histories. Porter contradicts Greenblatt's Foucauldian sense of "power" as itself essentialized, transcendental, and, when located in the classics, a transhistorical *episteme*.[20] Likewise, Timothy Murray notes that "much of this scholarship reasserts the force of the 'master narrative' by analyzing how texts generate singular 'master discourses.'"[21] Murray goes on to critique the very notion of period itself, as does Thomas Postlewait in "The Criteria for Periodization in Theatre History."[22] What I would like to note here is the move in this convergence toward the ever more materially specific theorization of power/text and toward the micro level in its configuration. Outside of a focus on the canon or on dominant history the growing heterogeneity of subjects—agents of the drama or history—accommodates different historical/cultural structures. Ethnic and female agencies finally configure into the literary and historical scholarship. Cornel West in his article "Black Culture and Postmodernism" notes how, previously, agency and subjectivity were configured according to the model of white culture. West posits an alternative sense of agency and form making. Instead of the traditional subject-hero-object domination narrative, the black subject deploys a kind of "kinetic orality—dynamic and energetic rhetorical styles that form communities" rather than create images of great individuals; "antiphonal styles" rather than the droning single voice of the narrator; "fluid, improvisational identities that promote survival at any cost" rather than the humanistic unified, stable subject; a "passionate physicality, . . . bodily stylizations of the world . . . that assert one's somebodiness in a society in which one's body has no public worth."[23] Black critics like Cornel West and postcolonial critics like Trinh Minh-ha have brought a more heterogeneous subject to theory and history, although from within the postcolonial, Third World position the very primacy of the subject position may signal First World privilege, as Gayatri Spivak has suggested.[24]

One of the notions in West's theory, "physicality," leads to an important site of the theory/history convergence—the body. Feminists, ethnic theorists, and Foucault have theorized the body into history, history onto the body, the body and institutions, and the body and representation. A whole new history and theory of the black woman's slave body is being written at this time.[25] It has prompted new investigations of legal systems, definitions of motherhood, new theories of social power matrices, and novels such as Toni Morrison's *Beloved.* In theater the body has become a site of what Raymond Williams called a "fully historical semiotics."[26] Elin Diamond's article on bodies and Caryl Churchill exemplifies this strategy.[27] Theorizing and historicizing the female actor's body and the black woman's slave body critically foregrounds the bodiless, essentialist quality of traditional history and critical theory. In spite of my own bodily metaphor of the primal scene of their convergence, the claim theory and history make toward truth and universal significance resides in their bodilessness—their transcendent status in proximity to Plato's pure Ideas; their pretensions to universal agency. In contrast, material history, here focused on the body, forgoes such claims and operates in local venues and specific contexts to inscribe oppressive operations of the ideal (read *ideo-logy*) in the flesh.

At this point in the history of scholarship these old bodiless pursuits are giving way to a full-blooded cultural materialism. Foucault suggests that the new history "is thus situated within the articulation of the body and history. Its task is to expose a body totally imprinted by history and the process of history's destruction of the body."[28] This new kind of history is no longer focused on the narrative of the heroic body, or the ideal body; it is focused instead on the fainting body, the feverish body, and, for feminist theorists, even the hysterical body and all that it implodes of the institutions of medicine and psychoanalysis, the practices of discourse and the frame of representation. In other words writing history and theory is, as Hélène Cixous once suggested, "writing the body."

In sum the new historian/theorists today no longer sound the old, wheezing one note of the seamless narrative style, nor do they record the exploits of the unified subject, traveling the worn axis of bipolar oppositions in his quest to discover and dominate. Instead, they play upon and are played upon by the keyboard of contiguities, microstrategies, and heterogeneous agents. This is not, however, a playful pluralism. The historical moment configures the interventions of dominant power and its institutions. Moreover, those of us who work within this convergence realize we are where we work and our ideas are where they are published. The material conditions of our own ideas make them what they are and what they will become in their reception.

After just reading Richard Symonds's book, *Oxford and the Empire,*[29] in which he details the interaction between Oxford and colonialism in the organization of the study of the classics, literature, and history and the major role Oxford University Press has played in this project, I received a copy of a new book published by that press which included a feminist article of mine. All the postmodern slippage, butch-femme masquerading, antiracist critique, and general feminist force I could muster could not adequately resist the history of that imprimatur upon my work. While hoping for change, I continue to note the process of my own assimilation. Still, I can hope that the scholarly pursuit and practice of heterogeneity/inclusion and an eye to material conditions, in the midst of strengthening hegemonic social and economic forces, may yet provide a laboratory for change.

NOTES

1. Marvin Carlson, on that same panel, wittily reversed my title to read "The Use of Critical Theory in History." His paper appears in *The Performance of Power: Theatrical Discourse and Politics*, ed. Sue-Ellen Case and Janelle Reinelt (Iowa City: University of Iowa Press, 1991), 272–79.

2. Elizabeth W. Bruss, "Suddenly, An Age of Theory," *Beautiful Theories* (Baltimore: Johns Hopkins University Press, 1982), 3–32.

3. Bruss, "Suddenly," 16.

4. Janice Price, the head of what used to be Methuen, once related to me a more depressing account of this phenomenon. She proposed that the people who had once been activists could no longer work satisfactorily in that way and retreated into writing it rather than doing it—thus, the burgeoning of a certain critique in the 1980s.

5. See Gauri Viswanathan, "The Beginnings of English Literary Study in British India," *Oxford Literary Review* 9, nos. 1–2 (1987): 2–26.

6. Gayatri Chakravorty Spivak, "Can the Subaltern Speak?" in *Marxism and the Interpretation of Culture*, ed. Lawrence Grossberg and Cary Nelson (Urbana: University of Illinois Press, 1988), 276–77.

7. See Minnie Bruce Pratt, "Identity: Skin Blood Heart," in *Yours in Struggle: Three Feminist Perspectives on Anti-Semitism and Racism*, ed. Elly Bulkin, Minnie Bruce Pratt, and Barbara Smith (Brooklyn: Long Haul Press, 1984), 10–63; and the theoretical reading of it in Biddy Martin and Chandra Talpade Mohanty, "Feminist Politics: What's Home Got to Do with It?" in *Feminist Studies Critical Studies*, ed. Teresa de Lauretis (Bloomington: Indiana University Press, 1986), 191–212.

8. I have discussed this process at length in my introduction to *Performing Feminisms: Feminist Critical Theory and Theatre* (Baltimore: Johns Hopkins University Press, 1990), 5–7.

9. See Jacques Derrida, *Dissemination*, trans. Barbara Johnson (Chicago: University of Chicago Press, 1981).

10. See Heiner Müller, "Reflections of Postmodernism," *New German Critique* 16 (Winter 1979): 55–57.

11. Michael Foucault, "The Discourse of History," in *Foucault Live*, ed. Sylvère Lotringer, trans. John Johnston (New York: Semiotext(e), 1989), 25.

12. Alice Rayner, "Harold Pinter: Narrative and Presence," *Theatre Journal* 40 (1988): 482–97.

13. Daniel Brewer, "Stages of the Enlightened Sublime: Narrating Sublimation," *Theatre Journal* 38 (1986): 5–18.

14. See Teresa de Lauretis, "Desire in Narrative," in *Alice Doesn't: Feminism, Semiotics, Cinema* (Bloomington: Indiana University Press, 1984), 103–57.

15. Phyllis Rackin, "Anti-Historians: Images of Femininity in Jacobean Tragedy," in *Performing Feminisms: Feminist Critical Theory and History*, ed. Sue-Ellen Case (Baltimore: Johns Hopkins University Press, 1990), 207–22.

16. Ibid., 211.

17. See Carolyn Porter, "Are We Being Historical Yet?" *South Atlantic Quarterly* 87, no. 4 (Fall 1988): 743–86.

18. Myra Jehlen, "Patrolling the Borders: Feminist Historiography and the New Historicism," *Radical History Review* 43 (1989): 33.

19. See Stephen Greenblatt, *Renaissance Self-Fashioning: From More to Shakespeare* (Chicago: University of Chicago Press, 1980).

20. Porter, "Are We Being Historical Yet," 755.

21. Timothy Murray, *Theatrical Legitimation: Allegories of Genius in Seventeenth-Century England and France* (New York: Oxford University Press, 1987), 4.

22. Thomas Postlewait, "The Criteria for Periodization in Theatre History," *Theatre Journal* 40 (1988), 299–318.

23. Cornel West, "Black Culture and Postmodernism," in *Remaking History*, ed. Barbara Kruger and Phil Mariani (Seattle: Bay Press, 1989), 93.

24. See Spivak, "Can the Subaltern Speak," 274–77.

25. See Hortense J. Spillers, "Mama's Baby, Papa's Maybe: An American Grammar Book," *Diacritics* (Summer 1987): 65–81.

26. Raymond Williams, quoted in Porter, "Are We Being Historical Yet," 748.

27. Elin Diamond, "(In)visible Bodies in Churchill's Theatre," *Theatre Journal* 40 (1988): 188–204.

28. Michel Foucault, "Nietzsche, Geneology, History," in *Language, Counter-Memory, Practice: Selected Essays and Interviews*, ed. D. Bouchard (Ithaca: Cornell University Press, 1977), 148.

29. Richard Symonds, *Oxford and Empire: The Last Lost Cause?* (London: Macmillan, 1986).

Ideology, Performance, and the Illusions of Demystification

Herbert Blau

Telling It Like It Is

Many years ago I thought I could get a performance out of an actor by naming his or her blindness. I prided myself on a certain analytical power, not only in respect to the text but to the textuality of the psyche. What went with that was, to be sure, the necessity of a director: skill at reading signs, signs of behavior, what made a performance and also undid it, habits, tics, giveaway reflexes, the pathology of a surface, as well as the fantasy text of a subtext, which was palpable self-evasion. As soon as I felt anything like that I would, as if with a Geiger counter on the originary trace, go right to the heart of the matter. It was like being a moral monitor at the level of the drives. If I could tell the actor precisely what was, in any appearance, being repressed, that ought to solve the problem.

Putting aside the onerous aspect of *getting* a performance out of anybody, there was reason to think I had misgauged the dimensions of an issue for which Brecht, defining it in other terms, had proposed another method. The subconscious has a bad memory, he had remarked, the actor's psyche so impaired by the production apparatus of a class-divided society, that it is "not at all responsive to guidance."[1] Which doesn't mean that it is merely quiescent, nor quite reducible to ideology, whose relation to performance I want to examine here. What I shall say about ideology is not meant to enter the proliferous debates on the matter among neo-Marxists ("a veritable deluge," as Stuart Hall has said of the early 1980s),[2] but to deploy a term that may, with its risks of reification, bear upon the materialities of performance, particularly in their resemblance. If this makes for somewhat looser-minded thought than stricter theory would allow, I trust it will be loose with the rigor of performance—especially as it is engaged with what memory wants to forget. (I shall be alluding here to certain performance events outside the structure of institutional theater, but what I have in mind at the moment is best considered there, in relation to the precarious art of acting, which in the theater as we mostly know it has a long investment in psychological depth.) Damaged, preempted, colonized, as it may be, the subconscious can also be stubborn, with the ingenuity of amnesia. In the more or less Nietzschean form of an active forgetting, that may be making ideological claims of its own.

This is an obscure if generic aspect of performance which is perhaps best characterized by the apparent resistance of the finest, most dutiful of actors to what seems inviolable in a text. Or, more obscurely, to the undeniable logic of a director's best conception with which the actor seems to be, and believes s/he is, in complete accord. Yet there s/he is, conspicuously if unconsciously, or with the minimal measure of hypocrisy requisite to acting, doing it another way. "No cause, no cause," says the unspecious Cordelia (*King Lear* 4.7.74), who *did* object to the conception, when her own stubbornness was justified by the humiliated king, whose original mise-en-scène went so horribly wrong. If we tend to think of an Iago (depending on how we think) as the most (un)canny or subtle of actors, there are also actors in whom, like Cordelia, the line between acting and being may be far more subtle yet. So it appears to have been with Eleanora Duse, who acted, we are told (by Rilke, among others), without any false rhetoric or rhetoric at all, no sign, no sign, in what seems to have been the pure unprotected semiosis of self-effacing performance. Or, what's even more perplexing, the materialization of performance in its emptying out, the nothing that comes of nothing: in the mirror without an image, the apotheosis of absence. This would appear to be as far from ideology as performance can imagine itself.

Or as deep into ideology as it can be without knowing it. For there is a sense in which "ideology curves back upon itself, creating outside of itself a void that cannot be explained because it is, precisely, nothing."[3] This is the space without boundaries in which ideology seems to merge with the structure of the unconscious, from whose (unimaginable) coign of vantage there is no frontier to cross because there is no geography, nor existence but its own. A null, a nothingness, it is an existence without a history, which is what Freud appeared to have had in mind when he proposed that "the unconscious is eternal." And it is precisely this metapsychological notion of Freud's which Althusser had in mind, "word for word," when he thought of history without a subject and ideology as eternal, that is, not transcendent nor without temporality, "but omnipresent, transhistorical and therefore immutable in form throughout the extent of history . . . , exactly like the unconscious."[4]

If there were times when the habits of an actor also seemed immutable in form, exactly like the unconscious (and nothing in its emptiness as lustrous as that of Duse), one of the things I had to learn is that repression in the actor has remarkable versatility or resources of displacement. Adept as I was at reading a text, what I'd missed at the outset was the sticking point in, say, the plays of Ibsen or O'Neill, the paradox of enlightenment, whose dubious brilliance not only informs and darkens the entire history of the canonical drama but is, in the avid ritual of exposure and self-discovery, the nervous threshold of every rehearsal. What I found myself discovering through countless rehearsals—and with every rehearsal, the recessive economy of revelation—is what should have been self-evident to begin with: telling it like it is can be a disaster. That seems inarguable enough after the exhaustive intimacies and calamitous truths of a Hickey or Gregers Werle. But even with Brechtian distance honesty is by no means the best policy. So the perverse pragmatics of the Brechtian text suggests, no less the perversity of a form which is—in either minimizing or emphasizing its own presence, letting you know it's theater or pretending that it's not—verified by or verifying illusion.

Over and over we learn, as it is in life so it is in theater, which in its reflexive mirror doubles the inadequacy of any truth. Regarded thus, theater is the instrumental virtue that gives the lie to life—in the doubly unjudgable sense of *giving:* refusing it as a lie and endowing it with falsehood at once. So it was with my own truth telling about the inadequacy of the actor's truth; it merely doubled the bind. It was particularly chastening to discover that, far from being the solution to this conundrum, I had with the blindness of insight in naming the blindness become an instrumental part of the actor's problem. Perhaps the most grievous part. Such is the aesthetics of candor, about which, and the illusions of demystification, we have been perhaps a little remiss in theory.

Credibility and Commodification

No matter that I wanted to maintain credibility with the actor. Aside from the risk that the desire for credibility is an effect of vanity, what accounts for it in performance remains elusive in method. Credible in respect to what? for whom? where? when? who speaks?—it is hard to say, though most of us instinctively say it even while, theoretically, denying we can speak for others or while dismantling the ideological frameworks within which judgments are made. Meanwhile, the actor, constrained to accept the fiction that it is the audience "in the last instance" which determines any truth, goes about establishing credibility in performance—at least within the structure of our theater—by duplicities of which even s/he is unaware. This meets its match (or *méconnaissance*) in the complicity of the audience. (In the mutual admiration society of certain forms of alternative theater—where alienation, camp, and ideology embrace—the acting may be broader and, in a masquerade of awareness, the complicity even thicker.) The history of the drama provides us with prototypes of the actor who, resisting the entire process, refuses to play the actor, making matters worse. So it is in the conception of Alceste by Molière, an actor himself with the acutest mastery of the idea of acting and a sense of its duplicity which goes much deeper yet, since it directs itself at the end of all honesty to the desperation of duplicitous *need.* "Pretend, pretend that you are just and true, / And I will do my best to believe in you."[5] Thus, Alceste to Célimène, who has no trouble pretending, but can't quite guarantee anything like that, even if Alceste, giving audience to her pretense, could keep his part of the bargain.

There is in any case a critical gap between repression and pretense, the construction of an appearance and, more or less overdetermined, the appearance of indeterminacy. If the character of Célimène moves through the play something like the principle of indeterminacy, submitting herself to the world's gaze, it is the actress who performs Célimène who is in this regard—the consistency of her caprice—more indeterminable yet. (Let me not complicate this with the possibility that she might be, in a disengendered theater, played by a man, and not only in the Theater of the Ridiculous, where the candor of the aesthetic, its *jouissance,* includes playing it in drag.) From the evidence of his texts what Molière understood is that, for all the display, the actor is accountable to the rites of repression. The crucial issue is *concealment*, as it is in ideology, linked as it has been, crucially, to the fetishism of commodities, with its grounding in appearances as seductive as Célimène, the factitious or phantasmic character of commodity form.

That the image of the woman has itself been linked, through the entire history of the theater, to the status of a commodity has been, we know, the ideological burden of much recent theory, as of all kinds of feminist performance, whether in compensatory drama on a conventional stage or in the more experimental hybrids of the gallery scene. So far as the theater, however, has perpetuated the image of woman as absence or empty signifier, it has also revealed in its concealment the historical, if not generic, reality of the actor: that there is, irrespective of gender, *no way of escaping the commodity form.* If that does much to explain, at least in the profession today, the psychopathology of the actor, the other side of the coin is that there are actors not blind to this at all, who never thought otherwise and, with the inarguable aura of expensive commodities, turn that knowledge into a stage presence that is, with the acquiescence of the audience, something more than a facsimile of power. Between such actors and the recessiveness of a Duse there is the very difficult question of what constitutes power in acting as well as an entire spectrum of attitudes about what the theater is and what it should be, with more or less conviction about the (ir)relevance of ideology or with more or less utopian vision of going, like Artaud's victim signaling through the flames, beyond ideology.

The Camera Obscura

Compared by Marx in its operations to a camera obscura, ideology has developed over the years an always questionable and erratic reputation, all the more so after the events in Eastern Europe, its apparent exhaustion there. (If usage of the term has also been erratic, Marx himself is partly to blame. For while it could be said that it was with *The German Ideology* that the concept came of age, it by no means arrived with any strict definition. As for the subsequent sparse or uneven commentary in Marx's later writings, it had nothing like the analytical rigor brought to labor, capital, surplus value, and the concept of fetishism as well.) Subsumed as it has been in the dimension of the Imaginary, we tend to think of ideology with a certain wariness or instinctive melodrama, if not as mere dogma, as an inverted image of life which can only be distrusted, and distrusted all the more if we accept Marx's proposition that the reality inverted has already been inverted by the relations of production, leaving us doubly deceived. As there are also actors, however, aware of their status as commodities, who struggle against the realities of the profession, so there is ideology that knows itself as such and which is, as we say, ideologically committed. It is, nevertheless, the habit of mind cultivated by our sense of reality *as theater* that makes us distrust all commitments as merely effects of partial knowledge. And so it is that, with self-reflexive attention to the politics of the unconscious and the theatricality of psychoanalysis, with its dramaturgy of the transference, we have come to distrust most the one who is presumed to know: the analyst, the director, those heuristic or specular figures expert at exposure while (at least in traditional practice) remaining concealed themselves.

What we learn, however, from the archetypal figures of the drama, Oedipus, Hamlet, who lent their names to psychoanalysis, is that the more the actor shows, the more might be in hiding. And the more I named it in the name of truth, the more it seemed that I had become a crucial element in the "given circumstances" (Stanislavski's term for what, in the play, grounds the rehearsal, repression's agency or double, the parlous ground of inhibition). Here one begins to feel more than a little like Alceste. *Must one see it and not say it?* As I put my unerring finger on the actor's secret drive, naming it for what it was, I had not thought much about the insidious power of naming.

Nor could I make anything like the distinctions involved in Freud's reading of signs, a conception of interpretation so discerning and bold that, as Lacan remarked in his seminar on "The Direction of the Treatment and the Principles of Its Power," it has been robbed by popularization "of its full mantic significance." What I hadn't quite caught on to in the exposure of a drive is that the drive in its appearance implies "the advent of the signifier," with "the great compulsive scenario" or slippery slope of the Symbolic and its "cryptographical tracing off" into the impasses of the Imaginary, where judgments are being made which are profoundly ideological but, like the interpretation going out of sight at the dream's navel, escape all ideological vigilance. Of course, we didn't think then, and directors are unlikely to think now, in either ideological terms or Lacanian language. But Lacan moves the issue into familiar territory when he remarks that what Freud has recovered in the exposure of a drive is "the subject's lines of fate" and adds that "it is the face of Tiresias that we question before the ambiguity in which his verdict operates."[6]

Statutes of Limitations

I actually staged a production of *Oedipus* quite early in my career, but, like those who think they resolve the complex by merely repeating its terms (which is, all told, what most productions do), it may have taken a while before the ambiguity registered. Or the ineluctable lesson about the illusions of exposure: that in attentiveness to the transparency of the symptoms there may be a failure to read the equivocating signs. For whatever the verdict was, I also thought at the time, with something like oedipal presumption, that there was not an actor living whom I couldn't make respond to the force of an *idea*. Or an image. Or some powerfully developed concept of what was, if he, or she, only *saw* it, possible in the role, though s/he not only didn't see it but couldn't even imagine it—or gave up believing years ago, if the truth were known, that such a thing was possible for her or him at all. I blush to think of the number of actors—actors who admired and even loved me—whom I tried to get to do things they could never do because *I* wanted them done (the prospect exhilarating! the conception brilliant!), and, what's more, that they tried to do, against their self-conceptions, *because* they loved or admired me or, as I did acquire the authority of a director (with all its job-giving power), because they were simply afraid. I believe that I learned over the years that what *is* possible for a given actor has to be determined by the actor's own sense of what in the most suggestive circumstances remains within range, so that possibility may be released at the farthest edge of limit. No idea will survive the unnameable stage fright of an actor who knows—with whatever desire, idealism, faith, determination, or self-surrender—that s/he is simply not up to it. Not now, here, under the circumstances materially given, (and with *you* present) perhaps never.

There is also the chastening point when ideas are not up to it either. Assuming to begin with a certain quality of mind, a seriousness about ideas, an engagement in a "community of the question,"[7] with the fact that there *is* a question, one can expect from ideas only certain limited possibilities under particular historical conditions. There is much talk about transgression in theory, but one sees very little of it in performance, either with actors or with ideas. Even the most audacious of actors needs the most auspicious of circumstances to leap boundaries. What we look for is the propitious meeting between history and desire, or as Artaud perceived the site of "essential theater," between dream and events. No more is possible to any given idea under constraints of time and objective conditions than is possible for a particular actor under constraints of training, psychological makeup, the director's presence, the other actors, the production scheme, the means and relations of production, the staging, the opening date, the deadline, and in the United States the still-marginalized profession itself, including the material conditions of (mostly) unemployment. As for the submerged ideas, half-ideas, half-baked ideas, mere guesswork, fantasies, ghosts of thought and fragments of apprehension, the phantom objectivity that in one of its definitions makes up ideology, one hardly knows what is possible to that—though Althusser suggests that just because such ideas are taken for granted, or "govern us without our consent,"[8] they are not necessarily invalidated, aesthetically or politically useless.

Any idea, fertile as it may have been, wears out its welcome, and some ideologies have been liberating for their little moment and lethal the next.[9] We all know that. It is the one truth that should be self-evident as we come to the end of the twentieth century, with its repertoire of ideological slaughter. I suppose, however, that if it *were* self-evident, then the very notion of revolution, with its promise of living truth—the belief that it could really happen, *must* happen—would not be possible. The necessity of this blindness—the discrepancy between what we know and what we may choose to forget—accounts in large measure for the ideological nausea in the mordancies of Heiner Müller, as in the bloodbath of *The Task* or the grotesquerie of his *Macbeth*. The mordancies were given another twist in the version I saw by the Stadttheater of Hanover at Experimenta 6 in

Frankfurt, where the grisly joke for a mostly young and already jaded audience, absorbing with mixed delight and derision the collapse of ideology along with the onerous Wall, was upon the "velvet" lining of the idea of revolution itself. It's as if they were taking for granted, even before the accelerated unification of East and West, the spontaneous reproduction of the Same.

This is not quite the same, however, as the subliminal accretions of ideology or ideology that like the common cold merely sneaks up on us, occluding the origin of value in the relative innocence of "false consciousness," which Althusser was trying to rescue, in his notion of an ideology "spontaneously lived," from mere self-deceit.[10] There are, to be sure, elements of false consciousness wherever in language we turn our thought. Yet, as we think of ideology in any committed sense, as a body of thought to which we give our bodies, it's well to remember another thing that memory tries to forget: if there is something mortifying in thought itself that is particularly deadened when institutionalized, that is all the more so when it turns, in the guise of a critical practice, into the great compulsive scenario of rectitude. As Müller obsessively shows, sometimes with a jaundice to the point of self-revulsion, there is no exemption in all this for revolutionary thought, and in the art of this century we have seen—out of the most admirable idealism *or* rigorous critique—liberating affinities with totalitarianism.

What Remains to Be Done?

"In the destructive element, immerse," said Conrad, enunciating the principle that gave subversive energy to high modernism. Immersed itself in a correct politics, the same principle seemed to congeal the thought of certain heroic figures who, in disjunct and fractured, exemplary forms of art, taught us to hold contradictory ideas in the mind at the same time. For some now engaged in the critique of modernism that was the problem to begin with: not the correct politics, but the wrong politics, marked by contradictions. There are any number of variants on the theme, but the lamentable binarism or schizoid split in the case of Ezra Pound may be read as a cautionary tale of an alienated culture virtually consumed by contradictions. "In Pound," wrote Charles Olson after his visit to St. Elizabeth's, "I am confronted by the tragic double of our day. He is the demonstration of our duality. In language and form, he is forward, as much the revolutionary as Lenin. But in social, economic, and political action he is as retrogressive as the Czar."[11]

But if Olson's view of the revolutionary in Pound seems a little hyperbolic, consider Gramsci on the futurists, who were sufficiently distressing to a socialist politics even, like Pound, before their affiliation with fascism. "What remains to be done?" Gramsci wrote in 1921—one of the landmark years of the modern—echoing Lenin. The answer is still being echoed by certain of the more schizoanalytical voices and radical practices of the postmodern: "Nothing other than to destroy the present form of civilization. . . . It means not to be afraid of innovations and audacities, not to be afraid of monsters." Pointing out that the futurists grasped the necessity for new forms, philosophy, behavior, and language, Gramsci identified this as a "sharply revolutionary and absolutely *Marxist* idea," in which socialists were not even vaguely interested, though they had, according to Gramsci, no idea of their own, not even political or economic. If the socialists were frightened at the prospect of having to shatter the machine of bourgeois power, the working class, which could hardly imagine it, would take a long time before it could do "anything more creative than the futurists [had] done."[12]

If this evaluation of the foresight of futurism was, at the time, not absolutely accurate, it was sufficiently on the mark. As we think of it now, however, what seems to me important in the sharply revolutionary and absolutely Marxist *idea* is the degree to which it turned by innovations and audacities into something else. Whereupon we might conclude, retrospectively, that it was not so sharp and absolute to begin with. Or too much so. And that the contradictions had always soiled or invalidated whatever truth there was in the idea, as with Marxism itself almost everywhere in the world. Particularly where it released the monsters. Which are always more tolerable in theory and fiction than they are in human form. Or, for that matter, in the human form of theater, as we may see on the edge of taboo in certain excesses of rehearsal, or in actual performance when something of that excess, the uncontrollable mystery, breaks the frame of pretense and is about to spill over the stage.

Yet if there is in all its diminished (or monstrous) truth one Marxist imperative that remains inarguable, that is the necessity to *historicize*. No doubt that process will be moving through habitual categories, the conceptual sediments in the dynamics of interpretation. With all due vigilance about our own reflexes, and the "intangible historicity"[13] with which, designating a context, we may confound it with origins, we must also remember that contradictions, too, are a matter of context. What appears to be systemic may only be so by hindsight. Or it may be more ambiguous than that, adventitiously subject to the course of events, a latency in the system released by history, though it mightn't have been released if it weren't *that* system. Thus, it might be said that certain ideas can give rise to certain pernicious effects in history, while it's hard to imagine others taking the same course.

But taking a cue from Ronald Reagan, let's "stay the course" for a moment by moving back in history, to one of the great periods in which politics and the image of statecraft were at the heart of theater, and vice versa: the early seventeenth century. There we can see another factor that is, in its analysis of power, at the anguished fault line of Jacobean drama, as in the cracked brain of Lear when he is weighing contradictions in the extremities of the sky (but with a material base in the body and economics as the last instance: "No eyes in your head, nor no money in your purse? Your eyes are in a heavy case, your purse in a light, yet you can see how this world goes" [4.6.145–48]). If it remains the task of ideological analysis to look for contradictions, it must also expect that contradictions will have, depending on who's in, who's out, and the predisposition of analysis (not quite the same as its intangible historicity), a more or less benign or inimical face. Despite contradictions and, like Adorno, an indisposition to certain new forms (nonhegemonic, like black music),[14] Gramsci himself is *in* with American intellectuals looking for ideas to justify a political function in the academy; but he came in just as he was going *out* with Italian intellectuals, who felt his ideas exhausted as a scriptural figure in the Communist party, which was even before the events in Eastern Europe thinking of changing its name. (At the time of this writing the loose gathering of its uncertain constituency is, through whatever ideological transition, temporarily called The Thing.)

Some of the intellectuals, whether "organic" (Gramsci) here or by "weak thought" (Vattimo) there, are also looking for ways ("nontotalizable") of thinking past contradictions or without contradictions. What makes things more complicated, however, is an unpurged sense of permanent crisis which was the constituting agency and legacy of modernism. Sustaining itself with more or less advanced paranoia, this crisis addiction of modernism certifies for its critics (Marxist, psychoanalytical, poststructuralist, feminist) that it is the symptomatic mirror image of advanced capitalism, divided to begin with in the apparent rationality of its logic of domination, tearing itself apart with contradiction. The most radical ambition, perhaps, of postmodernism is to shatter the mirror itself or, in a kind of homeopathy of hemorrhaging image, to void it like the Taoist mirror that is a reflective surface without an image. Meanwhile, the hemorrhage is unabating, and in the "society of the spectacle"—*capital* accumulating to such a degree that it comes an image[15]—we seem to be dealing with a hemophiliac. Or, for those who see the spectacle congealing in its dispersion, the arterial possibility of a massive clot.

An Immense Reality

Without laboring the mixed medicine or a diagnosis in the mirror, there was certainly good reason for the critique of modernism, and for searching out a counterlogic or alternative forms of thought. Nor is there any reason I can think of for art to remain the same, even if that may threaten, as it periodically has threatened, to dissolve the categories, collapse genres, and abolish the idea of art. One of the claims made over the last generation, in the debates over minimalism, is that it was not only the anesthetic global spectacle but also, more locally, the dematerialization of art into theatricality that threatened the death of art.[16] What has been, however, doubly perplexing to critique is, for all its contradictions, the durability of advancing capitalism, and, for all the collapsing of genres, the recurrence of categories and the stubbornness of art.

Yet if the art object is returning, it is returning with a high quotient, or consciousness, of theatricality, and performance itself as a somewhat autonomous phenomenon is in various mutations still on the scene, the (im)materiality of its passing strangeness having passed over into a theater of images (and from thence to MTV), which had very mixed feelings about escaping the hegemony of art. It was during this period of innovation and audacities, with its valorization of body language, that performance was for a time dissociated in experimental theater, and still in critical theory, from the (allegedly) repressive dramaturgy of the oedipal tradition. There are residual contradictions here that could be examined, but the idea of performance has become in theory, and in all the humanistic disciplines, an exemplary model or heuristic principle: a form of inquiry which is materialized in the bodily succession of signifiers which is emptied into thought, consuming itself thus and, so the theory goes, escaping commodification.

It is curious, however, that this seems to describe (in much the same words I used earlier) the acting of Eleanora Duse, whose destiny it apparently was in forsaking rhetoric to become a fetish. That's surely what she was to Rilke when he described the "unutterably touching" quality of a performance in which, "so slight, so bare, without pretext of a role," she virtually disappeared from the eyes of the audience as if, in a premonitory instance of recent film theory, she had read its specularity as an appropriative gaze. The power of theater has always been in the mystery of its vanishings; yet what are we to make of her hiding there, "as children hide," with her hair, her hands, or a spray of roses before the face "on which they preyed," or her fingers crossed in a sign to ward off the evil eye? Sublimely, subliminally, is it an escape or seduction? For, in Rilke's evocation, as her performance moved toward an "immense reality," still recoiling from (or with?) the "long gossamer threads" of the gaze, the spectators were "already breaking into applause: as though at the last moment to ward off something that would compel them to change their life."[17] Someone like Chekhov would say the odds are against it: except for appearances, nothing would change, or maybe a hundred years or a thousand years in the future, despite the sublimity of the performance or, in a peculiar inversion of the pure natural exposure of a self, its *alienation*. Whatever this memorable performance may have been—and we can only guess at a distance, or fantasize—it does suggest in a sort of tripled paradox of the mirror of production the suture between the image of woman as consummate absence, the idea of acting itself, as most accomplished when wholly consumed, and the empty or occulted nature of the commodity.

This immense reality has, of course, been the subject of severe distrust, while the notion of woman as absence has been, if not strategically adopted as the ironic virtue of an imposed defect, severely rejected as a historical burden. There is more to be said, however, about the variable manifestations of acting which appears, by method or mystique, other than acting and about the body, which (dis)appears in the ghostly procession of signifiers. (Or in a kind of parody of this spectral phenomenon, as when Laurie Anderson clones herself on PBS, enfolding the self's identity into the mediatized image, as if giving itself over not to the procession of signifiers but to "the precession of simulacra."[18]) For this is an ideological problem of some consequence in the ontology of theater, as one might expect it to be as well in "the postmodern condition," insofar as that is inseparable—through the crudest public display of the *bruitism* of heavy metal or the myriad gossamer threads of alluring image—from the commodified spectacle itself, or the spectacle as the pure venereal "nature" of commodification.

Subtext of the Spectacle

But we came to reflect upon that condition by way of the modernist obsession with crisis, which remains the ruptured and dismembered subtext of the spectacle. And while we continue to seek theoretical alternatives to a thwarting binarism or a phallic formalism, or the sovereign reach of modernist desire—its collusion with the principle of sovereignty itself—we are no further along, in the massive commodification of culture, in responding massively to the last of Marx's theses on Feuerbach: so much for interpretation, let's get on with change, unless it be, as in the immediate aftermath of revolution in Eastern Europe, the massive desire for commodities. I am not saying this ironically. In a recent colloquy at the Festival of Avignon (summer 1990), Ewa Walch, dramaturg of the Deutsches Theater in East Berlin, spoke discerningly and compassionately about precisely this development in relation to the future of the theater in what was the Deutsche Demokratische Republik (DDR). After years of unquestioned subvention and reliable audiences, there is now confusion in the repertoire and vast insecurity in the work force. "Today," she said, "our theaters are half empty. Since last October, the public has left the theater for the street. Very few of them have returned. The large majority have rather made the trip to the supermarkets of the West. It is unthinkable to condemn this attitude, but it is a true problem for the theater."[19]

Meanwhile, if there has been some change, revolutionary or otherwise, since the (somewhat indeterminate) advent of modernism, nothing recent in our given circumstances—from deconstruction to *perestroika* to the incursion on the economy of Japanese microchips—suggests that the situation of crisis has in any way abated, except as wish fulfillment. If there is something more than wish fulfillment in the emancipation of Eastern Europe, the euphoria has already abated into a host of new problems, from the economy and governance to ethnic minorities, tribal vendettas, latent fascism, and the perils of uneven development—not to mention the deflection of worldwide attention, weapons, and financing to the Middle East when, suddenly, unexpectedly, Iraq invaded Kuwait. At best we might be able to say—in the rhetoric of the postmodern, as in newer modes of performance or L=A=N=G=U=A=G=E poetry—that the situation of crisis has been put into the subjunctive. Nor has there been any appreciable change in the existential sense of impermanence itself, with pollution and ozone depletion threatening, among other perils, what American-Soviet negotiators call "the fifth basket" (beyond the usual agenda of arms control, human rights, bilateral relations, and regional conflicts). Aside from oil spills and radioactive waste, it's the collocation of the uncontrollable, what even in contemplation can make a basket case of us all, in ways that weren't even imagined in the most paranoid days of the Age of Anxiety: drugs and terror at every level, not only systemic but insidiously viral, and, with bootleg missiles and poison gas, a vengeful fundamentalism besides that may soon have, beyond its faithful masses and human waves, the technological resources to match its rage.

I'm not concerned at the moment with what's historically justifiable, what not, nor the sum of former depredations for which bourgeois imperialism will be held accountable by history, only the cumulative animosities staring us in the face, some of them, for whatever good historical reasons, almost demented. At the same time, what may be a saving grace or last-ditch defense against all this—aside from "the forces of moderation" everywhere— is not anything so spaced-out or conjectural as Star Wars. It is, rather, the multinationalization of capitalism itself, and the fact that with the unsteady dollar we nevertheless still own, with exponential growth, much of the fantasy life of the world. What I am referring to here has been the major focus of recent critique: the colonization of the unconscious on an international scale by American forms of desire, attached as they are to the supposedly defunct values of the bourgeois Enlightenment (a virtual litany of which we heard in the inaugural speech of Václav Havel as president of Czechoslovakia). That, and the blade-running impetus of cultural diffusion—most important of which is the deterrent presence on American soil of heavy investment from elsewhere, real estate holdings by Arabs and Japanese, with bankers-in-residence and other personnel—this may keep us, against the actuarial tables or animus of Saddam Hussein or the unburied curses of the Ayatollah, from the devastation we never experienced through two world wars, not to mention the defoliation of the jungles. Which is not to say that the pacifying effect of diffusion will not find more immediate and local reasons—including the unimaginable poverty no longer unimaginable, since, if it's not on television, it's right there on the streets—for further rage and murderous division.

Whatever the disinformation on the six o'clock news—or, as a postmodern manifestation, the dispersive effect of its spastic, incongruous, fragmented images—one thing would seem to have been documented conclusively: we still live in an age that seems to have been struck from history in the form of contradiction. And to return, on that "wobbling pivot" of a palpable truth (if I may use a Confucian phrase from Ezra Pound), to the issue about the durability of ideas under particular historical conditions: it would seem that contradiction has been absorbed as something more than myth (or mythology in Barthes's sense) into the ideology that is spontaneously lived, where it is, if politically or culturally useful at all (in Althusser's sense) more like the condition of its spontaneity. As for the instrumental promise of anything more consciously programmed, the formulation of models or "subject positions," no less doctrine, the datum would seem to be that no idea can be stable for very long, without contradiction, no less ideologically certified with an extended life expectancy. What remains to be done is still the major issue, but it hardly takes a commitment to modernist obscurantism to believe that Freud was as close as we're likely to come to the truth of thought when he said we must learn to live in uncertainty and doubt.

The Ideological Moment / Shadow of a Magnitude

If that doesn't mean there should be no ideological analysis, we are still left with the question of who is doing it? to what end? with what *predisposition*? and the degree to which the end assumes priority over the unrestricted movement of thought. True, there are times when, like the breaking of clocks for the renewal of history, it seems that the free flow of consciousness must have a stop. And there may be an ideological moment, a moment where thought is arrested, as in the ideographic fix of a Brechtian *gestus* or the emblematic still of an Eisenstein film or the temporal pulsation, the closing up of the unconscious, that is the "Gordian knot" of the transference.[20] But the knot is a sort of vortex or, with the obstructed torsive momentum of Hamlet's "mortal coil," a gathering of thought at its limit, where the thought that empowers thought is always escaping itself. What is sometimes forgotten, it seems, is that there is no guarantee in the autonomous movement of thought that it will escape in the right ideological direction.

Ideas may strike us with the force of the absolute, but in history they are of necessity provisional. "...all is a—(*he yawns*)—bsolute," says Hamm, in the *mise en abîme* that sets the scene for the aporias of Beckett's *Endgame*.[21] Speaking of contradictions, it is Beckett's drama more than any other which, while positing the question of what's to be done as a recursive non sequitur, turns the appearance of paralysis, the ubiquity of its exhaustion, into a sort of reversing warp of entropy which is a reflexive form of energy. Or it's as if, in the hapless labor of diminution, its "exhaustive enumeration," desire were drawing sustenance not from the growth but from the impoverishment of capitalist accumulation. (As a dividend in the process, the *work*, the "impossible heap"—what must be "finished, nearly finished,"[22] the surplus value of the *remainder*—keeps alive, with whatever nostalgia, the modernist question of the power of the aesthetic. Or is it a question, ideologically, of the power of nostalgia?) However mordantly fractured in Hamm's yawn, the idea of the absolute is still there in Beckett, not merely as conceptual bricolage or residues in the text, but in his insistence as well, in his own directing, on the *absoluteness of the music* in the discontinuities of the text.[23] From Plato through Artaud the imagination (imagination dead imagine) has been moved by the vast abstraction of this transcendent idea, the shadow of a magnitude, the absolute itself. But to all appearances—and this is the aleatoric substance of the Beckettian music—we live in a universe where transformation is the only law, and that appears to contain, however unfortunately, an immemorial statute of limitation on the salutary life of any thought. This does not preclude the possibility that the recession of any thought may undergo a historical rebirth in the return of the repressed. It is hard to think of anything worth thinking—including things that seem, at a given time, too absurd to think—

that does not thus return, though like the materials of the unconscious refigured in thought.

As it emerges from the unconscious, with which, in the bottoming out of intention, it remains forever merged, ideology is itself a temporal pulsation. It is not only a function of time but, as an activating source, *timing* as well. As the actor learns, timing may be acquired as a matter of technique, but it veers in practice back toward the metaphysical, if not in accession to an absolute (though one speaks of absolute timing like absolute pitch), shadowing the magnitude of the eternity of the unconscious. (I have written of this elsewhere, while examining the "origins," or ideological grounds, of my own theater work, whose metaphysics, I should add, was by no means theological.[24] Thus:) *Take time,* says the director, working against time, in what is for the actor (*take* time or take *time?*) his customary double jeopardy or, professionally and ideologically, another version of the double bind. Here we have, perhaps, the unassuageable contradiction, the contradiction of/in time, which escapes analysis in the name of history. This is at the level of praxis, the *making* of theater, what the drama has always known since it articulated in its emergent form— which Aristotle placed between philosophy and history—the appearance of a reality that *looked* like theater.

The forms of theater in turn depend on their attitude toward this appearance. With the ideological consciousness of the postmodern theater— where performance is more or less dissociated from theater—we have seen various attempts to minimize the look by exaggerating it or playing with it, if not insisting on its extrusion on behalf of demystification: *this* being theater, and *that* being reality. But the reality *is* immense, and like the slippage of the signifiers, not that, *this,* not this, *that,* the trouble with appearance is that it always gets in the way.

NOTES

1. Bertolt Brecht, "Alienation Effects in Chinese Acting," *Brecht on Theater,* trans. John Willett (New York: Hill and Wang, 1964), 94.

2. Stuart Hall, "The Toad in the Garden: Thatcherism among the Theorists," *Marxism and the Interpretation of Culture,* ed. and intro. Cary Nelson and Lawrence Grossberg (Urbana, Ill.: University of Illinois Press, 1988), 35.

3. Terry Eagleton, *Criticism and Ideology* (London: Verso, 1976), 95–96.

4. Louis Althusser, *Lenin and Philosophy and Other Essays,* trans. Ben Brewster (New York: New Left Books, 1971), 161.

5. Jean Baptiste Poquelin de Molière, *The Misanthrope* (and *Tartuffe*), trans. Richard Wilbur (New York: Harcourt, Brace, and World, 1965), 117.

6. Jacques Lacan, *Ecrits: A Selection,* trans. Alan Sheridan (New York: W. W. Norton, 1977), 236–37.

7. Jacques Derrida, "Violence and Metaphysics: An Essay on the Thought of Emmanuel Levinas," *Writing and Difference,* trans. and intro. Alan Bass (Chicago: University of Chicago Press, 1978), 80.

8. Louis Althusser, *For Marx,* trans. Ben Brewster (London: Allen Lane, 1977), 150.

9. "I do not think," as Michel Foucault remarked, "it is possible that one thing is of the order of 'liberation' and another is of the order of 'oppression'" ("Space, Knowledge, Power," trans. Christian Hubert, *The Foucault Reader*, ed. Paul Rabinow [New York: Pantheon Books, 1984], 245). If I stress this issue here, that's because there has come into the (mainly academic) theater, out of the energy of theory, a promising dissidence that is, however, acquiring a ready doxology, which may increasingly guarantee tenure but, for all the rhetoric of subversion, not the remotest facsimile of a new shape of power—nor even, in the quick acquisition of status, a markedly different behavior.

10. Althusser, *For Marx*, 150.

11. Charles Olson, *Charles Olson and Ezra Pound: An Encounter at St. Elizabeth's*, ed. Catherine Seelye (New York: Grossman Publishers, 1975), 53.

12. Antonio Gramsci, *Selections from Cultural Writings*, ed. David Forgacs and Geoffrey Nowell-Smith, trans. William Boelhower (Cambridge: Harvard University Press, 1985), 51.

13. Fredric Jameson, *The Political Unconscious: Narrative as a Socially Symbolic Act* (Ithaca: Cornell University Press, 1981), 9.

14. Gramsci is perhaps the paragon of Marxist thinkers who at some critical limit of their identification with the masses—as what he called "organic intellectuals" or "collective individuals"—can't quite manage their aversion to the cultural expression of the underclass and, against ideological commitment, turn out to be, as the result of intellectual development, organic elitists. There is evidence of that in the passage of his prison letters where, chastizing his wife for arresting the education of his son Delio, he expresses intolerance for "the unformed, indistinct complex of images and sensations," an infantile state that, if preserved, inevitably gives birth to some form, however interesting, of "intellectual disorder" (*Letters from Prison*, ed. and trans. Lynne Lawner [New York: Harper and Row, 1973], 162–63). While Gramsci anticipated the ideological analysis of popular culture by the questions he asked of popular novels, there is a reflexive distaste for any expressive form, whatever its origins in the lower classes, if it is inimical to the growth of rational and analytical powers. Thus, his aversion to the "grafting of Asiatic idolatry onto the stock of European Christianity" (122) and even more to "the Negro music and dancing that has been imported into Europe," winning over segments of the cultured population "to the point of real fanaticism." "It is inconceivable," he adds, "that the incessant repetition of the Negroes' physical gestures as they dance around their fetishes or that the constant sound of the syncopated rhythm of jazz bands should have no ideological effects" (123). And, as he hears it, the effects are bound to be deleterious, especially for the young.

15. Guy Debord, *Society of the Spectacle* (Detroit: Black and Red, 1983), 34.

16. See Michael Fried, "Art and Objecthood," in *Minimal Art: A Critical Anthology*, ed. Gregory Battcock (New York: Dutton, 1968), 116–47.

17. Rainer Maria Rilke, *The Notebooks of Malte Laurids Brigge*, trans. M. D. Herter Norton (New York: W. W. Norton, 1964), 196–97.

18. Jean Baudrillard, *Simulations*, trans. Paul Patton and Philip Beitchman, (New York: Semiotext(e), 1983), 1.

19. Quoted in *Libération*, 25 July 1990, 16.

20. Jacques Lacan, *The Four Fundamental Concepts of Psychoanalysis*, ed. Jacques-Alain Miller, trans. Alan Sheridan (New York: W. W. Norton, 1978), 129–30.

21. Samuel Beckett, *Endgame* (New York: Grove Press), 2.

22. Beckett, *Endgame*, 1.

23. This essay was written before Beckett's death.

24. See "Origin of the Species," in Herbert Blau, *Take Up the Bodies: Theater at the Vanishing Point* (Urbana, Ill.: University of Illinois Press, 1982), 78–144.

Contributors

Philip Auslander is Associate Professor in the School of Literature, Communication, and Culture at the Georgia Institute of Technology. He has written extensively on the theory of performance for *Drama Review* and other journals. His book *The New York School Poets as Playwrights* appeared in 1989.

Rosemarie K. Bank, Associate Professor of Theater at Kent State University, serves as associate editor of *Theatre History Studies, Theatre Studies, Theatre Annual,* and the *Journal of Dramatic Theory and Criticism.* In addition to numerous articles and reviews in those journals, she has published in *Nineteenth-Century Theatre, Theatre Research International, Essays in Theatre, Women in American Theatre, Feminist Rereadings of Modern American Drama,* and *On-Stage Studies.*

Herbert Blau, currently Distinguished Professor of English at the University of Wisconsin, Milwaukee, cofounded the Actor's Workshop of San Francisco and later served as codirector of the Repertory Theater at Lincoln Center in New York and as Artistic Director of the experimental group KRAKEN. Two of his books, *Take Up the Bodies: Theater at the Vanishing Point* (1982) and *Blooded Thought: Occasions of Theatre* (1982), received the George Jean Nathan Award in Dramatic Criticism. His most recent books include *The Eye of Prey: Subversions of the Postmodern* (1987) and *The Audience* (1990).

Marvin Carlson is Sidney E. Cohn Professor of Theatre Studies and Comparative Literature at the City University of New York Graduate Center. He previously served on the theater faculties of Cornell University and Indiana University and directed numerous productions there. He is the author of many books, including *Theories of the Theatre* (1984), *Places of Performance: The Semiotics of Theatre Architecture* (1989), and *Theatre Semiotics* (1990).

Jim Carmody, Assistant Professor of Theatre at the University of California–San Diego, is Head of the M.F.A. program in dramaturgy. He is particularly interested in the intersections of cultural politics, performance, and semiotics, and he is currently completing a book entitled *The Cultural Politics of Mise-en-scène: Molière, From Antoine to Vitez.*

Sue-Ellen Case is currently Professor of English at the University of California–Riverside. She is the author of *Feminism and Theatre* (1988) and editor of *Performing Feminisms: Feminist Critical Theory and Theatre* (1990), a selection of essays based on the articles that appeared during her editorship of *Theatre Journal* from 1985 to 1989; and (with Janelle Reinelt) *The Performance of Power: Theatrical Discourse and Politics* (1991). She has directed productions for the University of Washington–Seattle, the Berkeley Stage Company, the Julian Theatre of San Francisco, and Cal-Arts.

Dwight Conquergood is Associate Professor and Director of the Graduate Program in Performance Studies and a member of the Research Faculty, Center for Urban Affairs and Policy Research, Northwestern University. He is also Director of the Center for Interdisciplinary Research in the Arts at Northwestern. He has conducted ethnographic fieldwork in refugee camps in Thailand and the Gaza Strip, and with street gangs in Chicago. He has published (with Paja Thao) *I Am a Shaman: A Hmong Life Story with Ethnography Commentary* (1989) and coproduced two award-winning documentaries based on his fieldwork: *Between Two Worlds: The Hmong Shaman in America* (1985); and *The Heart Broken in Half* (1990).

Tracy C. Davis, Assistant Professor of Theater and English at Northwestern University, is the author of *Actresses as Working Women: Their Social Identity in Victorian Culture* (1991) and

447

co-editor of Routledge's series on Gender and Theater. She has published articles on nineteenth- and twentieth-century sexual politics, theater reception, the acting profession, historiography, popular culture, and feminist theater in a wide variety of journals and collections. Her current research focuses on the economic history of Victorian theater.

Kate Davy is Associate Professor of Drama and Women's Studies and Associate Dean of the School of Fine Arts at the University of California–Irvine. Currently the theater review editor of *Theatre Journal*, she is the former associate editor and managing editor of *Drama Review* and co-editor of *Theatre Design and Technology*. She is the author of *Richard Foreman and Ontological-Hysteric Theatre* and the editor of *Richard Foreman: Plays and Manifestos*. Her work has appeared in *Performing Arts Journal*, *Drama Review*, *Theatre Journal*, and *Twentieth Century Literature*, among others. Recently her attention has focused on the implications of gay theory, or "queer theory," for feminist and lesbian feminist performance.

Elin Diamond is Associate Professor of English at Rutgers University. The author of *Pinter's Comic Play* (1985), she has published articles on feminist and theater theory in *ELH*, *Theatre Journal*, *Modern Drama*, *TDR: A Journal of Performance Studies*, and *Art and Cinema*. She is completing a new book, *Feminist Stagings: Unmaking Mimesis*.

Jill Dolan is currently Assistant Professor of Theater and Drama and Women's Studies at the University of Wisconsin–Madison, where she recently codirected (with Phillip Zarrilli) a production of *A Midsummer Night's Dream*. She has served as managing editor of *Women and Performance Journal*, *Drama Review*, and *Theatre Crafts Magazine* and has published many articles addressing feminist and performance issues. She is the author of *The Feminist Spectator as Critic* (1988, rpt. 1991).

Ellen Donkin, Associate Professor of Theater at Hampshire College in Amherst, Massachusetts, has published essays on Bernhardt and Duse (*Turn-of-the-Century Women*) and on directing Gertrude Stein (*Theatre Three*) and is presently co-editing a book on feminist directing with Susan Clement and writing a book on late eighteenth-century women playwrights in London.

Jeanie Forte is an independent scholar, director, and dramaturg living in Palo Alto, California, and teaching part-time in drama and English. Her publications include articles and reviews in *Theater*, *Modern Drama*, *Theatre Journal*, *Women and Performance*, and *High Performance* and the soon-to-be-released book *Women in Performance Art: Feminism and Postmodernism* (1992).

Mohammad Kowsar is Associate Professor and Graduate Coordinator in the Theater Arts Department of San Francisco State University. He is the author of *The Critical Panopticon: Essays in the Theatre and Contemporary Aesthetics* (1992). Kowsar has also directed many plays in San Francisco, notably for Theatre Telos, a company whose stated objective is to present socially relevant and ideologically committed plays.

Bruce McConachie teaches theater and American studies at the College of William and Mary. He is co-editor of *Theatre for Working-Class Audiences in the United States, 1830–1980* (1985) and (with Thomas Postlewait) of *Interpreting the Theatrical Past* (1989), and author of *Melodramatic Formations: American Theatre and Society, 1820–1870* (1992).

David McDonald is Associate Professor of Drama at the University of California–Irvine. He was the founding Executive Director of the University of California Humanities Research Institute and is a former editor of *Theatre Journal*.

Jim Merod is Dean of Arts and Sciences at National University in San Diego. He has taught critical theory at Brown, Brandeis, Cornell, and Stanford universities and the University of California–Los Angeles. He is the author of *The Political Responsibility of the Critic* (1987). He has recently been a Fellow at the Humanities Research Institute at the University of

California, and he regularly writes about jazz for a variety of publications, including the *San Diego Union*, the *Jazz Link*, the *Los Angeles Times*, and the *San Diego Voice*.

James Moy is Associate Professor of Theater and Drama at the University of Wisconsin-Madison. His articles have appeared in *Theatre Journal*, *Theatre History Studies*, and *Theatre Survey*. He is a former editor of *Theatre Journal*.

Vivian M. Patraka, Professor of English at Bowling Green State University, has published work on feminist and political theater in *Theatre Journal*, *Modern Drama*, *Theatre Annual*, *Art and Cinema*, *Studies in American Drama, 1945 to Present*, and *Women and Performance*, and in the books *Making a Spectacle: Feminist Essays on Contemporary Women's Theatre* and *Performing Feminisms: Feminist Critical Theory and Theatre* (1990). She is currently writing a book on theatrical representations of fascism and the Holocaust.

Thomas Postlewait teaches in the Department of Theater and Drama, Indiana University. He is the author of *Prophet of the New Drama: William Archer and the Ibsen Campaign* (1986) and co-editor (with Bruce McConachie) of *Interpreting the Theatrical Past* (1989). His current projects include an edition of the letters of Bernard Shaw and William Archer and a book on the concept of periodization in cultural history. He is series editor for "Studies in Theatre History and Culture" at the University of Iowa Press.

Janelle G. Reinelt, Professor of Theater Arts at California State University–Sacramento, recently edited (with Sue-Ellen Case) *The Performance of Power: Theatrical Discourse and Politics* (1991). Her book on Brecht and the contemporary British theater is forthcoming from the University of Michigan Press, and she is the new co-editor of *Theatre Journal*. Her most recent work as a director was a production of Simone Benmussa's *The Singular Life of Albert Nobbs* (1990).

Sandra L. Richards is Associate Professor of Theater and African-American Studies at Northwestern University. She has directed productions at Stanford University and in Nigeria. Her articles have appeared in such periodicals as *Theatre Journal* and *Brecht Yearbook*, and she is currently completing a study of the plays of Femi Ọṣọfisan.

Joseph R. Roach, Professor of English at Tulane University, is the author of *The Player's Passion: Studies in the Science of Acting* as well as articles on the history and theory of theater in *Theatre Journal*, *Theatre Survey*, *The Encyclopedia of Communication*, and *Discourse*. His most recent stage appearance was in Henry Fielding's *The Tragedy of Tragedies; or, the Life and Death of Tom Thumb the Great* (1989), in which he played the footnotes.

David Román is Assistant Professor of English at the University of Washington–Seattle and a member of ACT UP (AIDS Coalition To Unleash Power). His essay is part of a book-in-progress that examines the relationships between contemporary U.S. theater, gay male performance, and AIDS.

John Rouse is Associate Professor in the Department of Theater and Dance at Tulane University, where he directs the Master of Arts Program. He is the author of *Brecht and the West German Theatre* (1989) and articles on Brecht, Robert Wilson, and the contemporary German theater. He is Vice President of the International Brecht Society. His current projects include a collection of interviews with people who worked with Brecht at the Berliner ensemble and a study of the plays of Heiner Müller.

Richard Schechner is Professor of Performance Studies at the Tisch School of the Arts, New York University. He is the editor of *TDR: A Journal of Performance Studies*, and he is a theater director whose productions with the Performance Group include *Dionysus in 69*, *Mother Courage and Her Children*, *The Tooth of Crime*, *Oedipus*, and *The Balcony*. In 1989 he directed Sun Huizhu's *Tomorrow He'll Be out of the Mountains* (in Chinese) at the Shanghai

People's Art Theatre. His books include *Between Theater and Anthropology* (1985), *Performance Theory,* (1988), *By Means of Performance* (1990), coedited with Willa Appel, and *The Future of Ritual* (1992).

Bert O. States is Professor of Dramatic Arts at the University of California–Santa Barbara. He is the author of *Irony in Drama* (1971), *The Shape of Paradox: An Essay on Waiting for Godot* (1978), *Great Reckonings in Little Rooms: On the Phenomenology of Theater* (1985), and *The Rhetoric of Dreams* (1988).

Phillip B. Zarrilli is Associate Professor of Theater and Drama and South Asian Studies at the University of Wisconsin–Madison, where he also directs the Asian / Experimental Theater Program and the interdisciplinary Folklore Program. He recently codirected (with Jill Dolan) a production of *A Midsummer Night's Dream* (1990). His books include *The Kathakaḷi Complex: Actor, Performance, Structure* (1984) and (with Farley Richmond and Darius Swann) *Indian Theatre: Traditions of Performance* (1988). His *Paradigms of Practice and Power* is forthcoming.

Index